SEEING WILD

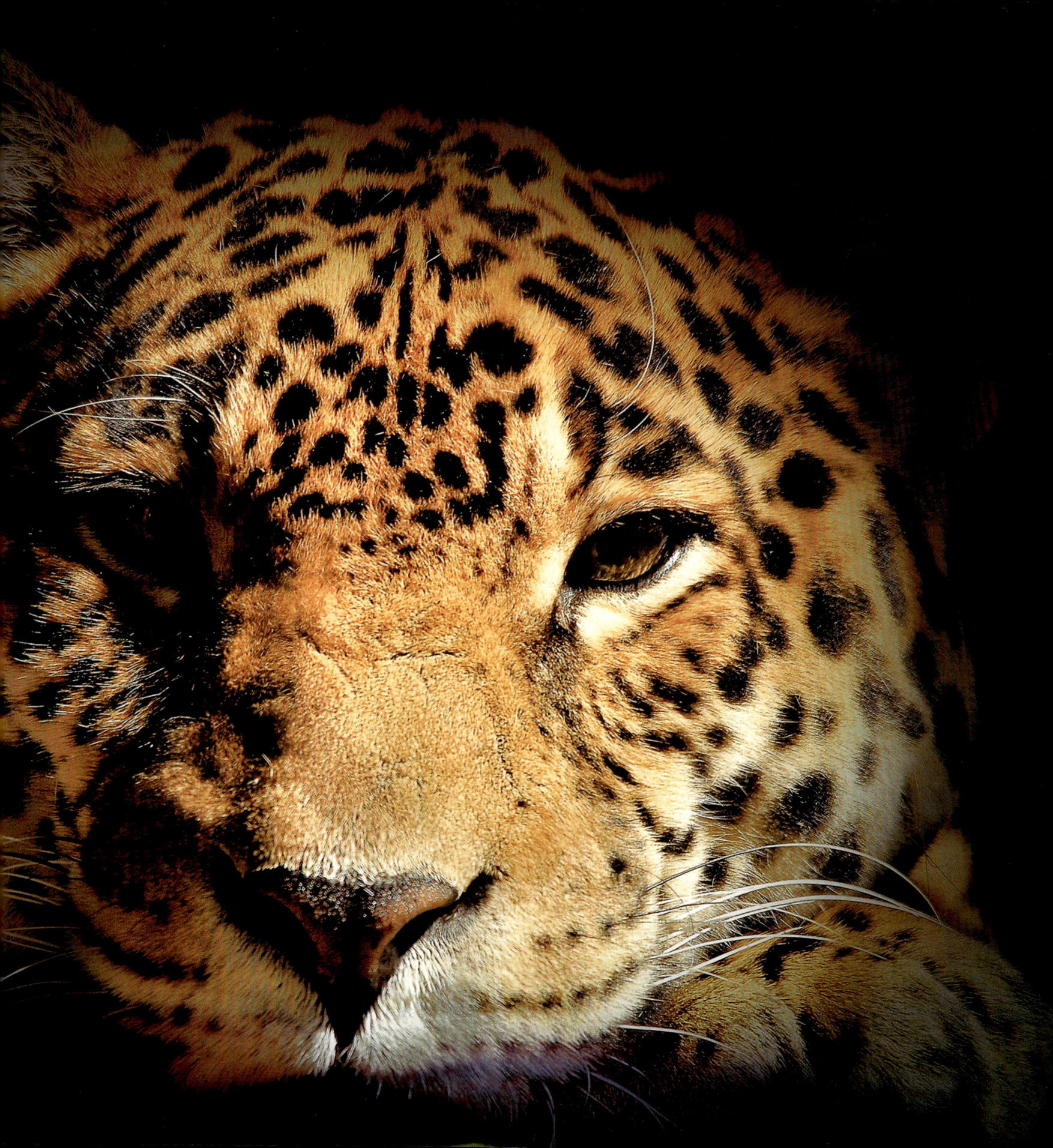

SEEING WILD

WILDLIFE PHOTOGRAPHY

Dennis Stewart

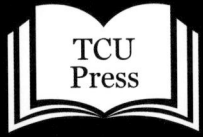

TCU
Press

FORT WORTH, TEXAS

LCCN: 2025001739

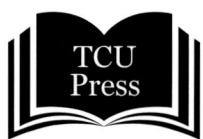

TCU Box 298300
Fort Worth, Texas 76129

www.tcupress.com

DEDICATION

Pursuing a dream is never easy, and it is only with the support of a special few in our lives that we can achieve greatness. I dedicate this wildlife book to my wife, Rebecca: without her unending love and support, it would not have been possible. I also dedicate this book to all my children, grandchildren, brothers, sisters, and most notably my parents, Esther and William, who encouraged me at an early age to find a passion in life and never let go of it.

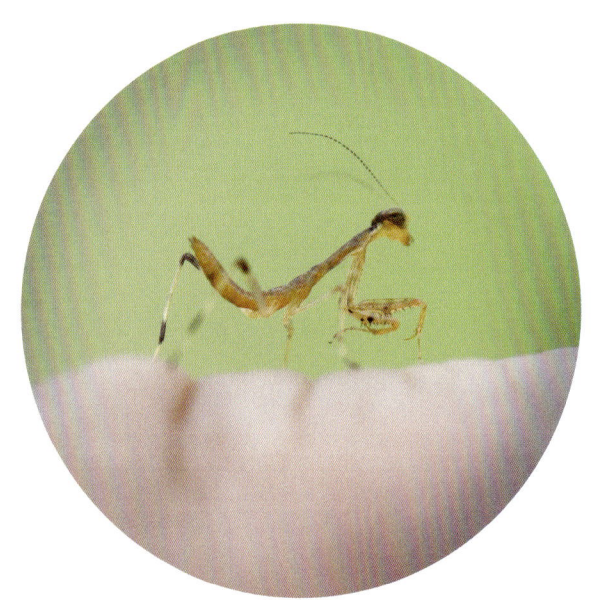

"*The true mystery of the world*
is the visible, not the invisible."

OSCAR WILDE

CONTENTS

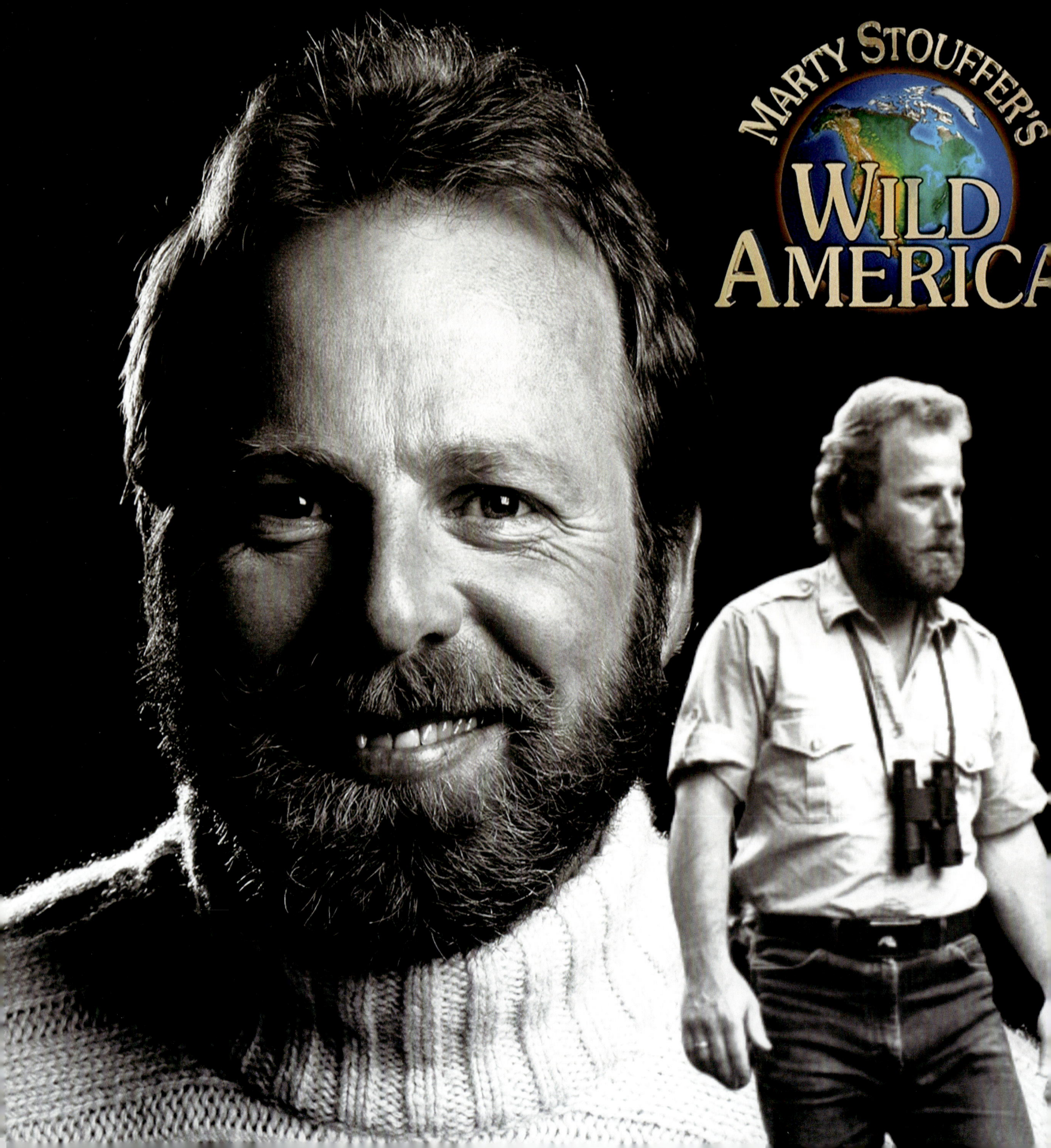

MARTY STOUFFER'S
WILD
AMERICA

FOREWORD

Life, death, and the rebirth of all species is the quintessential circle of life which links us all together. It's a never-ending story that invokes pain, passion, sorrow, and wonderment of our natural world. I am Marty Stouffer, and for more than half a century I have observed and filmed wildlife all across America. My television series *Wild America* allowed me the unique opportunity to witness animal behavior as never before seen. From the lofty peaks of the Rocky Mountains to the fertile swamps of a Louisiana bayou, the sheer abundance of life all around us has always provided me with great elation. I never know what I will encounter as I traverse that next high ridge, tranquil meadow, or soggy river bottom. From the majestic American bald eagle to the elusive wolverine, I have spent countless hours exploring, observing, and chronicling the behavior of wildlife in America. And I love making it available for all to see firsthand just how very astonishing the world around us truly is. Discovering the natural world is a spiritual awakening that will enhance your senses, enrich your mind, and lead you to a lifetime of fulfilment to which no therapy can ever compare. I love inspiring others to follow in my footsteps, and to preserve, protect, and cherish our great natural treasures. This has and will always be my most esteemed accomplishment. Join me, as I present to you *Seeing Wild*, as seen through the lens of my good friend Dennis Stewart. His photography will take you on a personal journey of our incredible natural world.

Marty Stouffer

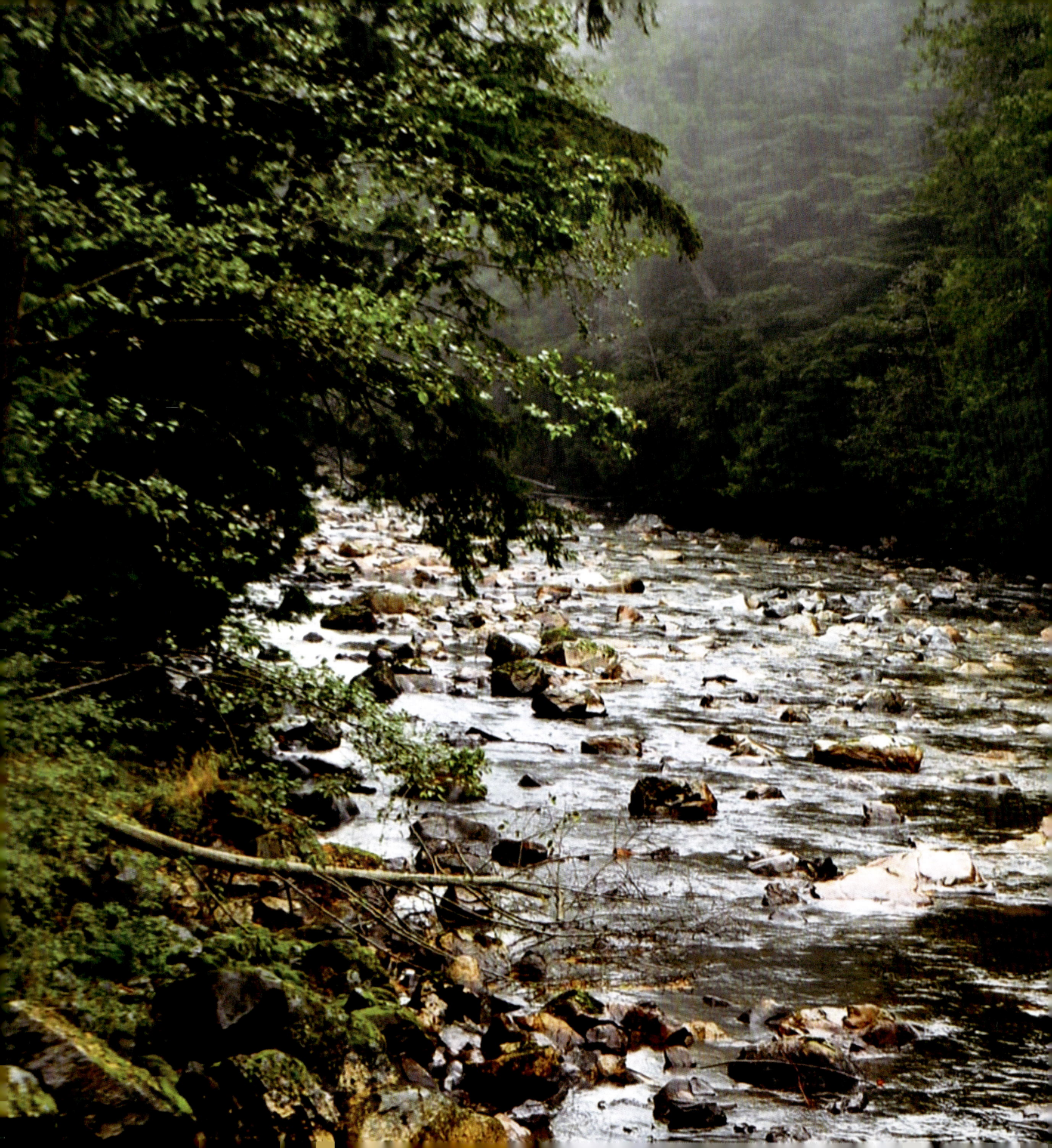

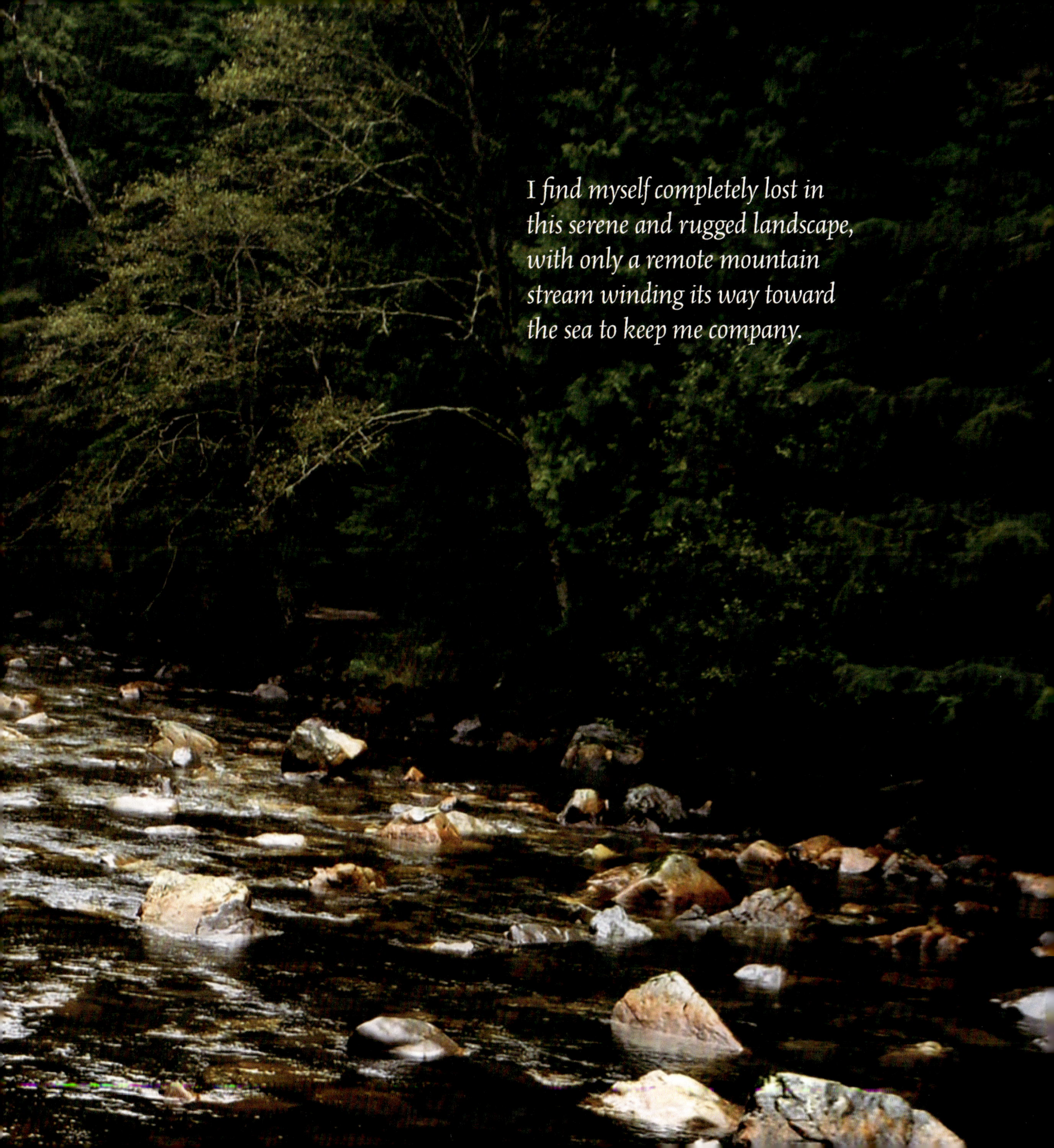

I find myself completely lost in this serene and rugged landscape, with only a remote mountain stream winding its way toward the sea to keep me company.

The silence of the mountains
is deafening to my ears, and
it is wonderful to behold.

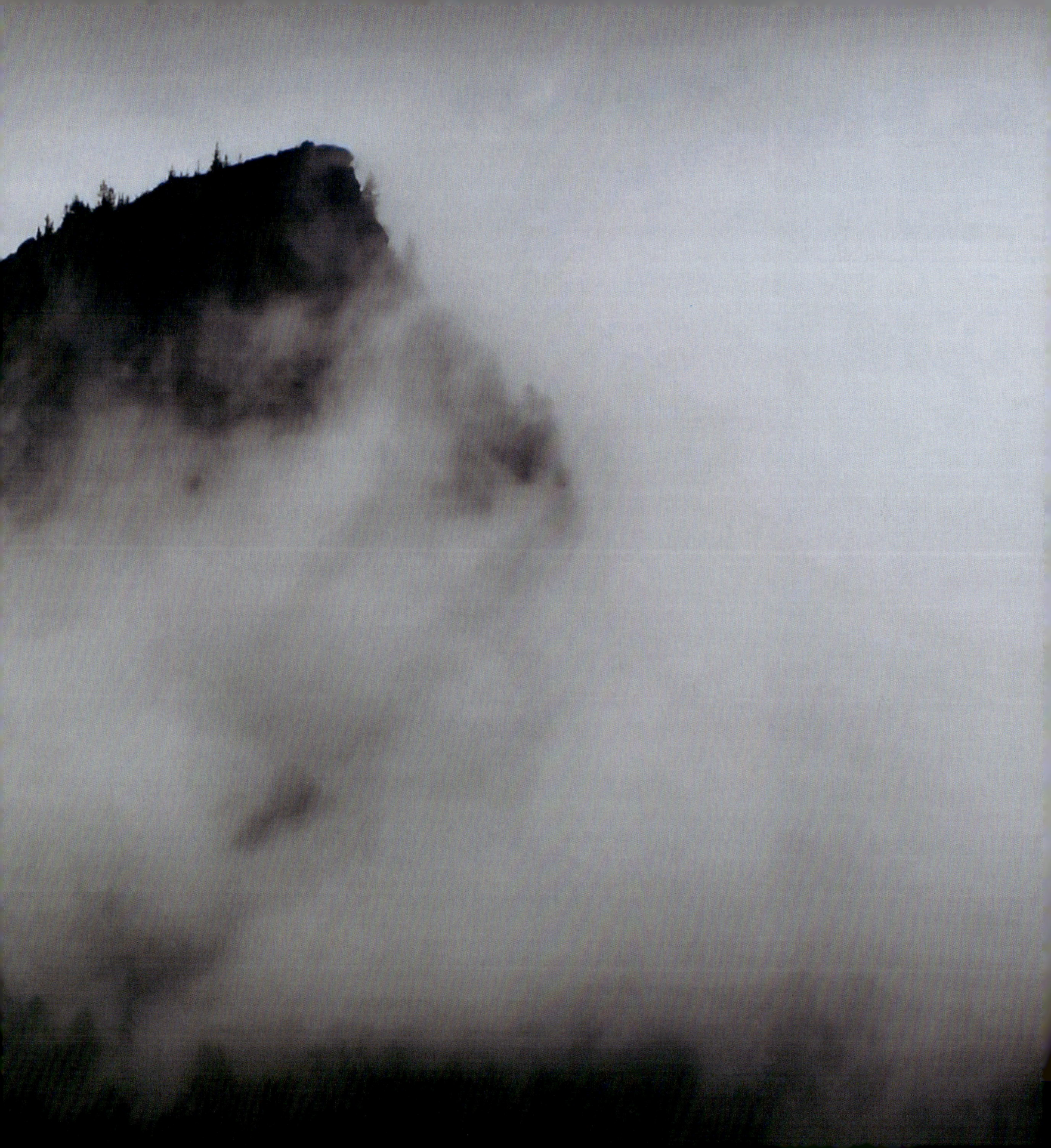

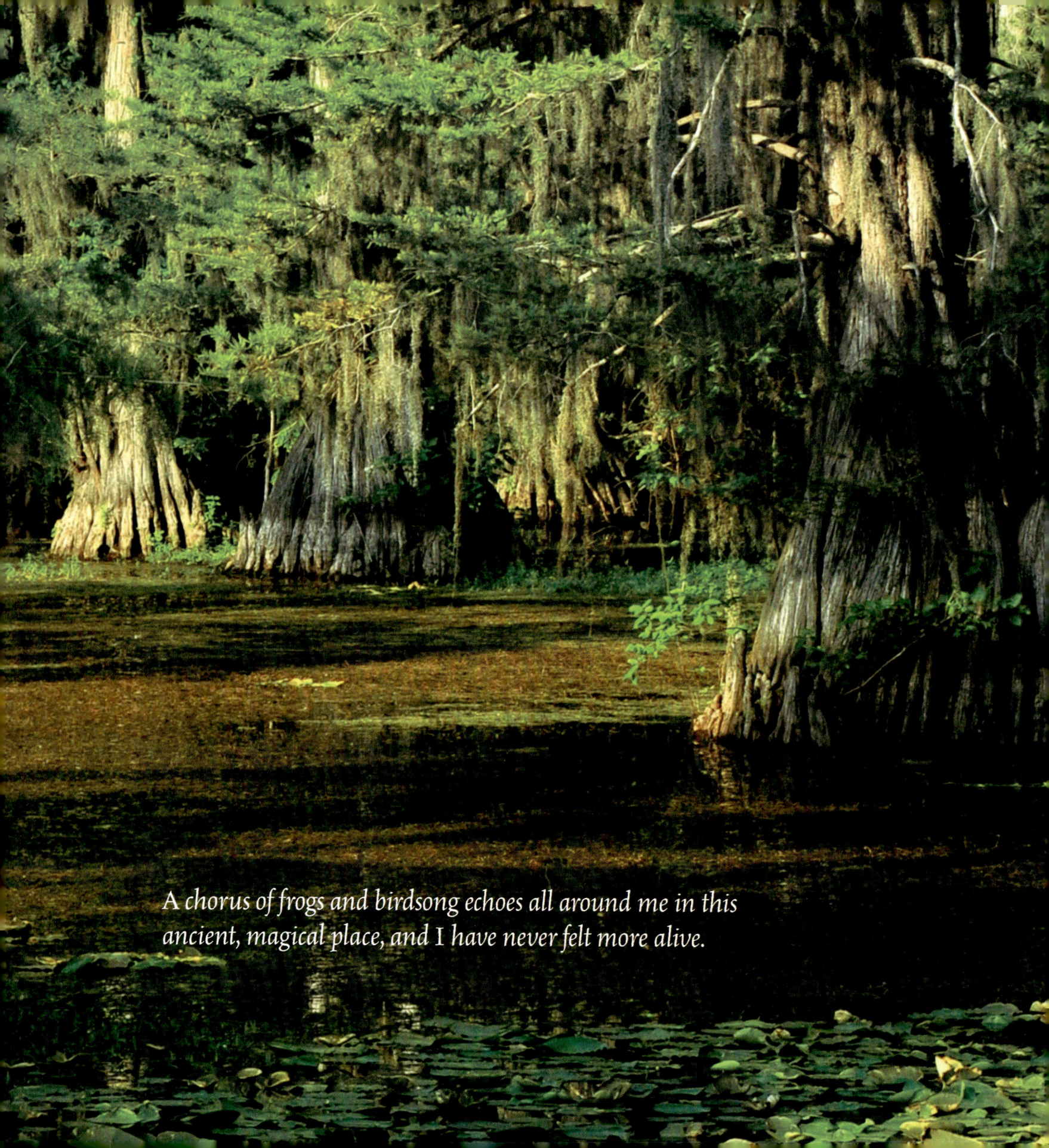

A chorus of frogs and birdsong echoes all around me in this ancient, magical place, and I have never felt more alive.

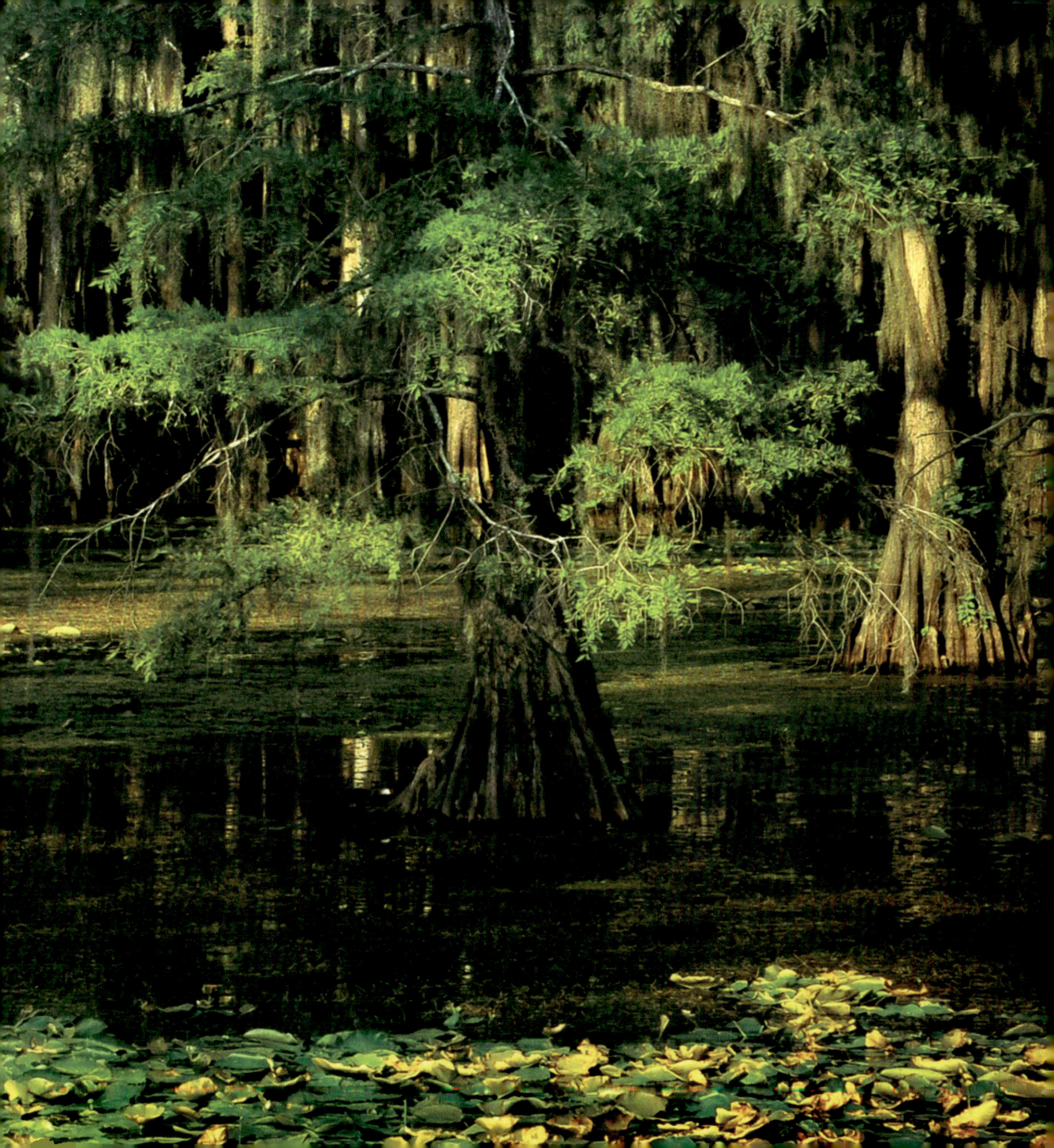

The Masai Mara whispers to me as storm clouds gather on the horizon, poised to quench the relentless thirst of this ancient land.

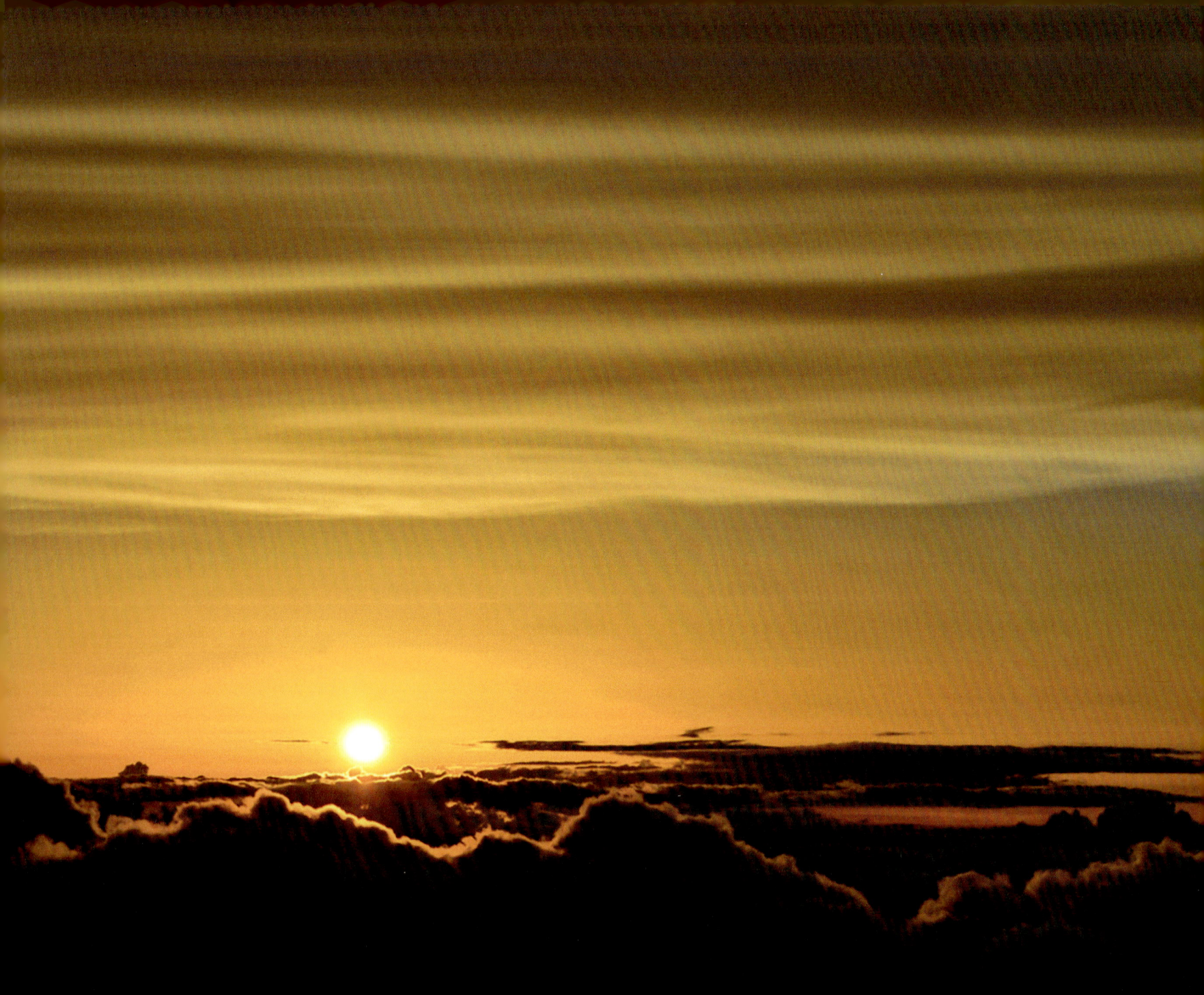

Atop the summit of Haleakalā, an ancient shield volcano
on the Island of Maui, you can still hear the spirits whisper
of a time long ago and a place like none other on Earth.

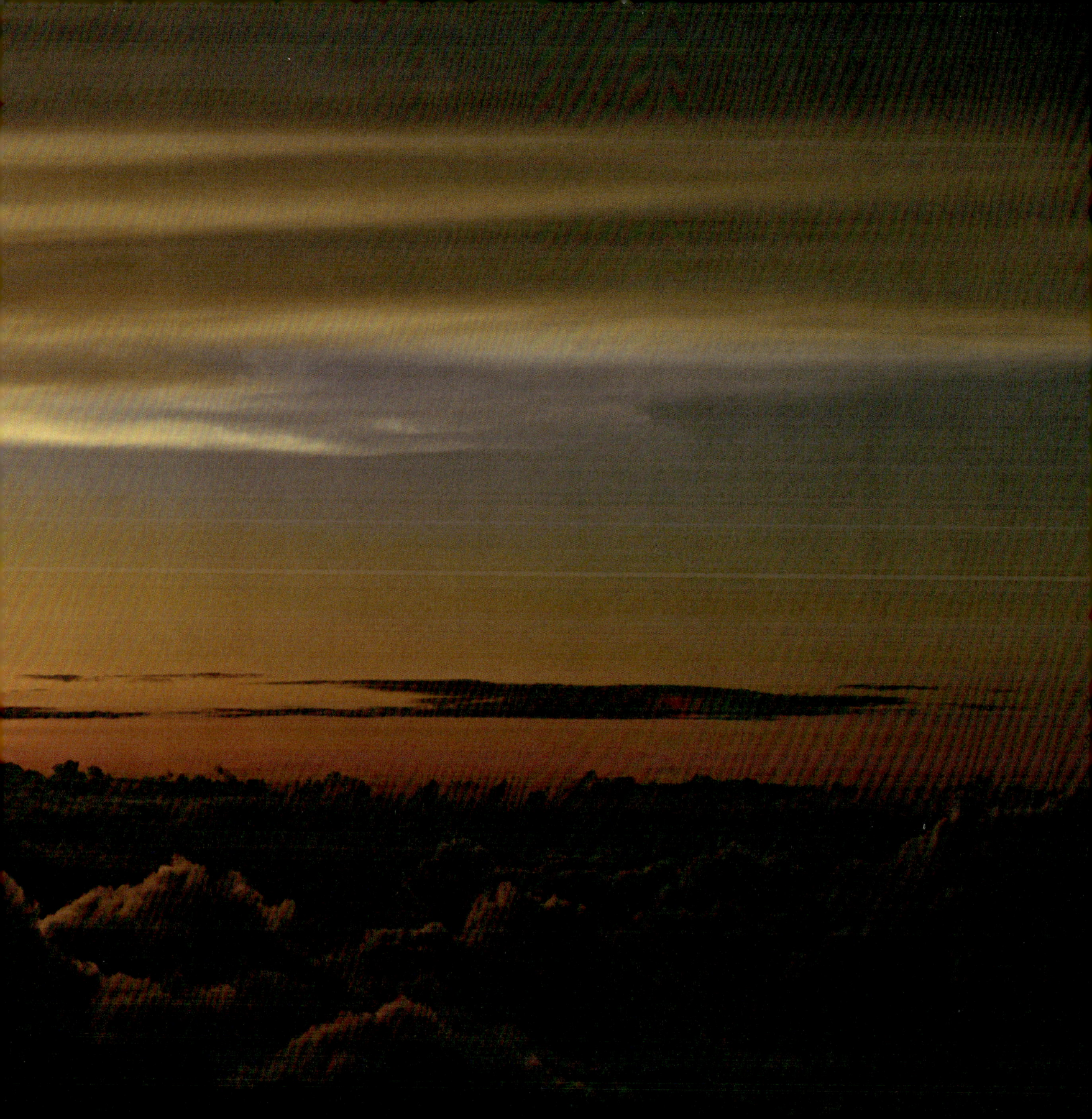

THE PEACE OF WILD THINGS

WENDELL BERRY

When despair for the world grows in me

and I wake in the night at the least sound

in fear of what my life and my children's lives may be,

I go and lie down where the wood drake

rests in his beauty on the water, and the great heron feeds.

I come into the peace of wild things

who do not tax their lives with forethought

of grief. I come into the presence of still water.

And I feel above me the day-blind stars

waiting with their light. For a time

I rest in the grace of the world, and am free.

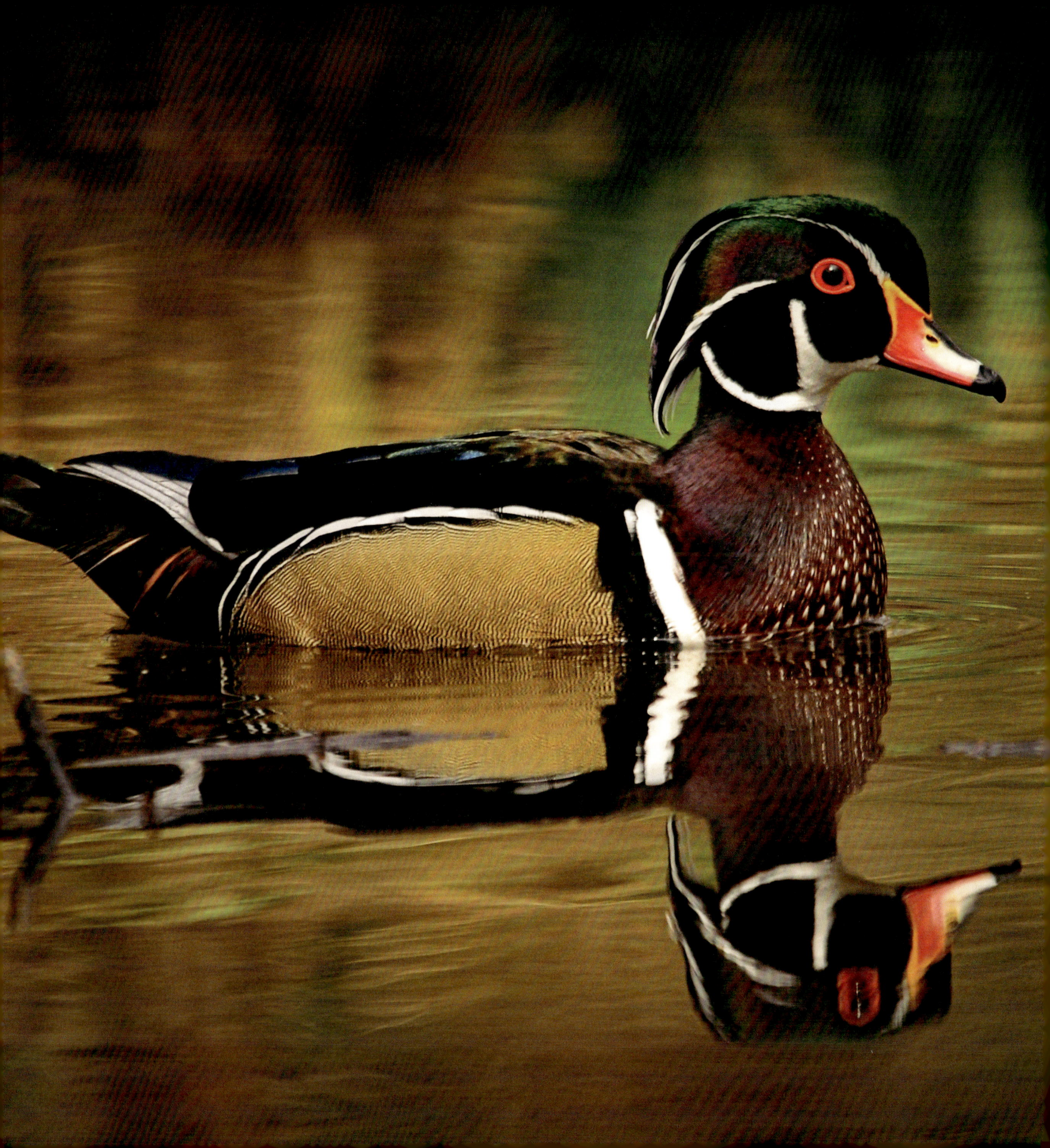

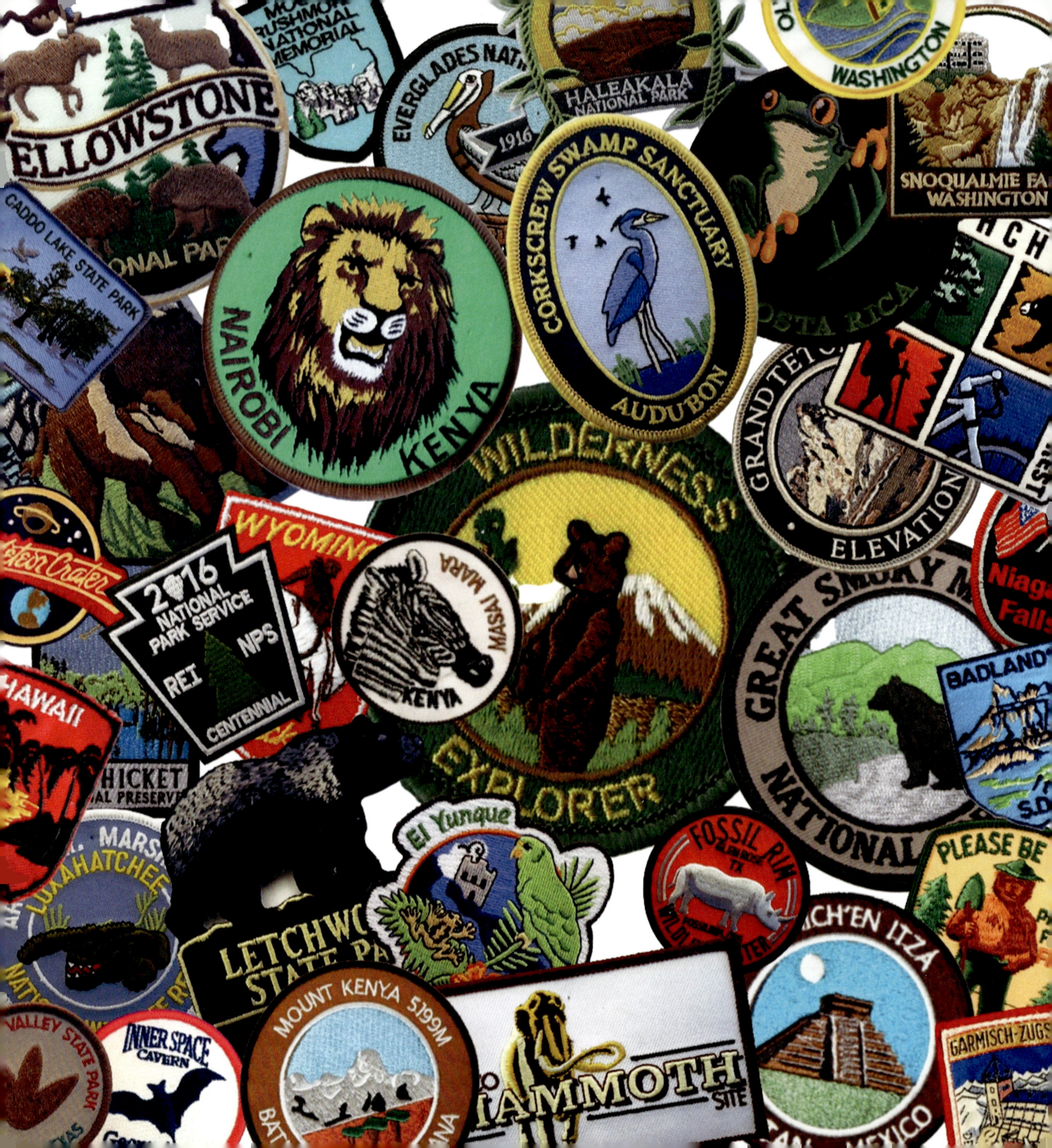

INTRODUCTION

Photographing nature and wildlife is not for everyone. It is a passion; it is an obsession; it is a never-ending journey of discovery that can thoroughly and relentlessly exhaust every fiber of your mind, body, and soul. Your subjects are typically uncooperative, finicky, and sometimes won't even show up for work. Still, when the day is done, and the bug bites are treated, there is absolutely nothing more pleasurable to me in life, nothing that I would rather be doing. I welcome and invite you to come into my world, if only for a brief moment in time. The wildlife images presented in this book represent over twenty years of fieldwork spanning three continents, multiple national parks, untold numbers of wildlife refuges, and the great state of Texas. Every image has been purposefully selected by me to best illustrate the beauty and splendor of the natural world that exists all around us, from the infinitesimally small damselfly to the immensely big African elephant. It is my incredible honor to present *Seeing Wild:* a collection of wildlife images as seen through my lens.

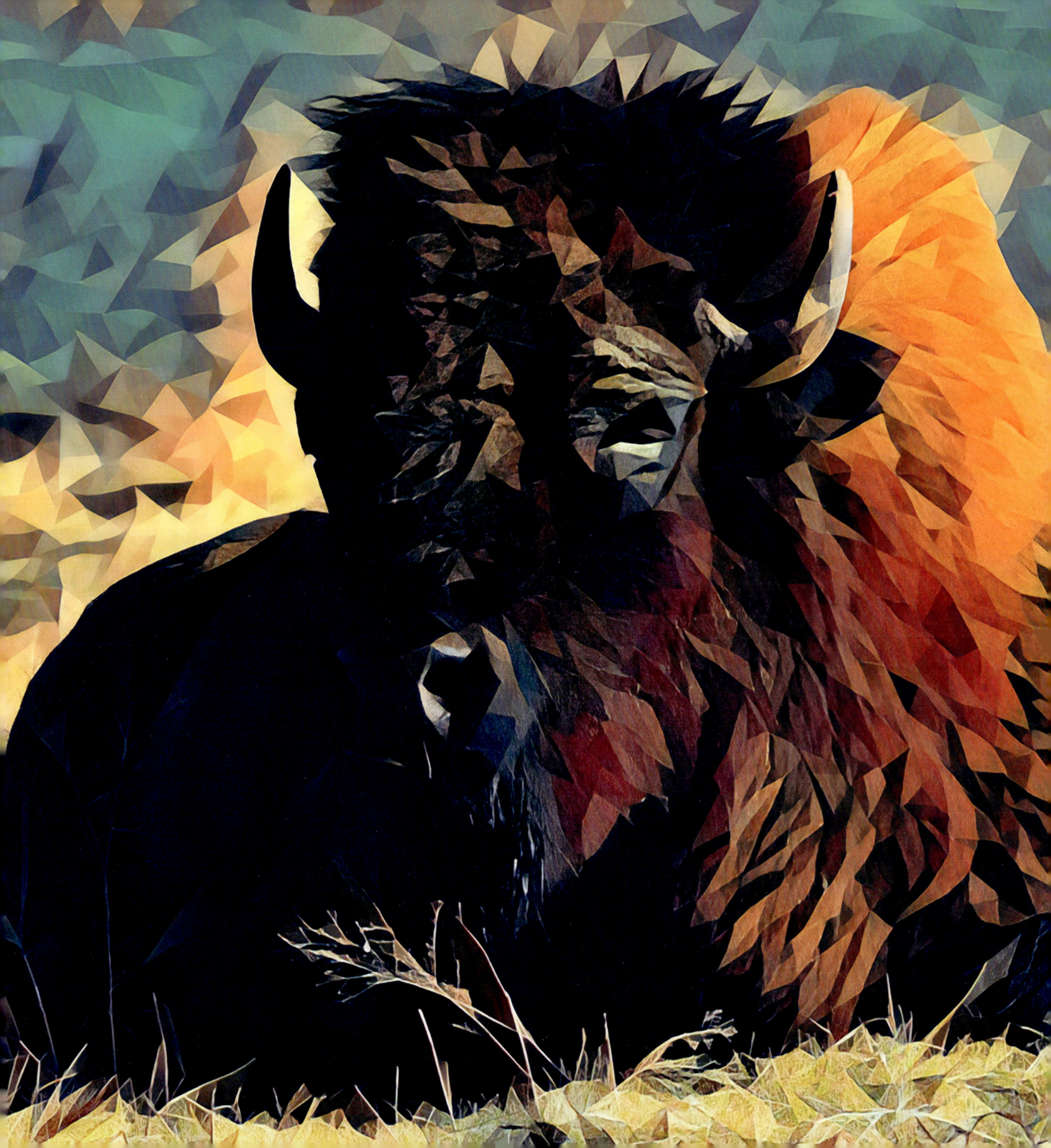

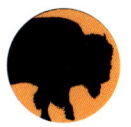

AMERICAN WEST

Majestic mountains, enchanted waterfalls, lush emerald valleys, and wide-open spaces. These are but a few select words to describe what is the American West, a place like no other on Earth. From the mighty Mississippi River to the shores of the Pacific Ocean, the American frontier stretches for thousands of miles in every direction. Where life abounds and losing yourself into nature is a distinct and real possibility. Long gone are the great herds of American bison that once thundered across the Great Plains, numbering in the countless millions. Yet still they can be found, protected and thriving in wondrous preserves like Yellowstone, our world's first national park. Photographing wildlife and observing the natural world in the American West is a journey that would take you a lifetime to pursue, and still leave you only wanting more. It will nurture your spirit, soothe your soul, and alter your perspective on the vital role we all have been given to conserve and safeguard this wondrous land now and forever. As you turn the next few pages, I hope my photography transports you into this world. Each picture is a life, and where there is life, there is always hope for a better tomorrow.

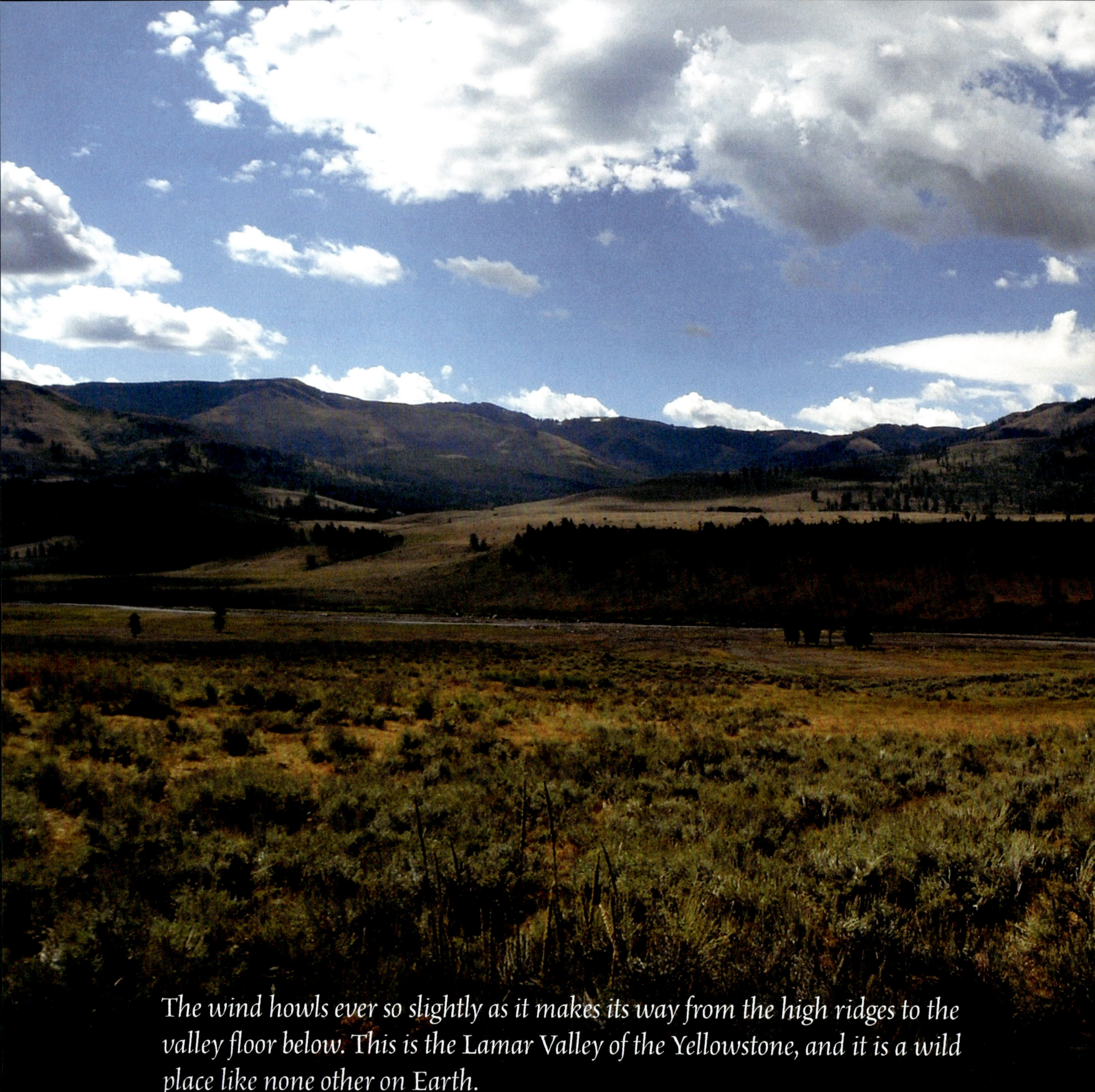

The wind howls ever so slightly as it makes its way from the high ridges to the valley floor below. This is the Lamar Valley of the Yellowstone, and it is a wild place like none other on Earth.

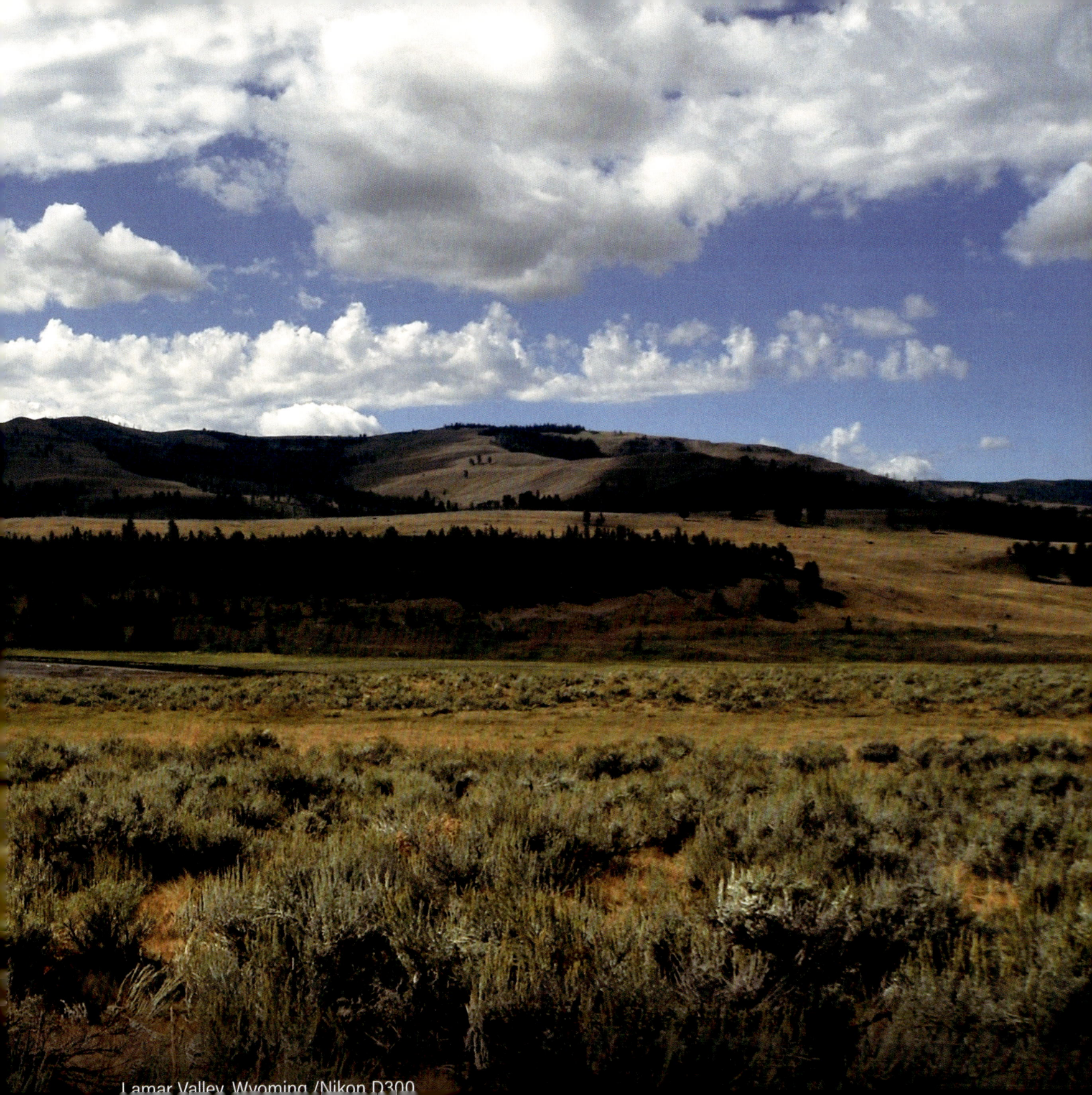

Lamar Valley, Wyoming /Nikon D300

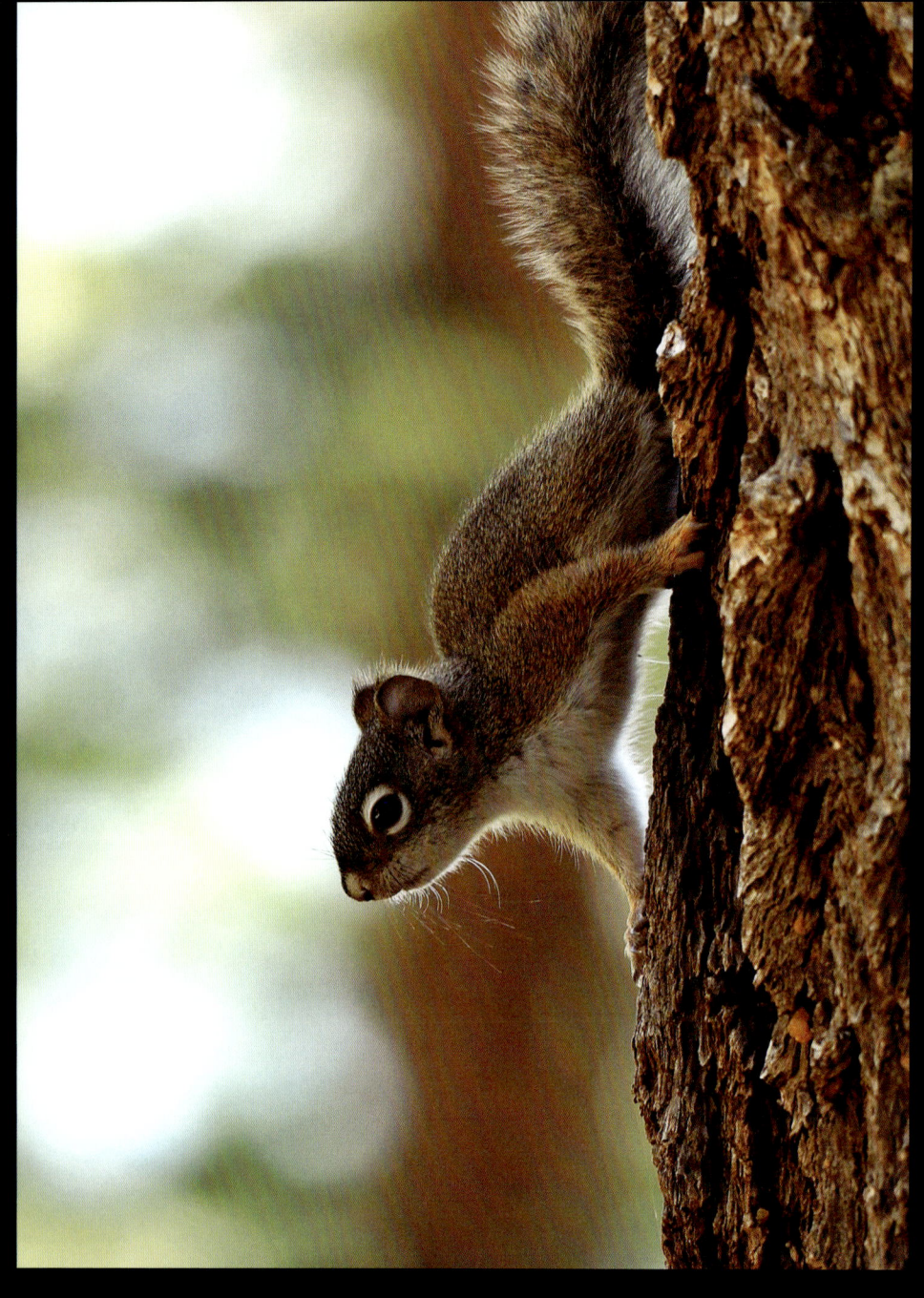

Atop a lodgepole pine, high above the lower falls of the Yellowstone River, a red squirrel lives its life in the tranquility of nature, oblivious to everything except the beauty that surrounds him.

Above: Red Squirrel, Yellowstone NP /Nikon D300
Opposite: Lower Falls, Yellowstone NP /Nikon D300

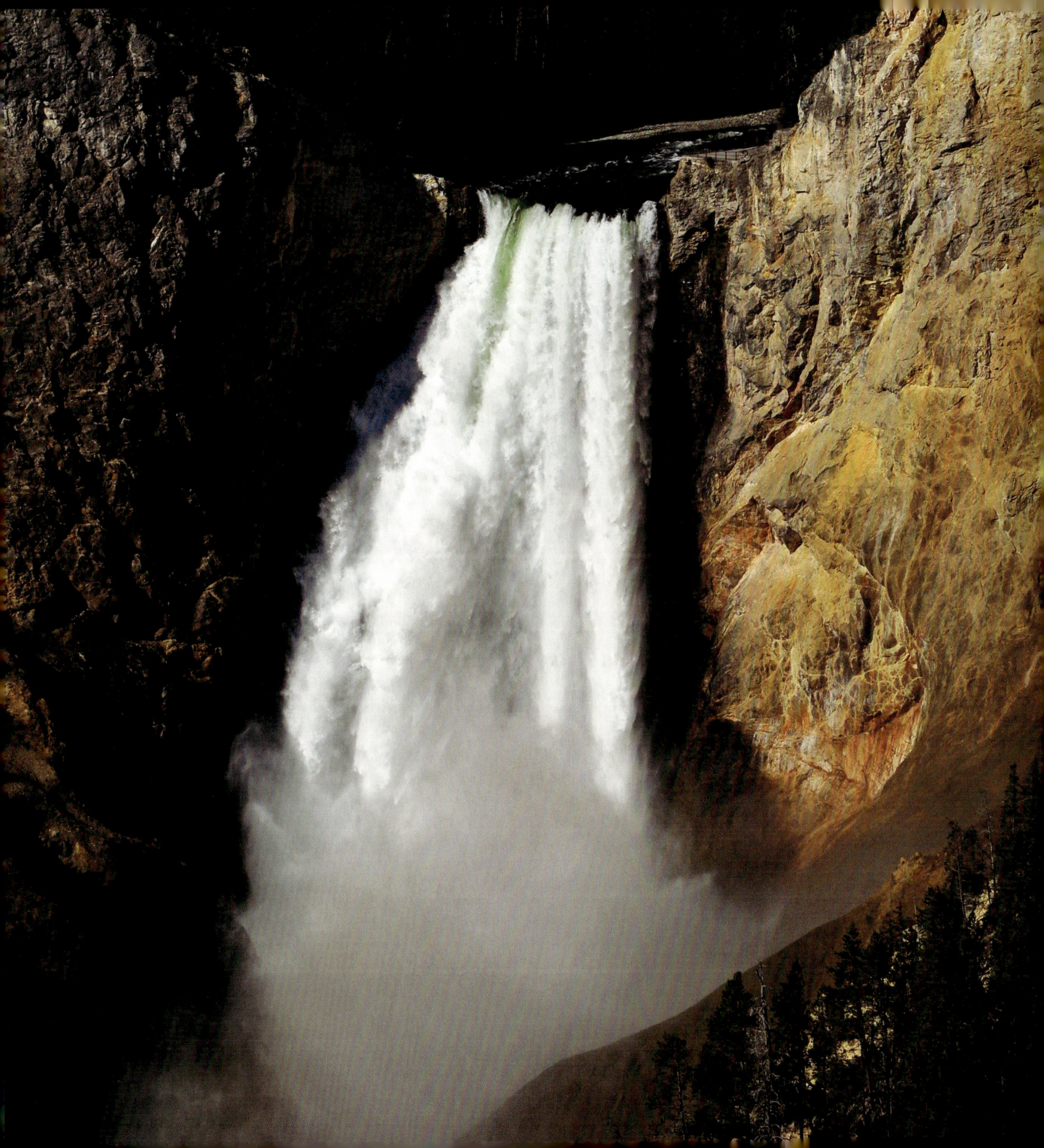

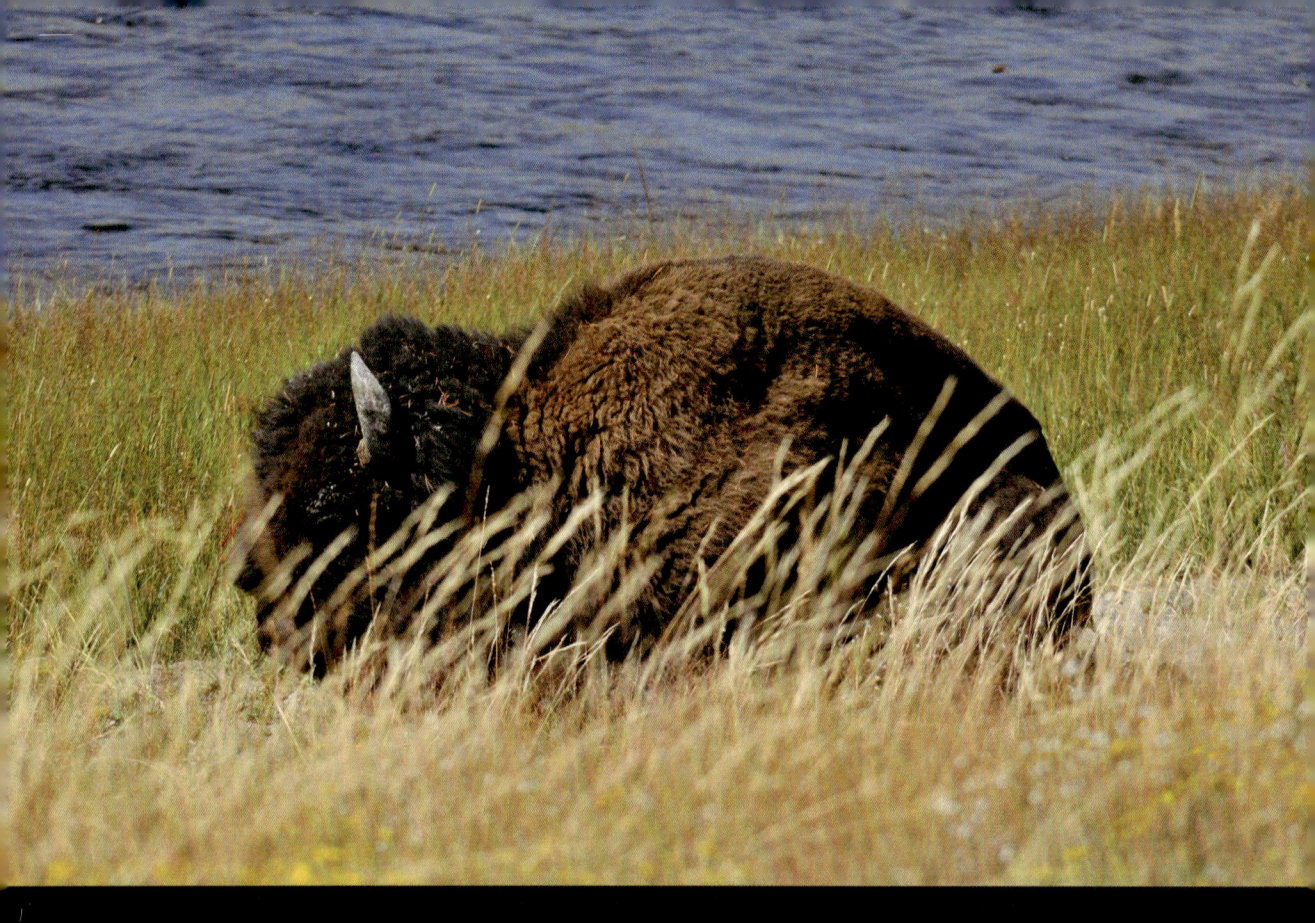

No tale about the American western frontier would be complete without including the bison in its narrative. They once numbered in the millions and roamed the great plains of America, serving as an indelible symbol of what once was and a warning to us all about how quickly animal species can become extinct—or almost extinct—if we allow it.

Above and opposite: American Bison, Yellowstone NP (Nikon D300

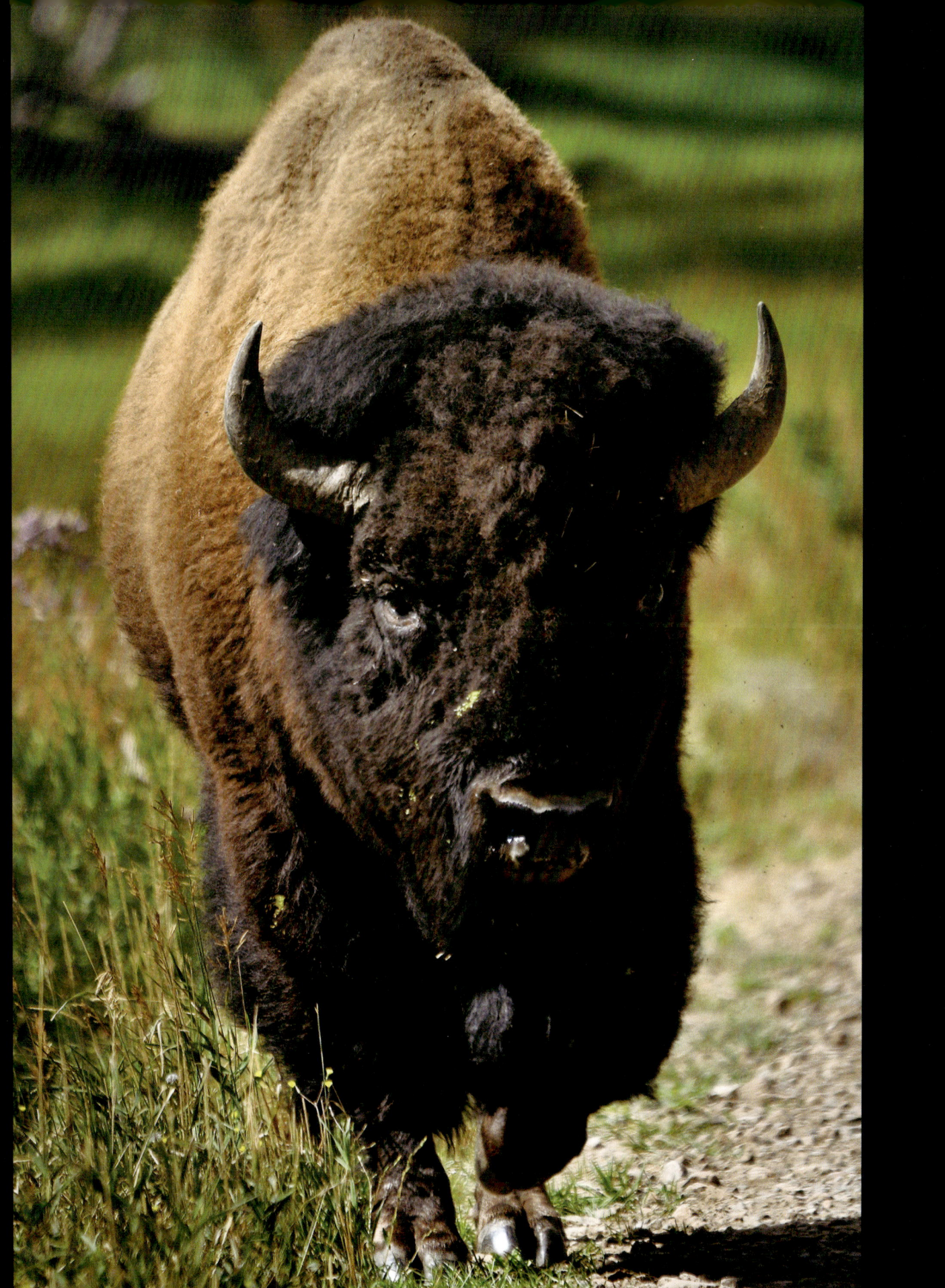

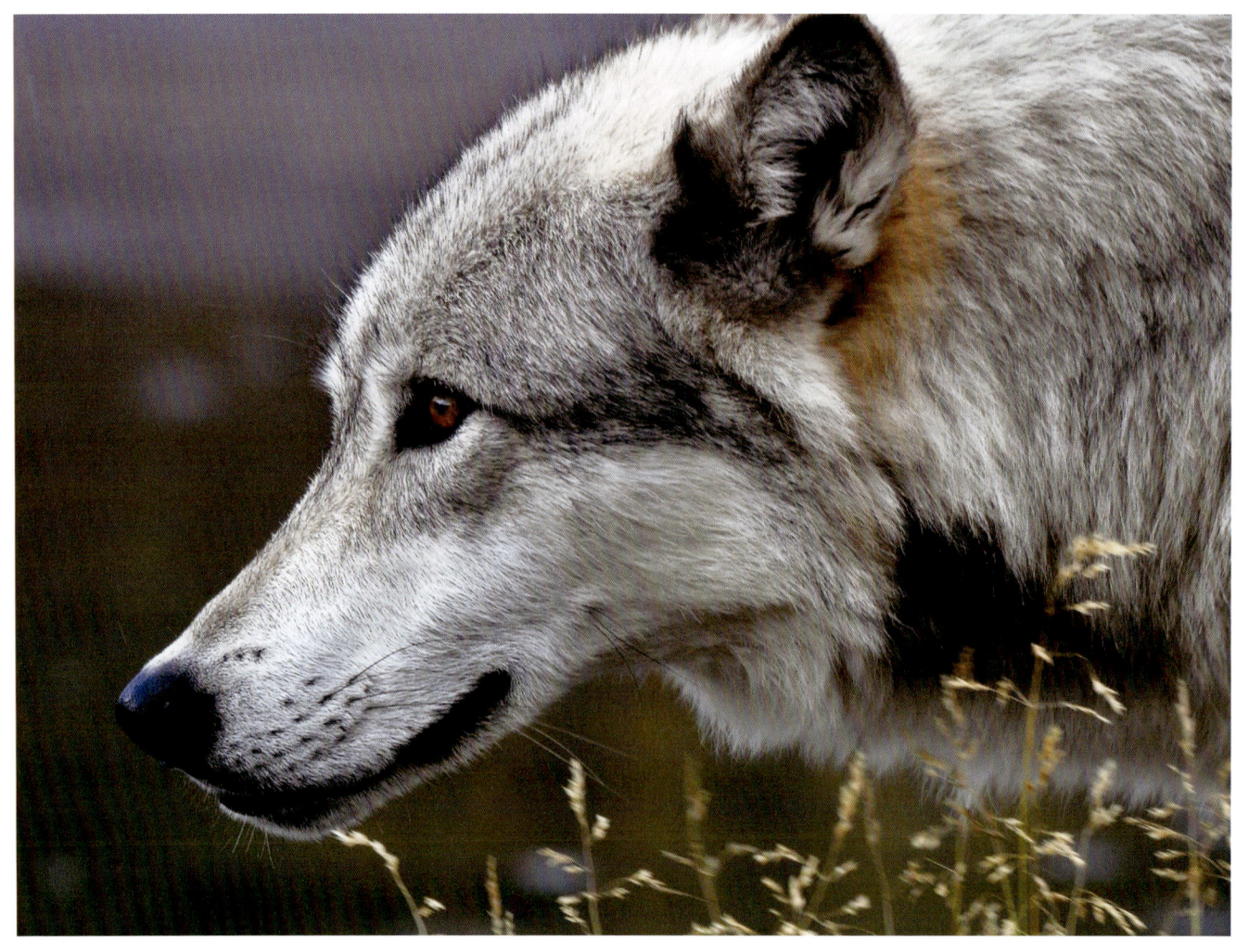

The sound of wolves howling amid Yellowstone's immense wildness fills me with an emptiness that is difficult to describe. They are mythical beings that are both enigmatic and elusive, and I find it impossible to fathom a world without them.

Above and opposite: Gray Wolf, Yellowstone NP /Nikon D300

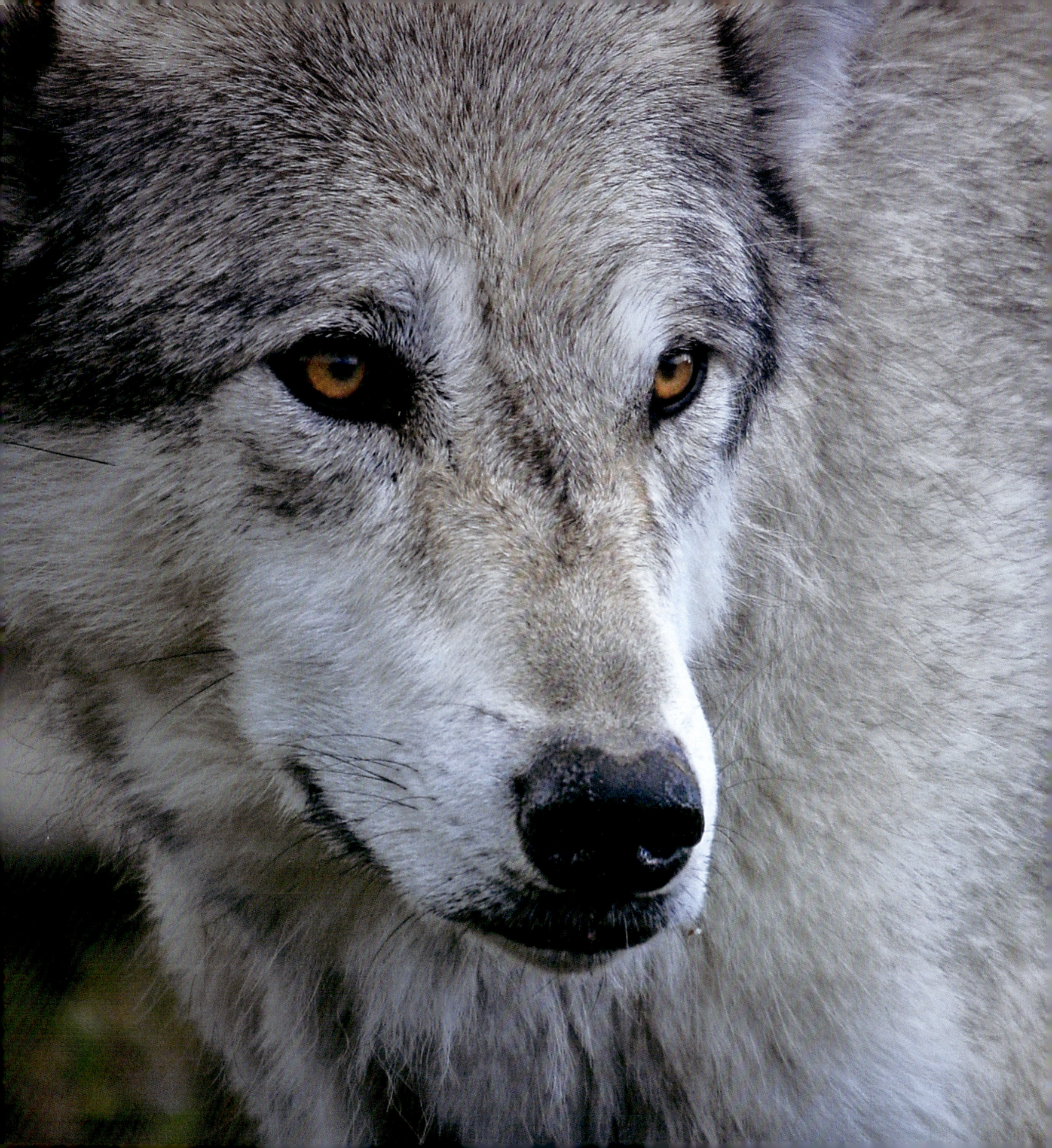

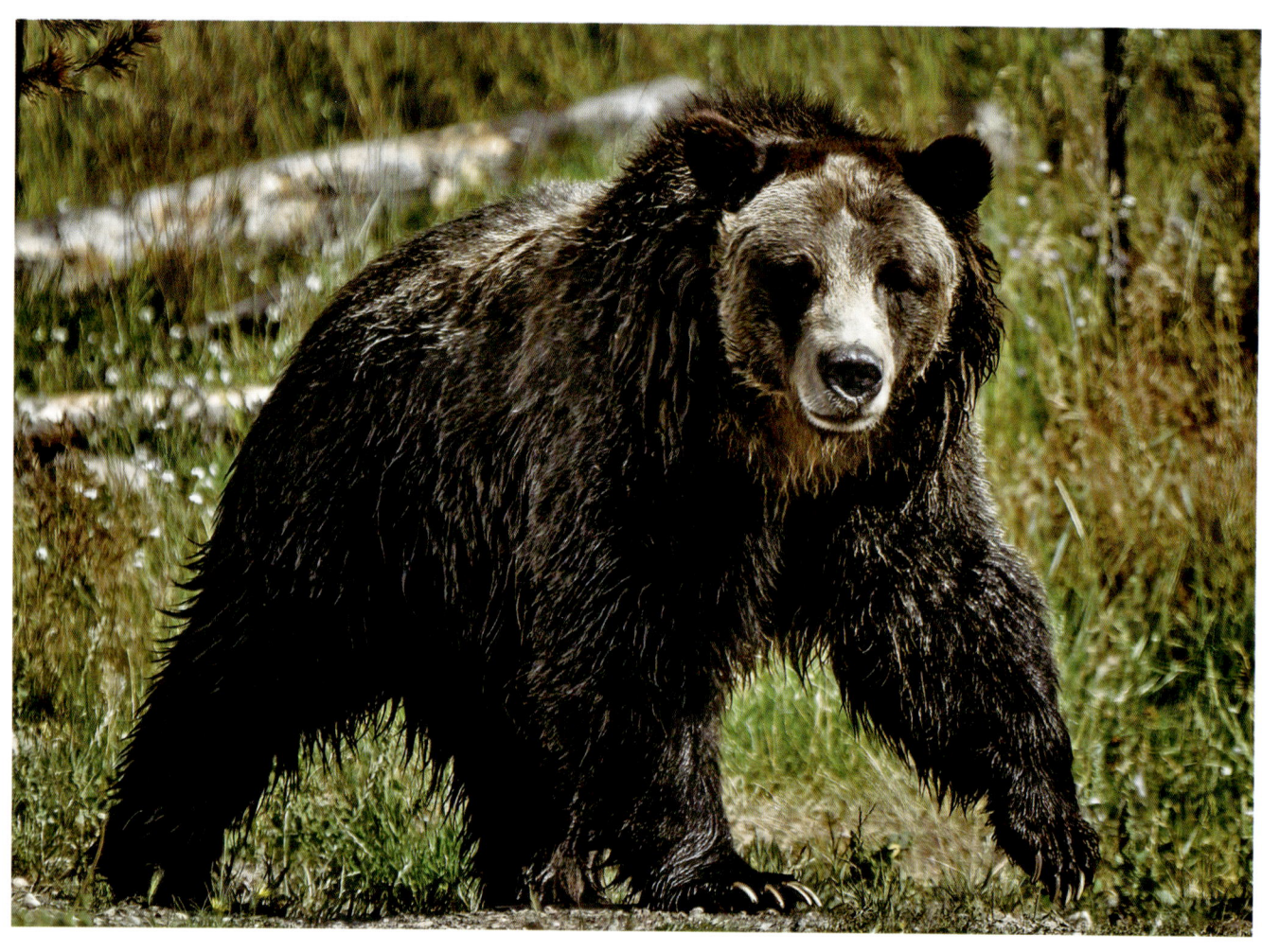

Yellowstone National Park is unlike any other place on this planet. Where deep canyons, towering waterfalls, majestic mountains, and wildlife abound. It is a place of such sheer grandeur that one can truly lose oneself in its imposing embrace.

Above: Grizzly Bear, Yellowstone NP /Nikon D300
Opposite: Lower Falls Canyon, Yellowstone NP /Nikon D300

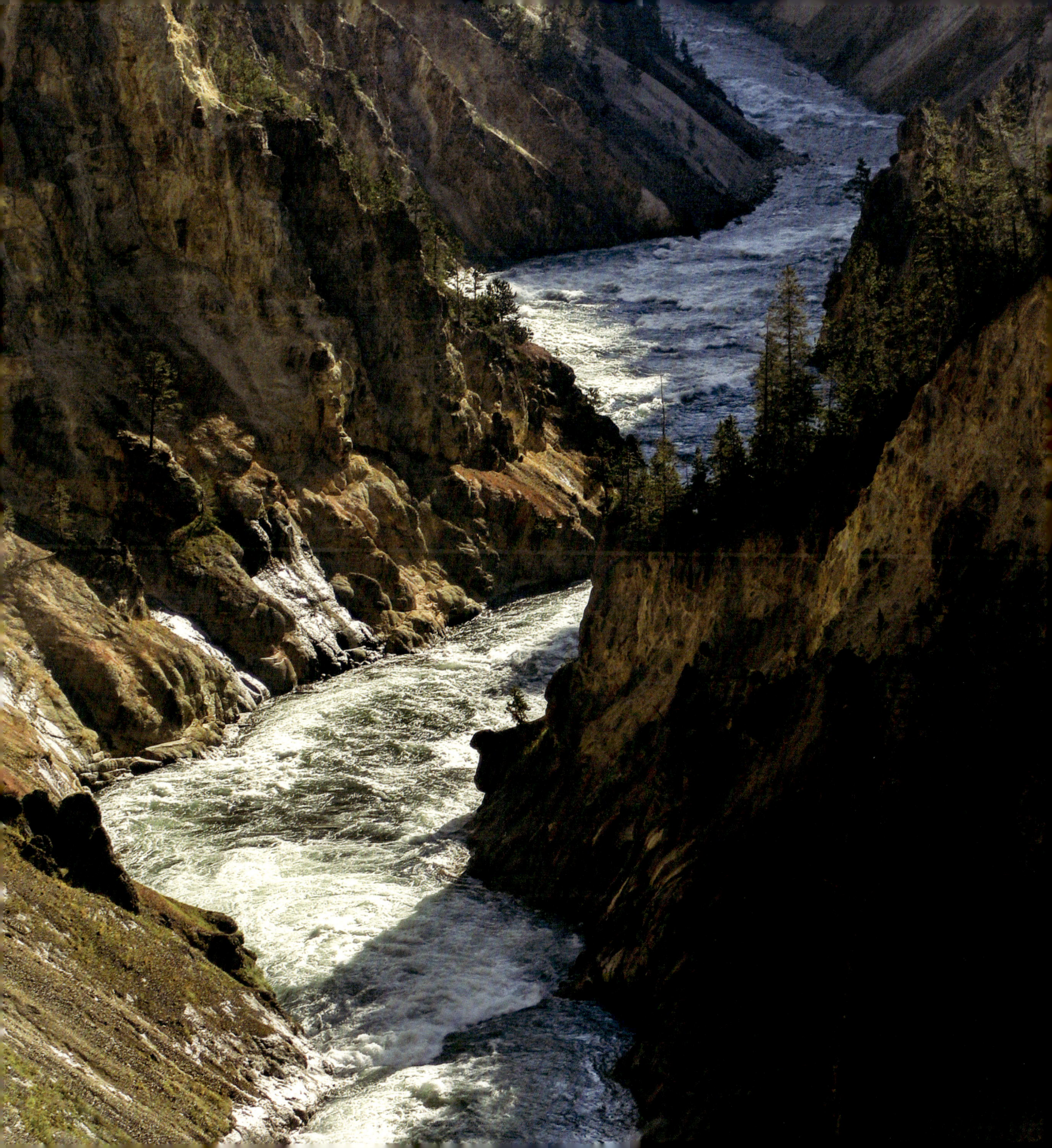

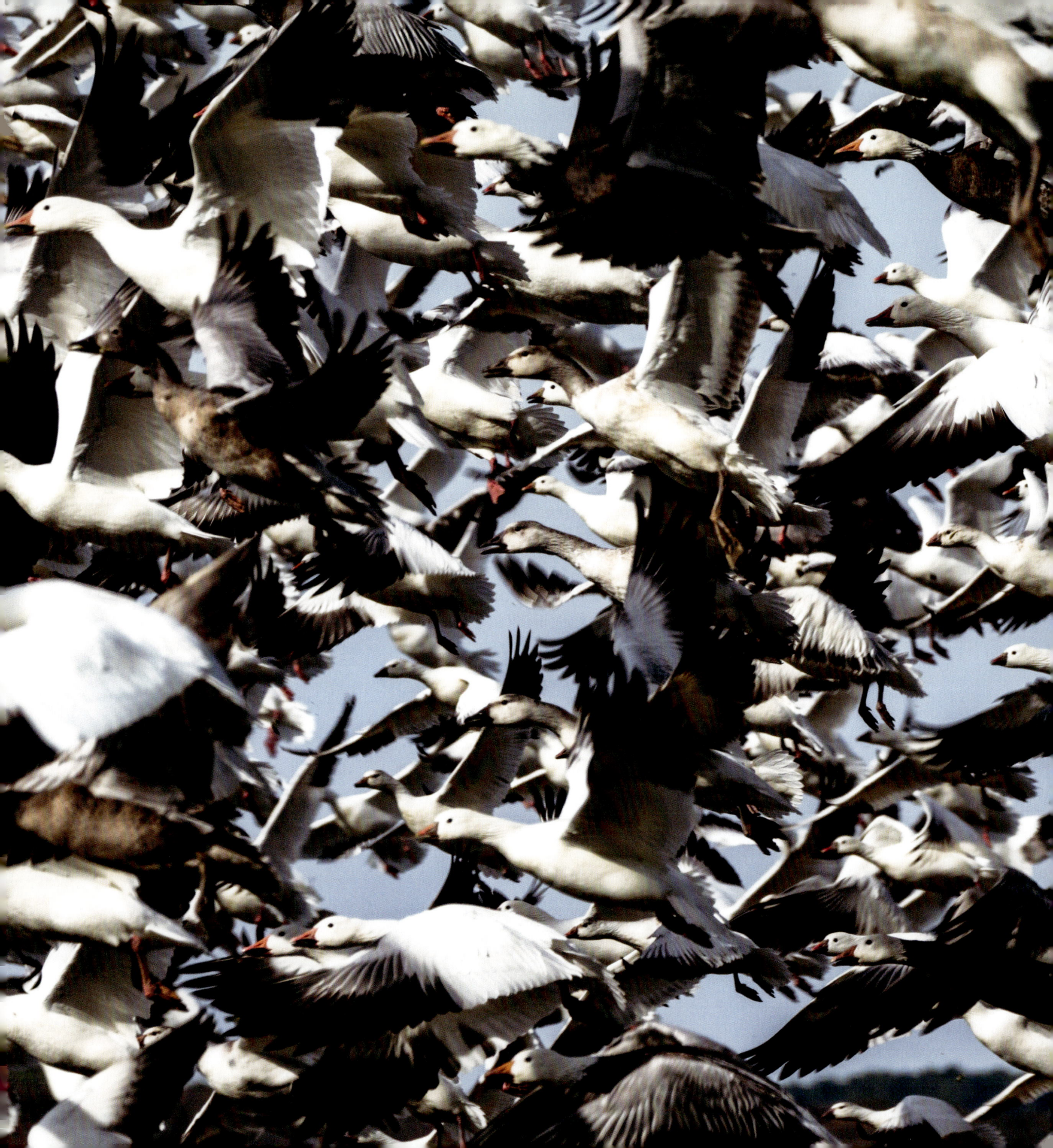

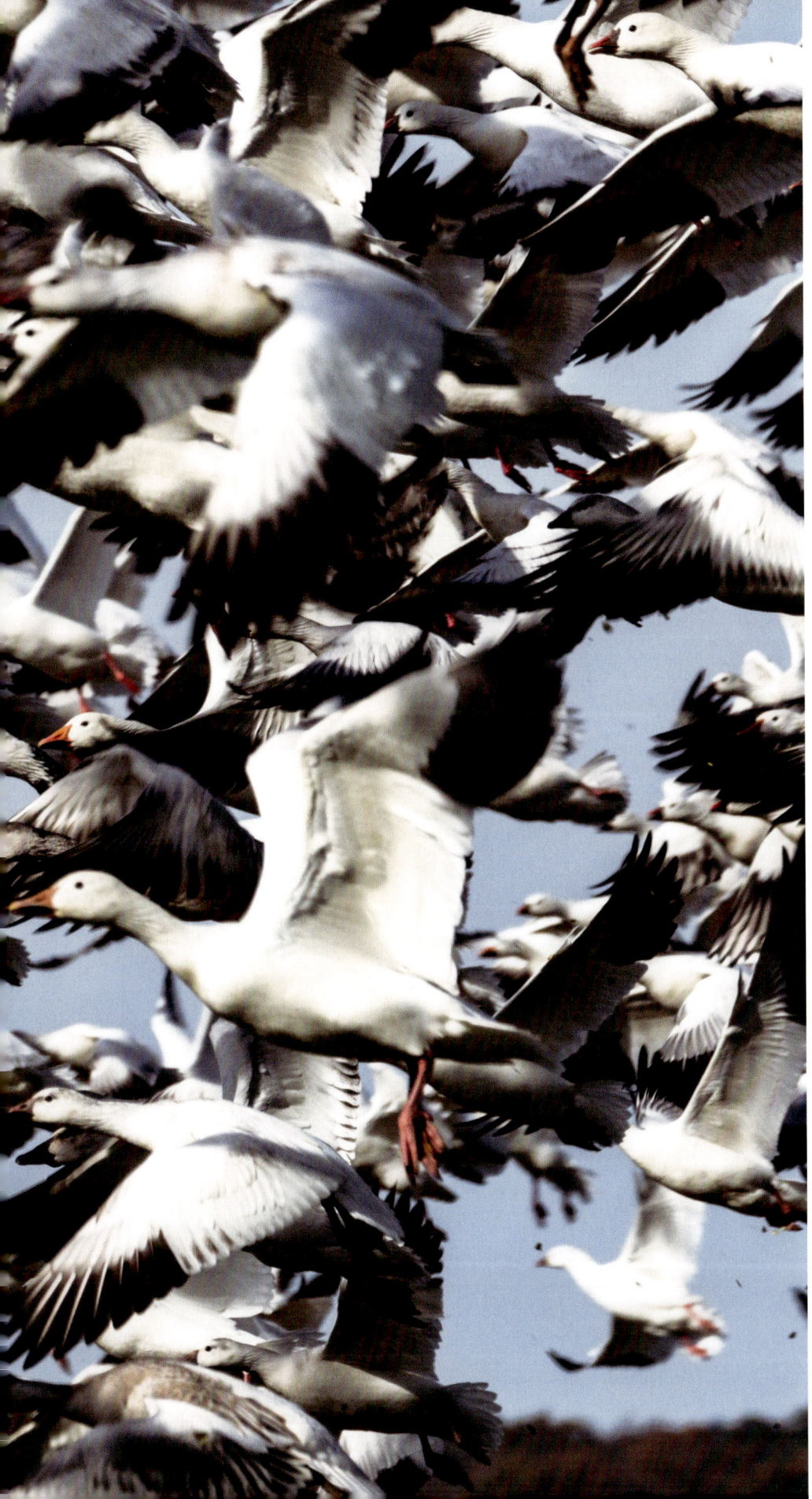

Their journey south has been long and arduous, but they have finally arrived safely at the refuge, their new home for the long winter months ahead. The sheer sound of tens of thousands of snow geese taking flight is a true revelation of nature that can easily overwhelm your senses and capture your imagination like never before.

Snow Geese, Texas /Nikon D810

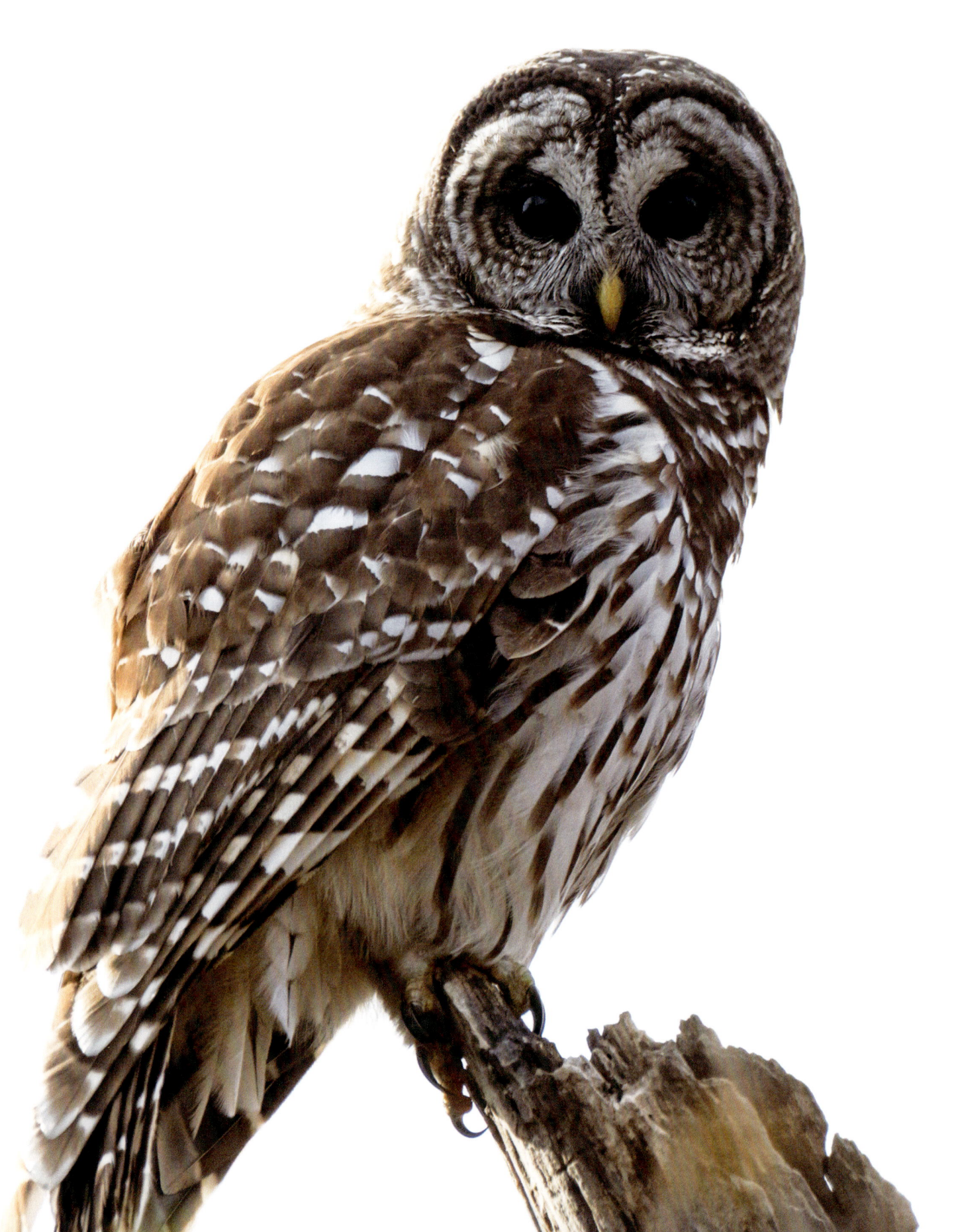

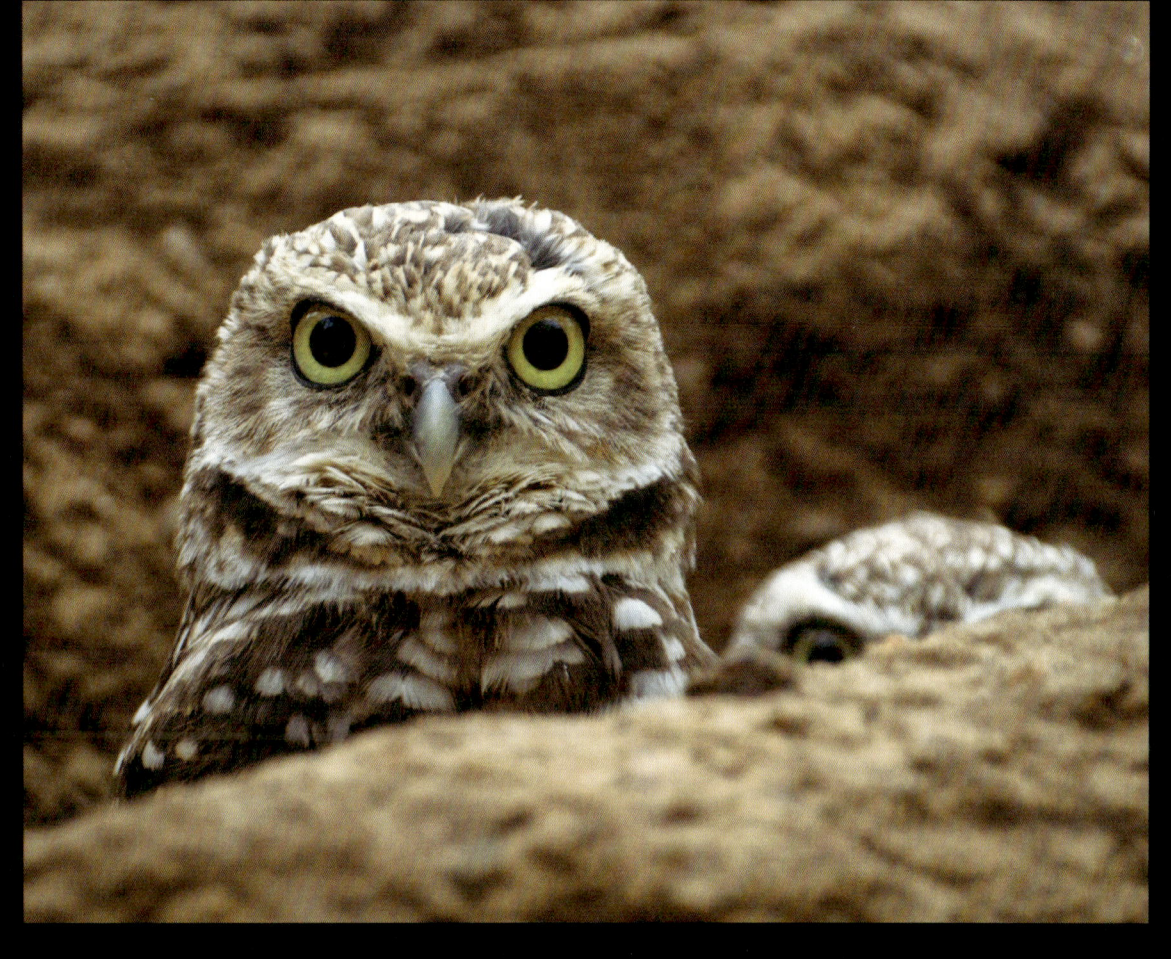

Seeing an owl instills a mysterious sensation within you. They are creatures of myth. They inhabit both dark woods and open meadows, and their callings can bring shivers to the soul and curiosity to the mind.

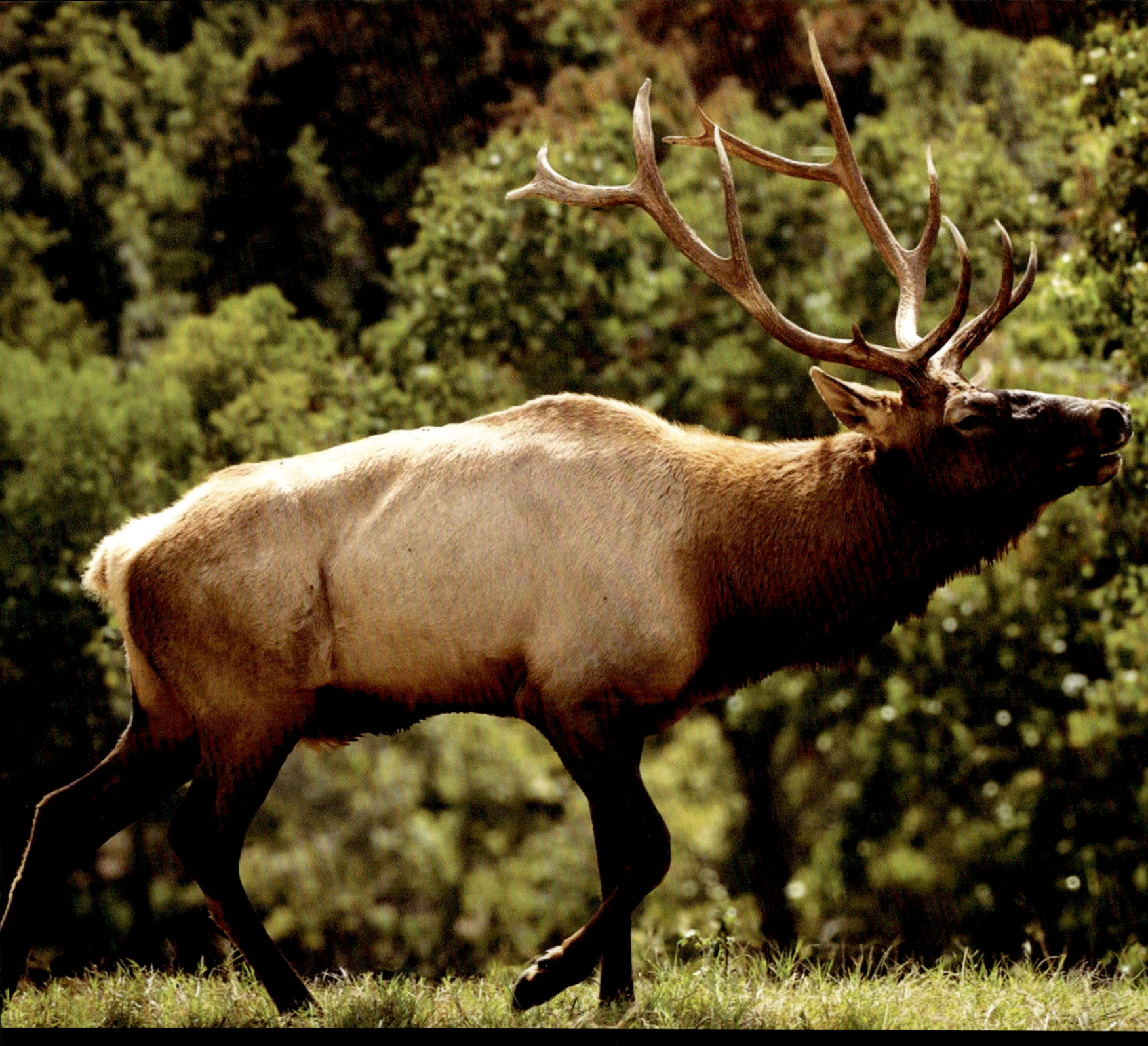

The days are getting shorter, and the desire to mate is growing stronger. The male elk, with magnificent antlers, bugles his tune throughout the park, ready to take on all comers.

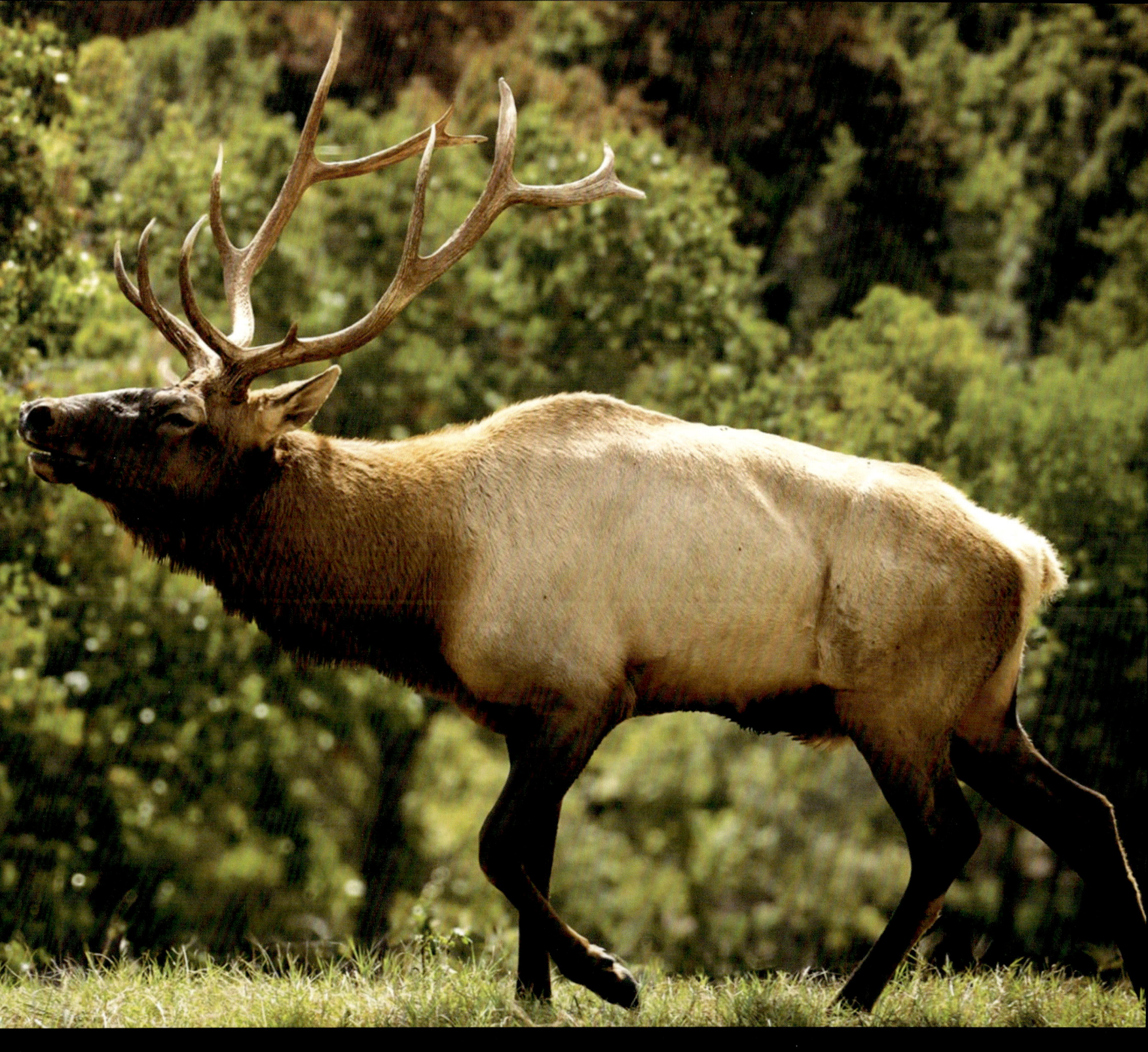

American Elk (mirrored image), Yellowstone NP /Nikon D300

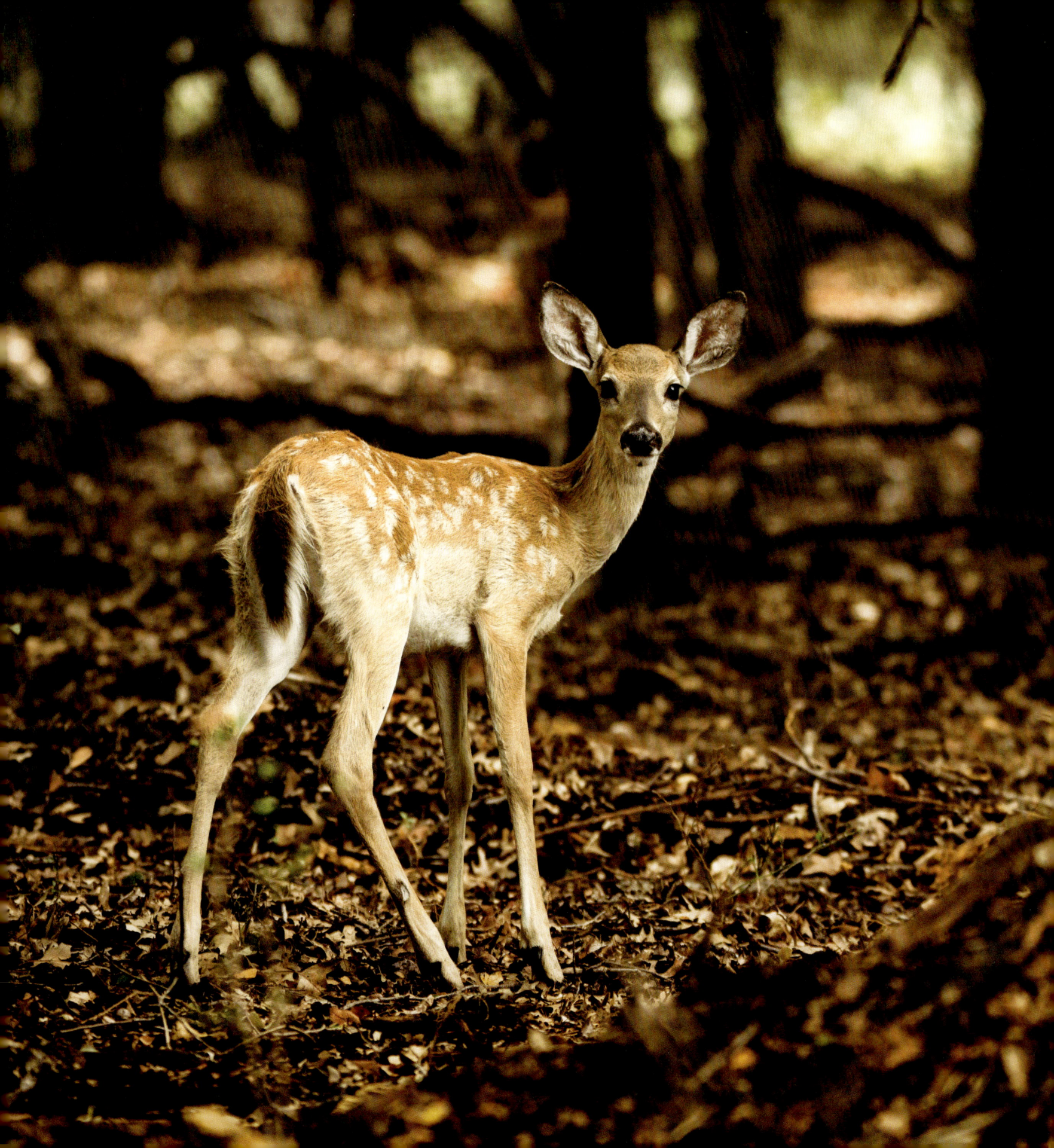

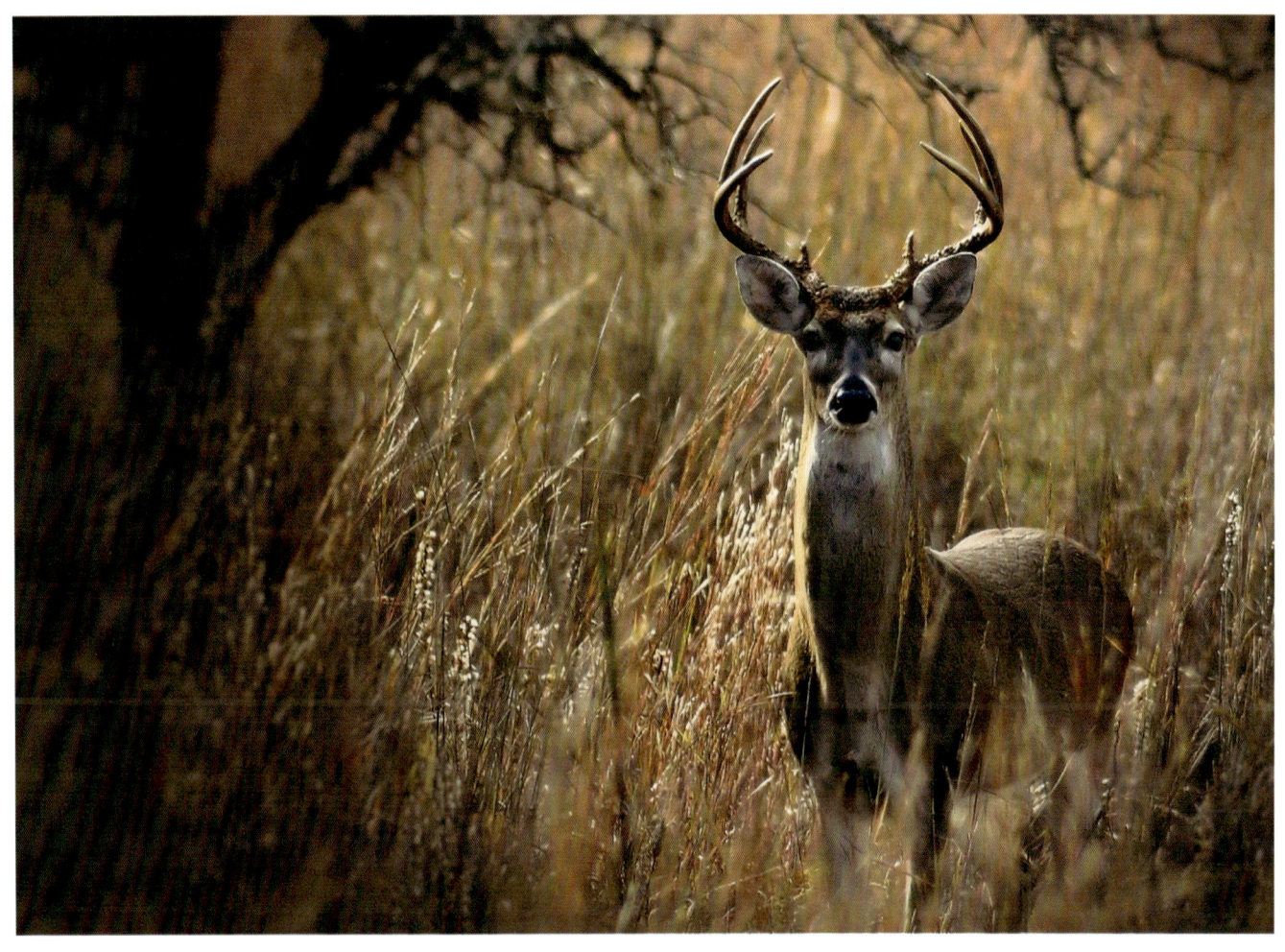

My excursions into the woods would never be complete unless I saw a stoic white—tailed deer alerting the world to my presence in a tall grass meadow. Knowing they are there comforts me, even when I can't see them through the thick forest veil that surrounds me.

Above and opposite: White-Tailed Deer, Texas /Nikon D810

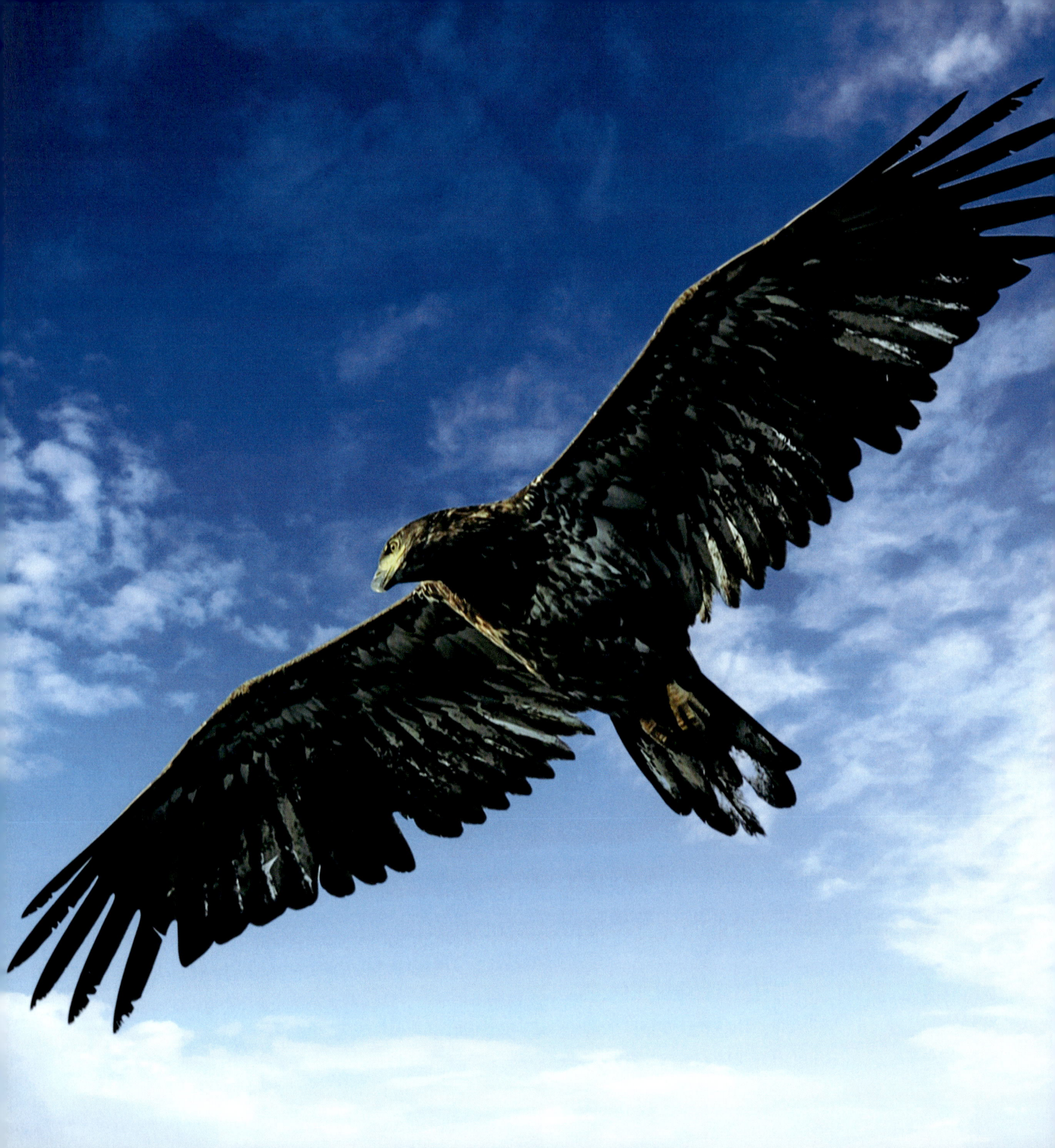

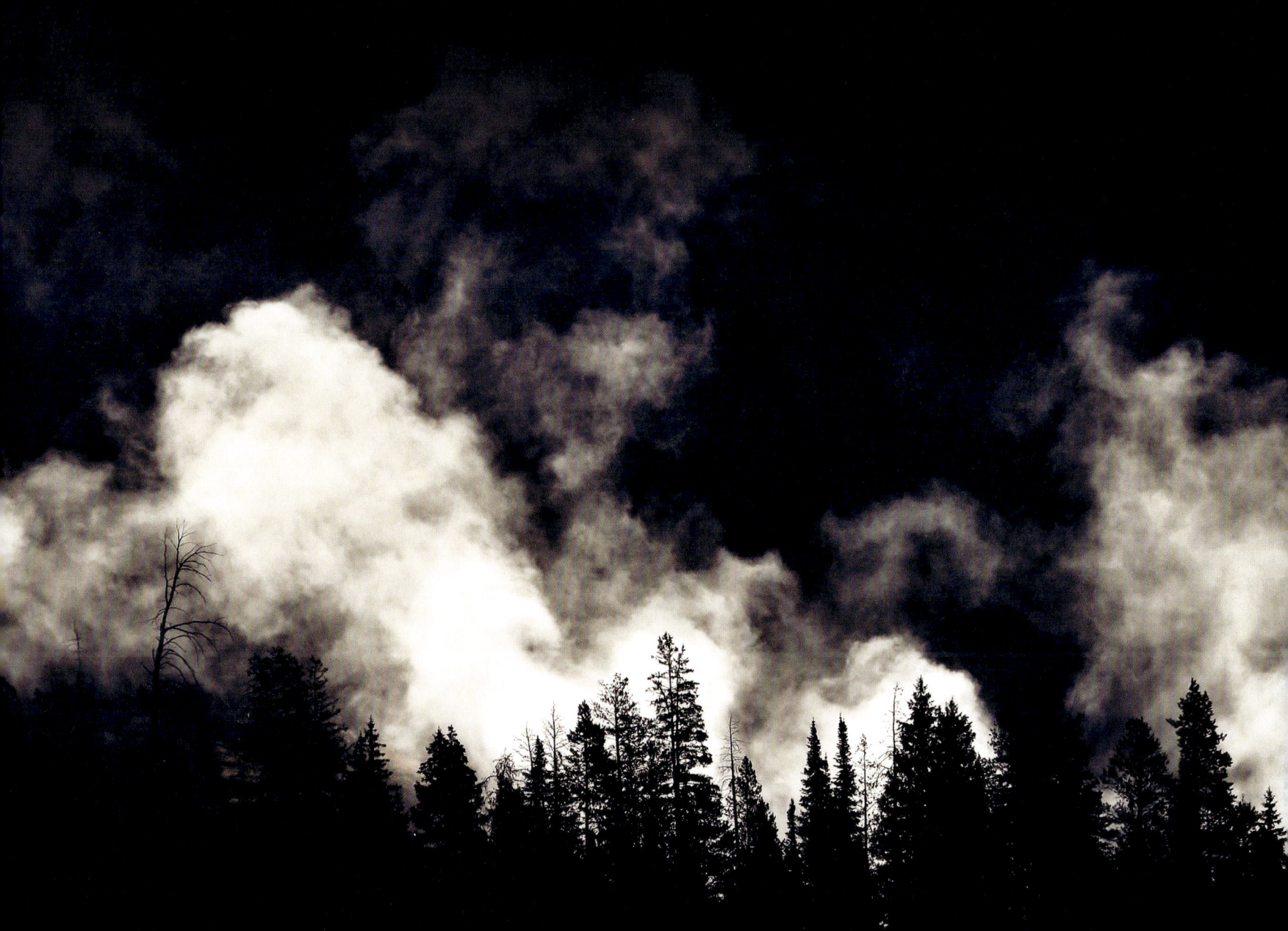

A young bald eagle soars high above, catching a glimpse of the world that I've always wanted to see, and what a magnificent vista that must be in Yellowstone. Our time together was brief, as is the case with most things in nature, but I can only hope that his wings took him far and wide, to even more amazing places than I could ever dream.

Above: Smoldering Geysers, Yellowstone NP / Nikon D300
Opposite: Juvenile Bald Eagle, Yellowstone NP / Nikon D300

The prairie plains seemed to stretch on forever as I drove down a rural country road. As I pulled over to reorient myself, I had the distinct feeling I was being watched, and who should appear but an inquisitive rabbit who was . . . well, all ears.

Opposite: Black-Tailed Jackrabbit, Oklahoma /Nikon D600

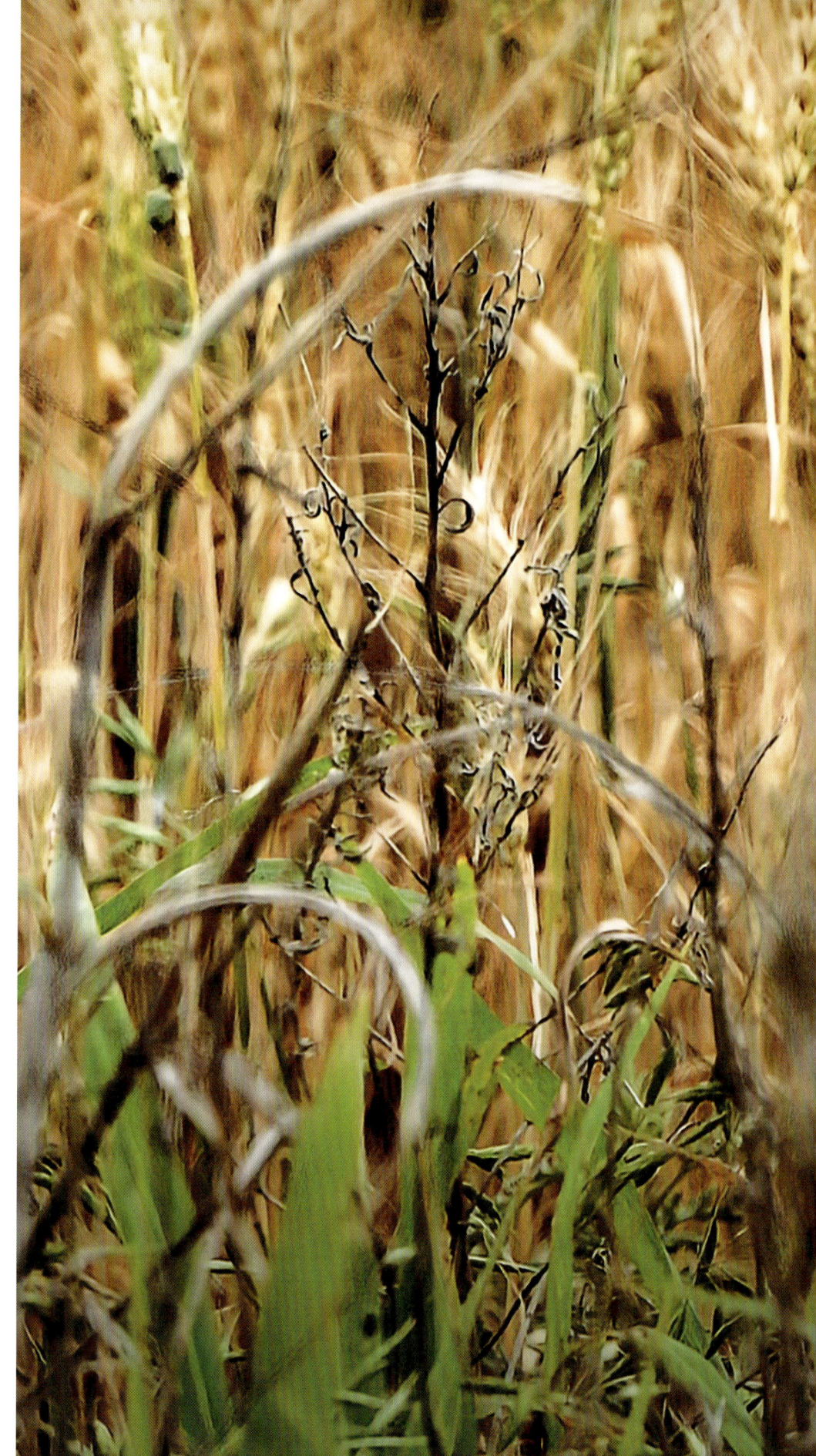

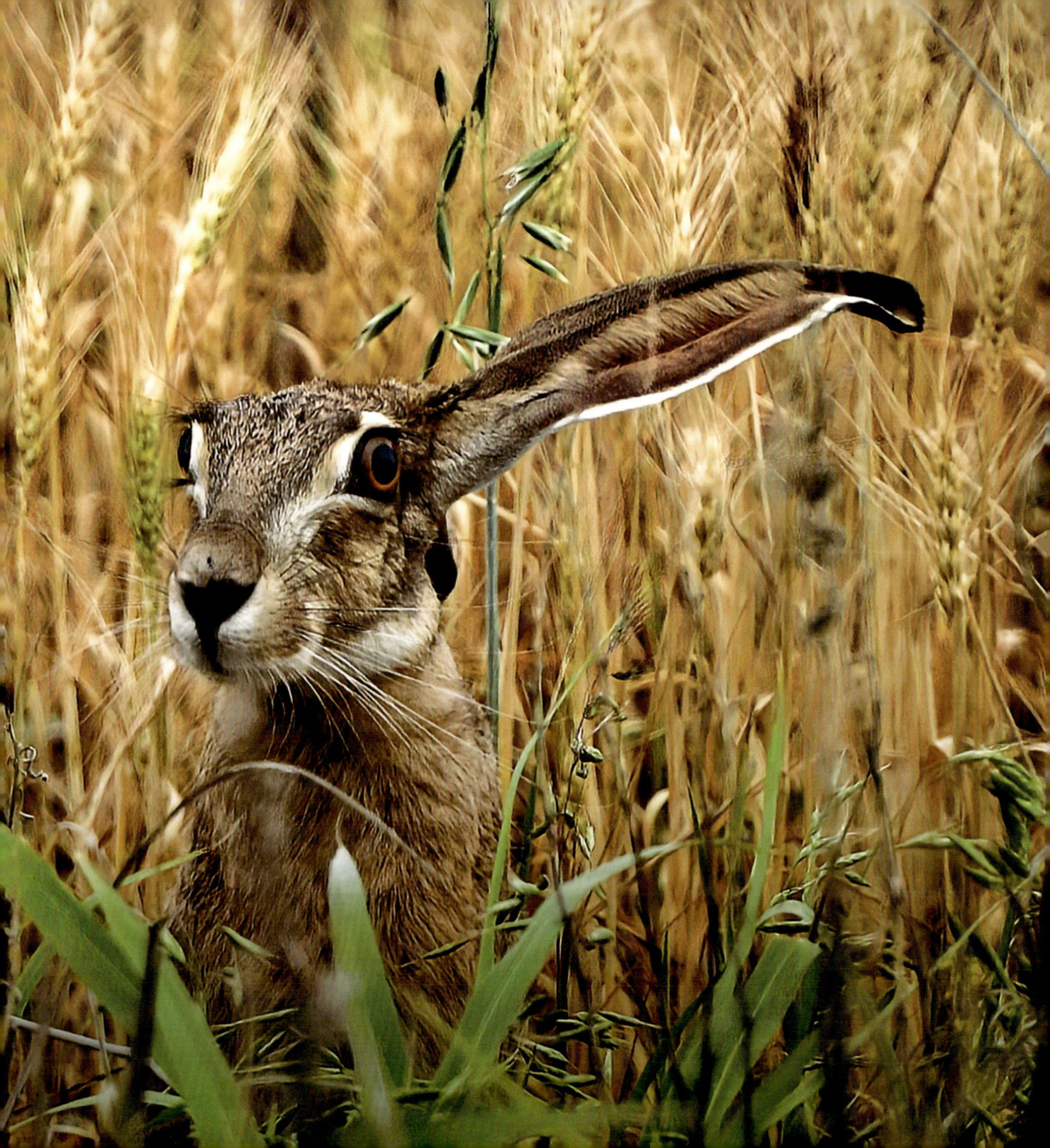

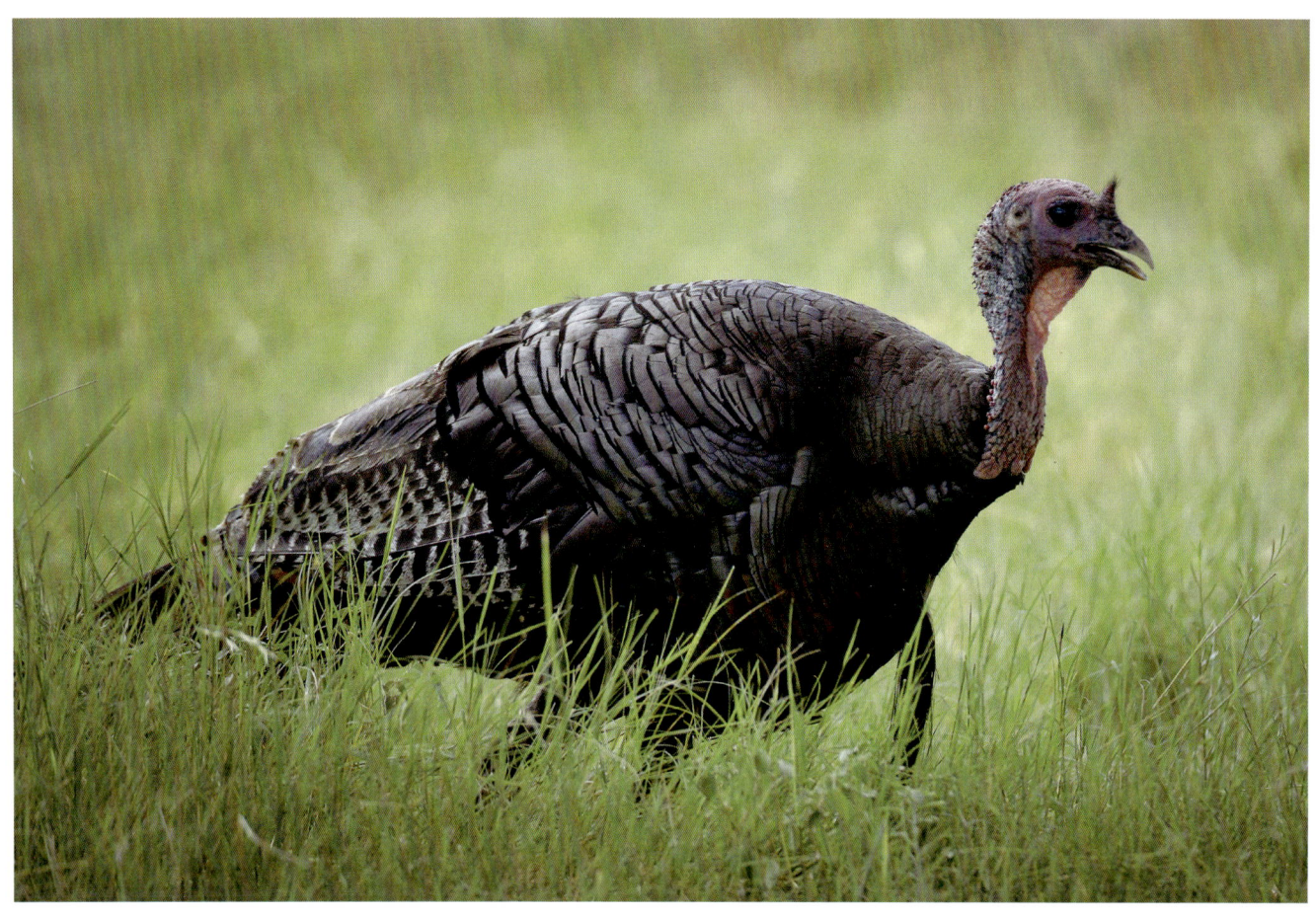

Two American bird species were in competition to be the symbol of American freedom. Both are worthy opponents, but in the end the bald eagle came out victorious, and thankfully so, as nothing is more striking to see in the wild than this iconic bird of prey.

Above: Turkey, Texas /Nikon D600
Opposite: American Bald Eagle, Texas /Nikon D300

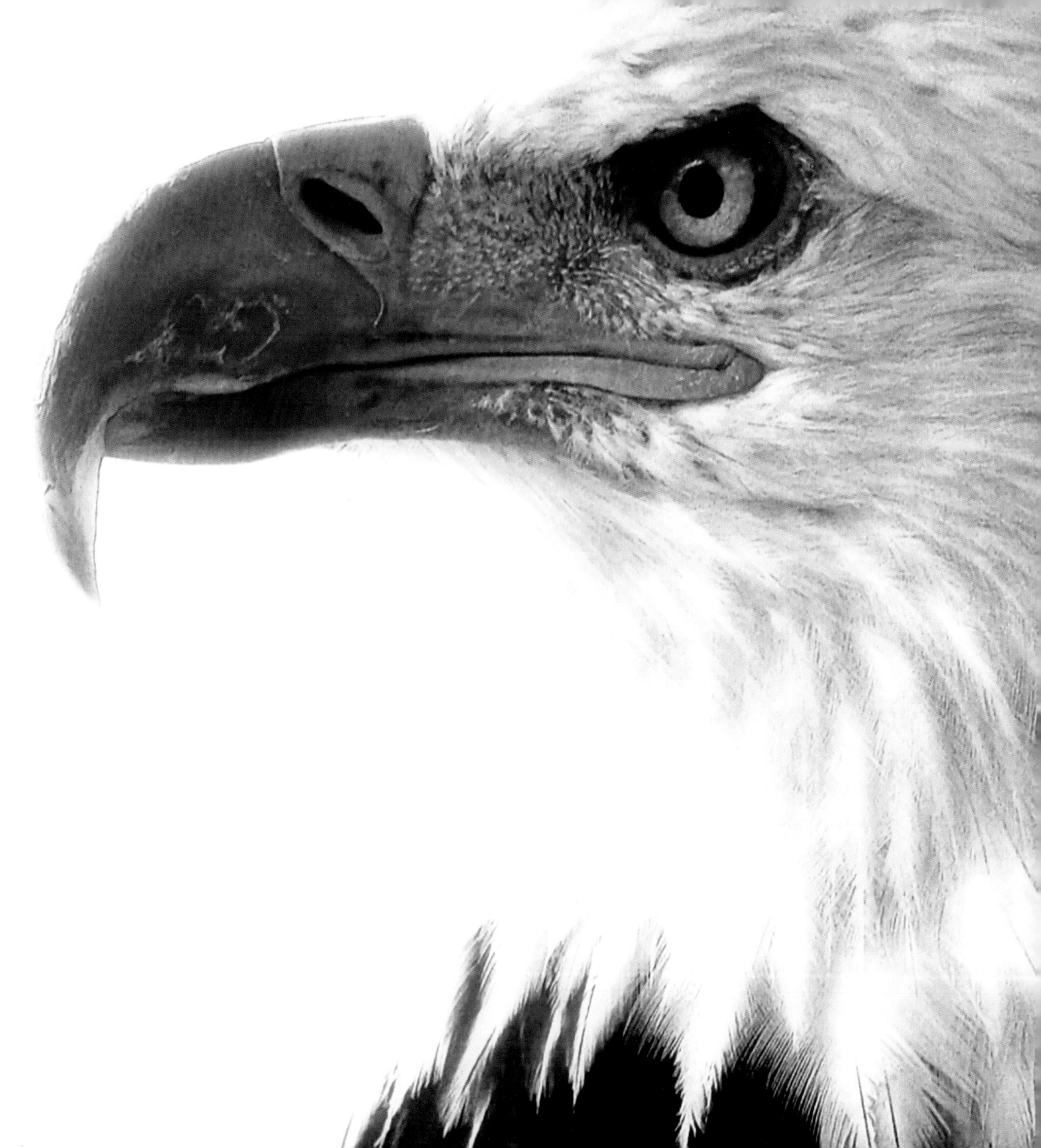

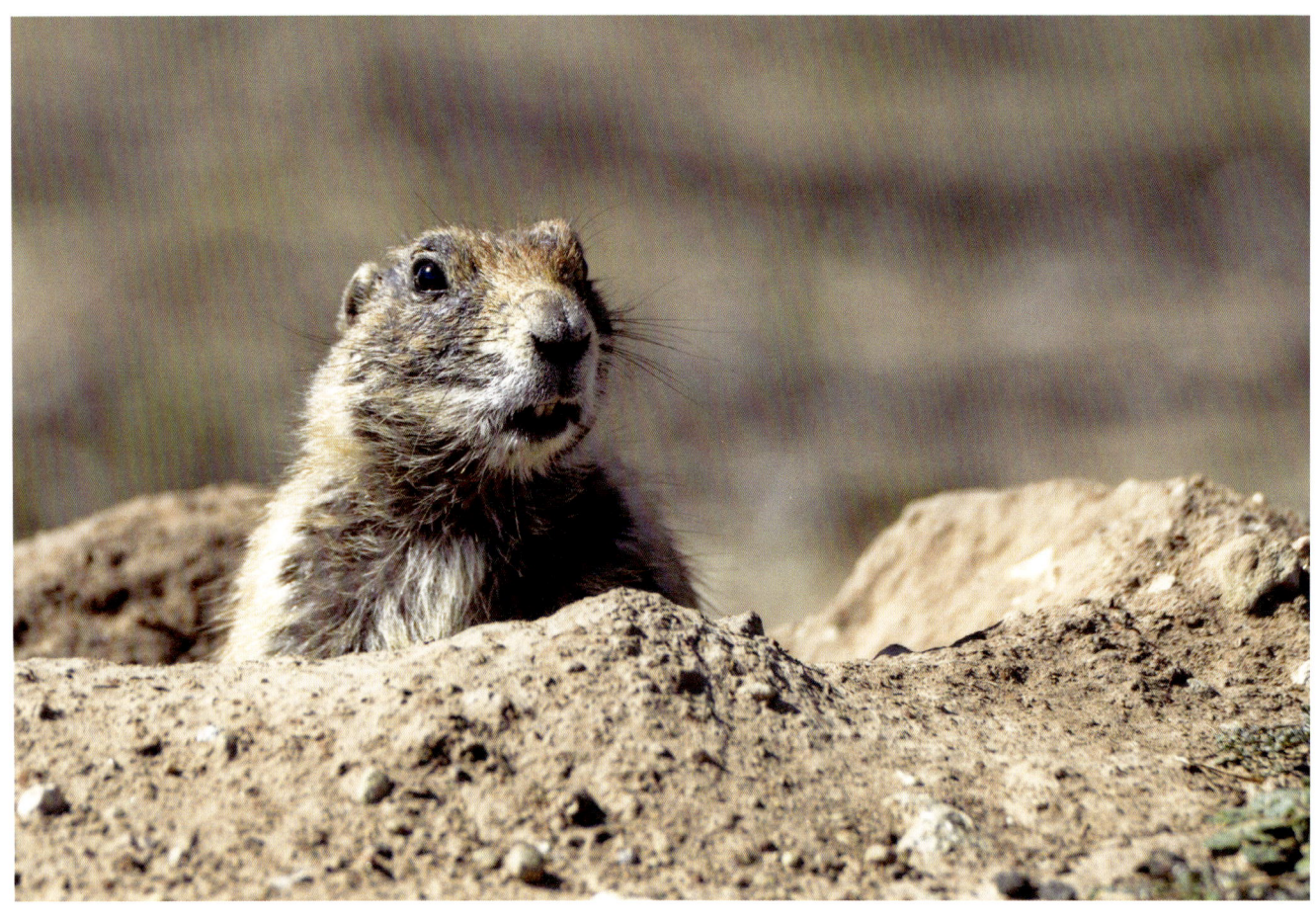

Given the enormous threat that predators pose to the prairie dog town, sentinels remain on high alert for any signs of danger that could potentially threaten the tranquility and peace of their windswept prairieland paradise.

Above: Black-Tailed Prairie Dog, Texas /Nikon D810
Opposite: Western Diamondback, Texas /Nikon D300

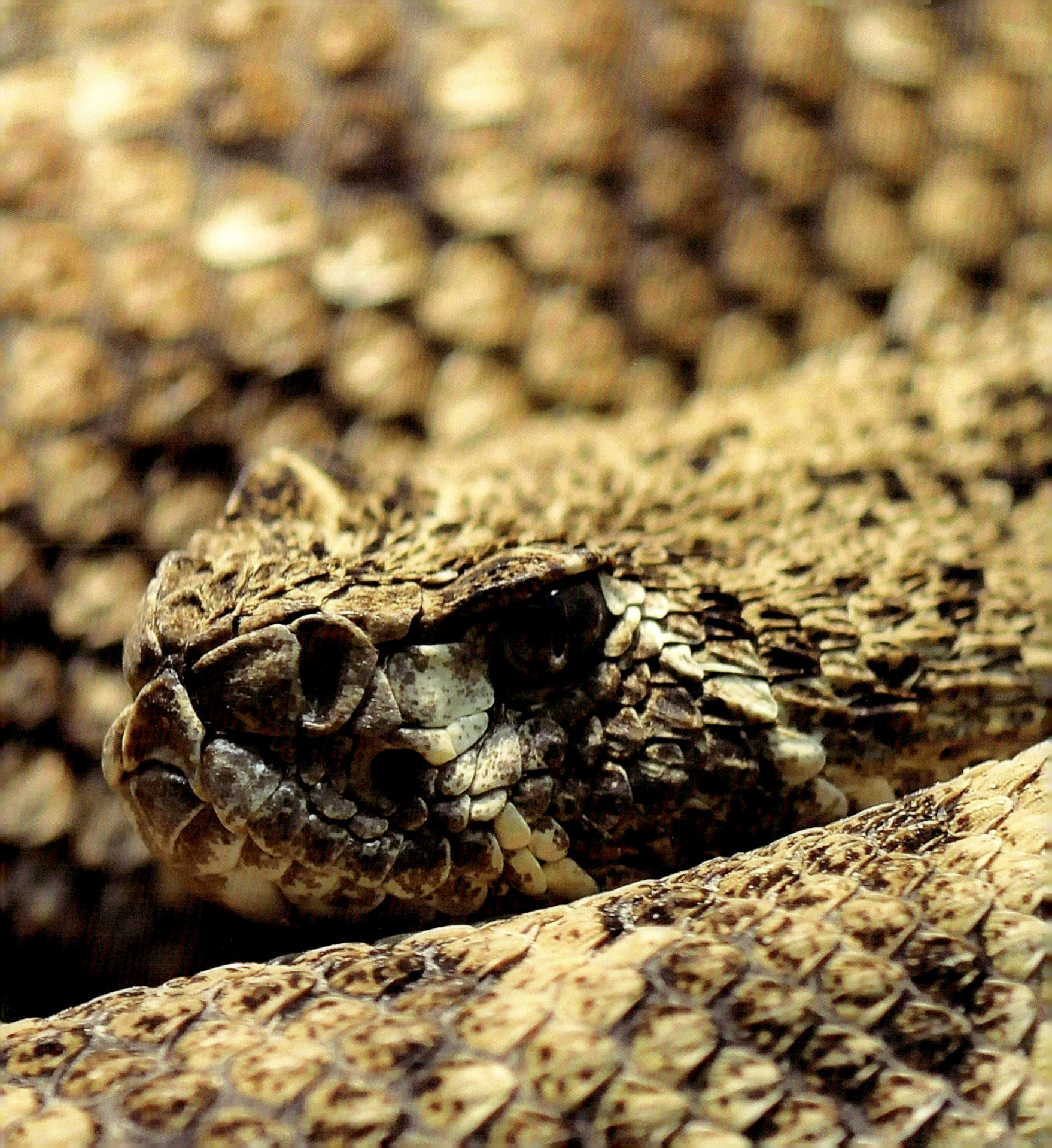

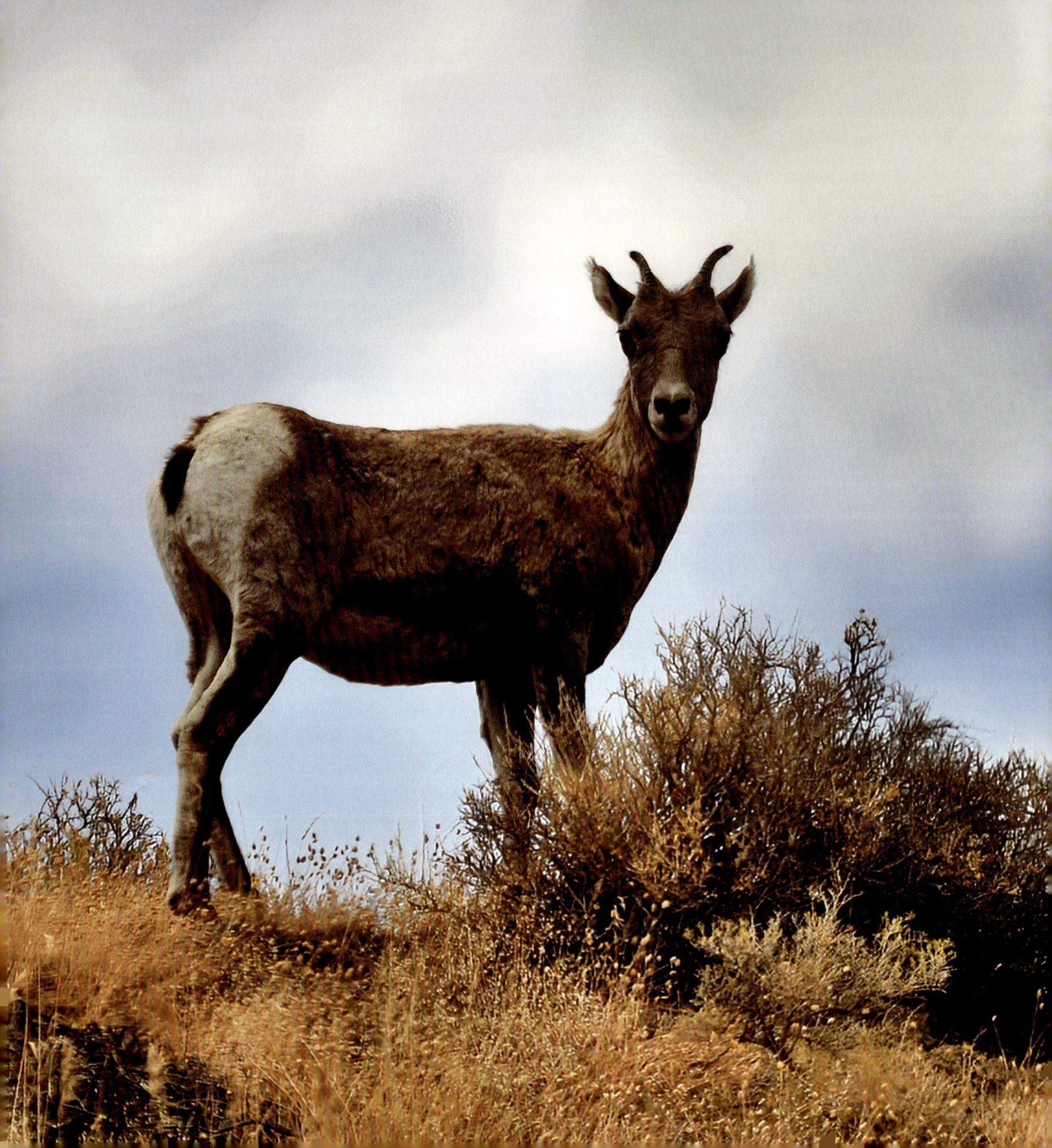

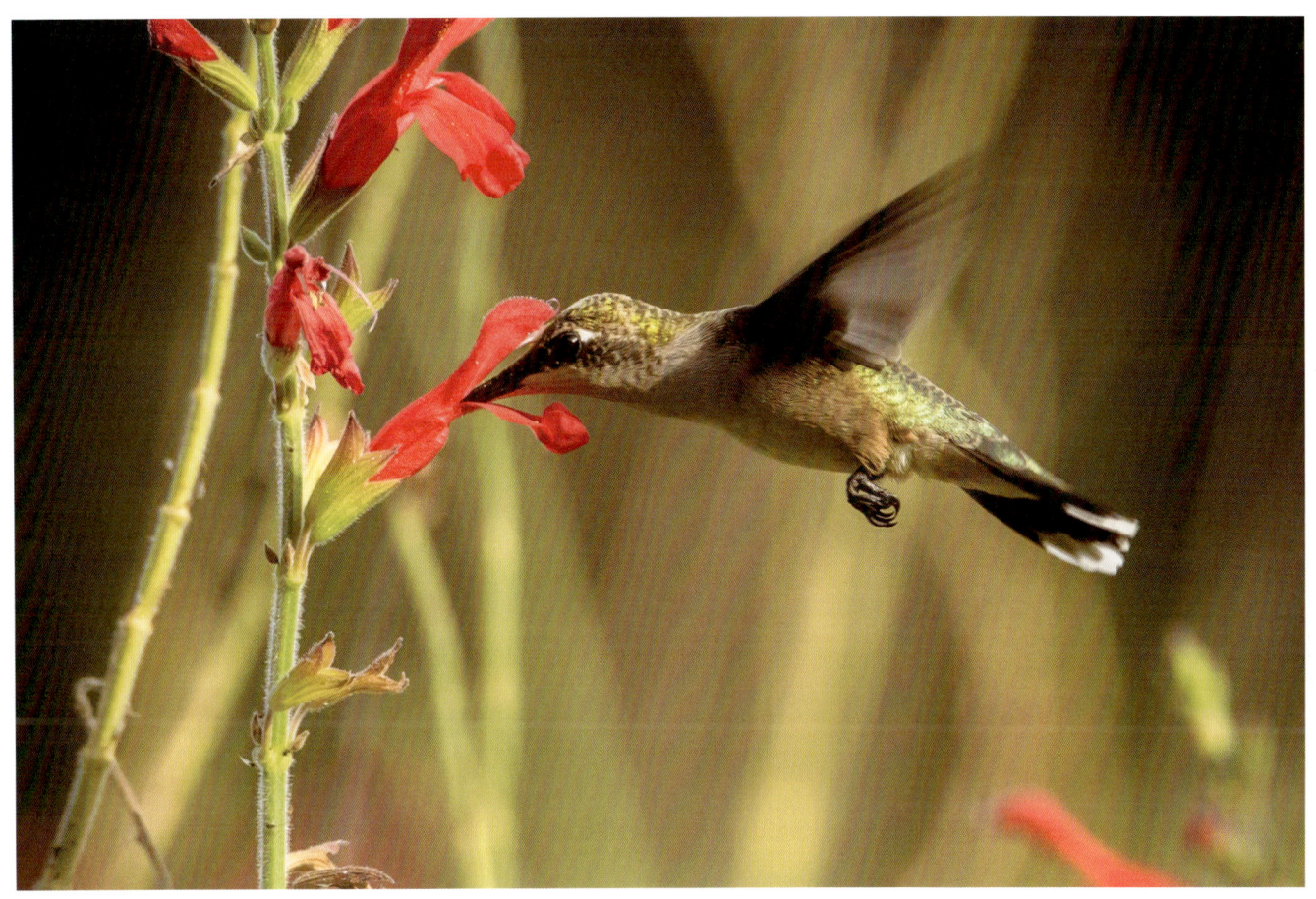

A *female bighorn sheep seeks refuge on a high ridge in Yellowstone, watching my every move as she scales the steep hills with scarcely a rest in between. Her climbing skill is incredible, and keeping up with her is virtually impossible.*

Above: Hummingbird, Texas /Nikon D300
Opposite: Bighorn Sheep, Yellowstone NP /Nikon D300

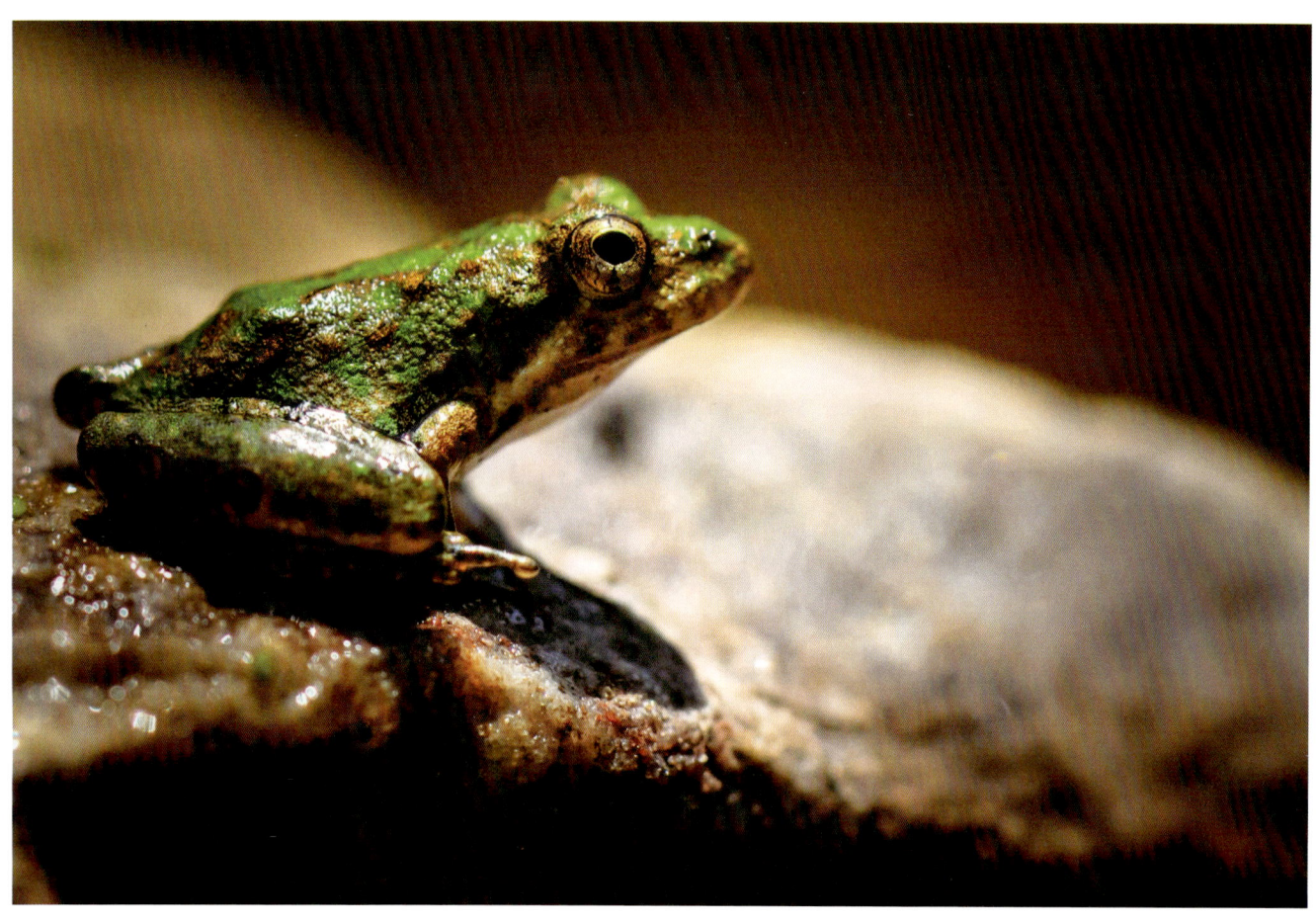

Hiking along a swampy trail that runs along the Texas-Louisiana border always refreshes my soul. The earth is always wet, the water a deep brownish hue, and life just seems to swirl all around me. From the little cricket frog to the ancient snapping turtle, there is so much to see in this place that I find myself utterly lost in time, if only for a short while.

Above: Blanchard's Cricket Frog, Texas /Nikon D600
Opposite: Common Snapping Turtle, Texas /Nikon D810

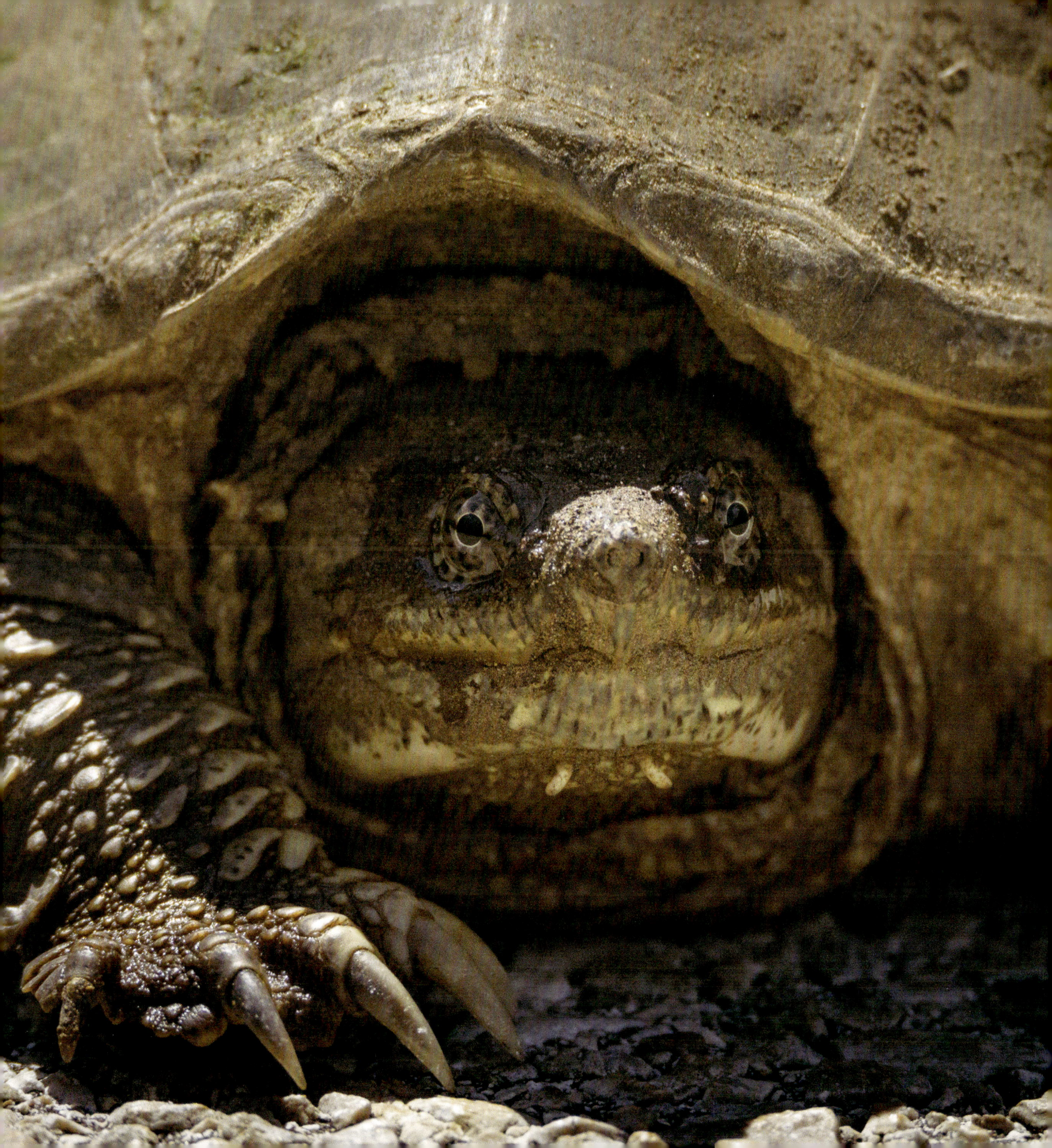

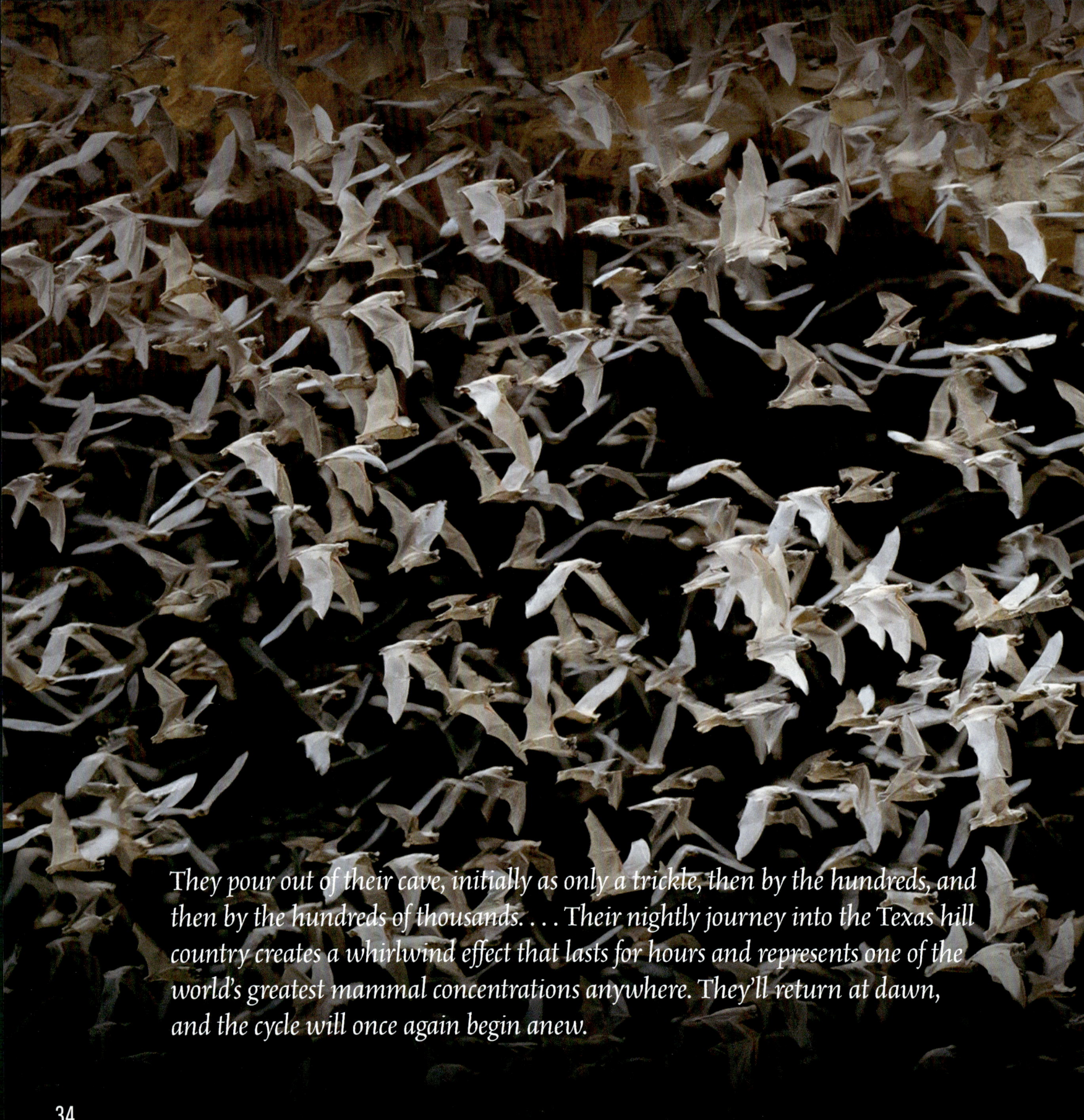

They pour out of their cave, initially as only a trickle, then by the hundreds, and then by the hundreds of thousands. . . . Their nightly journey into the Texas hill country creates a whirlwind effect that lasts for hours and represents one of the world's greatest mammal concentrations anywhere. They'll return at dawn, and the cycle will once again begin anew.

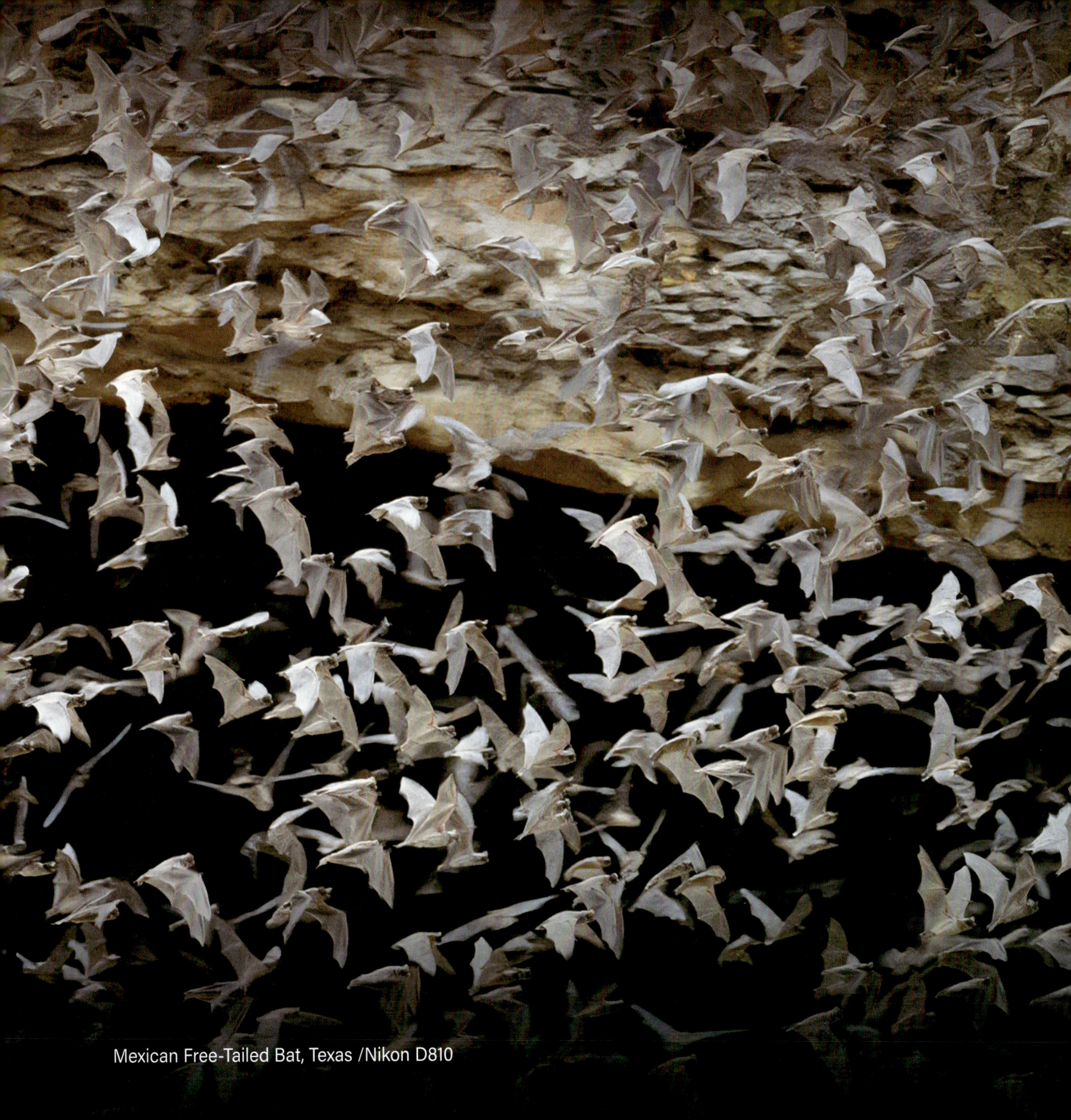

Mexican Free-Tailed Bat, Texas / Nikon D810

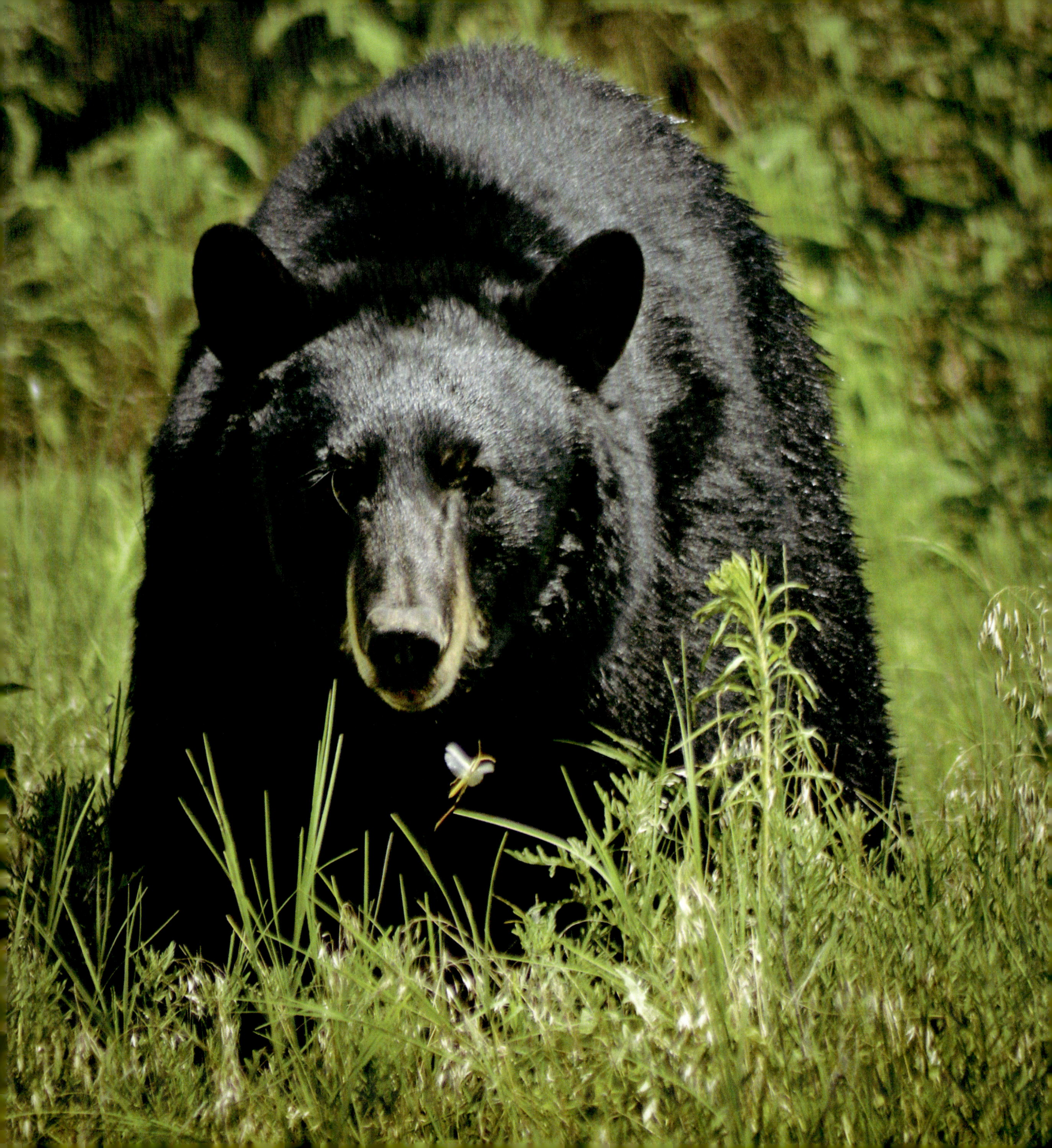

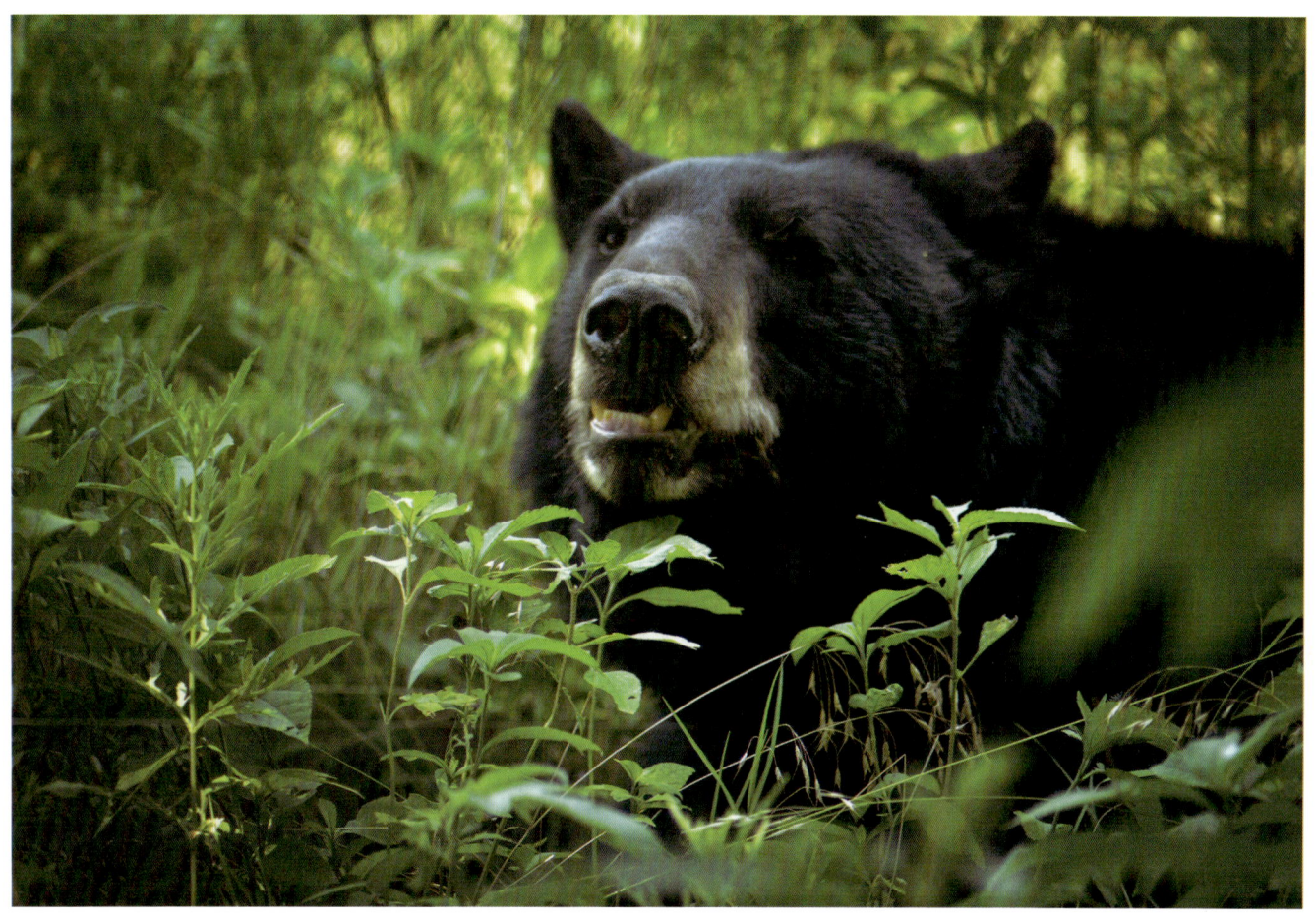

Deep within the Ouachita Mountains of western Arkansas, a curious black bear decided to pay my campsite a special visit to say hello. Being caught off guard, my initial reactions were probably somewhat unwelcoming, to say the least, but I did seem to have the wherewithal to take a few images of our little encounter before he departed to whereabouts unknown.

Above and opposite: American Black Bear, Arkansas /Nikon D600

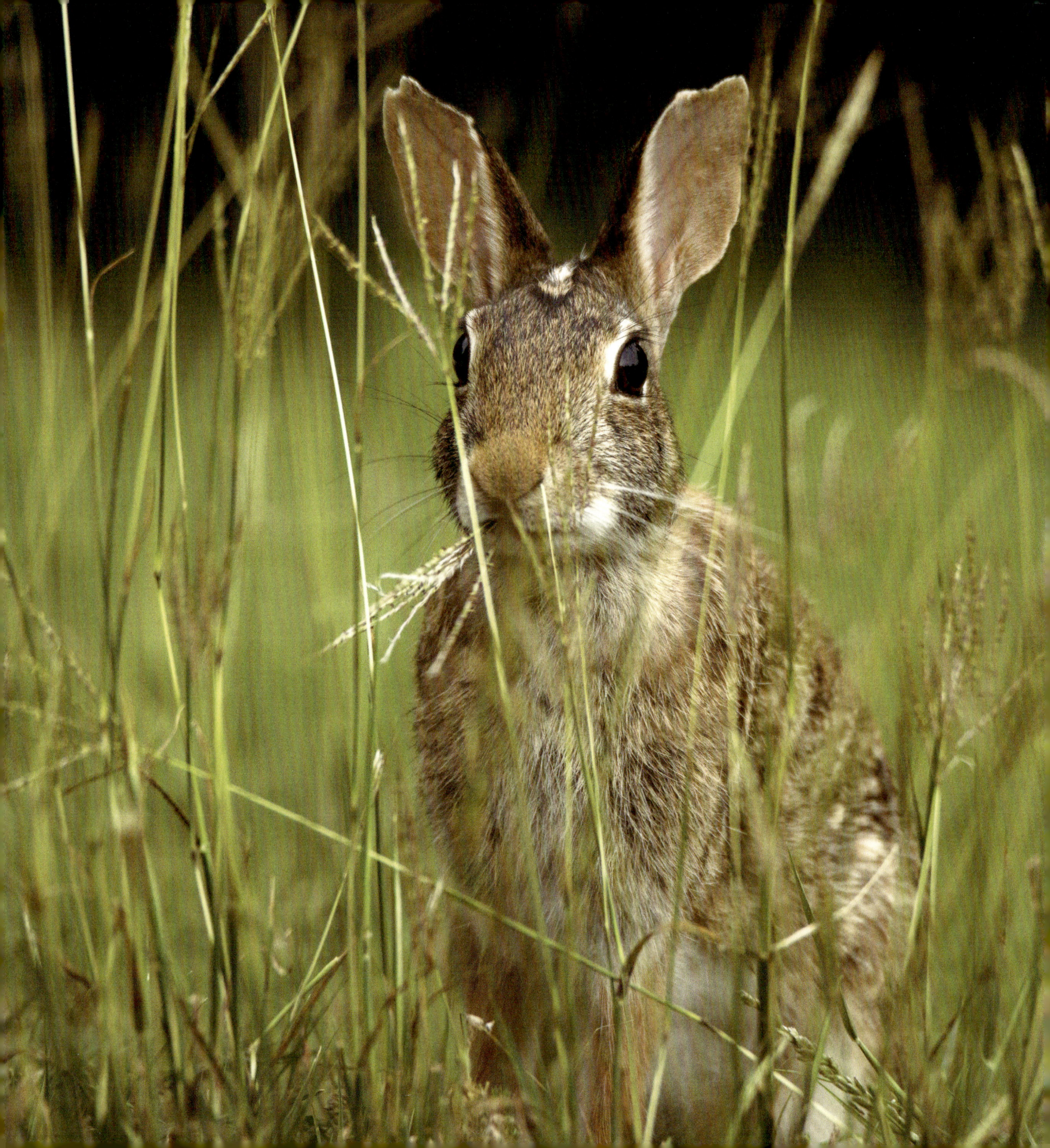

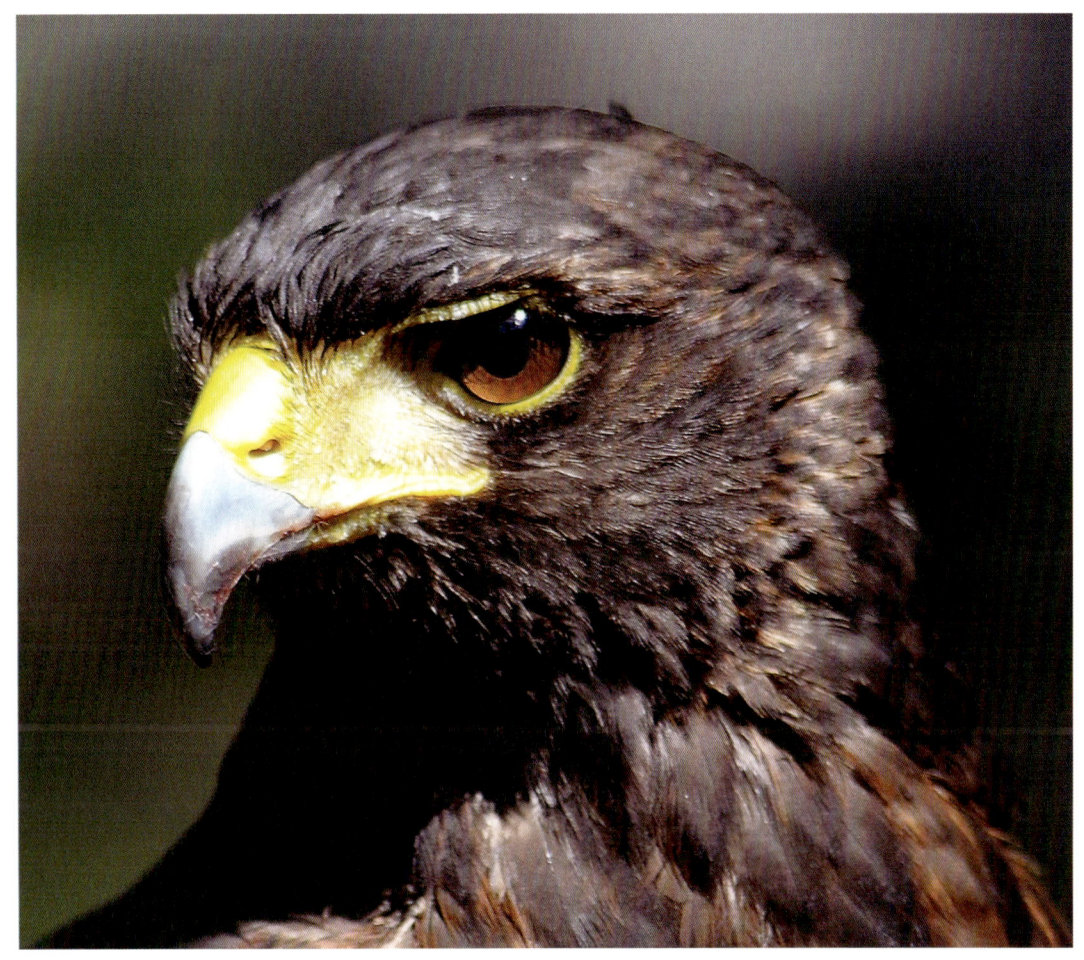

Many factors influence the survival of wild animals in nature, but none is more crucial than their staying vigilant—whether to detect danger or to seize an opportunity for prey. Raptors, with their remarkable bird's—eye view of the world, seem to hold a distinct advantage. Yet in the perpetual cycle of life, even their success is never assured.

Above: Harris Hawk, Texas /Nikon D300
Opposite: Cottontail Rabbit, Texas /Nikon D810

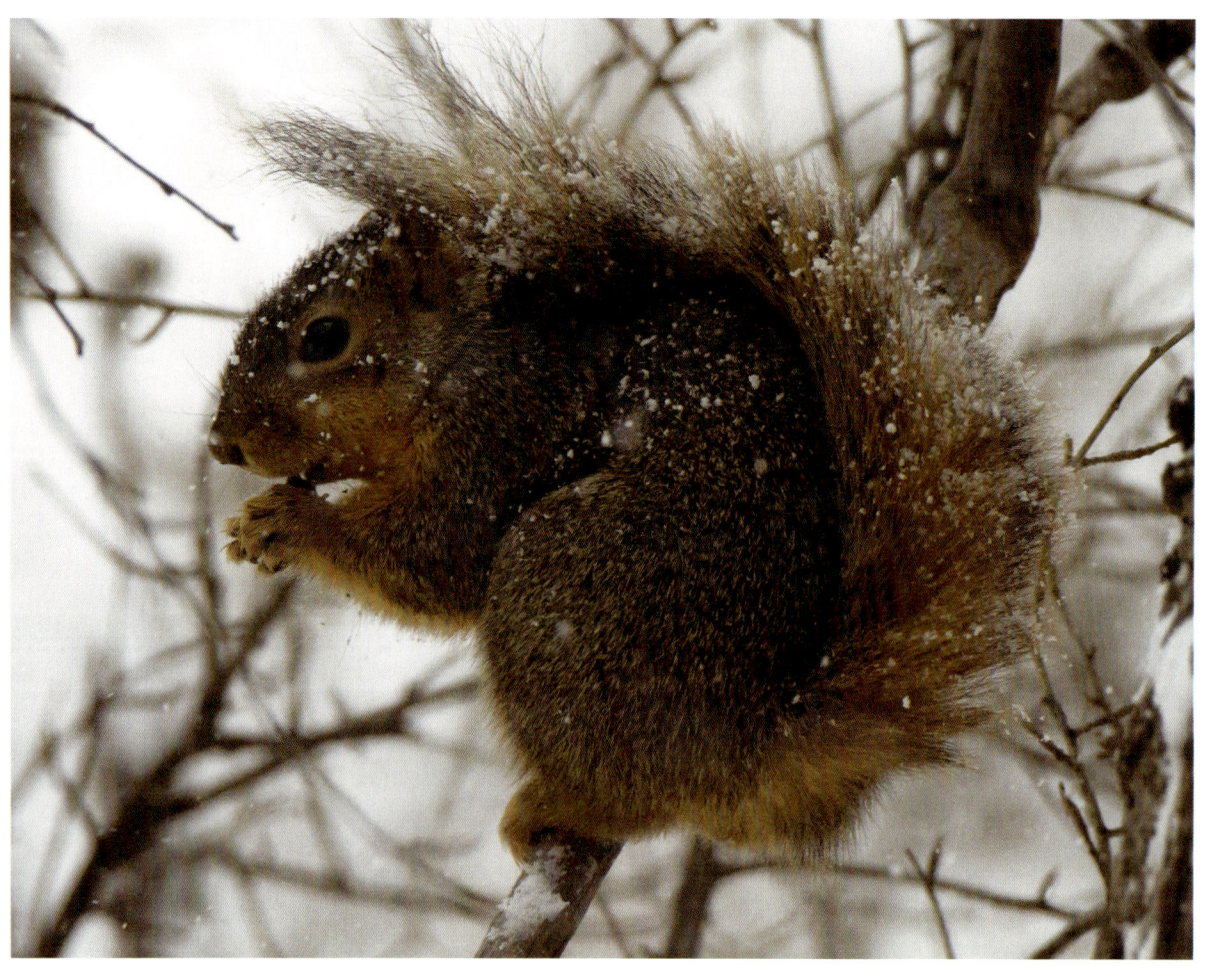

Inclement weather can really make an everyday shot something truly extraordinary, if you have the discipline to view wildlife year-round, and not just when conditions are optimal for you.

Above: Fox Squirrel, Texas /Nikon D810
Opposite: Mallard Duck, Texas /Nikon D600

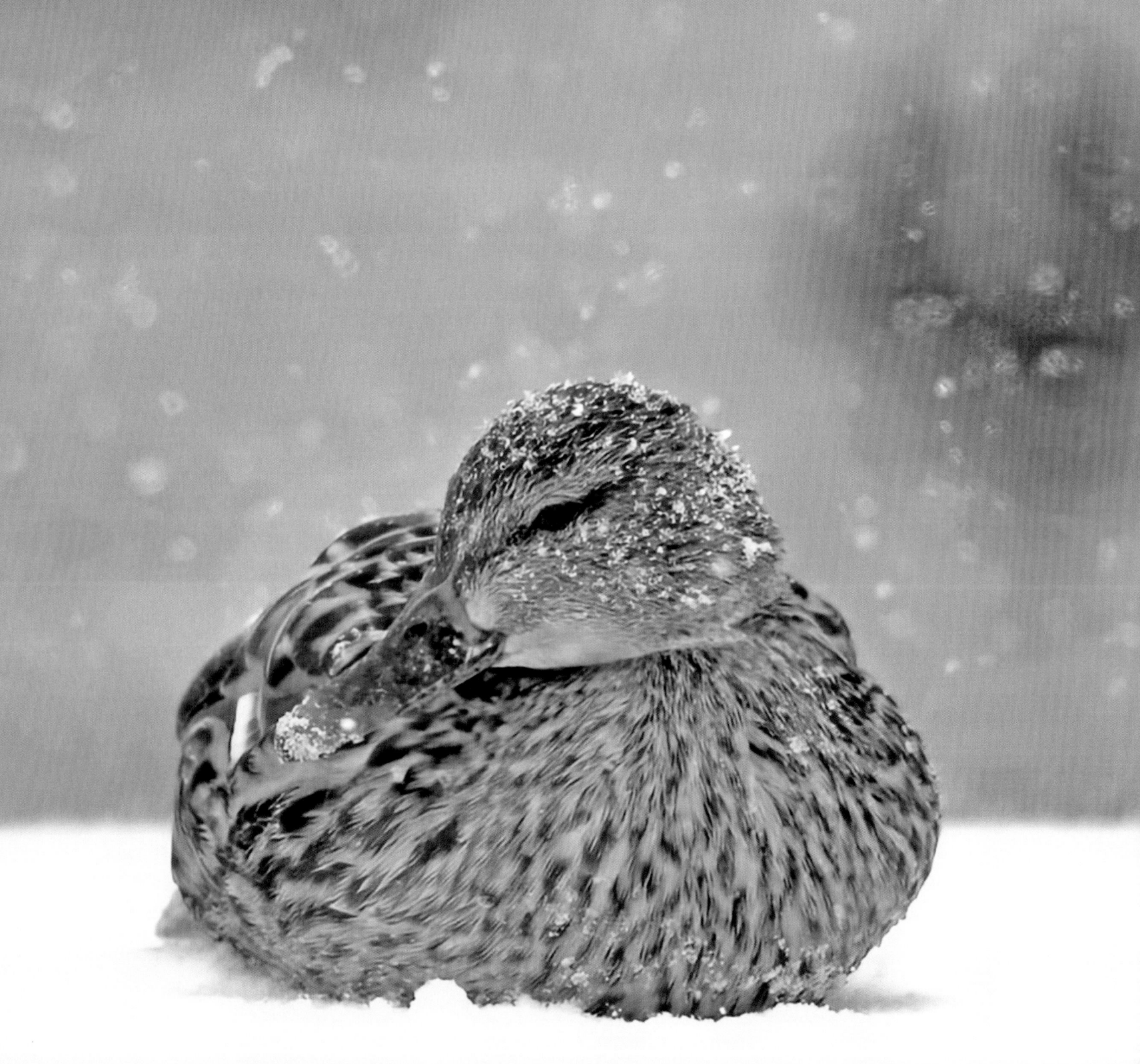

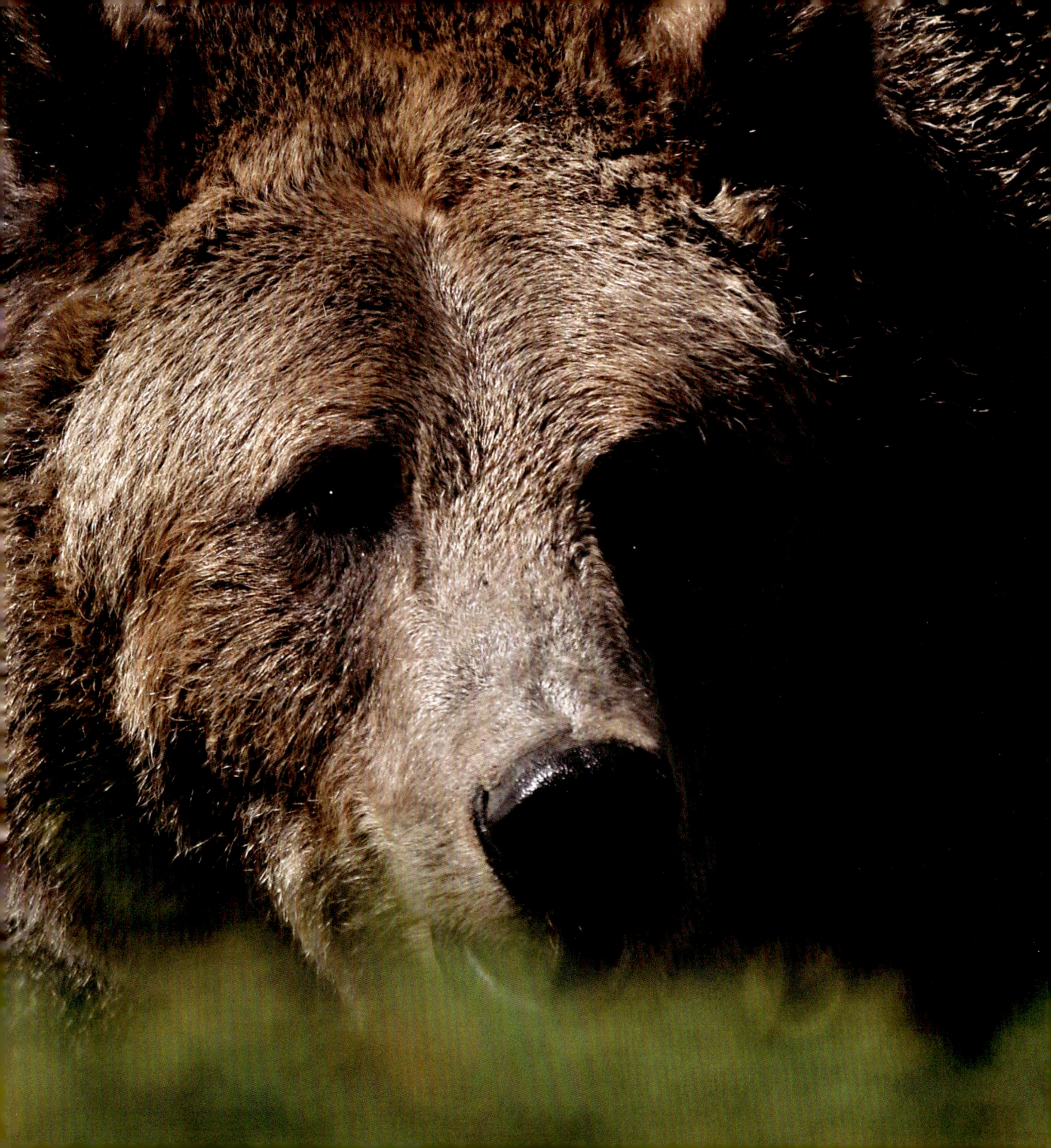

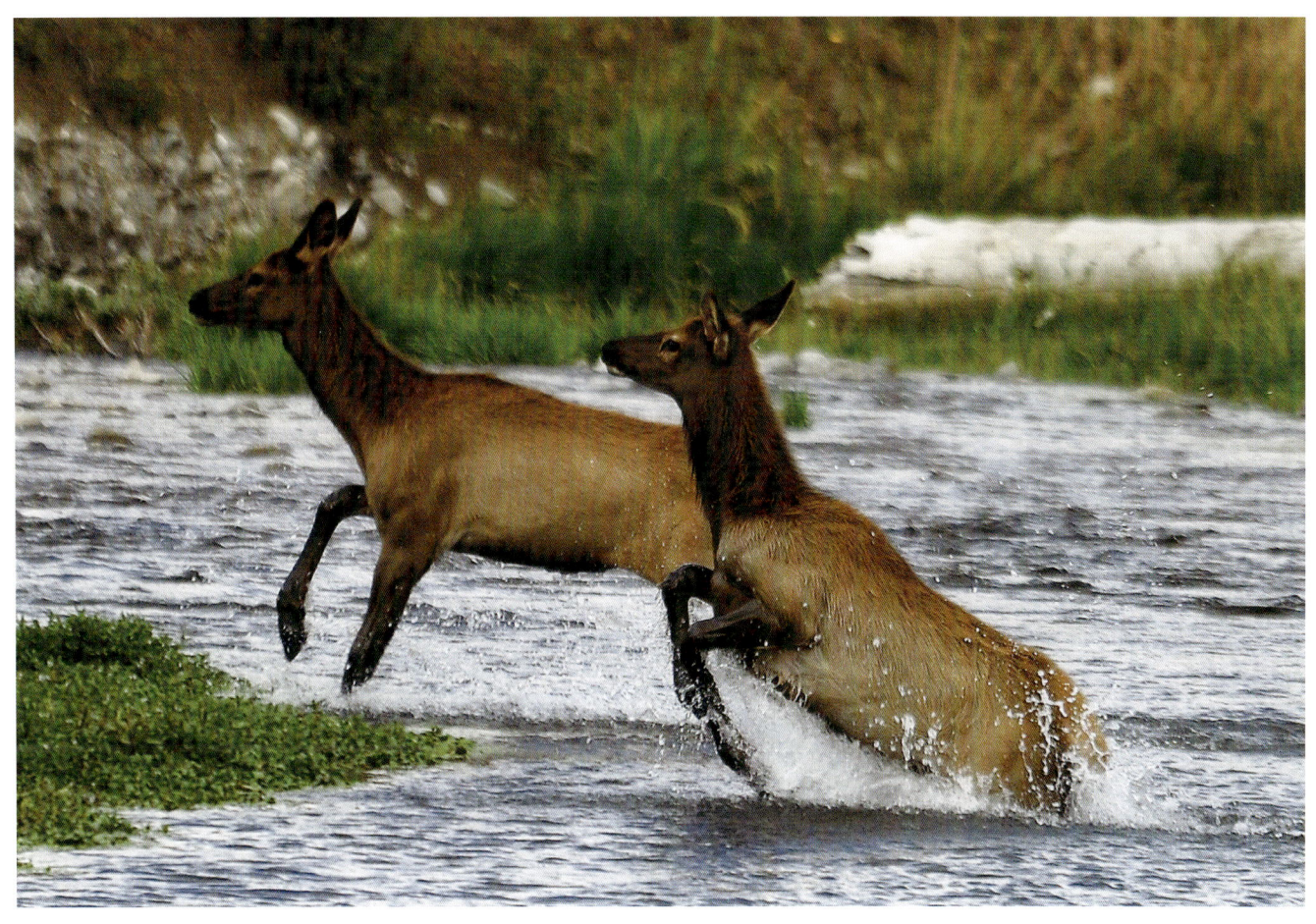

The words "grizzly bear" cause great anxiety in many individuals, which is quite understandable, since the grizzly has a fearsome reputation as one of North America's top predators. Even from afar, viewing one in the wild may be so captivating that you forget how dangerous they can truly be, until the bear notices you and heads in your direction.

Above: American Elk, Yellowstone NP /Nikon D300
Opposite: Grizzly Bear, Yellowstone NP /Nikon D300

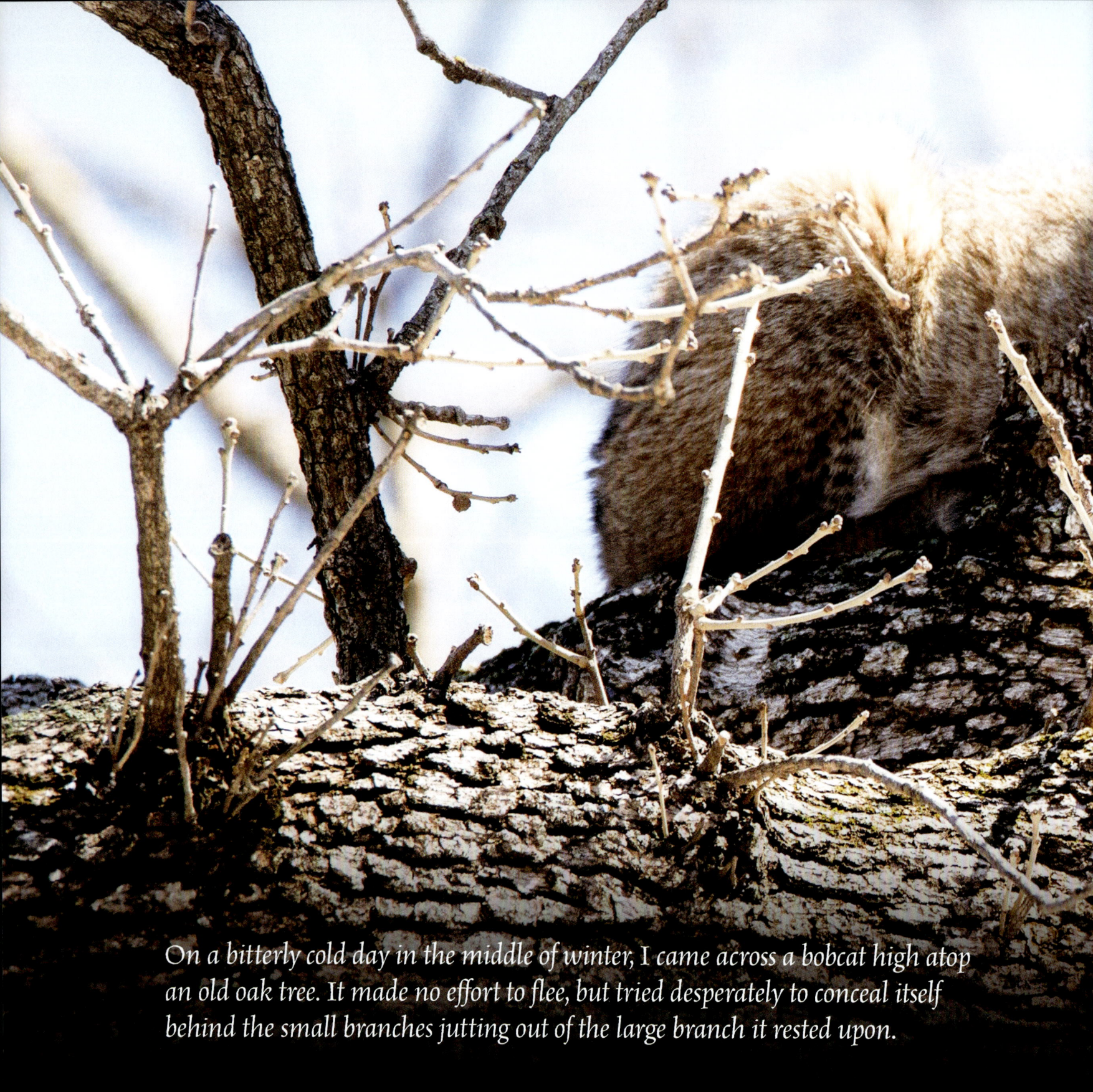

On a bitterly cold day in the middle of winter, I came across a bobcat high atop an old oak tree. It made no effort to flee, but tried desperately to conceal itself behind the small branches jutting out of the large branch it rested upon.

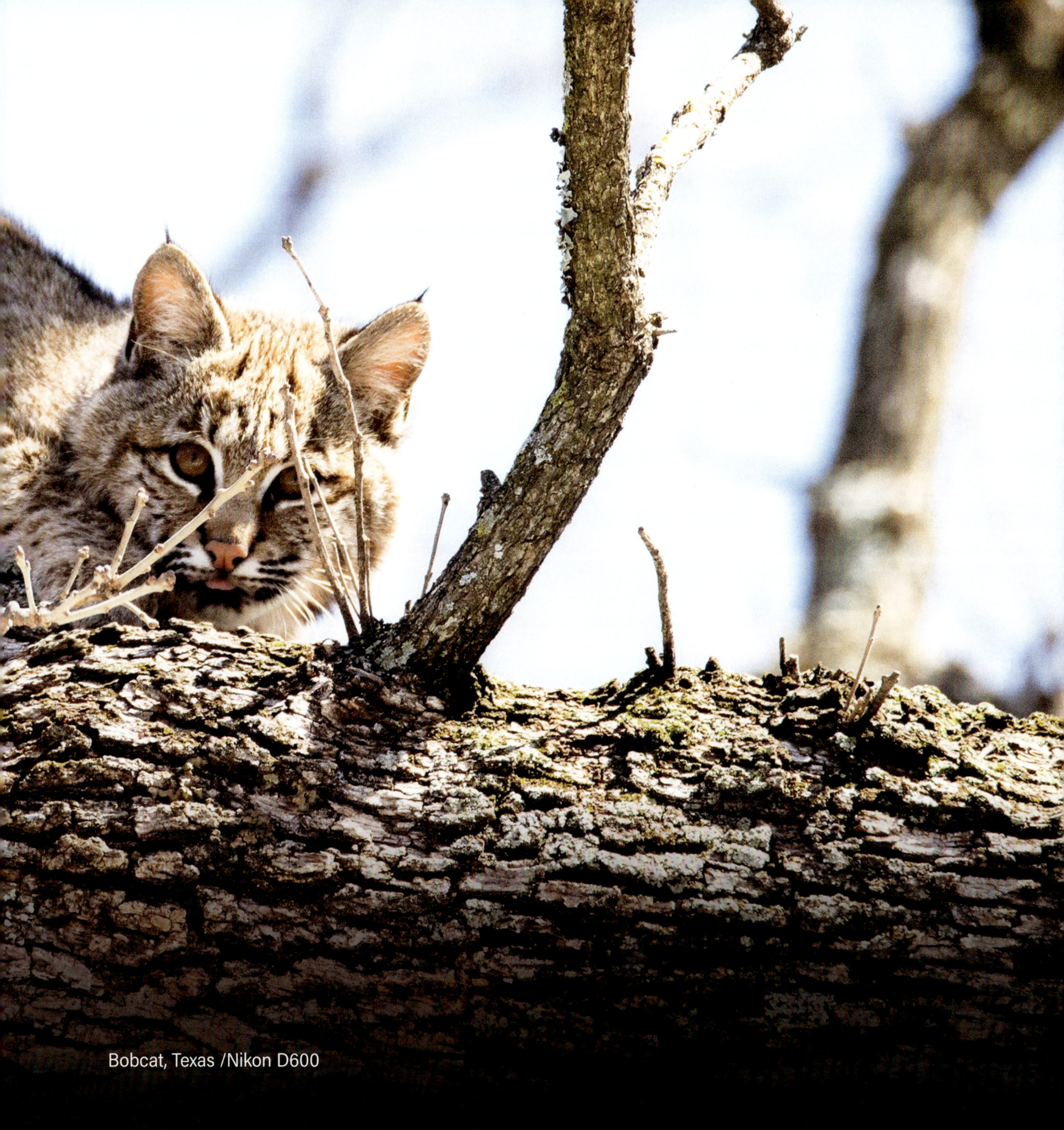

Bobcat, Texas / Nikon D600

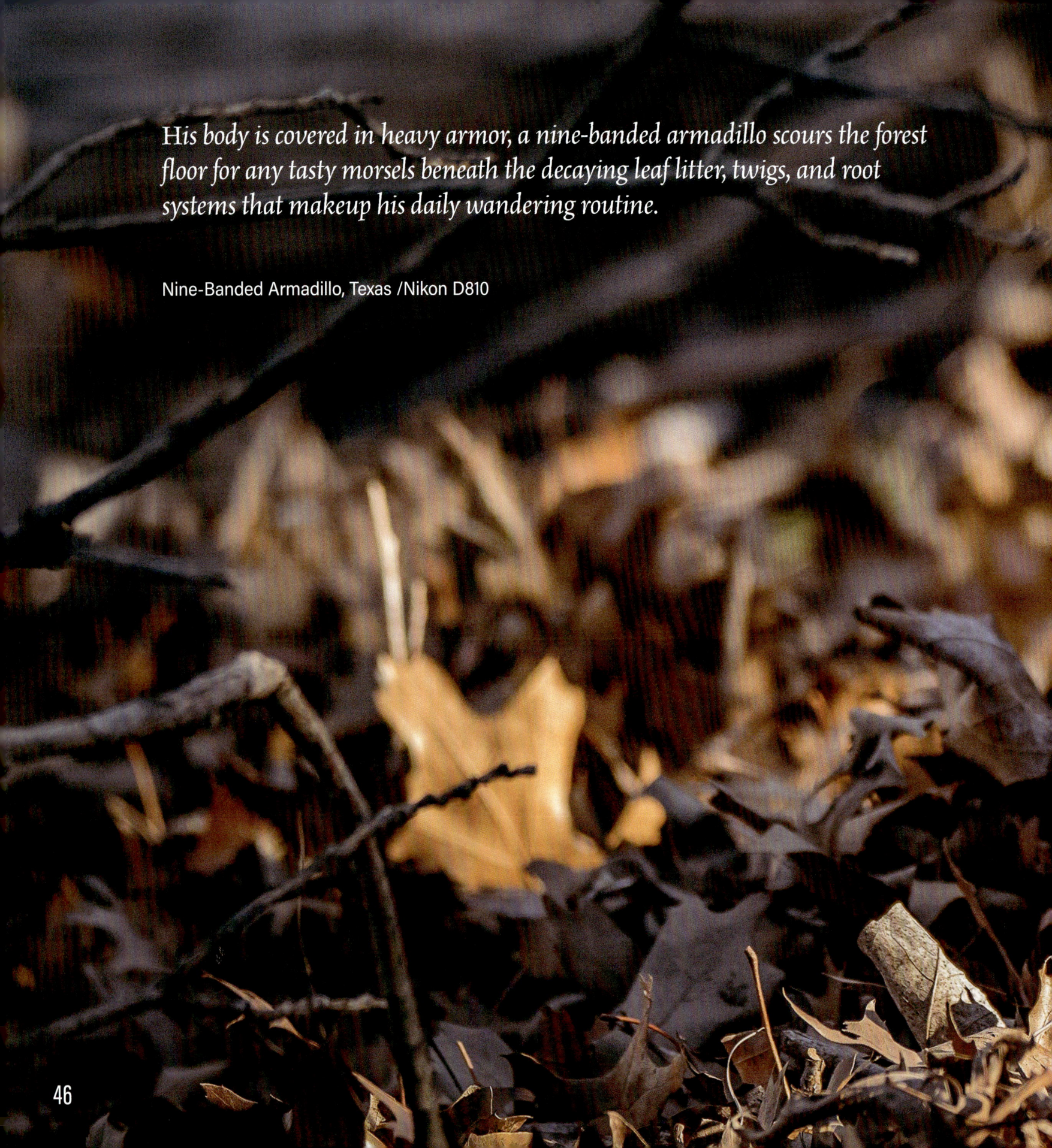

His body is covered in heavy armor, a nine-banded armadillo scours the forest floor for any tasty morsels beneath the decaying leaf litter, twigs, and root systems that makeup his daily wandering routine.

Nine-Banded Armadillo, Texas / Nikon D810

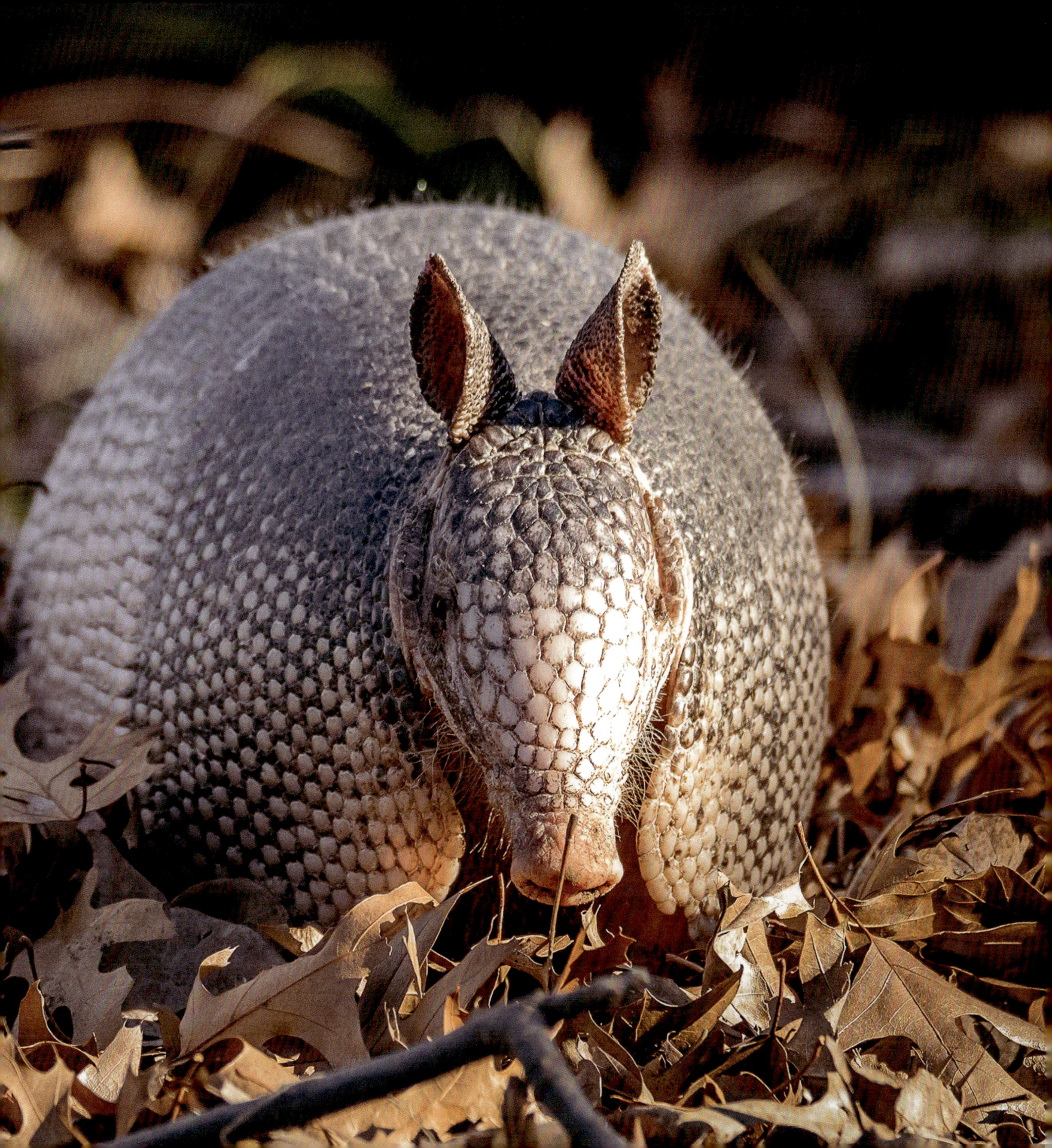

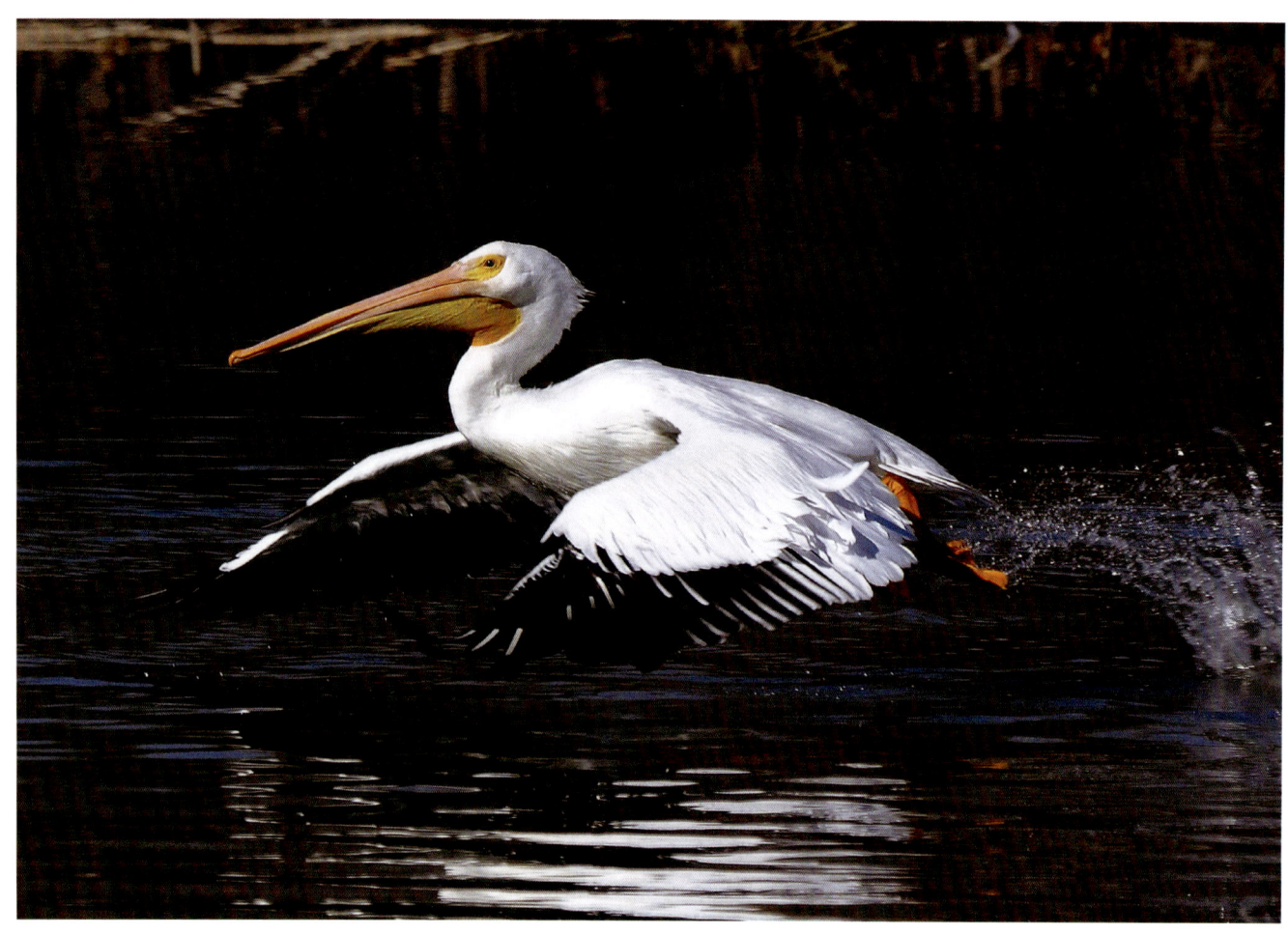

Despite their vast differences, the pelican reminds me of the long-extinct pterodactyl that once roamed Earth millions of years ago. My vivid imagination wanders on occasion, which is one of the reasons why the natural world fascinates, intrigues, and appeals to me.

Above & Opposite: White Pelicans, Texas /Nikon D300

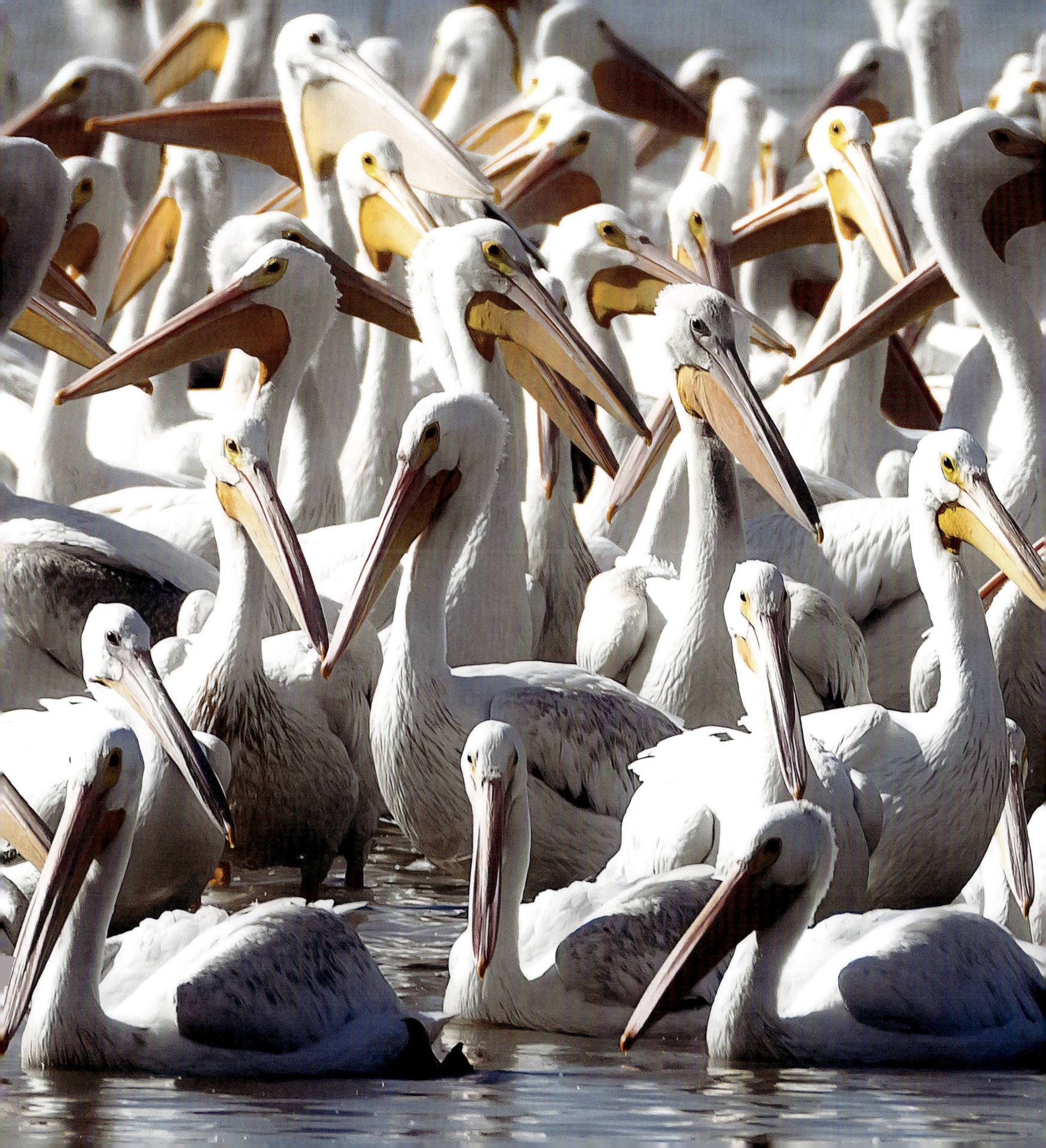

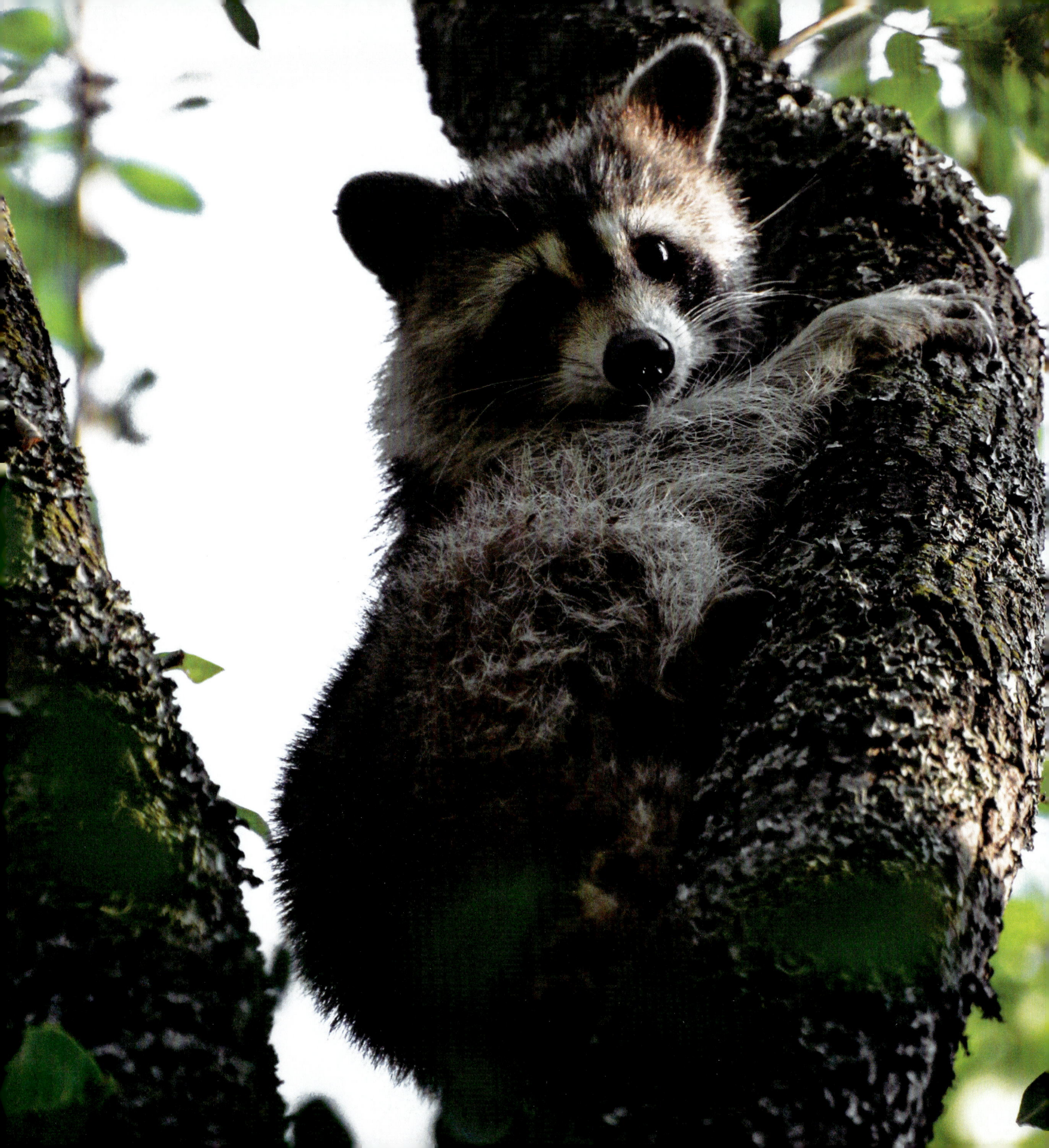

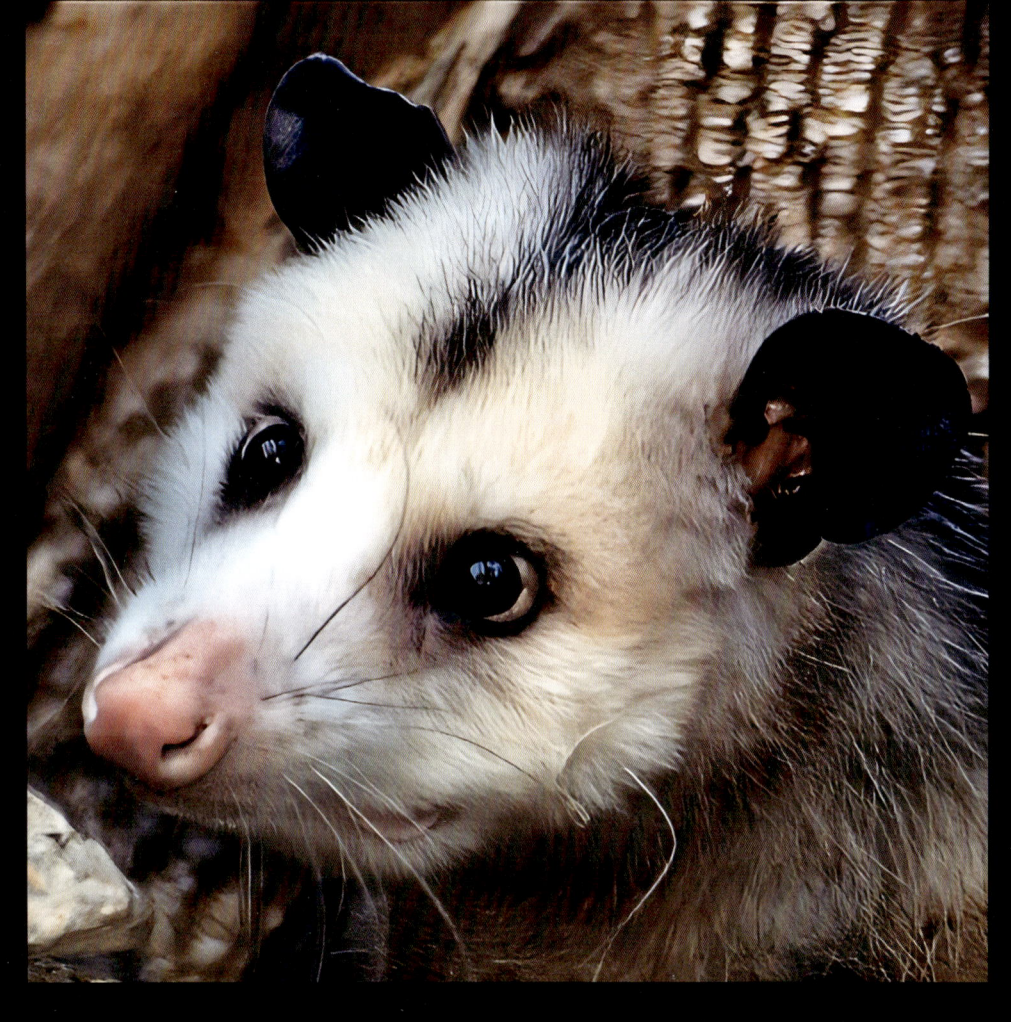

The cloak of darkness conceals the location and movement of many wildlife species in nature, so it is always a pleasant surprise to cross paths with one of these (mostly) nocturnal animals during my frequent hikes through the woodland forest of Texas . . . although I am uncertain if the feeling is mutual.

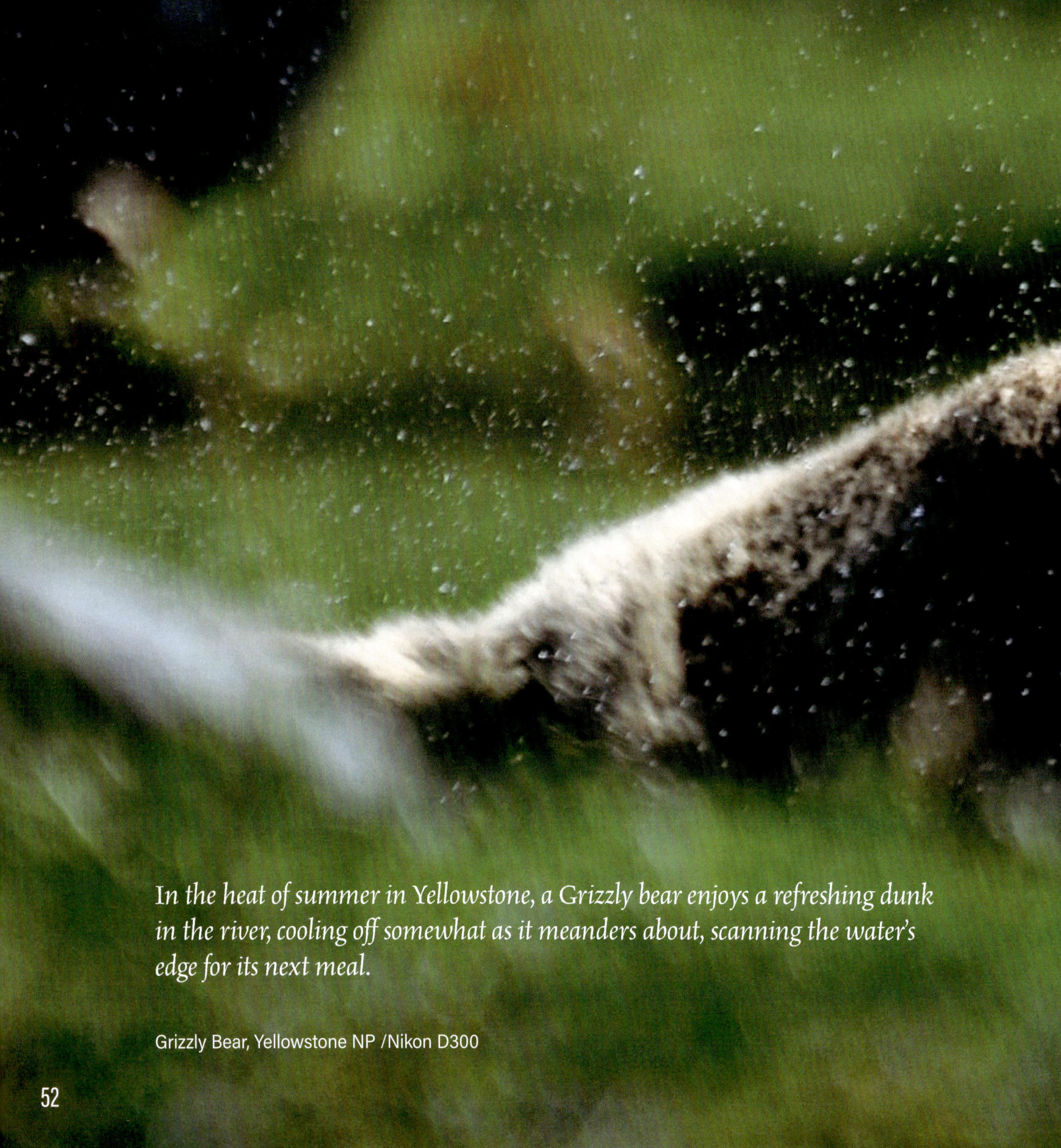

In the heat of summer in Yellowstone, a Grizzly bear enjoys a refreshing dunk in the river, cooling off somewhat as it meanders about, scanning the water's edge for its next meal.

Grizzly Bear, Yellowstone NP /Nikon D300

52

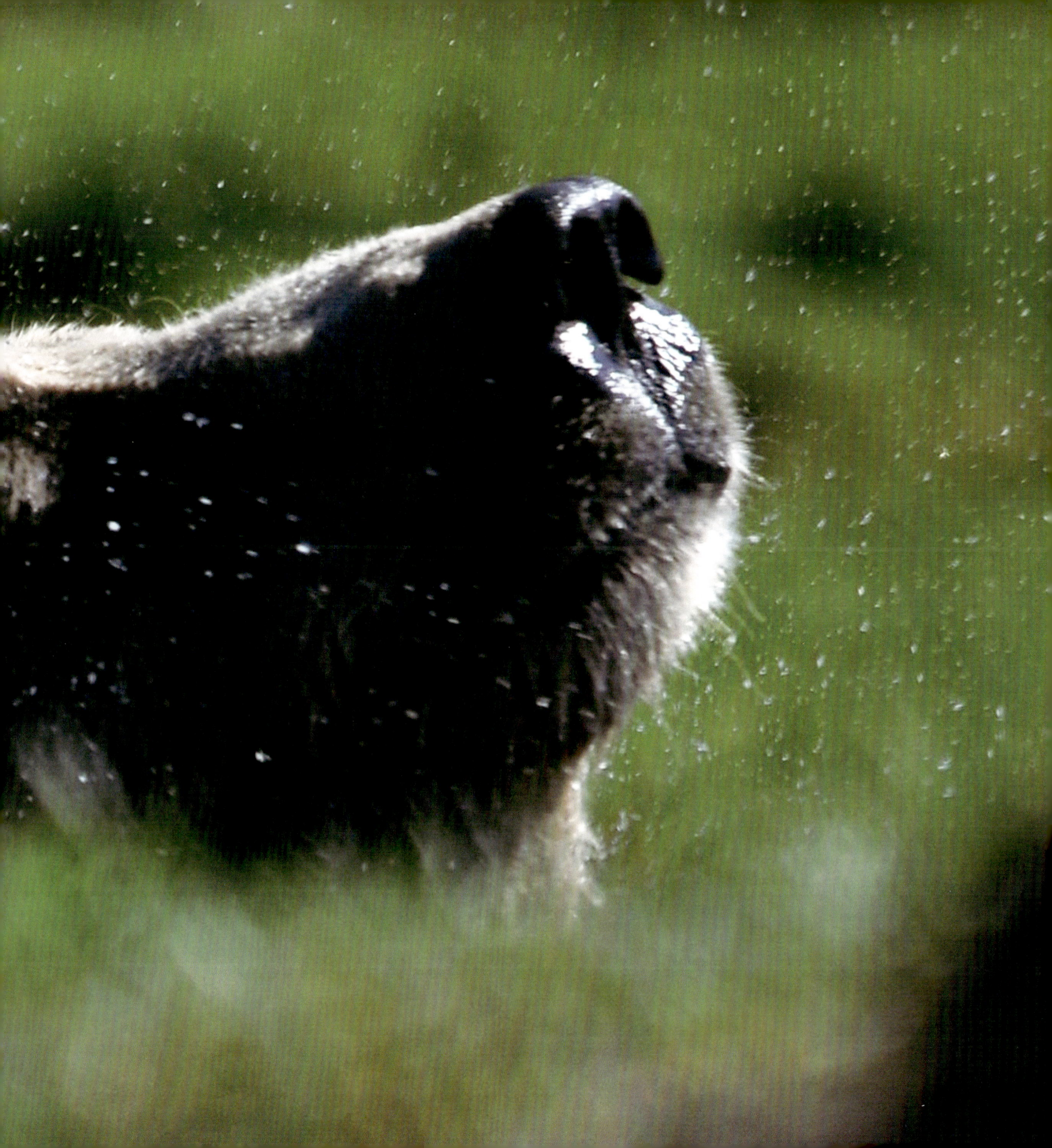

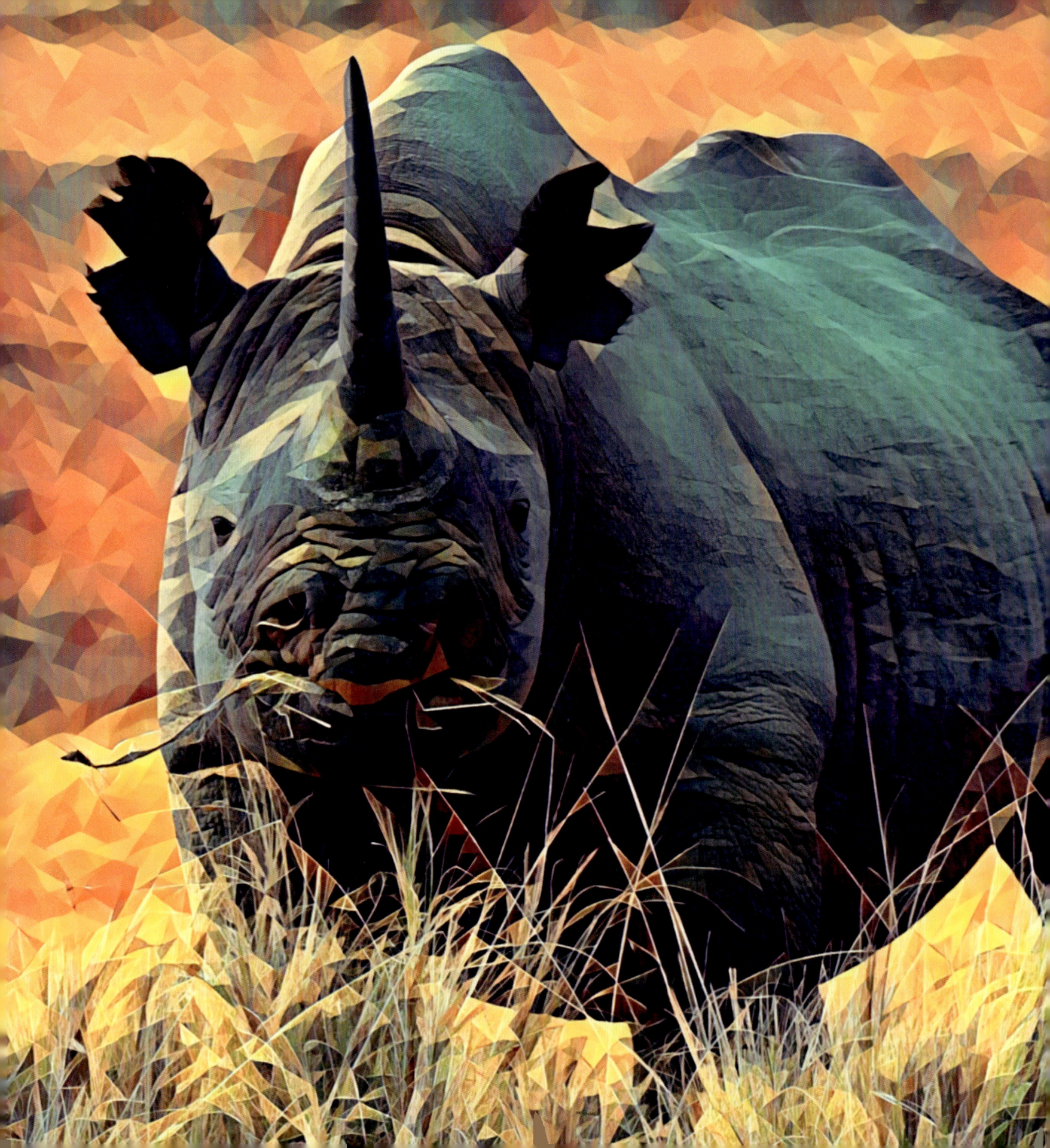

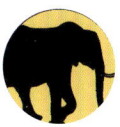

AFRICAN PLAINS

Nowhere else in our world conjures up visions of wildlife existing on such an unprecedented scale. A continent so vast in size that the largest desert on Earth can be found there, and jungles so dense that they have yet to be even explored by man. Africa, a place that has captivated my imagination since I was a child, watching National Geographic Specials with my father so many years ago. In my mind, I have walked the Serengeti, climbed Mount Kilimanjaro, and ballooned across the Great Rift of Africa more times than I can count. I always knew somehow, someday, I would visit this majestic place and was confident that all that I had envisioned would be much more than I could have ever imagined. I finally made my journey to Africa, along with a dear friend and mentor of mine. Our safari expedition took us throughout the heart of Africa, from the rocky outcrops of Mount Kenya to the shores of Lake Nakuru, and ever downward into the vast savannas of the Maasai Mara. The beauty of the land, the abundance of wildlife, and the generosity of the local Maasai tribes made this an adventure never to be forgotten but sure to be repeated. These photographs are in honor of my friend Bill, who died shortly after our trip.

As the African sun begins to paint the morning sky with its magical brush, darkness begins to slowly fade, allowing the ancient outline of Mount Kenya to emerge once again for all to see.

Mount Kenya, Kenya / Nikon D810

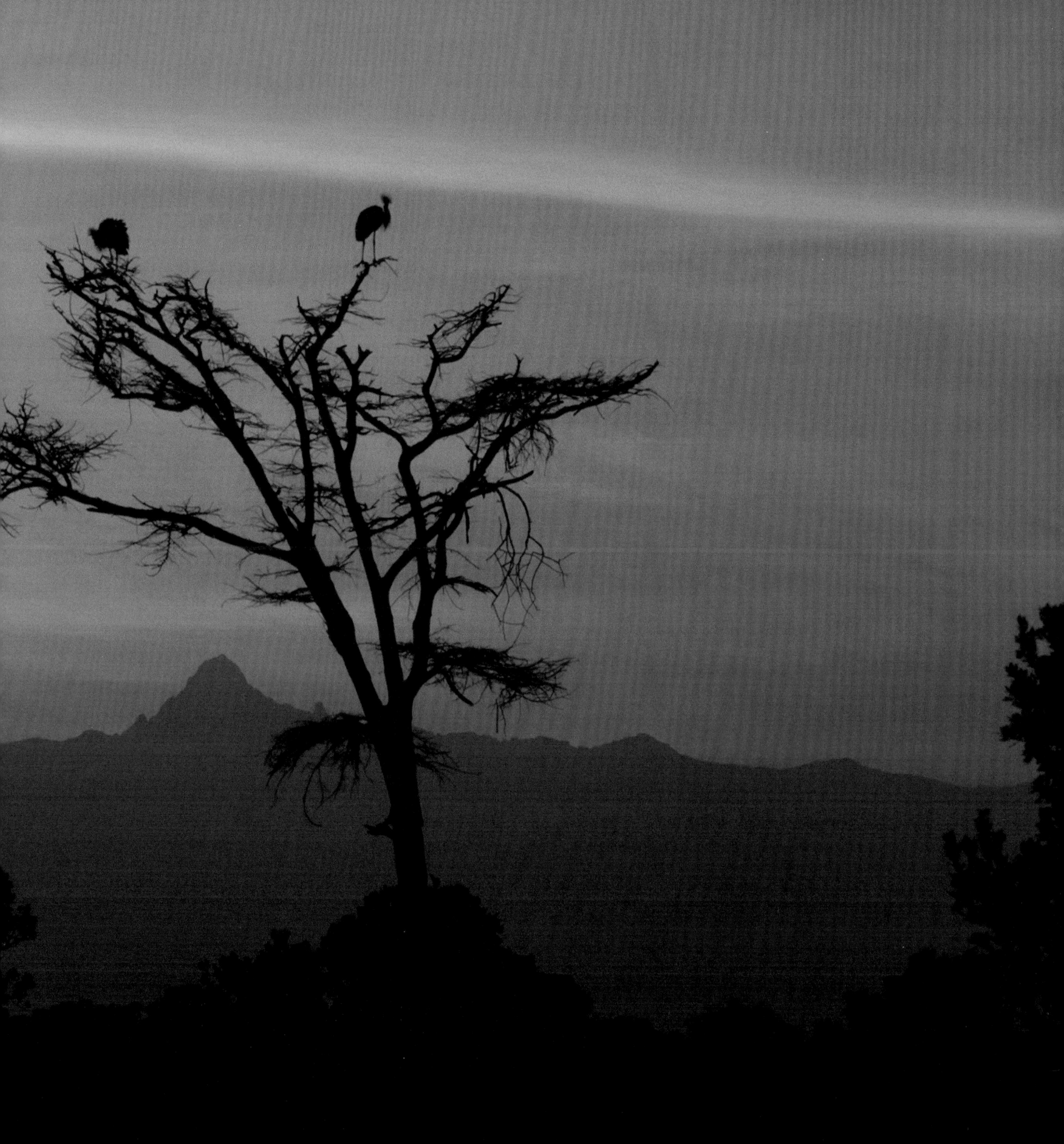

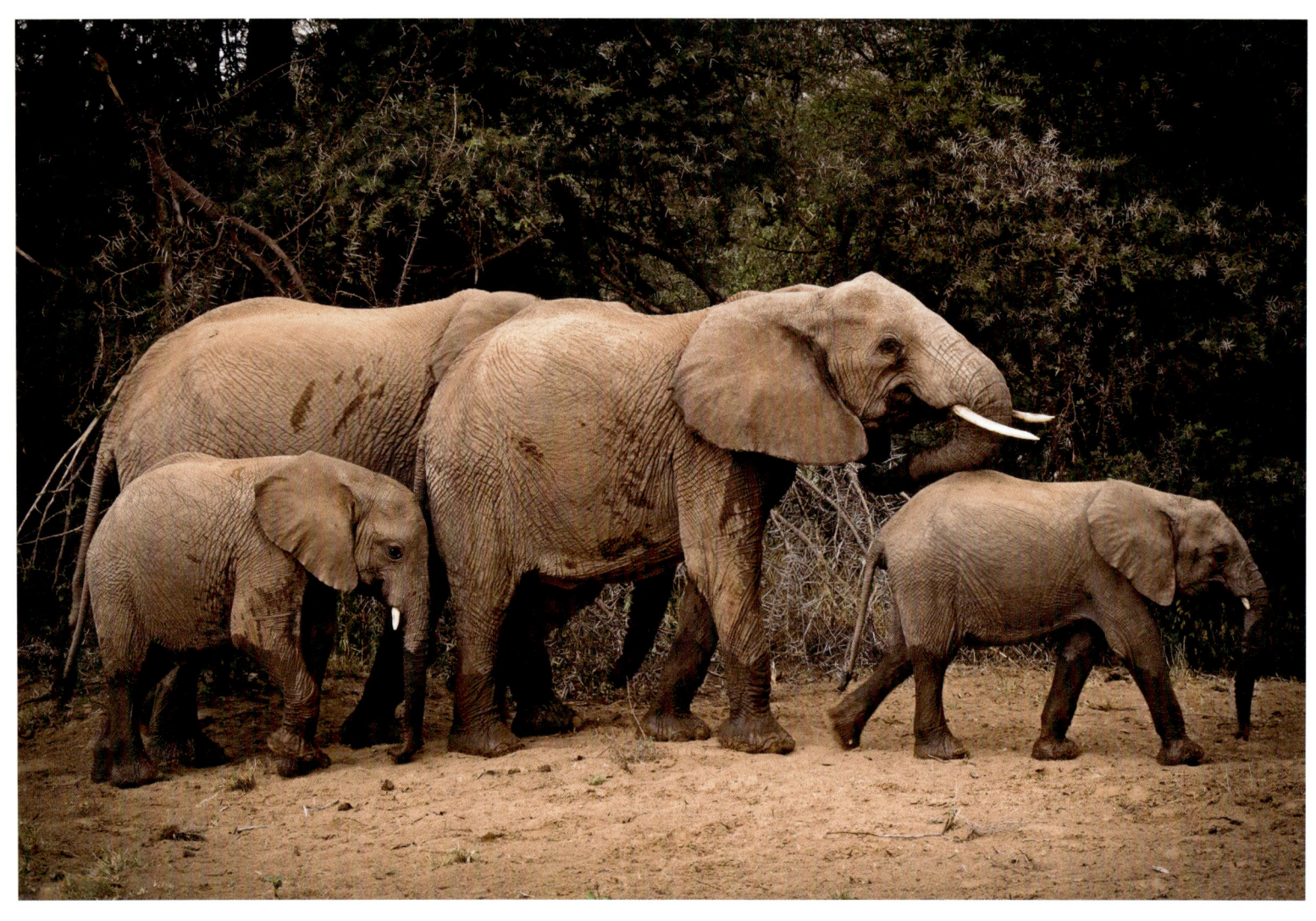

A large female African elephant with an adolescent calf crosses the very muddy Ewaso Ngiro River as they make their way into the Samburu National Reserve. Fed by seasonal rains and melting glaciers atop Mount Kenya, the Ngiro River is a permanent water source sustaining wildlife in a very arid part of northern Kenya.

Above and opposite: African Elephant, Kenya /Nikon D810

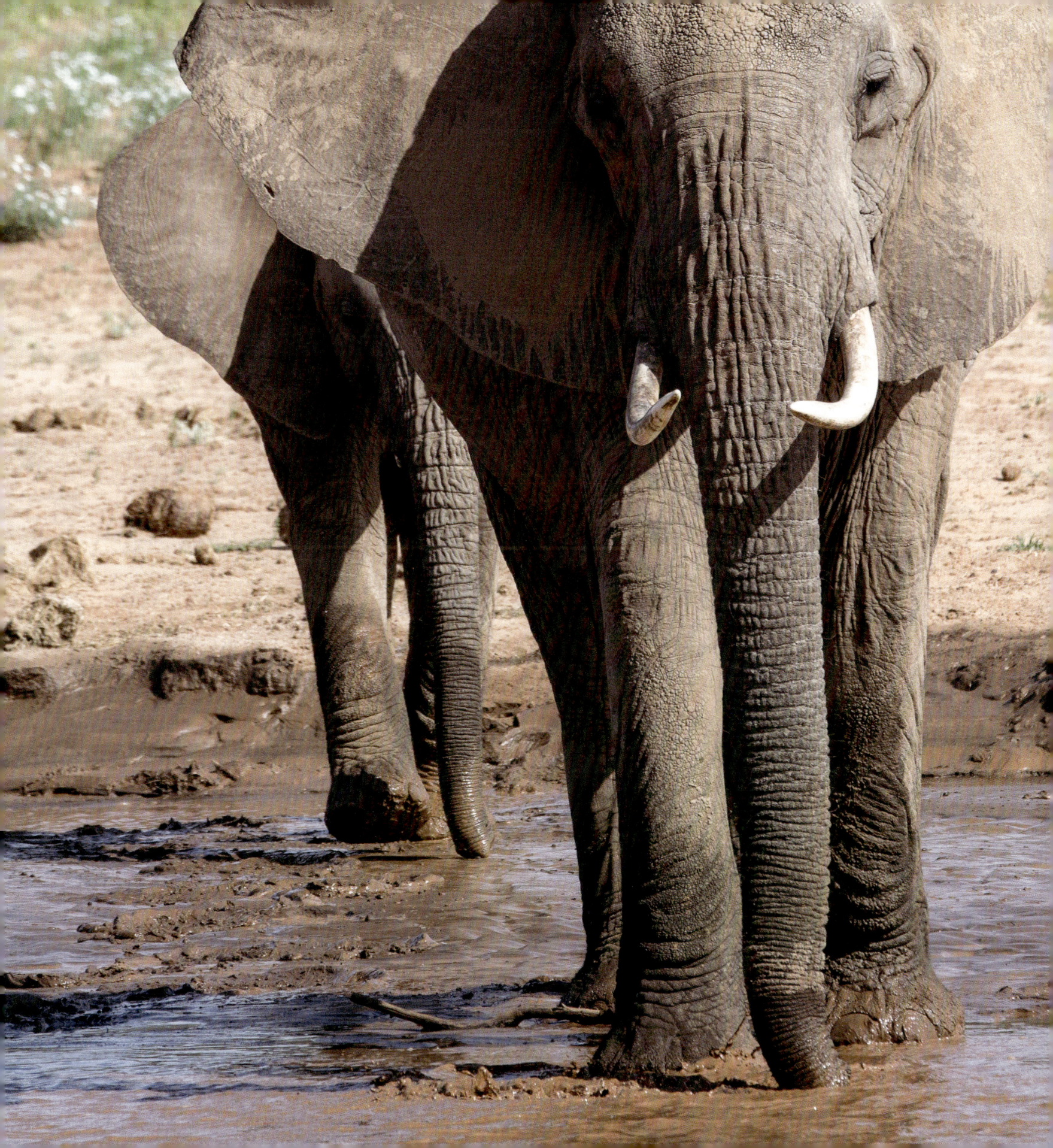

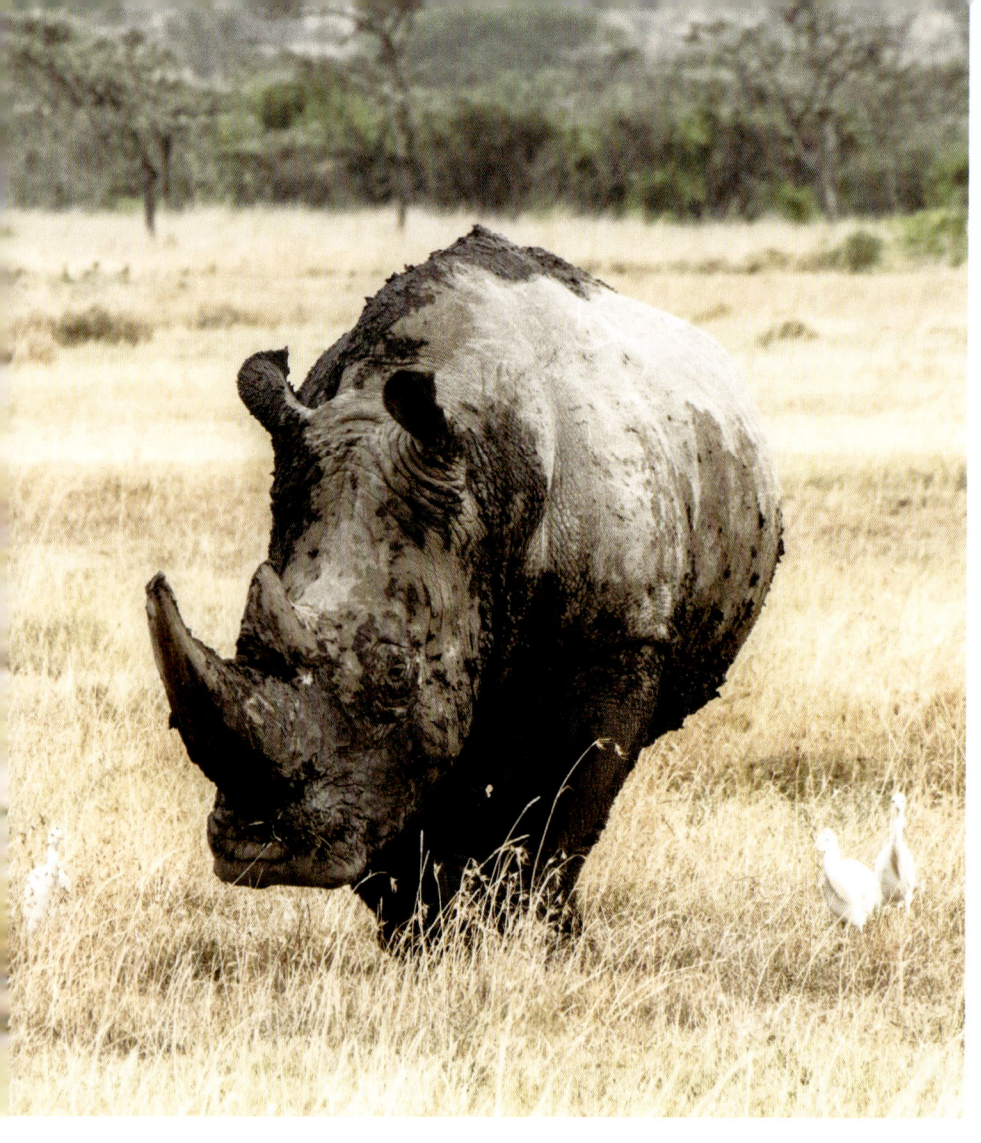

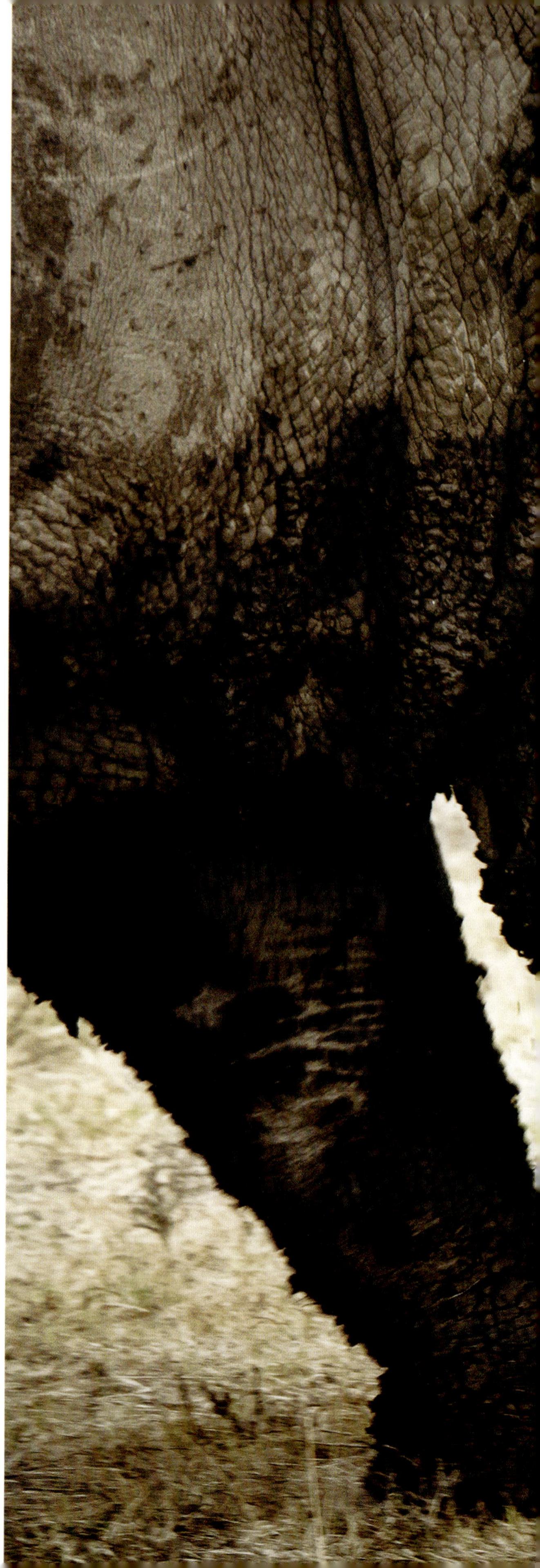

His mud bath now complete, a massive white rhino casually makes his way across an open African plain toward a distant watering hole to quench his thirst as the day grows long.

Above and opposite: White Rhino, Kenya /Nikon D810

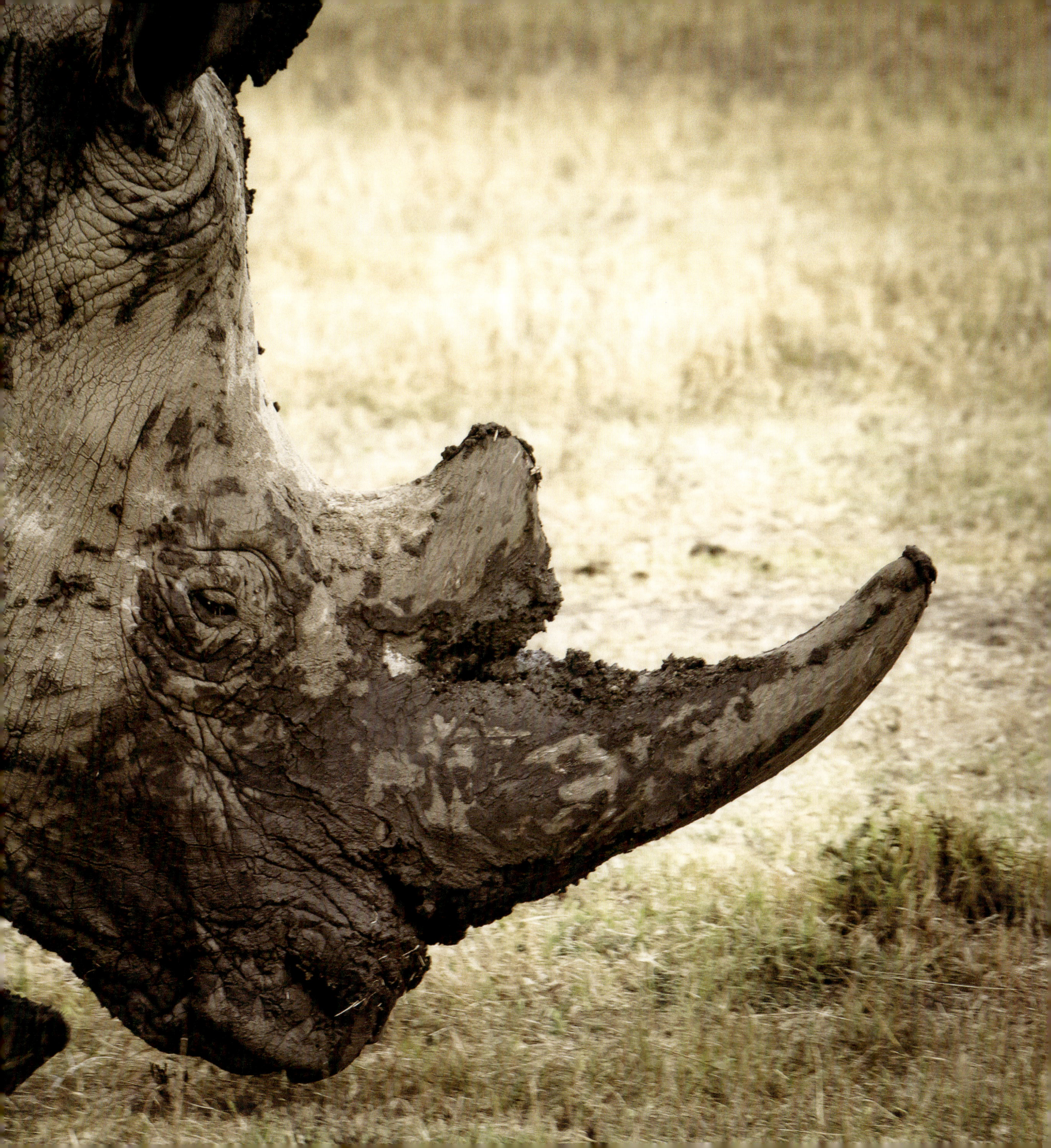

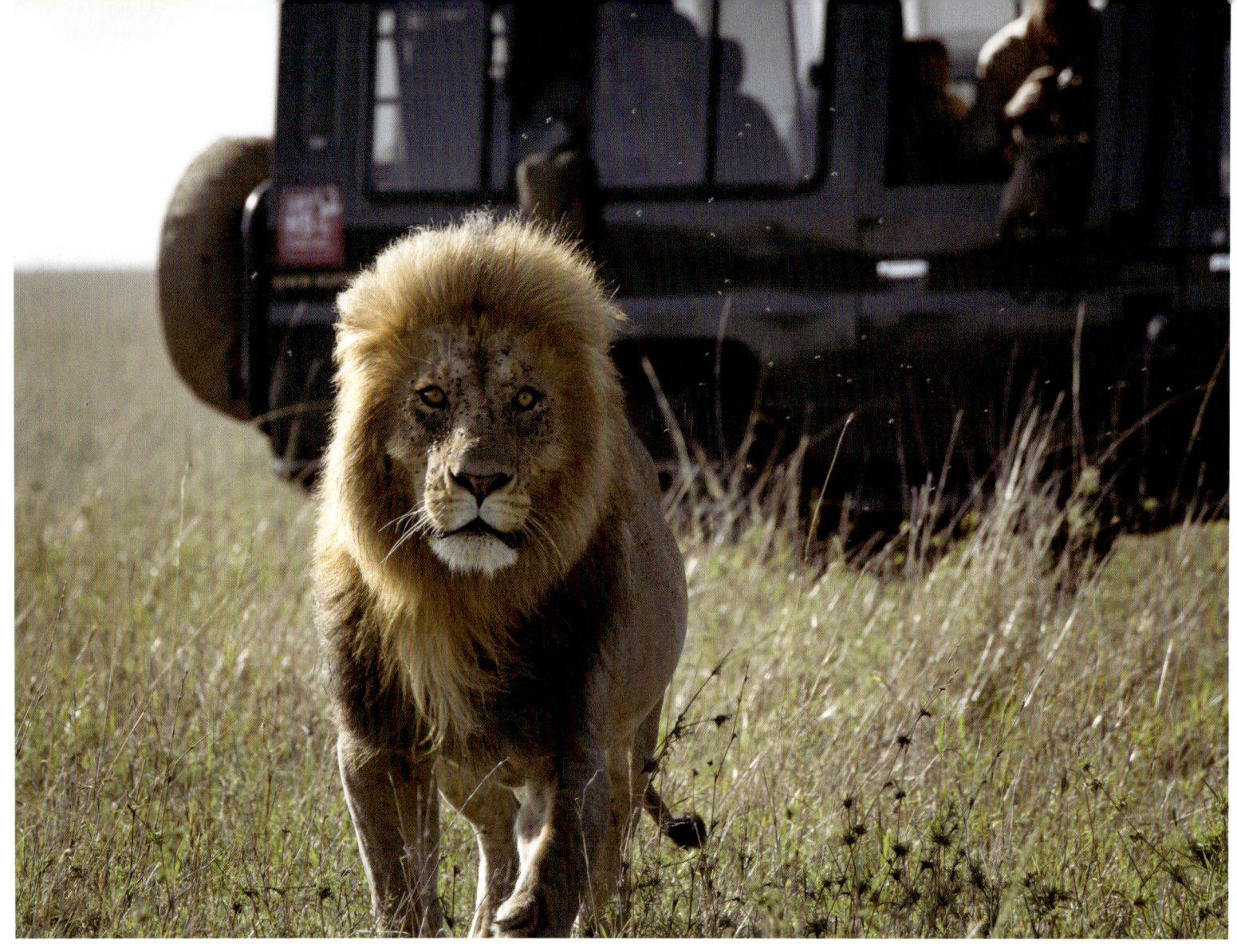

His power undeniable . . . he is the Lion King, and the Mara is the realm over which he rules. This mesmerizing image taken in the Maasai Mara captures the crossroads between humans and wildlife, and the fragile balance between them.

Above and opposite: African Lion, Kenya /Nikon D810

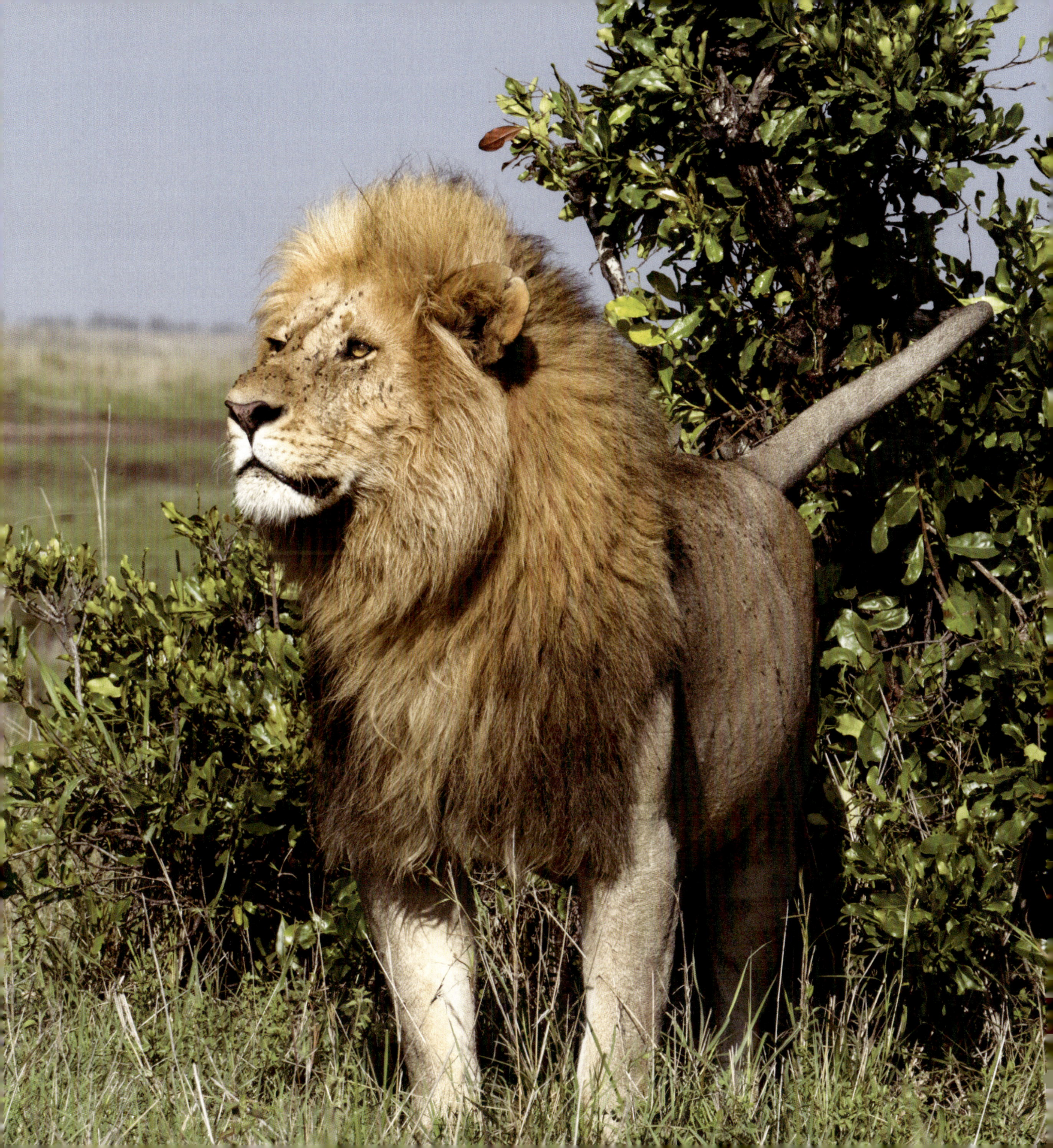

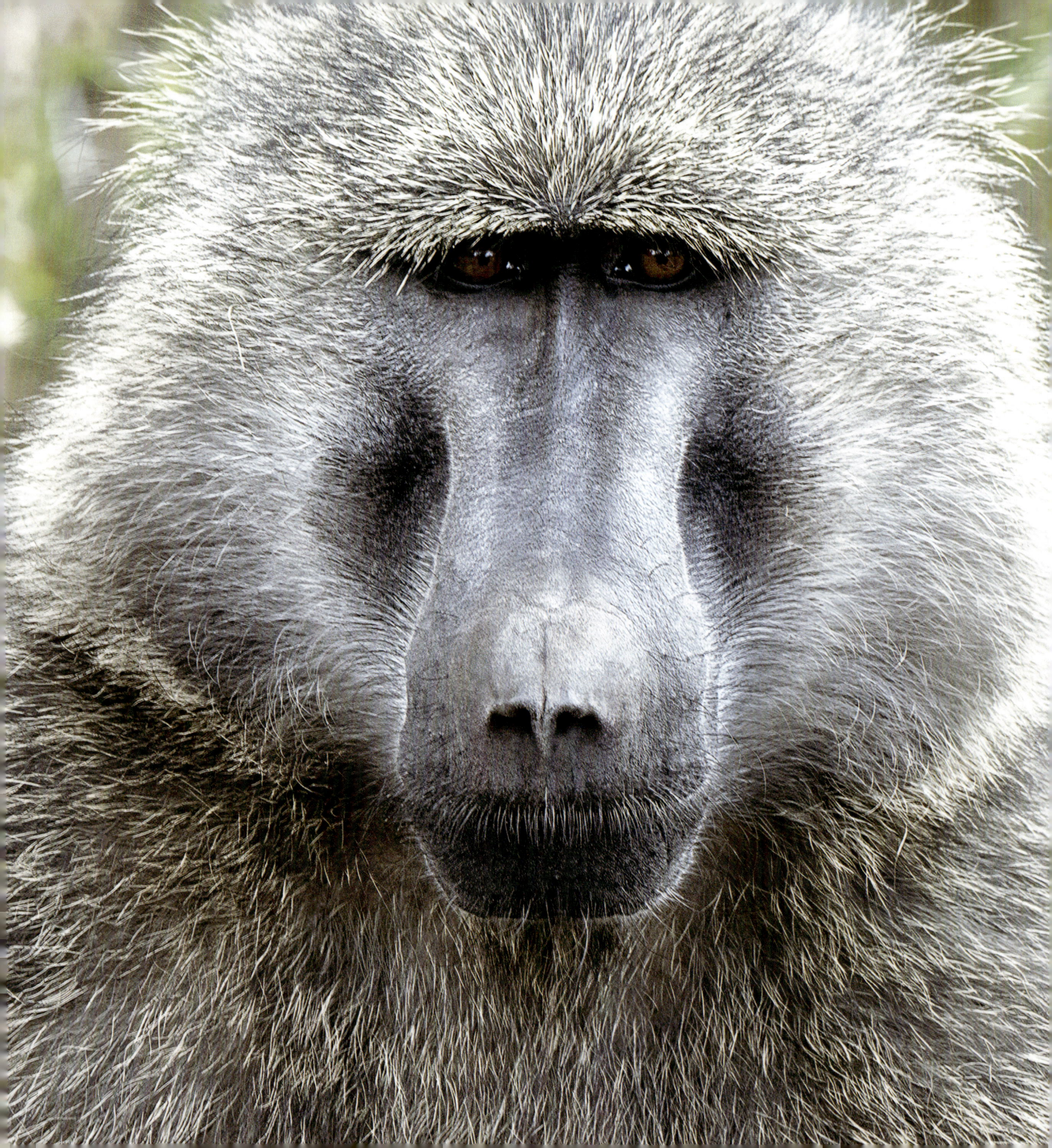

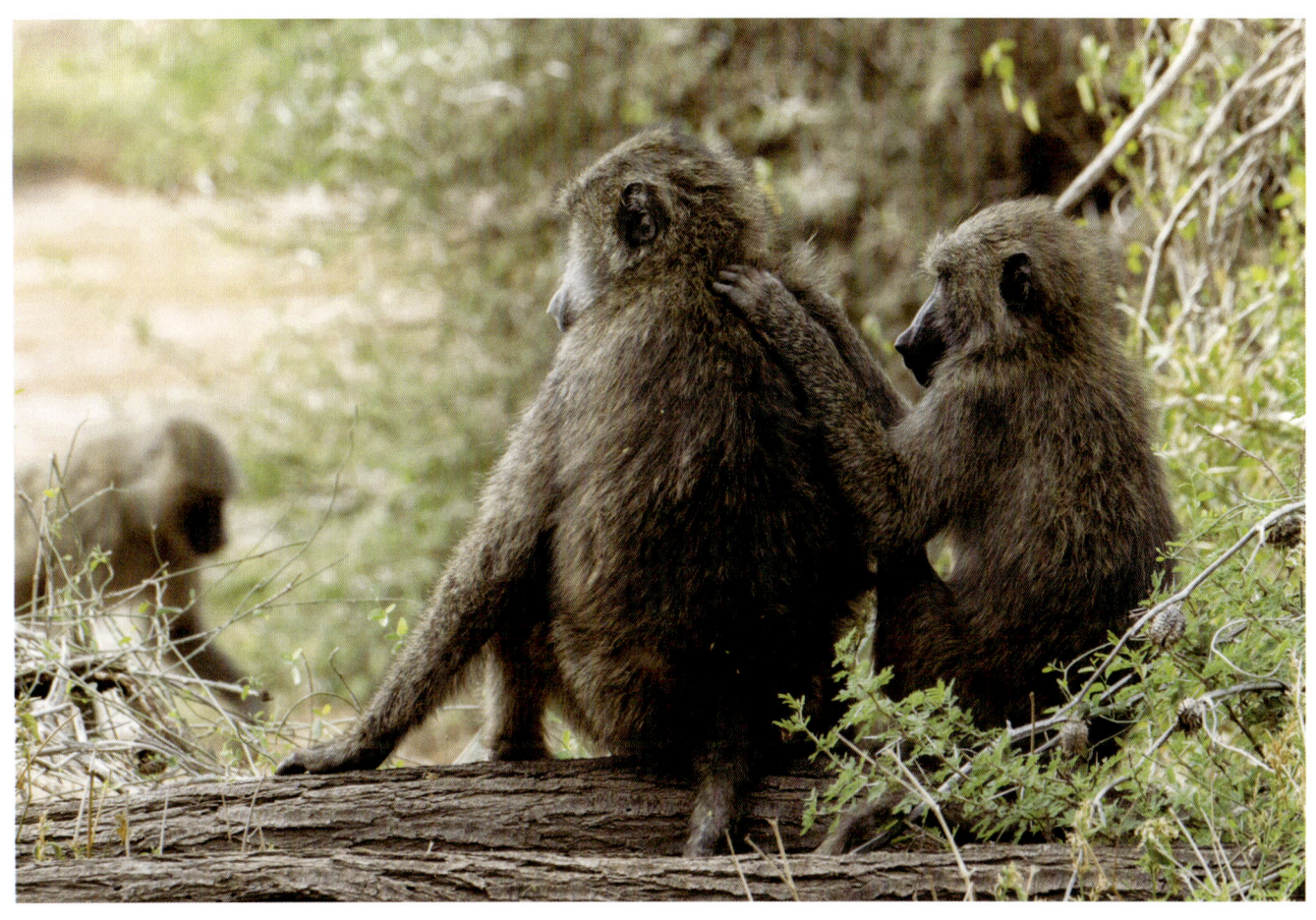

Sometimes an image resonates deep within you in a way you truly had not expected. The gazing eyes of an olive baboon pierce my camera lens, as if wanting desperately to tell me more about his life than I could ever have thought possible.

Above and opposite: Olive Baboons, Kenya /Nikon D810

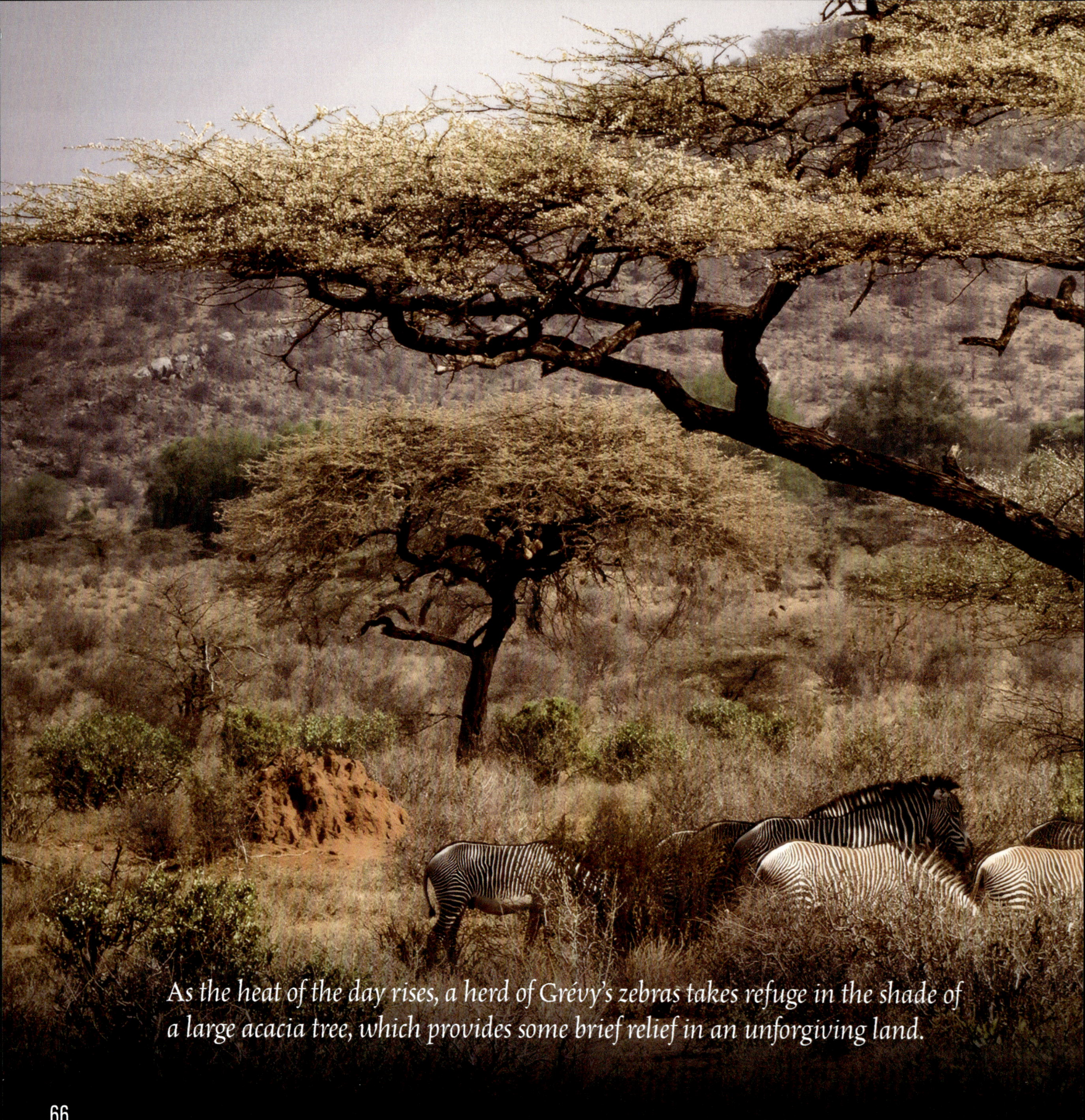

As the heat of the day rises, a herd of Grévy's zebras takes refuge in the shade of a large acacia tree, which provides some brief relief in an unforgiving land.

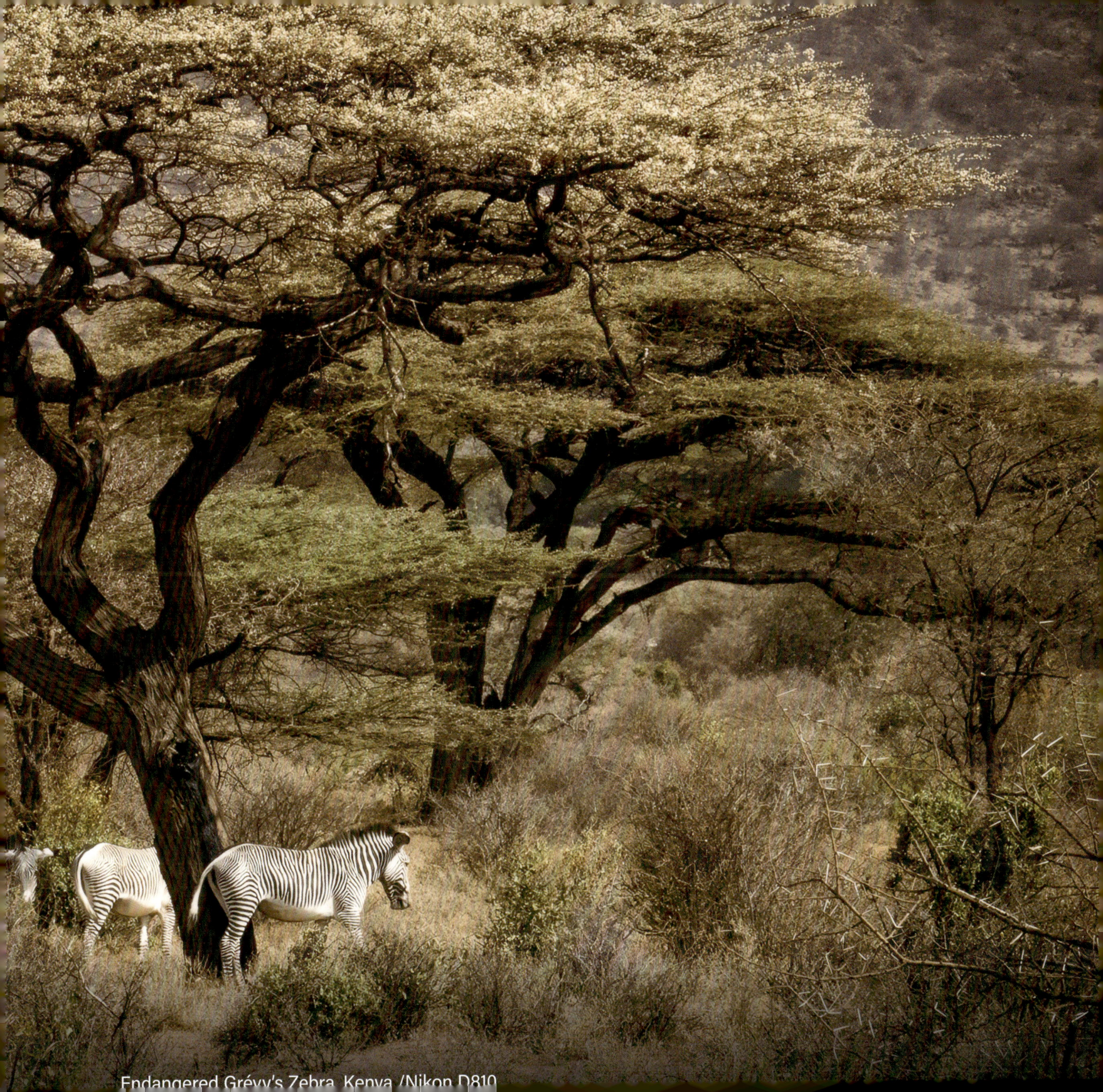

Endangered Grévy's Zebra, Kenya /Nikon D810

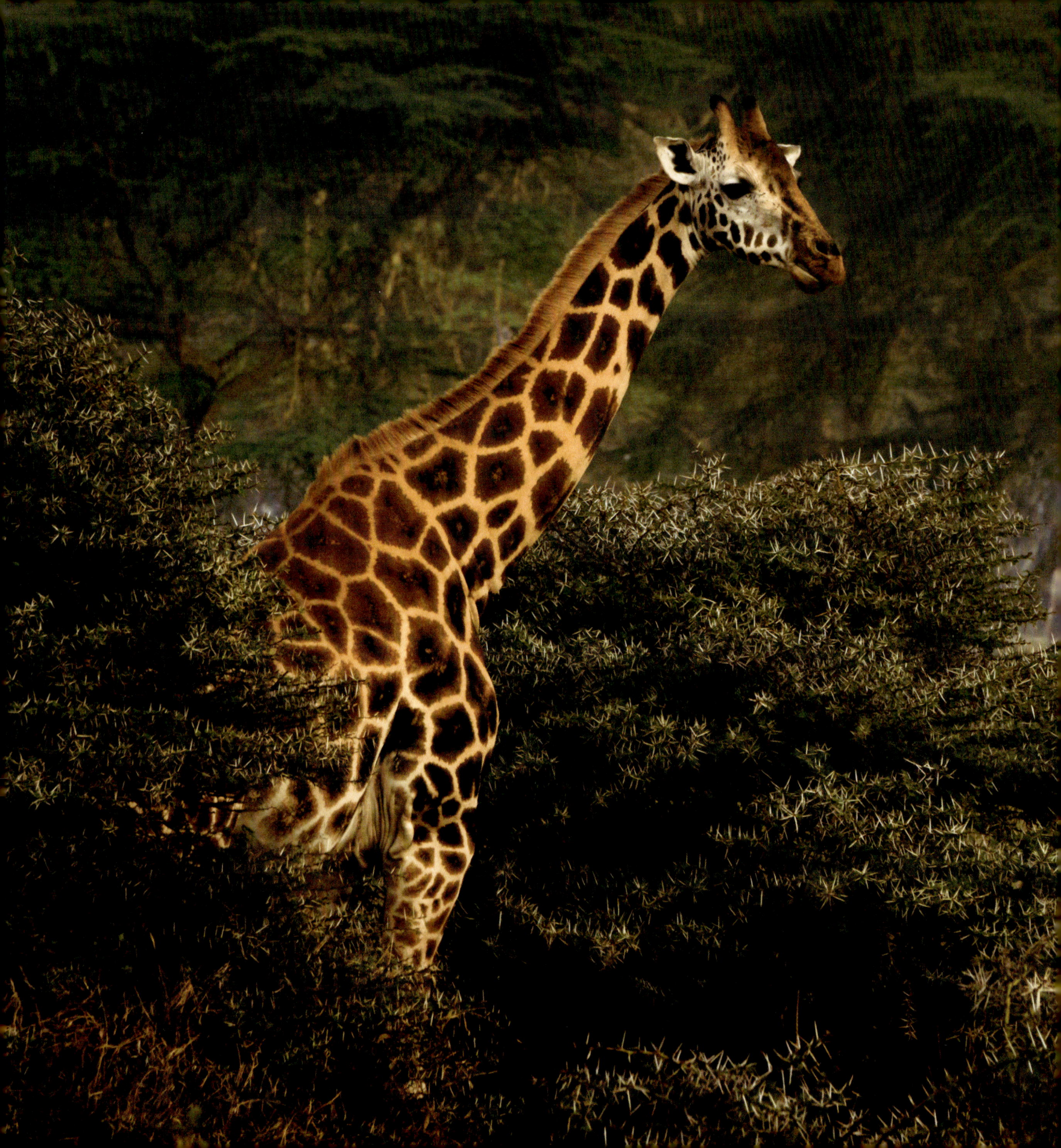

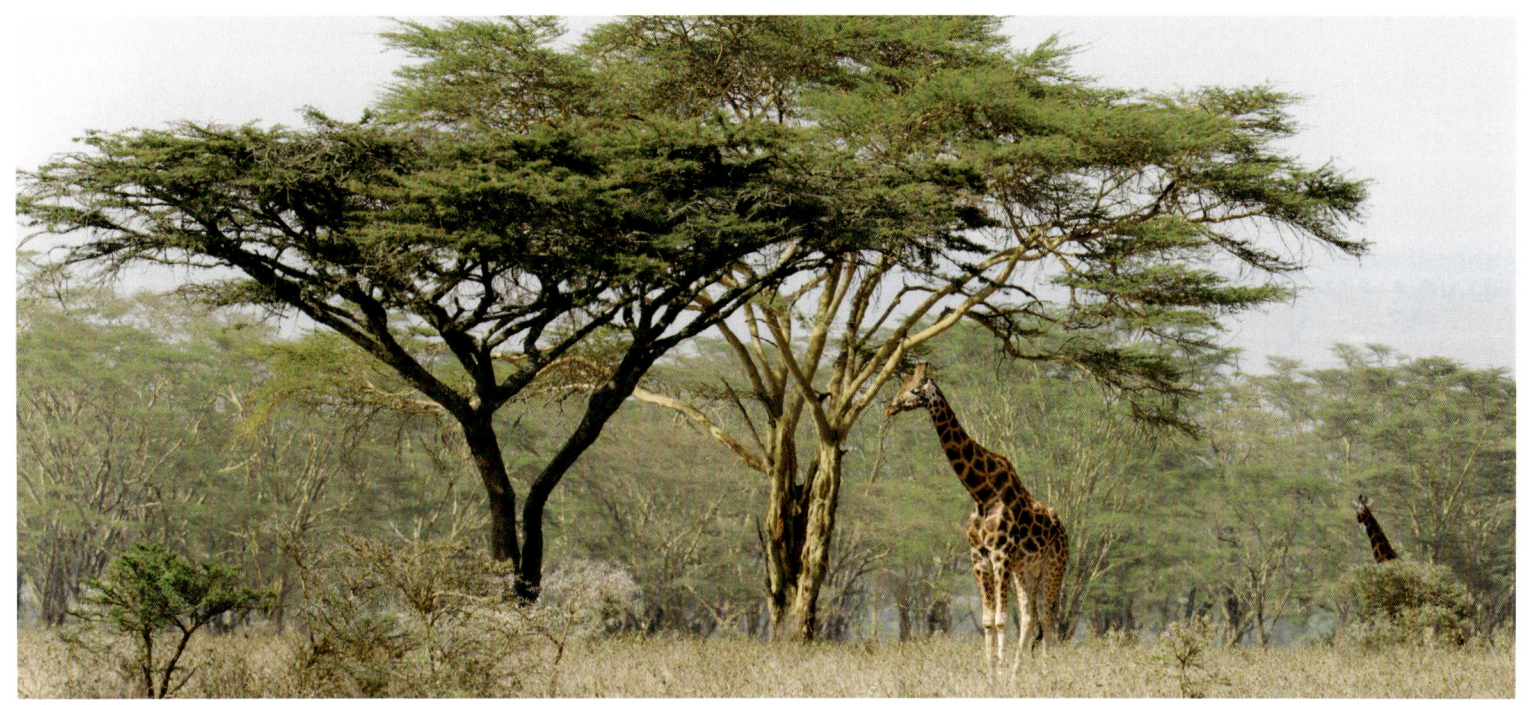

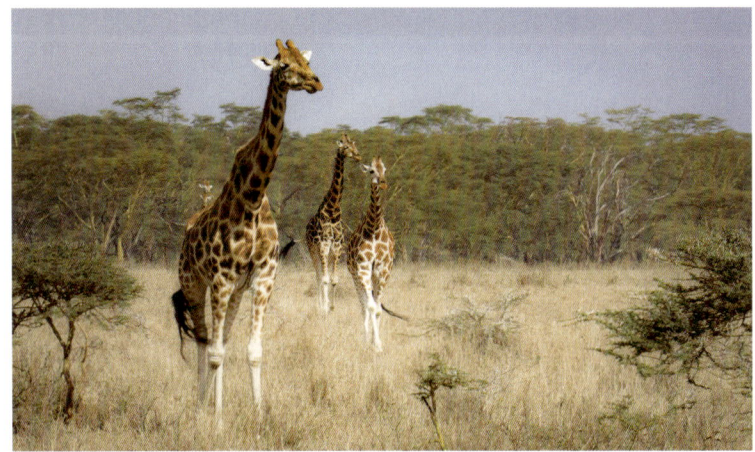

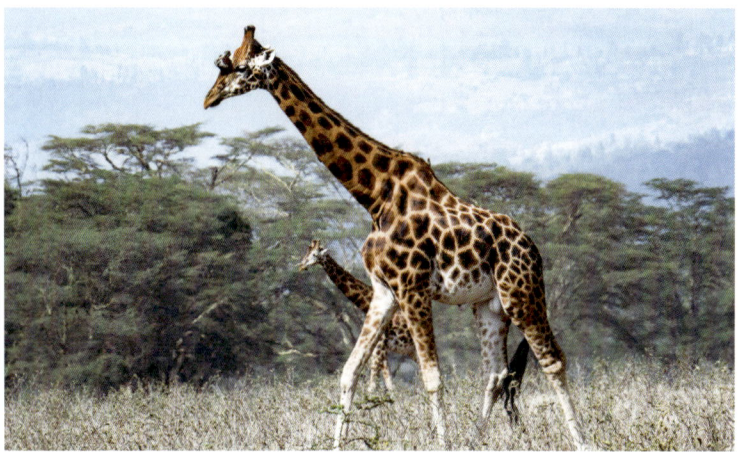

Like a mirage in the desert, giraffes of unparalleled grace and grandeur suddenly appear through the thorny bush and acacia trees that make up this harsh yet enchanted African landscape.

Above and opposite: Giraffe, Kenya /Nikon D810

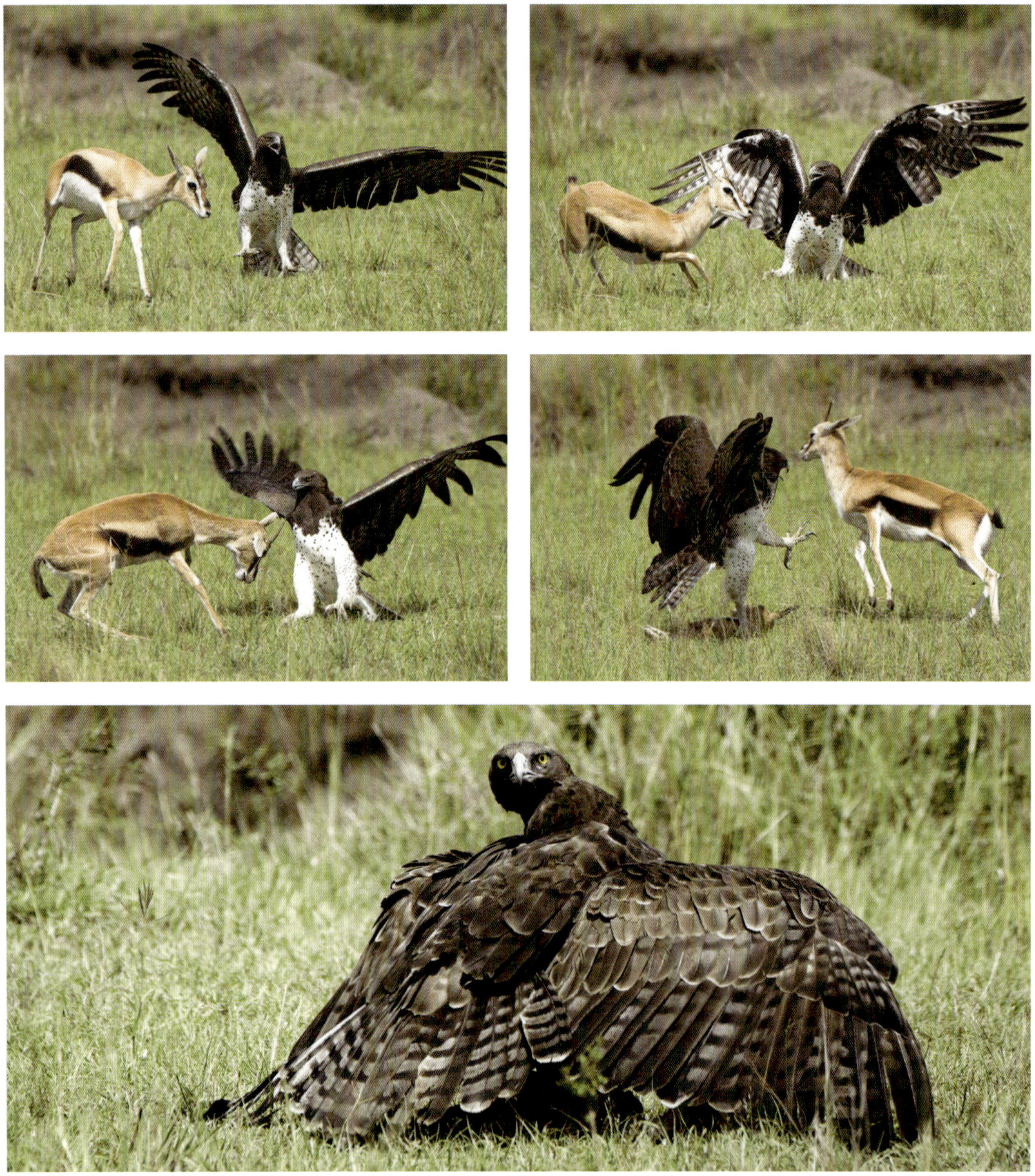

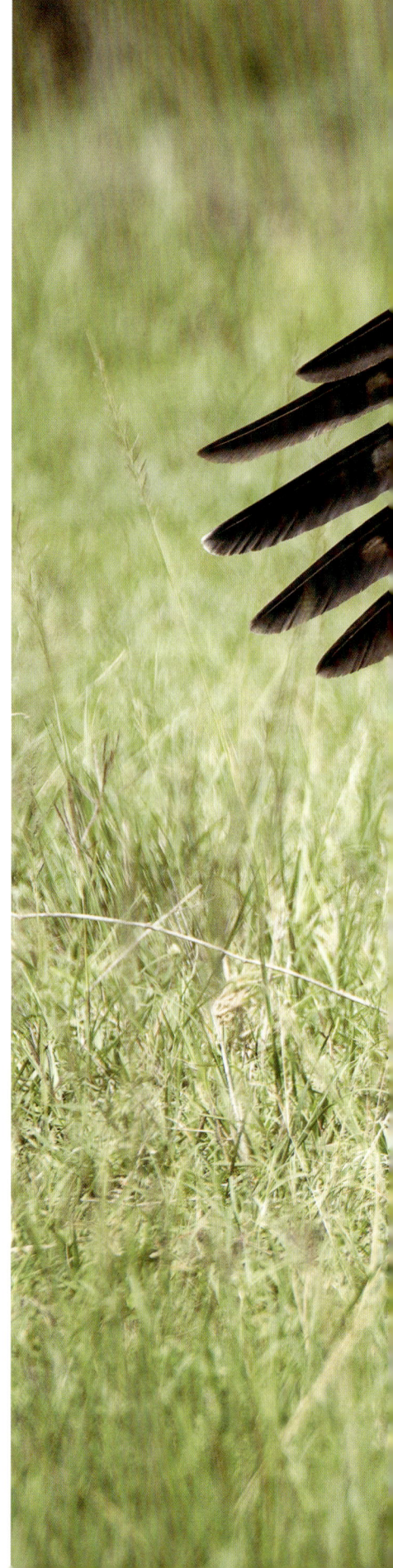

A life-and-death struggle between a martial eagle and a mother's love for her newborn fawn on the plains of the Maasai Mara.

Above and opposite: Martial Eagle, Kenya /Nikon D810

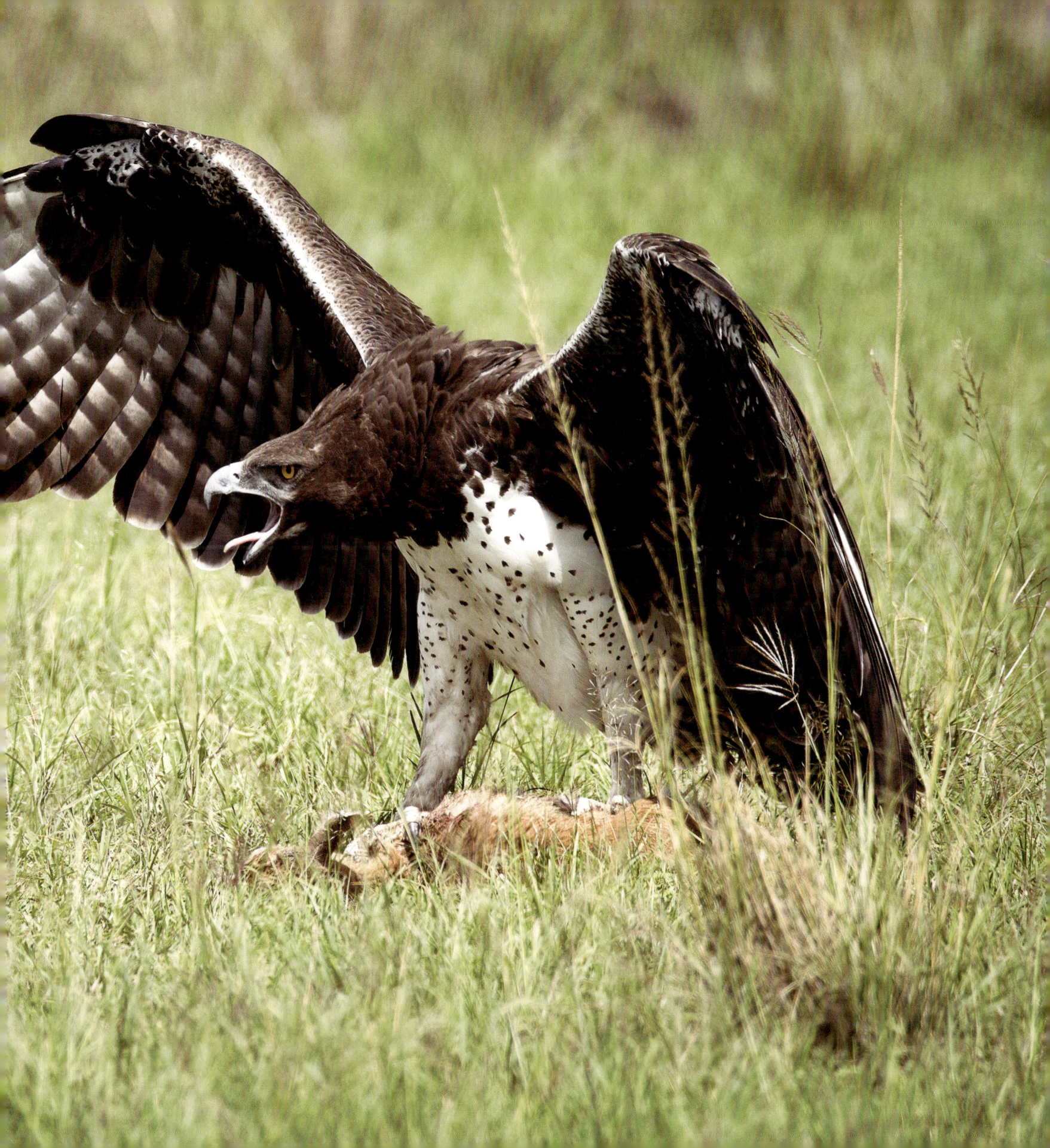

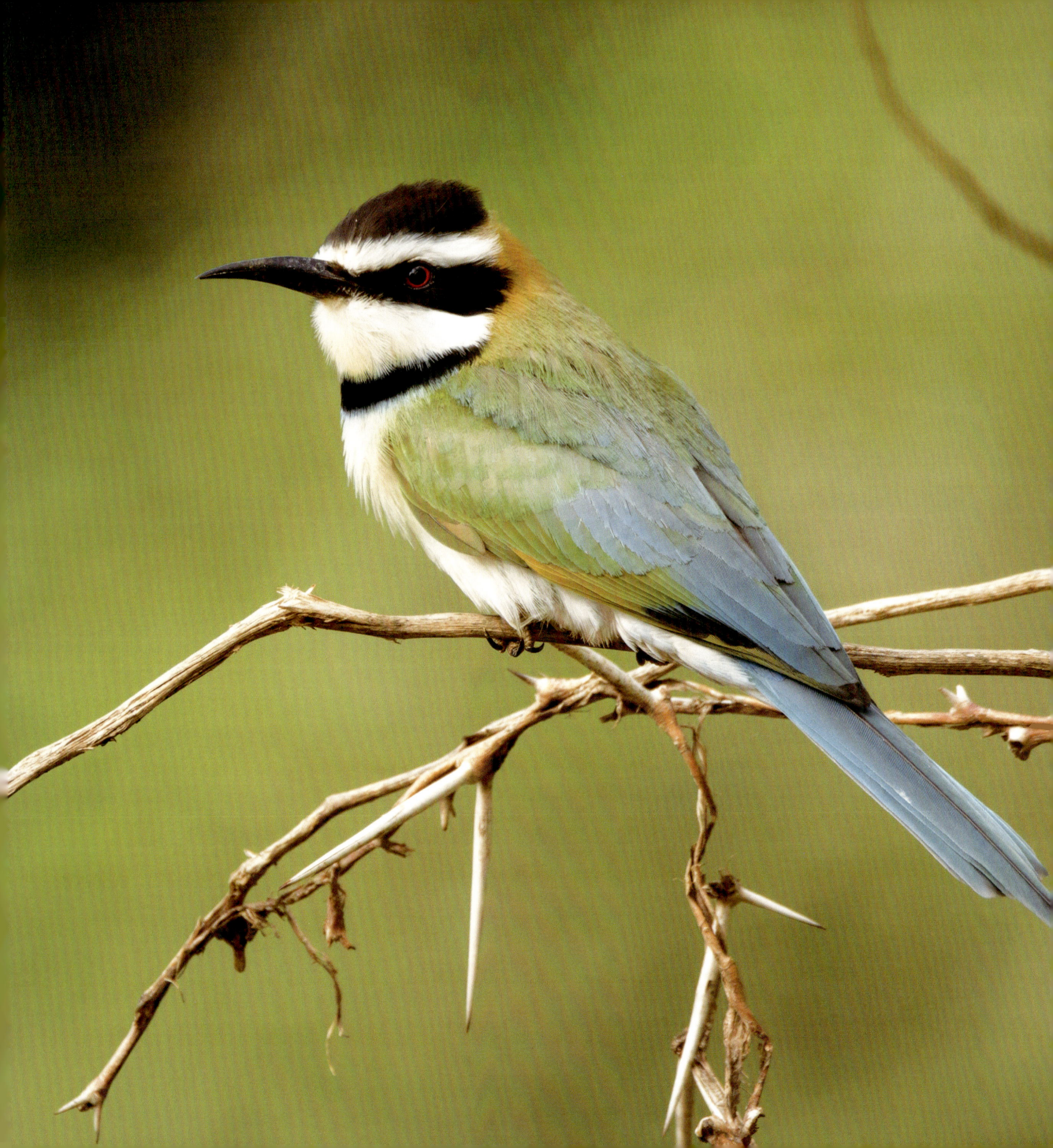

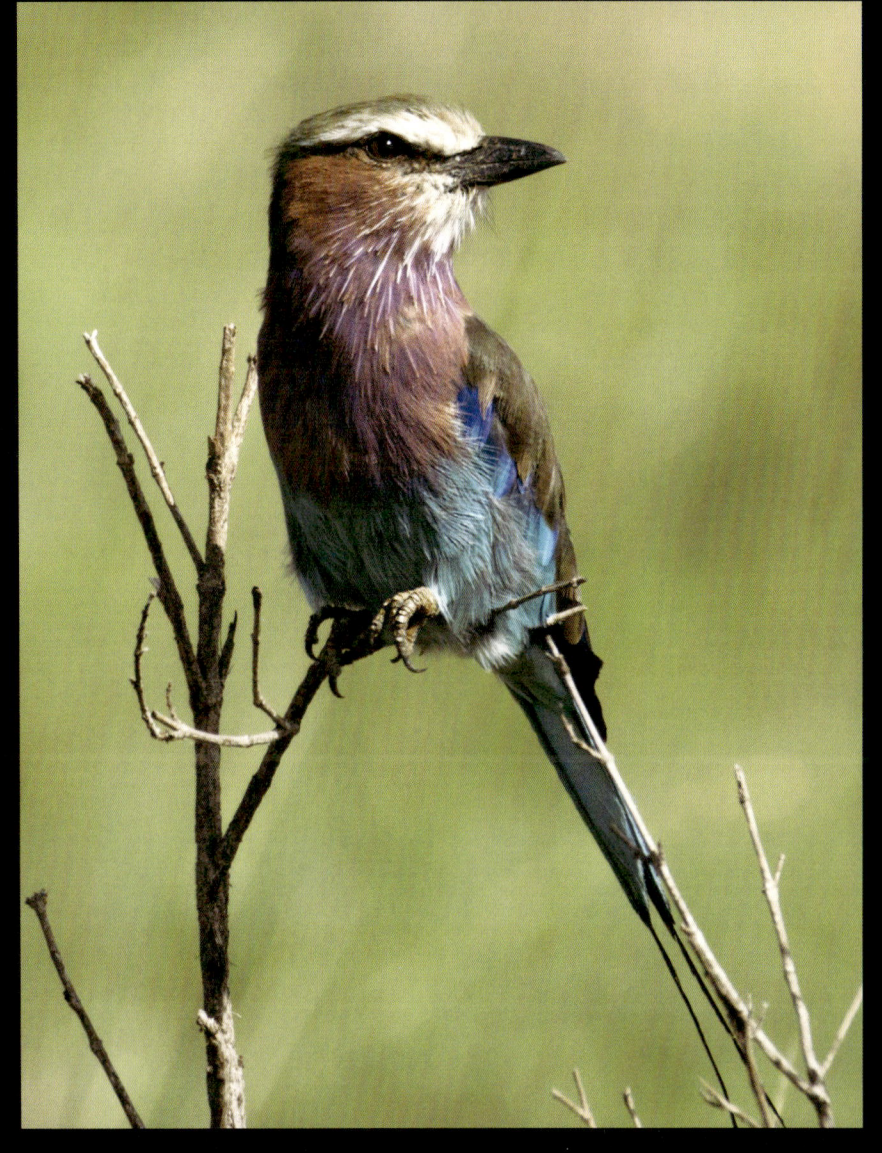

As the morning light chased away the long African night, I was greeted by a few of its more colorful residents who had gotten up early to sunbathe before breakfast

Above: Lilac-Breasted Roller, Kenya /Nikon D810
Opposite: White-Throated Bee-Eater, Kenya /Nikon D810

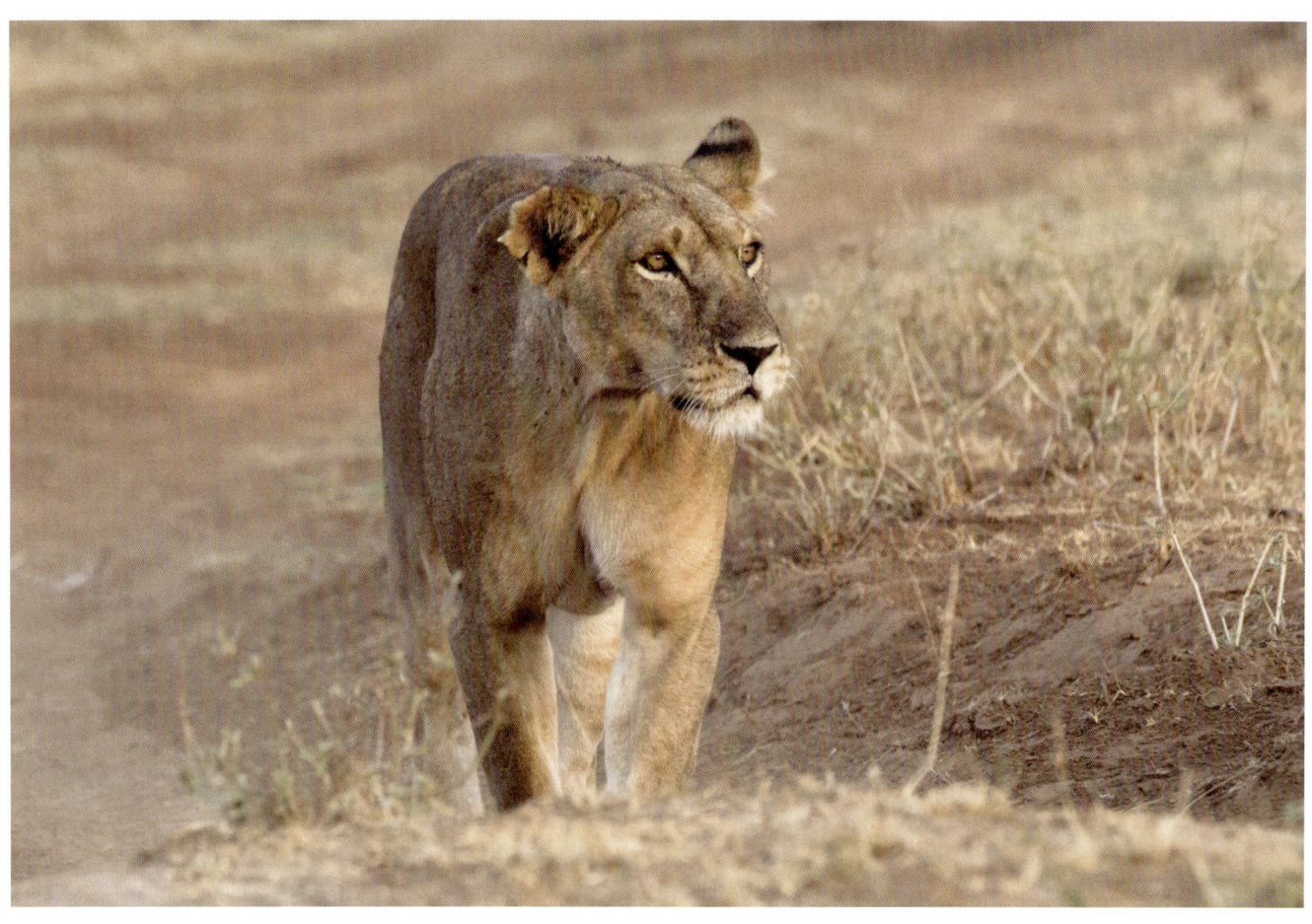

Her thoughts are unknown, her direction unclear, but she walks like a queen . . . confident, strong, and focused. The pride is hers to feed, so she must find prey or they will go hungry this day. She is the Mother of Kings and Lioness Supreme.

Above and opposite: African Lioness, Kenya /Nikon D810

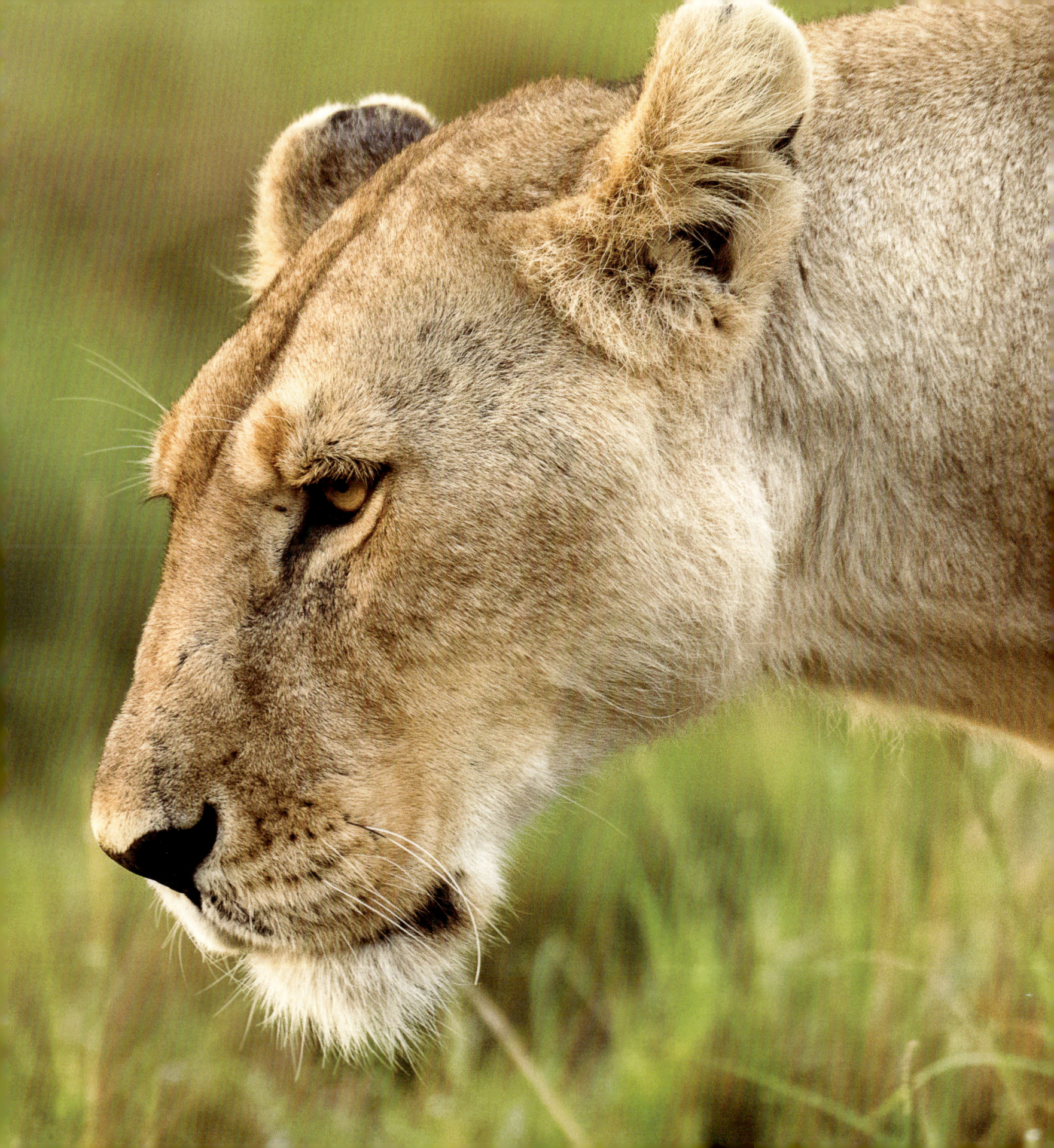

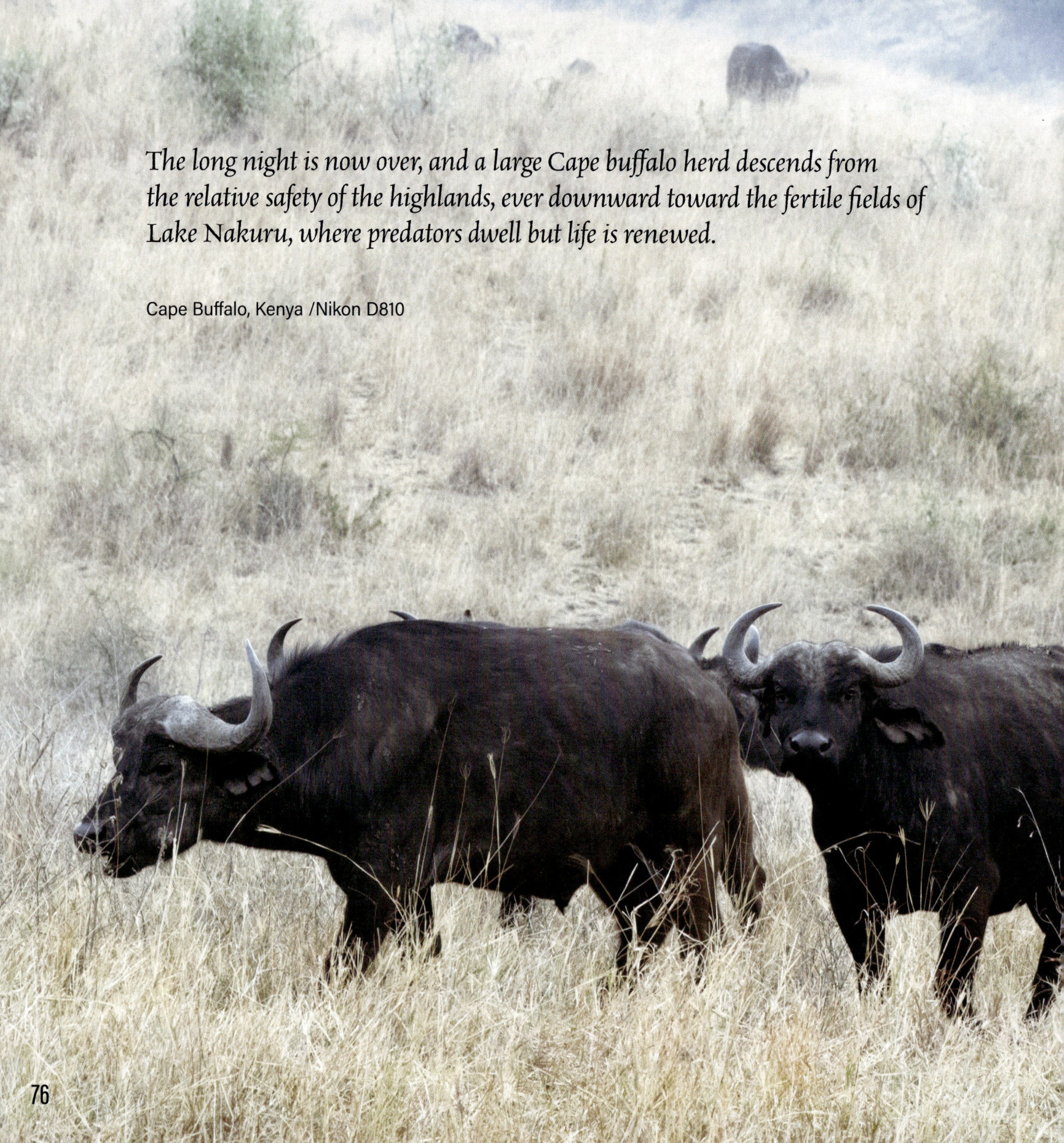

The long night is now over, and a large Cape buffalo herd descends from the relative safety of the highlands, ever downward toward the fertile fields of Lake Nakuru, where predators dwell but life is renewed.

Cape Buffalo, Kenya / Nikon D810

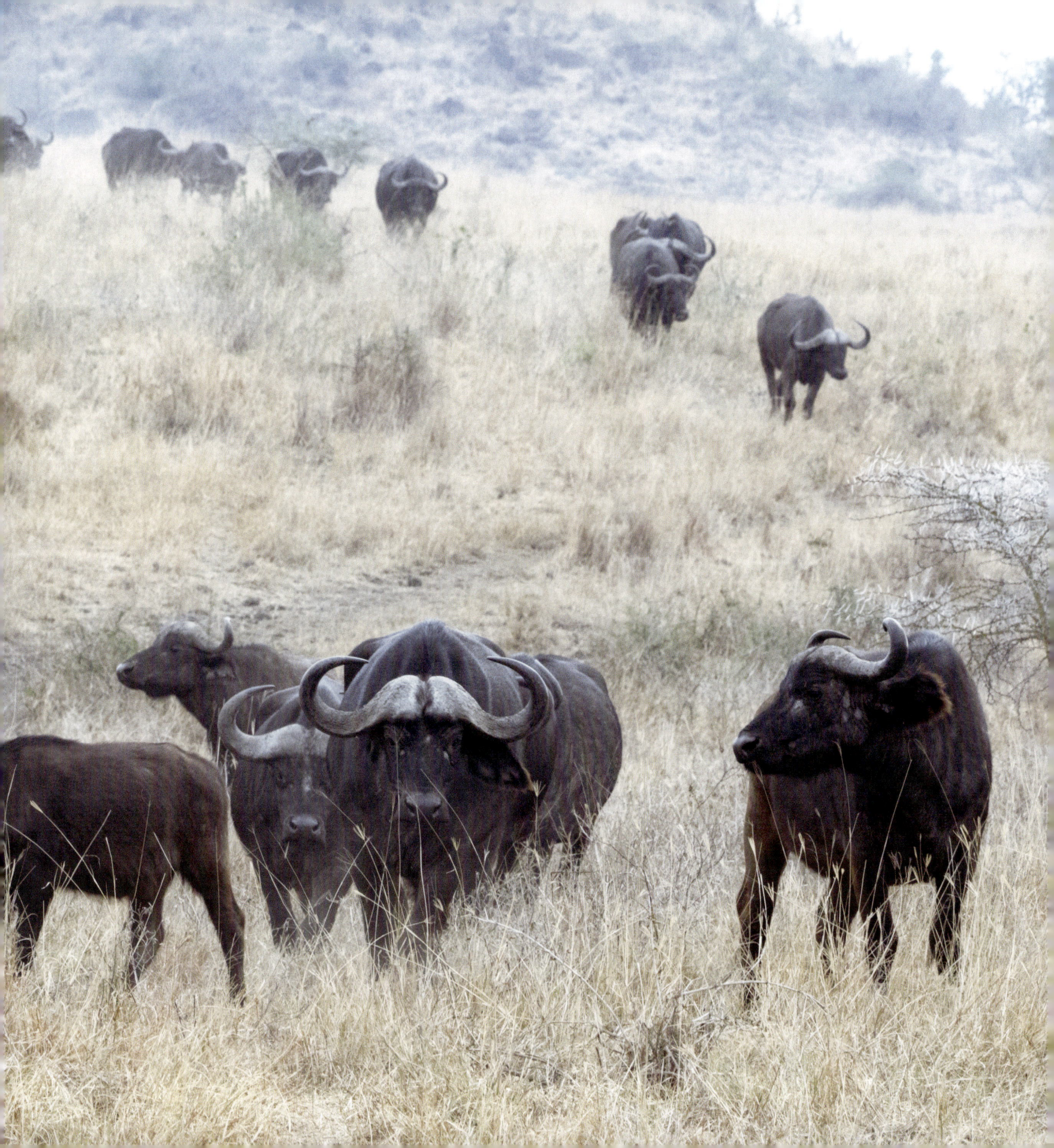

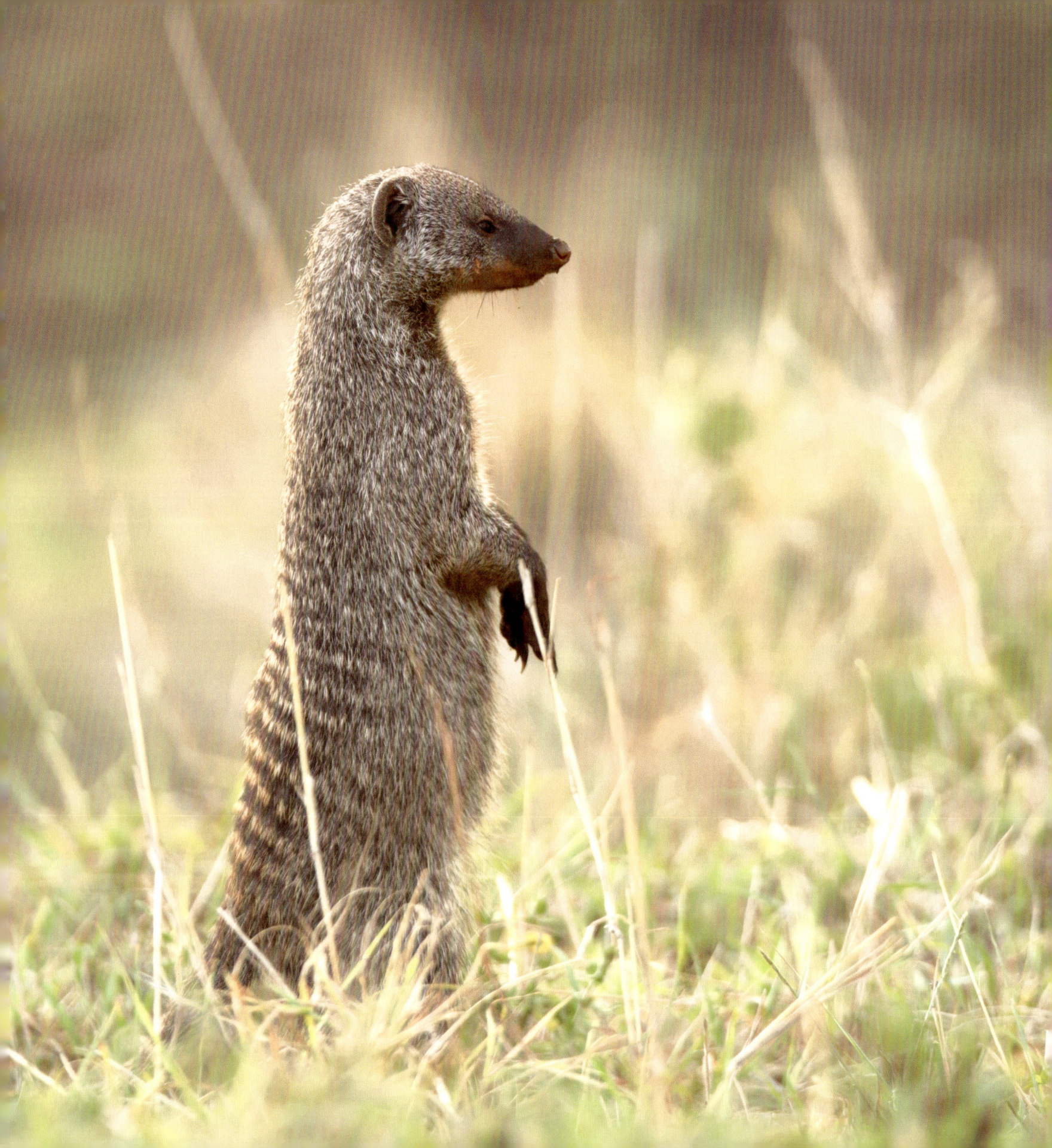

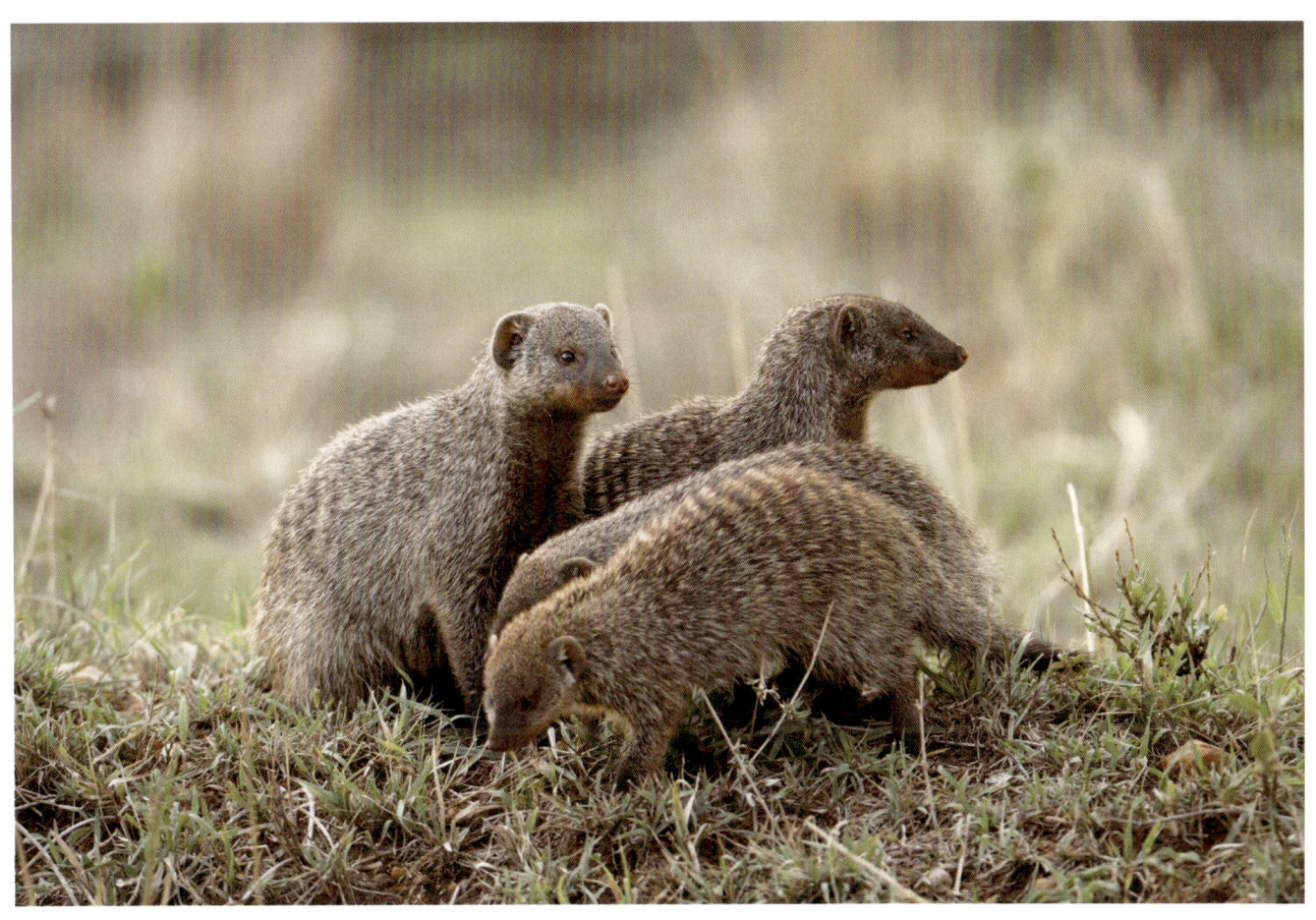

Unlike the comparable giants who dwell within the Mara, this mongoose family is small in scale but large in life. They carefully make their way each and every day, always on guard, always on alert, and always together.

Above and opposite: African Mongoose, Kenya / Nikon D810

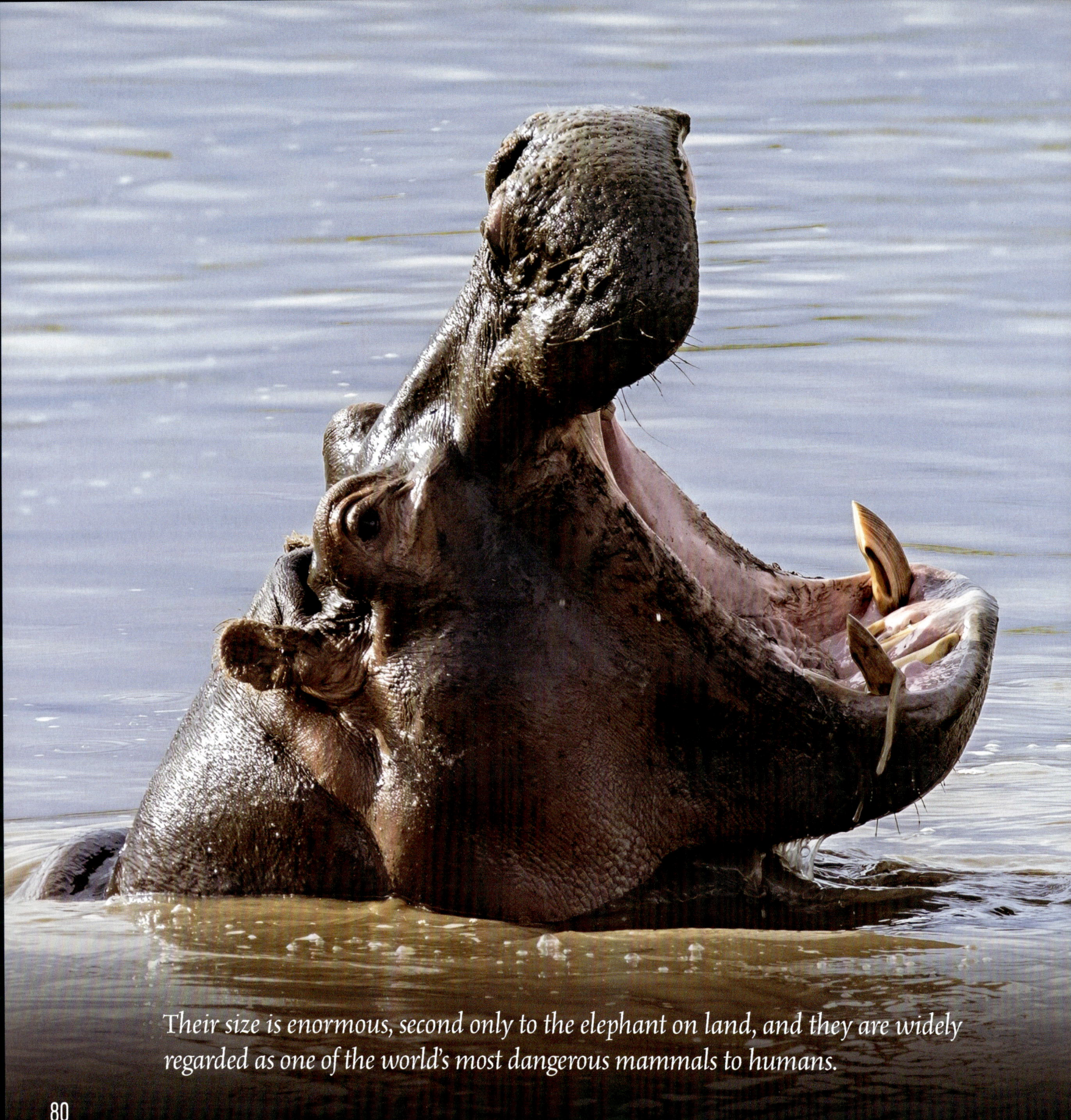

Their size is enormous, second only to the elephant on land, and they are widely regarded as one of the world's most dangerous mammals to humans.

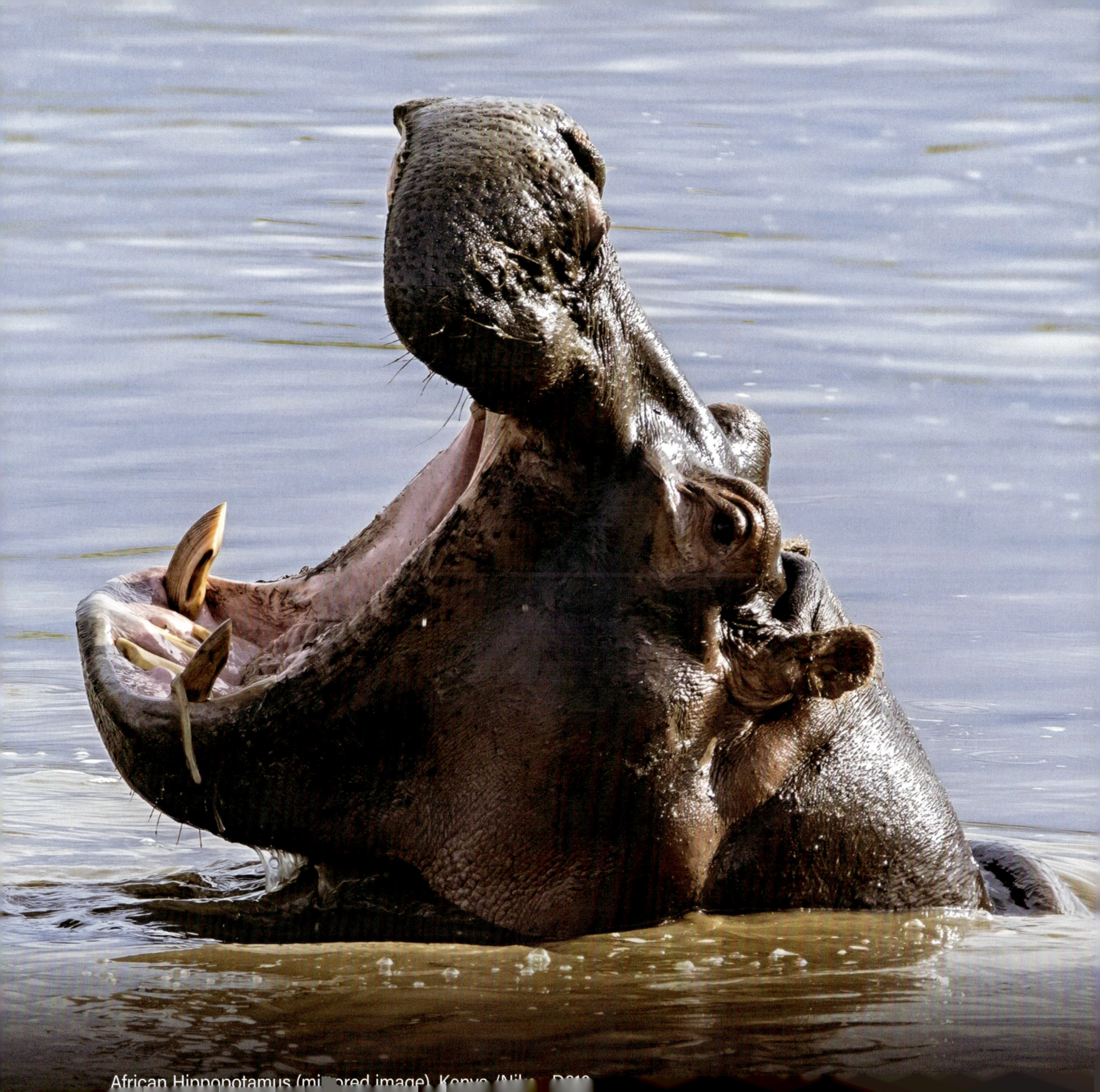

African Hippopotamus (mirrored image), Kenya (Nikon D810)

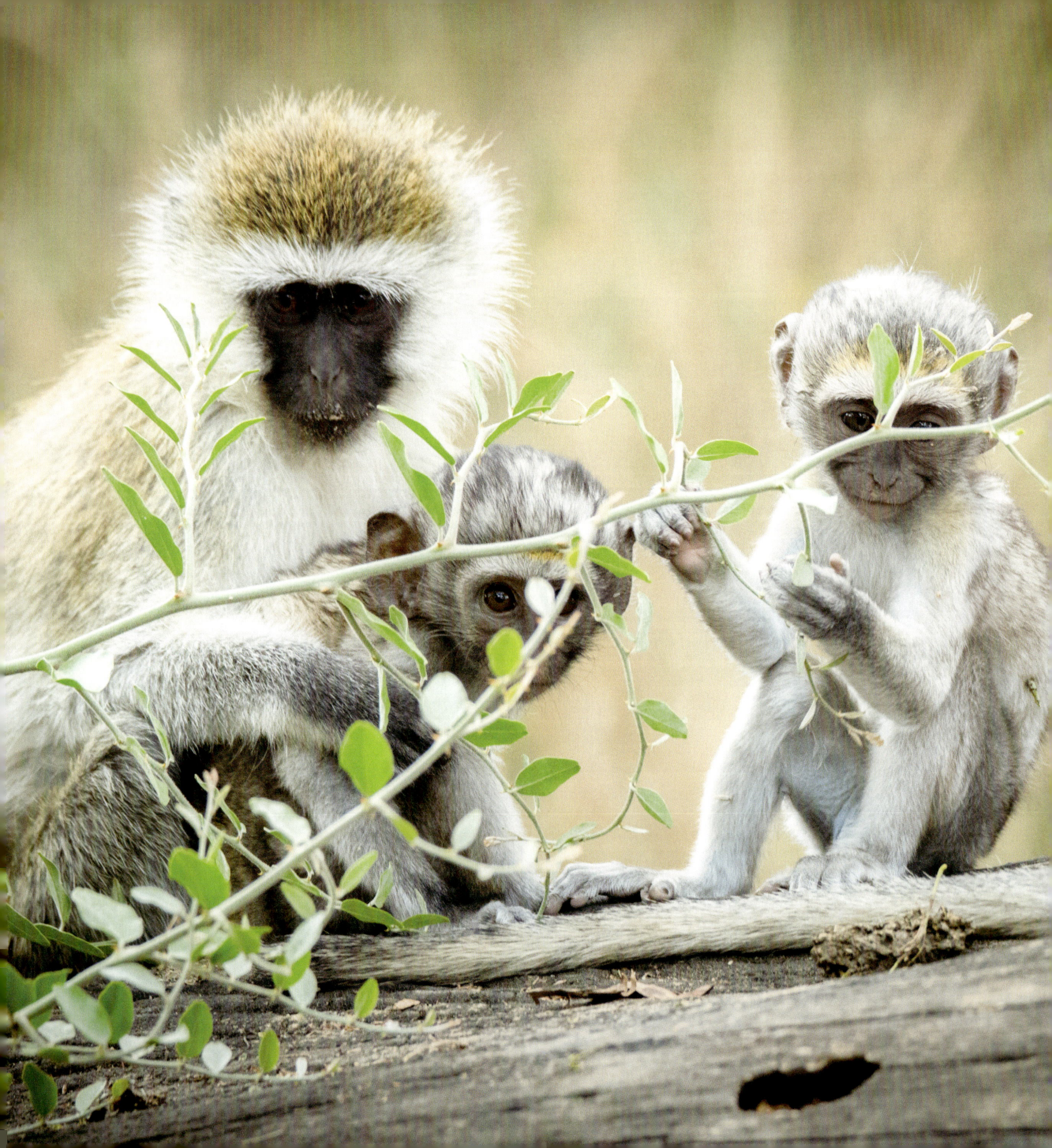

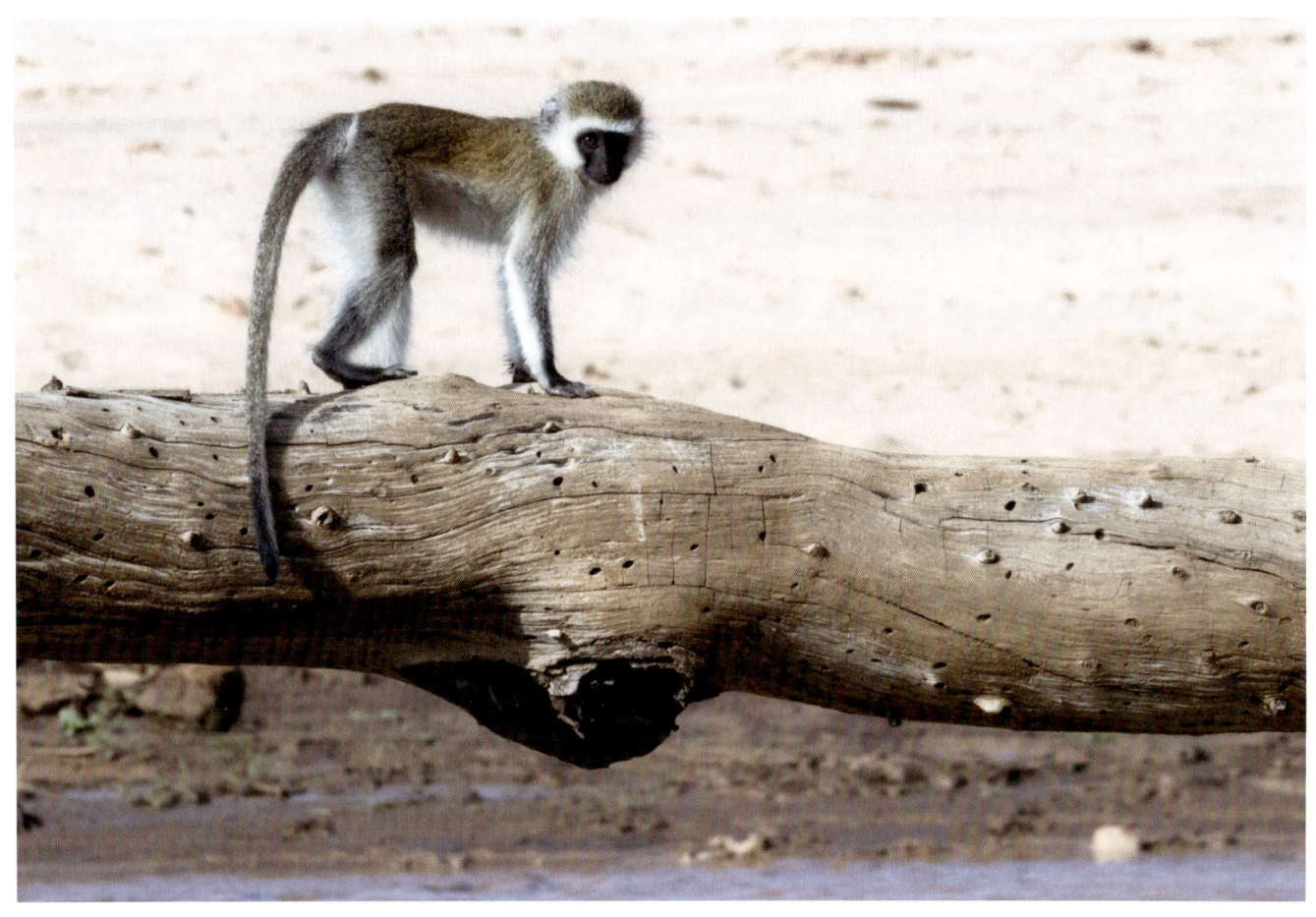

Young vervet monkeys stare at my presence with absolute wonder and curiosity, held at bay only by their mother's touch.

Above and opposite: Vervet Monkeys, Kenya / Nikon D810

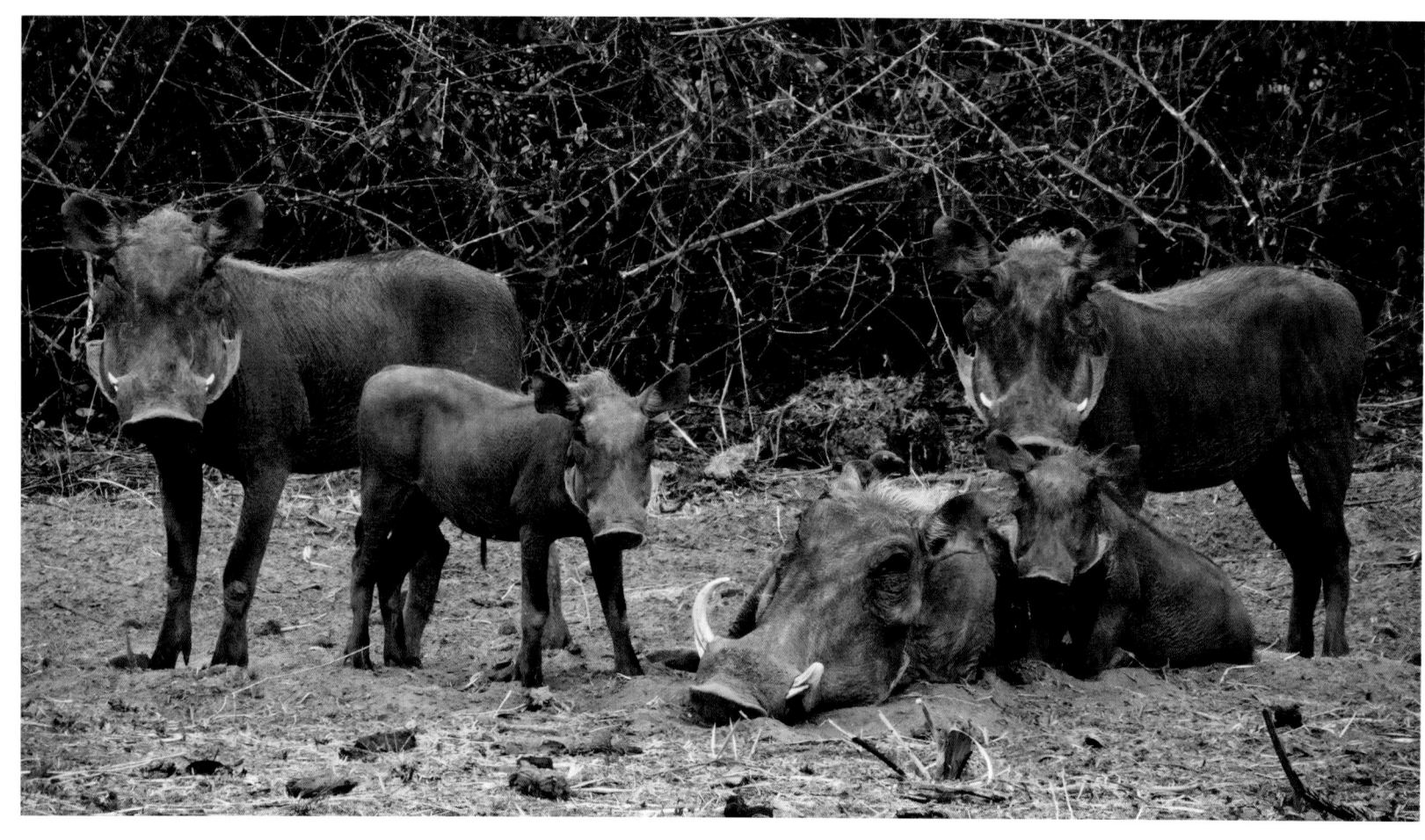

Intelligent, strong-bodied animals with a fierce reputation for invoking pain upon their enemies is the best way to describe the African warthog; one of Africa's most interesting animals to never win a beauty pageant.

Above and opposite: Warthogs, Kenya Africa /Nikon Africa D810

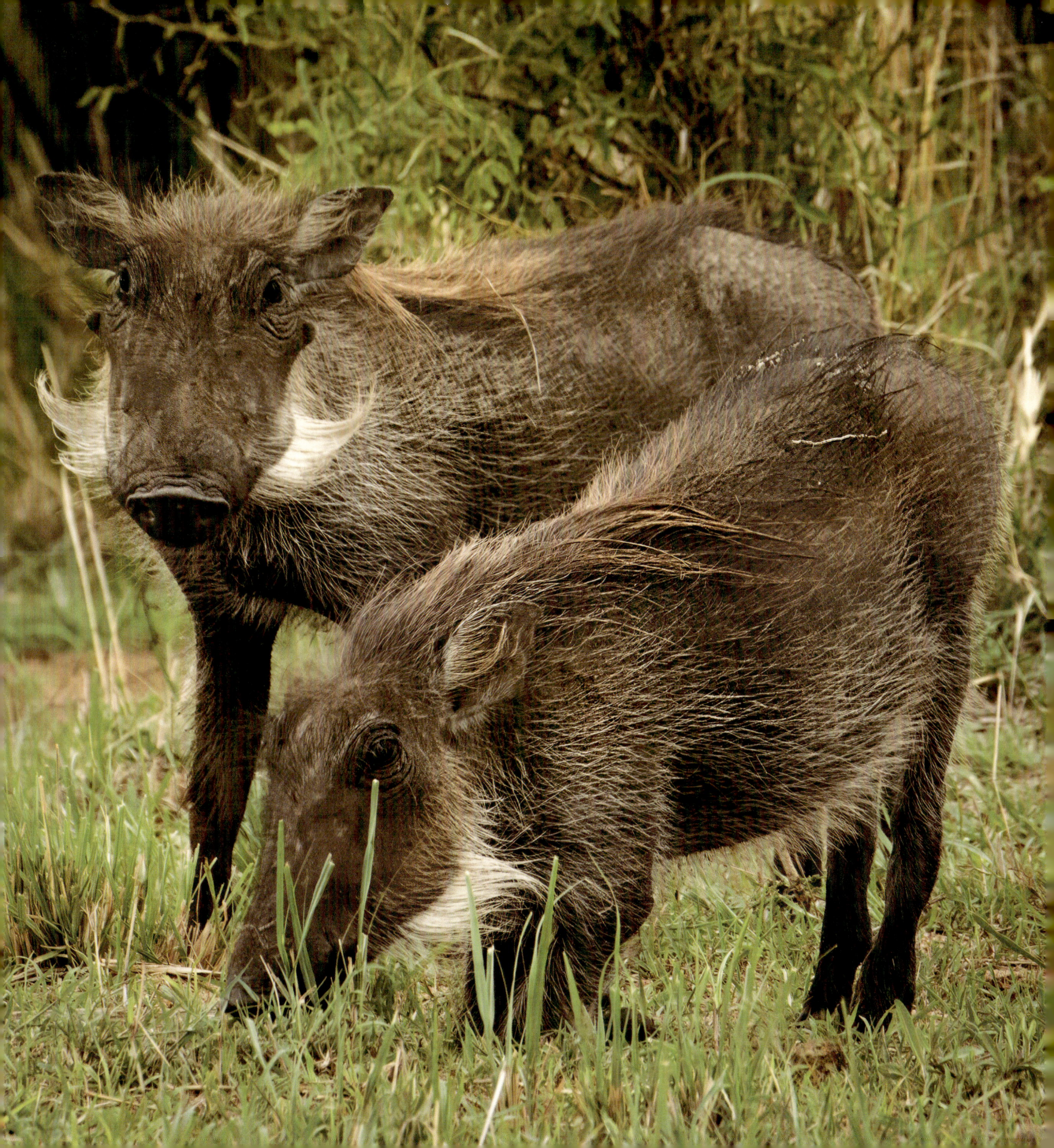

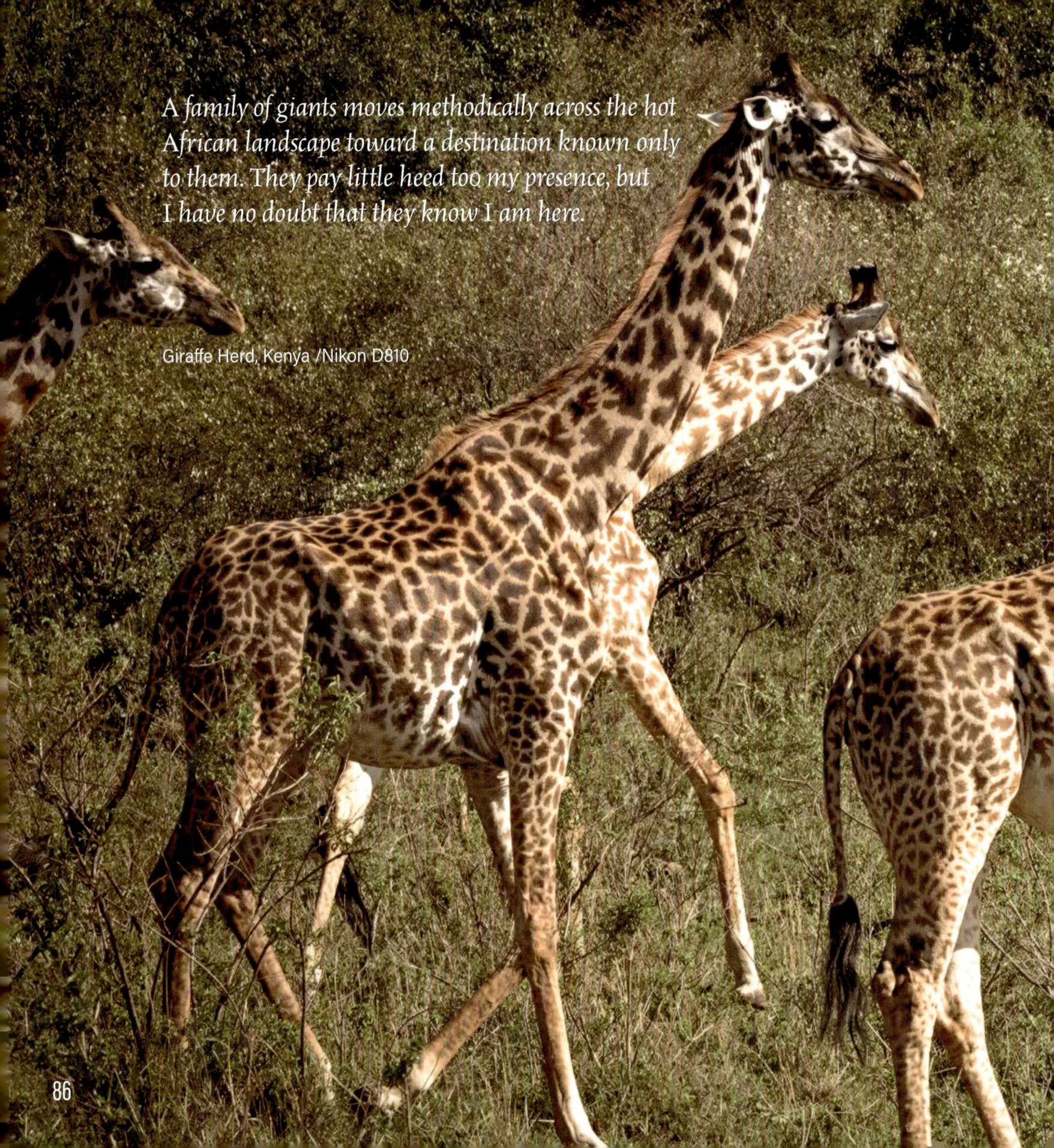

A family of giants moves methodically across the hot African landscape toward a destination known only to them. They pay little heed too my presence, but I have no doubt that they know I am here.

Giraffe Herd, Kenya / Nikon D810

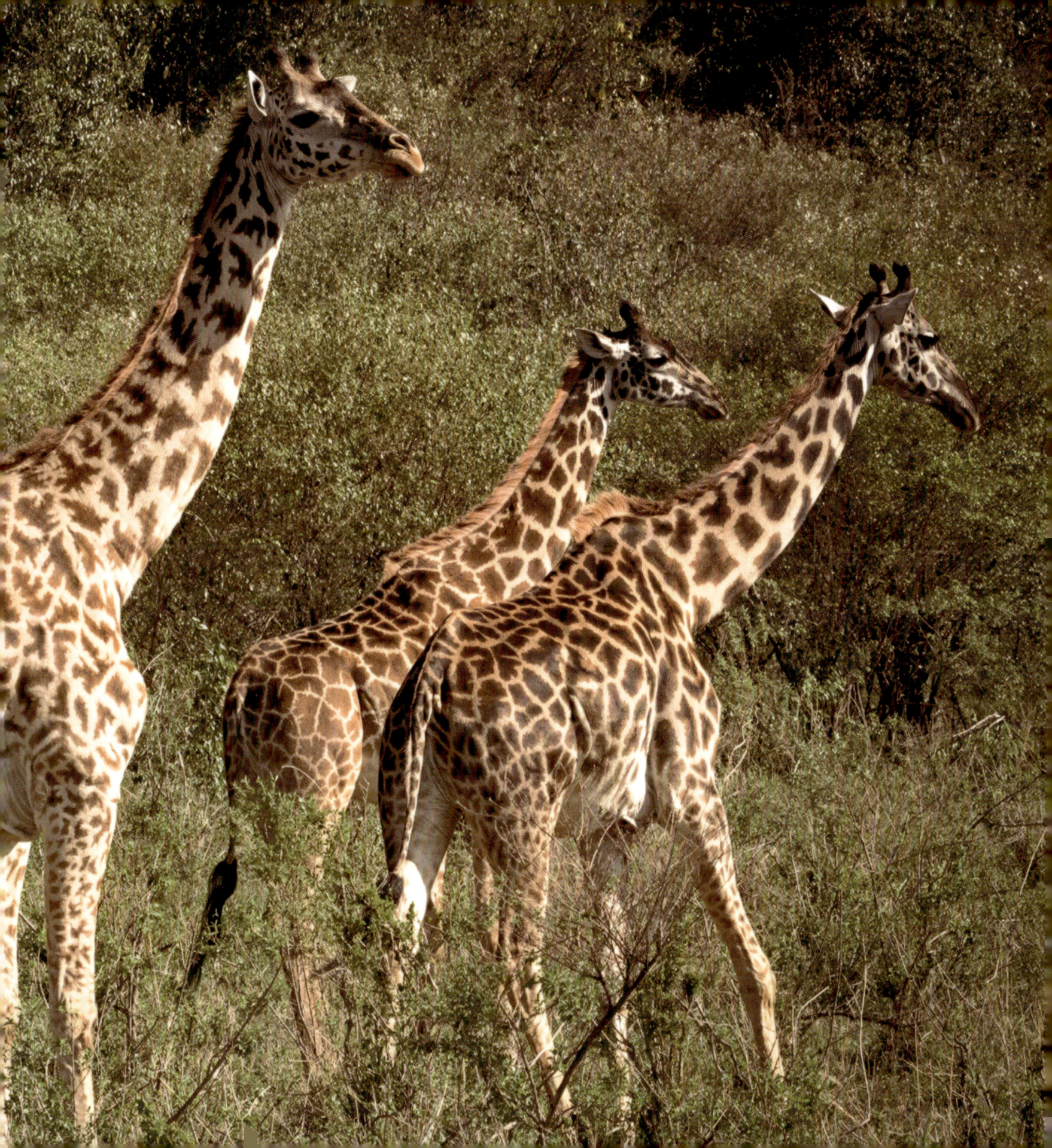

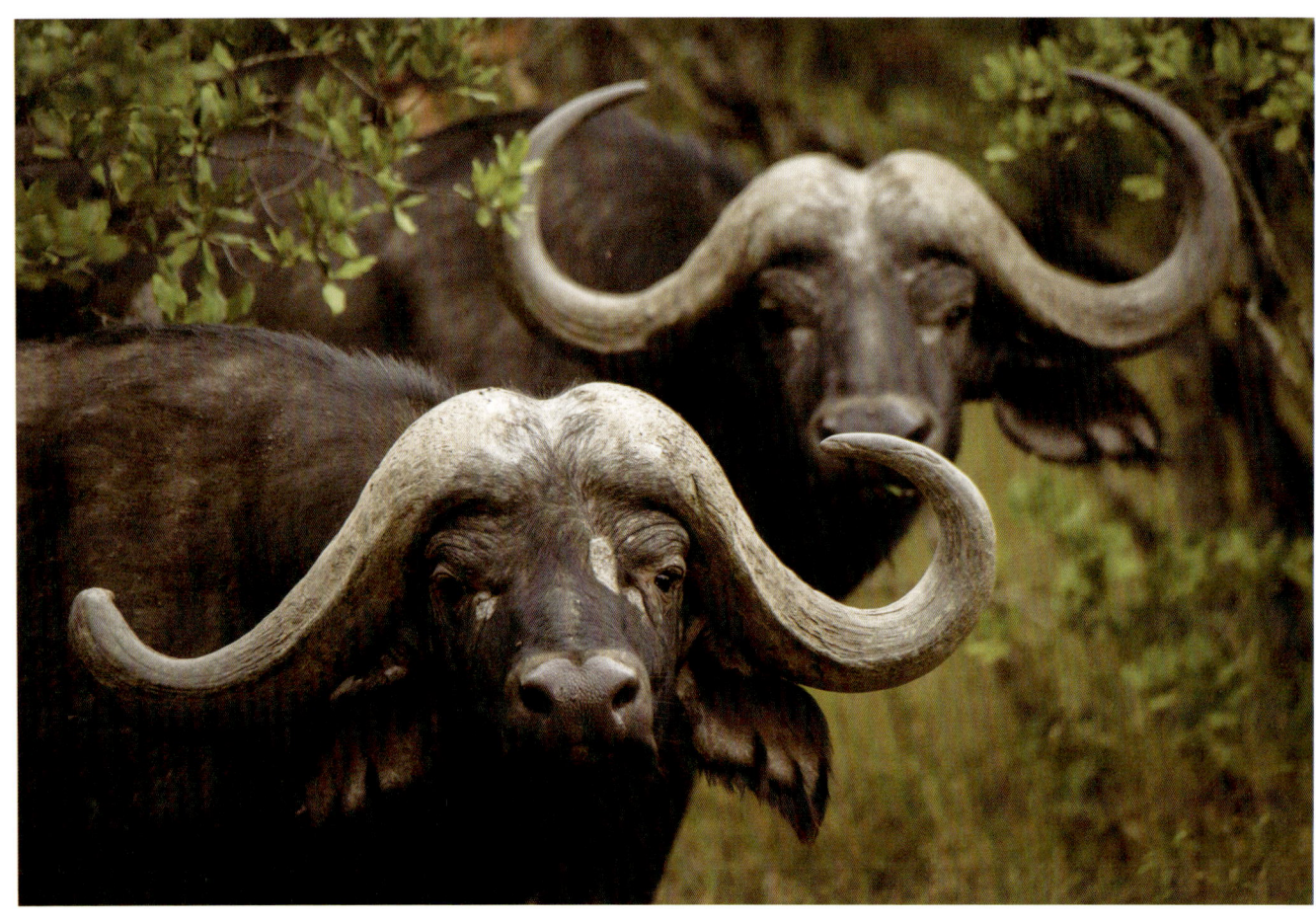

One of Africa's most dangerous animals, the Cape buffalo can invoke fear in even the hardiest of predators. Their sheer power can overwhelm, and when the herd moves as one they are virtually unstoppable.

Above and opposite: Cape Buffalo, Kenya /Nikon D810

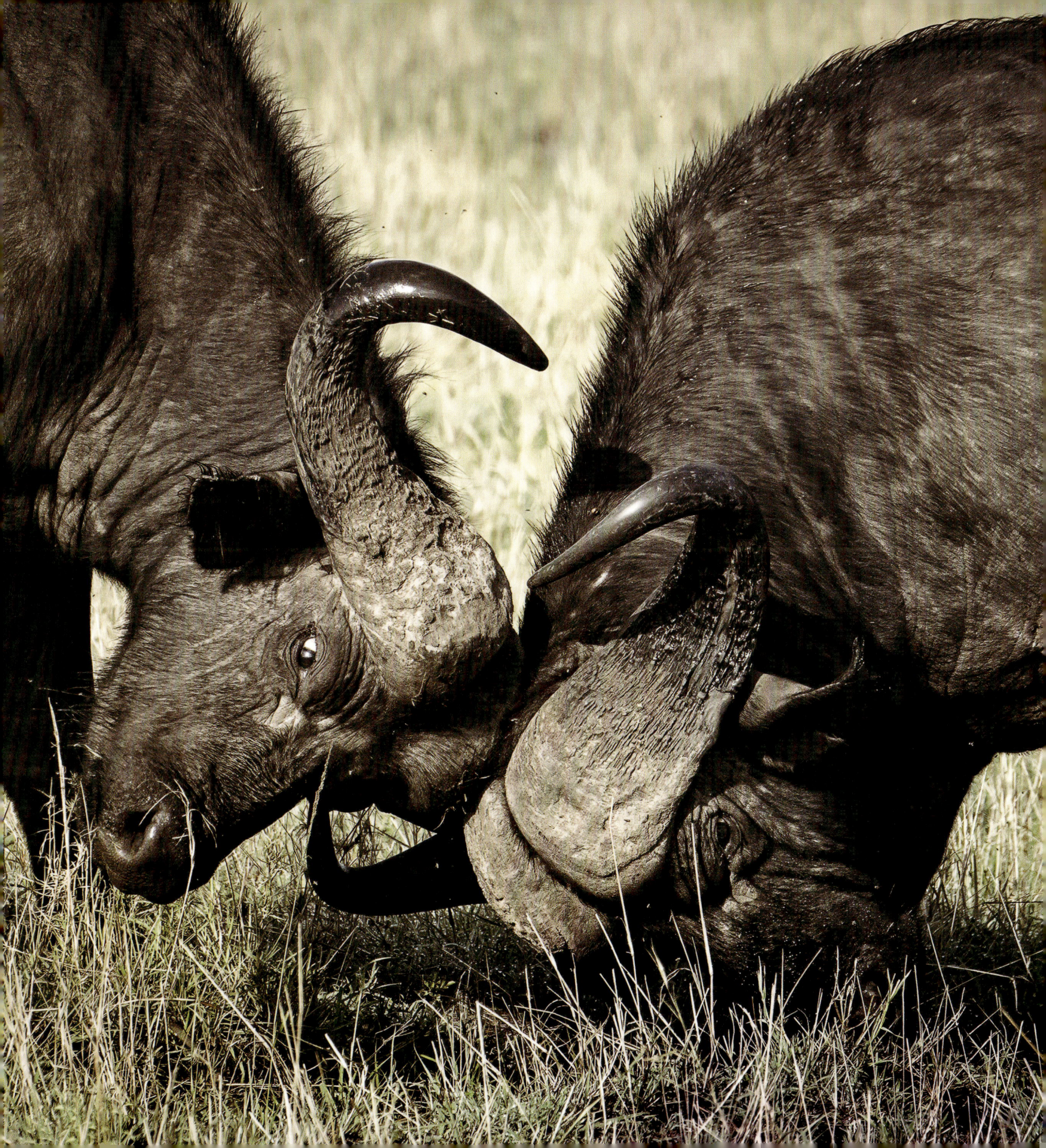

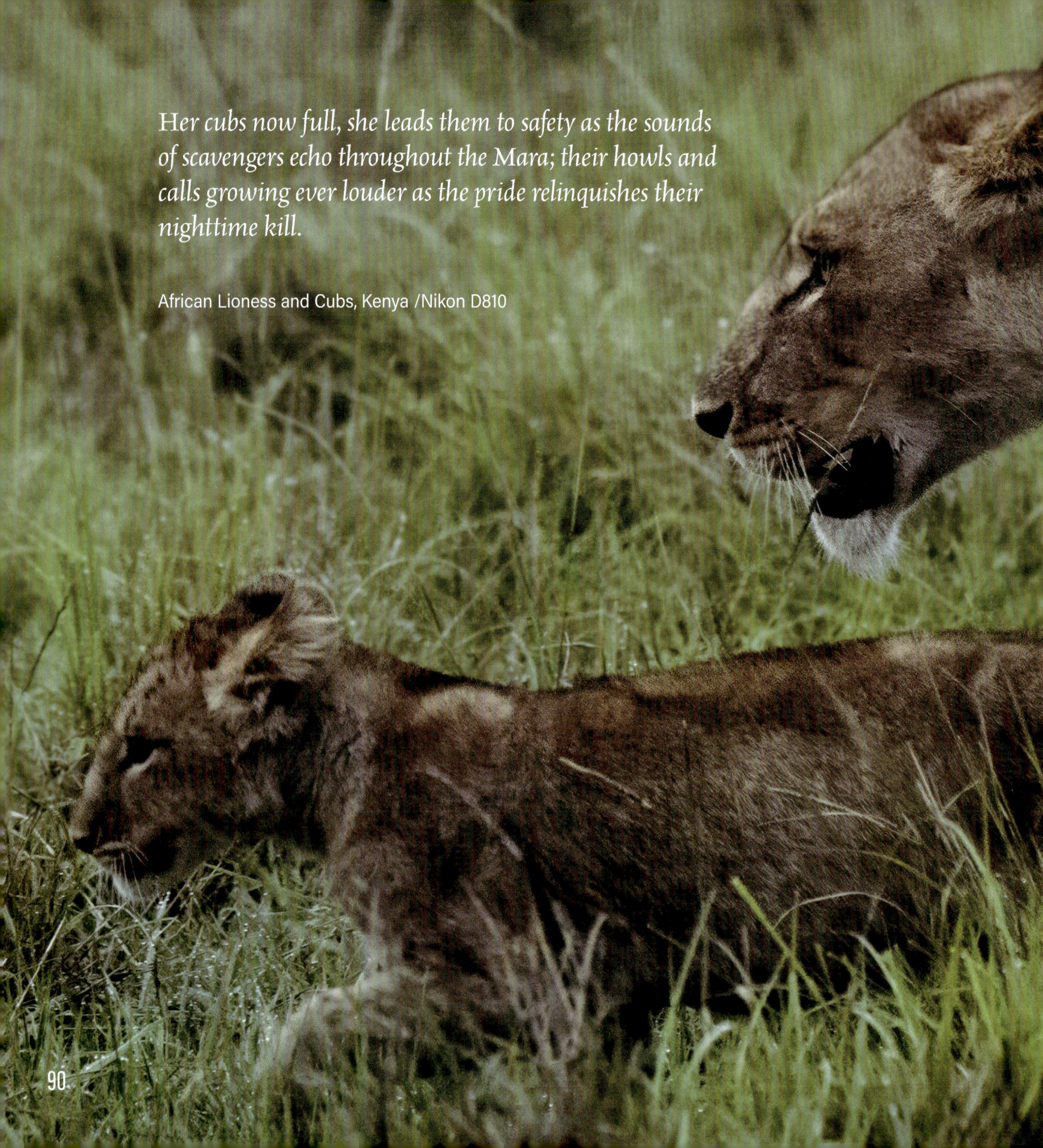

Her cubs now full, she leads them to safety as the sounds of scavengers echo throughout the Mara; their howls and calls growing ever louder as the pride relinquishes their nighttime kill.

African Lioness and Cubs, Kenya /Nikon D810

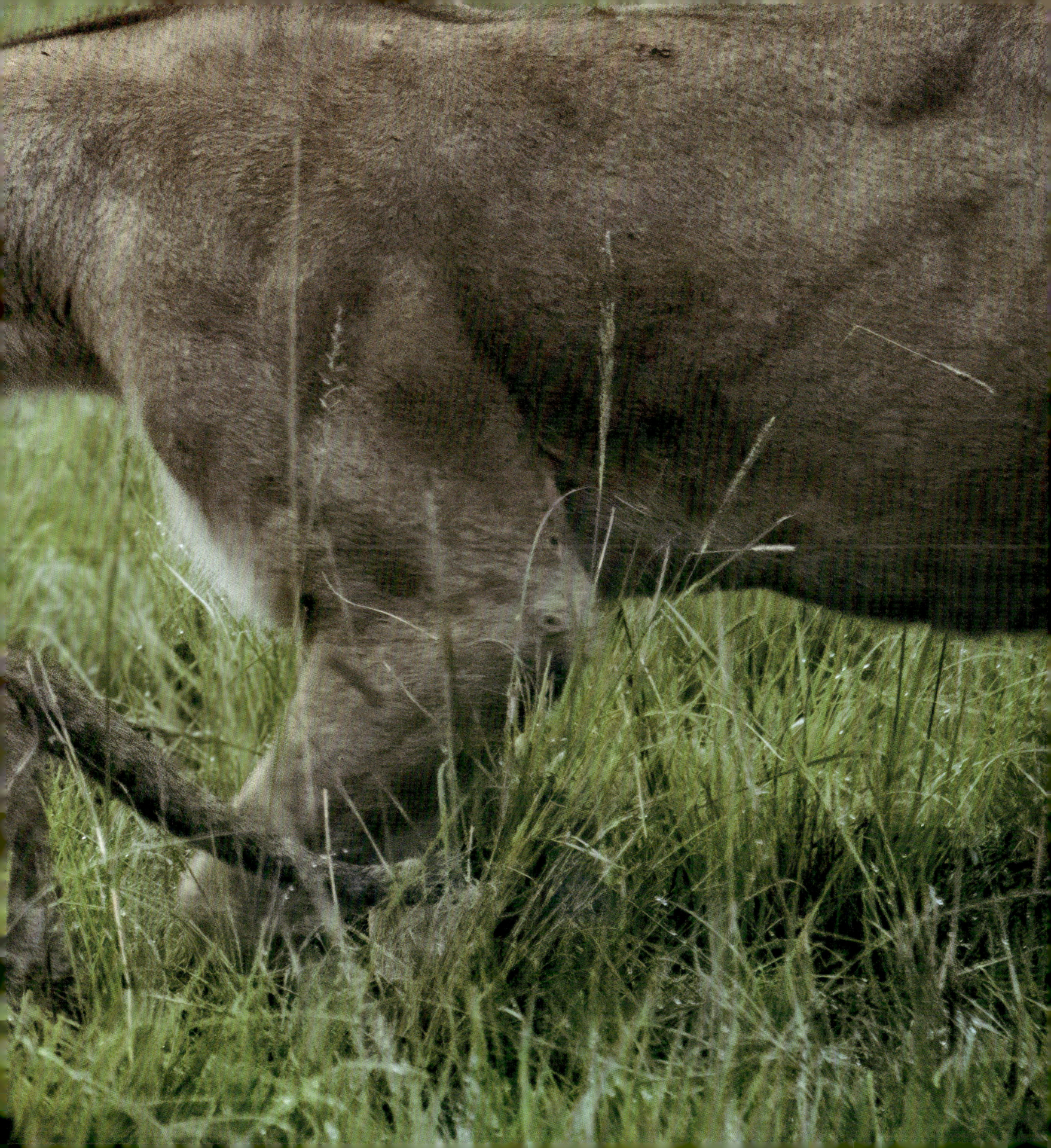

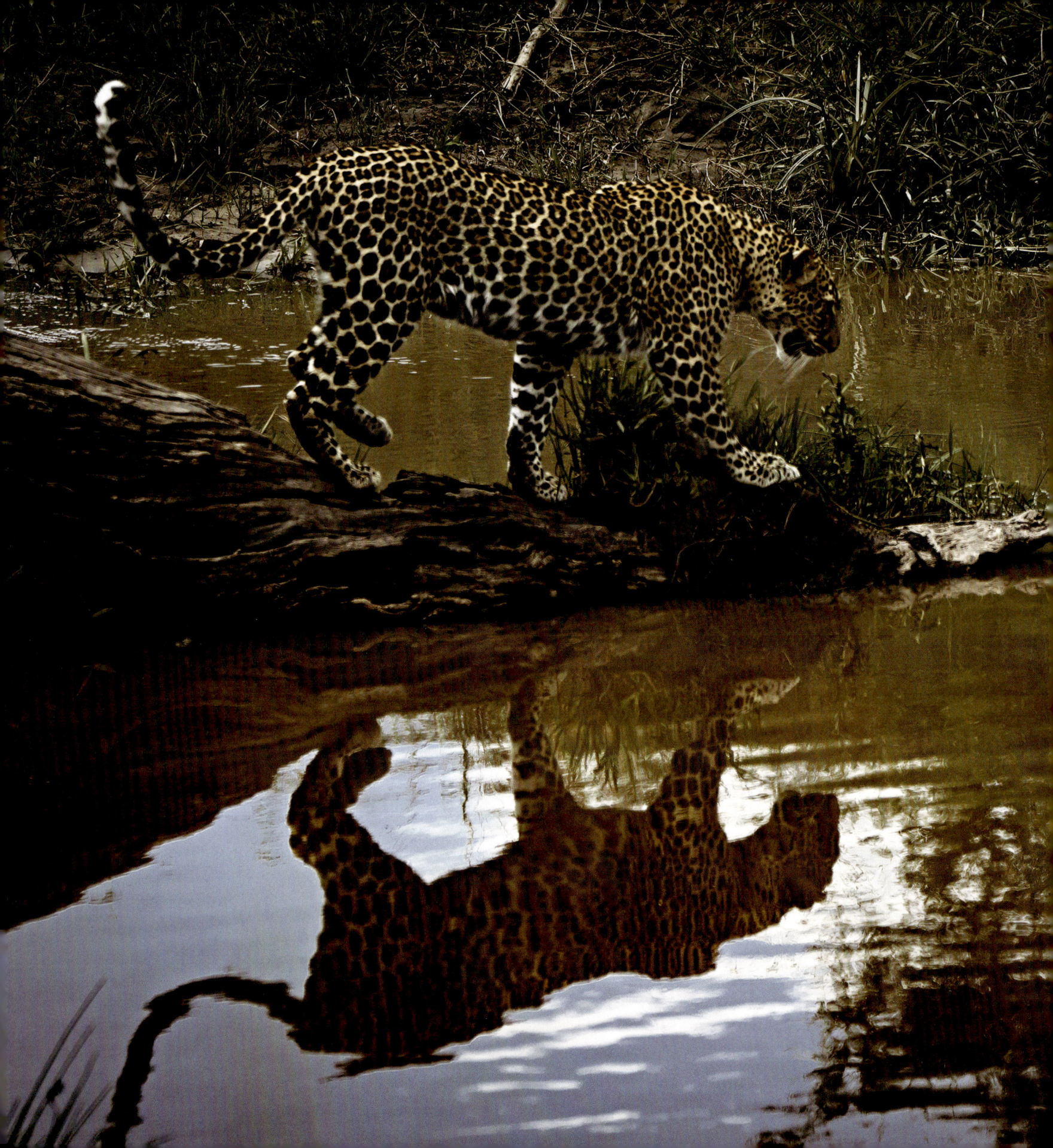

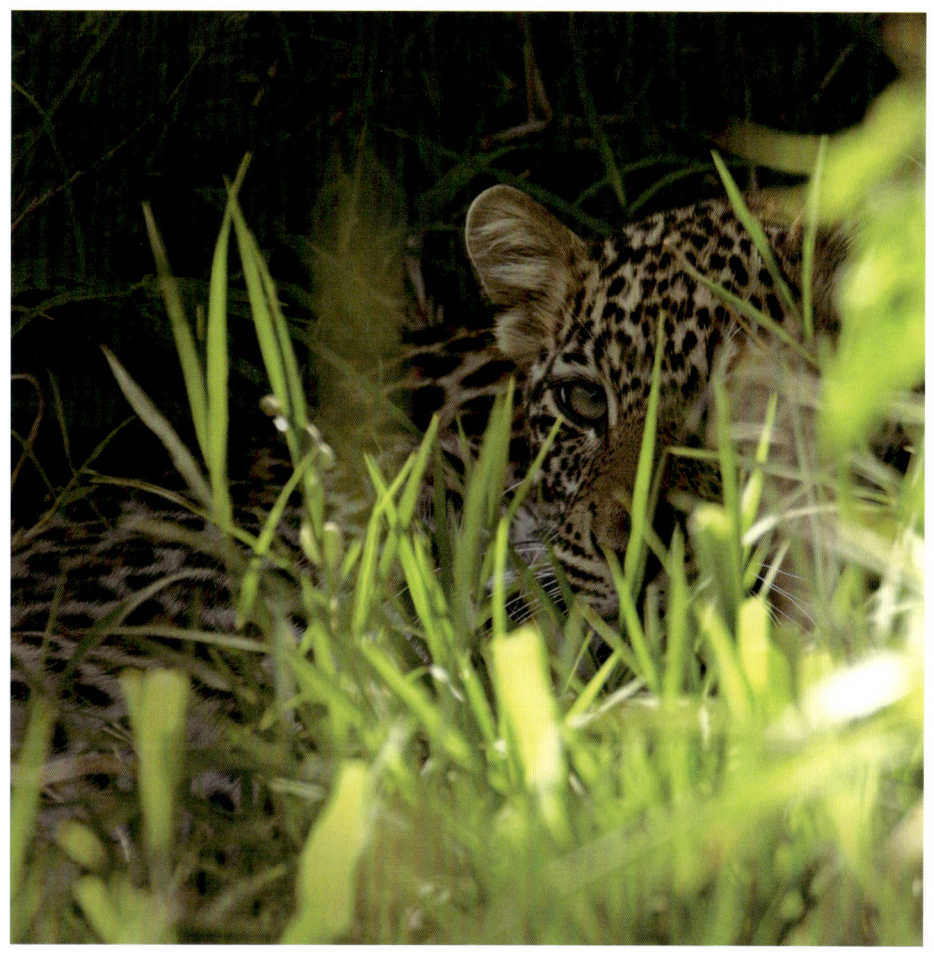

Silently moving through the shadows and embankments of the River Mara, a lone leopard heads out for the hunt once more, using her stealth and all her years of experience to guide her in her quest for prey.

Above and opposite: African Leopard, Kenya /Nikon D810

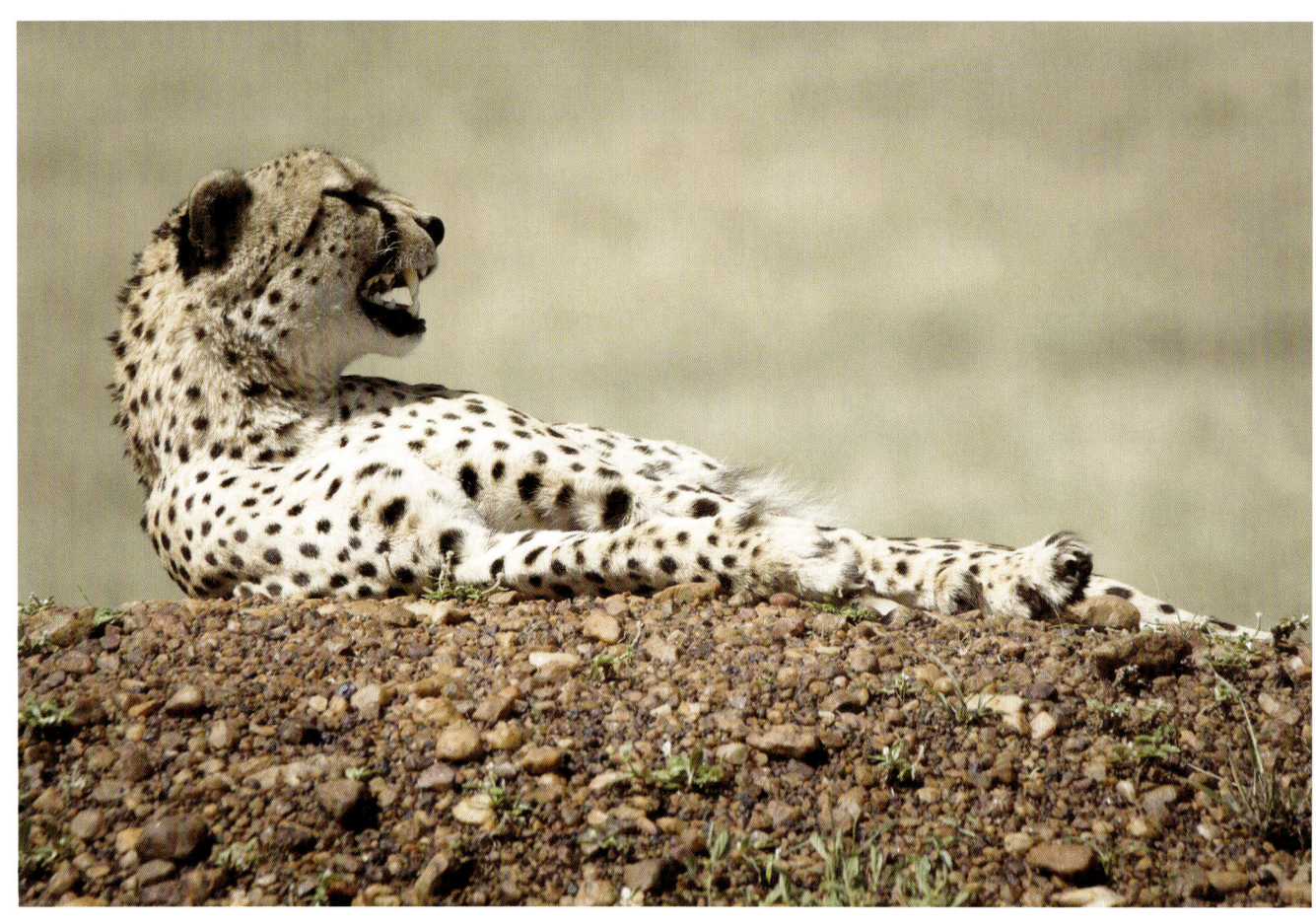

Flat grasslands as far as the eyes can see prevail within the Mara, making any high ground a preferable choice for this young cheetah to closely observe both predator and prey in the vastness of this ancient wilderness.

Above and opposite: African Cheetah, Kenya /Nikon D810

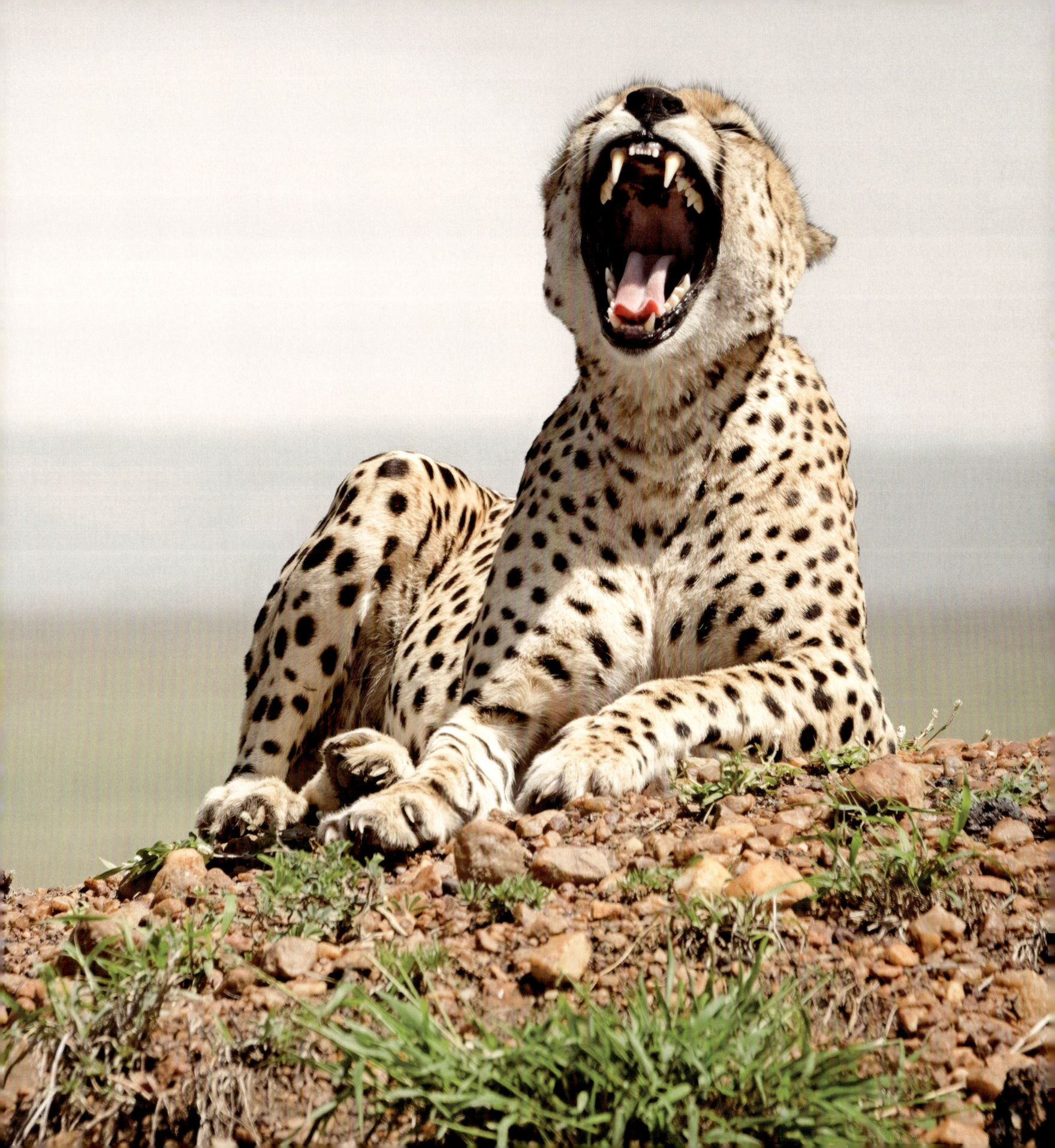

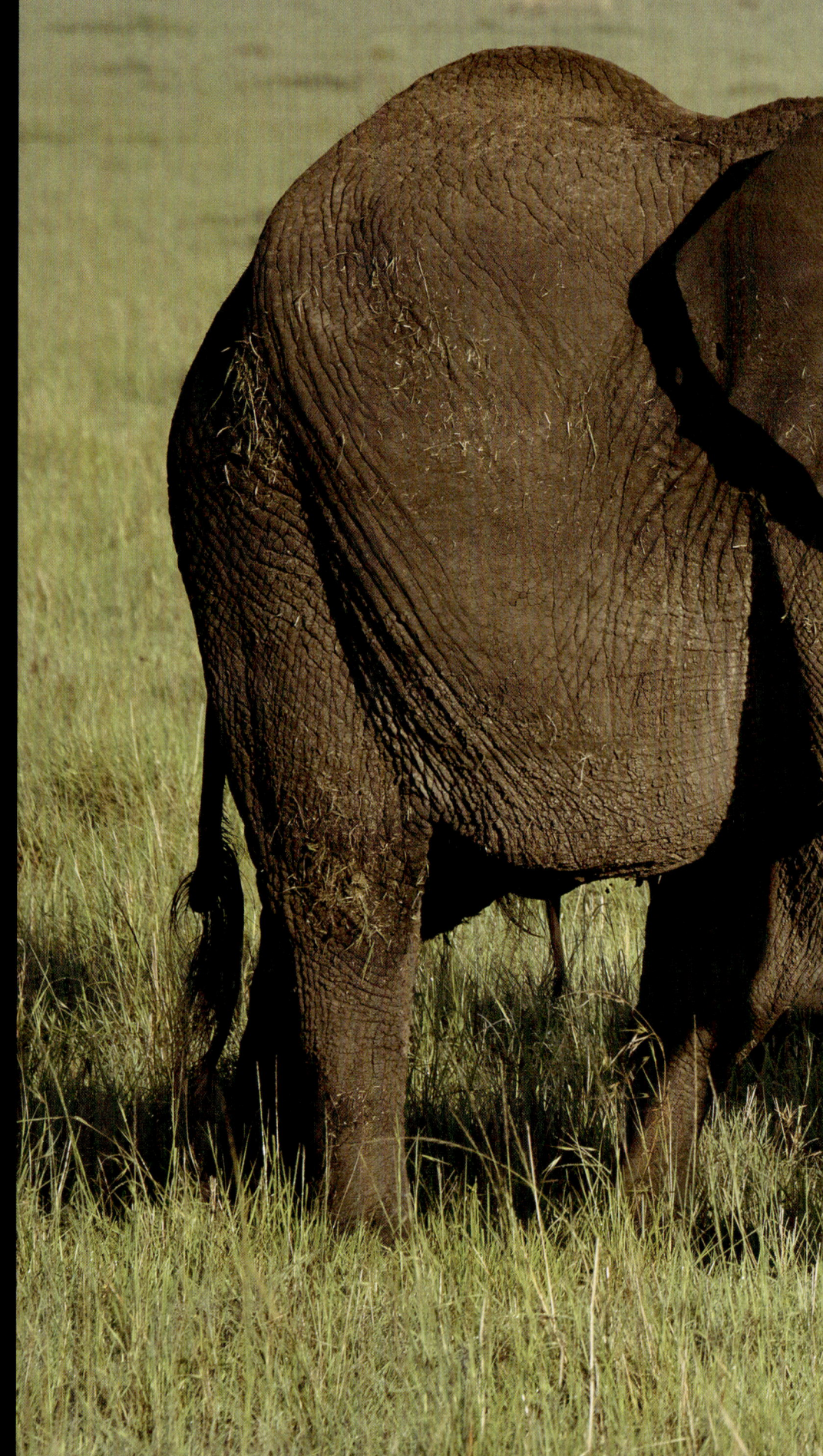

As the midday heat rises, she leads her family to a distant waterhole known only to her. She is the Matriarch, and their thirst will be quenched and life rejuvenated as a direct result of her care and understanding of this magnificent place called Africa.

African Elephant, Kenya / Nikon D810

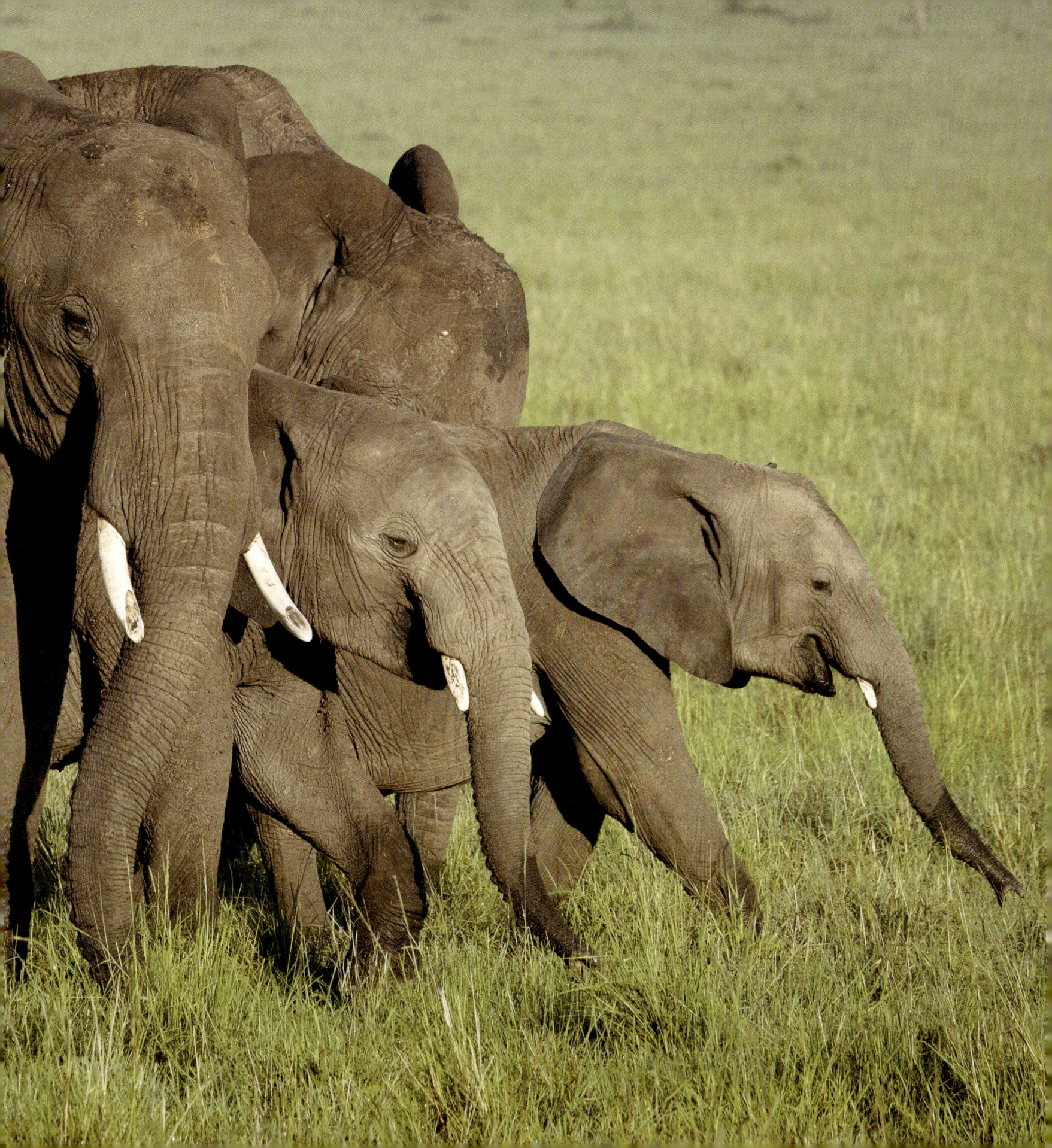

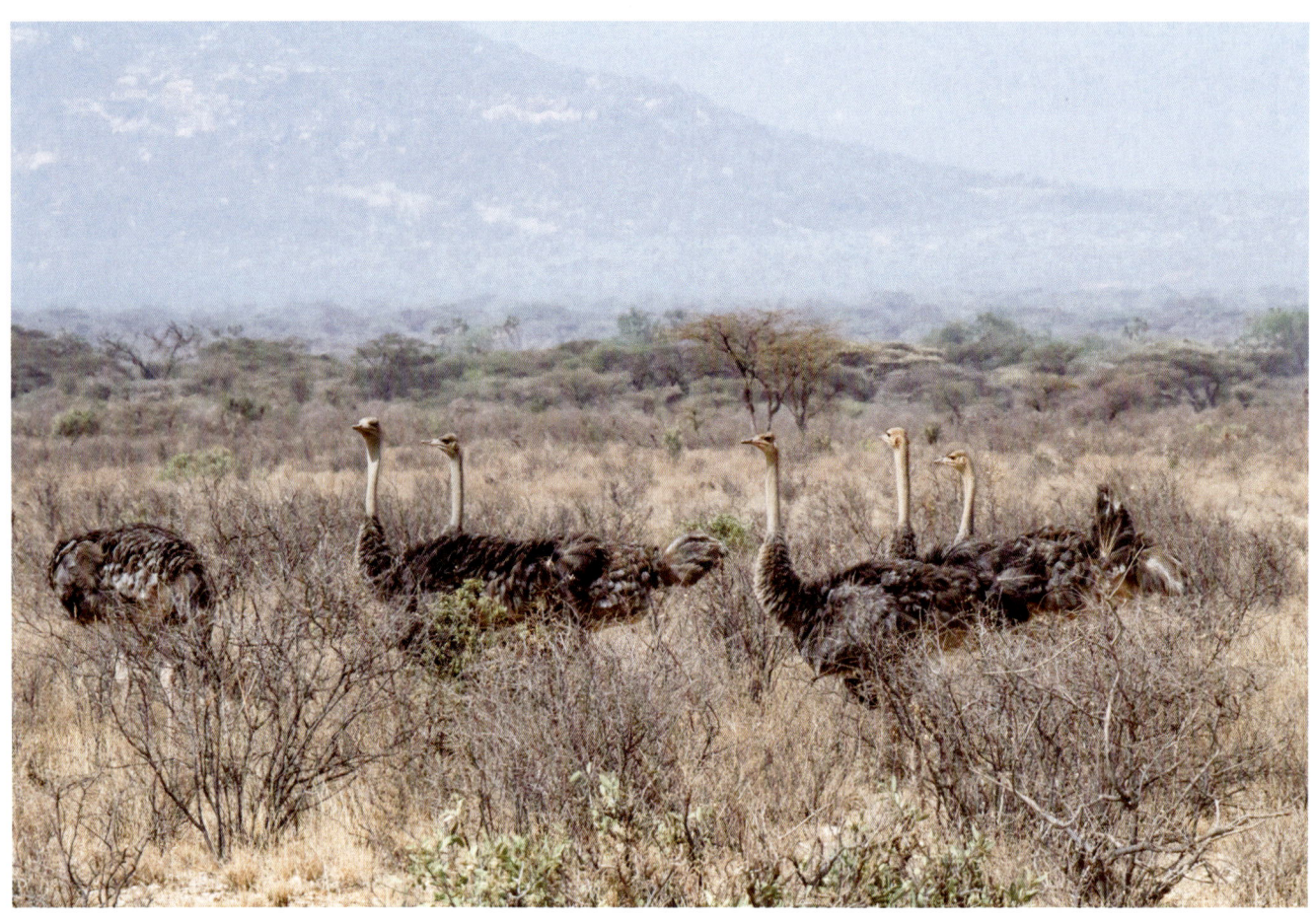

Ostriches have roamed here for as long as anyone can remember, with the arid African landscape providing perfect camouflage to raise their families. Still, they remain vigilant to the possible danger lurking within the tall grass and scrubland that surrounds them, as one misstep could be their last.

Above and opposite: Ostriches, Kenya /Nikon D810

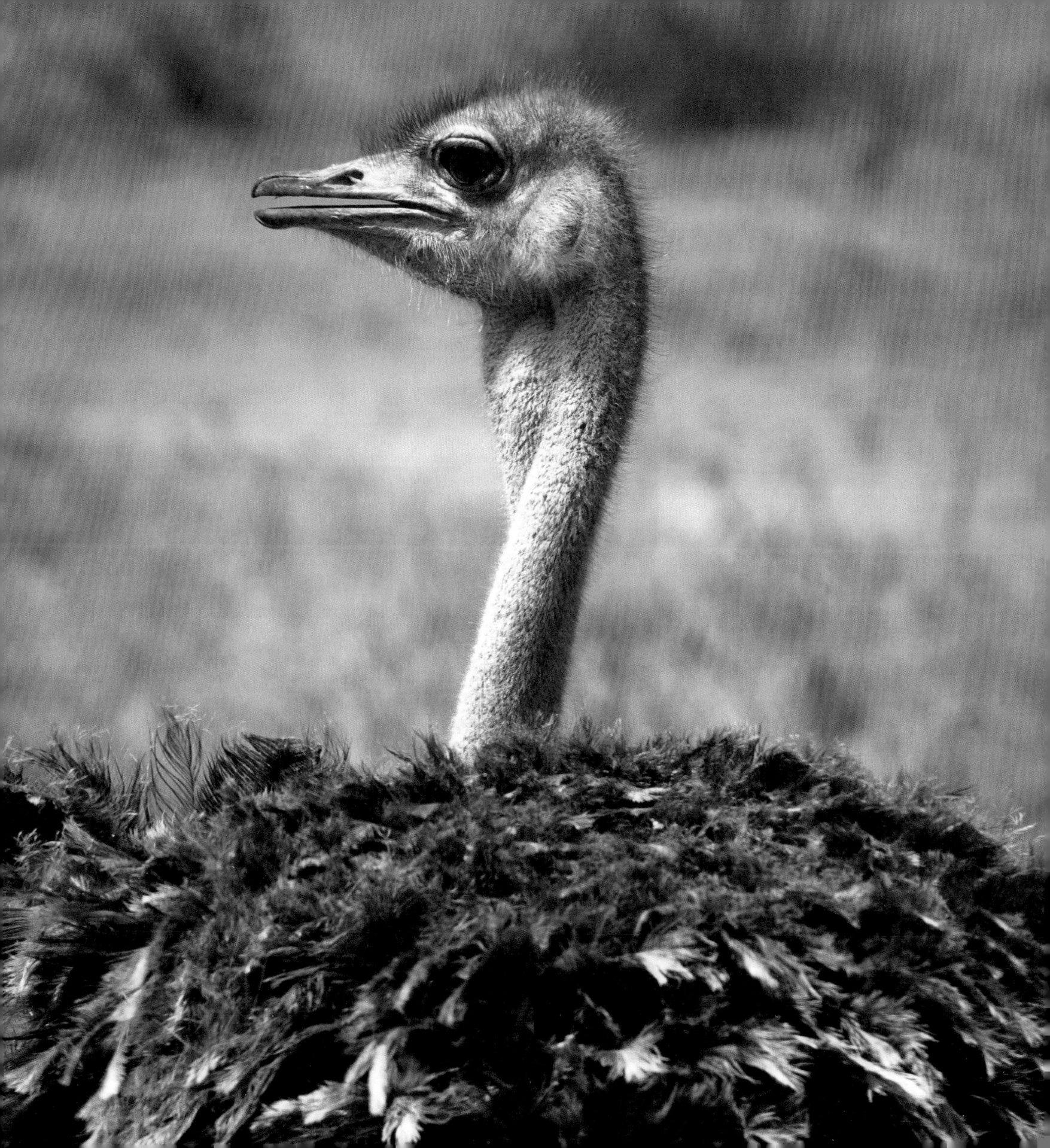

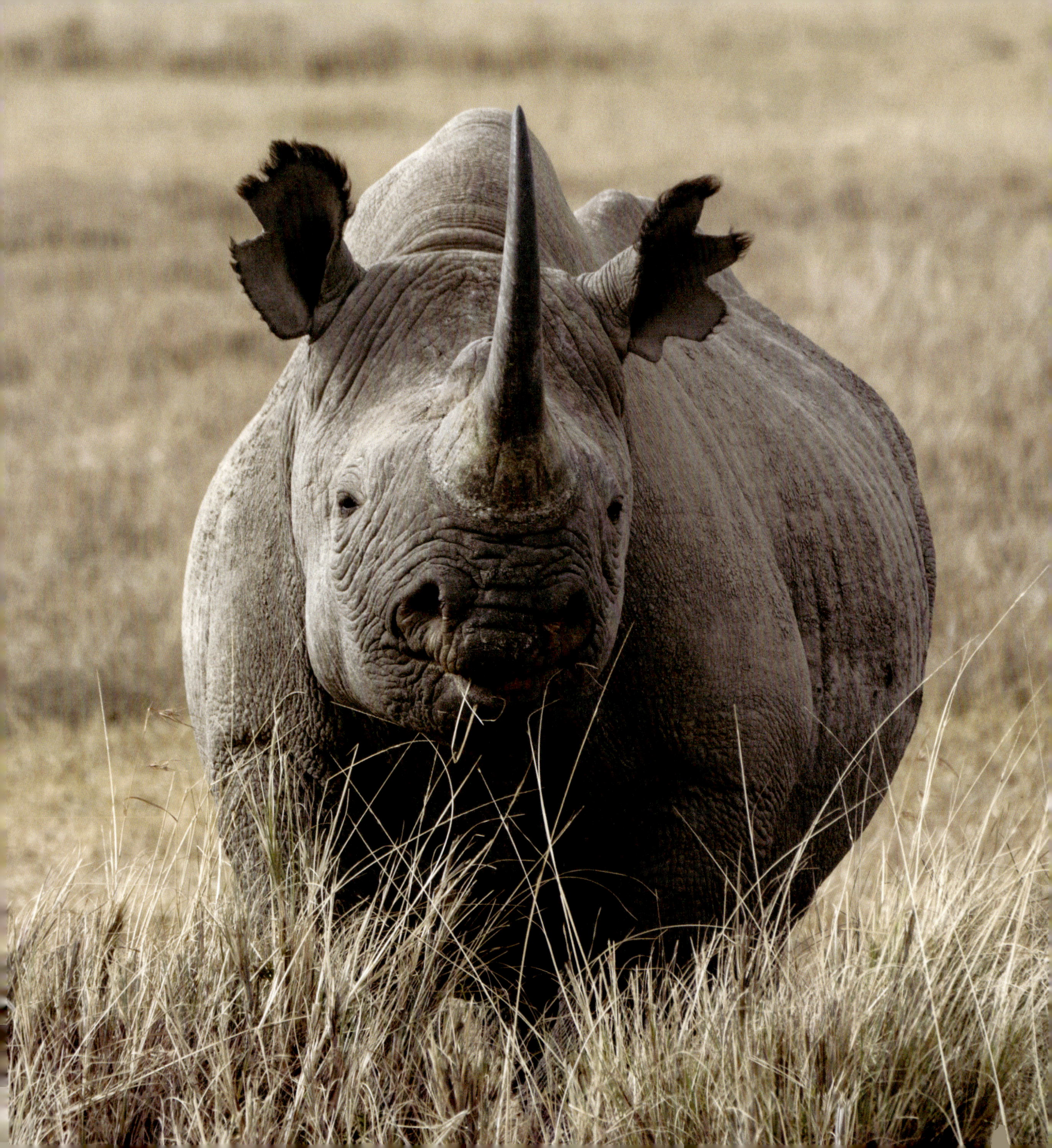

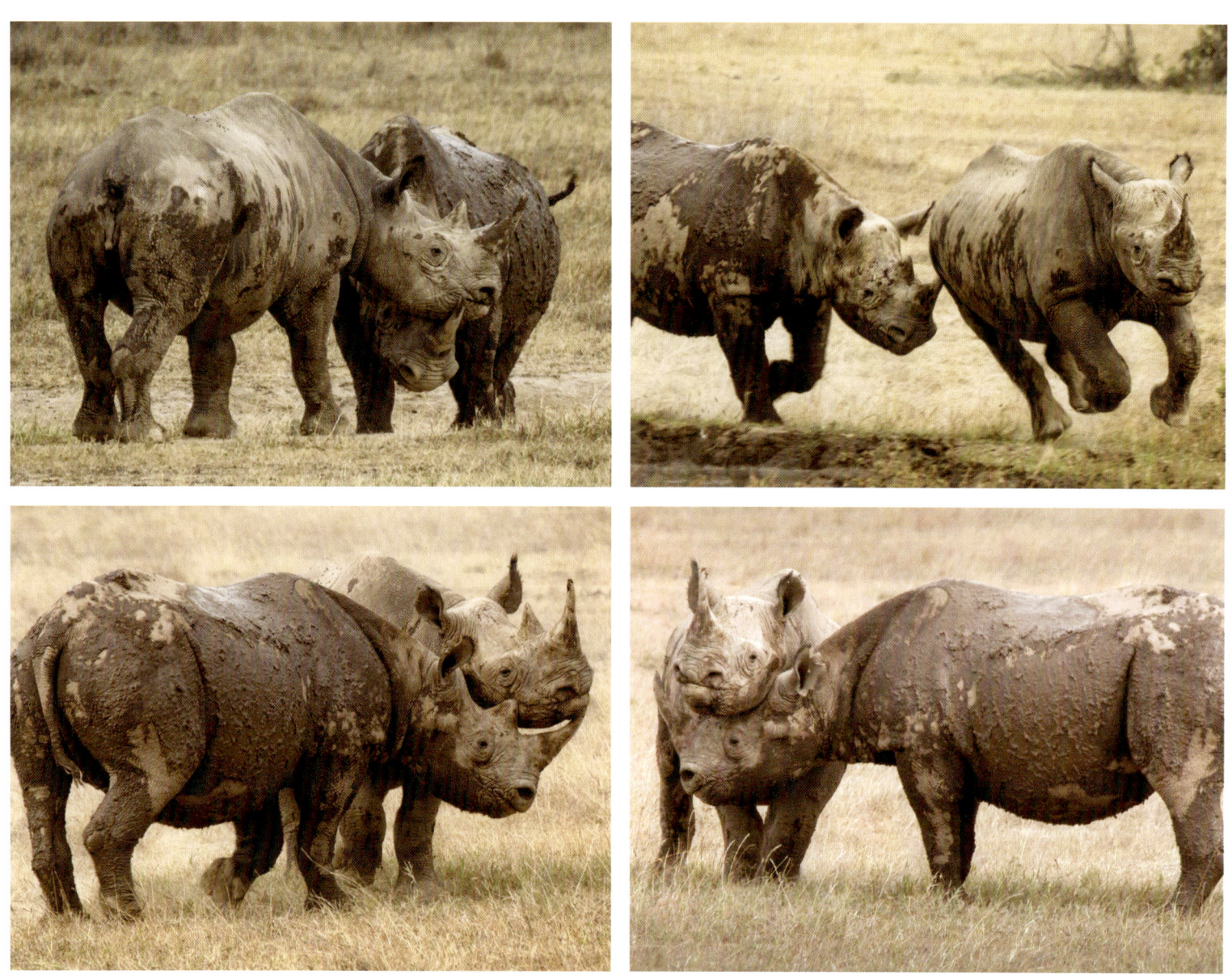

Two highly endangered black rhinos engage in a display of strength, stamina, and endurance that may one day decide who shall have territorial dominance over the other.

Above and opposite: Black Rhinoceros, Kenya /Nikon D810

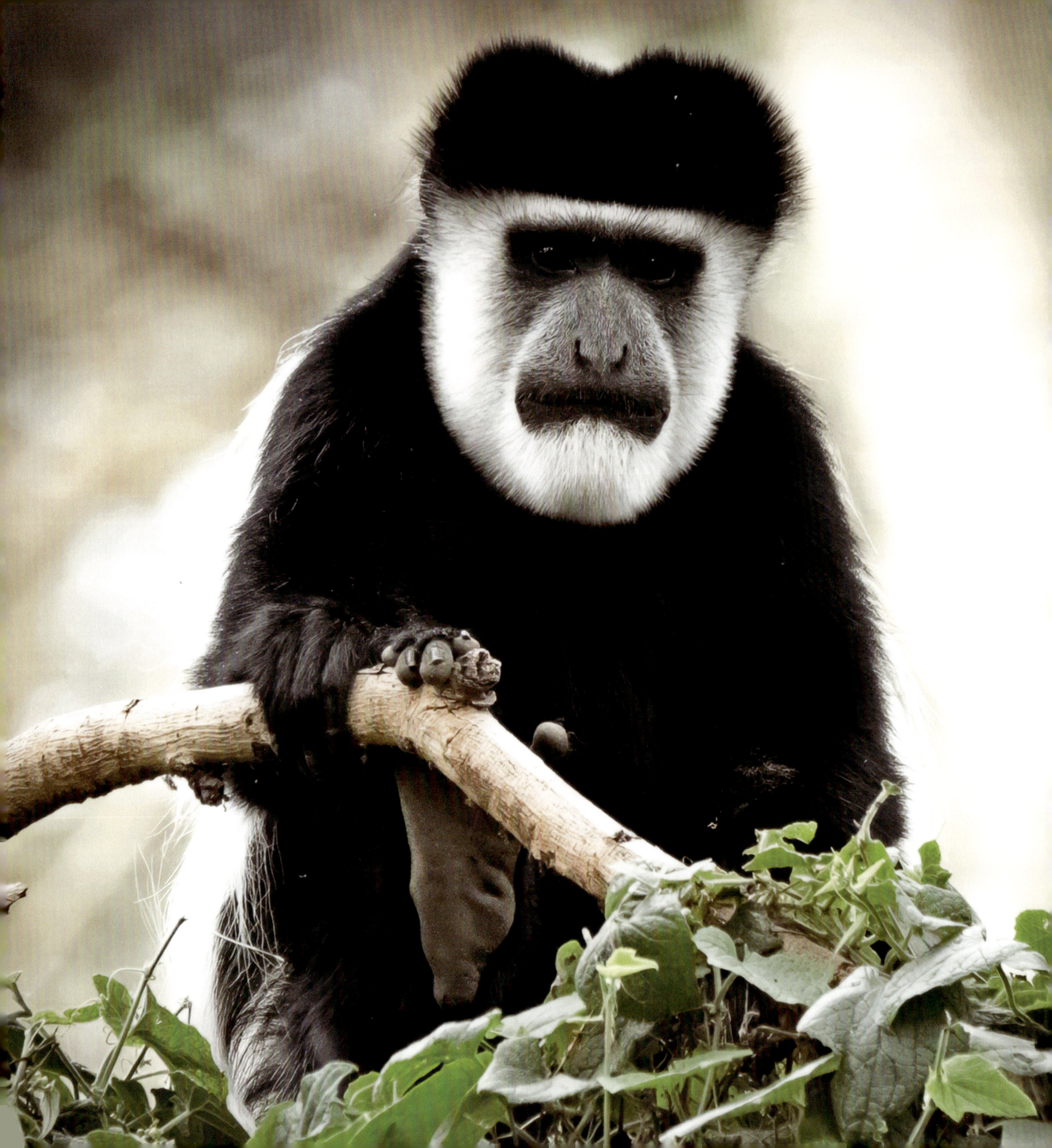

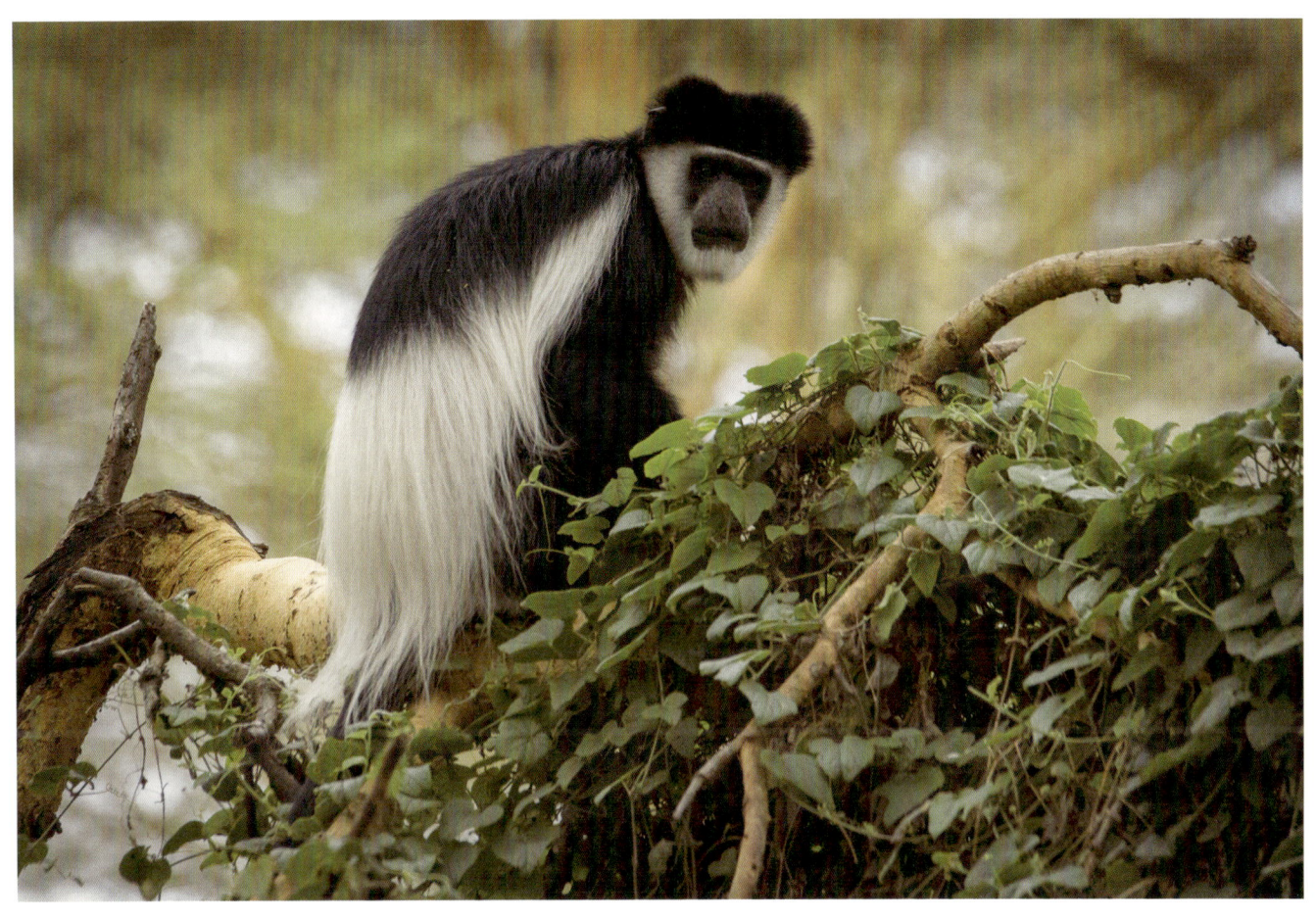

High atop the yellow acacia trees on the shores of Lake Nakuru, a troop of colobus monkeys gather to closely observe and monitor my every move as I unknowingly intrude upon their hidden domain.

Above and opposite: Black and White Colobus Monkey, Kenya /Nikon D810

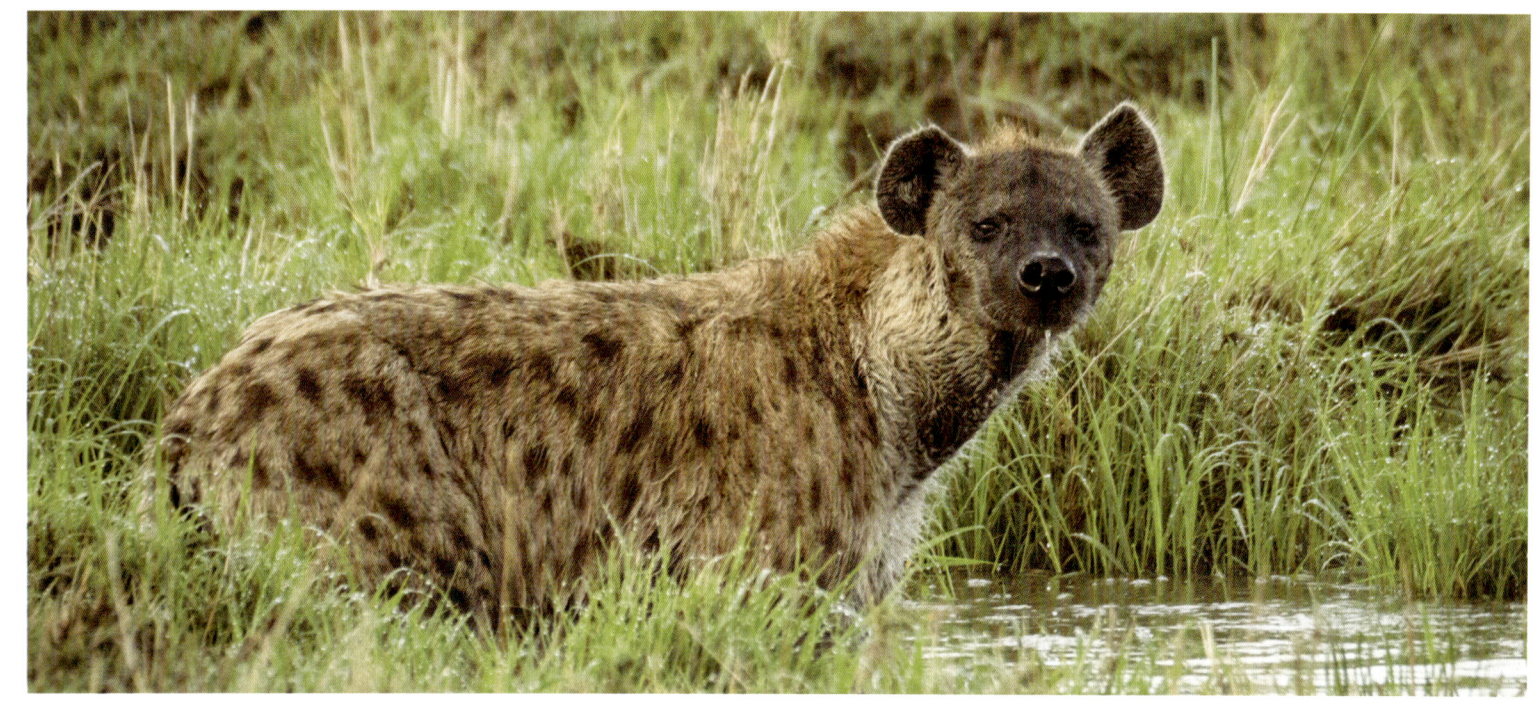

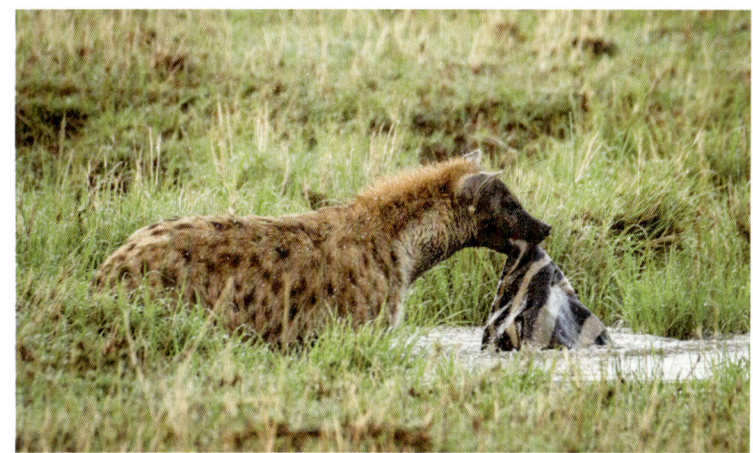
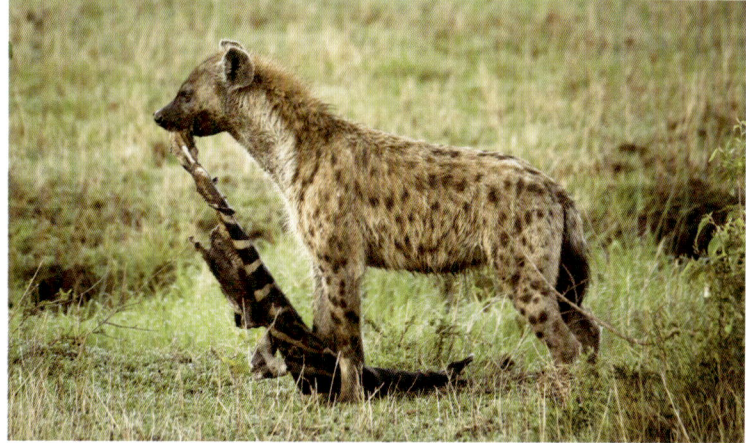

At a remote African waterhole, a lone hyena retrieves a zebra hide long hidden in the murky water to fill the gnawing hunger within, if only for just awhile.

Above and opposite: Spotted Hyena, Kenya / Nikon D810

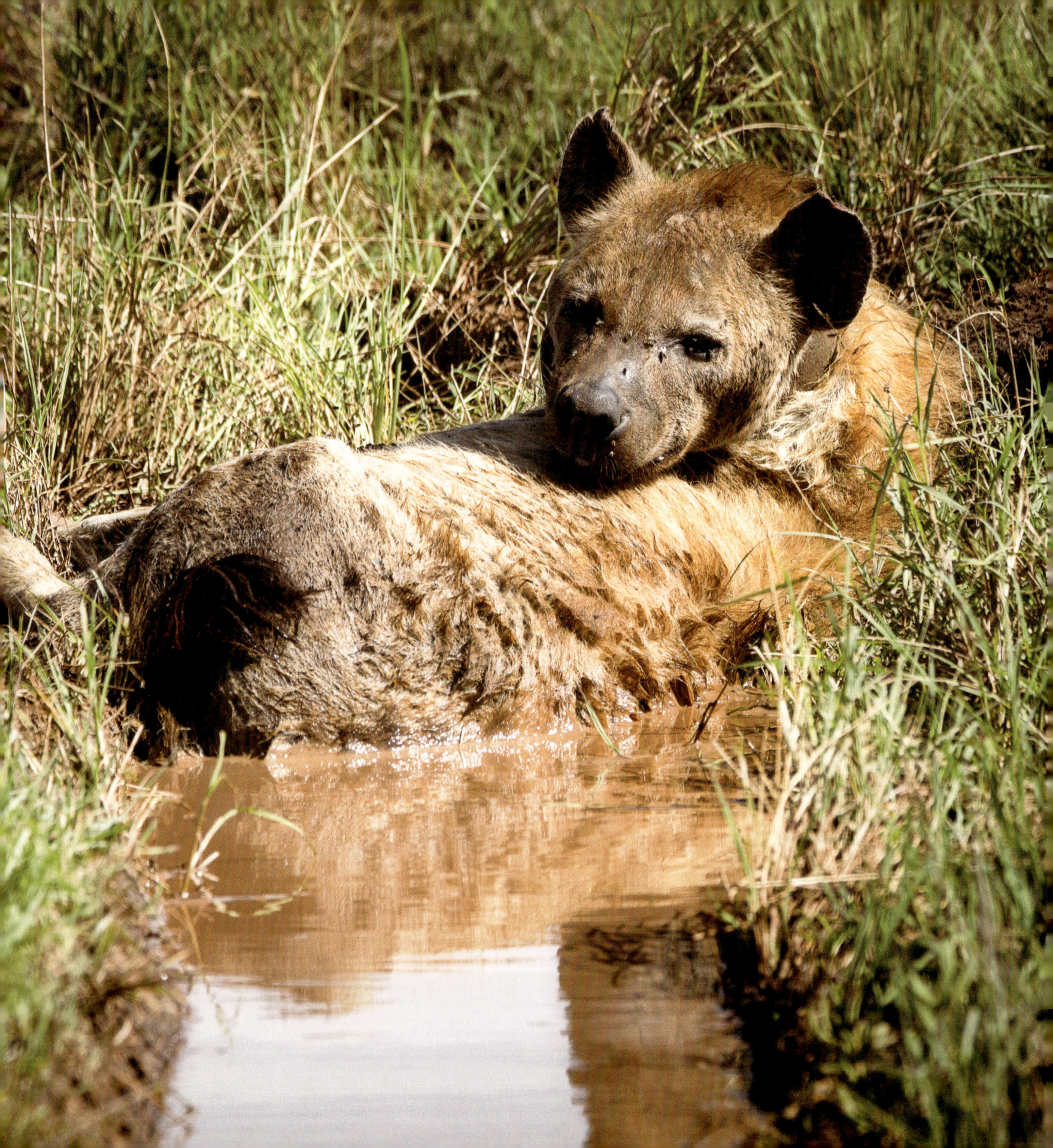

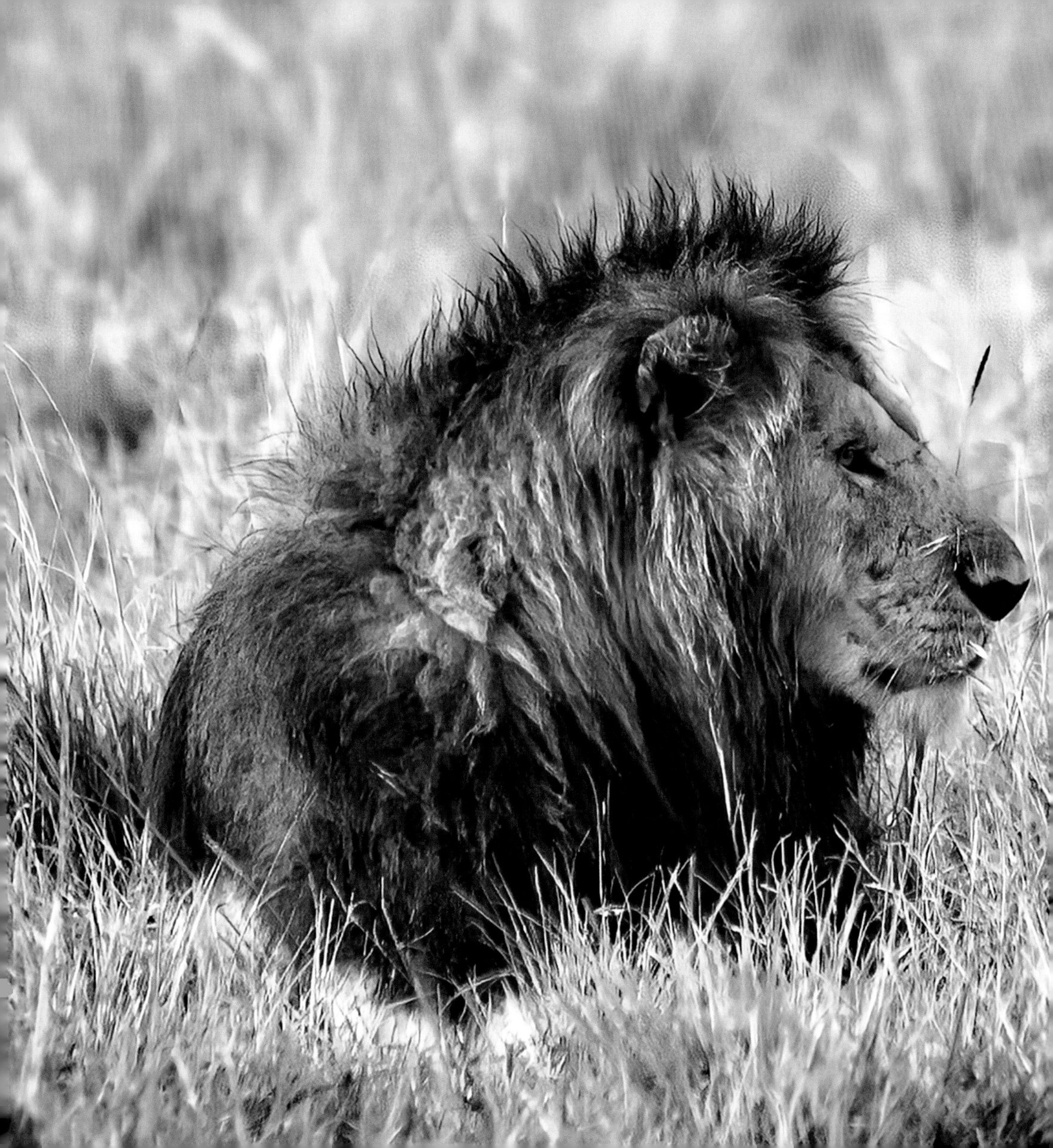

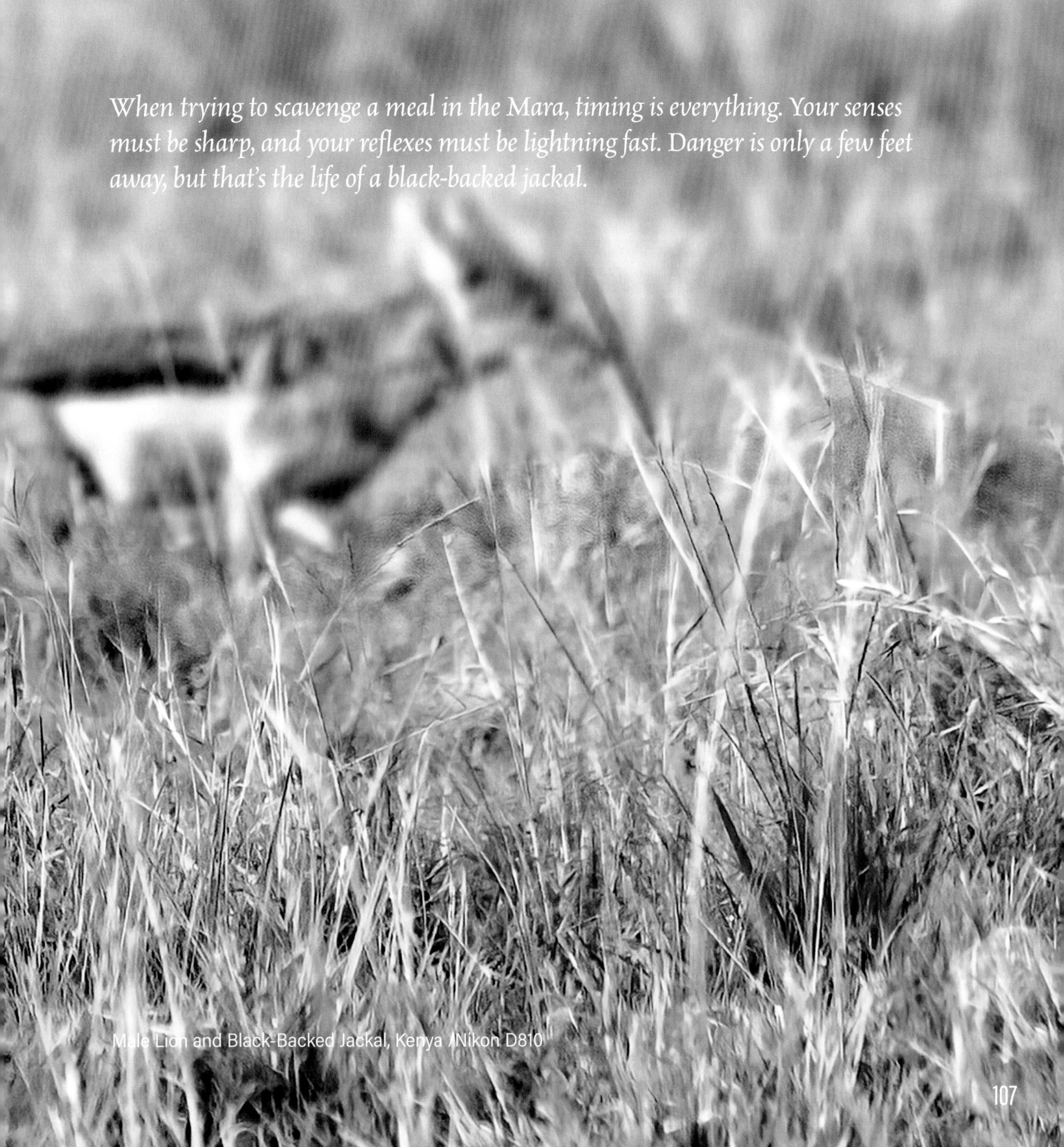

When trying to scavenge a meal in the Mara, timing is everything. Your senses must be sharp, and your reflexes must be lightning fast. Danger is only a few feet away, but that's the life of a black-backed jackal.

Male Lion and Black-Backed Jackal, Kenya / Nikon D810

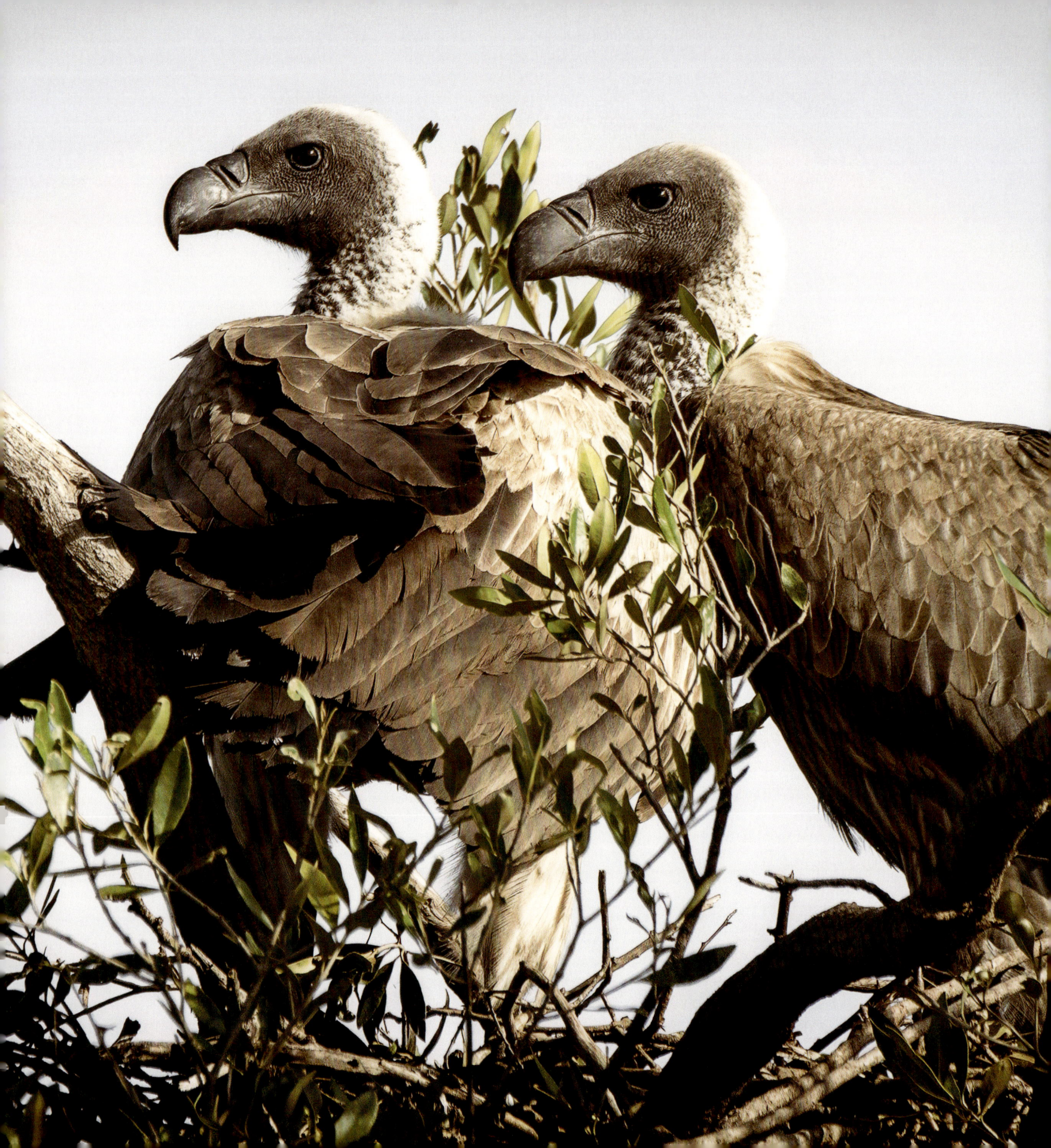

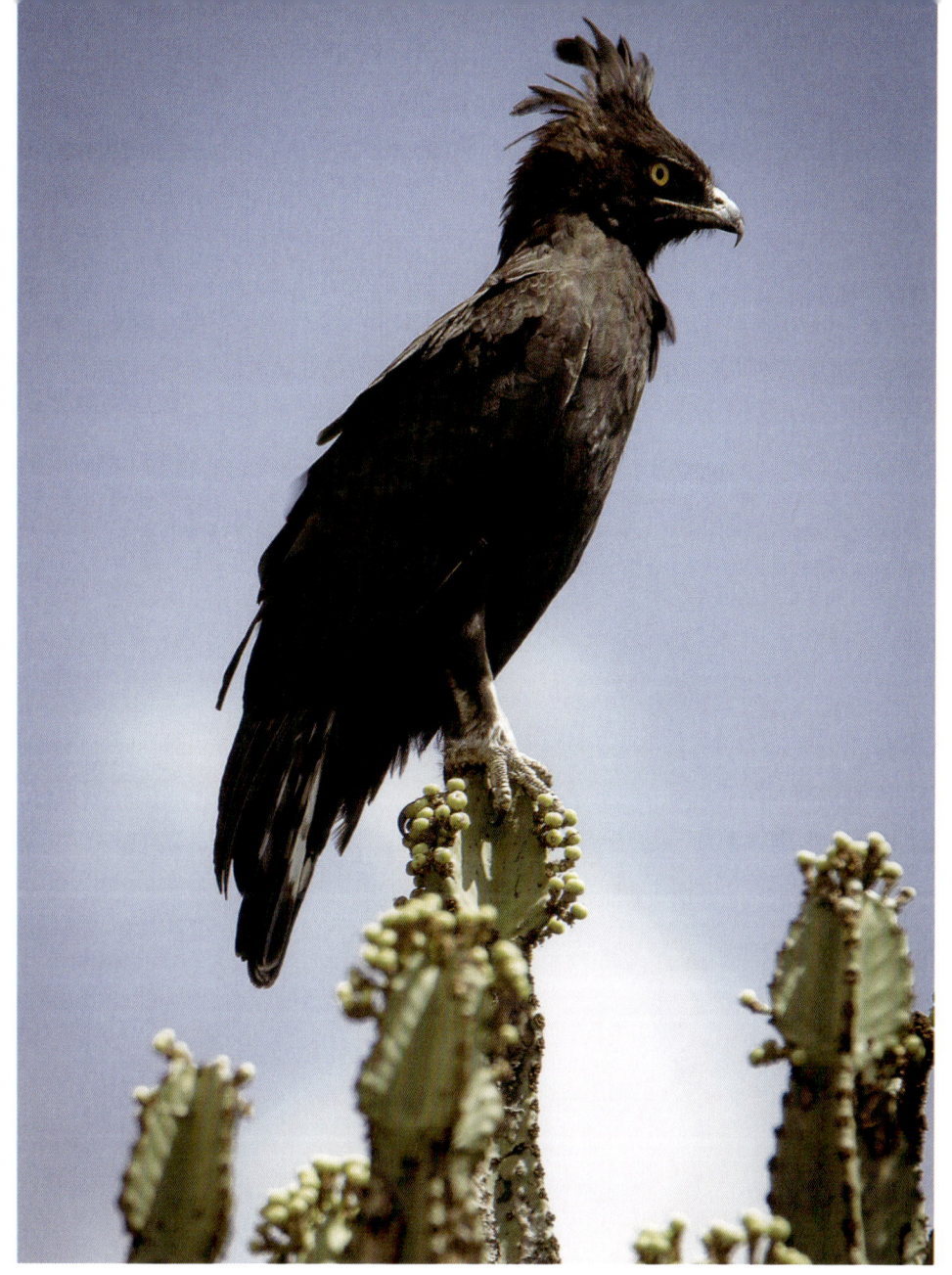

A pair of griffon vultures, typically depicted eating the rotting flesh off the remains of animals killed on the African savanna, readies their nest for the next generation, displaying a more nourishing characteristic for my lens.

Above: Long-Crested Eagle, Kenya /Nikon D810
Opposite: A Pair of White-Backed Vultures, Kenya /Nikon D810

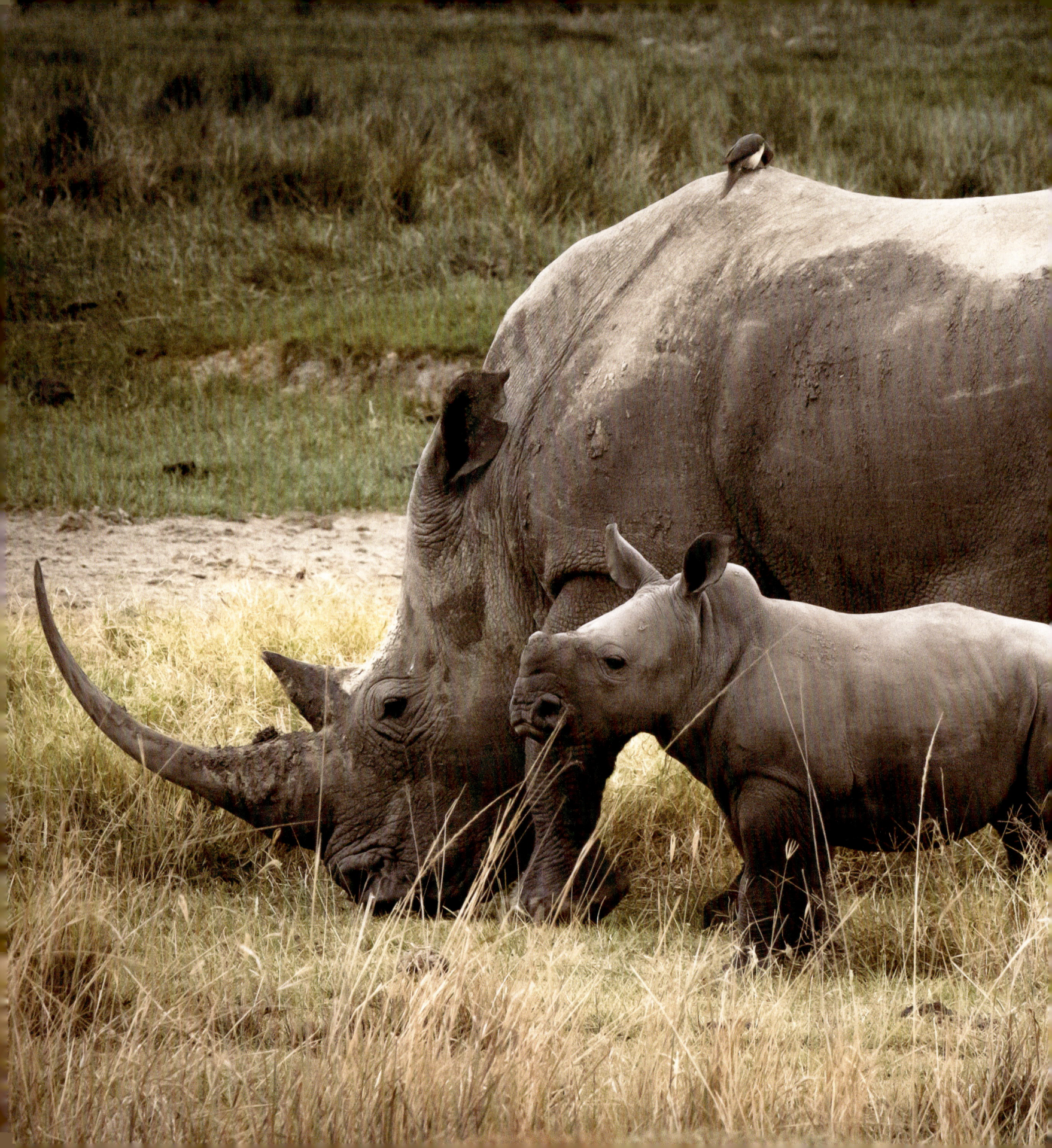

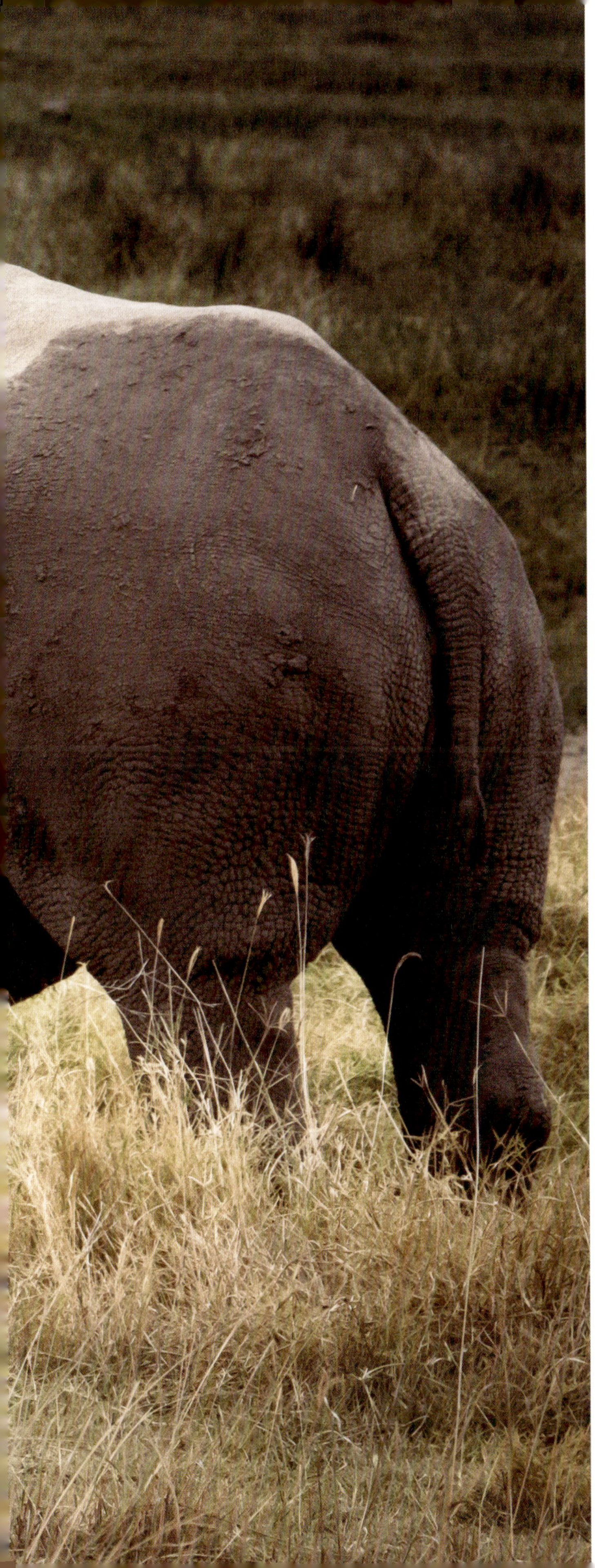

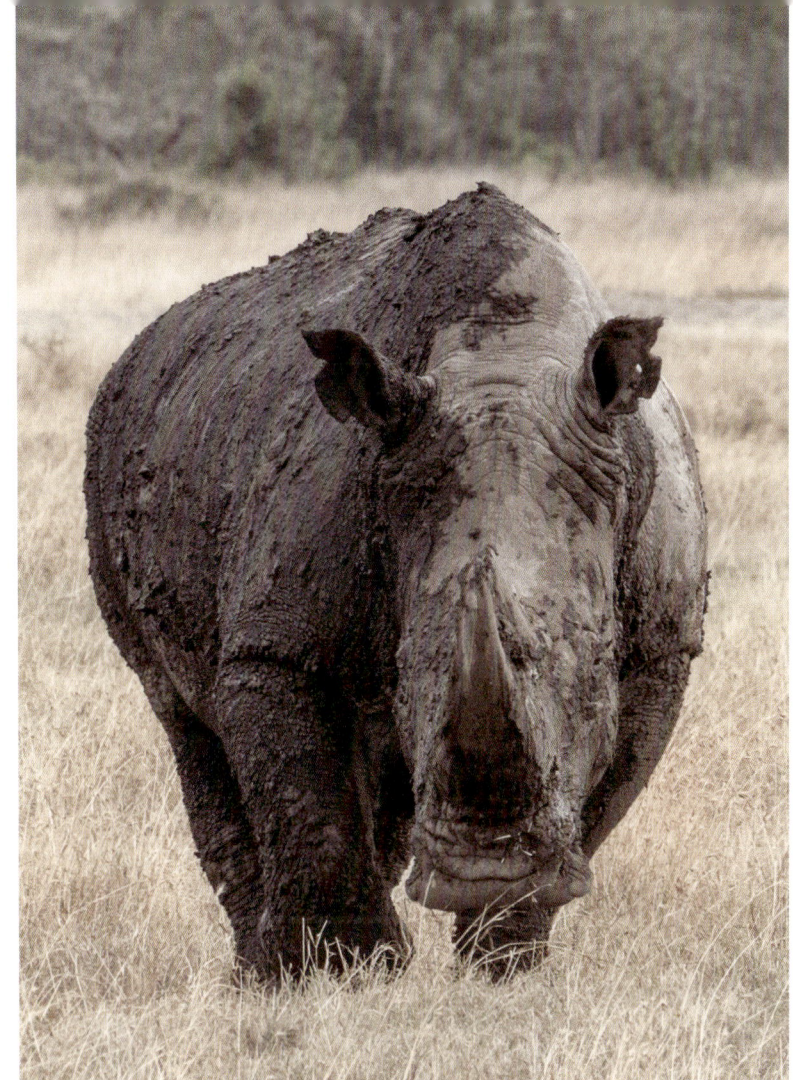

A juvenile white rhino, well protected by his mother's mass and power, possesses the characteristics of a fearless warrior even at a young age. He is a ray of hope for a species that has been cruelly slaughtered for nothing more than the magnificent horn that one day, with luck, he will proudly display for all the world to see.

Above and opposite: White Rhinoceros, Kenya / Nikon D810

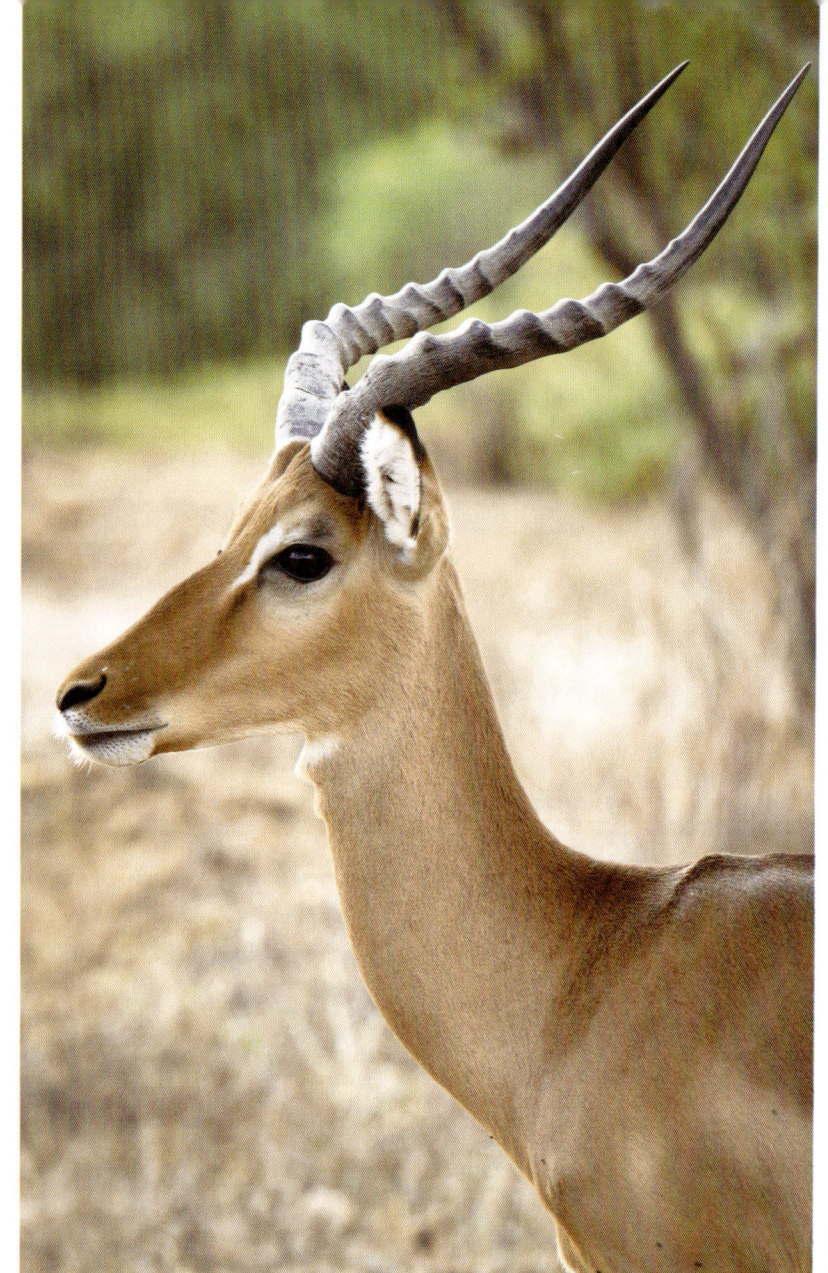
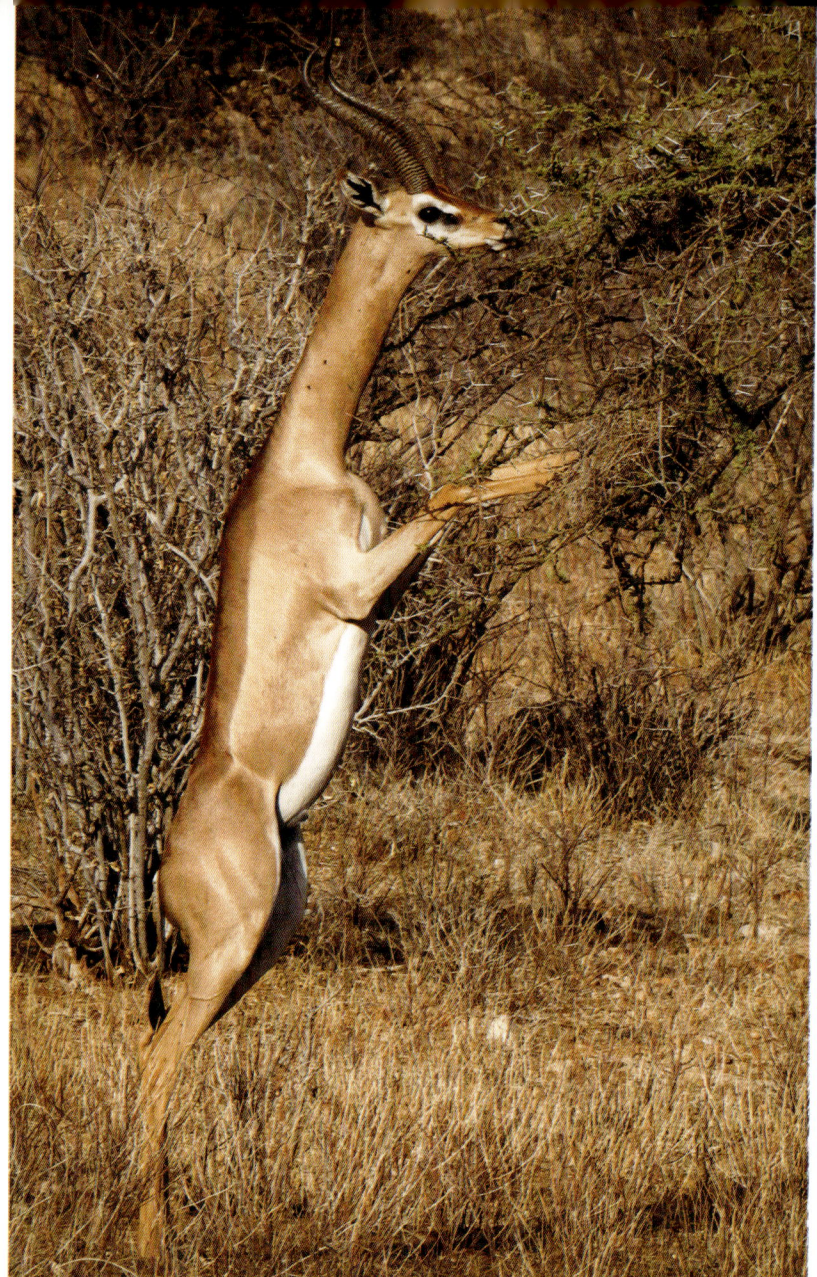

They are but a few of the many species of antelope that inhabit the African subcontinent. Swift, agile, and always on alert, they are all wondrous designs of nature, each adapted to survive and thrive in an unforgiving yet enchanted landscape.

Above (*left*): Impala, Kenya /Nikon D810
Above (*right*): Gerenuk, Kenya /Nikon D810
Opposite: Waterbuck, Kenya /Nikon D810

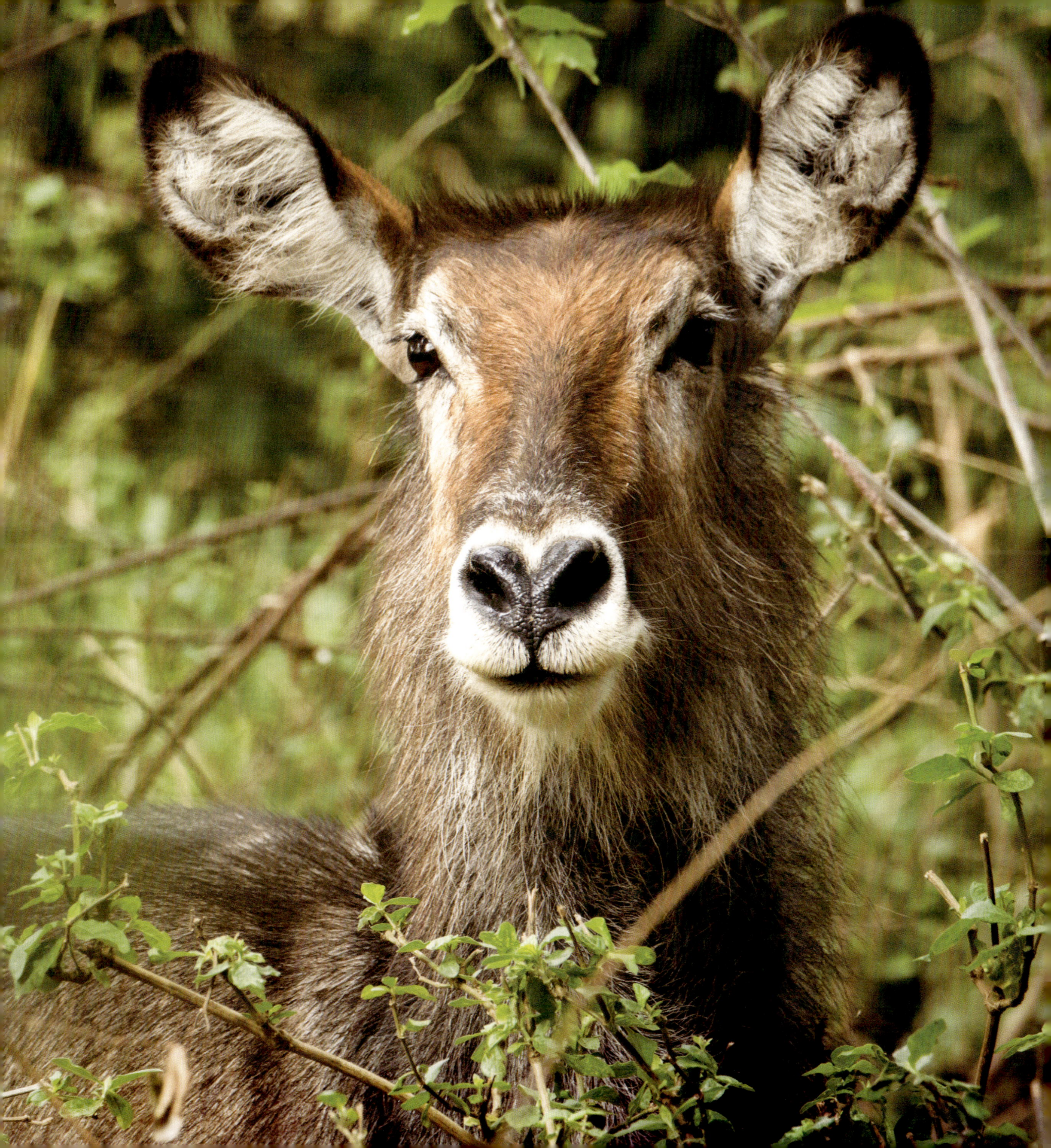

The day bids farewell to the night as the African sun sinks below the Mara's westernmost reaches, accompanied by a cacophony of sounds that foreshadow its impending arrival.

African Sunset with Elephants, Africa / Nikon D810

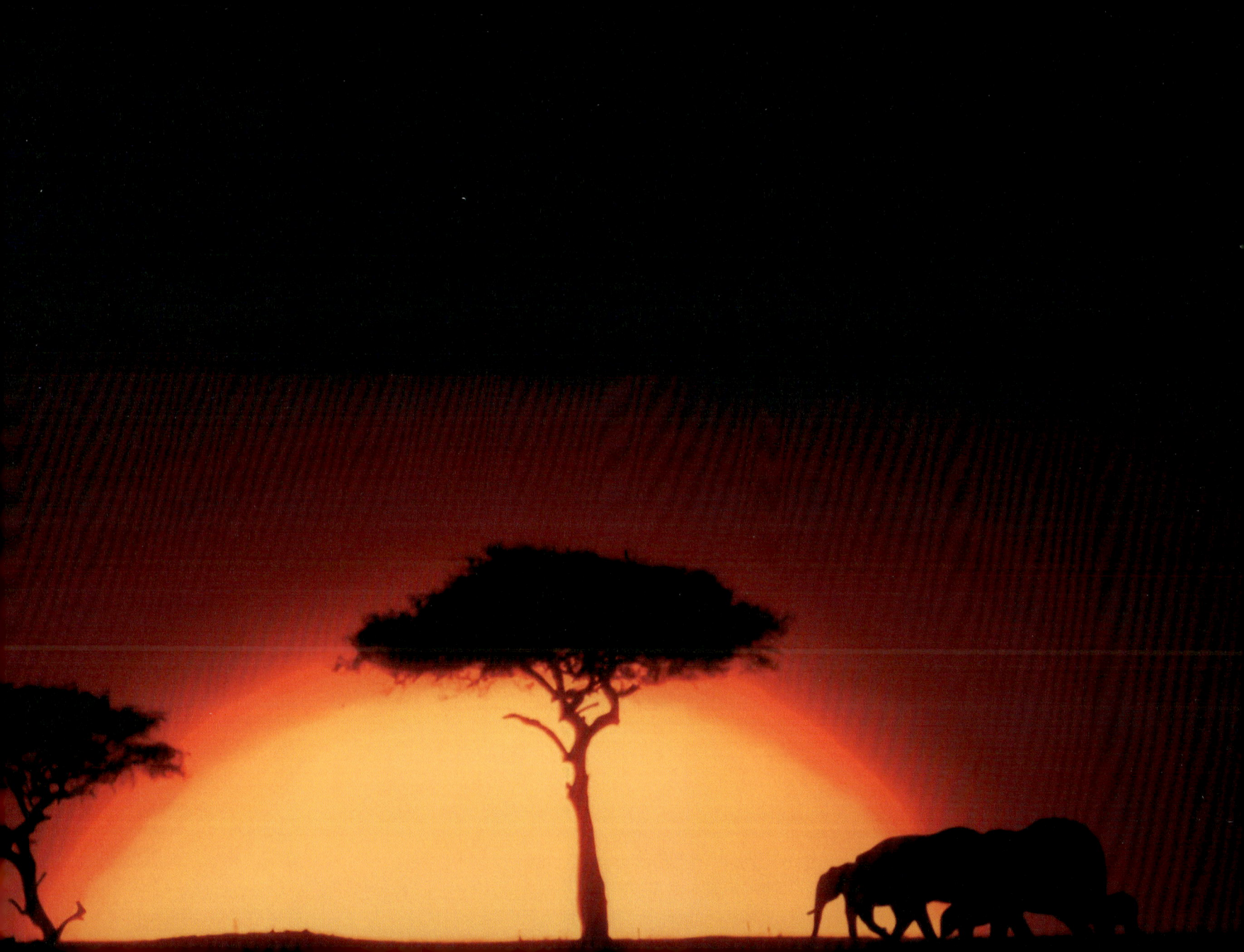

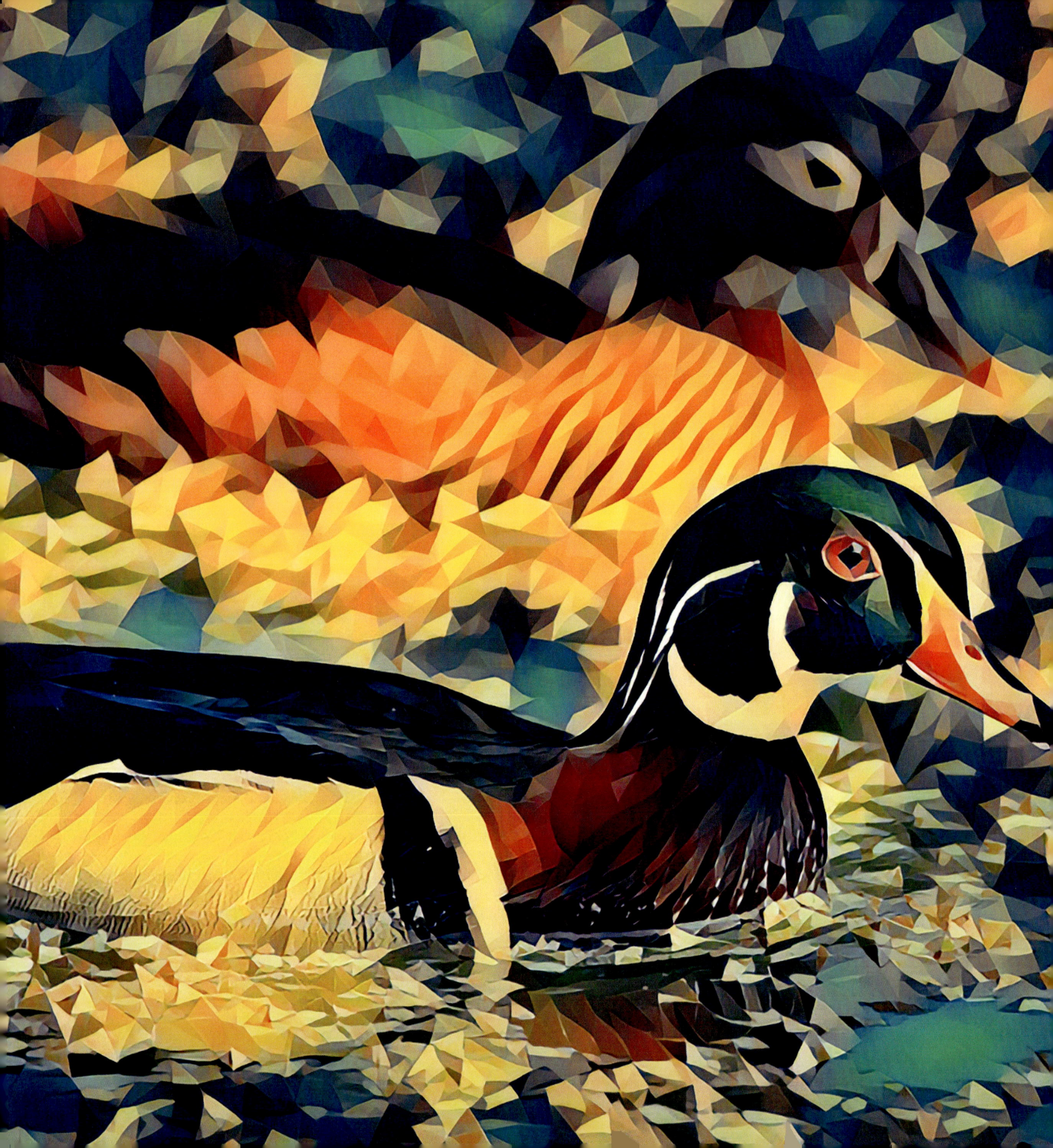

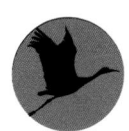

WETLANDS

Where there is water, there is life. No truer statement has ever been made. Our wetland areas have and forever will be the sustenance that feeds our natural world. They are found all over, with each being a unique ecosystem unto itself, sheltering millions of wildlife species, some of which are found nowhere else on Earth. To visit a wetland area, be it a murky swamp or an idyllic lake, is to invoke a sense of adventure as to all of the amazing things you might encounter: aquatic lily pads adorned with water droplets glistening in the afternoon sun; flocks of pelicans scouring the water's edge; the distant rattling of a kingfisher letting you know of his presence. Every step taken offers a new view into these watery realms, and I have been privileged to travel many steps to capture these fleeting moments for all to enjoy. Preserving and protecting our wetlands is of paramount importance, and each of us has an obligation and a responsibility to speak for those species that have no voice. The balance of life must be sustained at all cost, or life as we know it will be forever changed, forever lost.

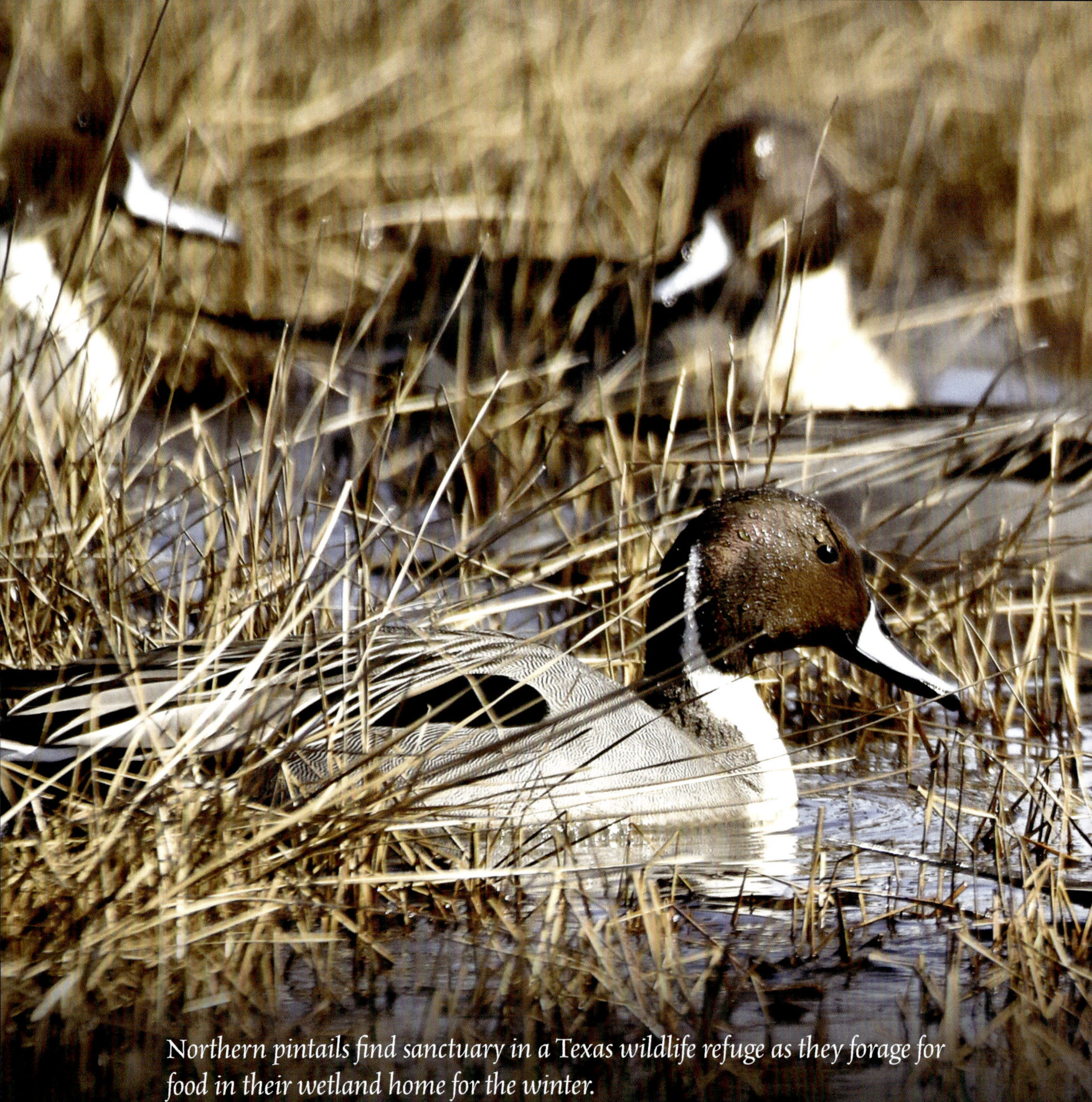

Northern pintails find sanctuary in a Texas wildlife refuge as they forage for food in their wetland home for the winter.

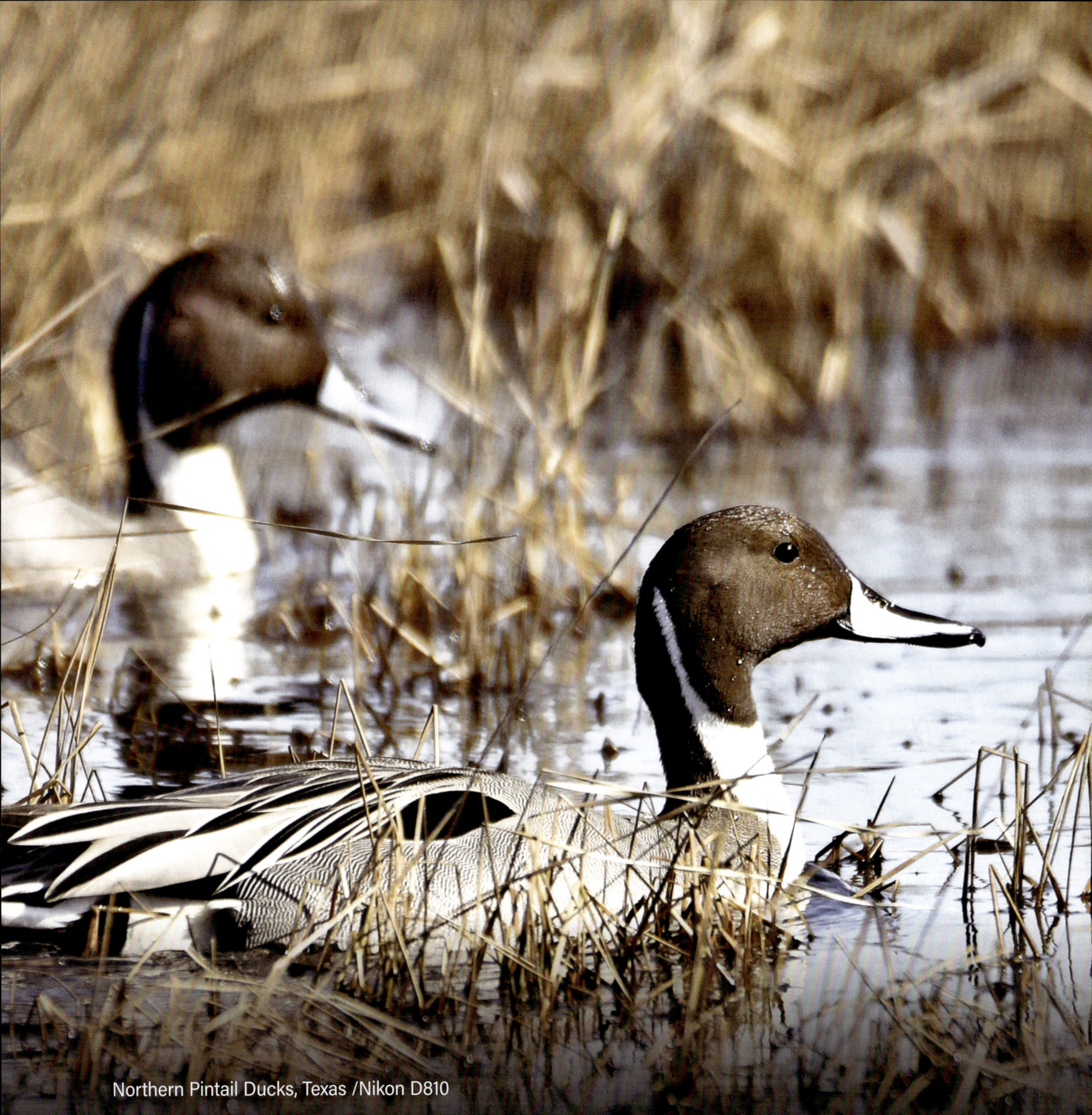
Northern Pintail Ducks, Texas / Nikon D810

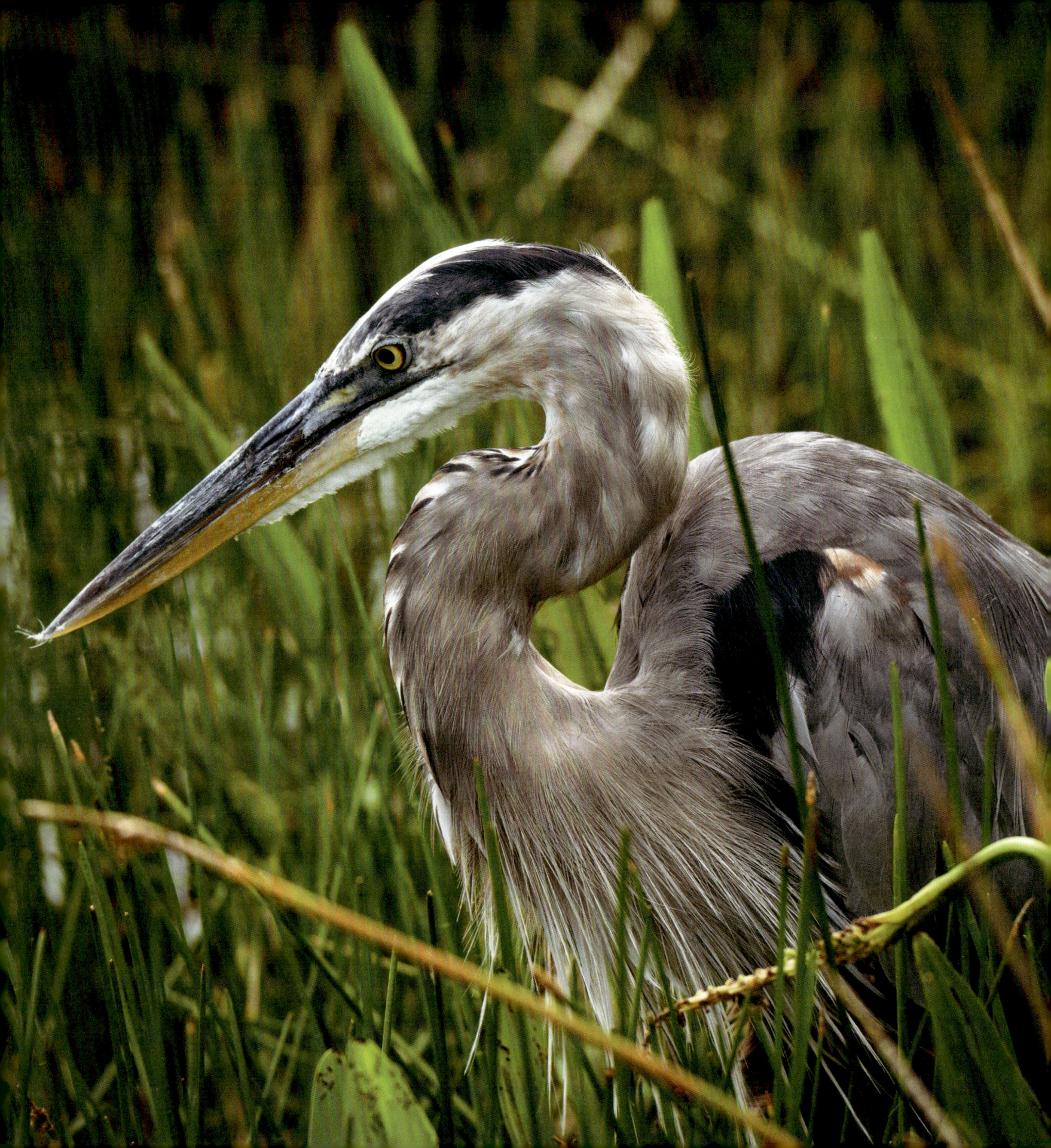

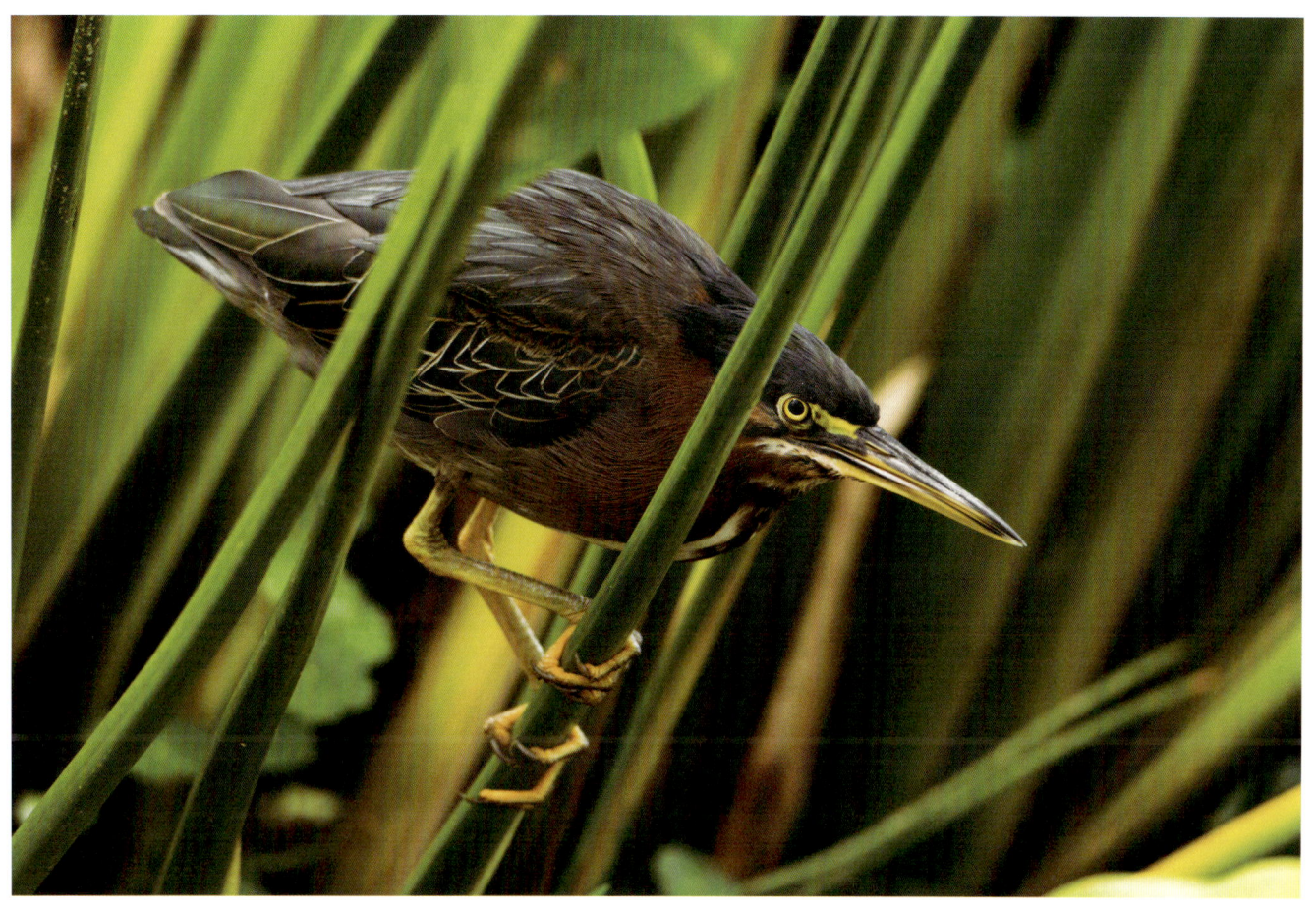

Deep within the slow-moving murky waters of the Everglades, an ever-observant great blue heron and green heron lie motionless within a high thicket of swamp reeds awaiting the arrival of breakfast.

Above: Green Heron, Florida /Nikon D810
Opposite: Great Blue Heron, Florida /Nikon D810

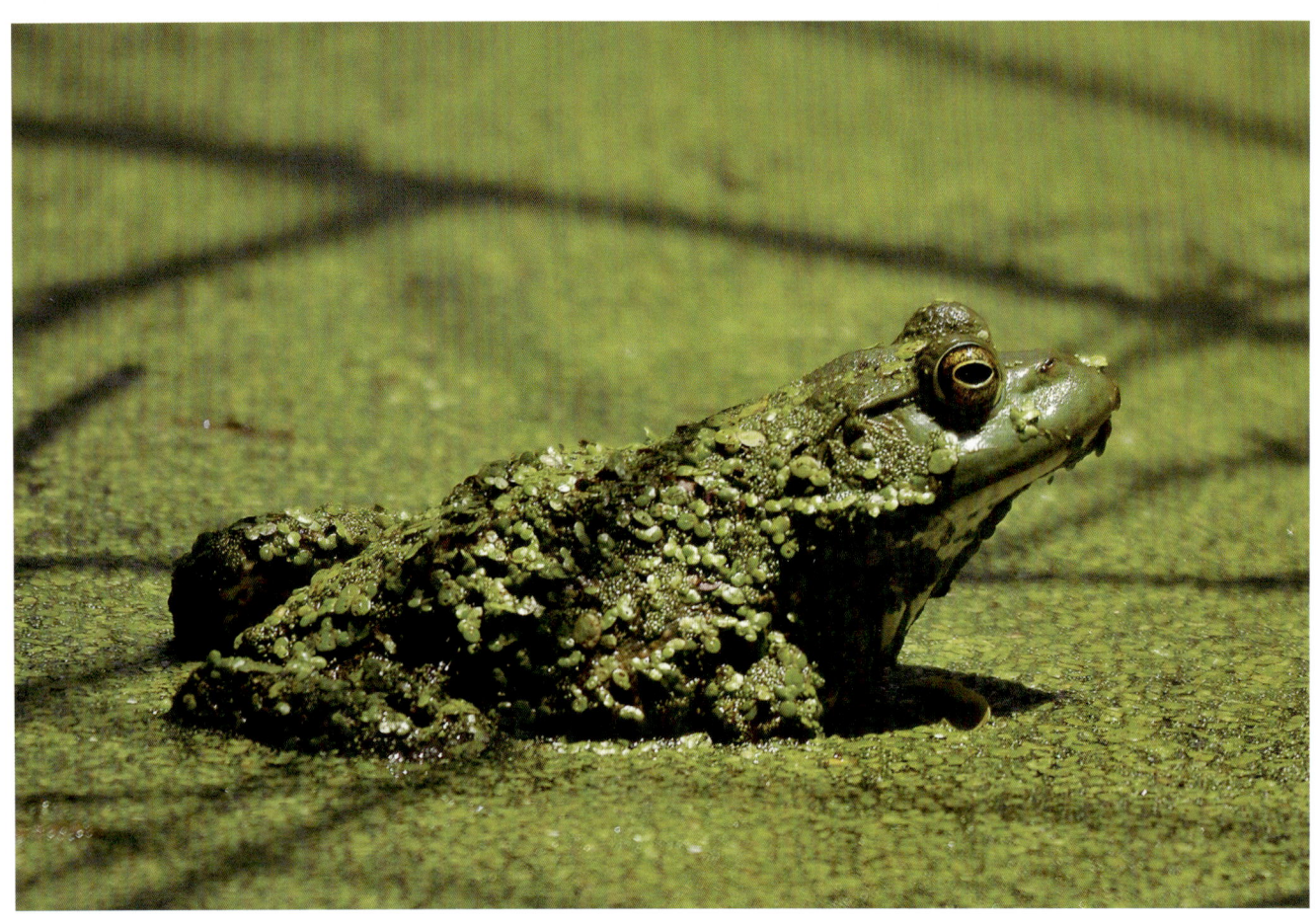

Perfect camouflage is nature's most prevalent means of playing "hide and seek" in the never-ending circle of life all around us. Two very different frog species, both perfectly concealed within their watery marshland realms.

Above: American Bullfrog, Texas /Nikon D600
Opposite: American Green Tree Frog, Texas /Nikon D810

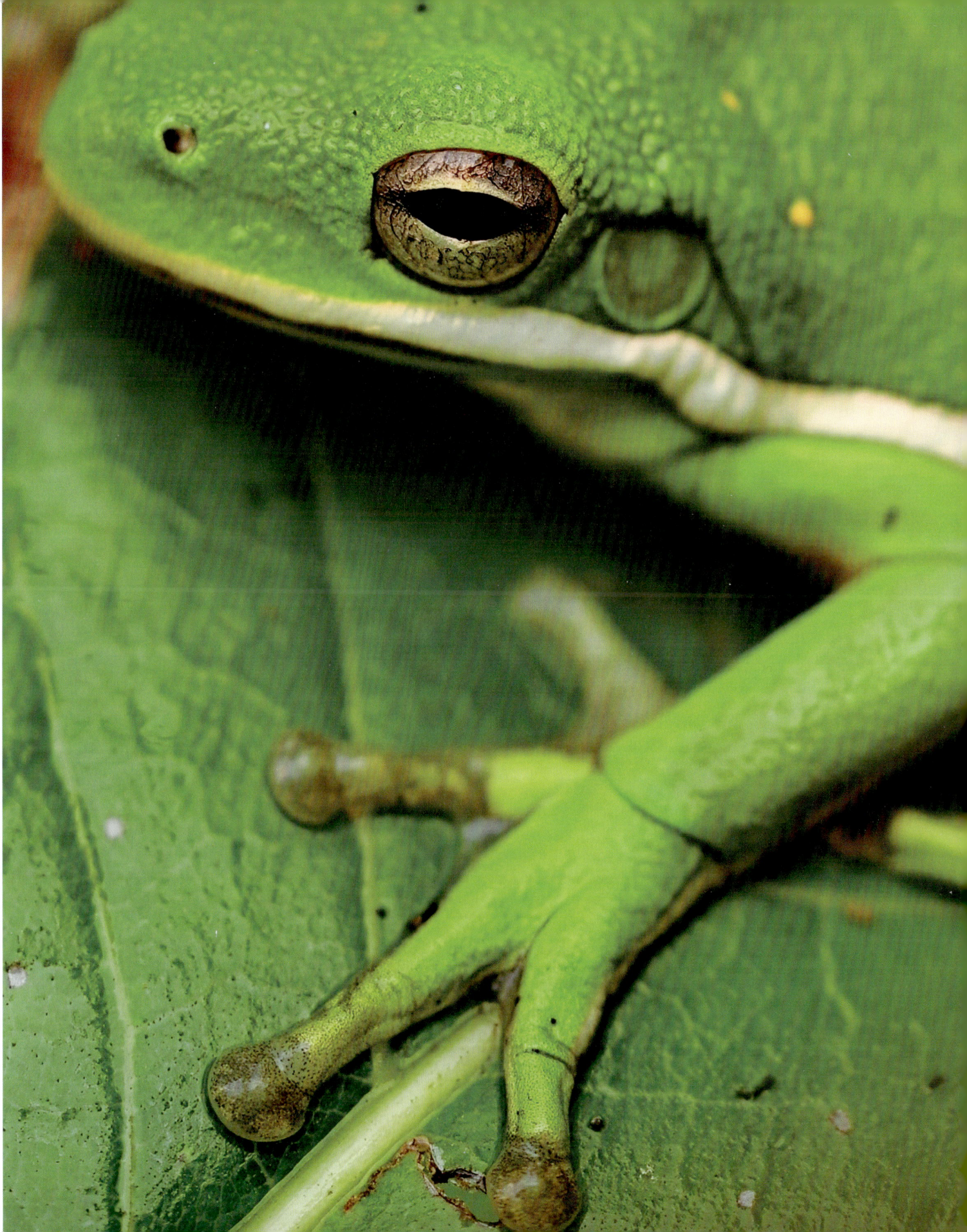

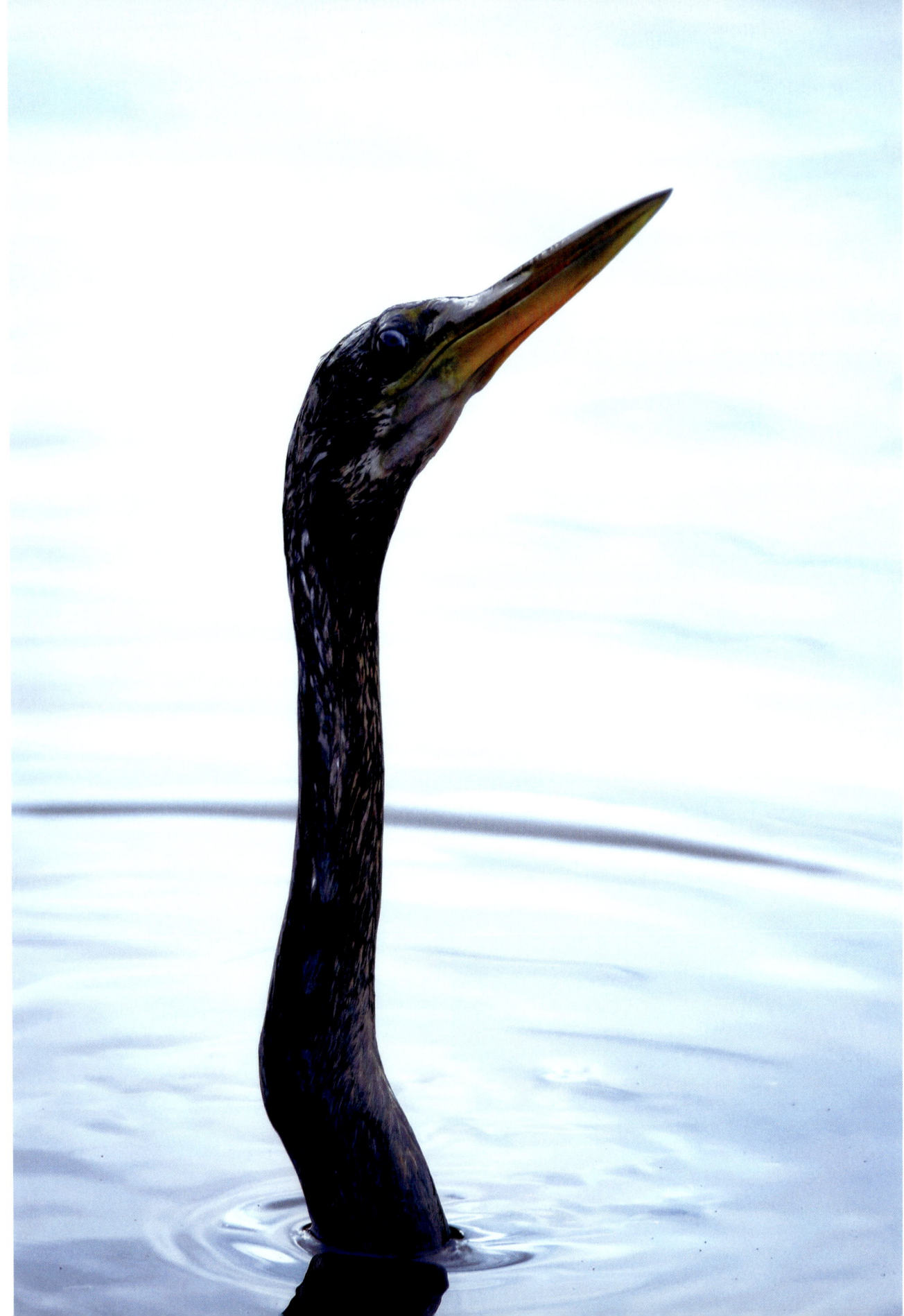

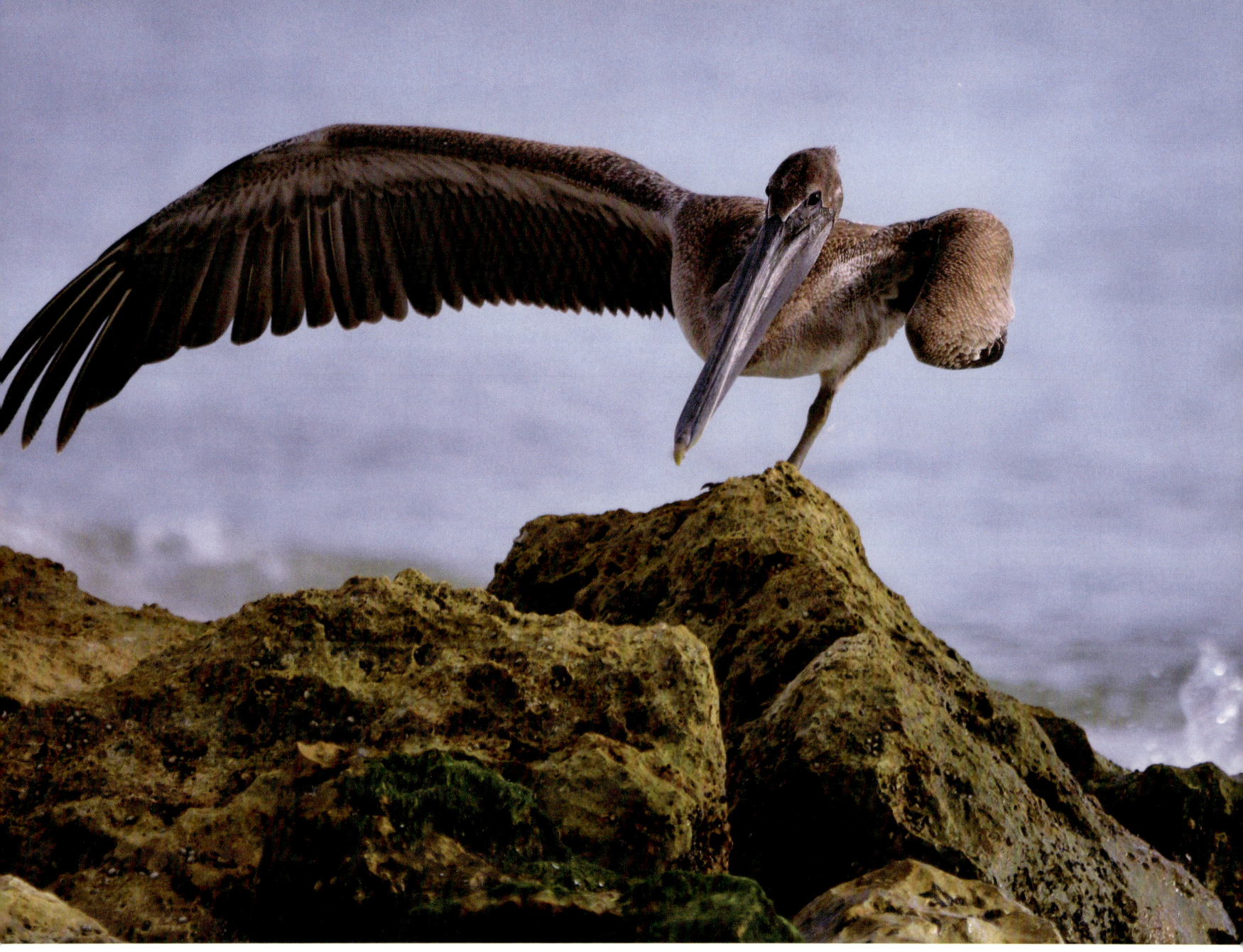

The "snake-bird" of the southern waterways, an anhinga, rises from the depths to greet me personally as I ready my camera for a quick close-up.

Early morning aerobics are on the agenda for this brown pelican, who certainly knows how to balance on a rock much better than I ever could.

Opposite: Anhinga, Florida /Nikon D810
Above: Brown Pelican, Florida /Nikon D810

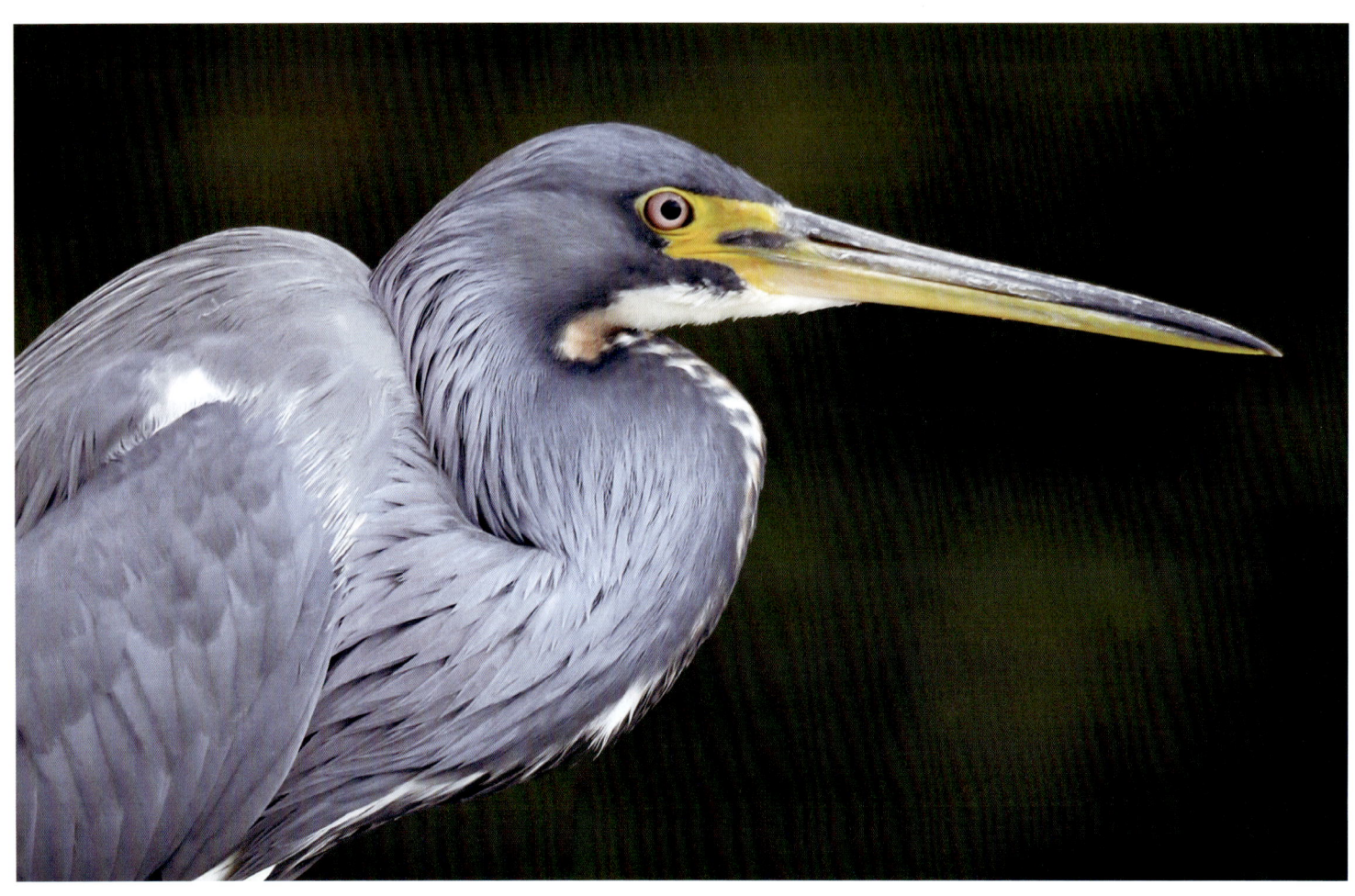

In the heart of the Florida Everglades, where danger lurks in every shadow, a female alligator fiercely guards her nest. She is the sole protector of her offspring's fragile future. Nearby, a tricolored heron perches stoically on a marsh boardwalk, offering me a stunning profile—a quiet reward for my patience and respect for this wild domain.

Above: Tricolored Heron, Florida /Nikon D810
Opposite: American Alligator, Florida /Nikon D810

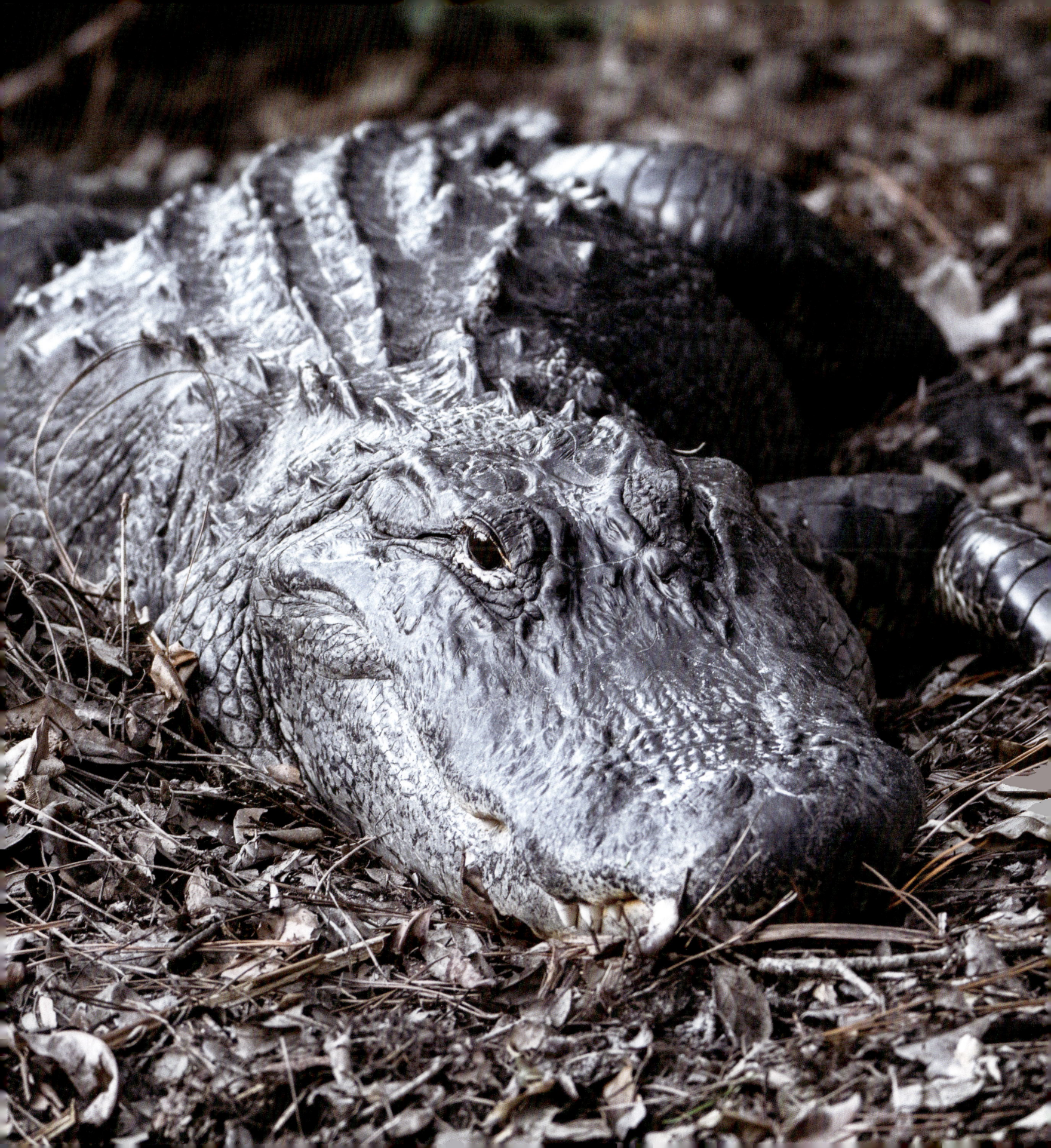

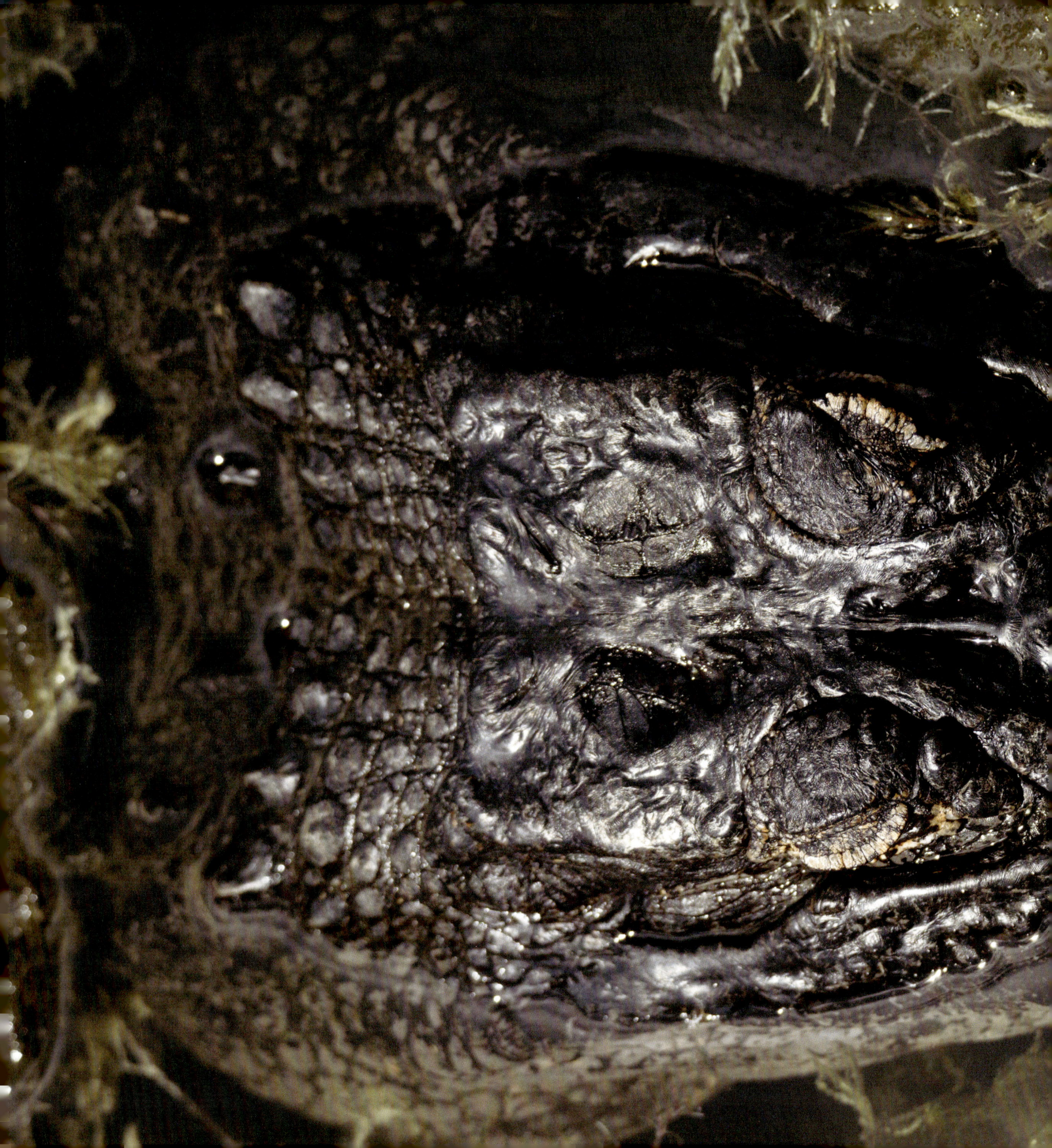

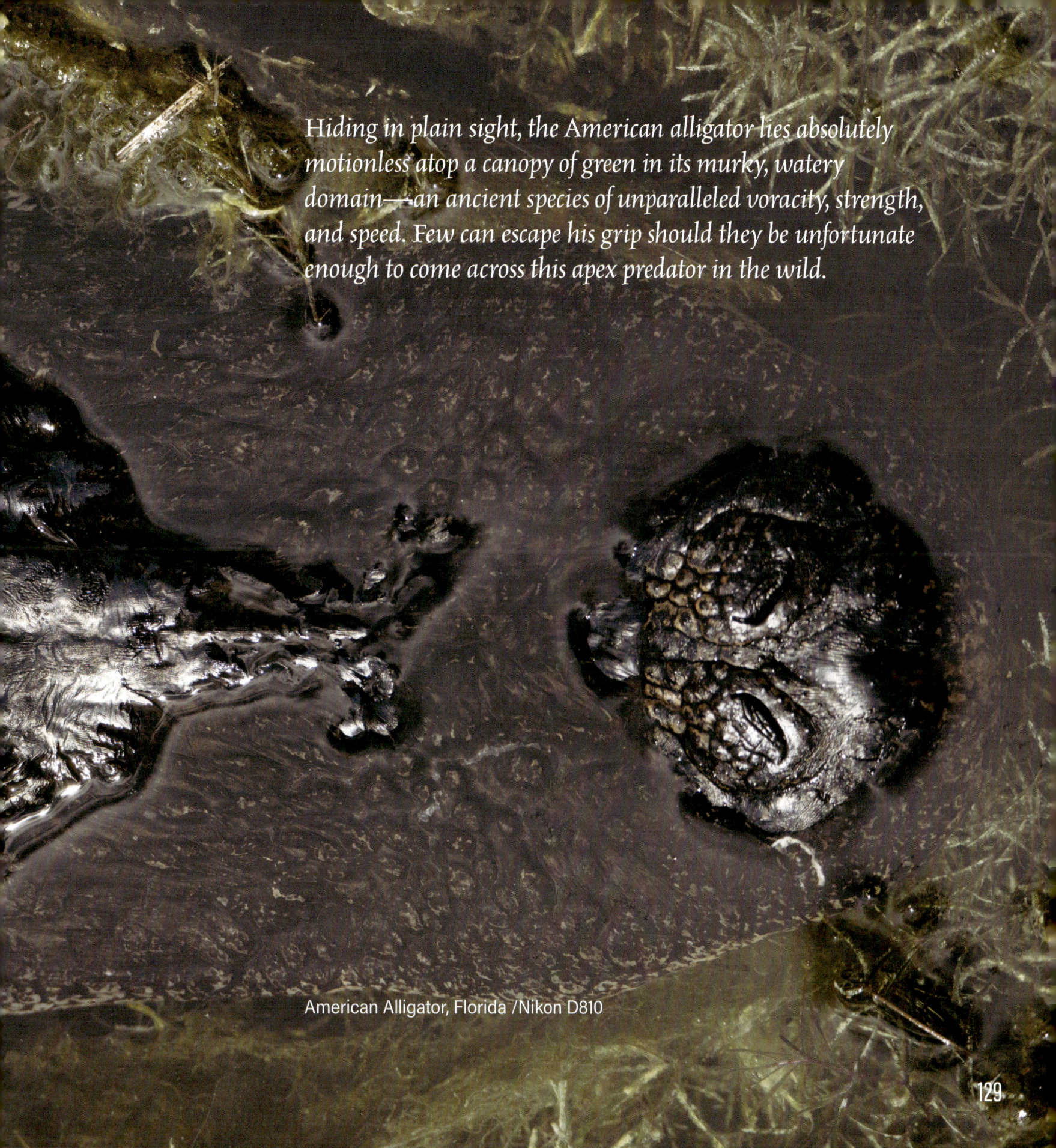

Hiding in plain sight, the American alligator lies absolutely motionless atop a canopy of green in its murky, watery domain—an ancient species of unparalleled voracity, strength, and speed. Few can escape his grip should they be unfortunate enough to come across this apex predator in the wild.

American Alligator, Florida /Nikon D810

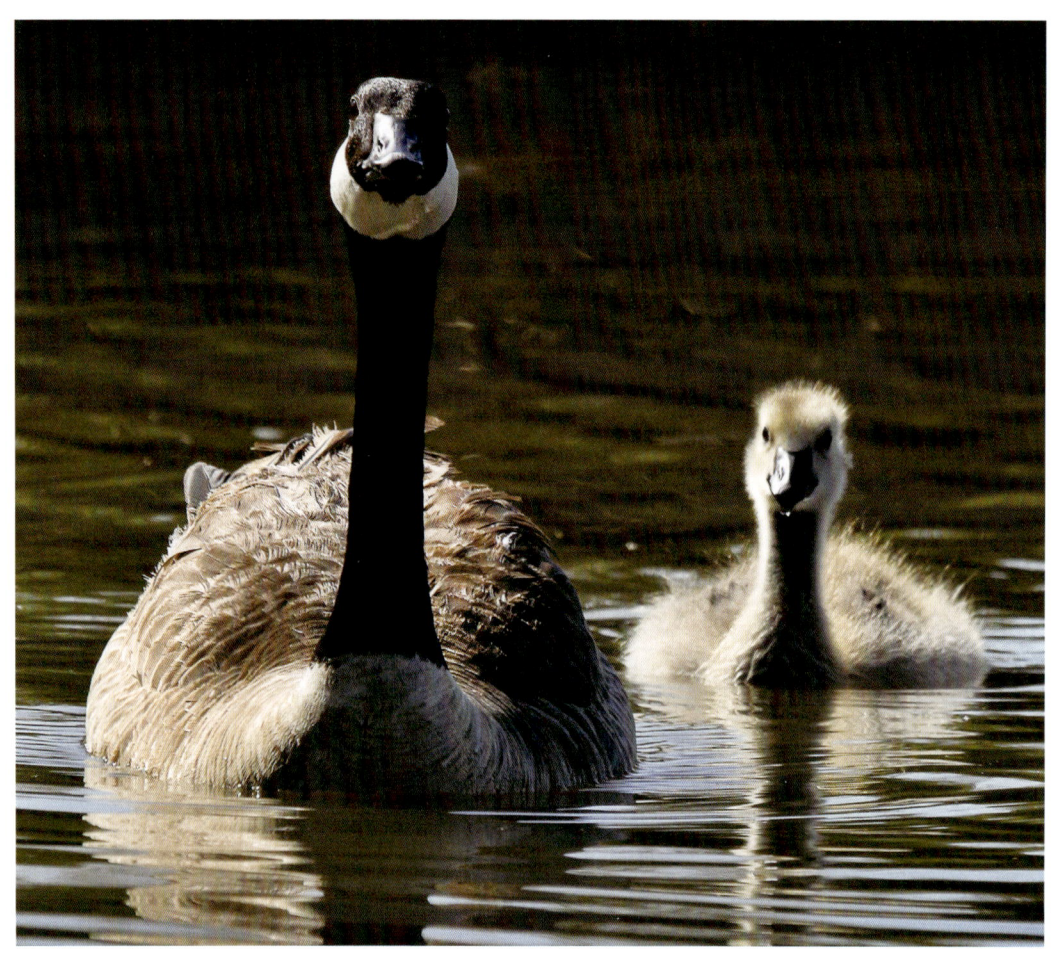

On the island of Maui, rain droplets accumulate atop the head of a black-crowned night heron, patiently waiting for the sudden tropical shower to pass.

Above: Canada Goose, Texas /Nikon D300
Opposite: Black-Crowned Night Heron, Hawaii /Nikon D600

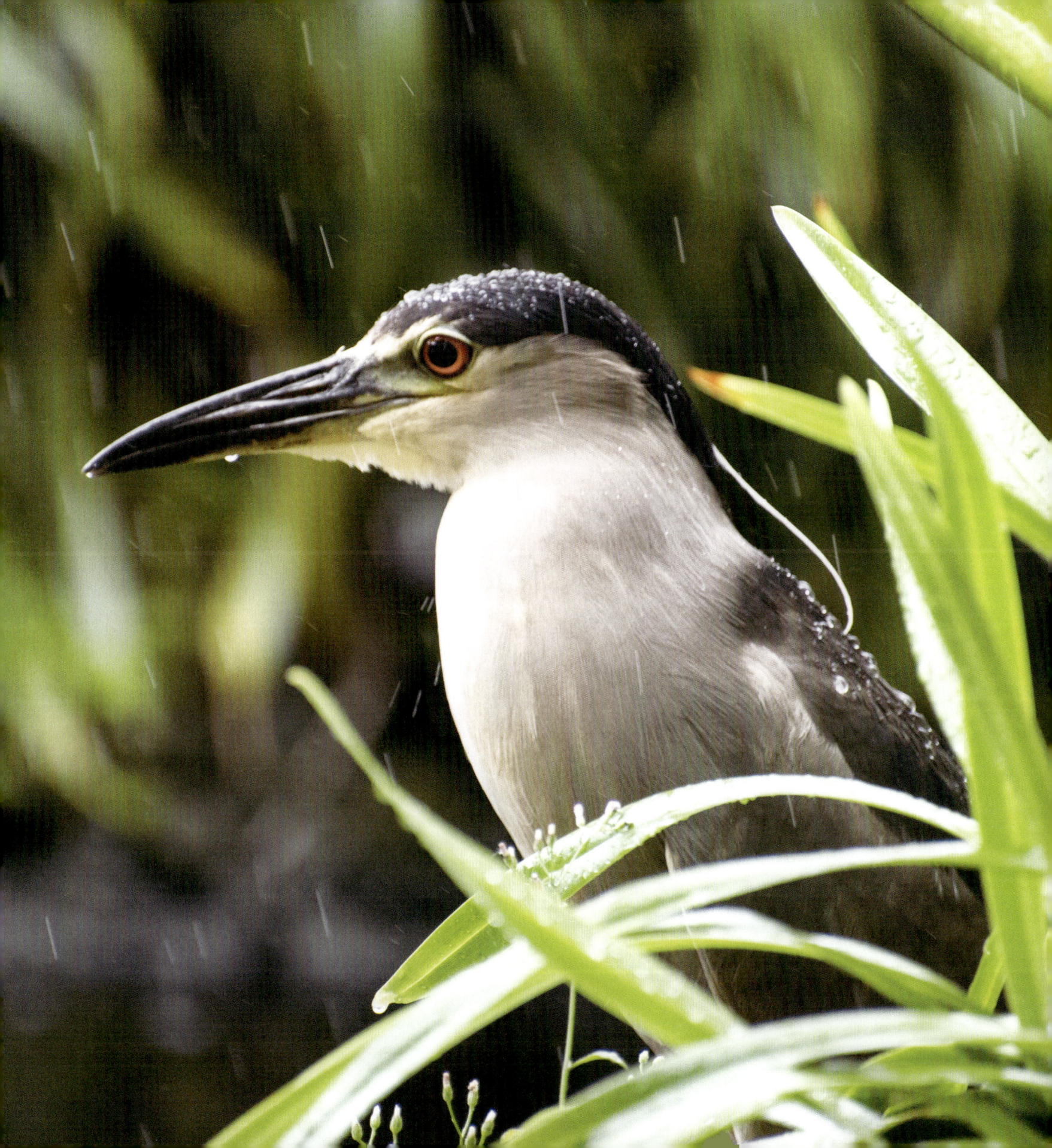

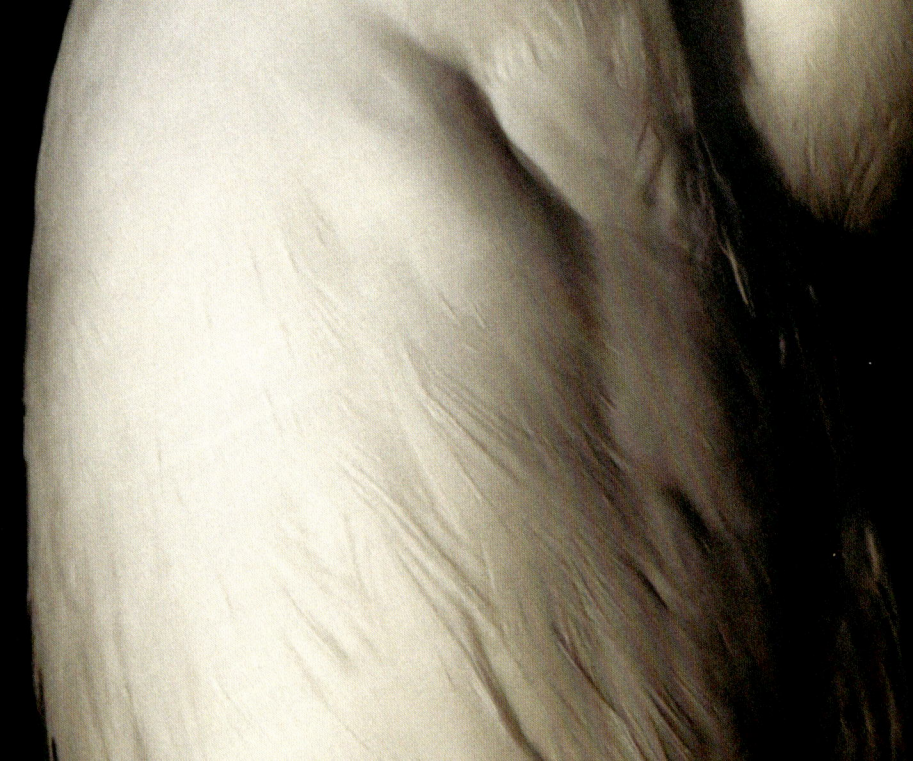

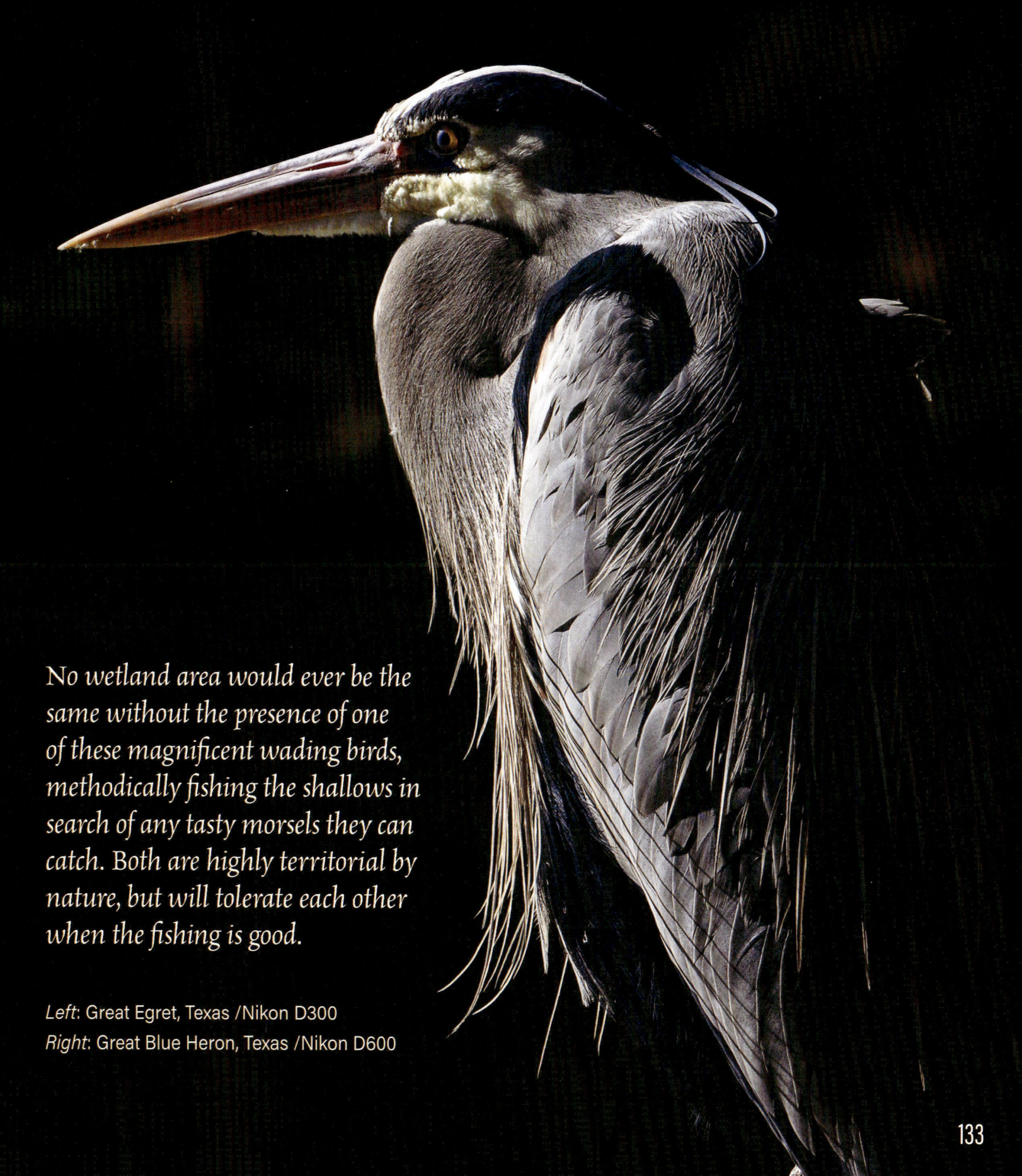

No wetland area would ever be the same without the presence of one of these magnificent wading birds, methodically fishing the shallows in search of any tasty morsels they can catch. Both are highly territorial by nature, but will tolerate each other when the fishing is good.

Left: Great Egret, Texas /Nikon D300
Right: Great Blue Heron, Texas /Nikon D600

133

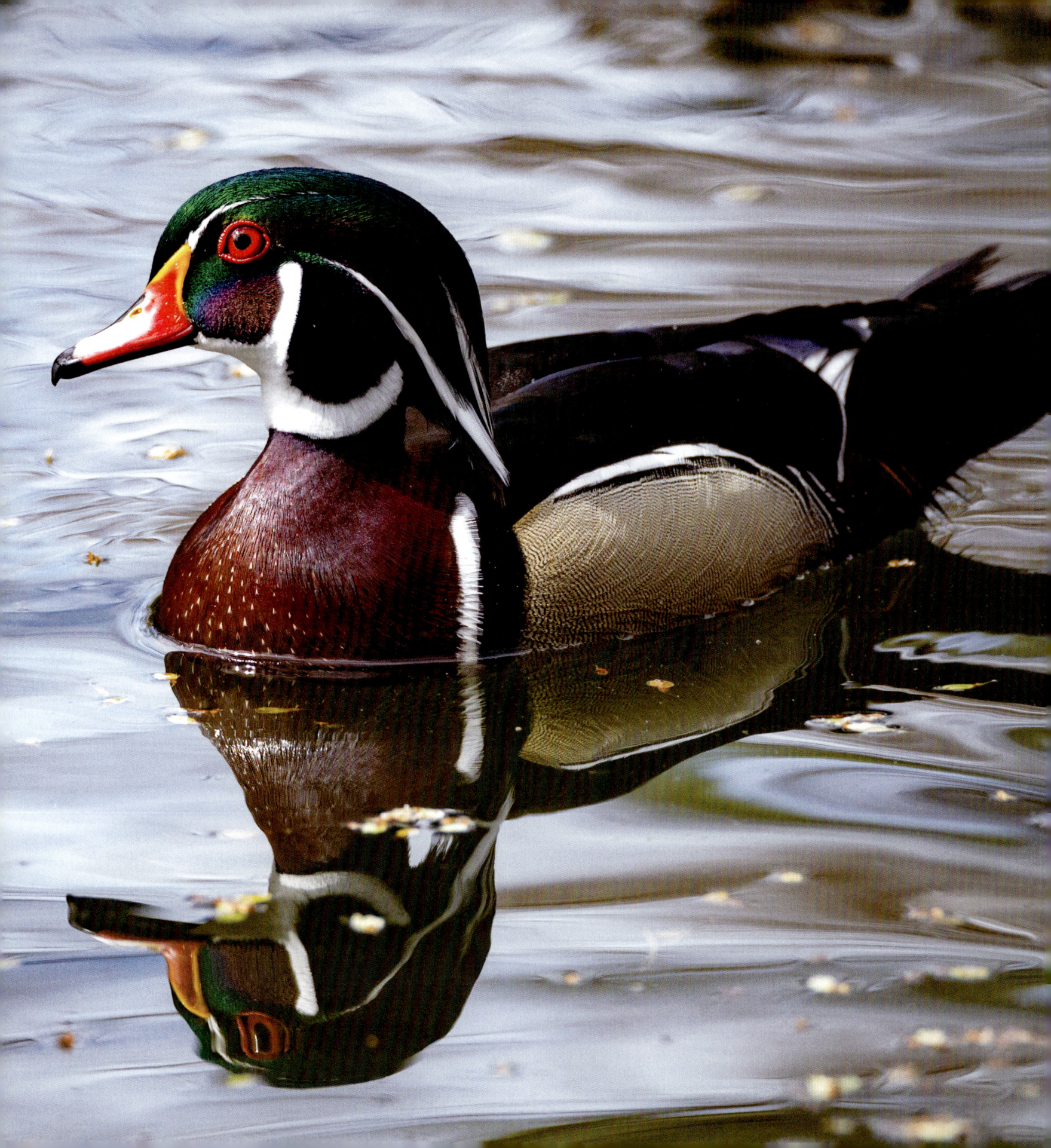

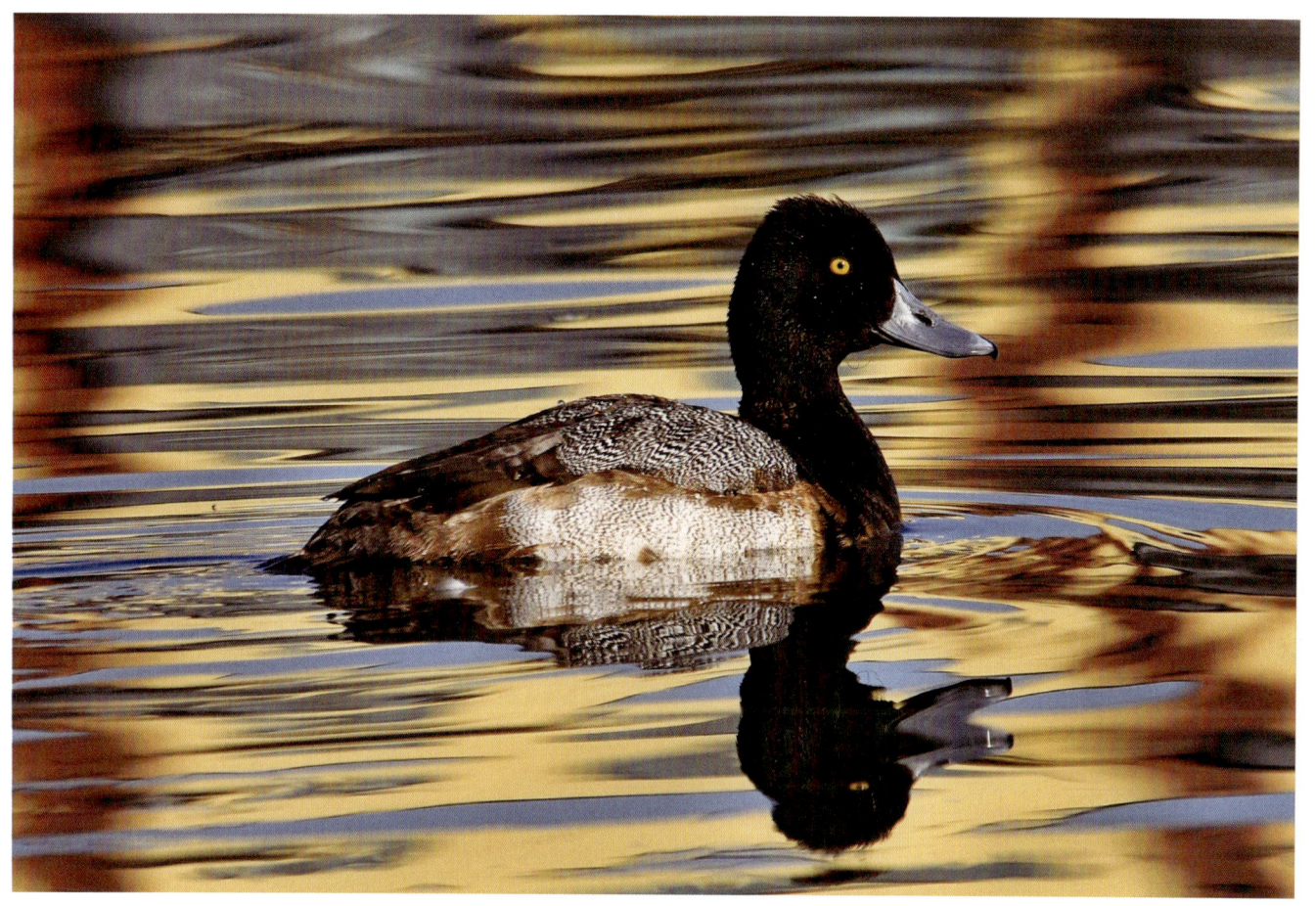

Wild ducks are naturally wary, and photographing them requires a true, determined effort, as well as a very long lens. The brightly colored wood duck is especially wary of his surroundings, and getting a good shot often takes a lot of time and patience.

Above: Lesser Scaup Duck, Texas /Nikon D600
Opposite: Wood Duck, Texas /Nikon D300

Hundreds of double-crested cormorants follow a large school of fish into the shallows, turning a blissful day into a feeding frenzy and a true spectacle of nature.

Above and opposite: Double-Crested Cormorant, Texas / Nikon D810

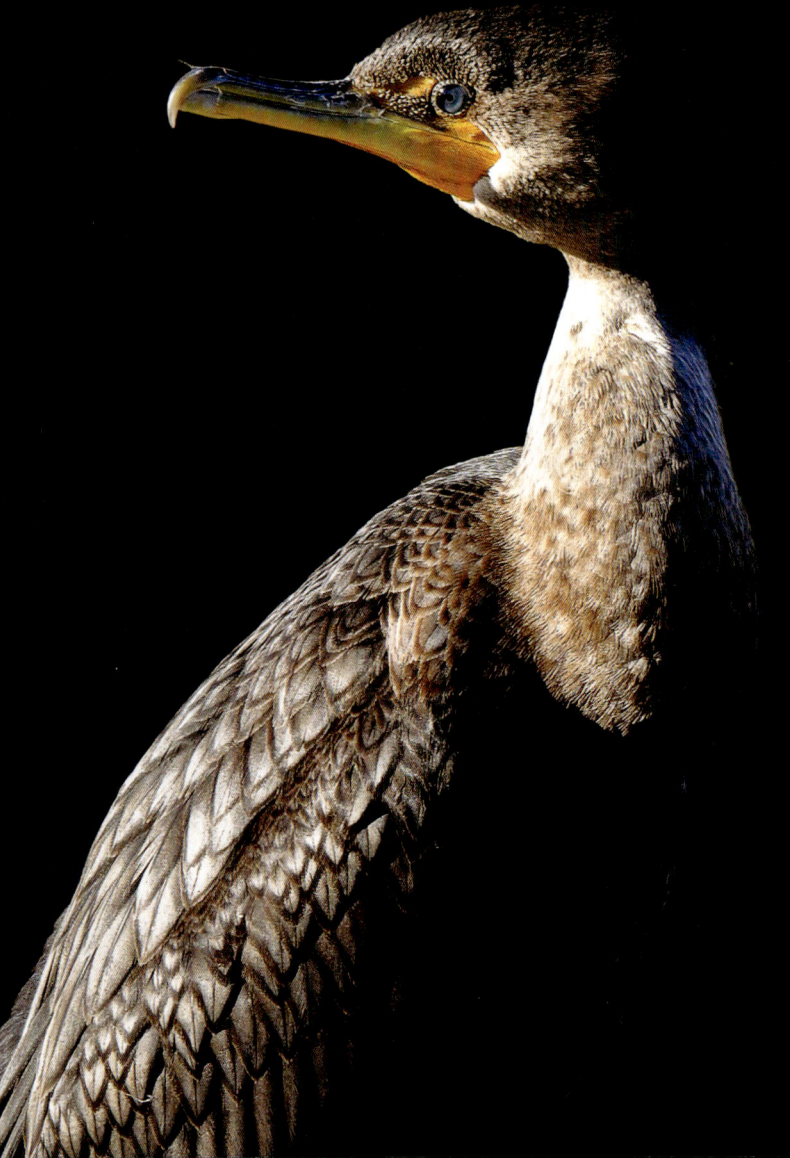

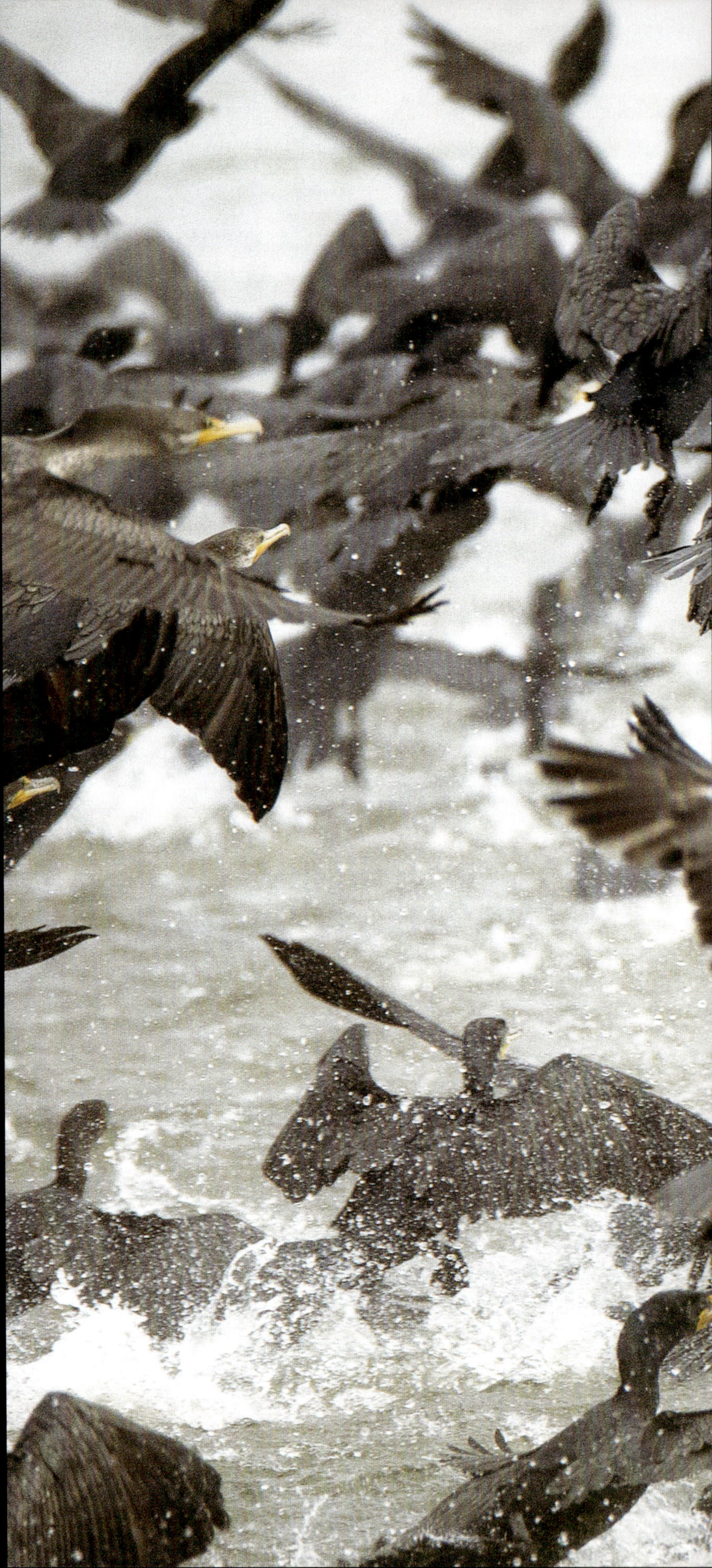

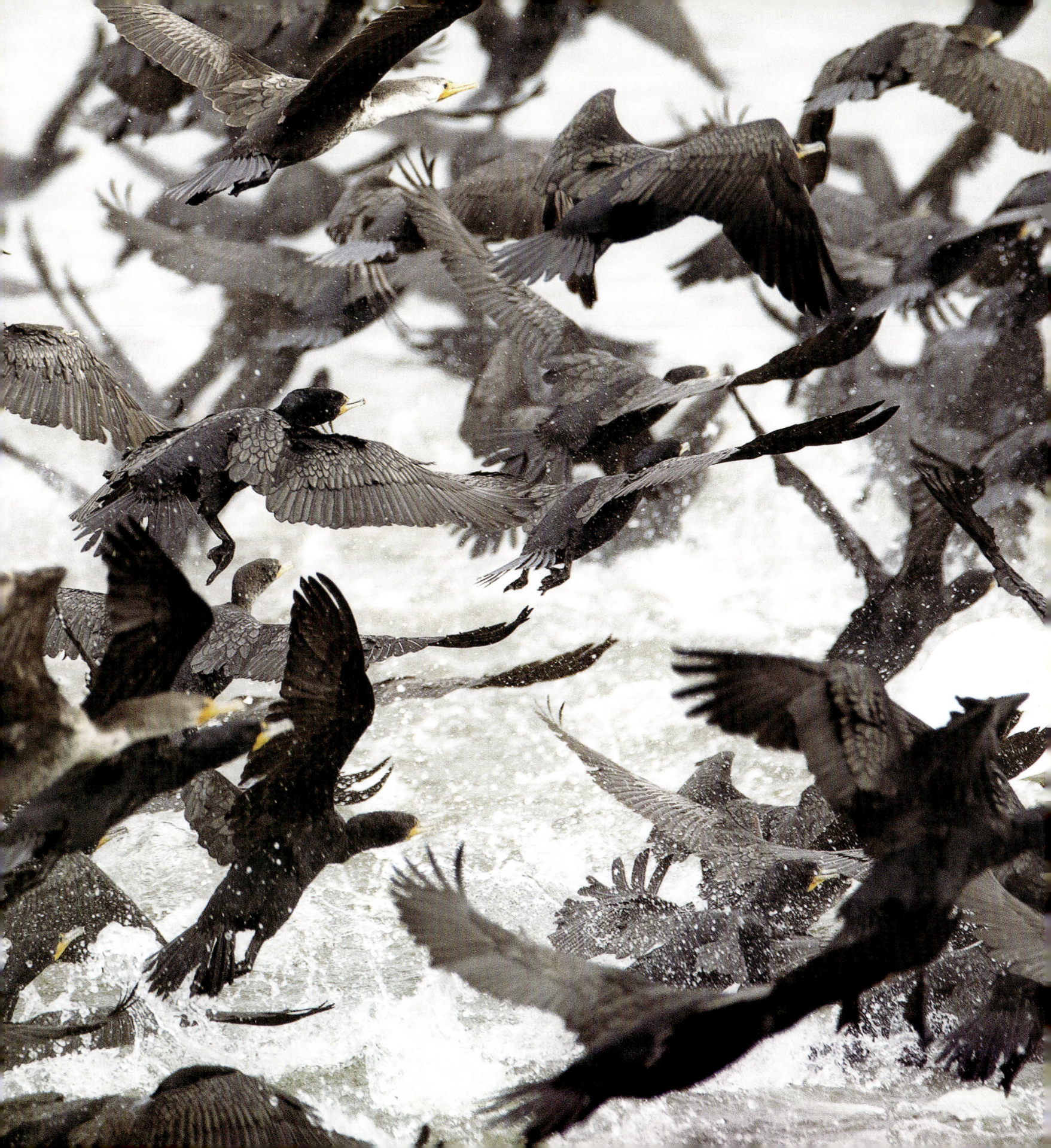

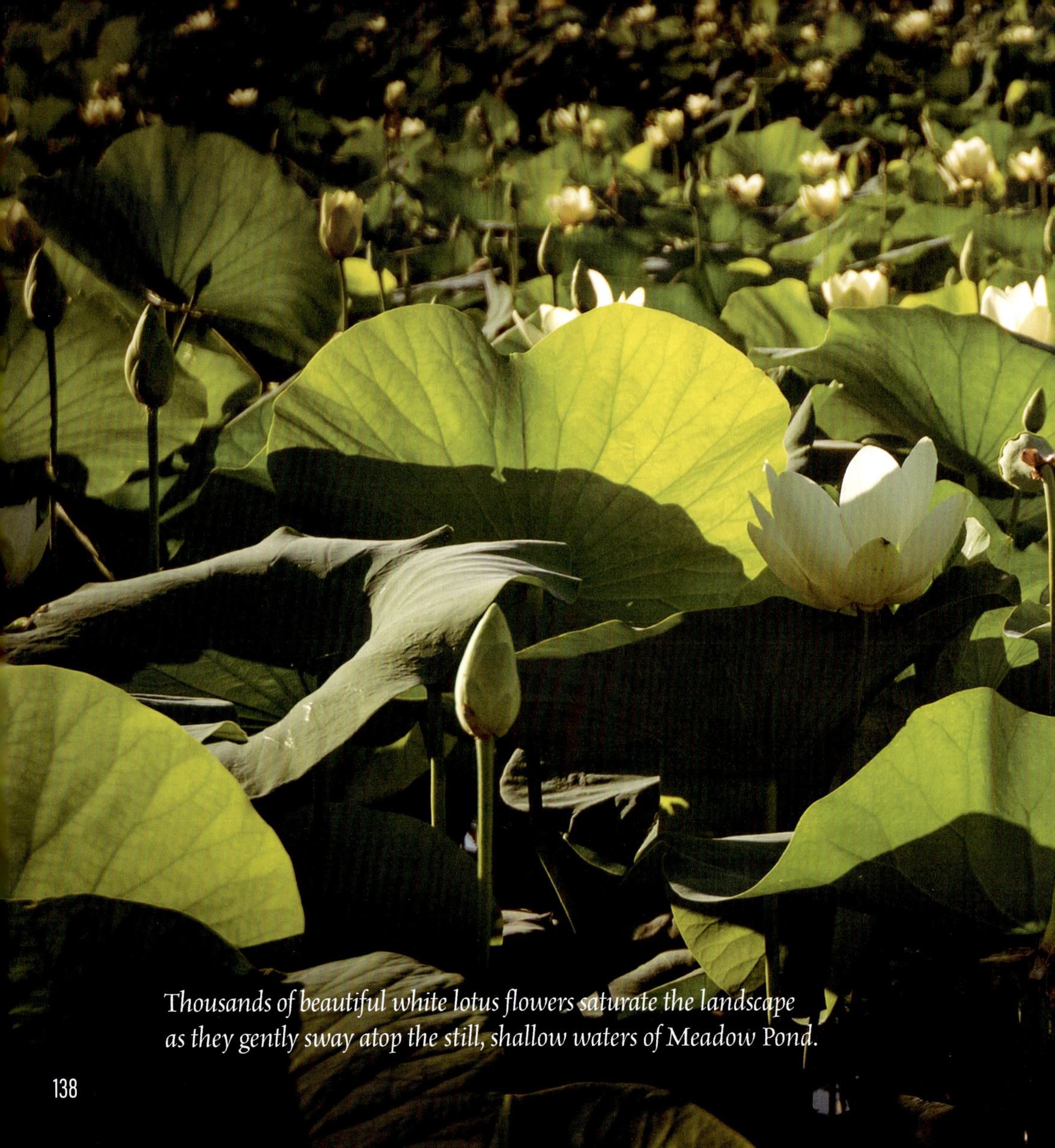

Thousands of beautiful white lotus flowers saturate the landscape
as they gently sway atop the still, shallow waters of Meadow Pond.

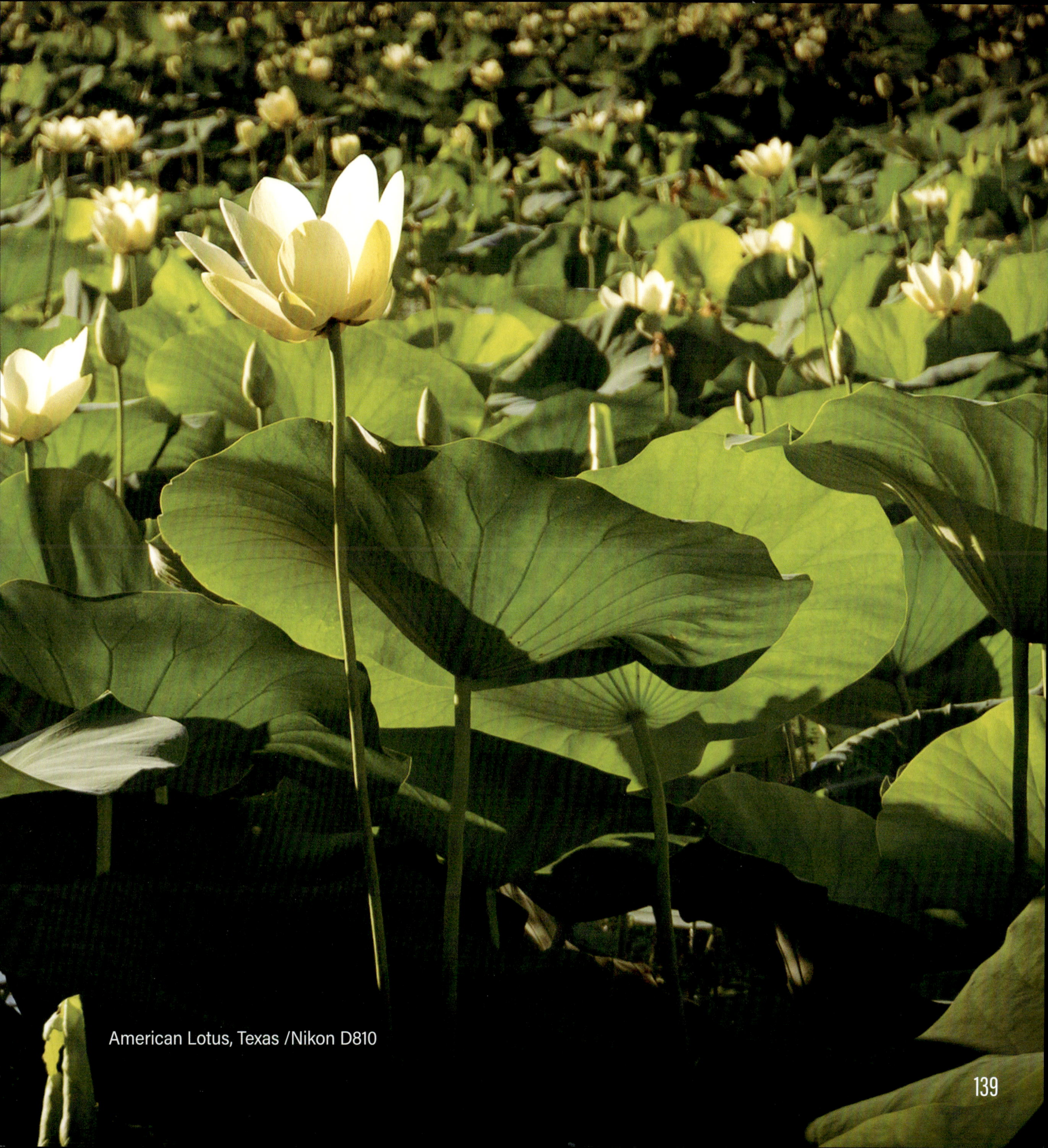

American Lotus, Texas /Nikon D810

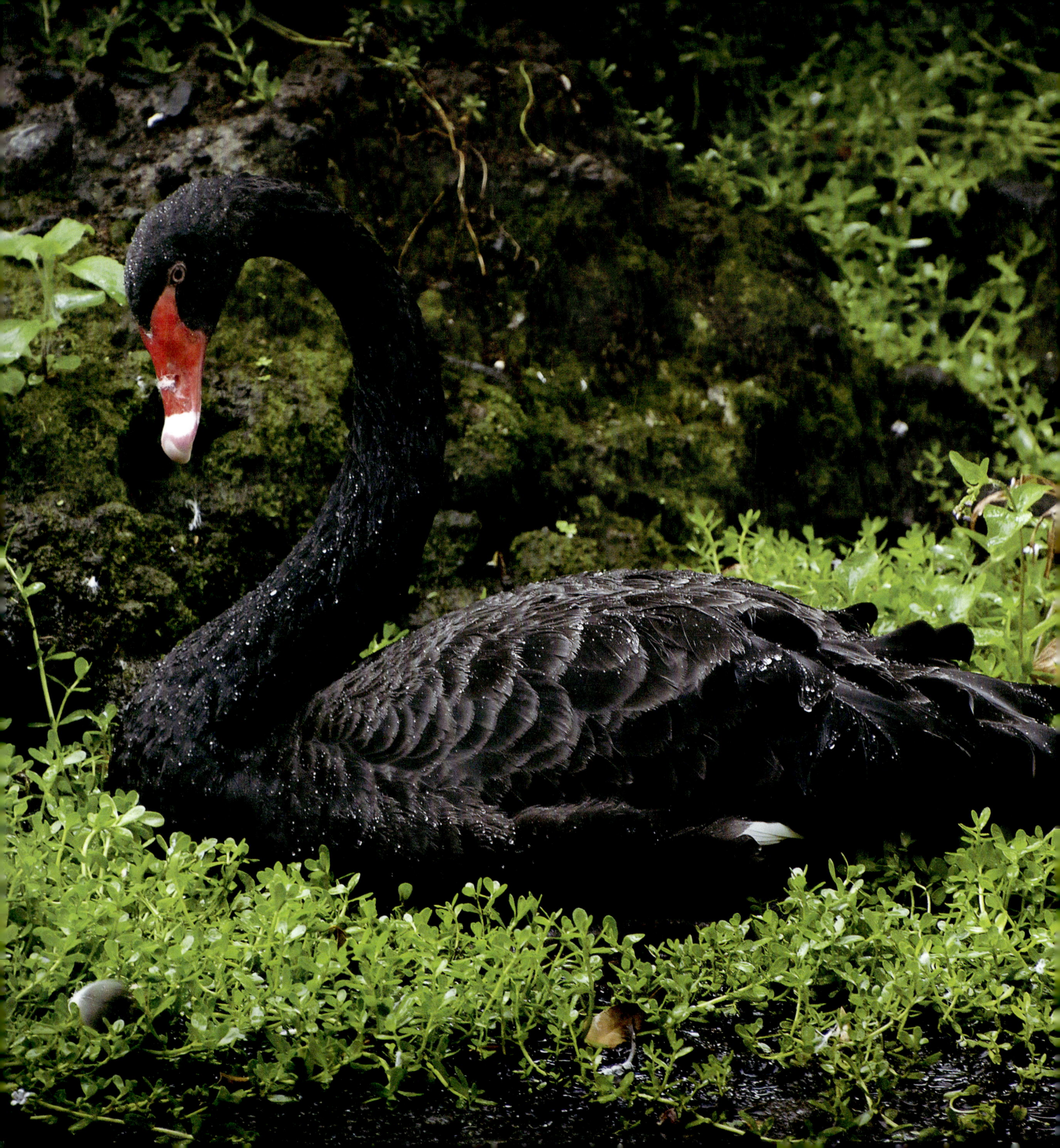

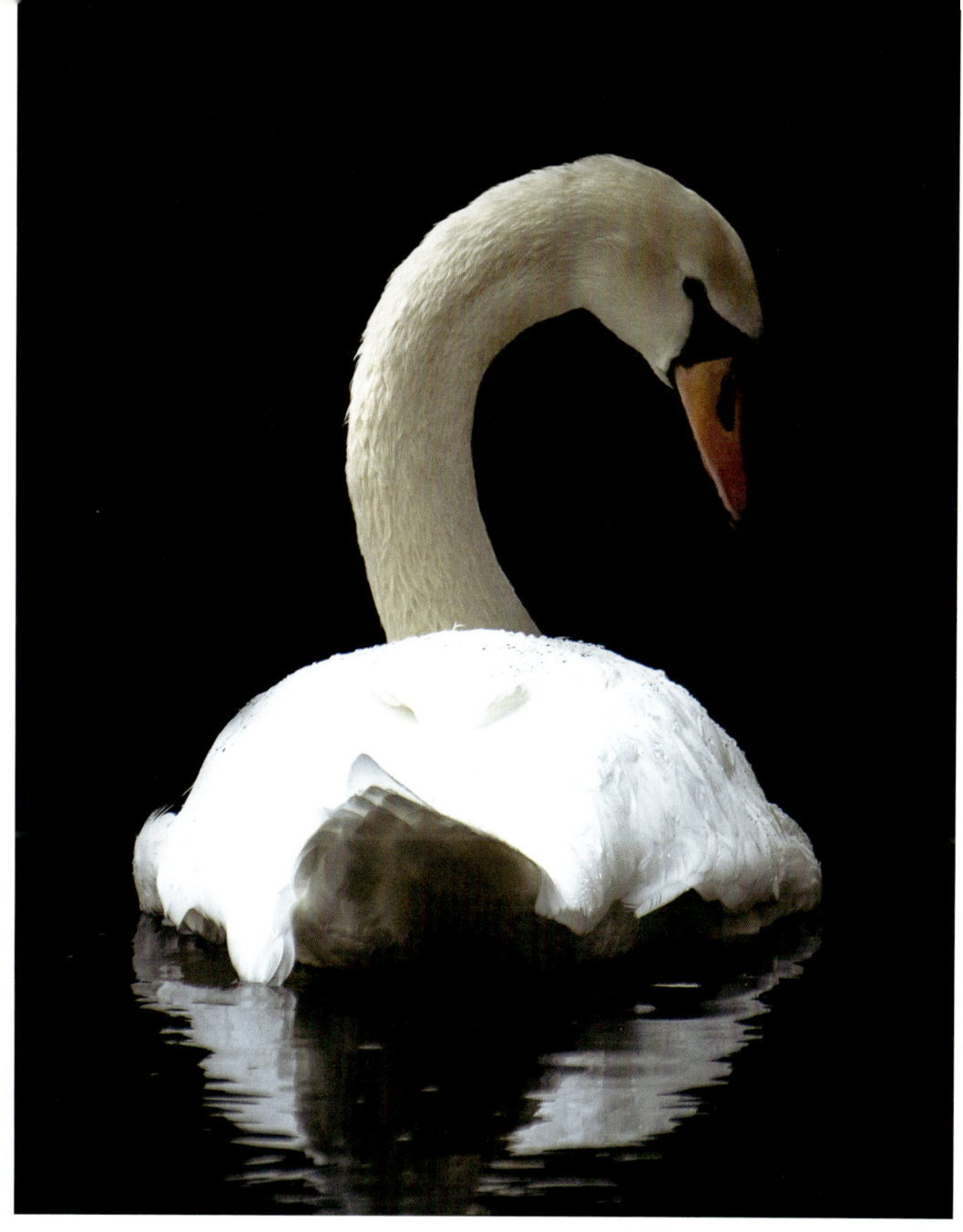

Swans, whether black or white, are one of the noblest animals on the planet, and their innate grace and elegance have inspired many a story.

Above: White Swan, Illinois /Nikon D600
Opposite: Black Swan, Hawaii /Nikon D600

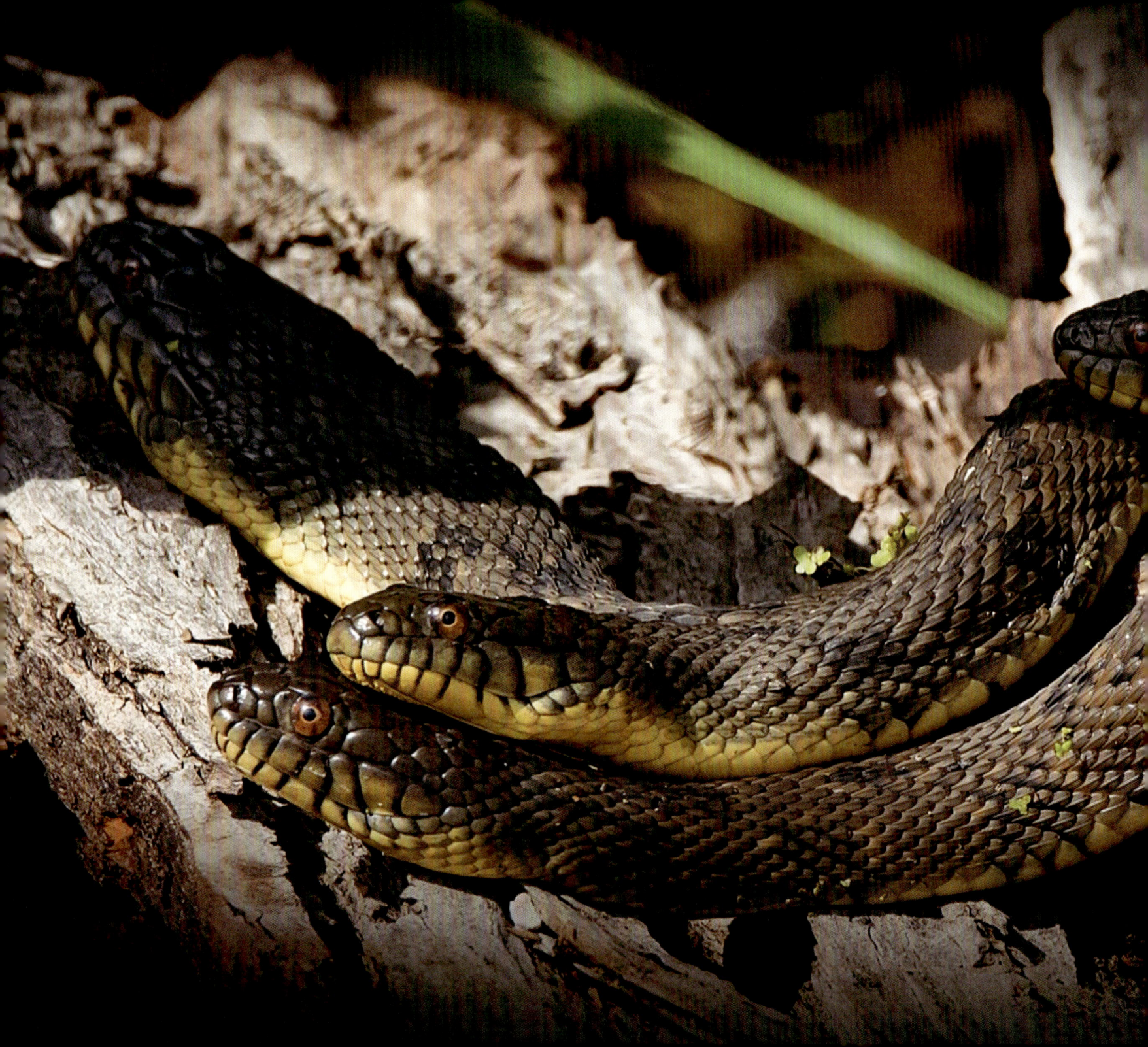

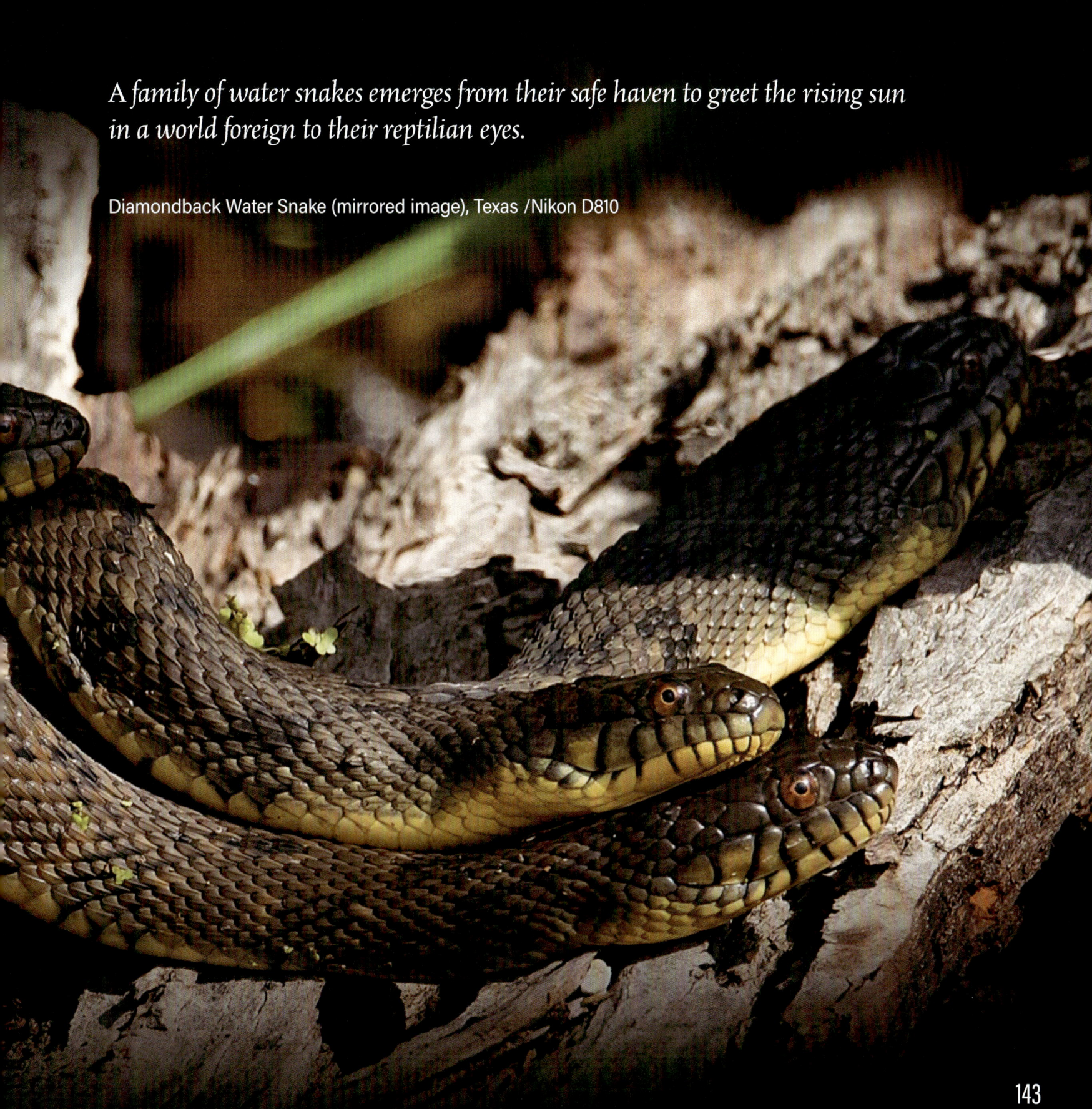

A family of water snakes emerges from their safe haven to greet the rising sun in a world foreign to their reptilian eyes.

Diamondback Water Snake (mirrored image), Texas /Nikon D810

143

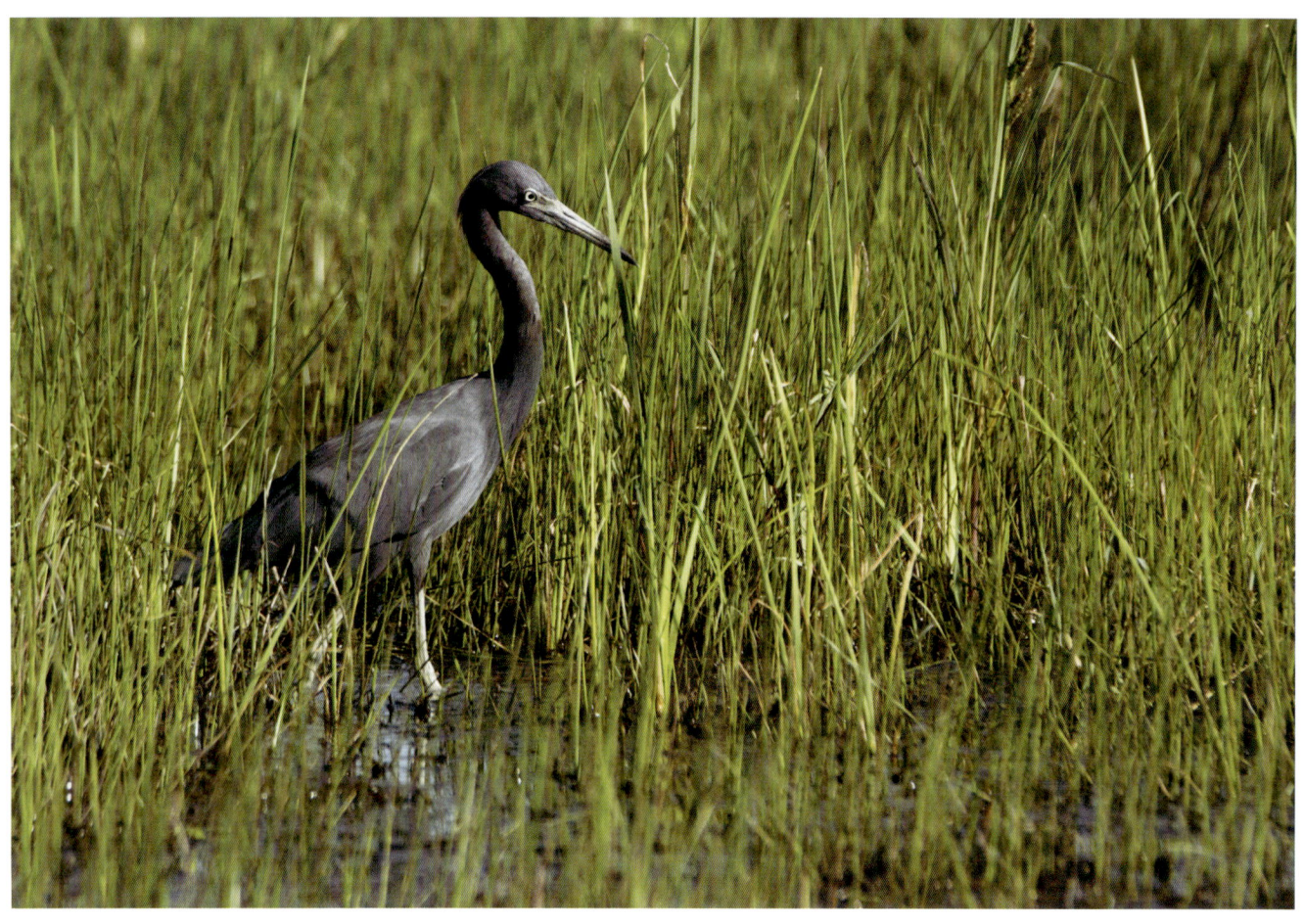

Wading birds live in perfect harmony with nature from the inland marshes to the coastal shoreline. Their presence always captivates me, as they are methodical in their behavior and so very beautiful to behold.

Above: Little Blue Heron, Texas / Nikon D600
Opposite: White Ibis, Florida / Nikon D600

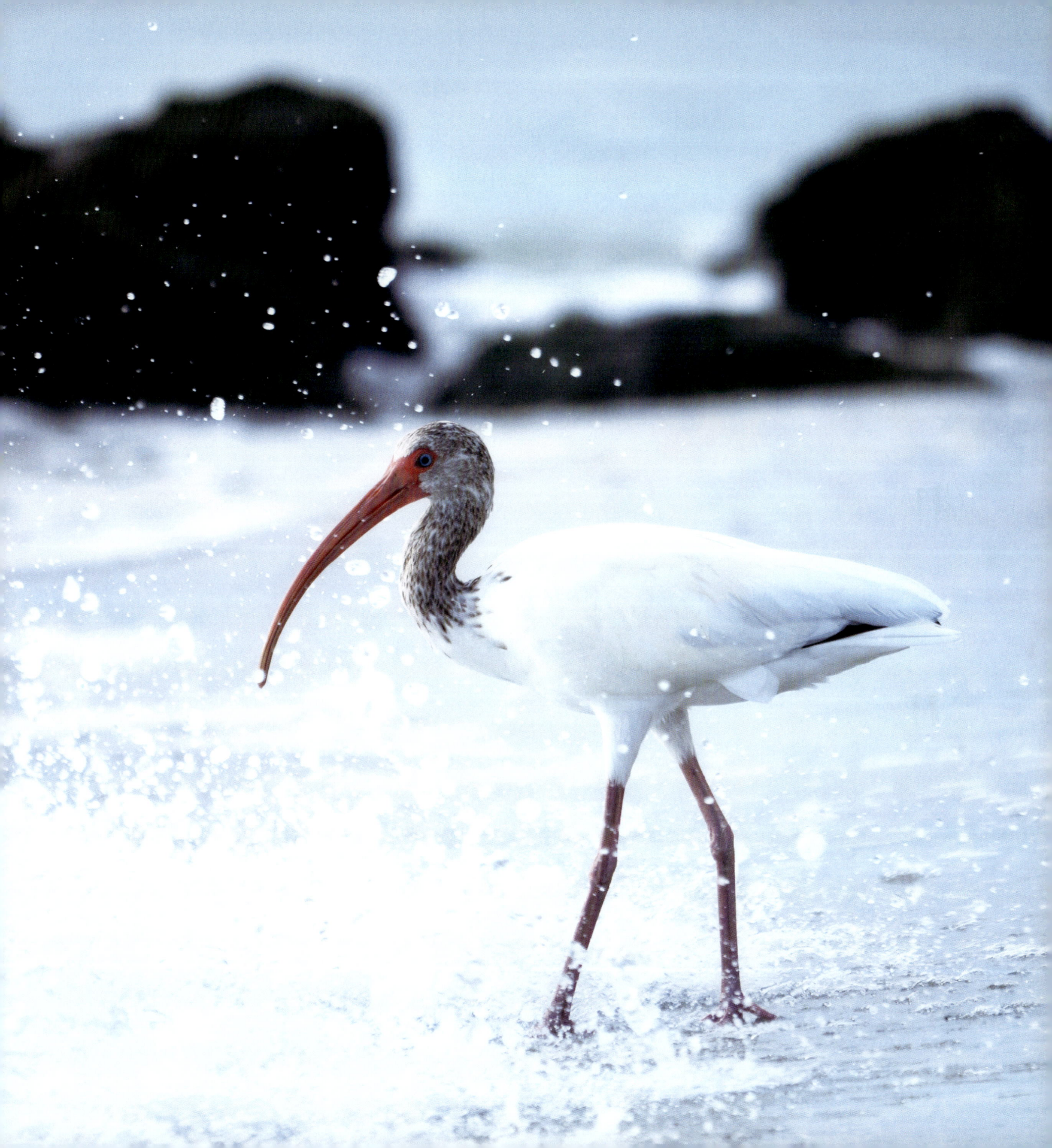

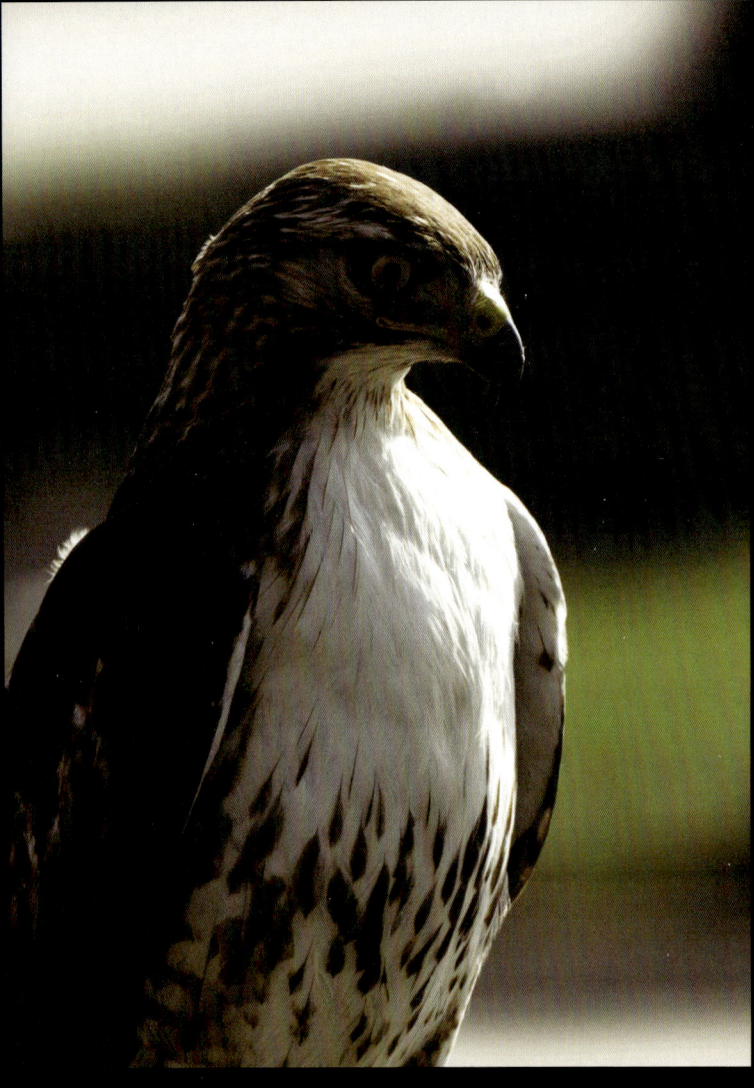

While I was hiking on a damp, boggy trail near the Florida Everglades, a tiny marsh rabbit appeared from the thicket. Seemingly out of place in this wetland realm, no doubt teeming with predators all around, his only defenses are camouflage, speed, and the unexpected ability to swim well should all other options fail.

Above: Red-Tailed Hawk, Texas /Nikon D810
Opposite: Marsh Rabbit, Florida /Nikon D810

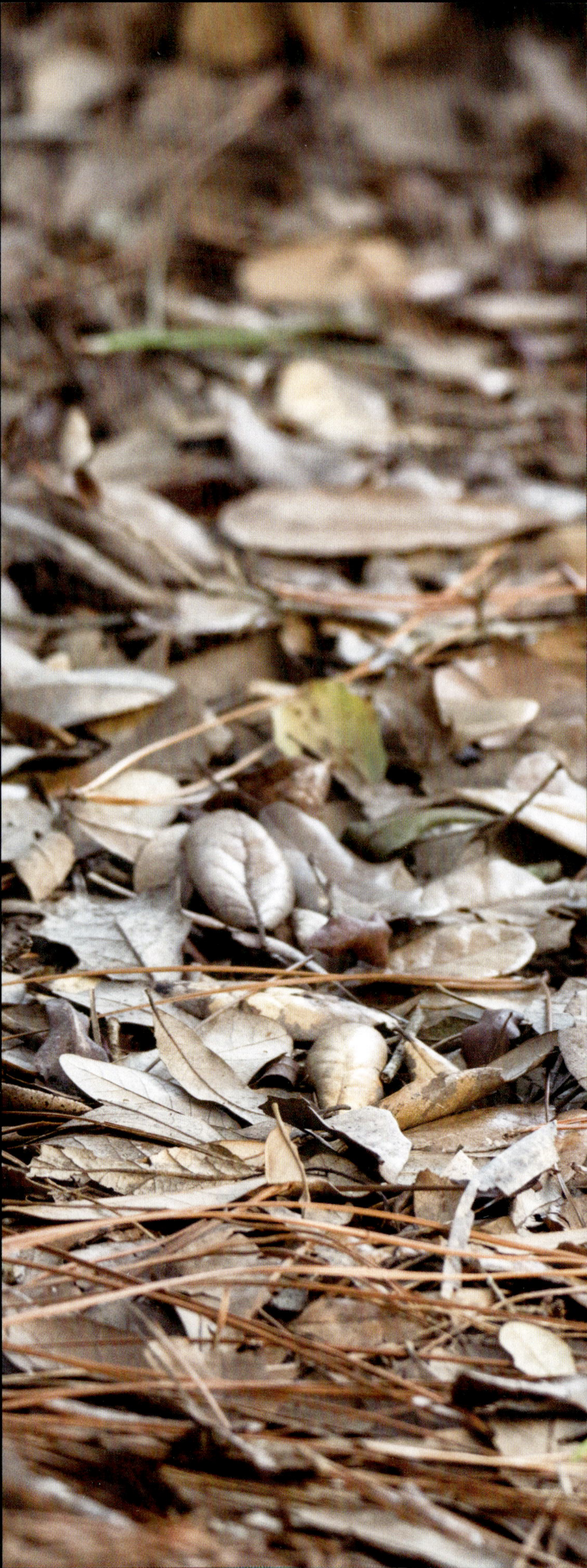

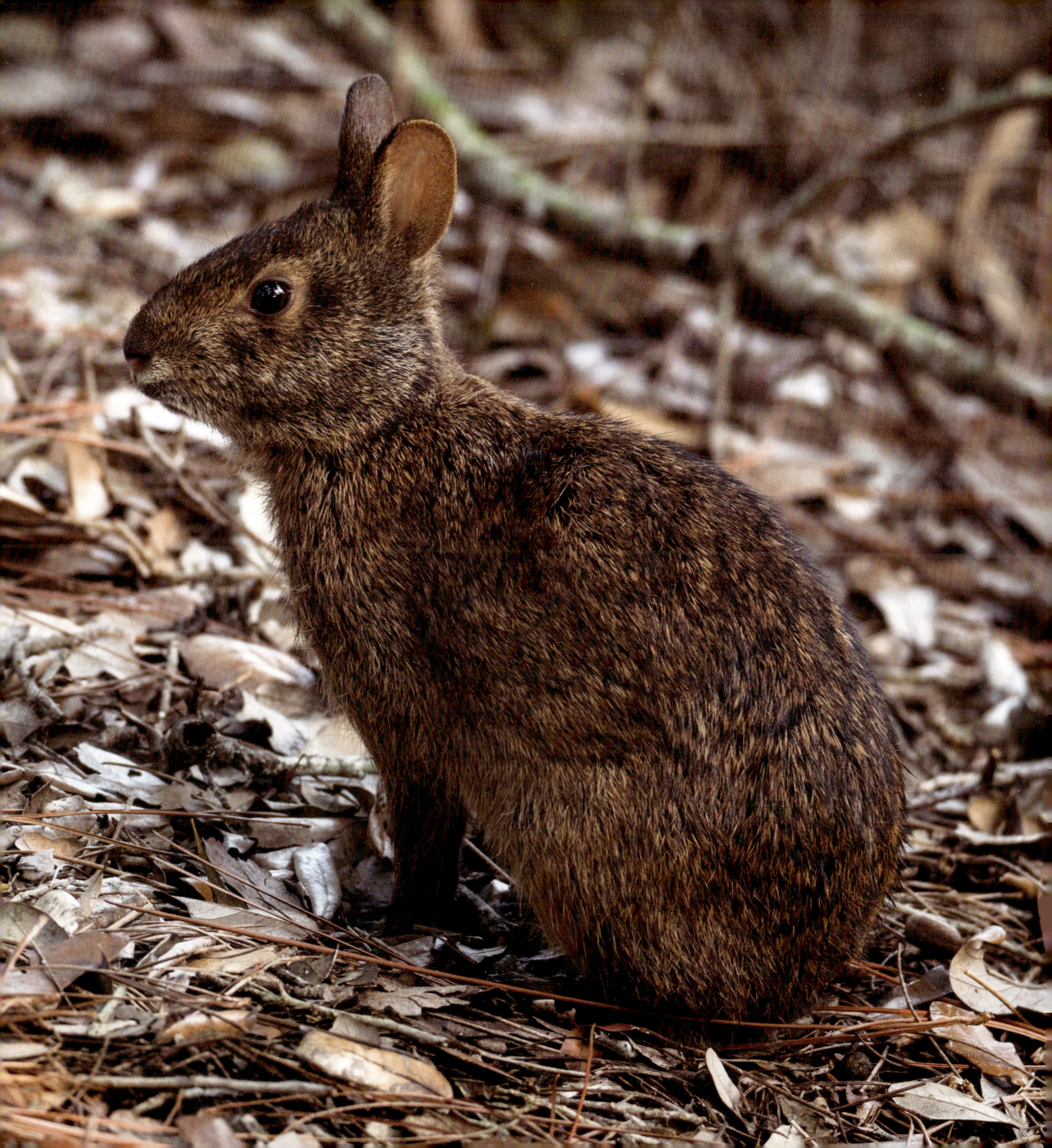

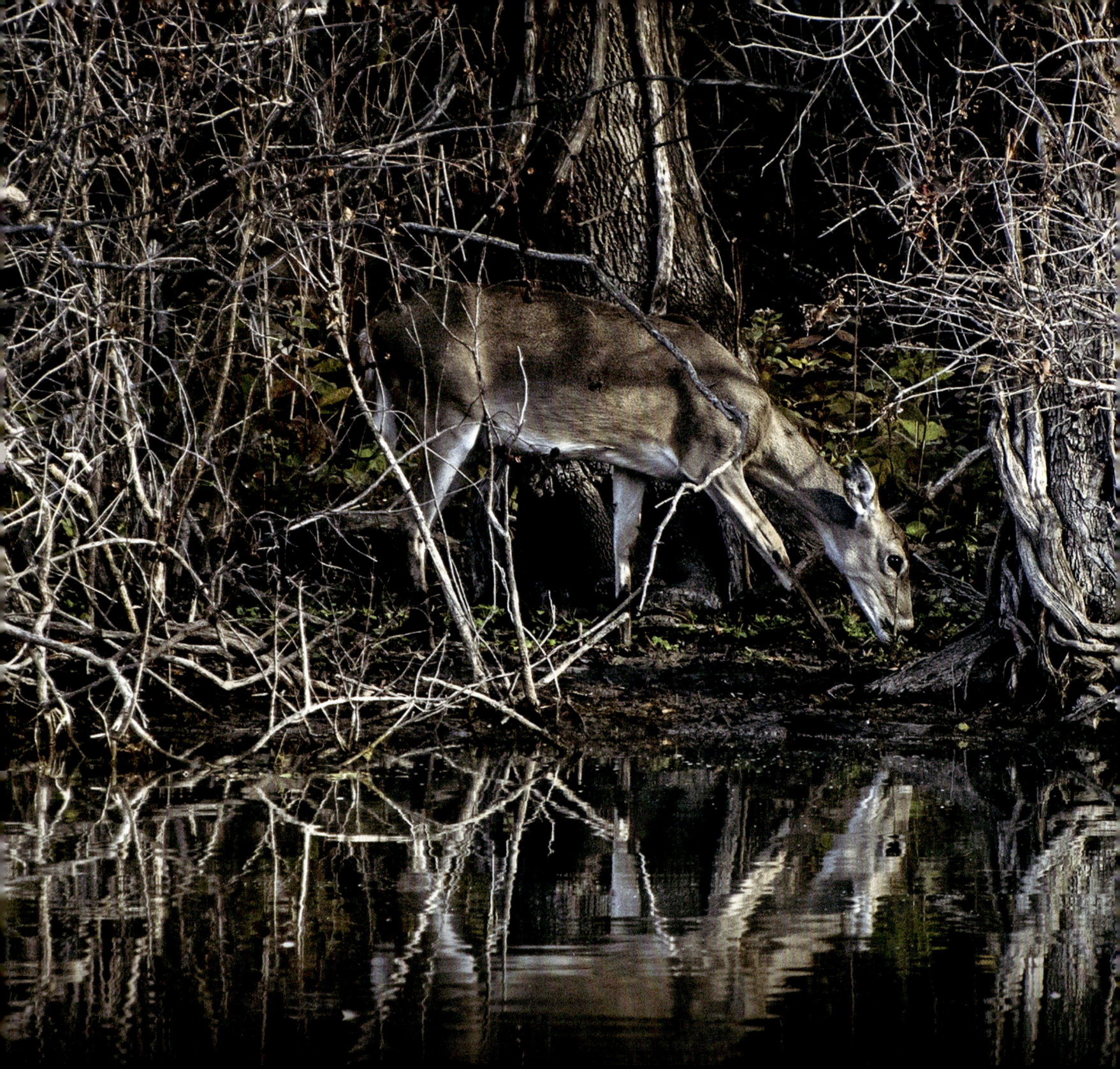

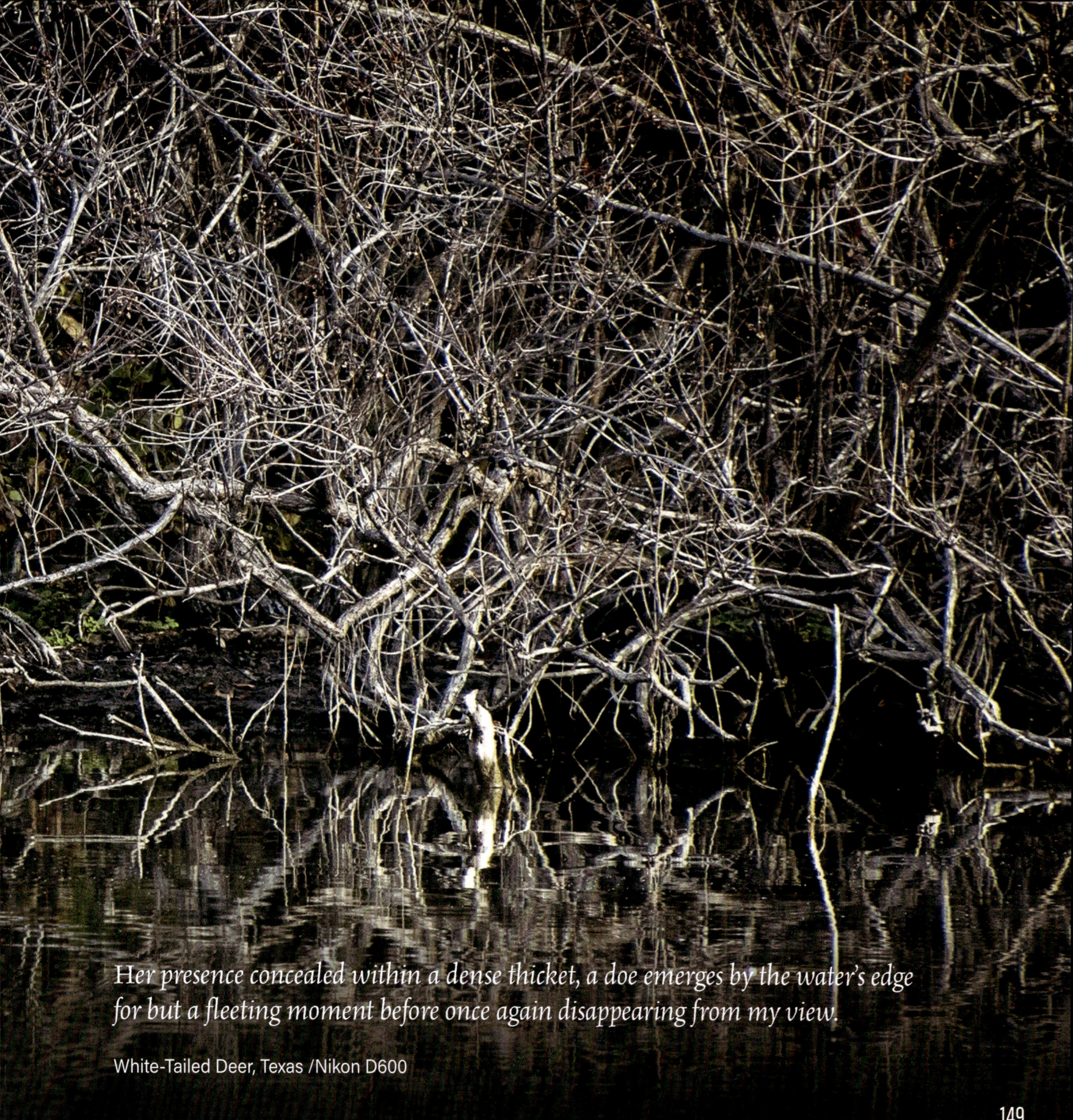

Her presence concealed within a dense thicket, a doe emerges by the water's edge for but a fleeting moment before once again disappearing from my view.

White-Tailed Deer, Texas / Nikon D600

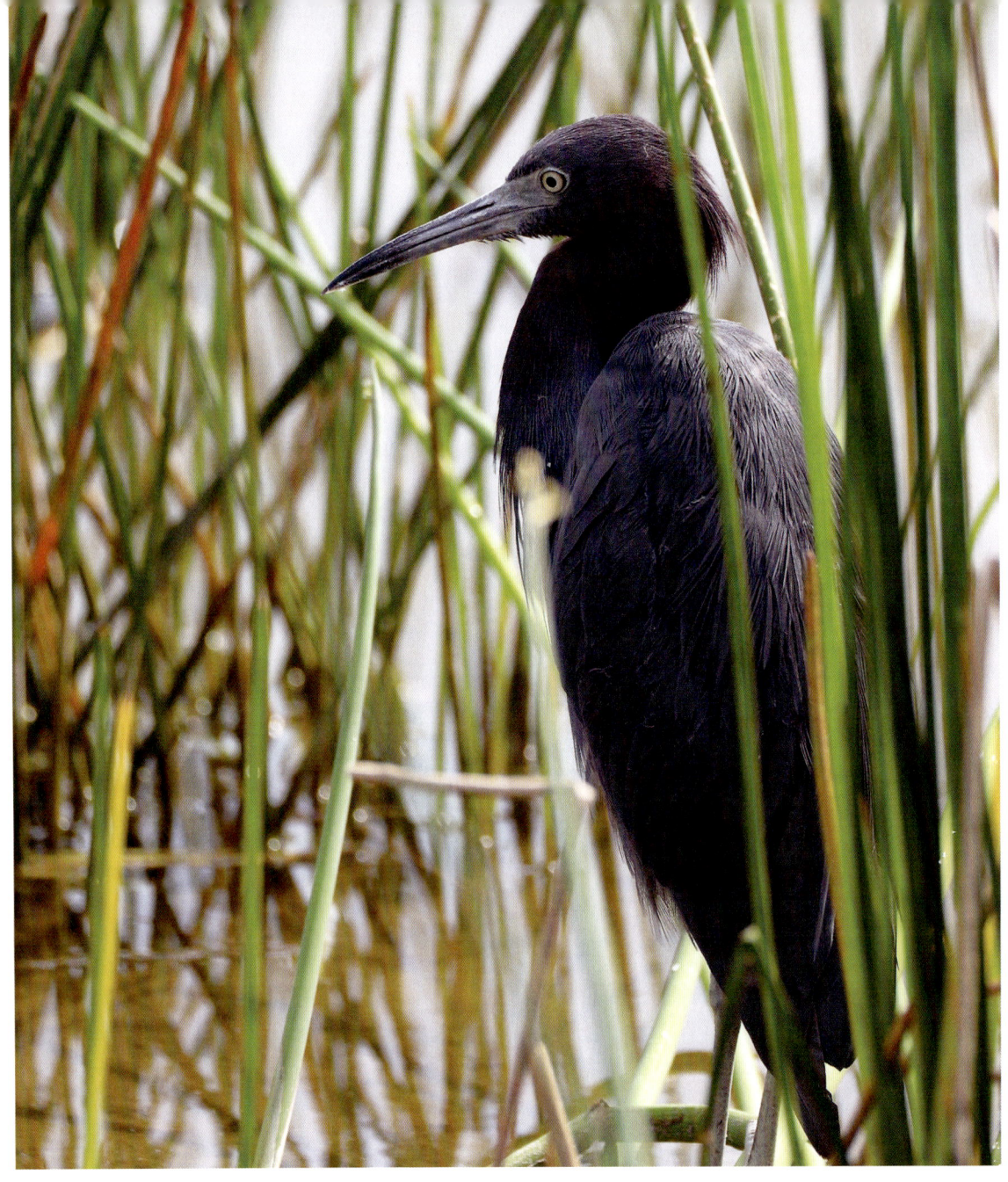

More like a submarine than a bird, the aquatic grebe rises to the surface, curious to my presence in her wetland home. I decided to call her the "Lady of the Lake," a designation most befitting our brief and solitary encounter.

Above: Little Blue Heron, Florida /Nikon D300
Opposite: Pied-Billed Grebe, Texas /Nikon D600

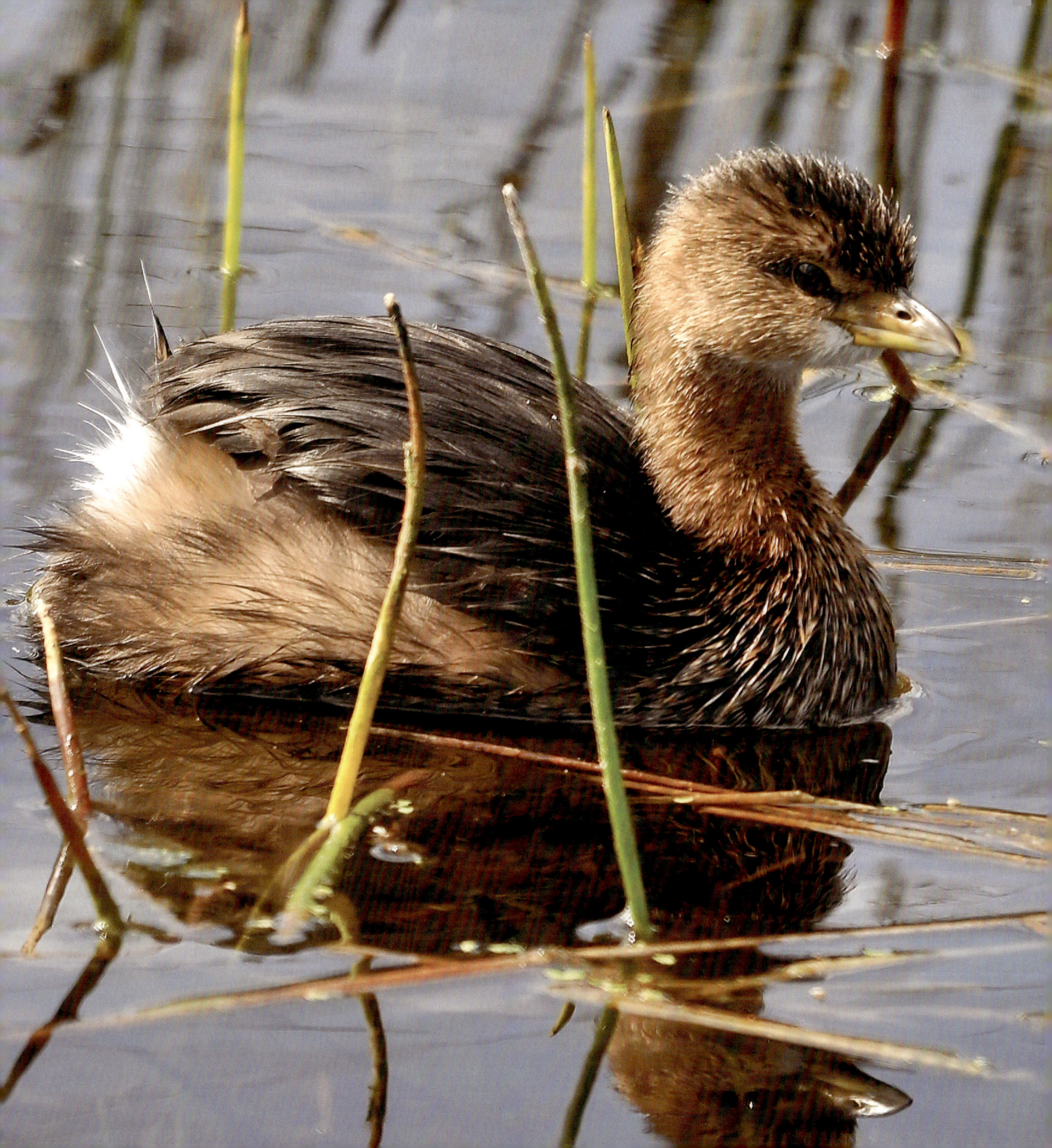

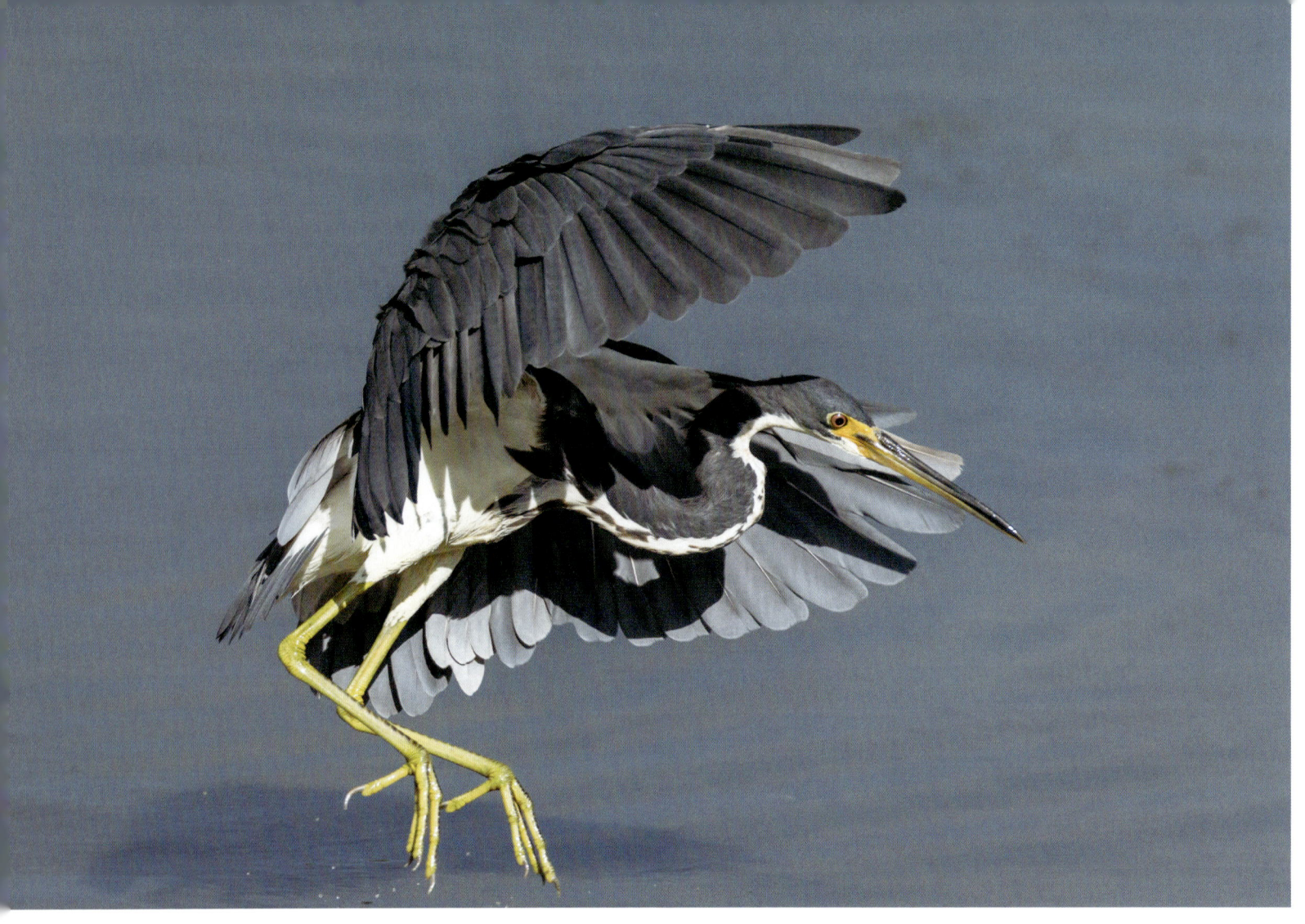

Brilliant tones of purplish blue permeate the early morning light as a purple gallinule calls out to its young in a wetland refuge located deep within the Florida Everglades.

Above: Tricolored Heron, Florida /Nikon D810
Opposite: Purple Gallinule, Florida /Nikon D300

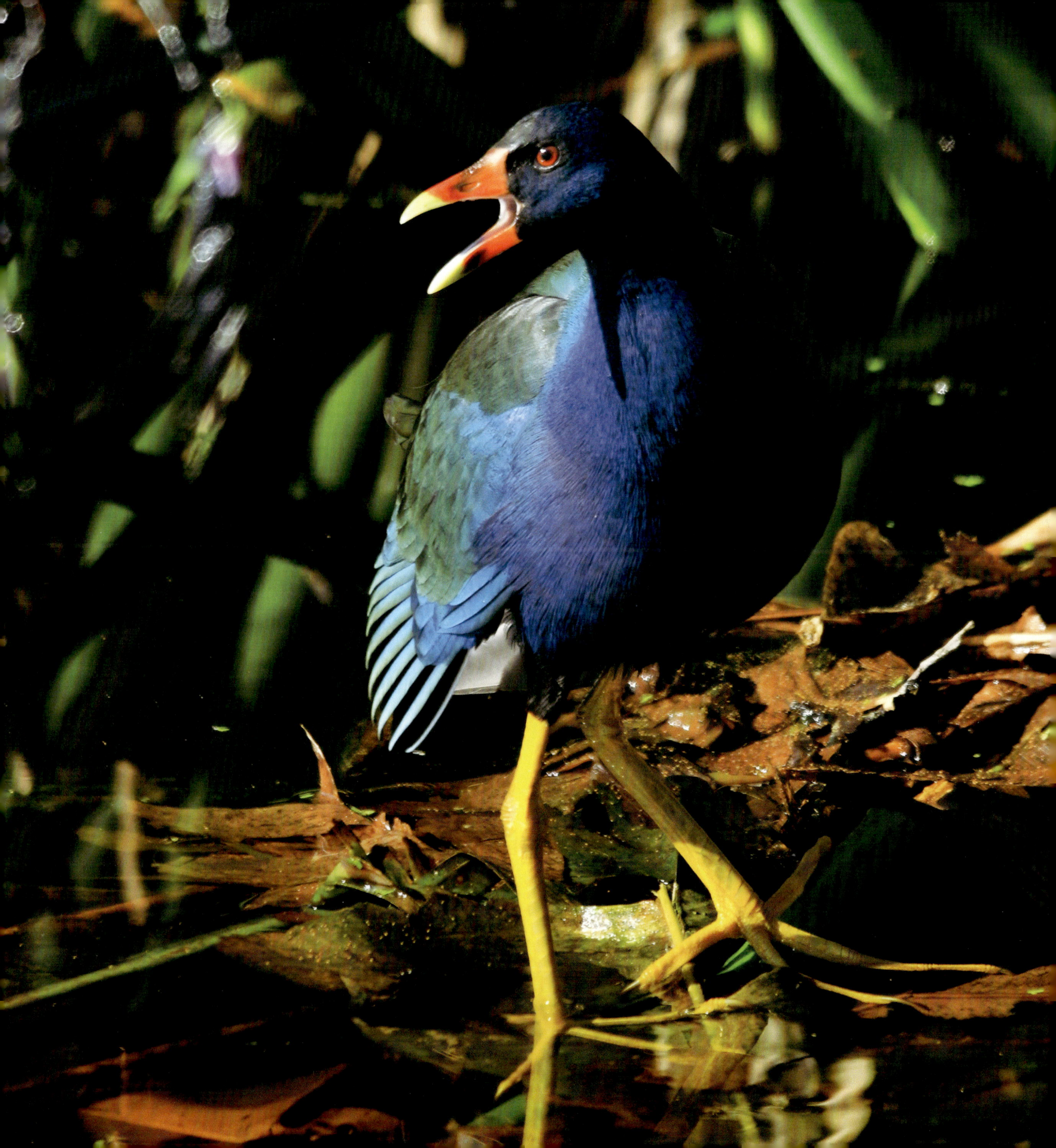

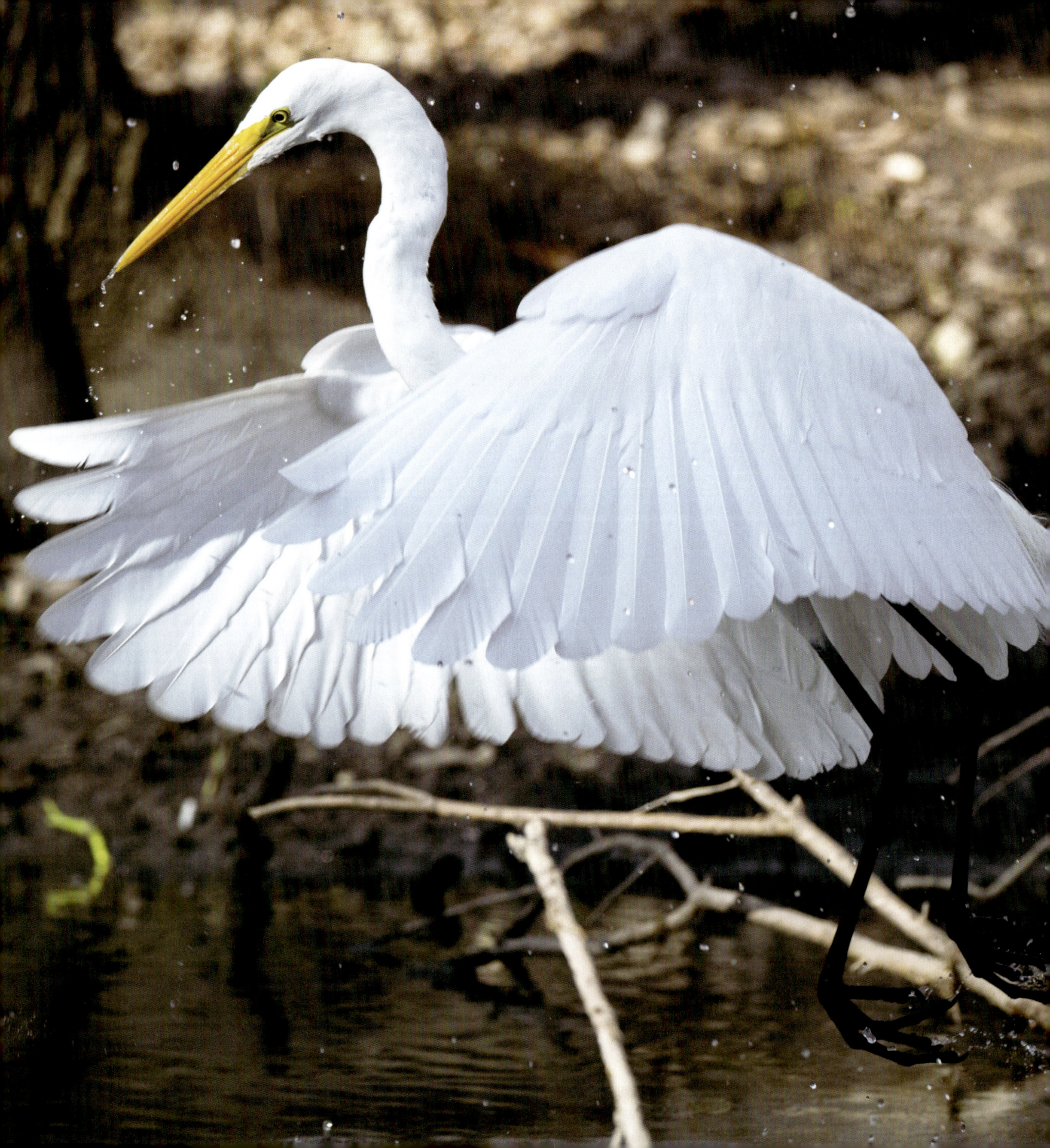

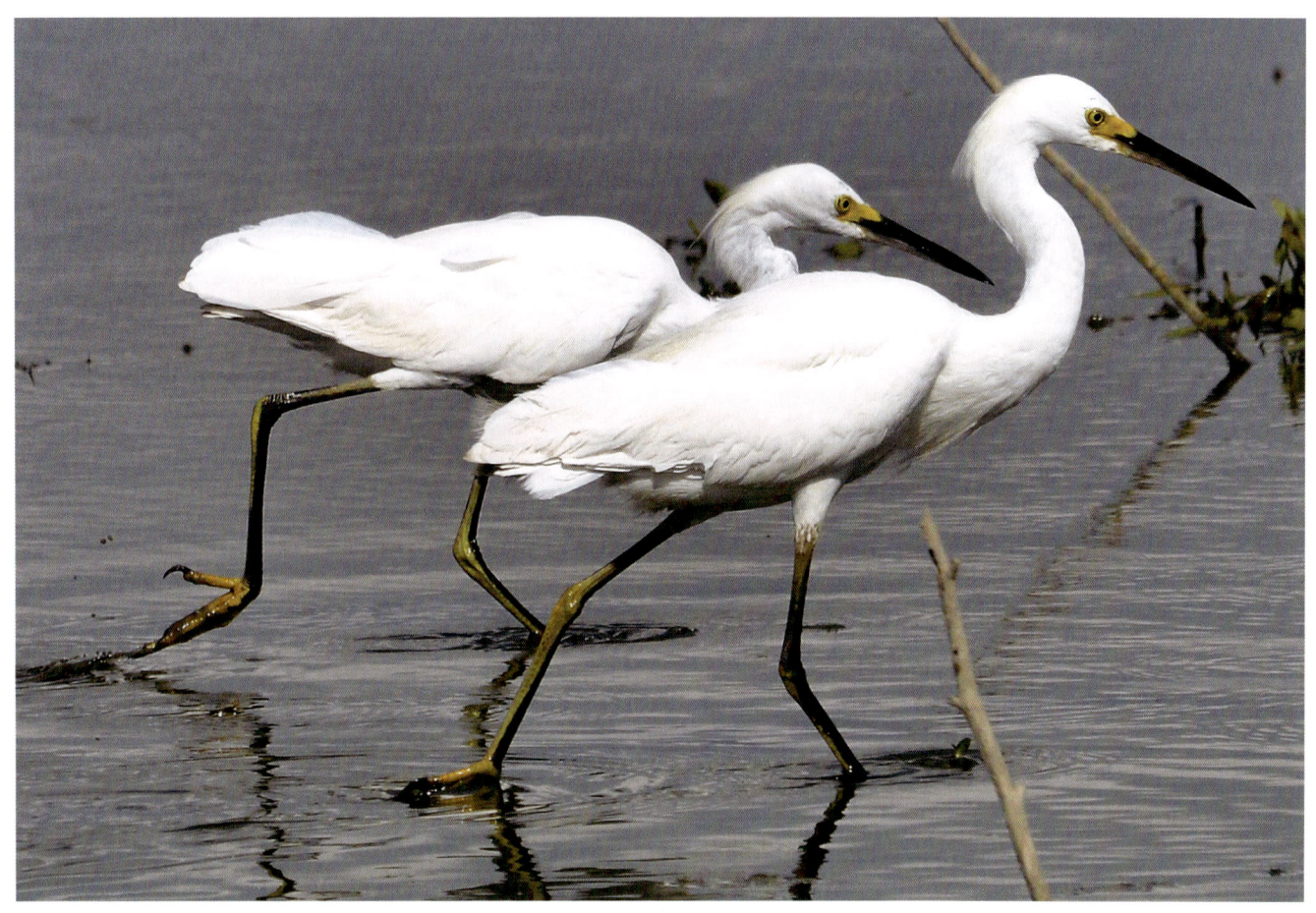

Although their unusual techniques may differ slightly, the stealthy great egret and snowy egret are both highly successful predators in wetland habitats located all over the world.

Above: Snowy Egrets, Florida /Nikon D300
Opposite: Great Egret, Texas /Nikon D600

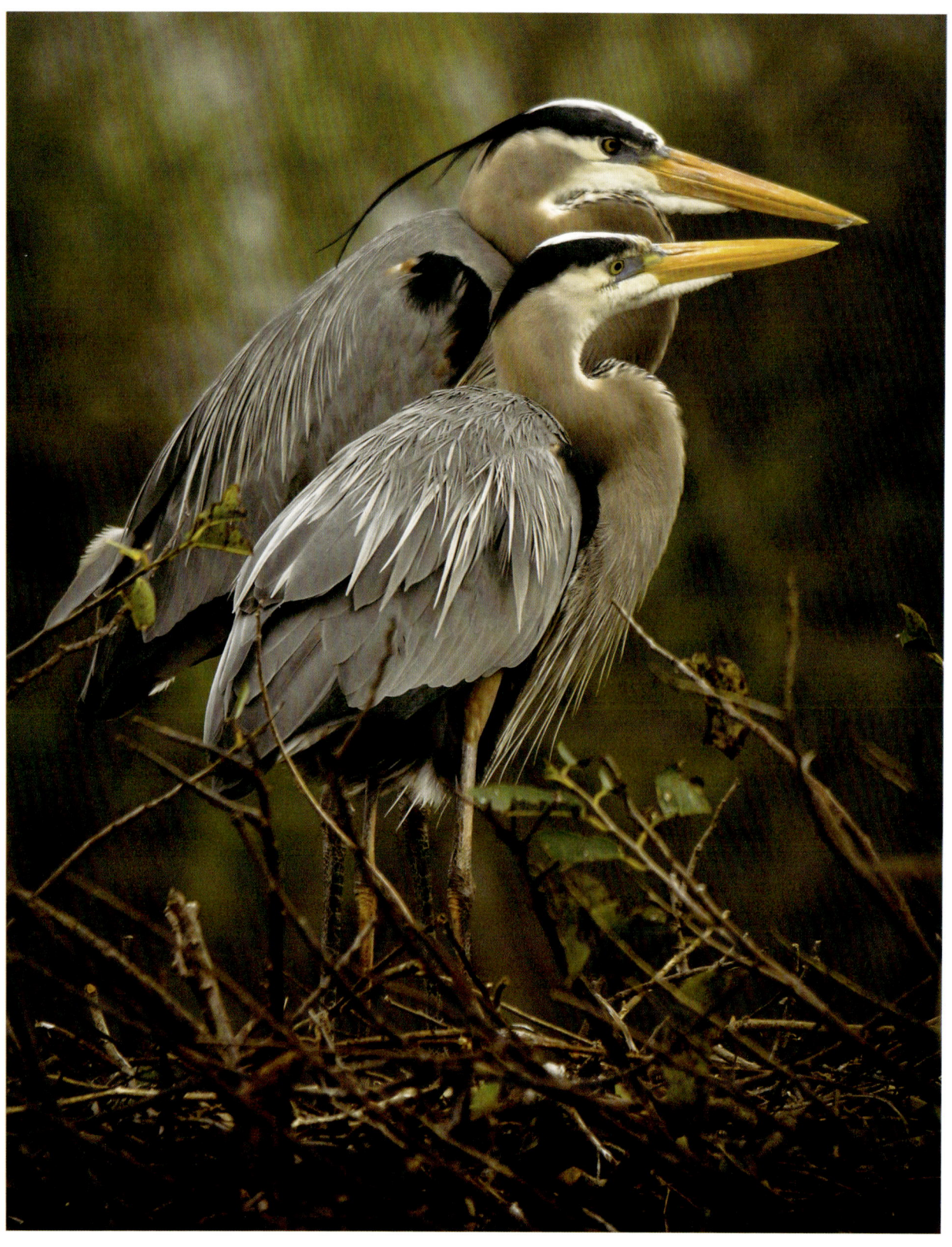

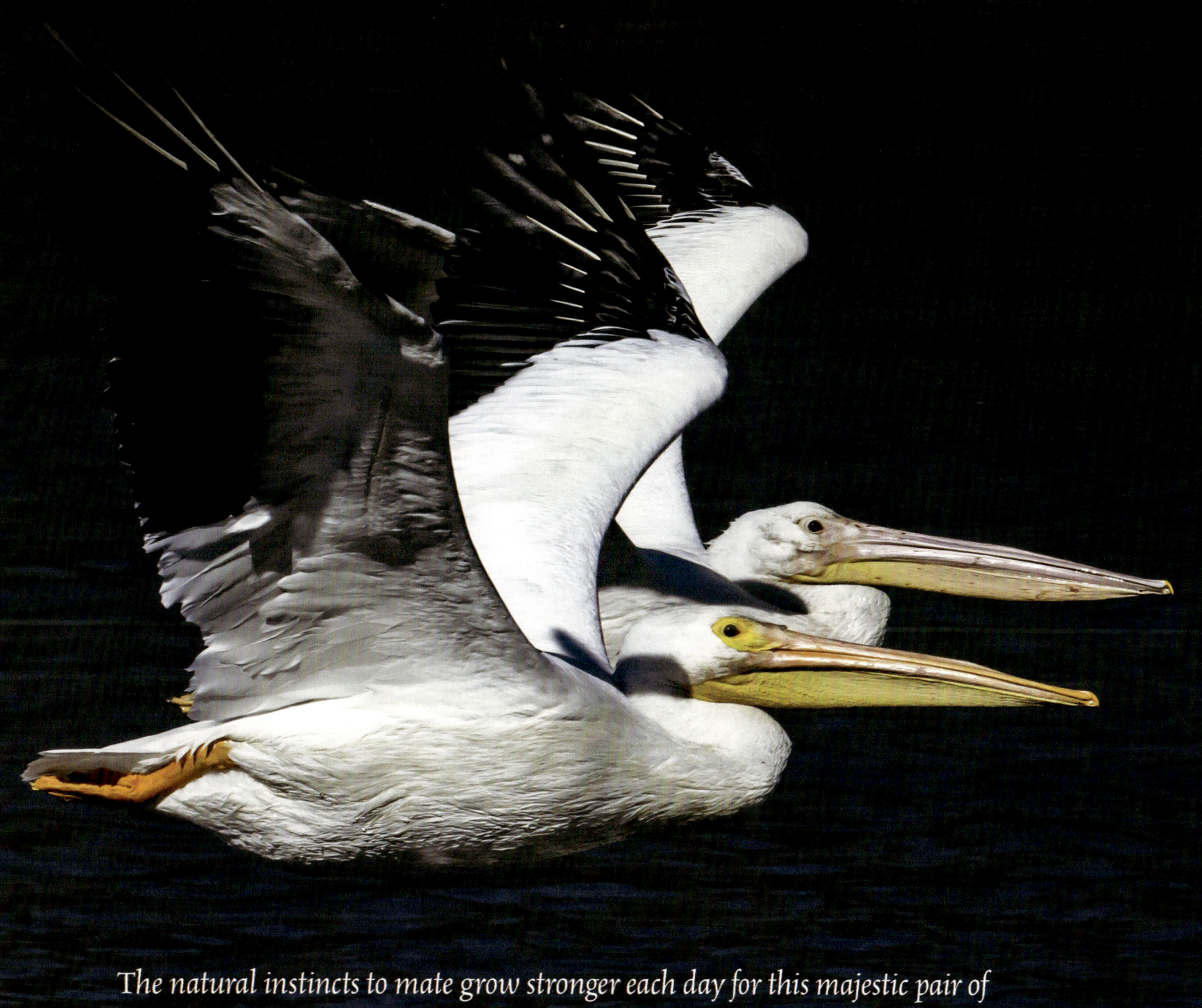

The natural instincts to mate grow stronger each day for this majestic pair of great blue herons. The nest, now complete, is strong and will make a perfect home to rear the next generation.

Above: White Pelicans, Texas /Nikon D810
Opposite: Great Blue Heron, Florida /Nikon D300

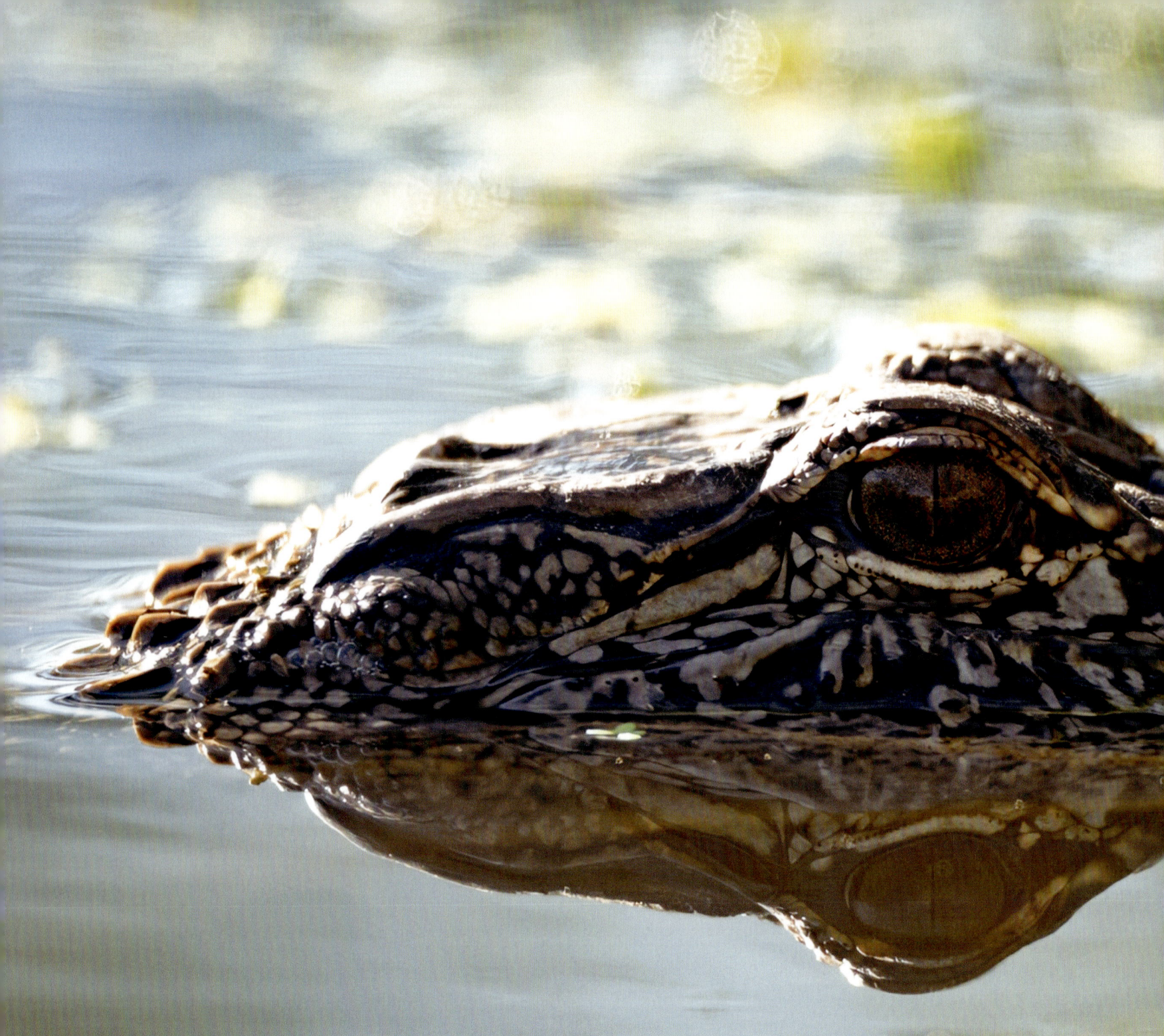

A young alligator breeches the water's surface to better view his wetland realm. Given ample time, he'll become an apex predator, but for now, staying in the shallows and remaining concealed is the best way to assure his continued survival.

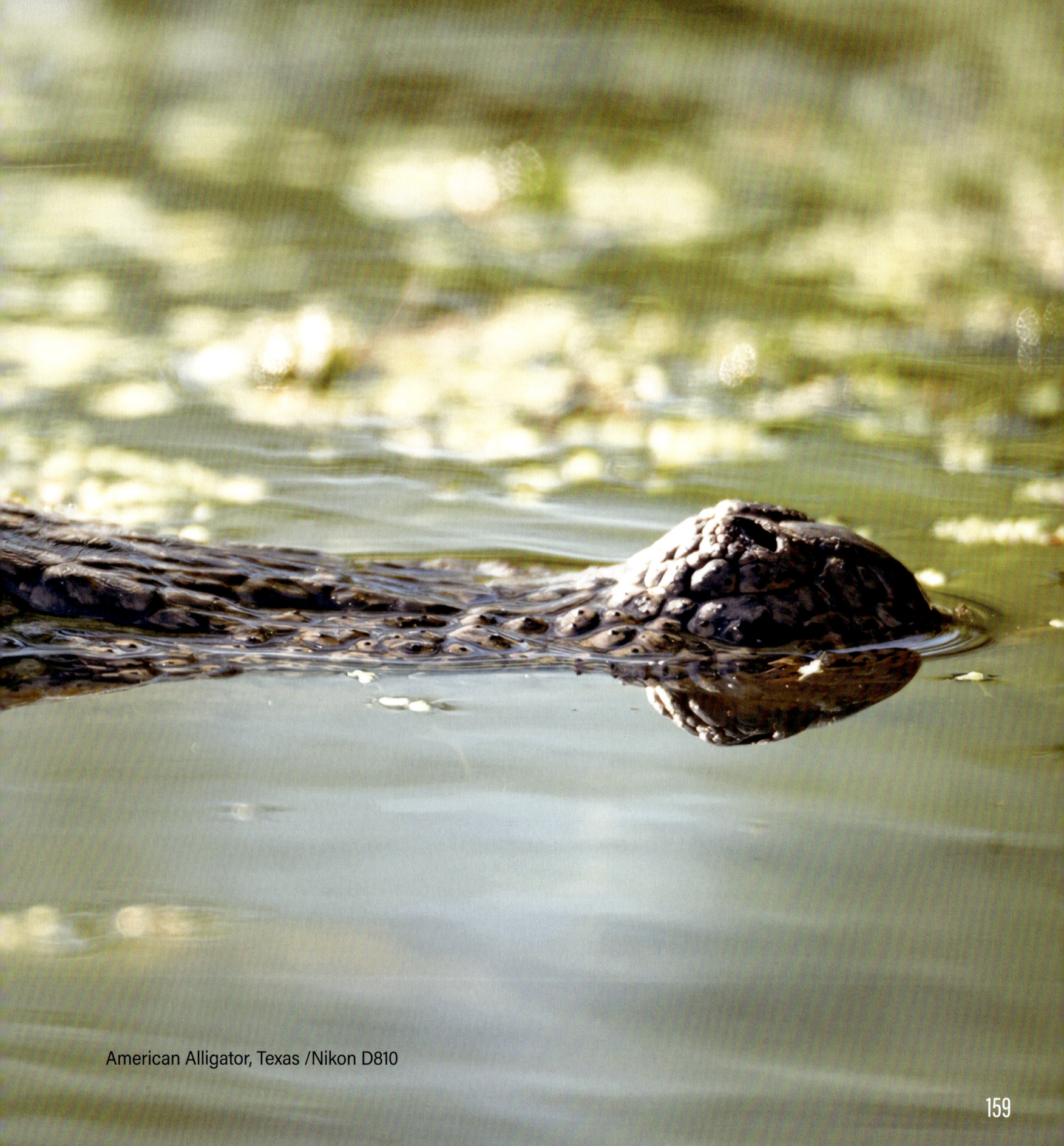

American Alligator, Texas / Nikon D810

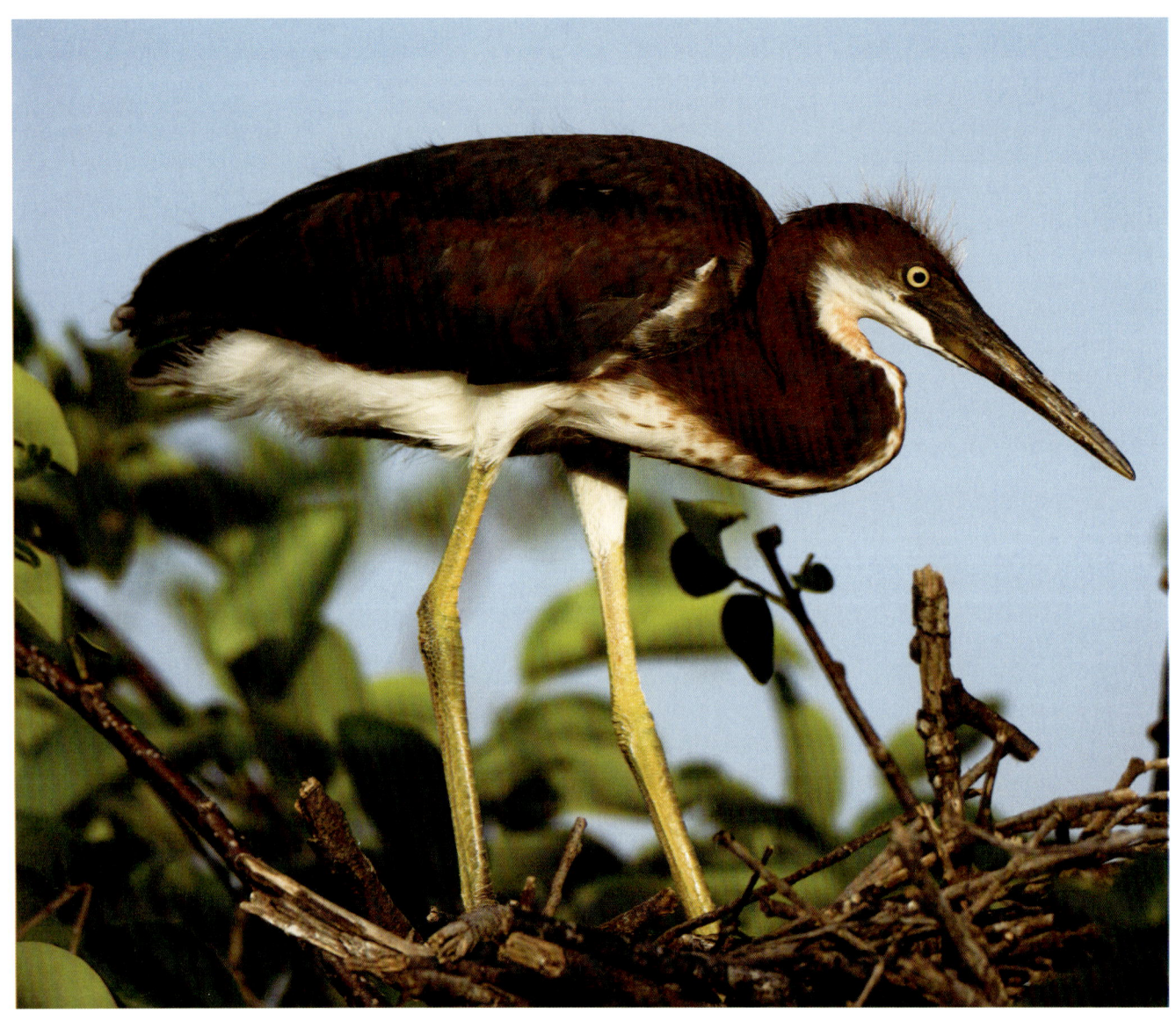

A green iguana slowly approaches the nest of a fledgling tricolored heron. These large reptiles, an invasive species in the Florida Everglades, have been known to destroy nests and eat any unhatched eggs still within, but it is late in the season on this day, and the squawks of the young heron deter him for the moment.

Above: Tricolored Heron, Florida /Nikon D810
Opposite: Green Iguana, Florida /Nikon D810

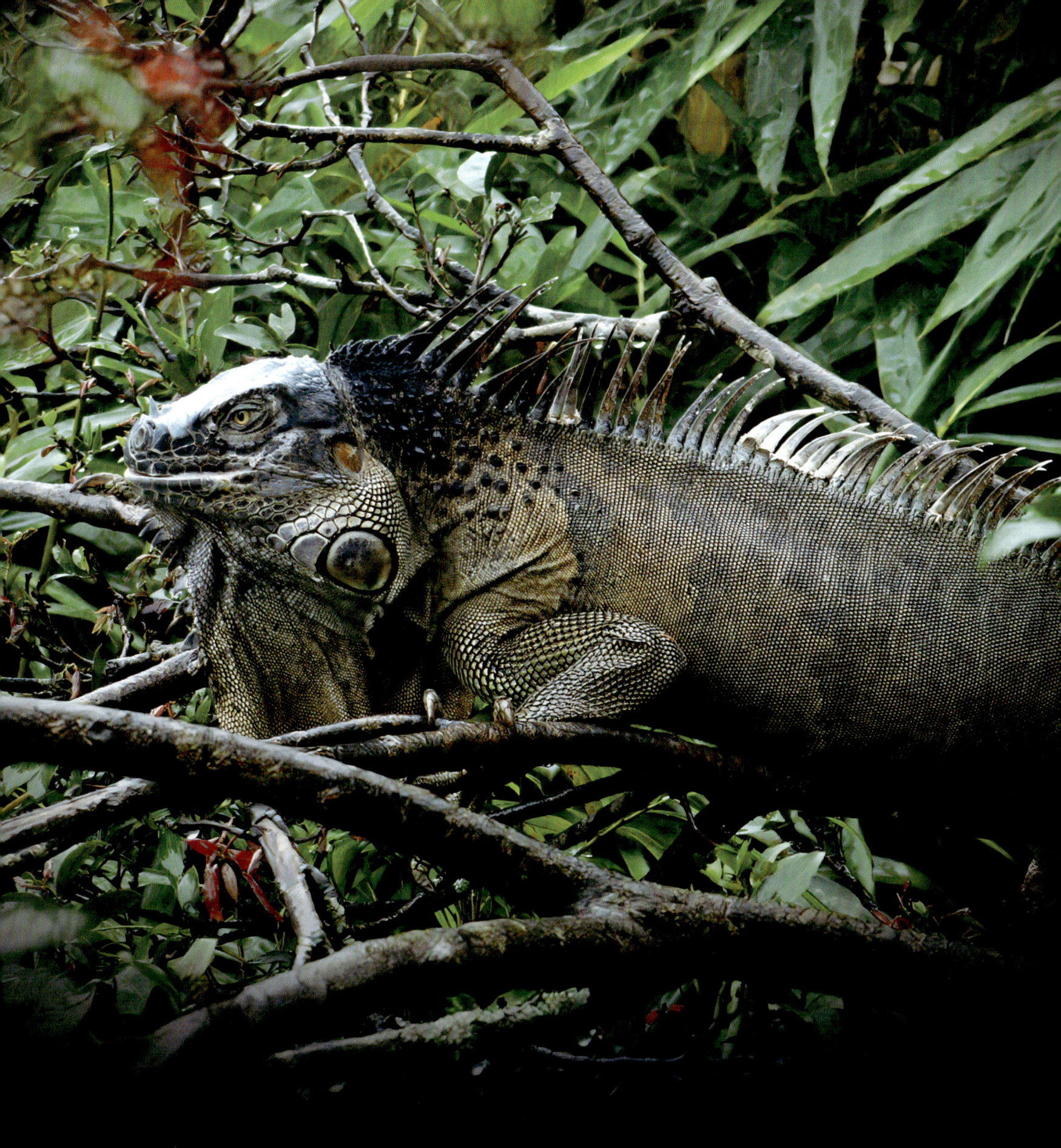

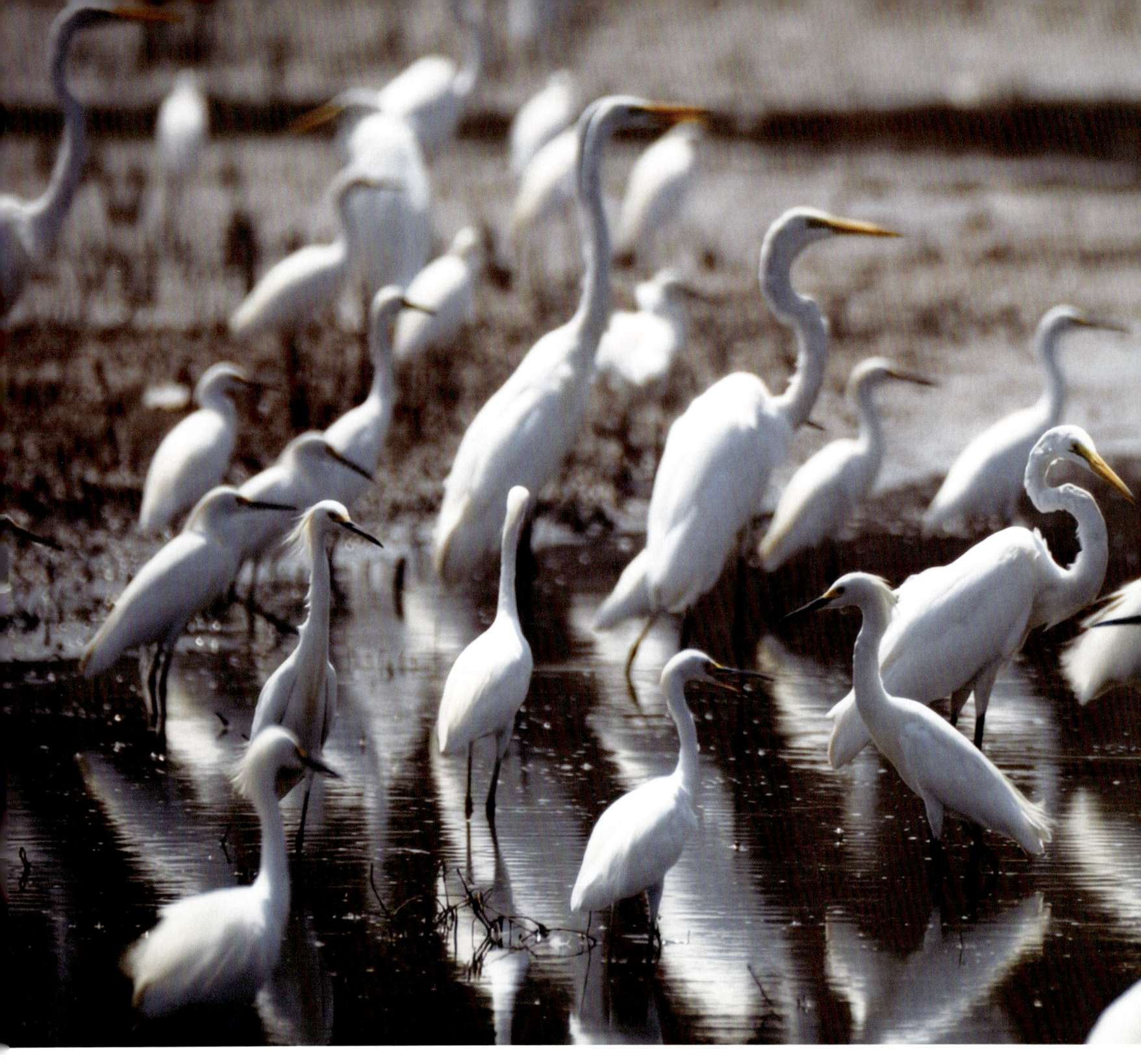

As the flood waters recede, wading birds flock in great numbers to share in the abundance of fish now struggling in the shallows with nowhere to go.

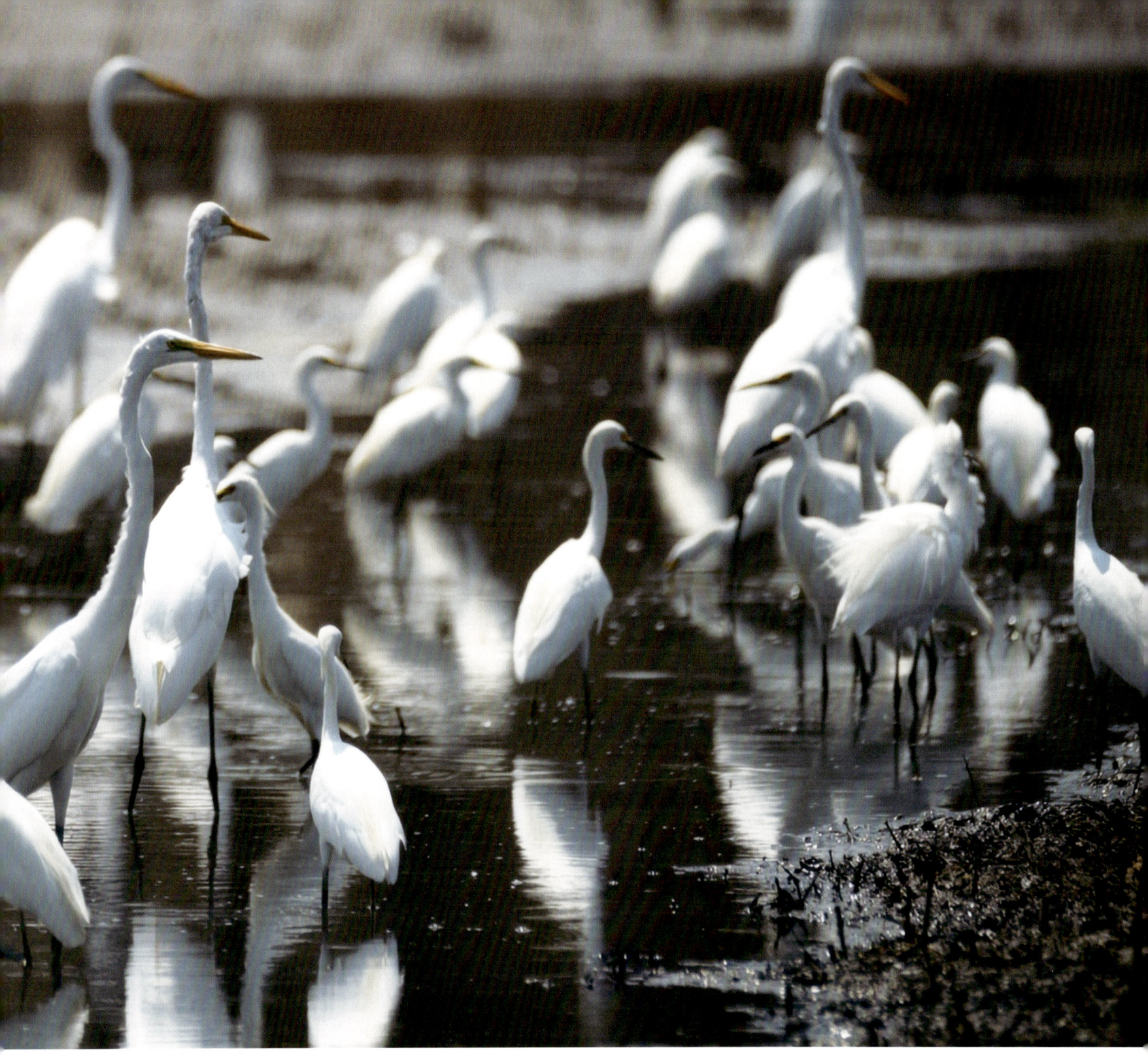

Morning in the Marsh, Texas /Nikon D810

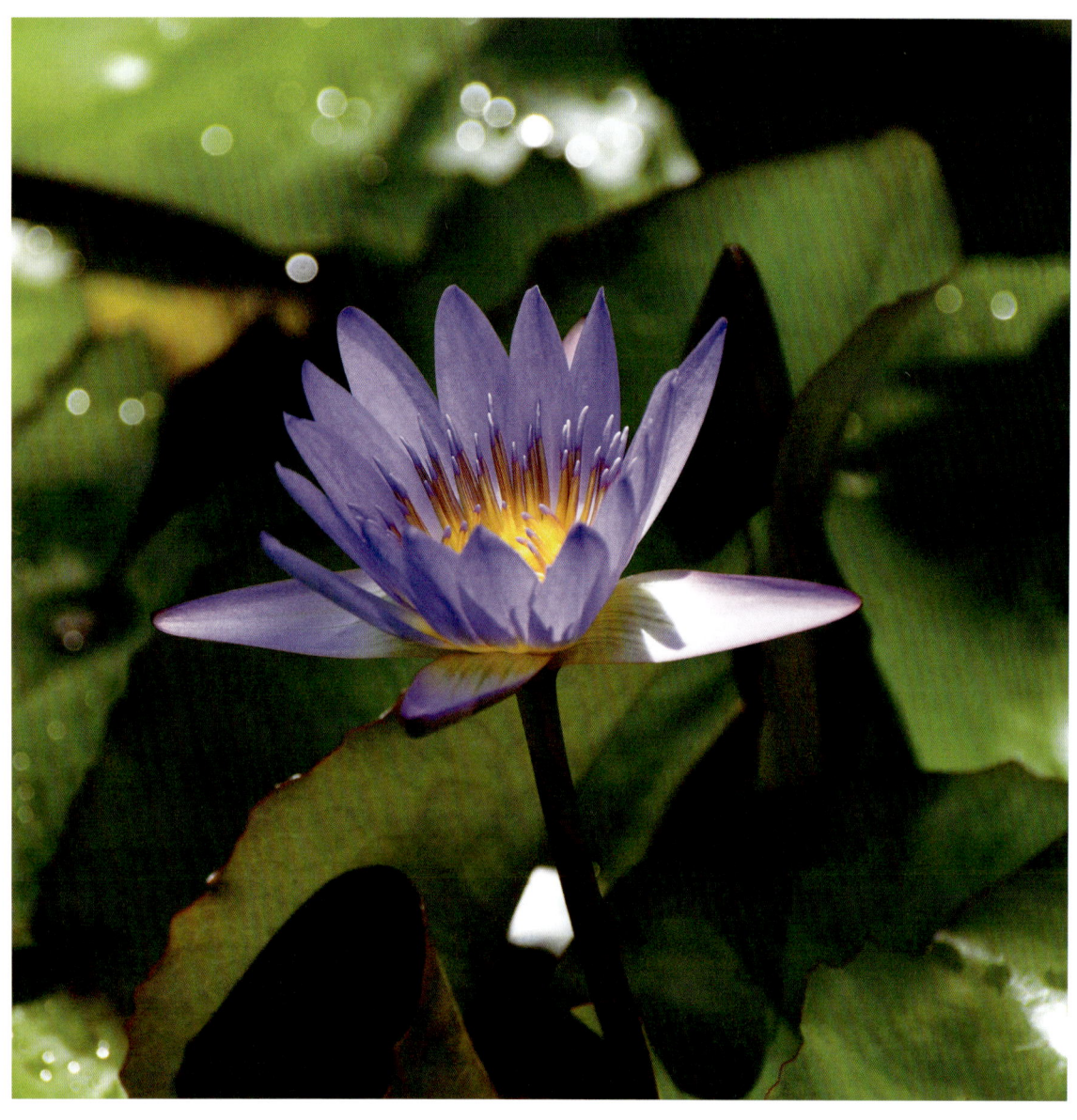

Wetland areas are nature's refuge. Water is life, and life flourishes here in the most dramatic, beautiful, and inspiring ways.

Above: Lotus Flower, Hawaii /Nikon D600
Opposite: Red-Eared Slider Turtle, Texas /Nikon D600

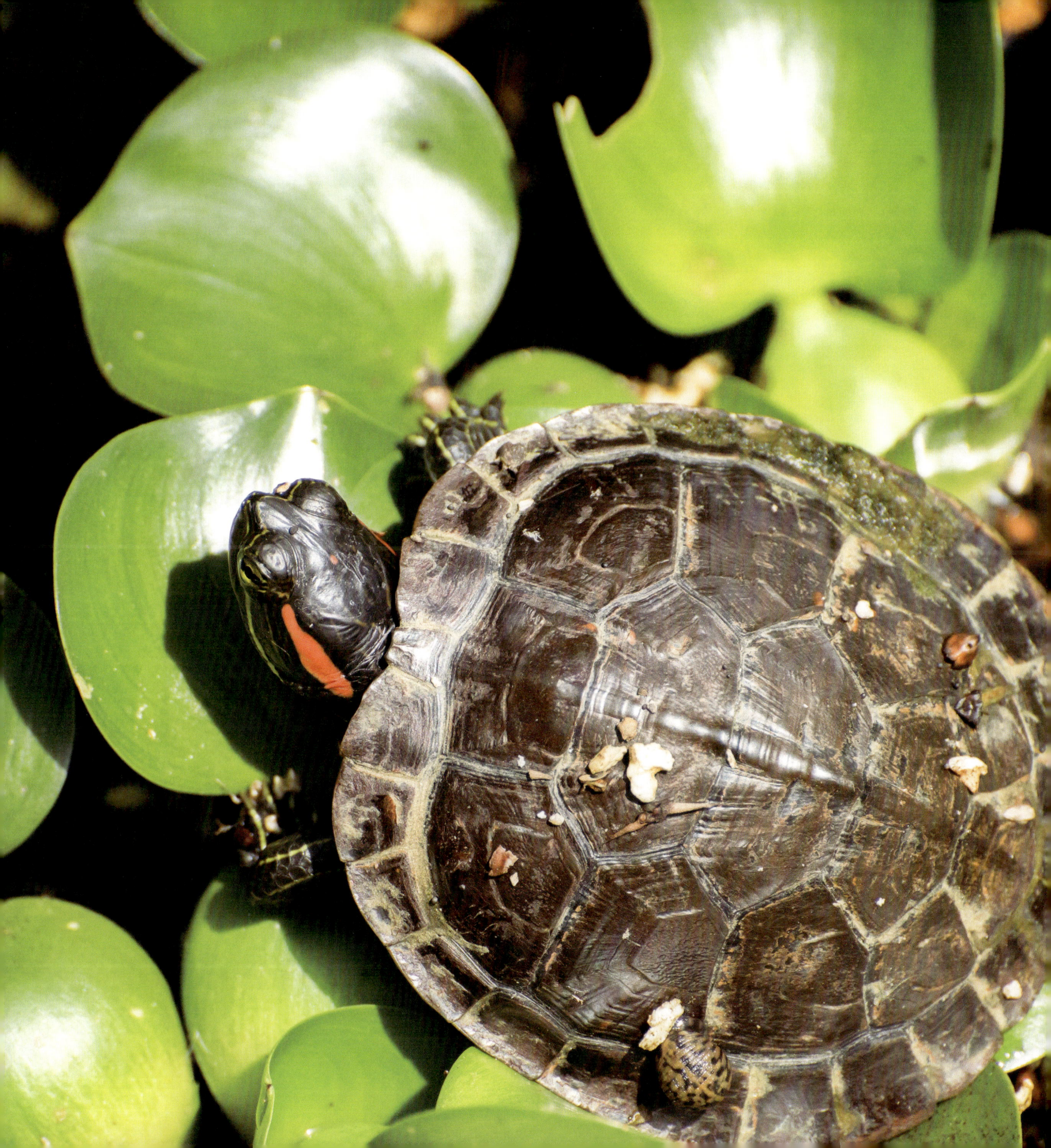

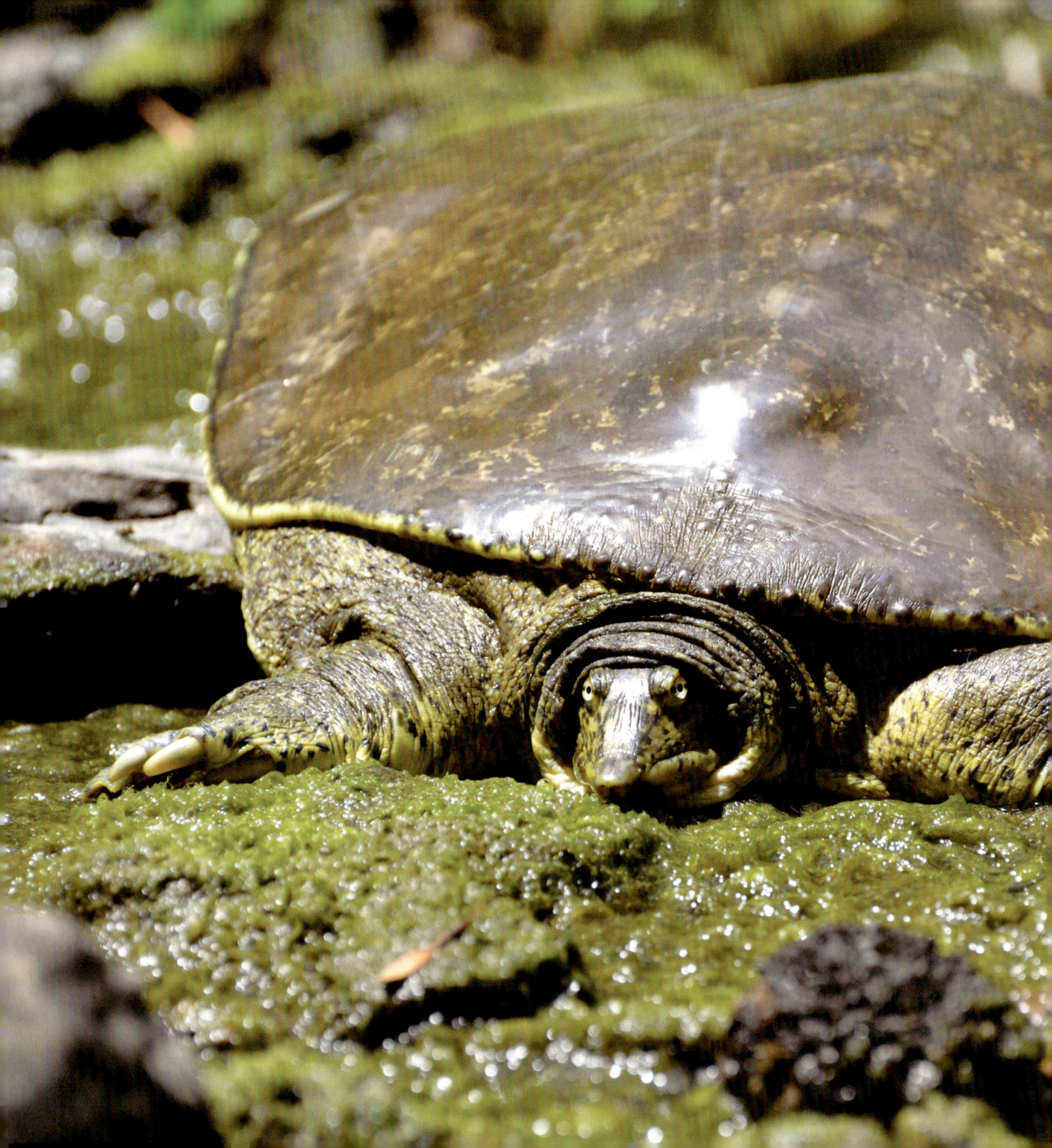

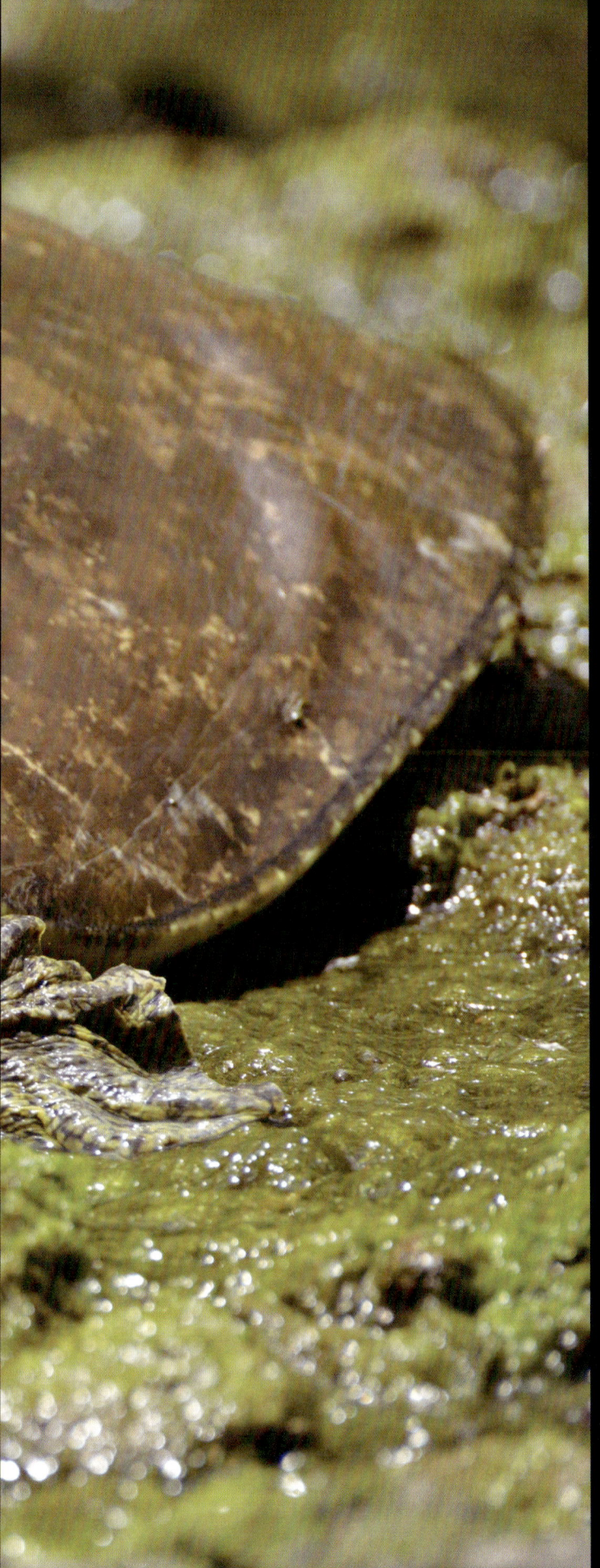

I came across this charismatic, large turtle resting deep within a Texas creek on an exceptionally hot and muggy day, making no effort to evade my approach. He sat there absolutely motionless, surrounded by a sea of greenish muck that no doubt was refreshingly cool to his sizeable frame. We quickly parted ways, but I'll never forget our brief but intriguing encounter.

Spiny Softshell Turtle, Texas /Nikon D300

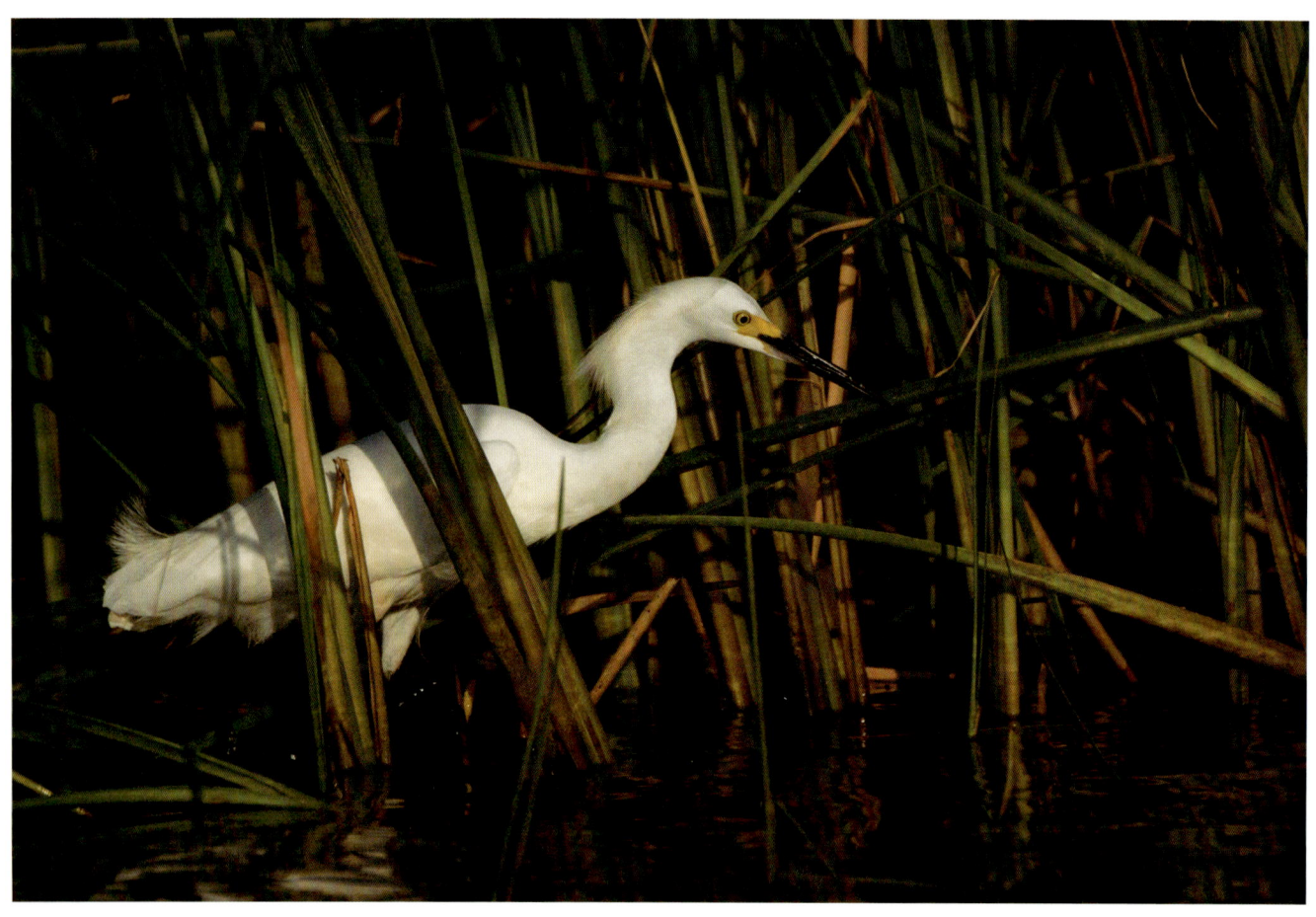

The calls of the kingfisher are easily identifiable, as he is unrelenting in patrolling his territory against all who intrude. He is the aerial dive bomber who rarely misses his prey, and, oh, did I mention, he is also, so very regal. Just look at that amazing crown.

Above: Snowy Egret, Florida /Nikon D810
Opposite: Kingfisher, Texas /Nikon D810

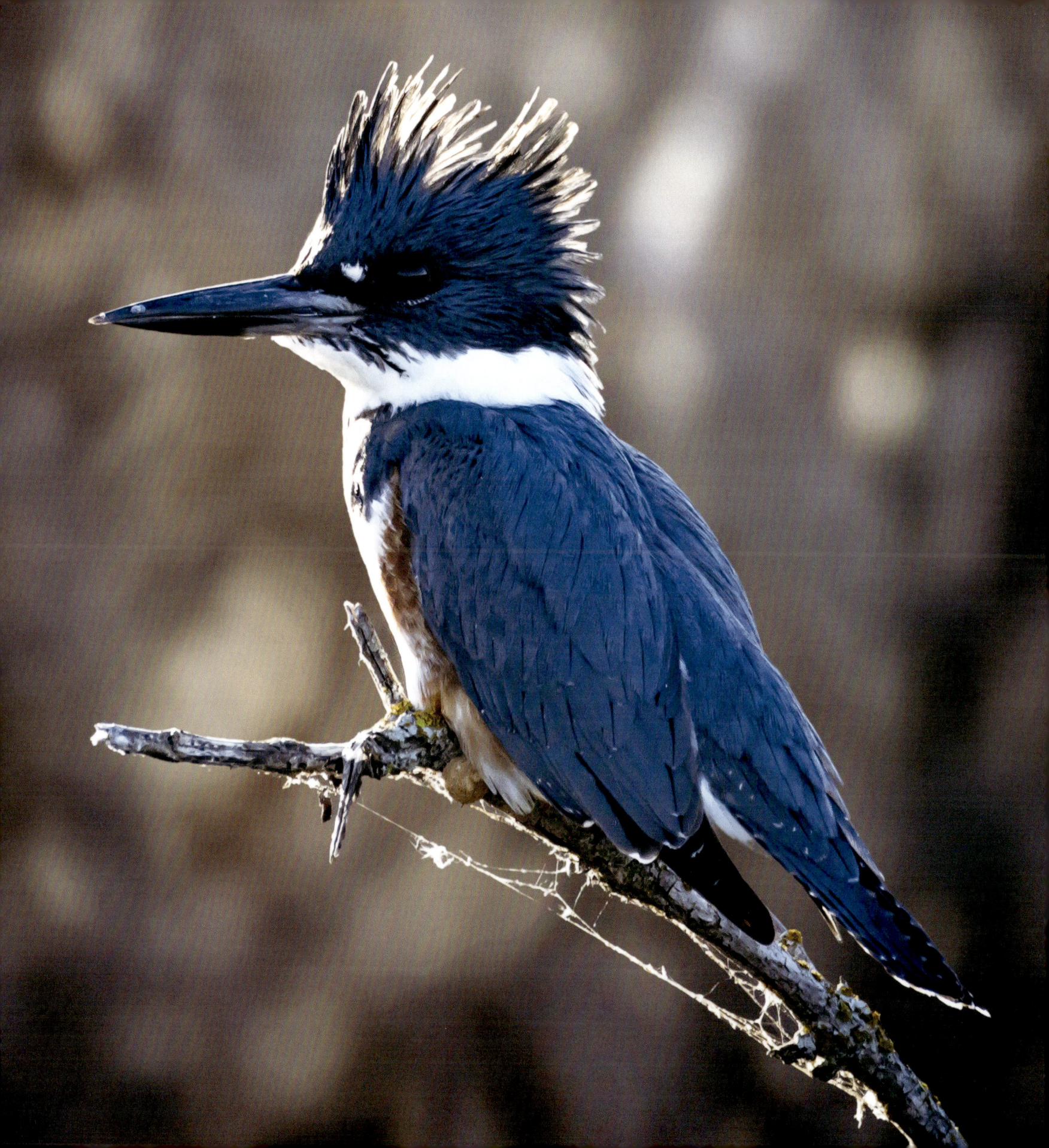

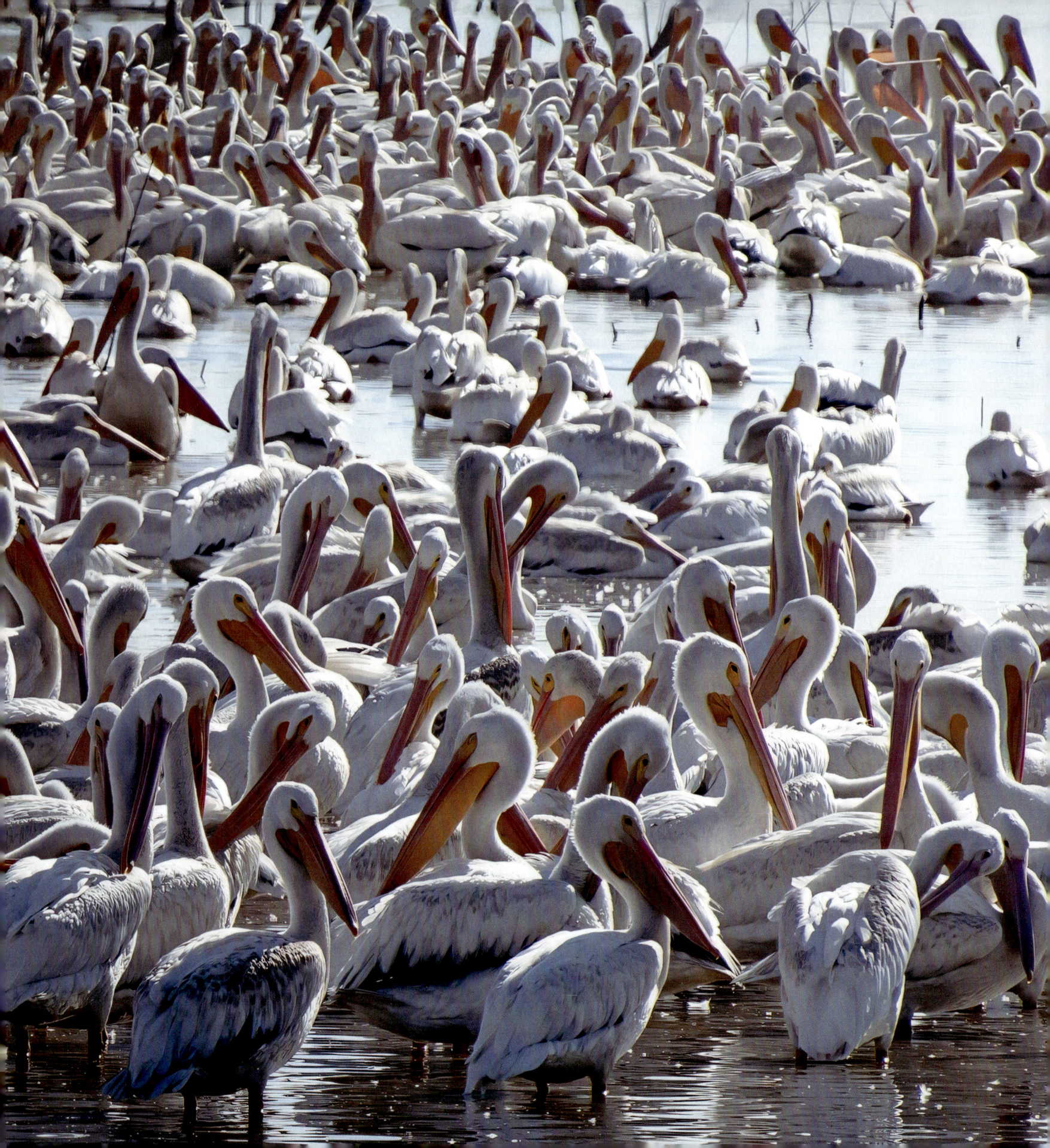

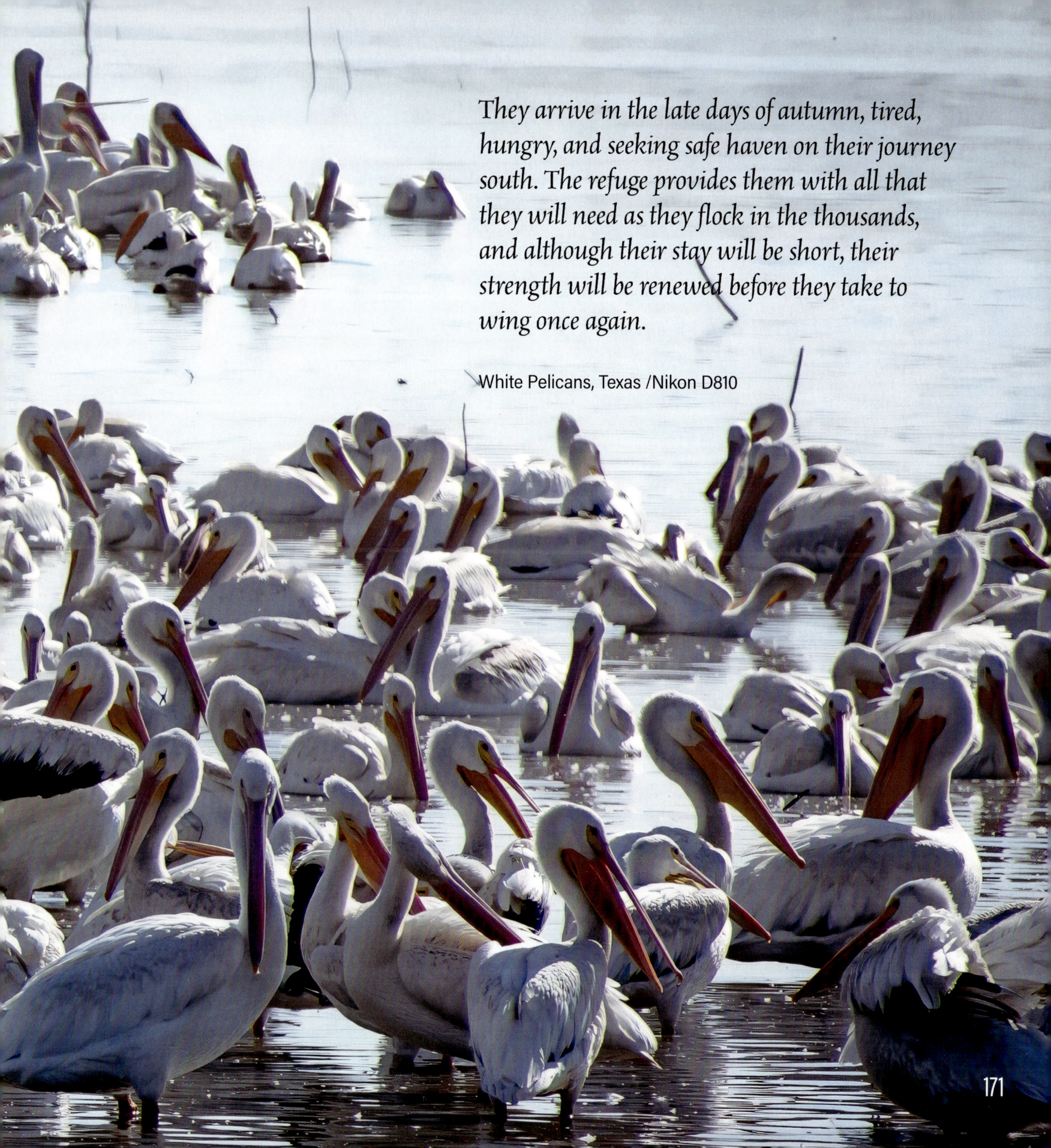

They arrive in the late days of autumn, tired, hungry, and seeking safe haven on their journey south. The refuge provides them with all that they will need as they flock in the thousands, and although their stay will be short, their strength will be renewed before they take to wing once again.

White Pelicans, Texas /Nikon D810

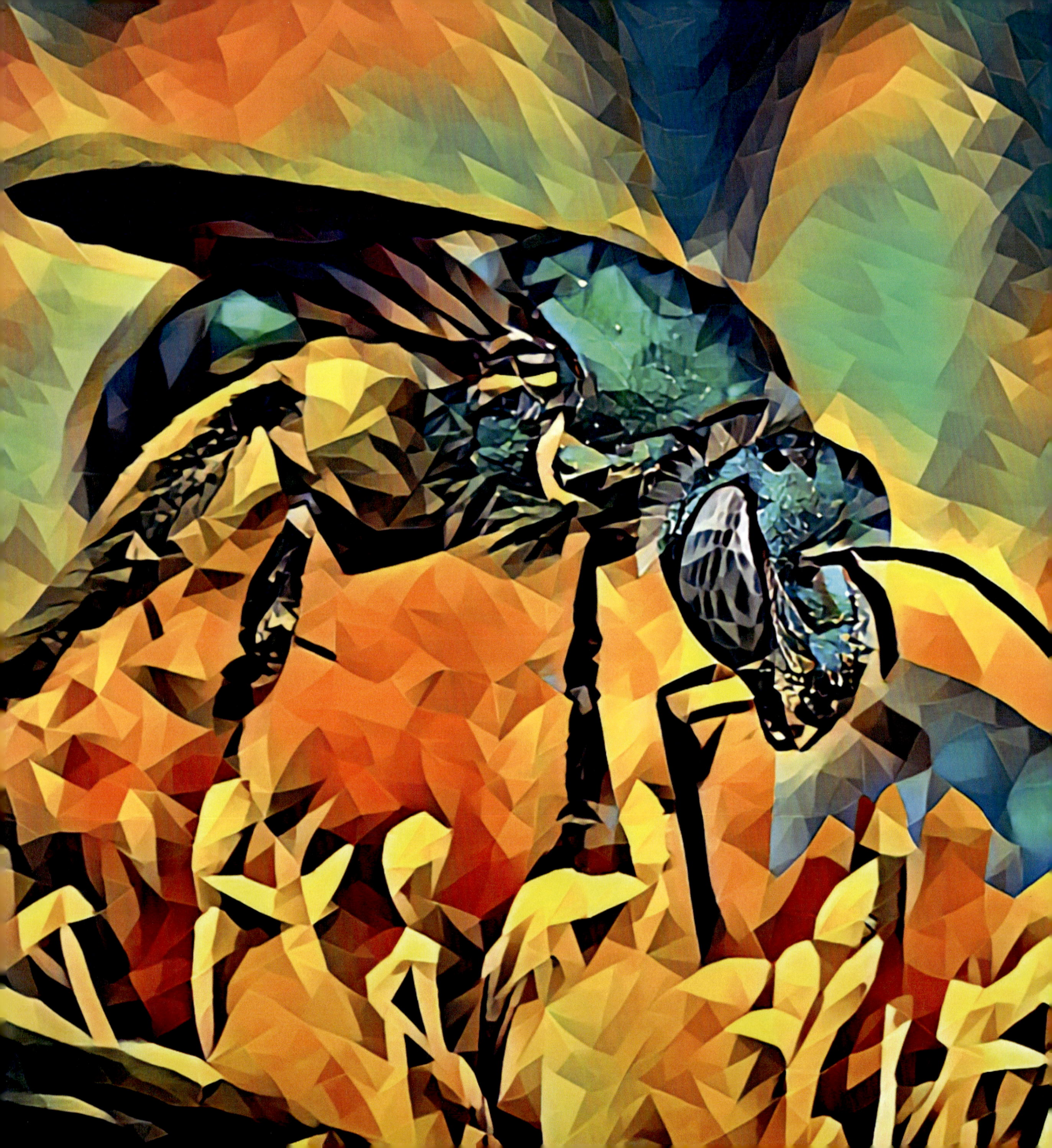

MACRO WORLD

The world abounds with wonders beyond the imagination. To see it, you simply have to open your eyes to what lies all around you and immerse yourself in hidden realms of the rarely observed. My journey into wildlife photography started here, and it continues to be one of my preferred means of escape from the reality of life as we all view it to be. To turn my lens downward toward this awe-inspiring place summons an immense anticipation as the veil of obscurity is lifted before me to see life in all of its grandeur. Peering closely into the eyes of a dragonfly reminds me that we humans are but one species of millions existing on this beautiful blue planet called Earth. Species of unparalleled complexity and variety. Tiny lives are intertwined with ours in our homes, our gardens, our parks, and everywhere we go. Most go unnoticed; some are invited, many are not. Macro photography provides us a window: a glimpse into a world truly unknown, a world full of alien creatures, alien landscapes, and inexplicable marvels the likes of which we have rarely seen. My voyage has only just begun, and I invite you to come with me as we enter into the wonders of the macro world.

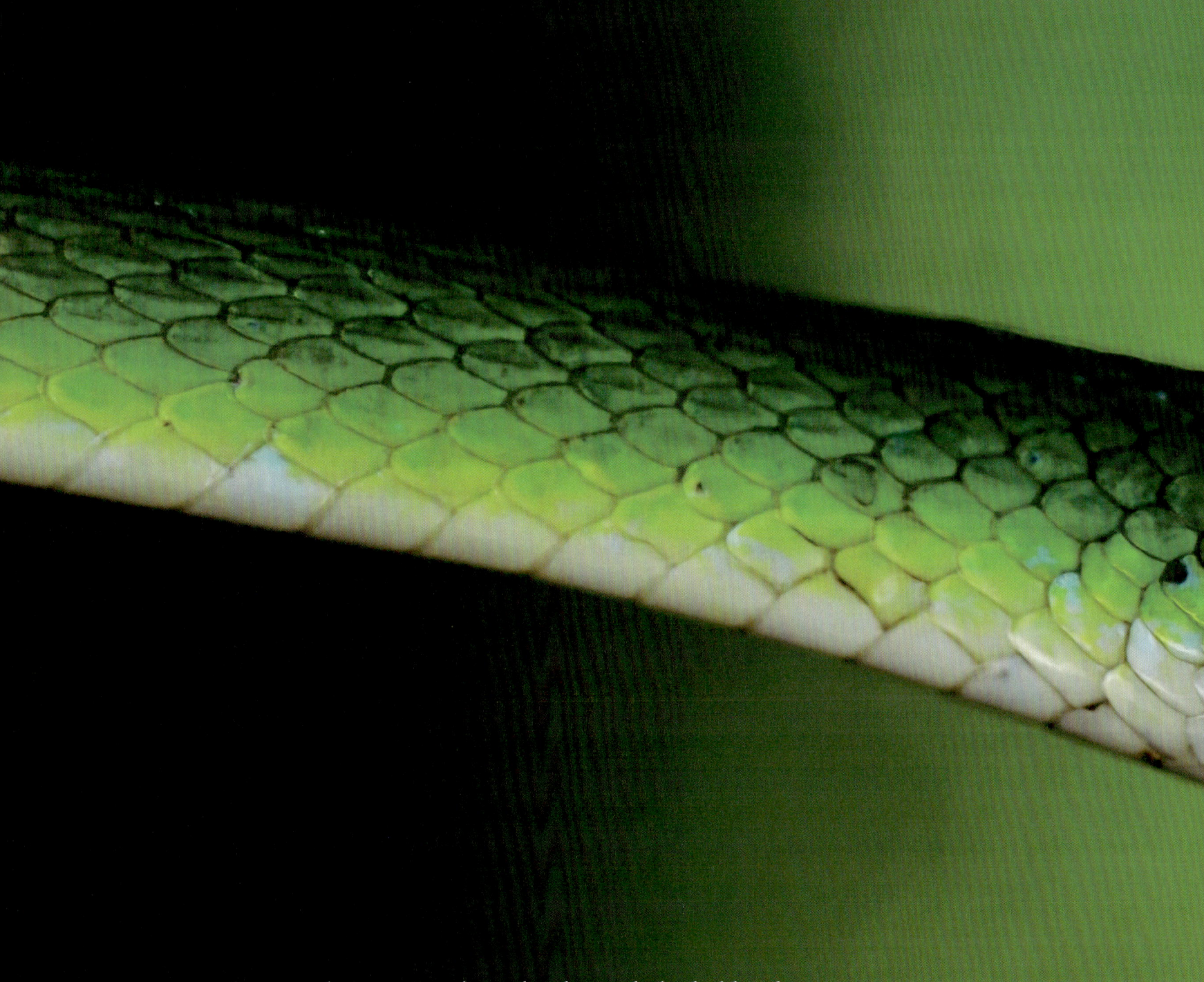

Barely as wide as a pencil, its slender scaly body blends into its environment with absolute perfection. Close your eyes for only a moment, and it will be gone, yet still be there in plain sight.

Rough Green Snake, Texas / Nikon D300 with 105mm lens

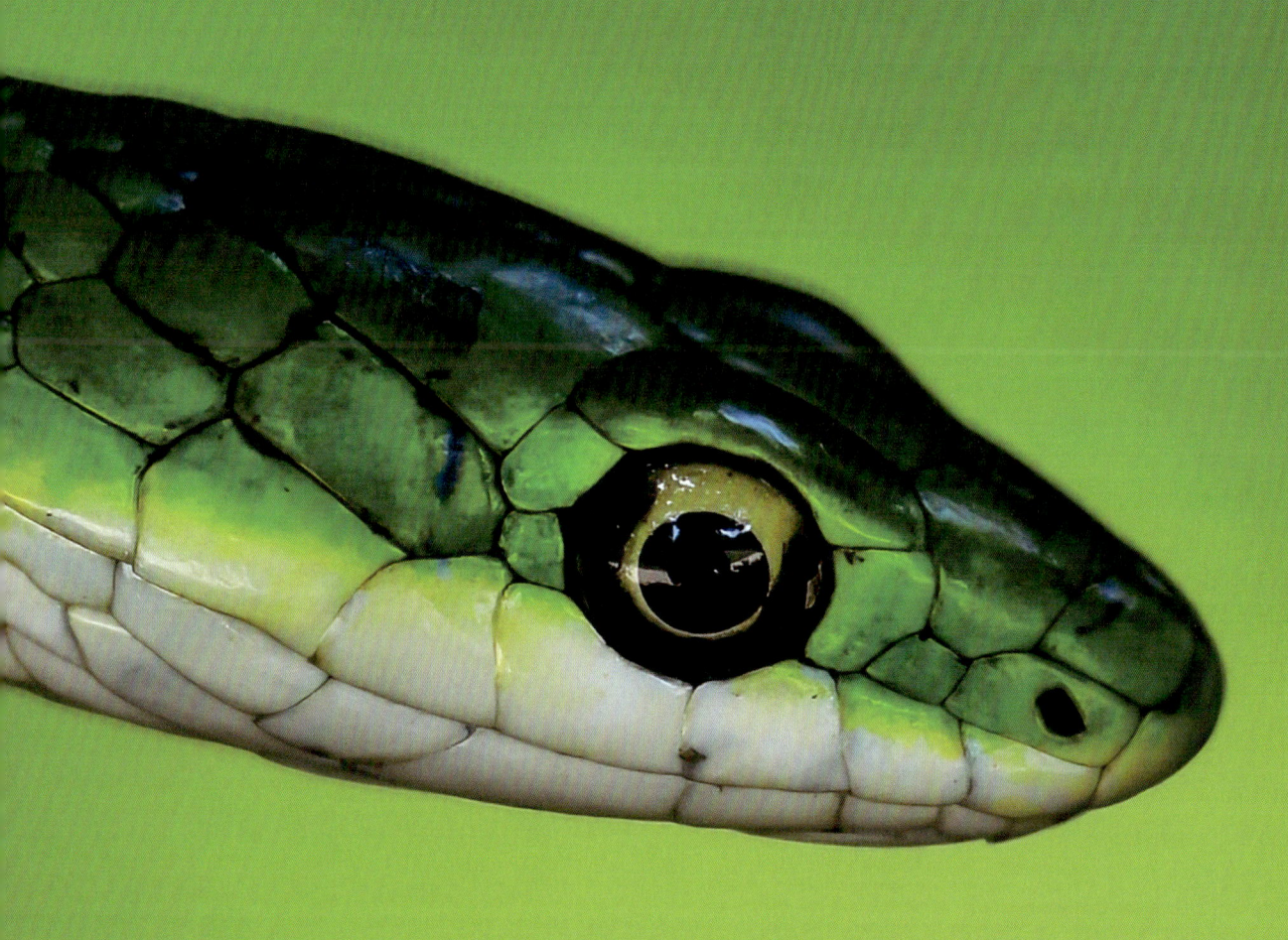

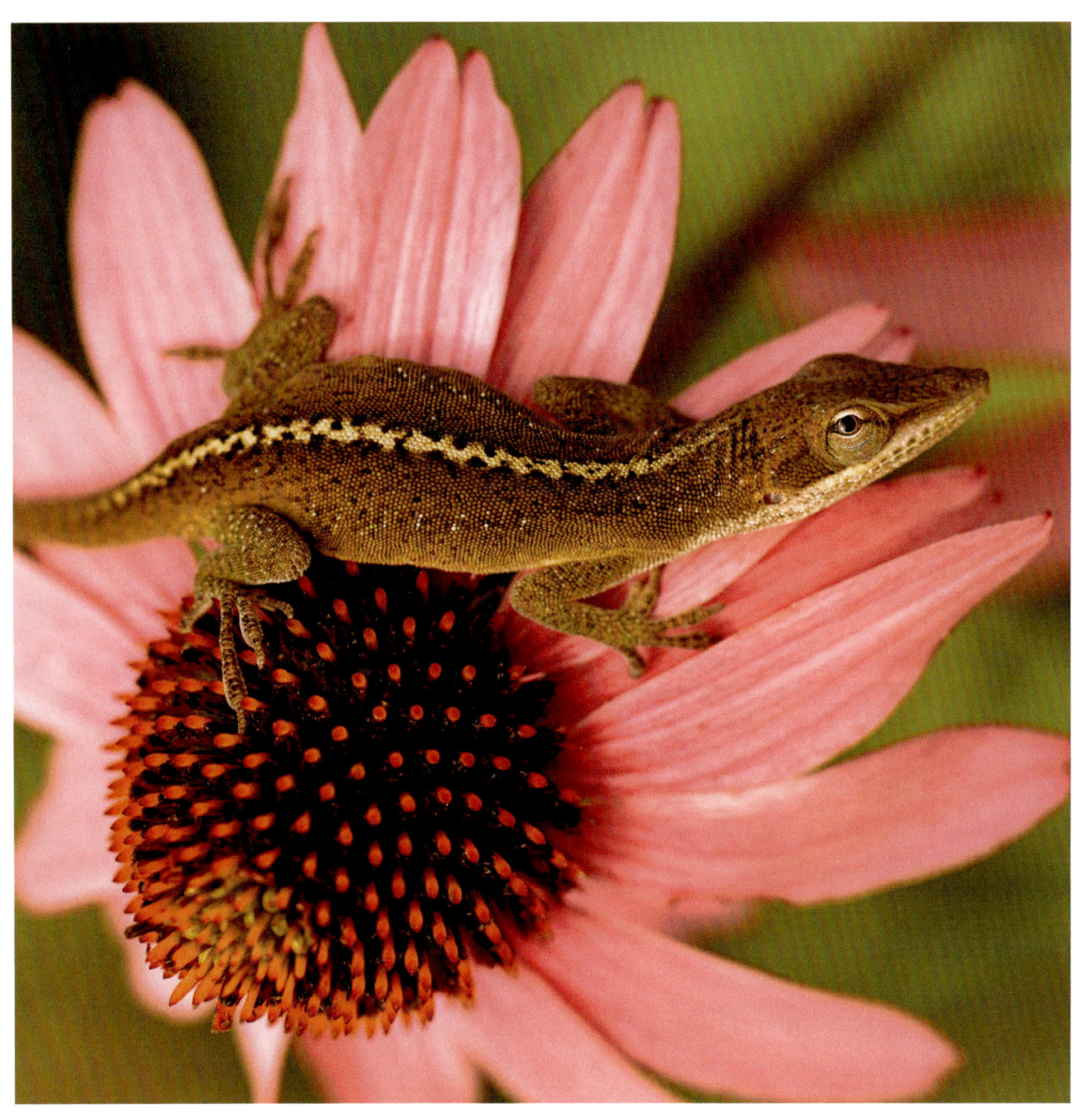

I *frequently wonder what they must see. Is the world around them vast from their vantage point of only a few inches tall? A simple flower garden must be a veritable wilderness to this small anole, and a farm pond, an endless ocean for a frog to explore.*

Above: Green Anole, Texas /Nikon D600
Opposite: Green Frog, Texas /Nikon D810

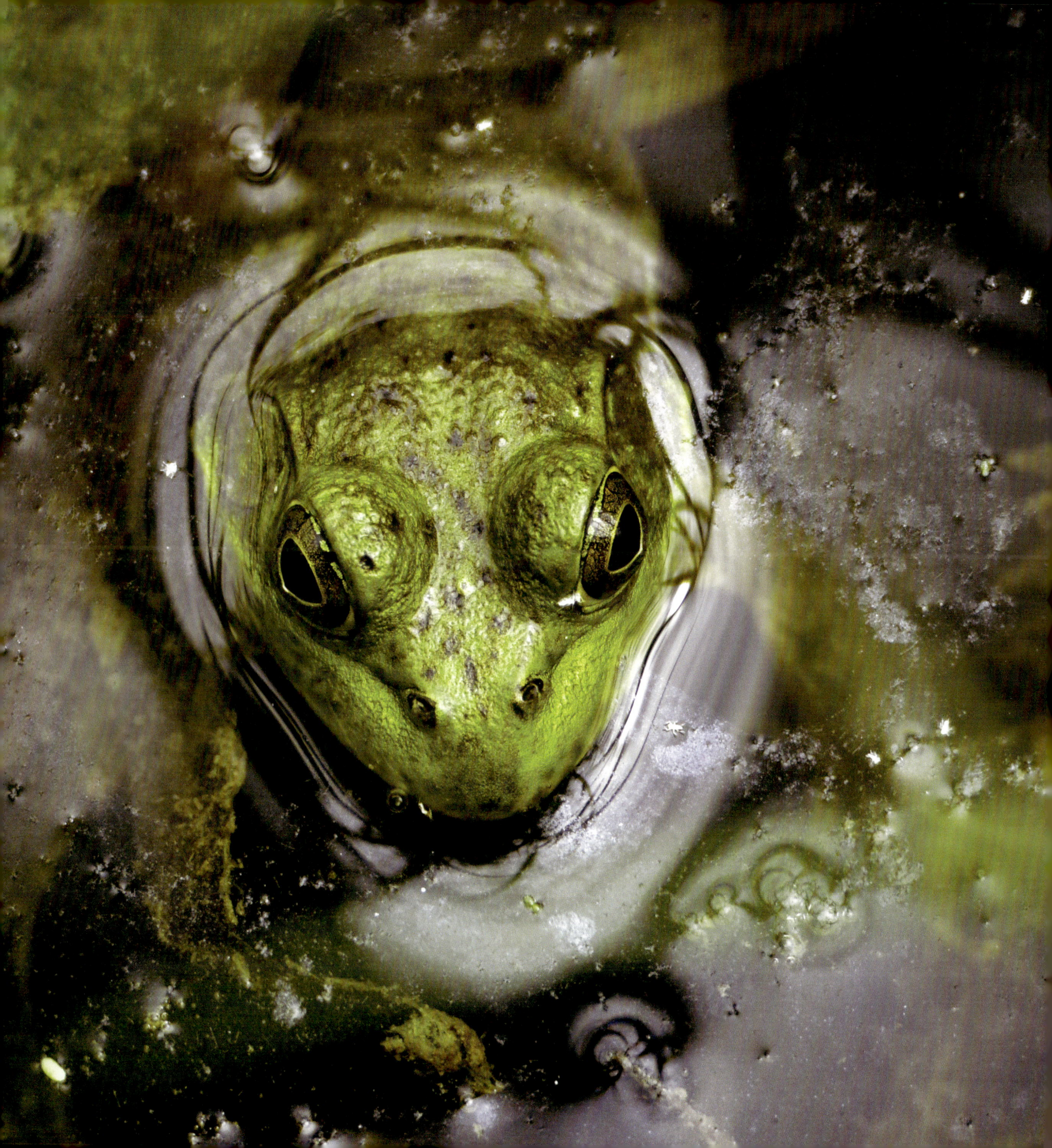

Upon looking into the eyes of this ancient species, I found myself mesmerized, as if I were gazing into the vastness of space and the billions of stars and galaxies that lie within. Mystery, magic, and wonder can sometimes be so powerful that the image leaps off the page and transports you into a place known only within your imagination. This image, taken in 2009, has inspired artists, naturalists, and photographers all over the world to see life in a whole new light.

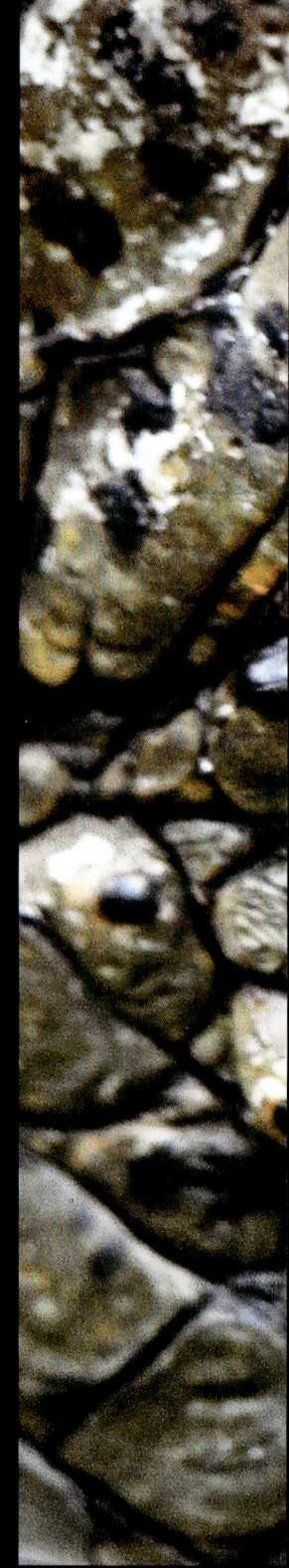

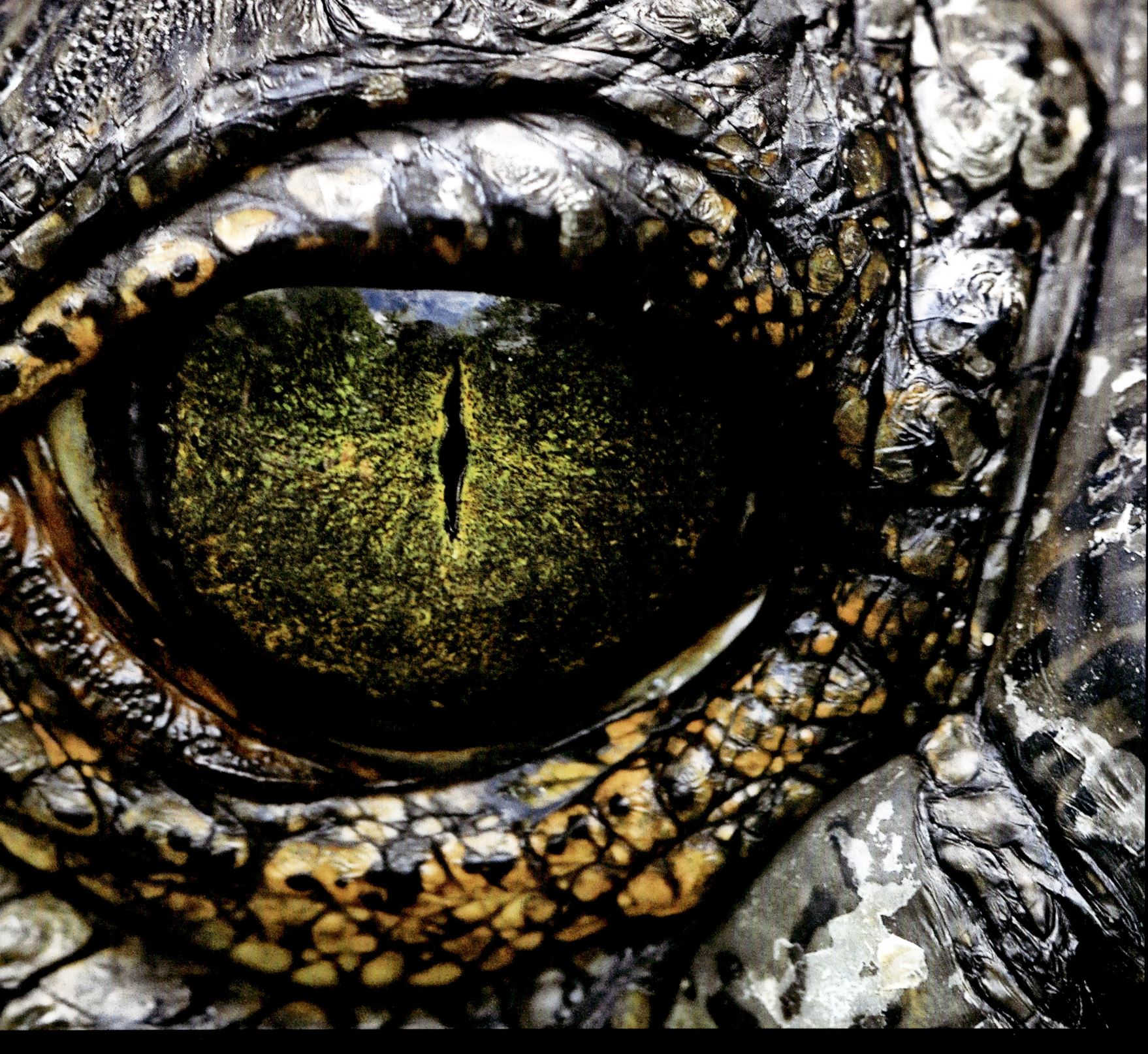

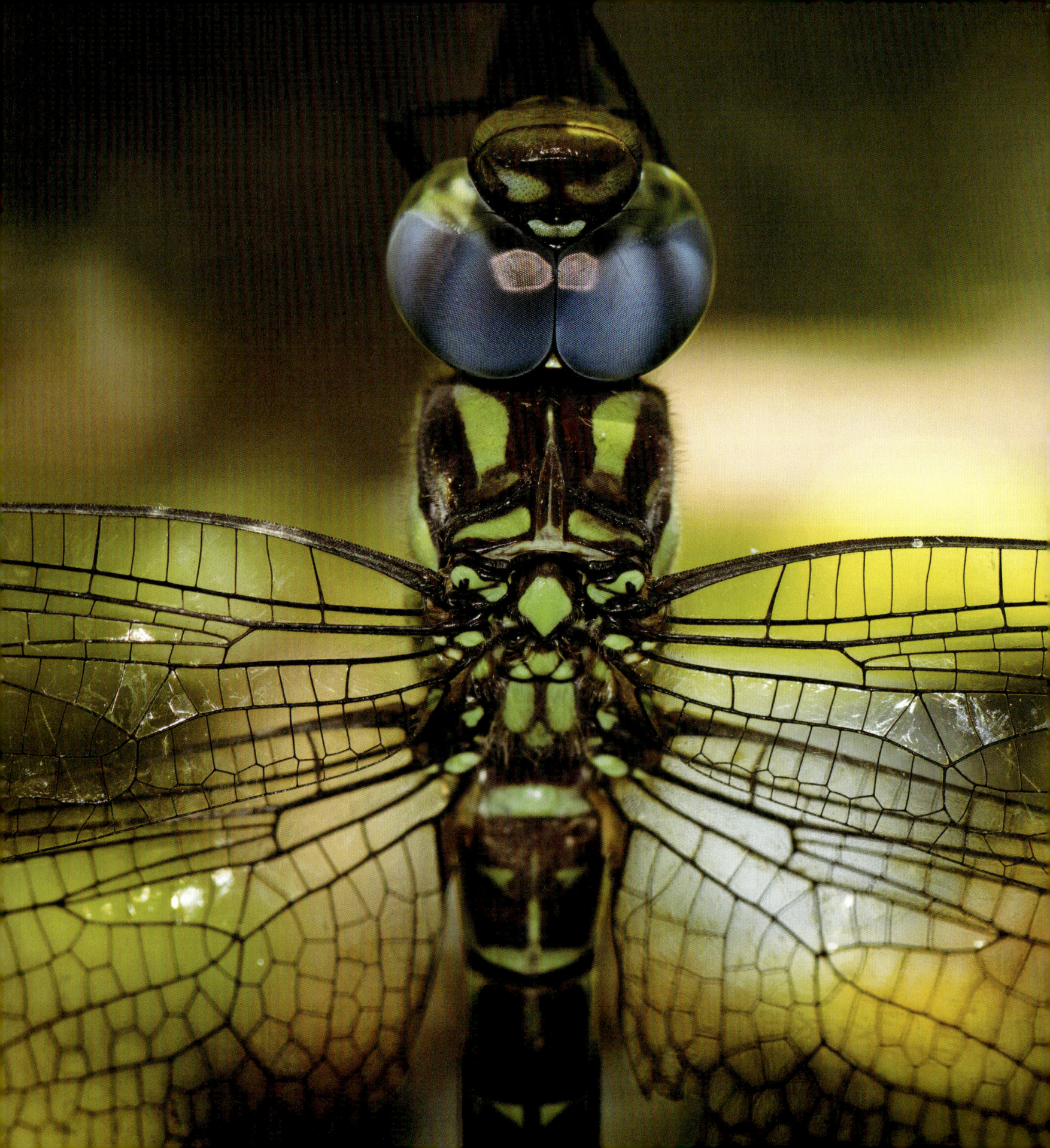

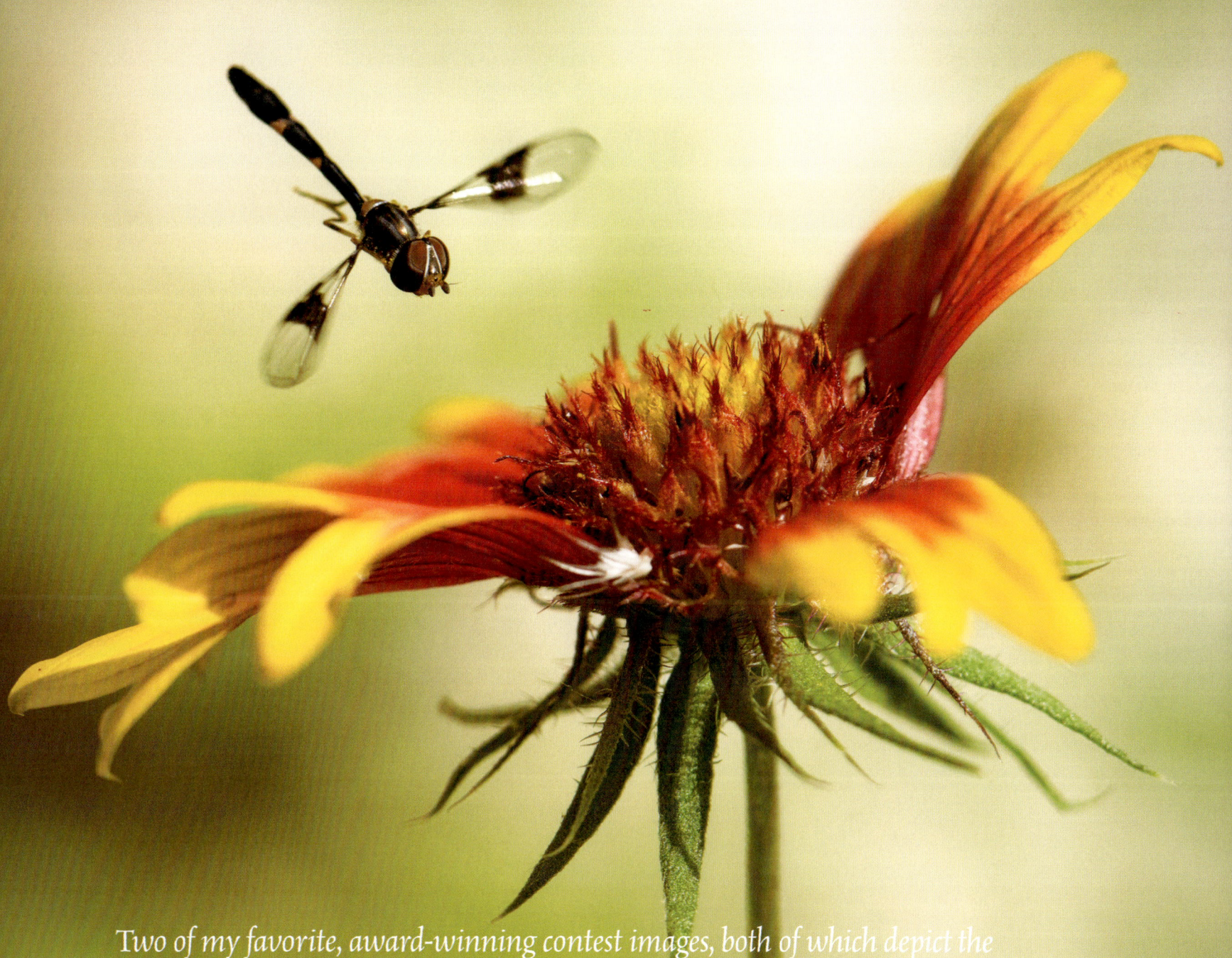

Two of my favorite, award-winning contest images, both of which depict the beauty of life that surrounds us each and every day. These insects mostly go unnoticed, but knowing they exist and that we are better off as a result gives me great comfort.

Above: Syrphid Fly, Texas /Nikon D810
Opposite: Blue Darner, Texas /Nikon D810

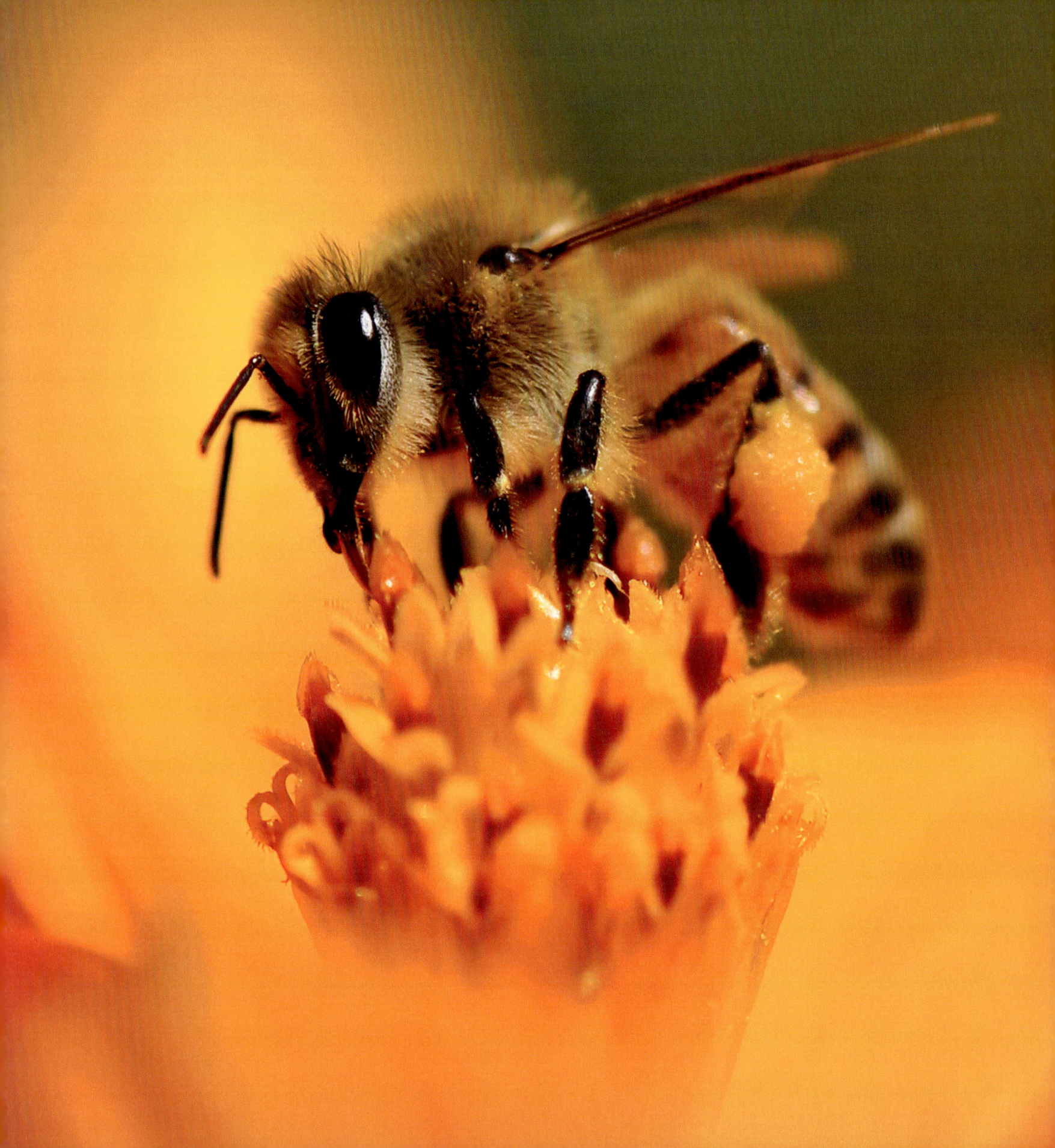

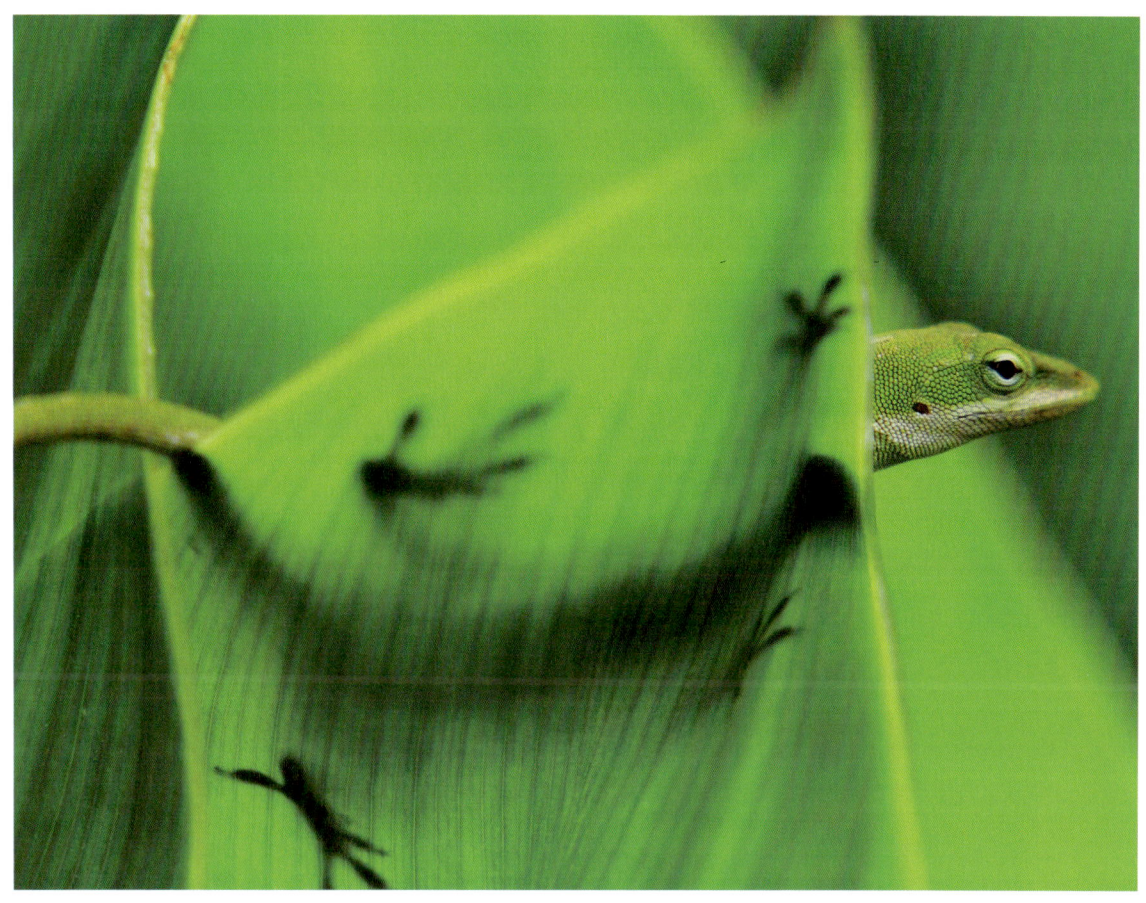

As springtime begins anew, a Texas honeybee hurriedly feeds upon the sweet nectar of a beautiful orange blossom, packing the pollen onto tiny hairs located on its hind legs to eventually carry off to the hive.

Above: Green Anole, Texas /Nikon D300
Opposite: Honeybee, Texas /Nikon D300

On the surface, a garden is a haven of delightful quiet, brimming with vibrant flowers, peace, and the delicious scent of springtime in the air . . . then a spider came along to remind me that appearances can be deceiving.

Green Lynx Spider, Texas / Nikon D810

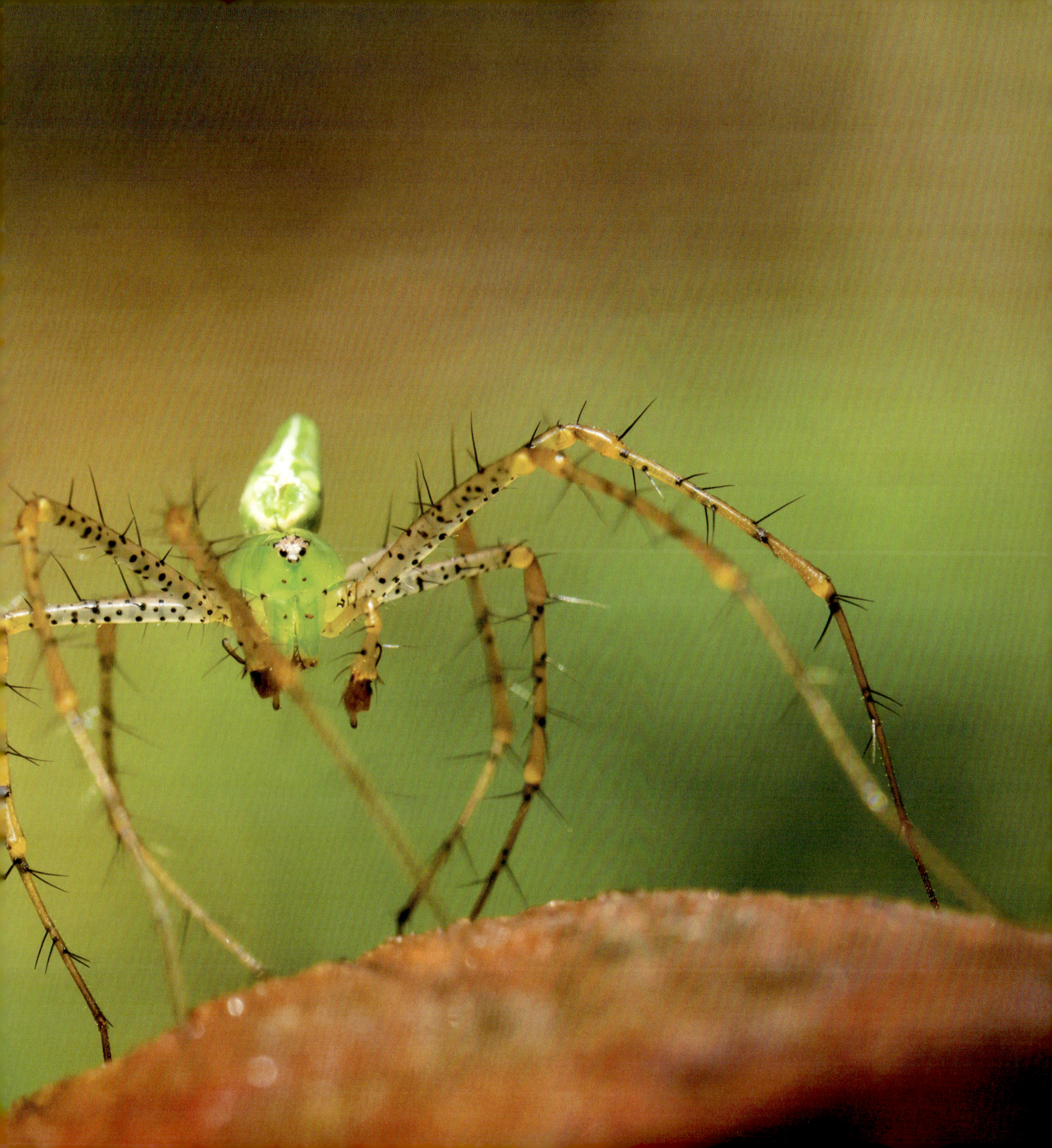

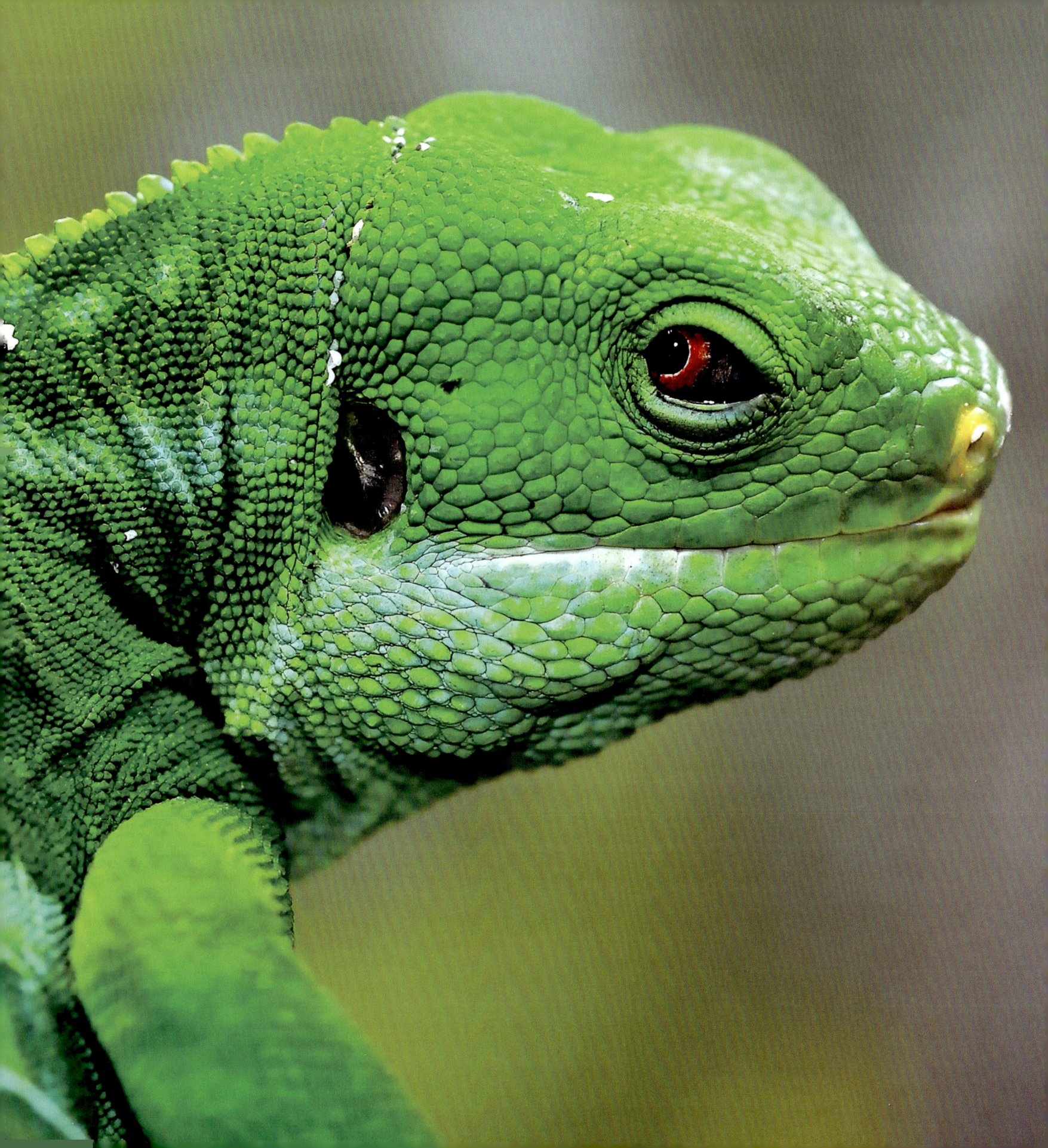

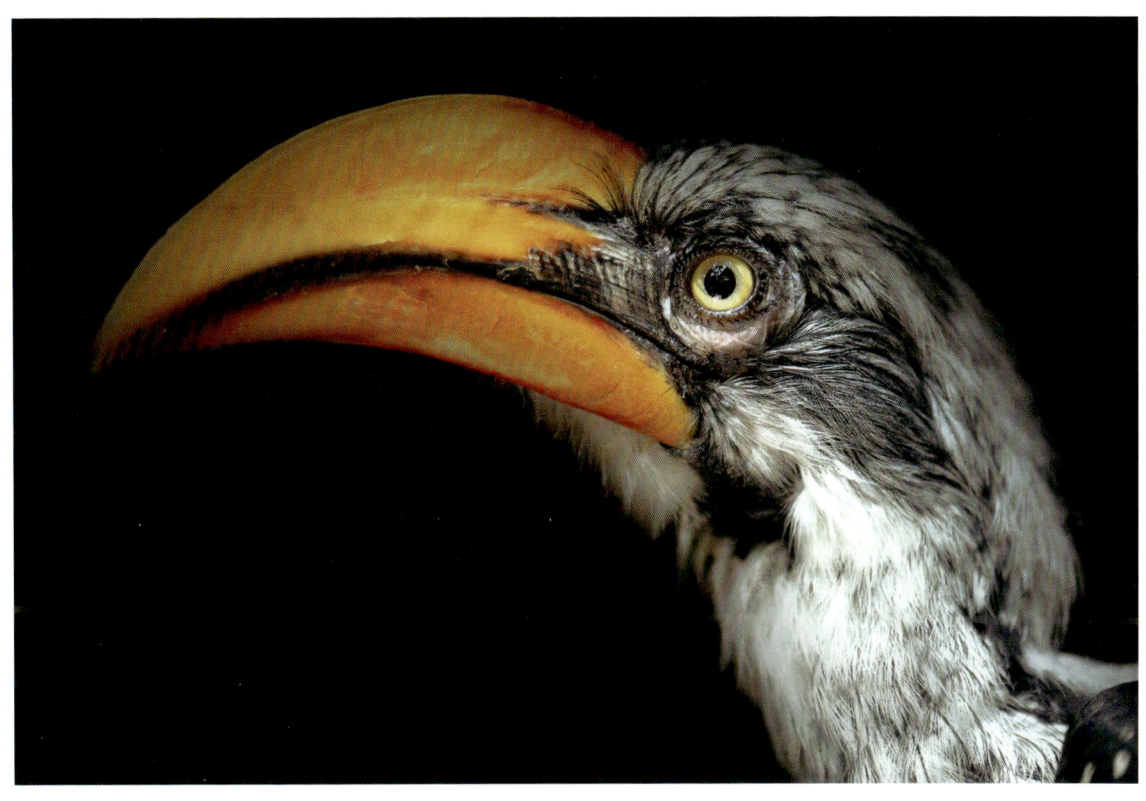

Two very diverse species, located thousands of miles apart, each displaying captivating behavior during our short time together. If I were to choose a favorite, though, it would be the iguana, whose own natural curiosity really made for a great day of photography.

Above: Eastern Yellow-Billed Hornbill, Kenya /Nikon D810
Opposite: Fiji Banded Iguana, Island of Fiji /Nikon D300

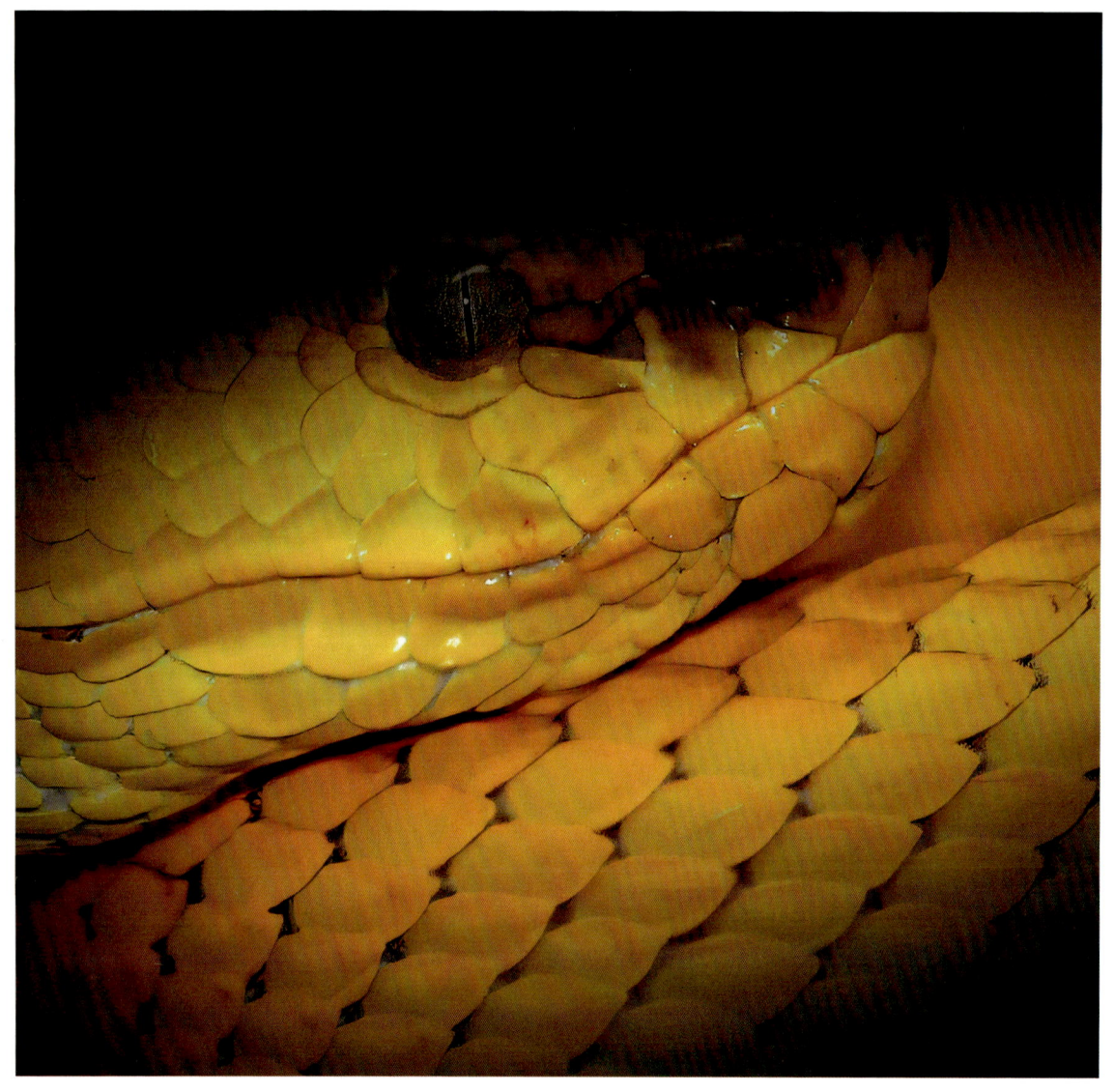

Snakes' interconnecting scales and rich, brilliant hues are a geometric marvel when it comes to their overall symmetry and ability to blend in with their natural surroundings. Most people, however, rarely have the opportunity or desire to get close enough to appreciate these endearing characteristics.

Above: McGregor's Pit Viper, Philippines /Nikon D300
Opposite: Bushmaster Snake, Costa Rica /Nikon D300

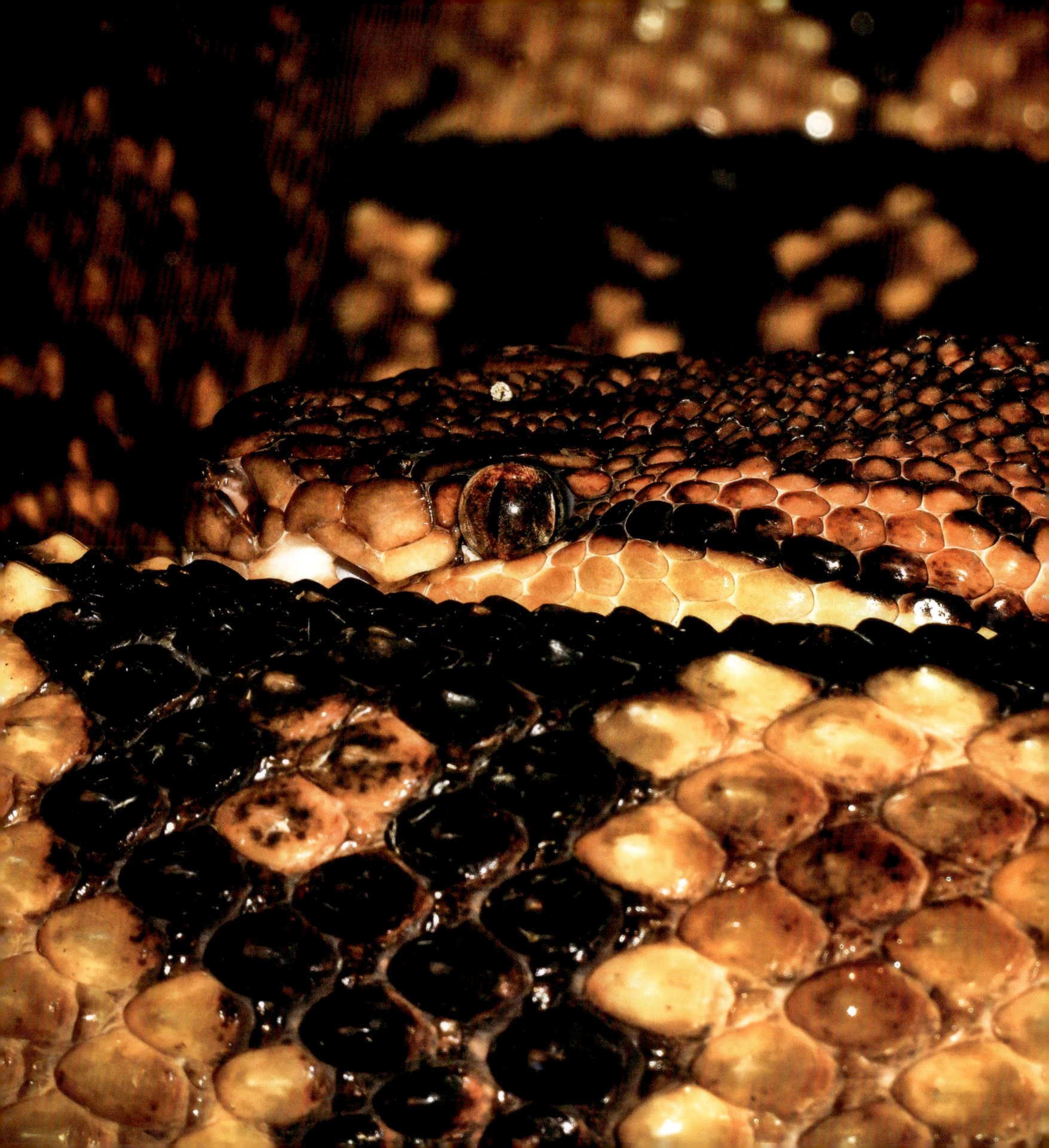

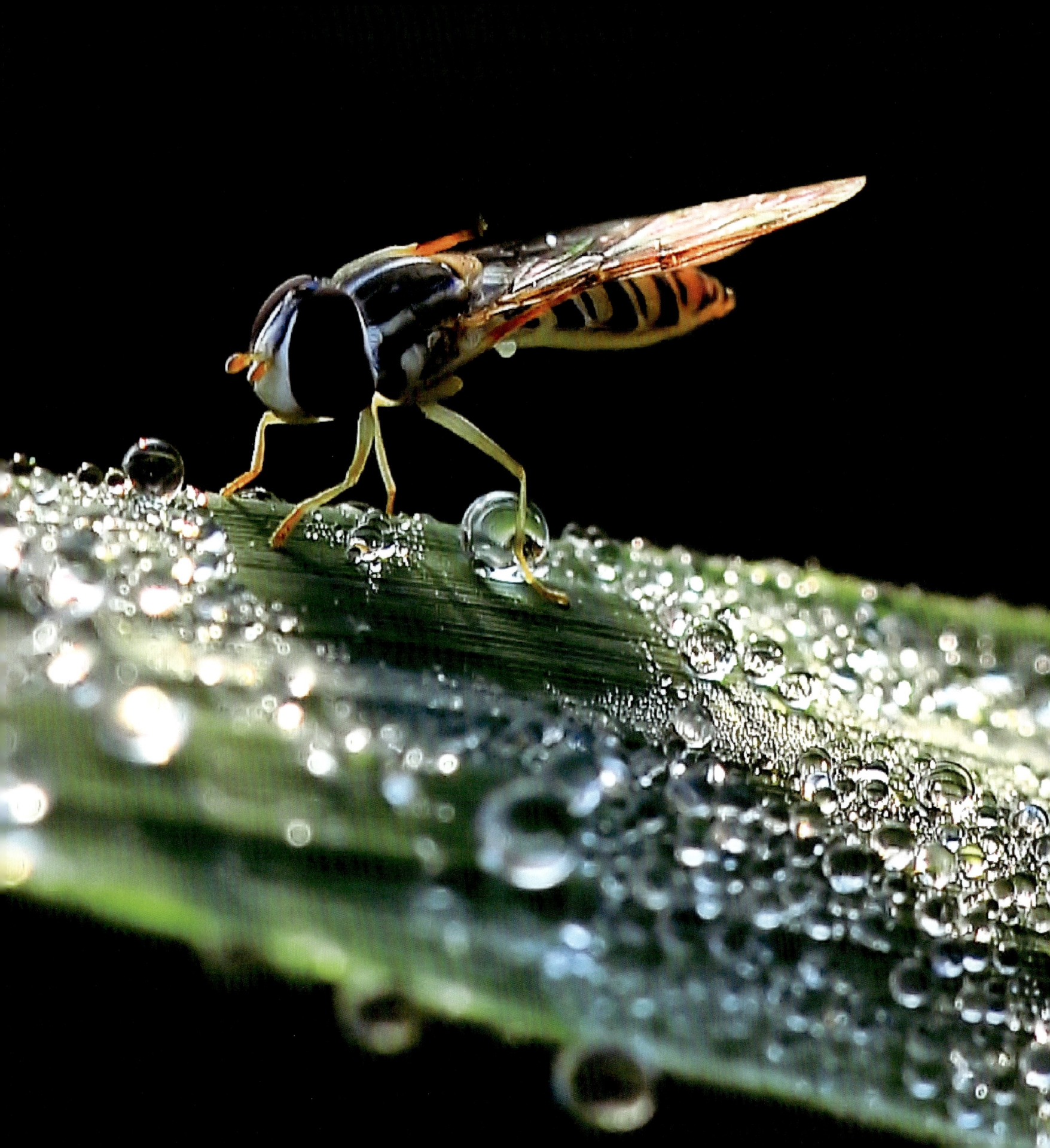

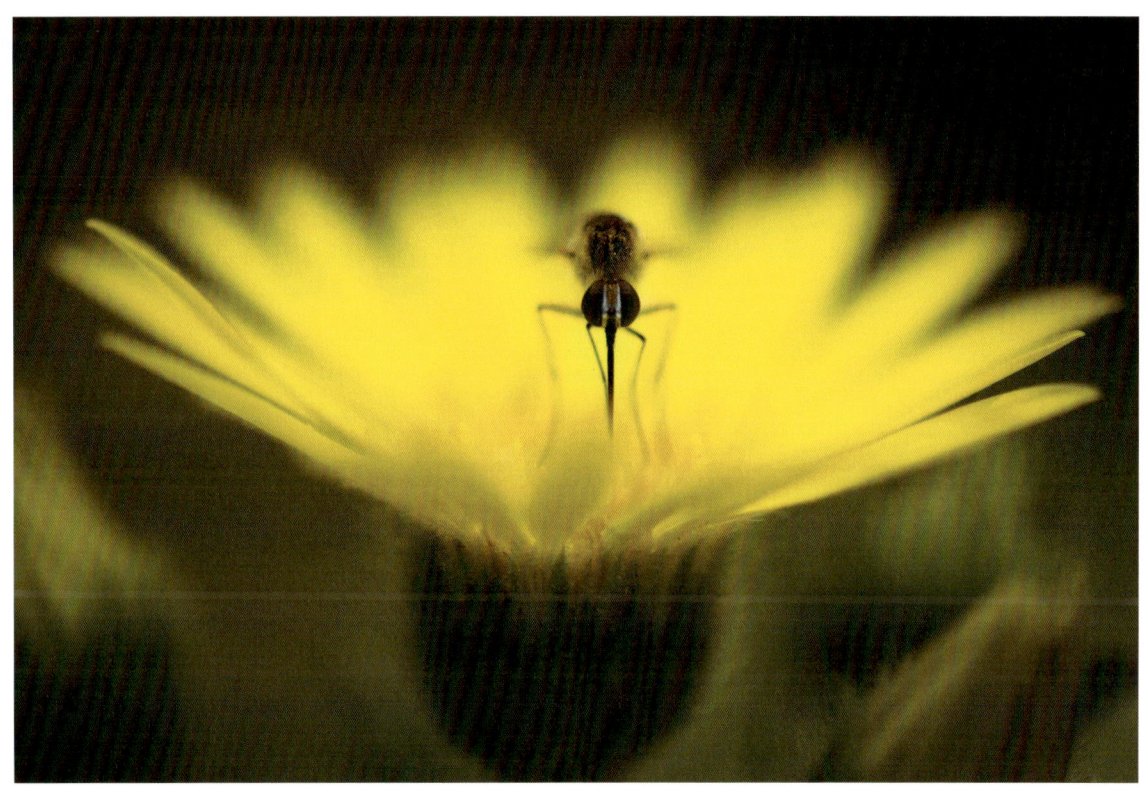

The phrase "It's a Small World" is the only way I can describe the two images depicted, yet still they are huge in comparison to the infinitesimal small life that constantly eludes our senses and stretches our imagination to its utmost limits.

Above and opposite: Syrphid Fly, Texas /Nikon D810

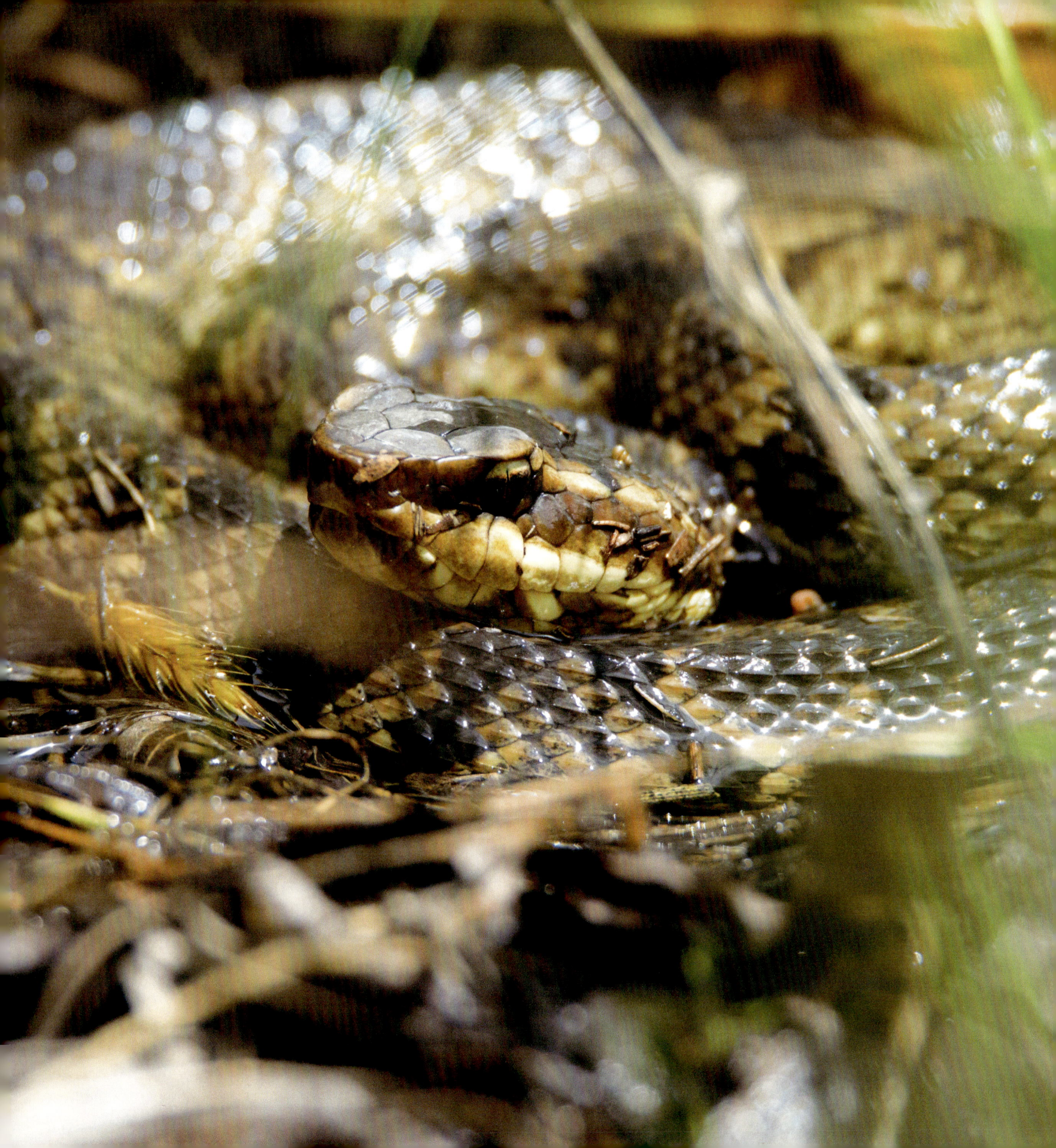

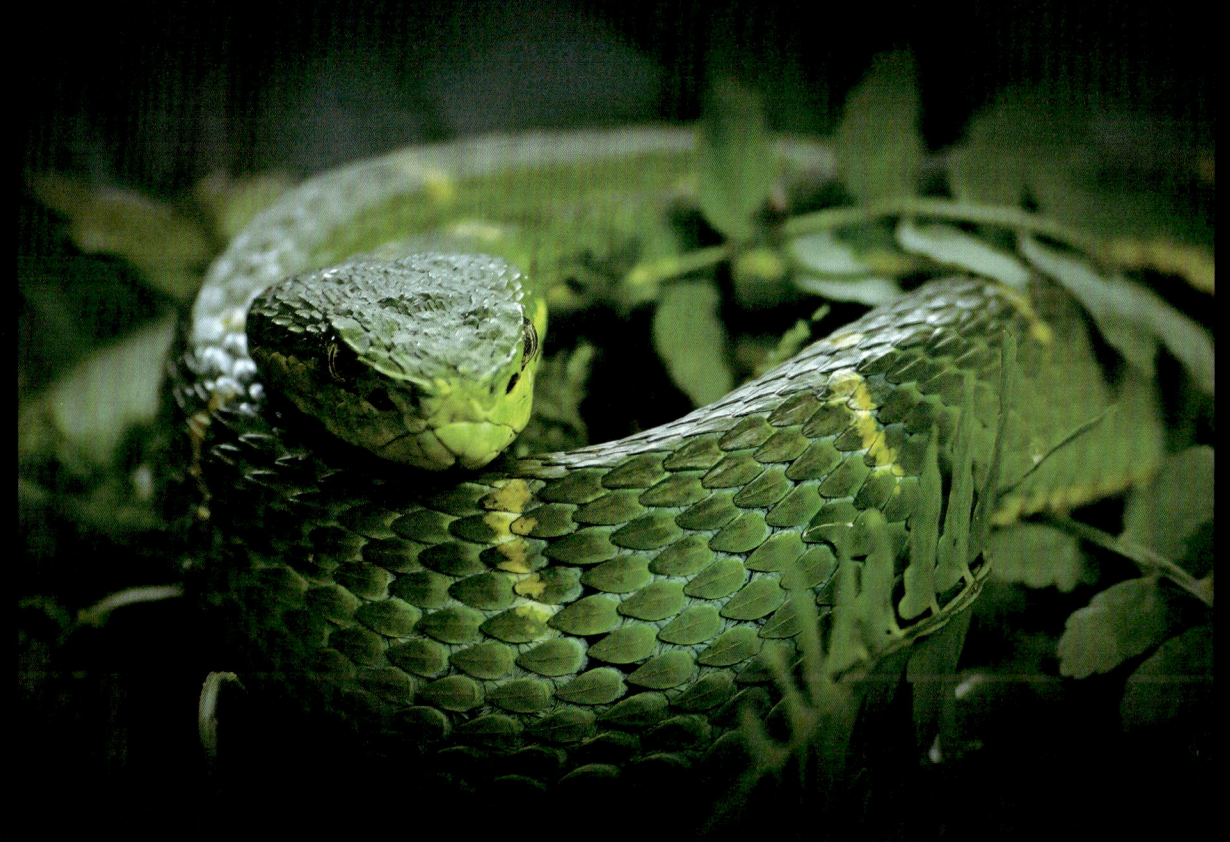

To genuinely appreciate life on Earth, I believe you must learn to take the time to see how incredible it is. Whether it's a snake, a frog, or an elephant, each is a unique creature that has evolved over millennia to become what you see today.

Above: Side-Striped Pit Viper, Costa Rica /Nikon D300

Opposite: Cottonmouth Snake, Texas /Nikon D810

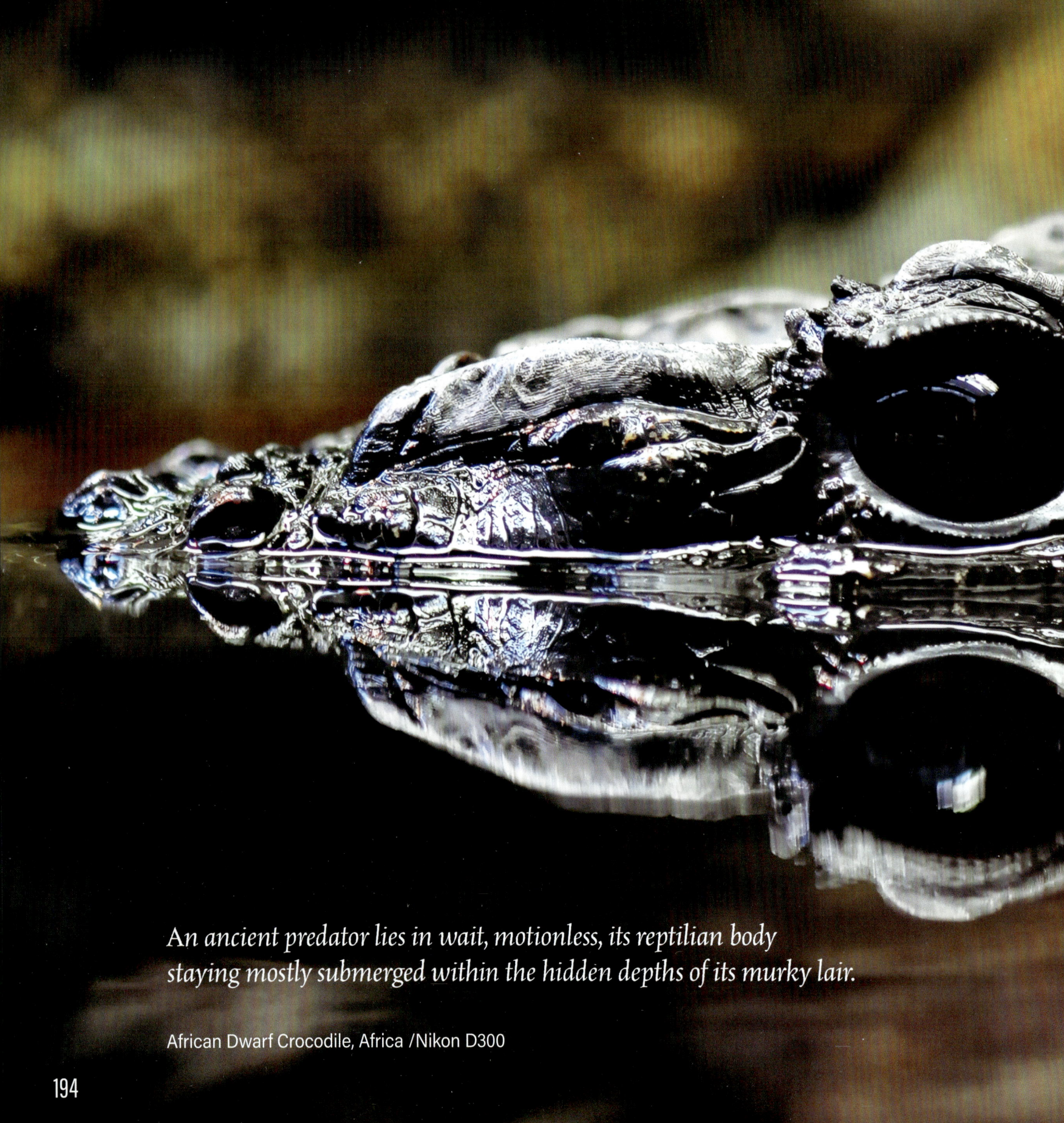

An ancient predator lies in wait, motionless, its reptilian body staying mostly submerged within the hidden depths of its murky lair.

African Dwarf Crocodile, Africa / Nikon D300

194

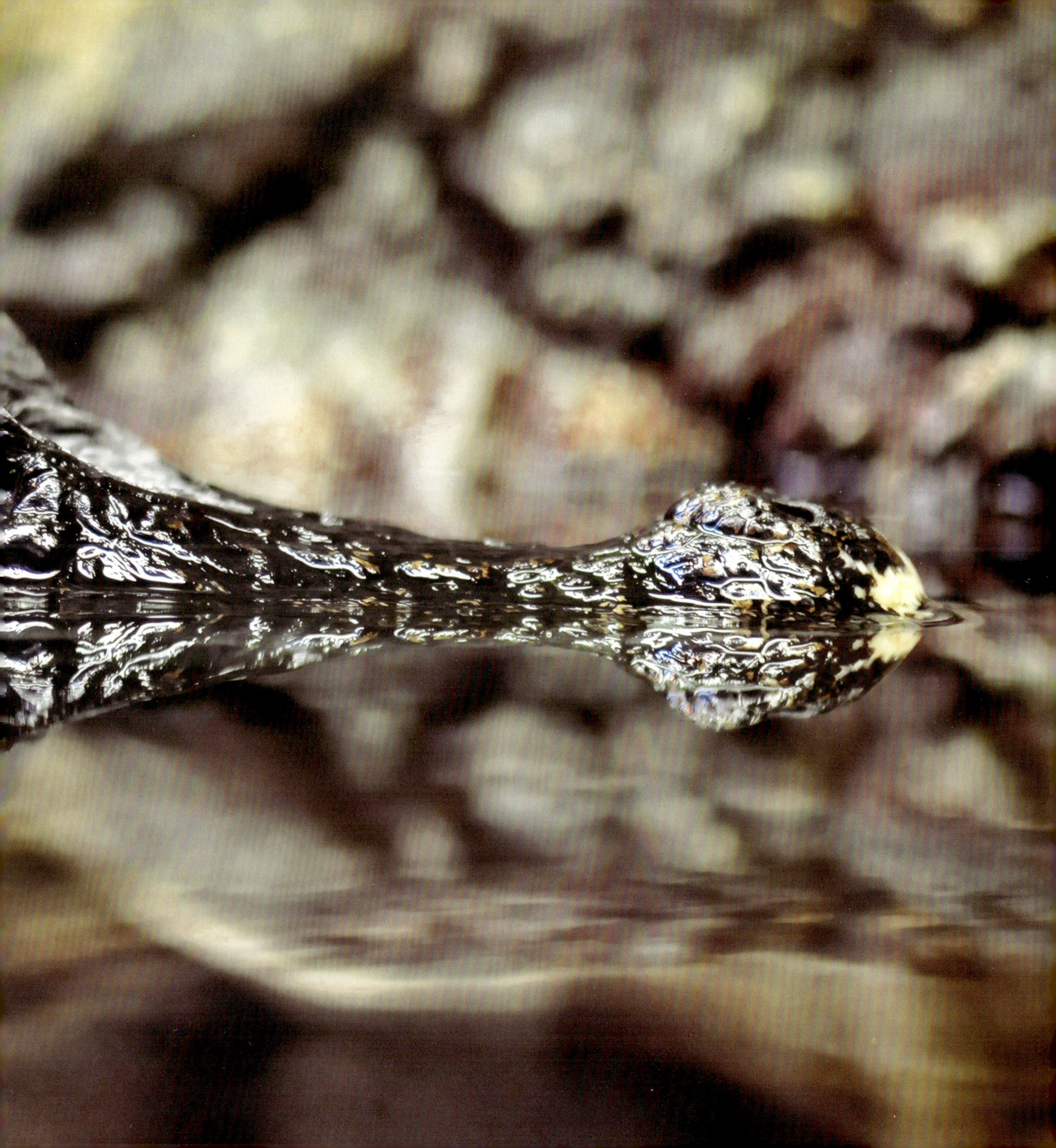

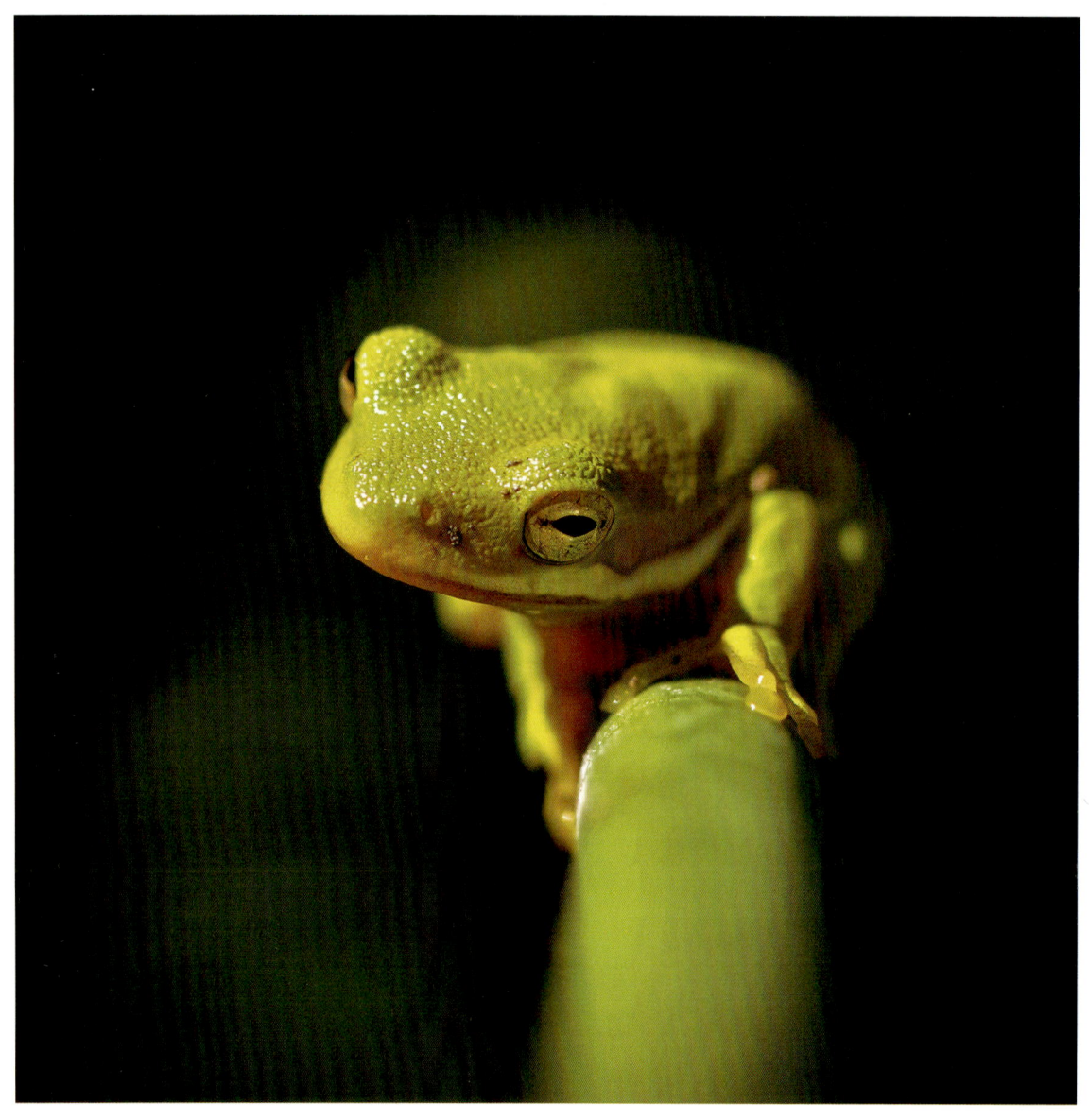

Color and light collide to complement the intricate beauty of life all around us, as everyday creatures suddenly become extraordinary to behold.

Above: American Green Tree Frog, Texas /Nikon D300
Opposite: Honeybee, Texas /Nikon D300

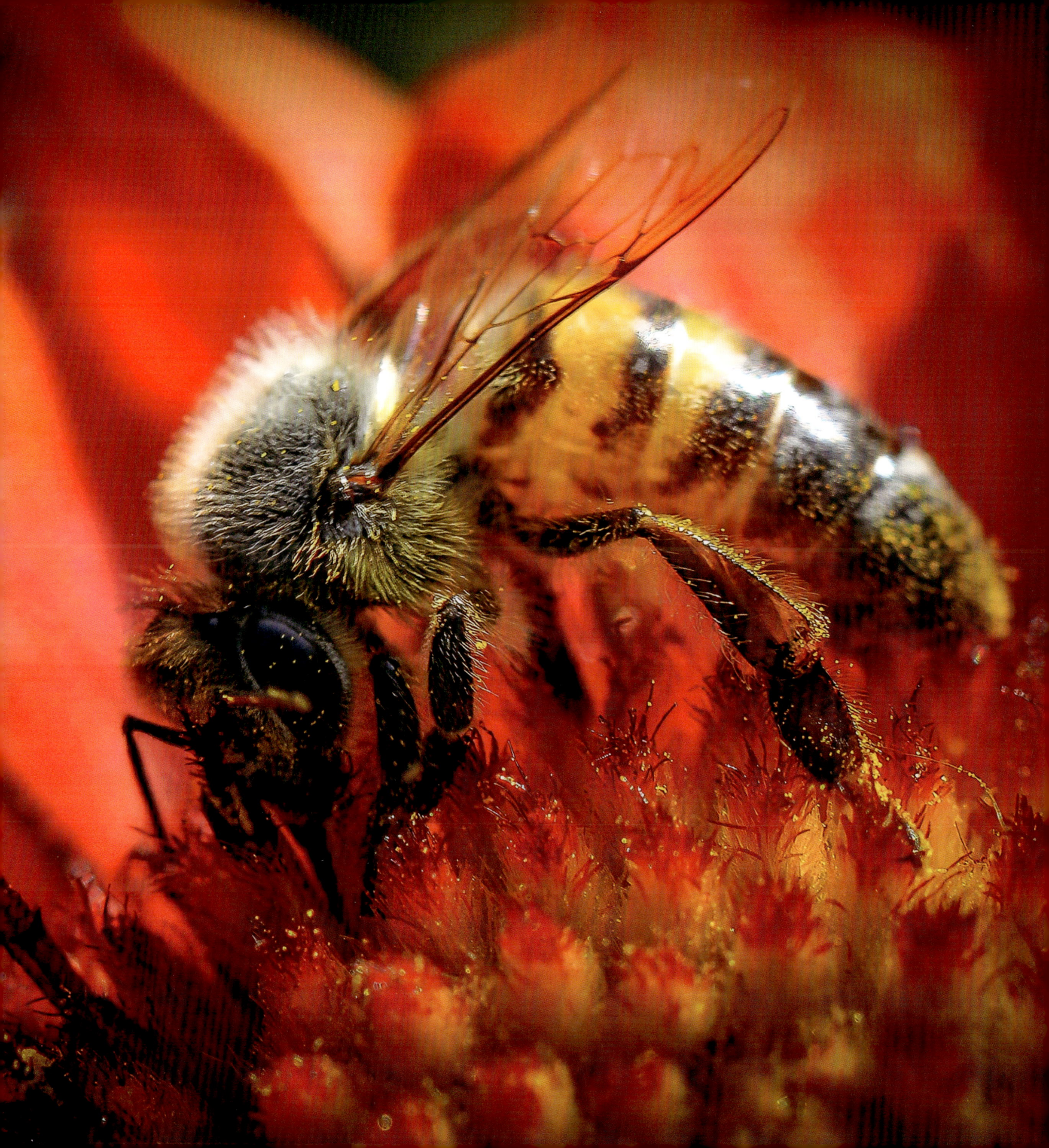

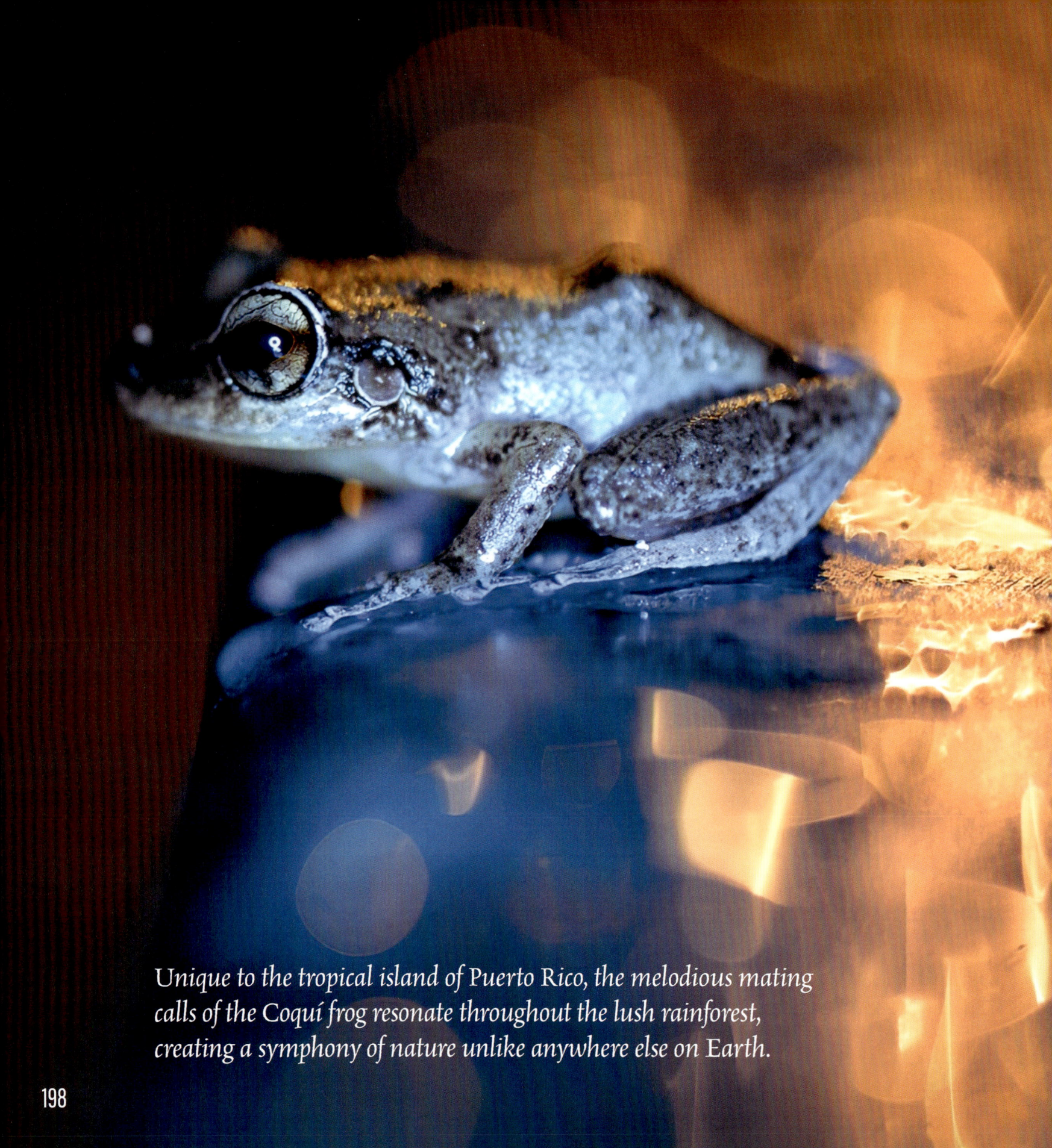

Unique to the tropical island of Puerto Rico, the melodious mating calls of the Coquí frog resonate throughout the lush rainforest, creating a symphony of nature unlike anywhere else on Earth.

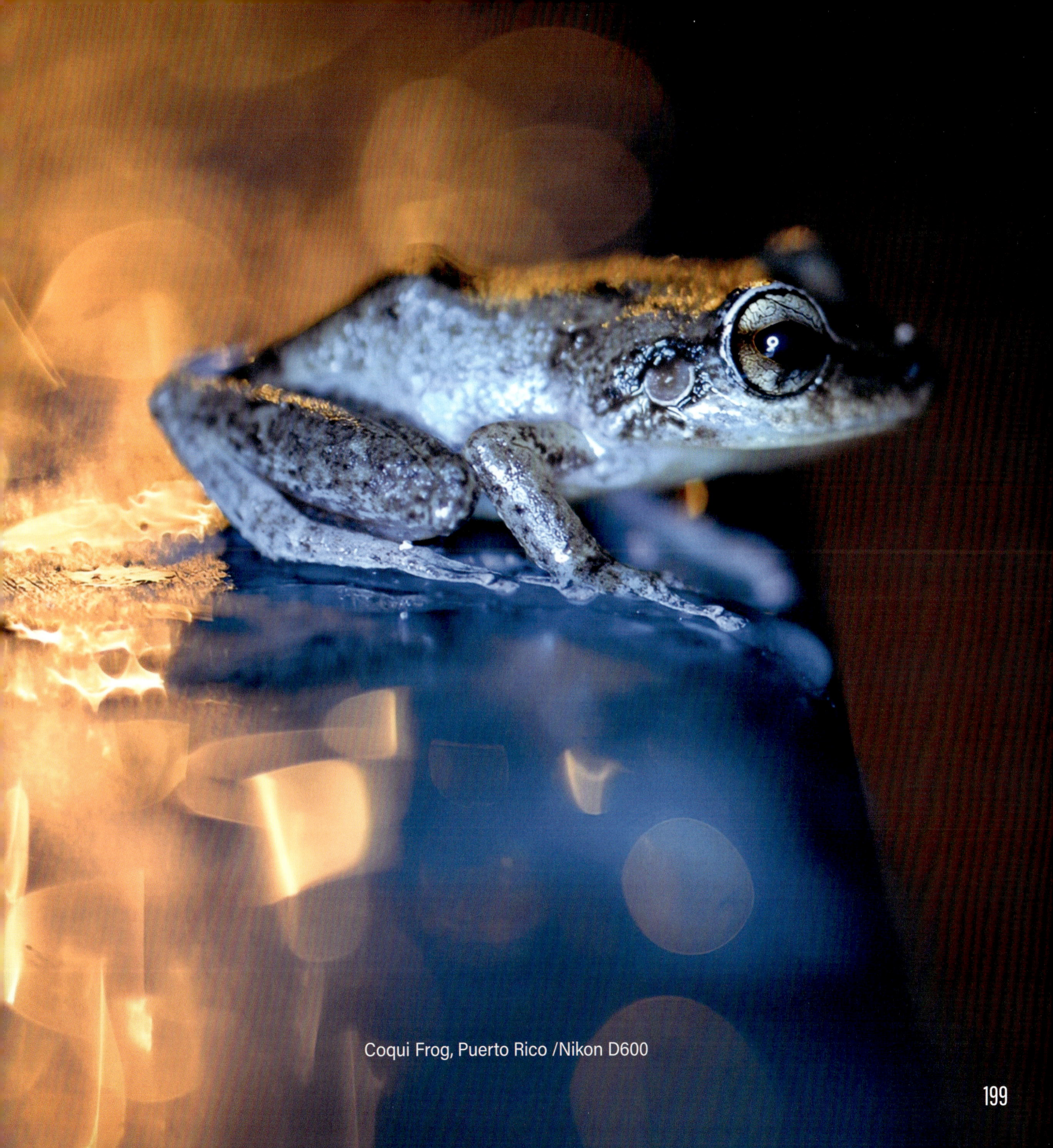

Coqui Frog, Puerto Rico /Nikon D600

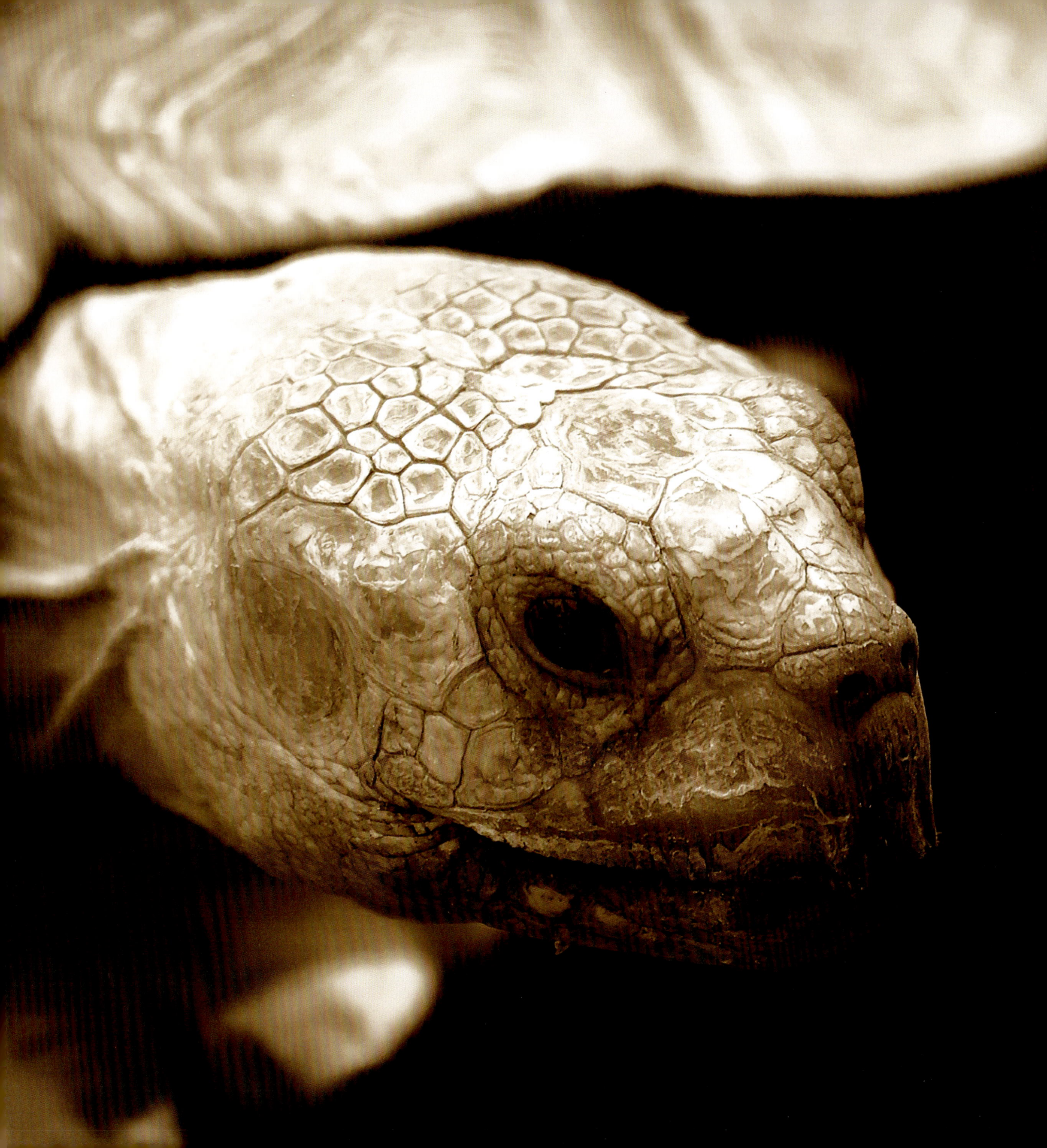

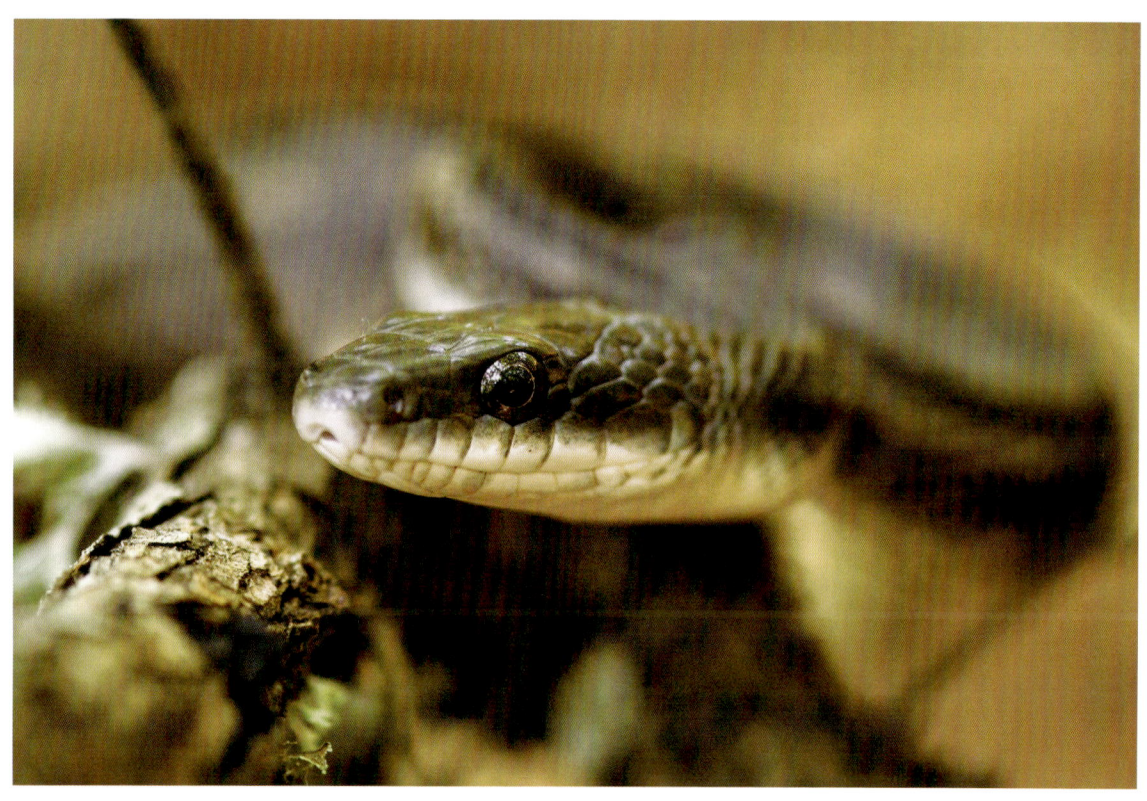

The wrinkles of time gone by are notably evident when looking into the face of an Aldabra tortoise. Very long-lived, their stories could have begun well before the US Civil War of 1861, making them living fossils for all the world to see.

Above: Western Rat Snake, Texas /Nikon D600
Opposite: Aldabra Tortoise, Texas /Nikon D300

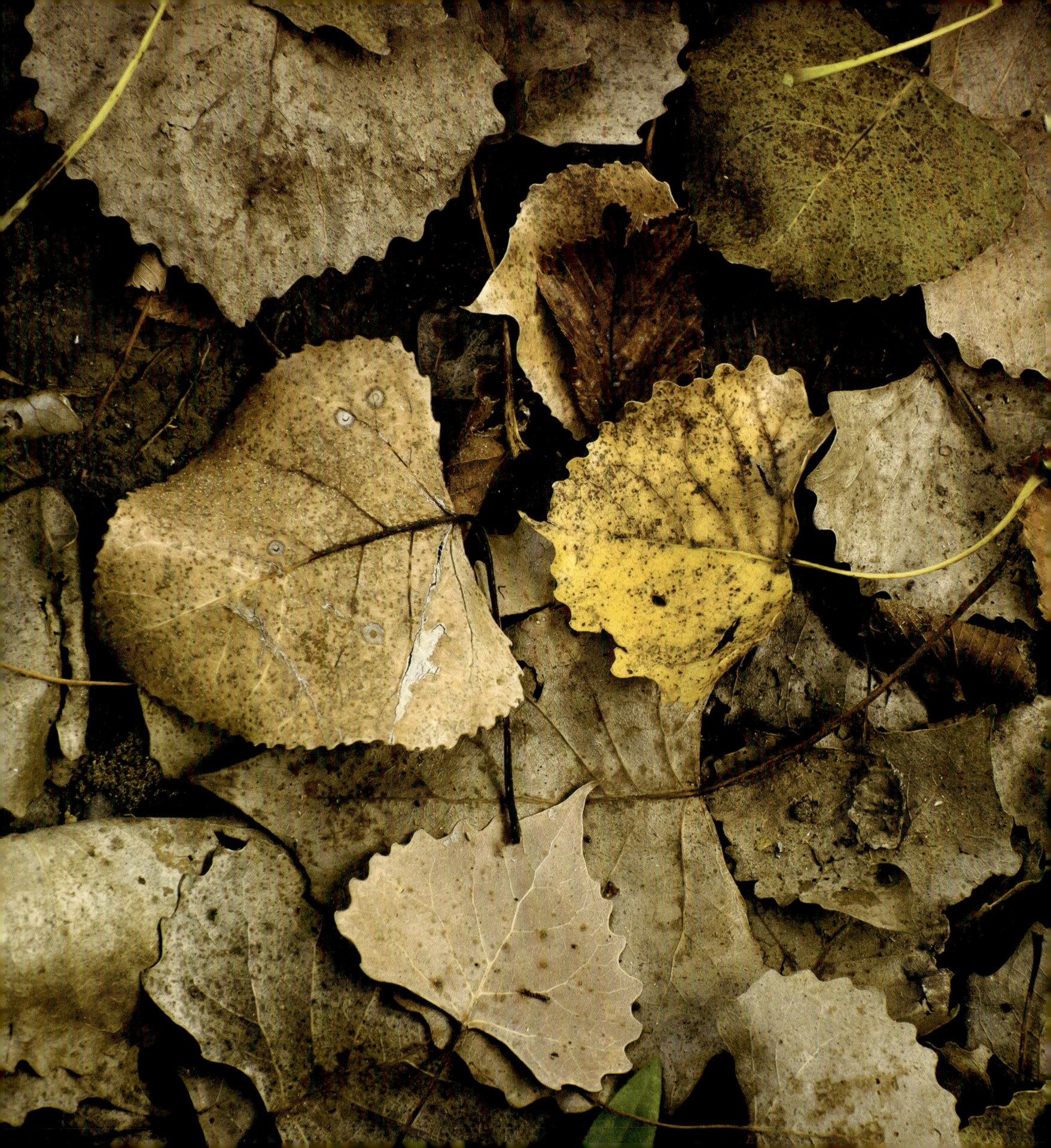

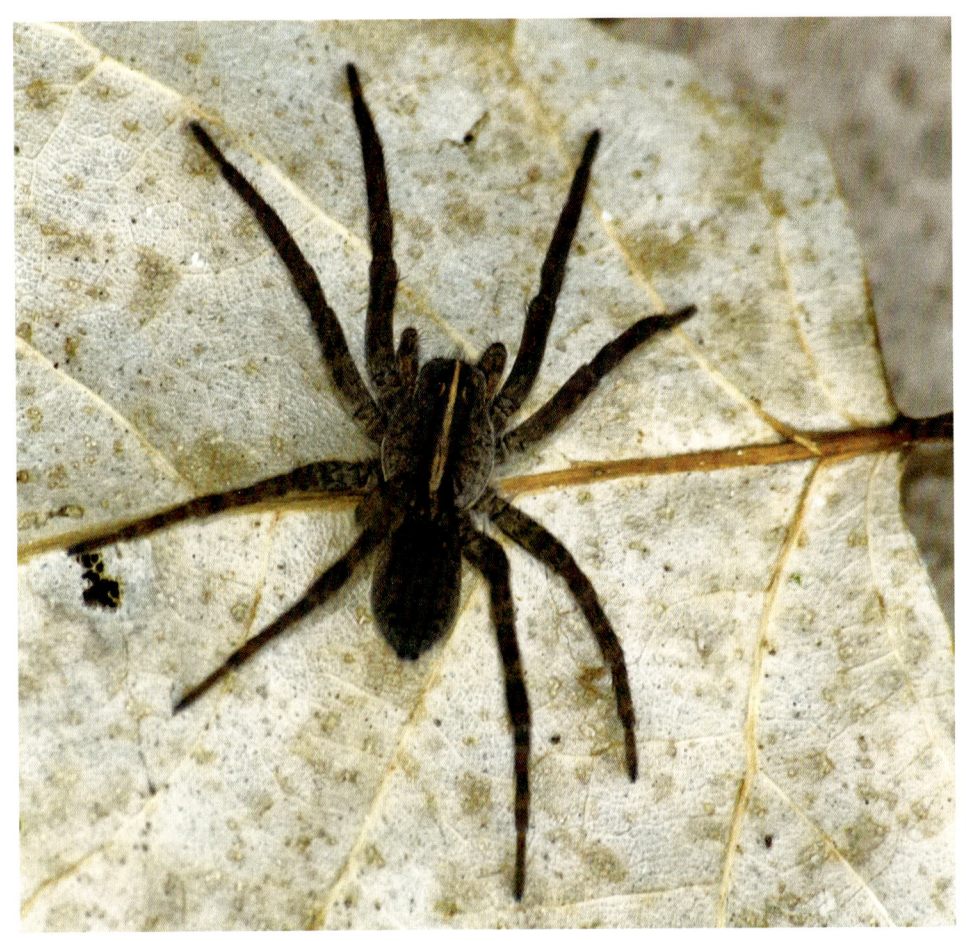

The Texas woodland floor conceals a plethora of life hidden deep within its shadowy embrace, as mighty sentinels such as live oak, elm, and sycamore trees drop thousands of leaves each season to help sustain and nourish it.

Above: Wolf Spider, Texas /Nikon D300
Opposite: Woodland Floor, Texas /Nikon D810

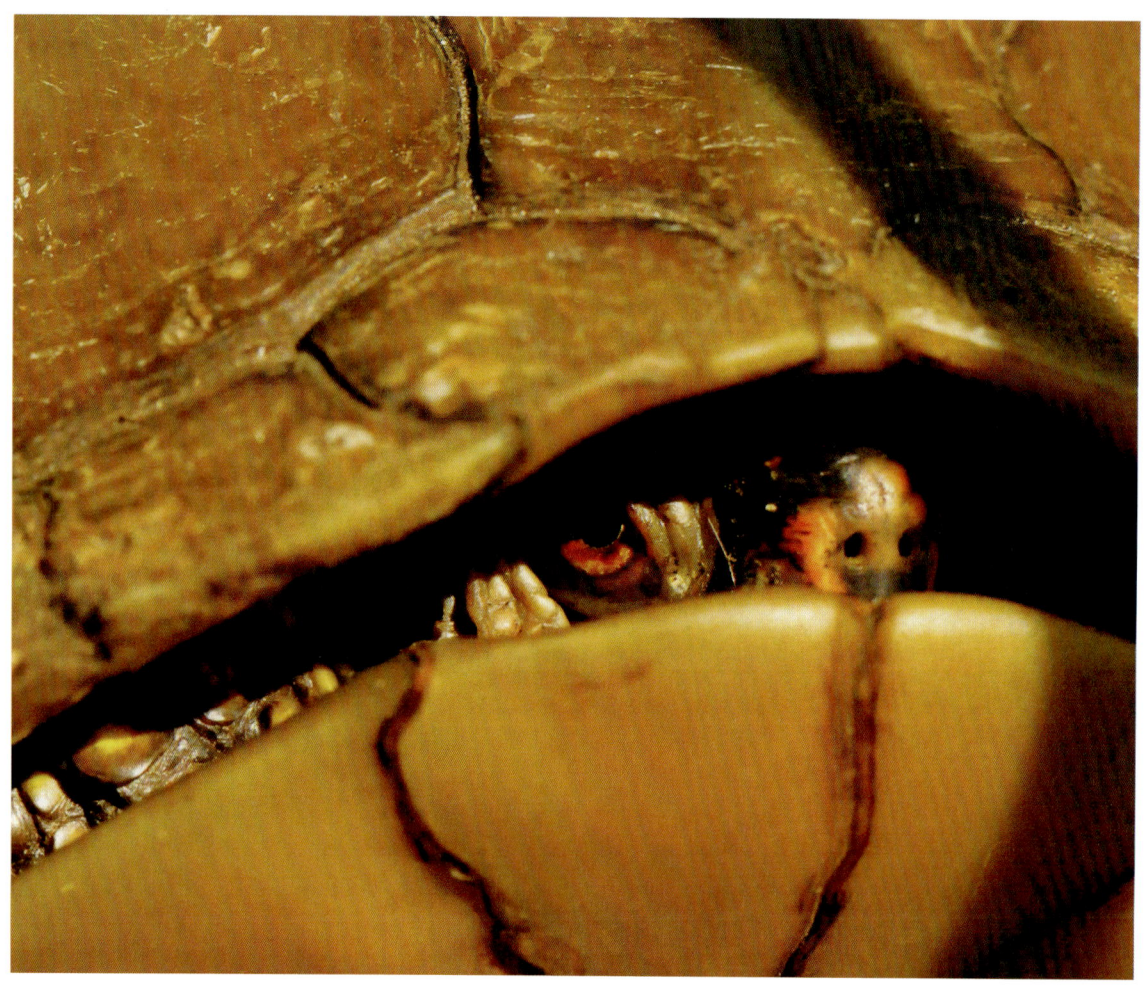

For some animals, avoiding danger is literally built into their DNA. The box turtle retreats into his fortified safe haven, while the armadillo, with its heavy coat of arms, shields himself well from most would-be intruders.

Above: Box Turtle, Texas /Nikon D300
Opposite: Nine-Banded Armadillo, Texas /Nikon D300

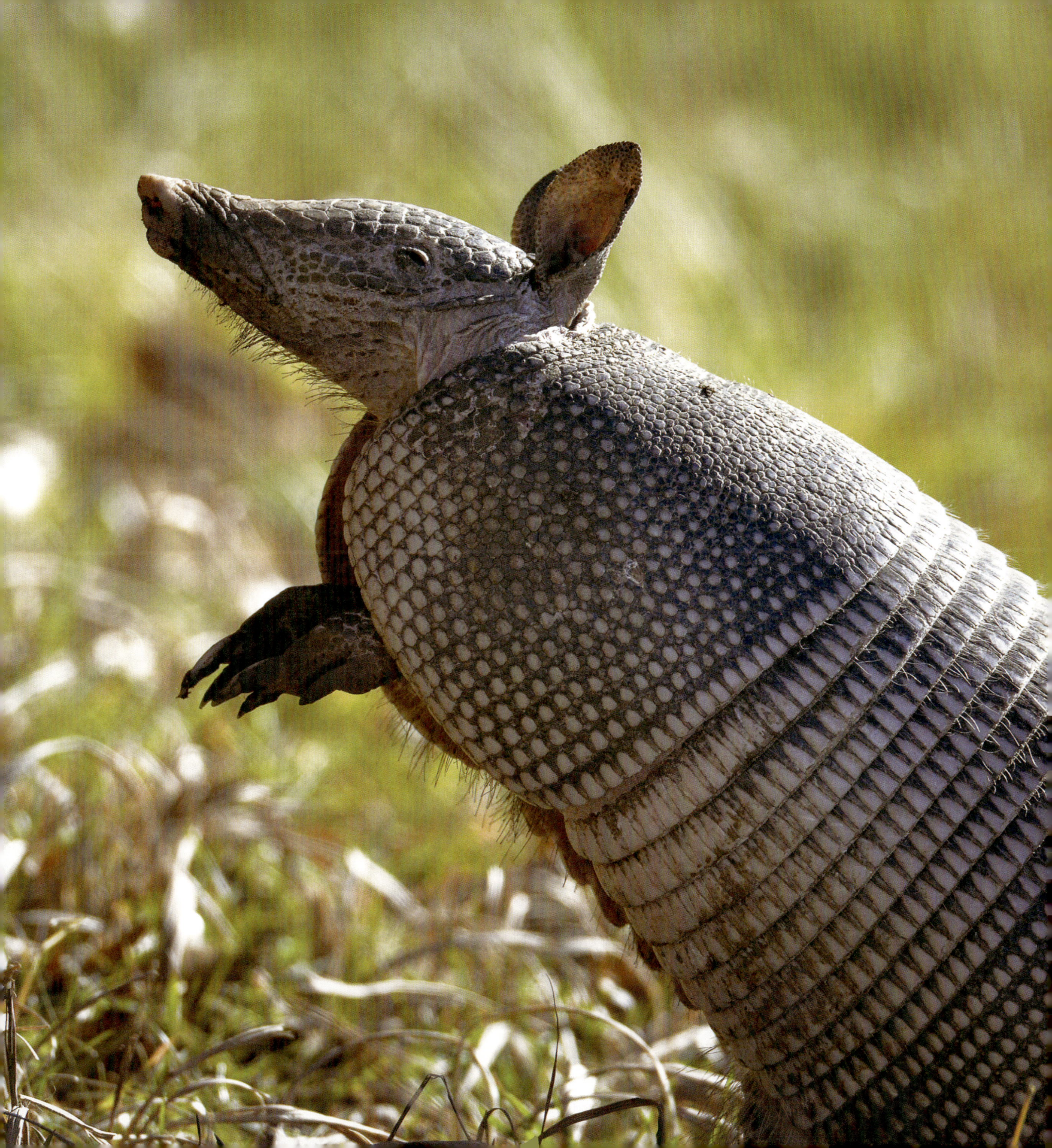

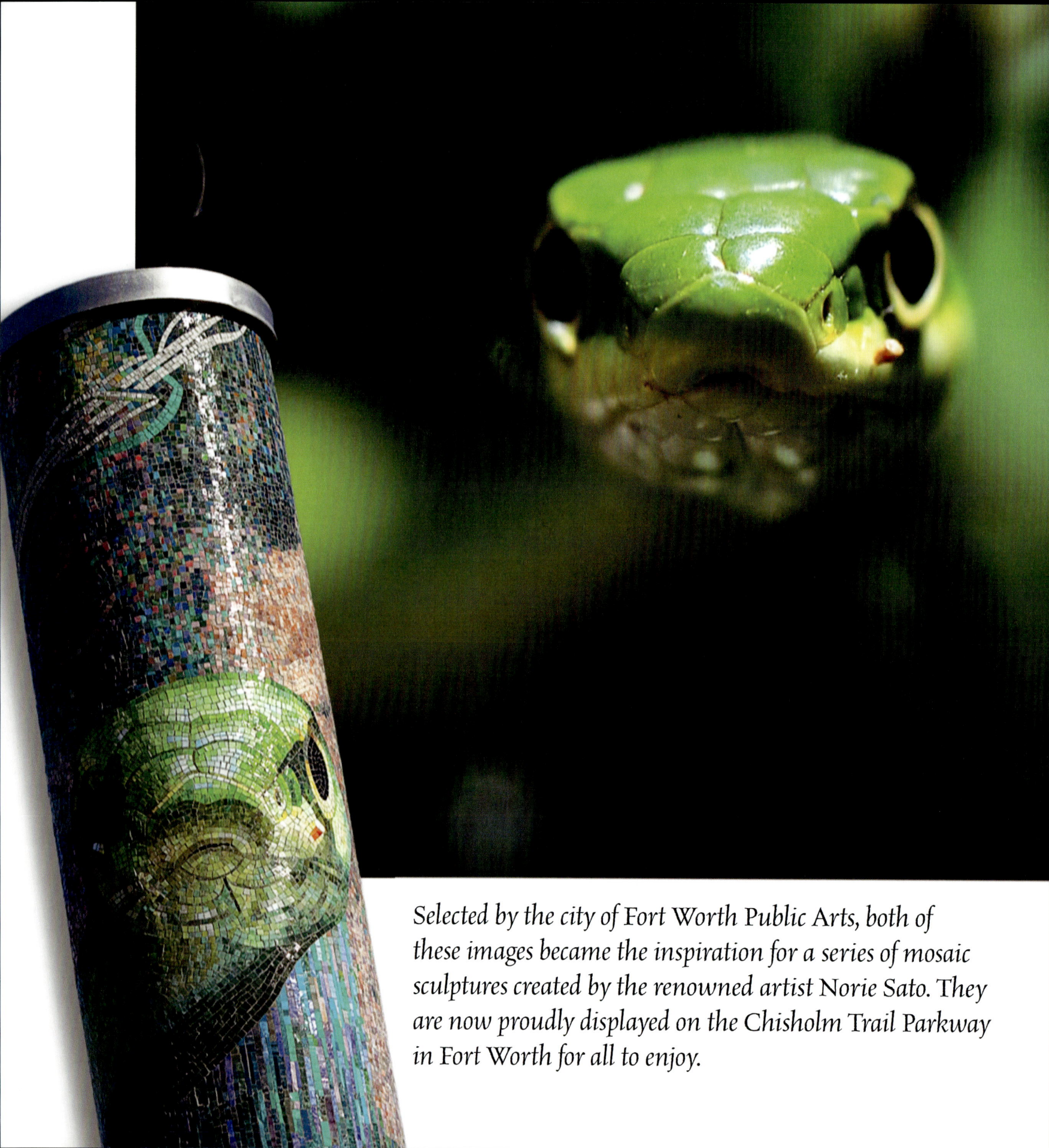

Selected by the city of Fort Worth Public Arts, both of these images became the inspiration for a series of mosaic sculptures created by the renowned artist Norie Sato. They are now proudly displayed on the Chisholm Trail Parkway in Fort Worth for all to enjoy.

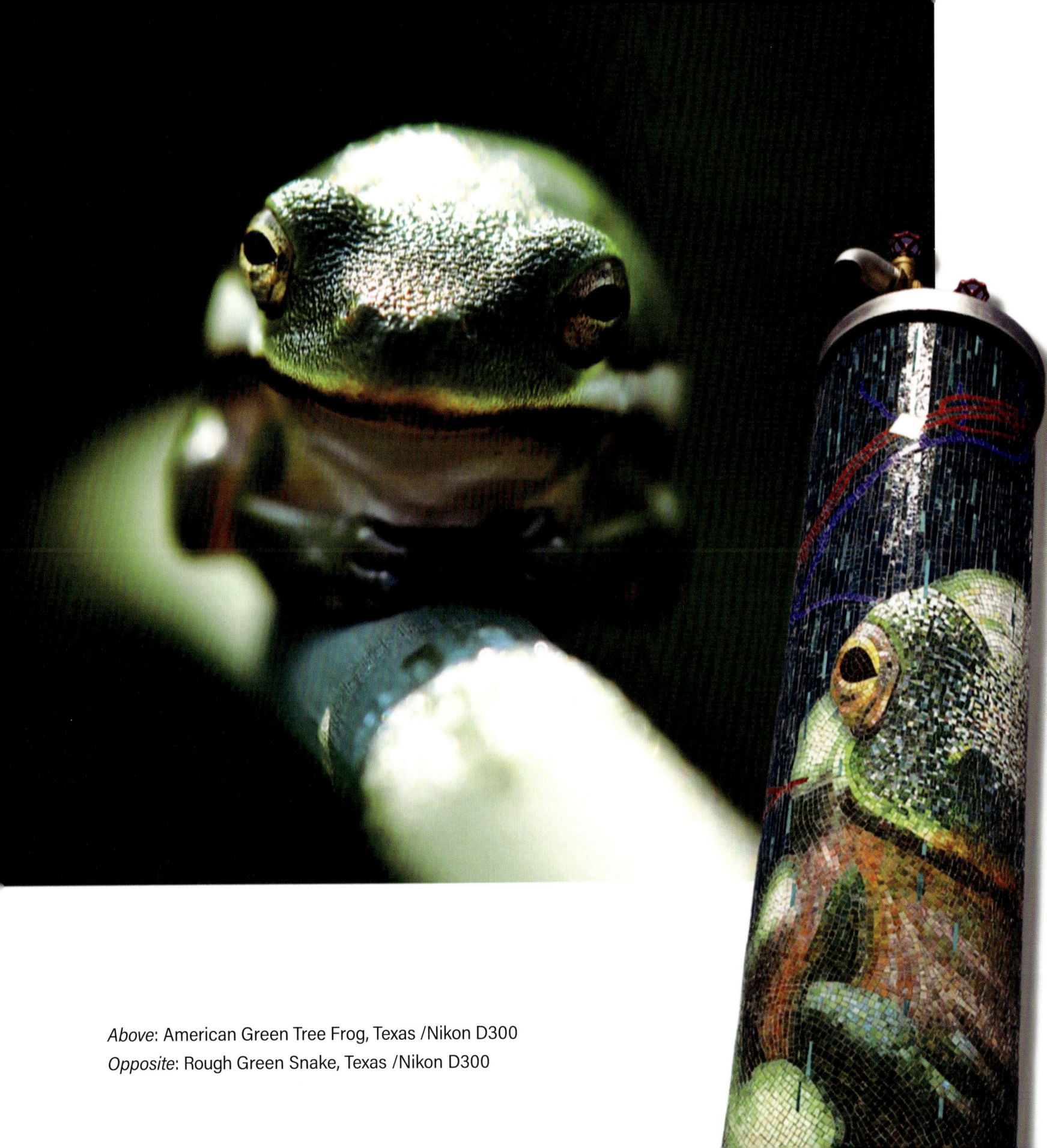

Above: American Green Tree Frog, Texas /Nikon D300
Opposite: Rough Green Snake, Texas /Nikon D300

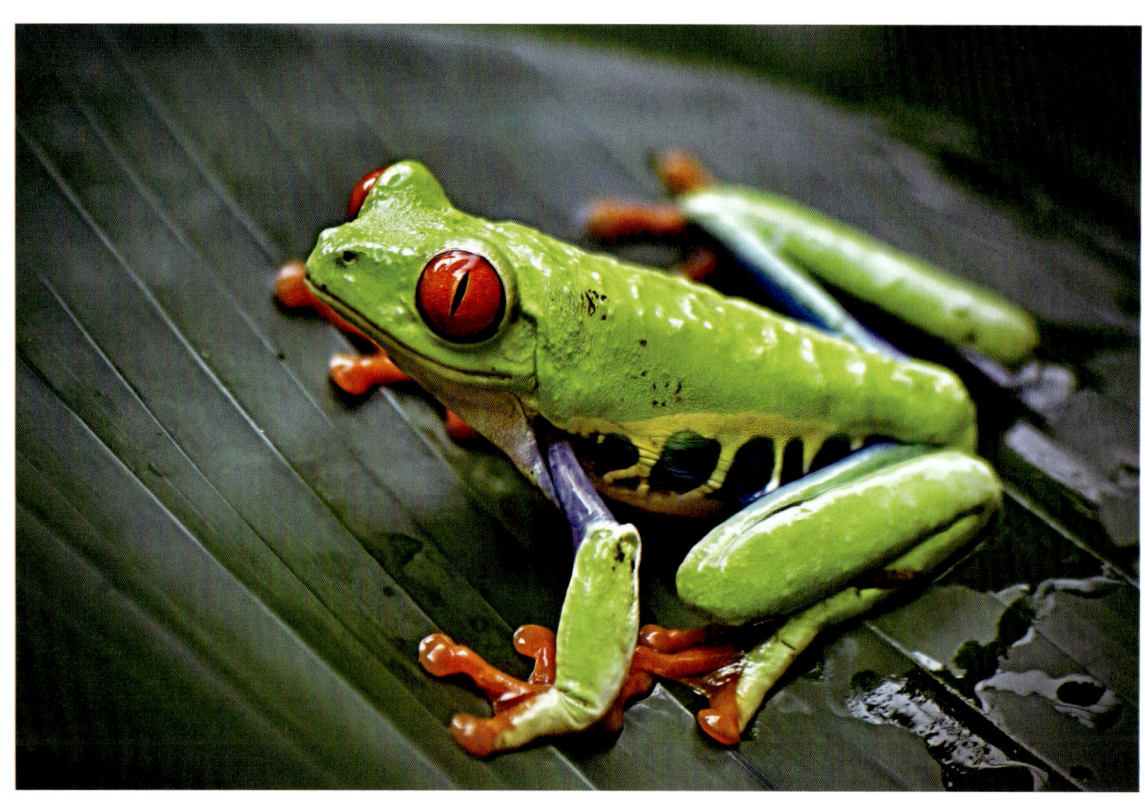

Vibrant color in nature is one of the very first things I take notice of, as life has this uncanny ability to both stand out and blend in when you least expect it. The key to survival for many species is knowing when to be still, as locations can be compromised with but the slightest movement

Above: Red-Eyed Tree Frog, Costa Rica /Nikon D300
Opposite: Halloween Pennant Dragonfly, Texas /Nikon D300

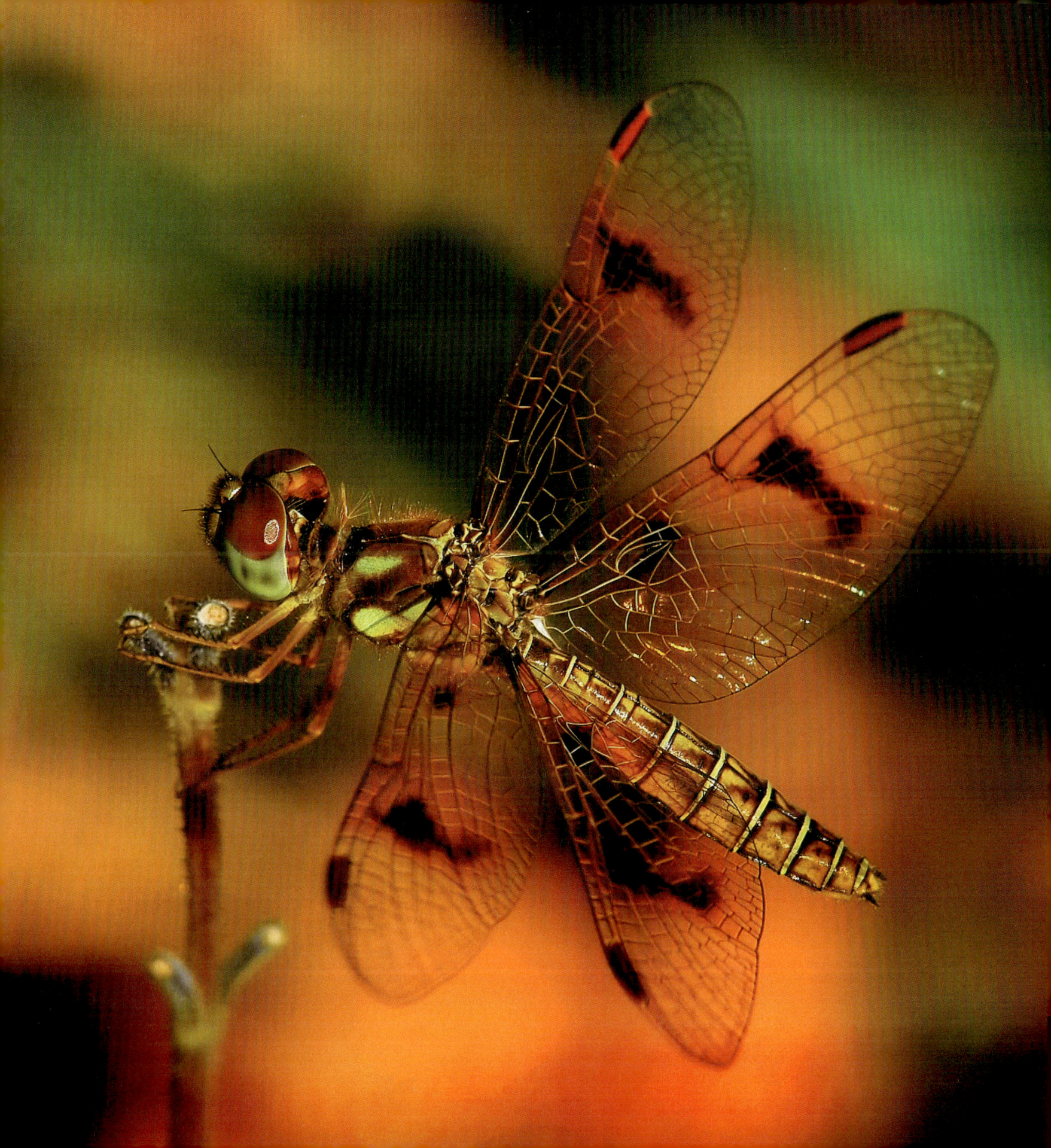

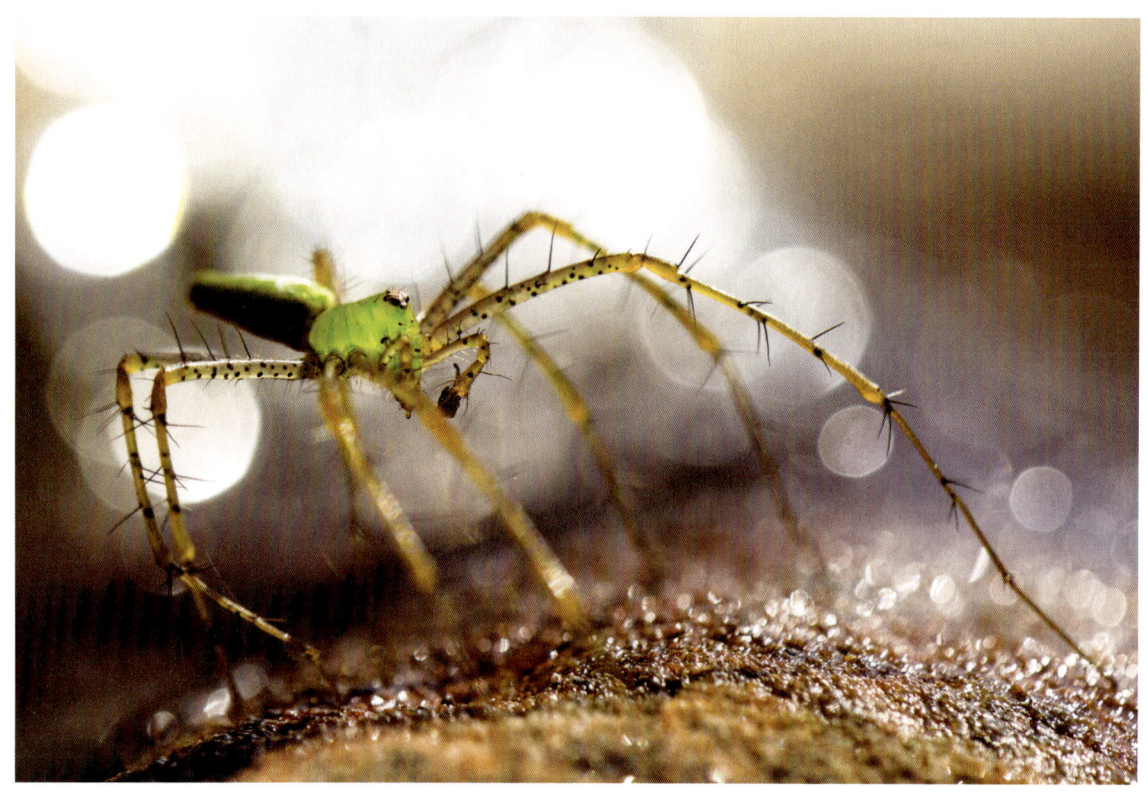

As I *hover above these small, wonderful, alien creatures in such close proximity, I often wonder how they see me. Most appear completely enthralled by my lens, even intrigued, which is something I never expected.*

Above: Green Lynx Spider, Texas /Nikon D810
Opposite: Green Darner Dragonfly, Texas /Nikon D300

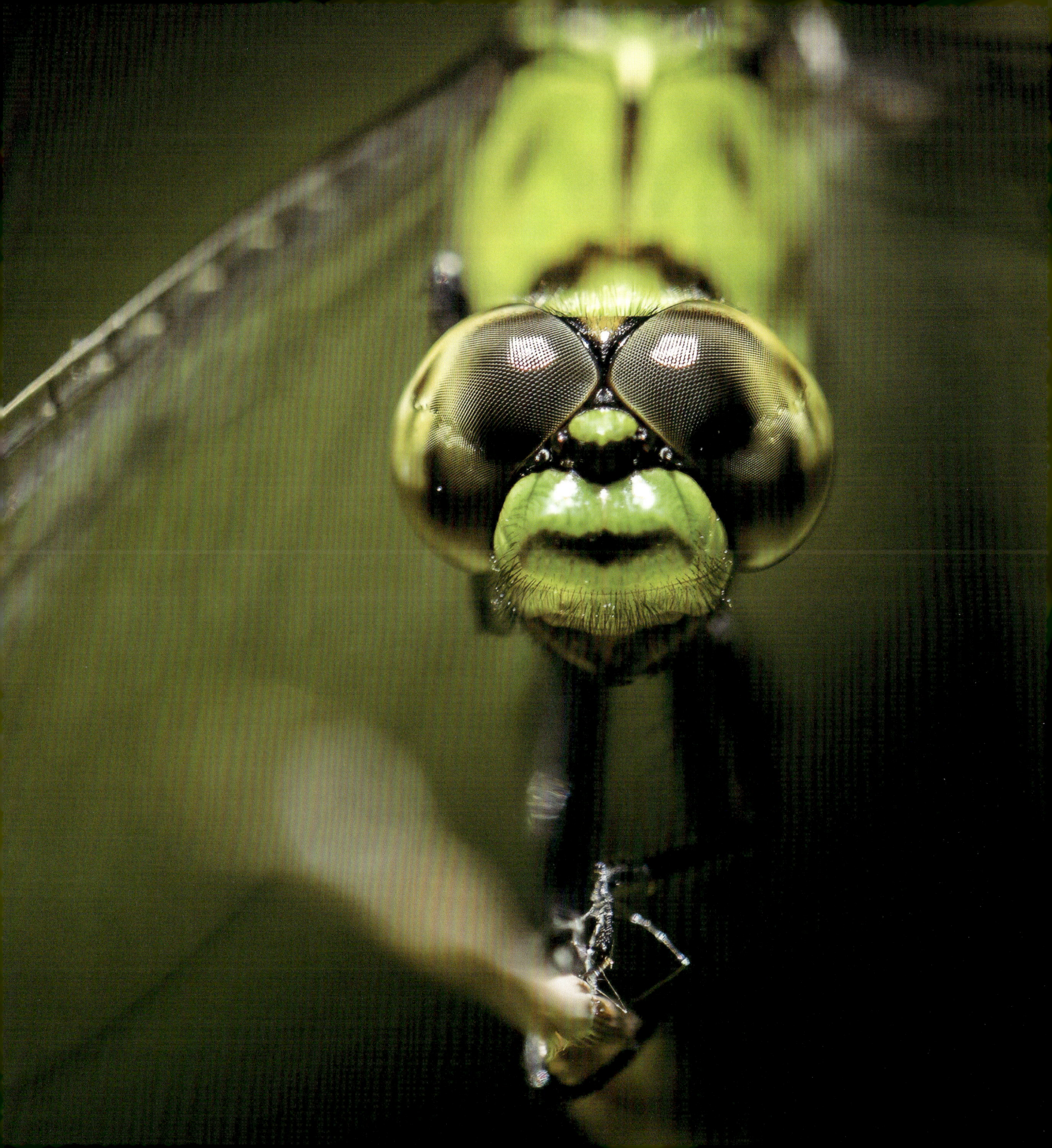

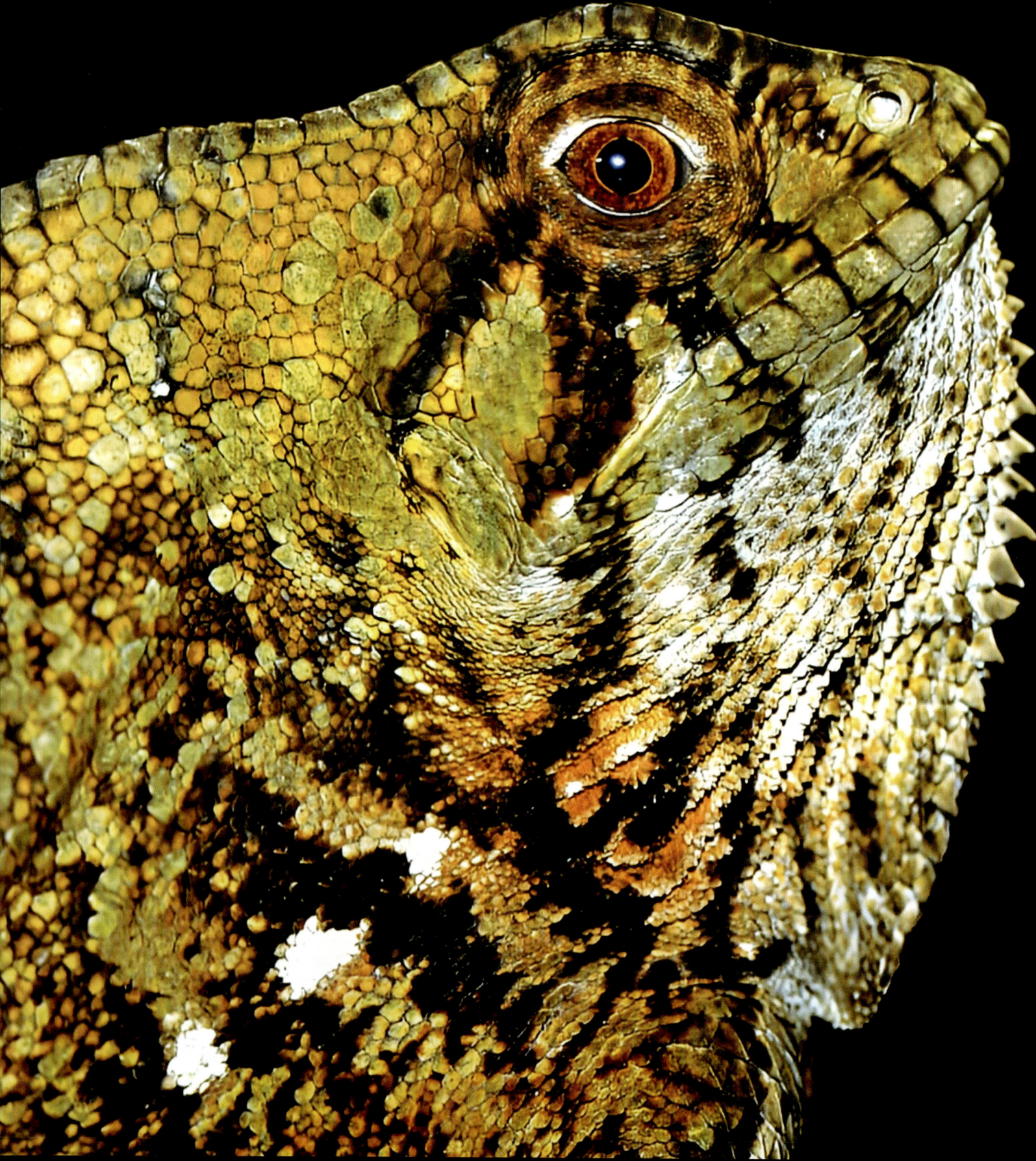

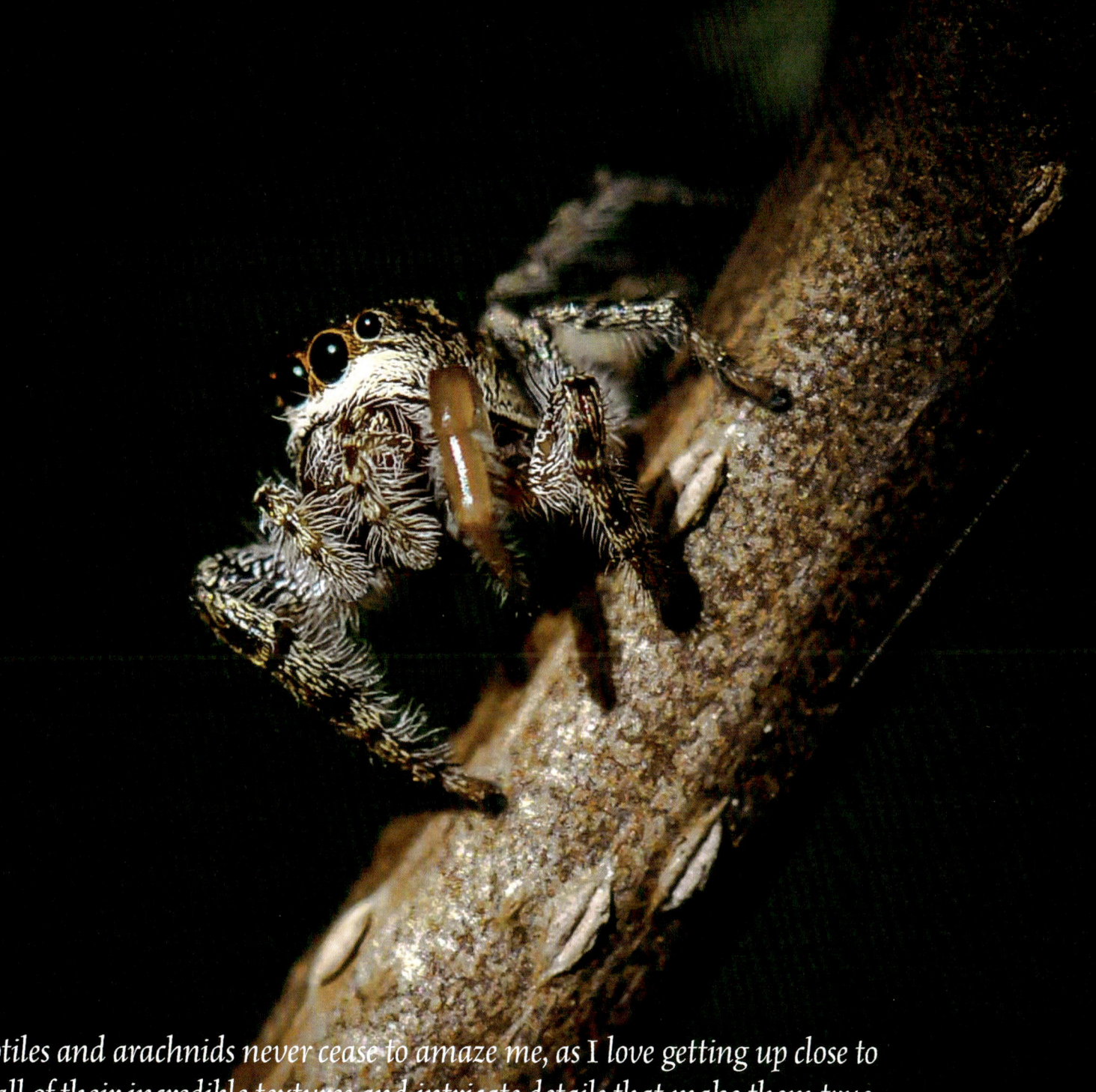

Reptiles and arachnids never cease to amaze me, as I love getting up close to see all of their incredible textures and intricate details that make them true wonders of our natural world.

Above: Jumping Spider, Texas / Nikon D300
Opposite: Frilled Lizard, Texas / Nikon D300

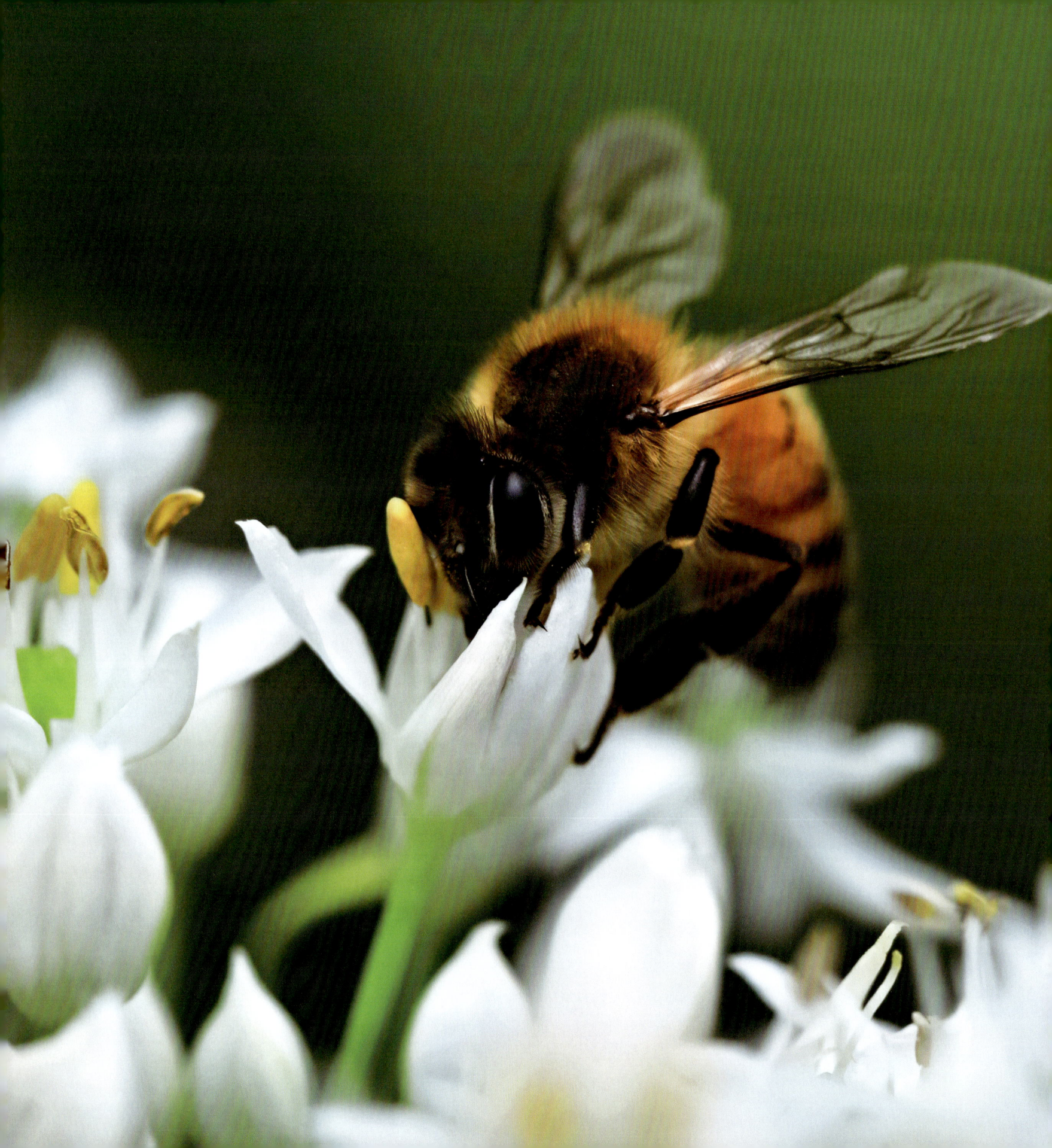

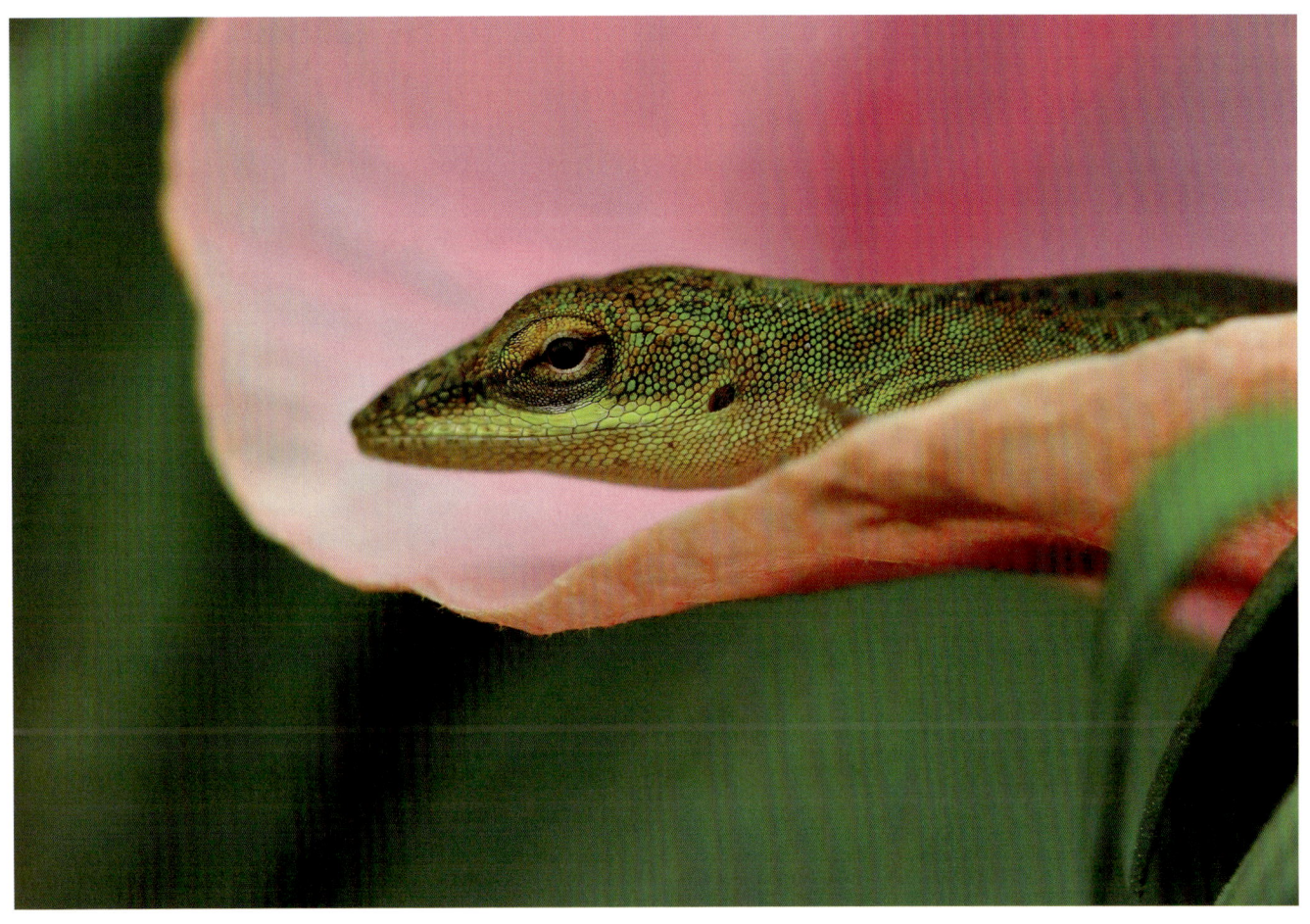

He is a living dinosaur, albeit a very small one in comparison to his long-gone Jurassic forefathers, but his mere presence can still unnerve his busy garden neighbors.

Above: Green Anole, Texas /Nikon D300
Opposite: Honeybee, Texas /Nikon D300

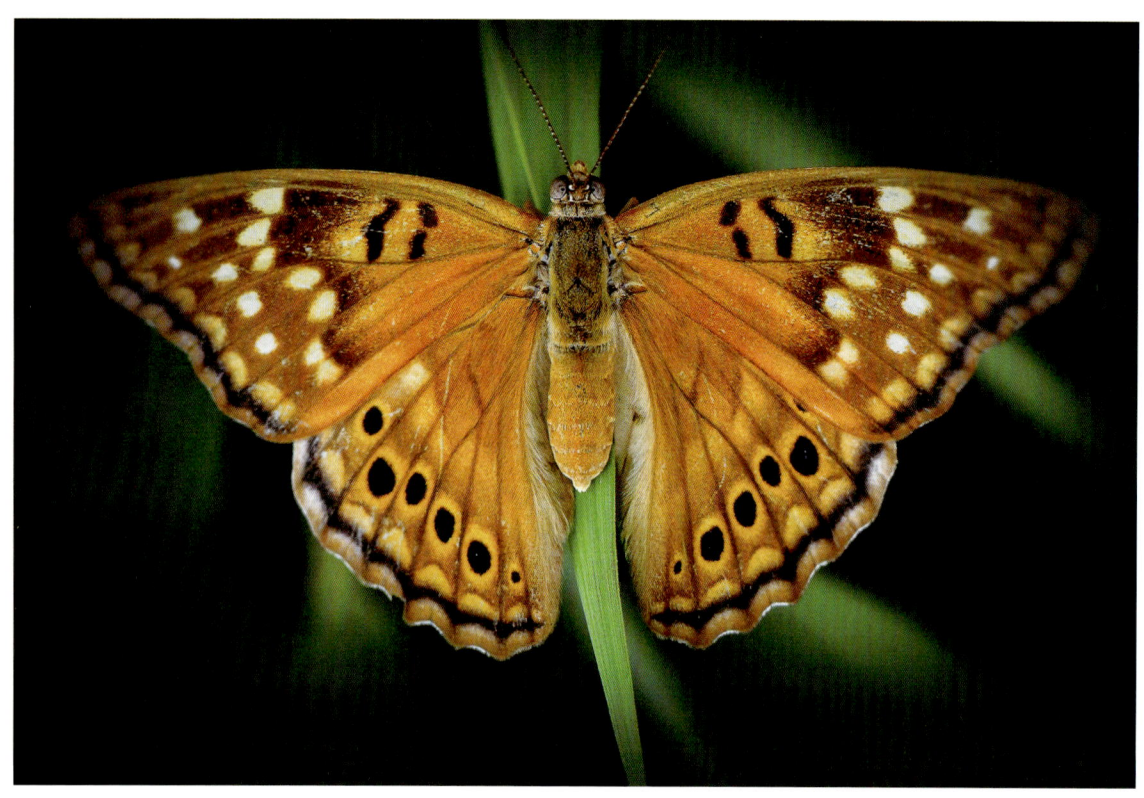

Some creatures simply exude beauty, and while I do my utmost to capture it with my camera lens, nothing compares to viewing life with your own eyes, as an image will only leave you wanting for more.

Above: Tawny Emperor Butterfly, Texas /Nikon D300
Opposite: Flamingo, Florida /Nikon D300

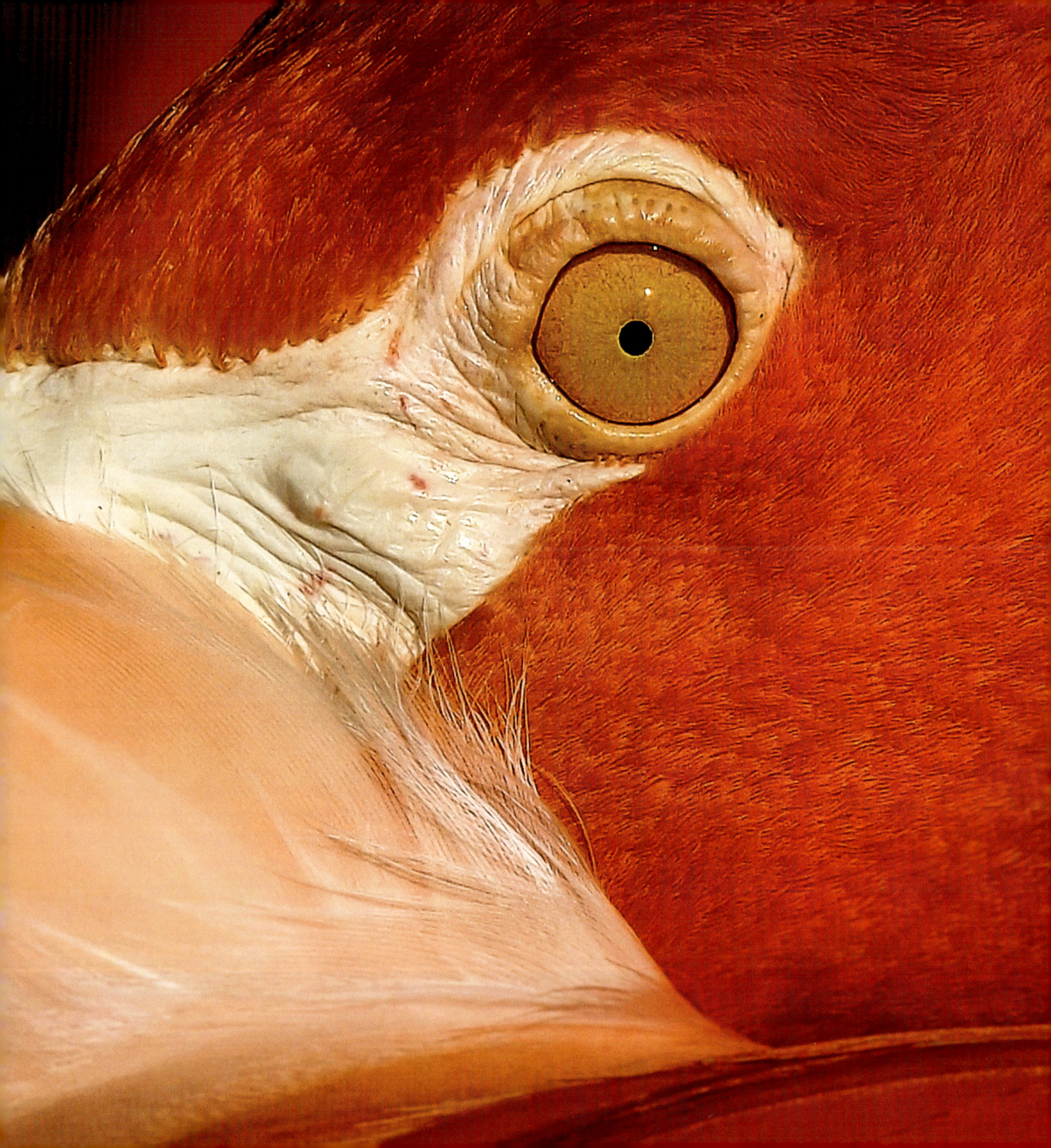

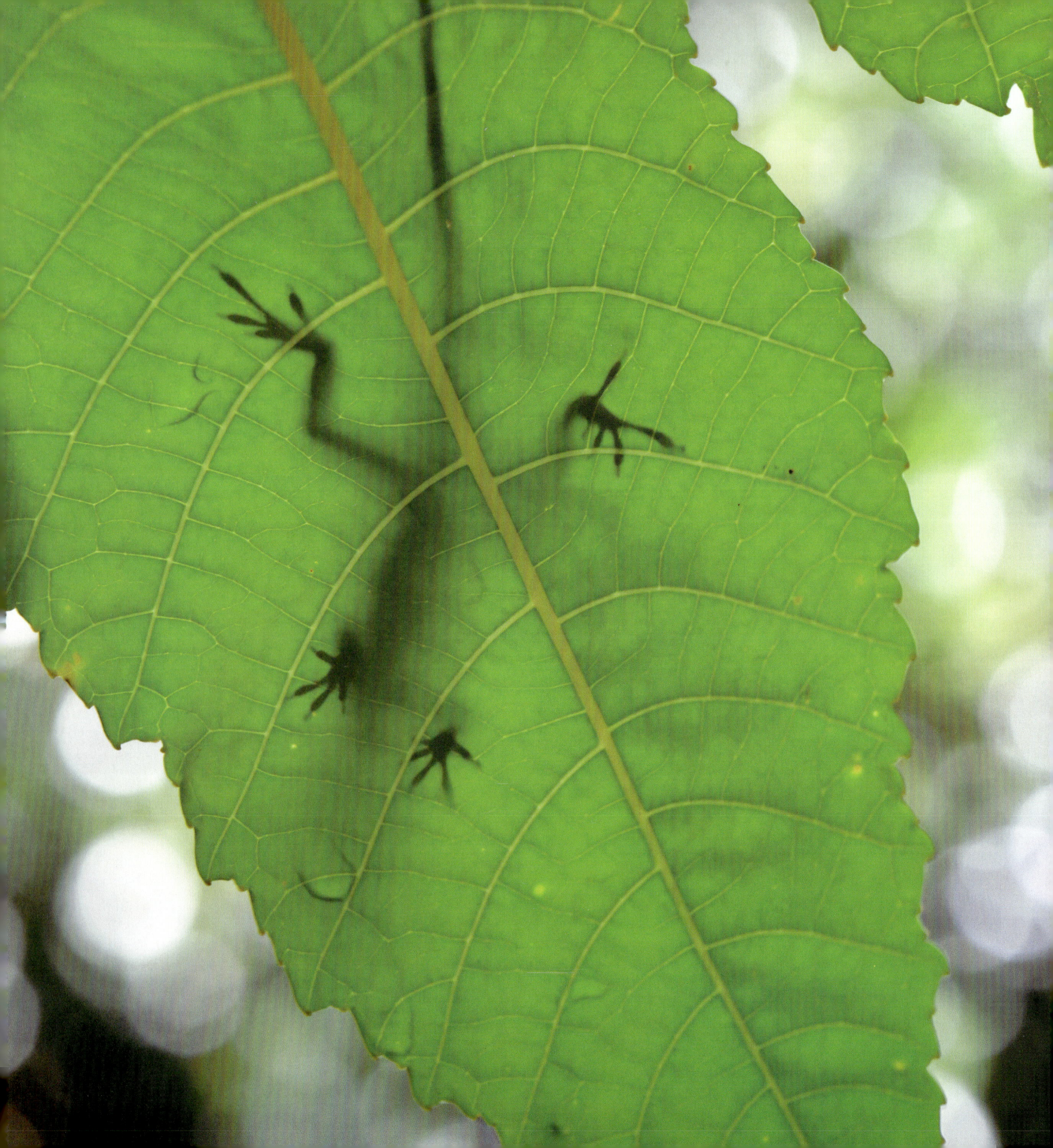

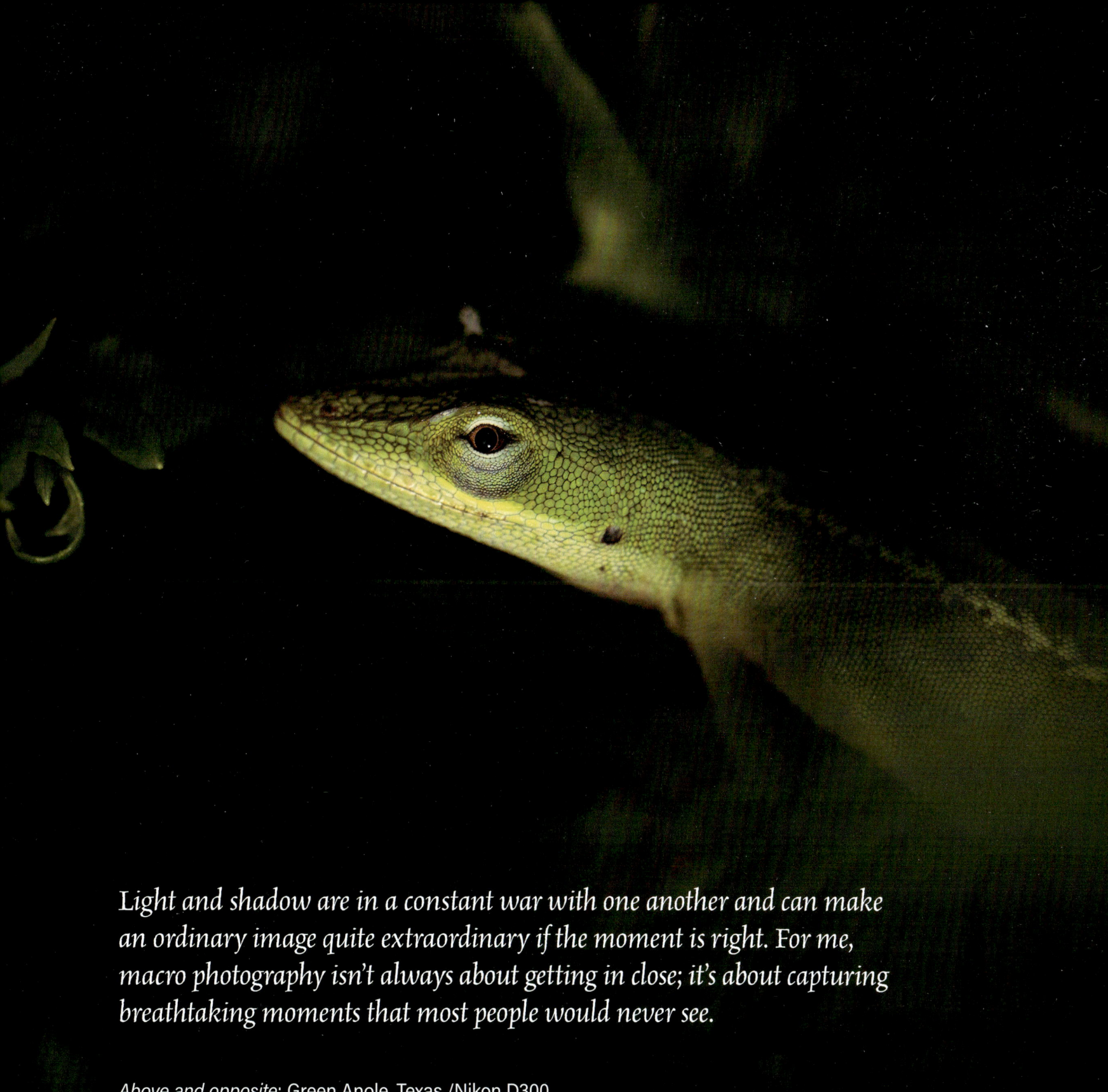

Light and shadow are in a constant war with one another and can make an ordinary image quite extraordinary if the moment is right. For me, macro photography isn't always about getting in close; it's about capturing breathtaking moments that most people would never see.

Above and opposite: Green Anole, Texas /Nikon D300

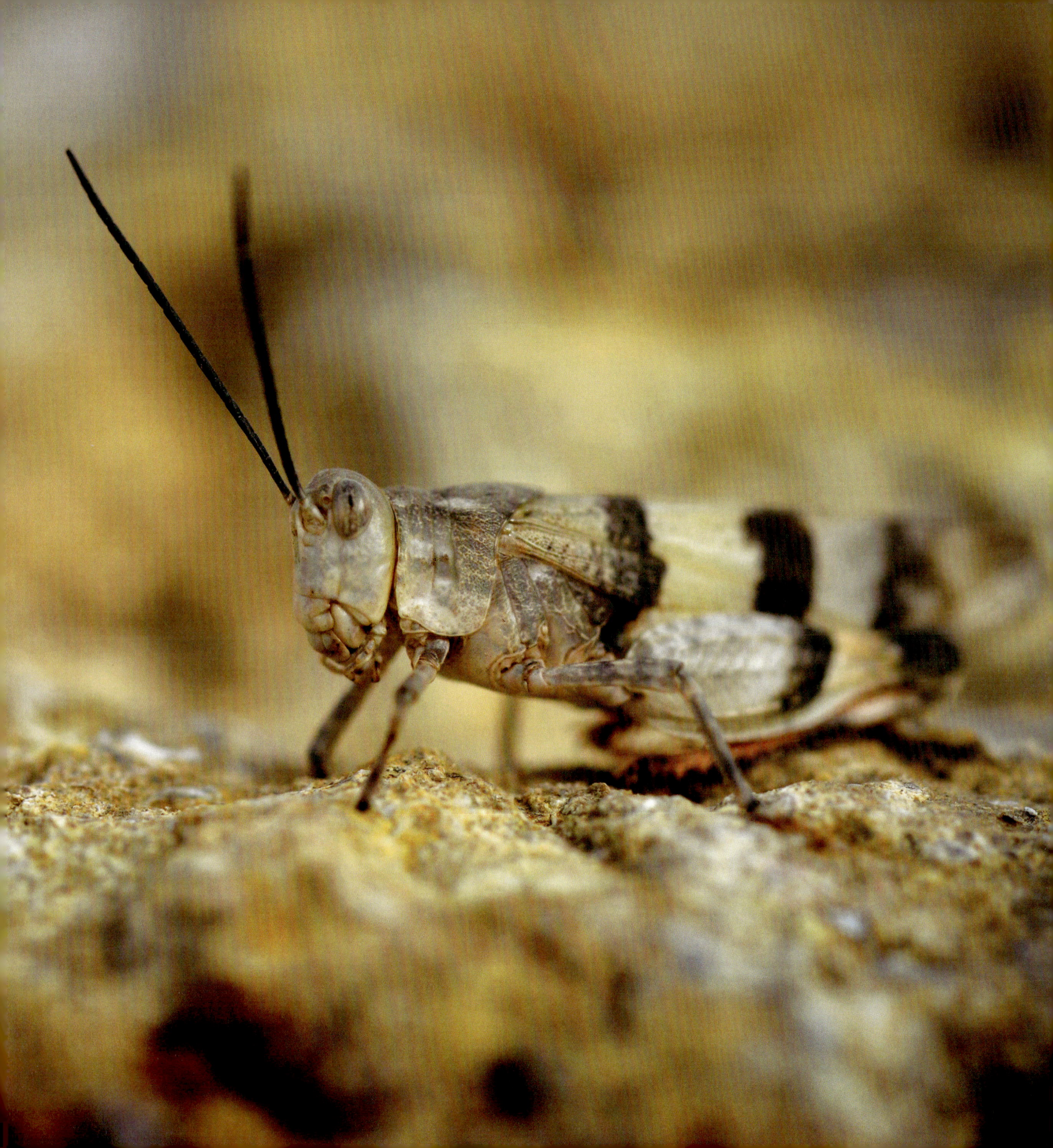

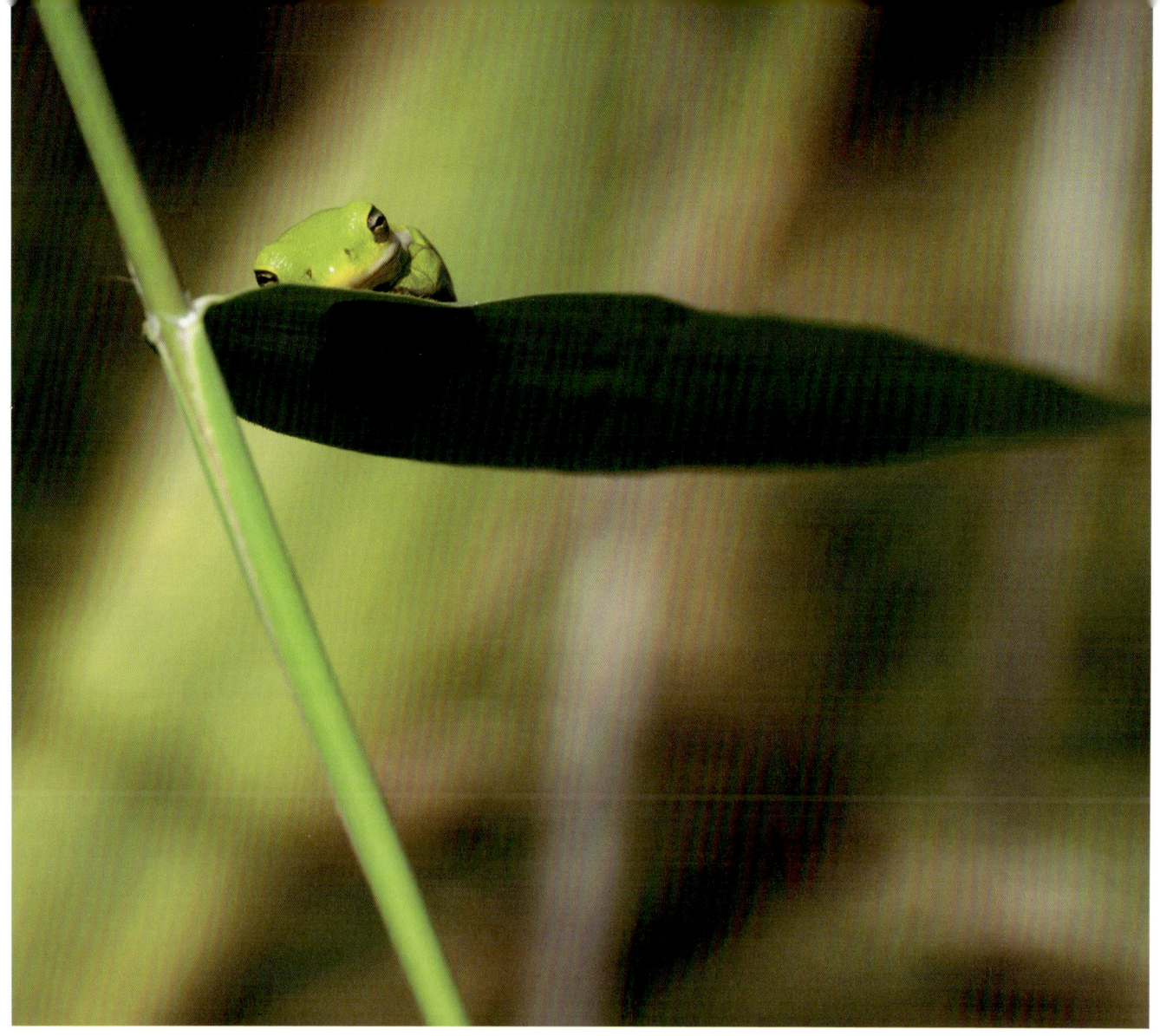

Camouflage is nature's best means of survival for many animal species, so being able to see camouflaged creatures can be difficult to say the least. The journey of discovery within the natural world can be challenging, but it can also enrich, enlighten, and entertain you in ways you cannot imagine.

Above: American Green Tree Frog, Texas /Nikon D600
Opposite: Grasshopper, Texas /Nikon D300

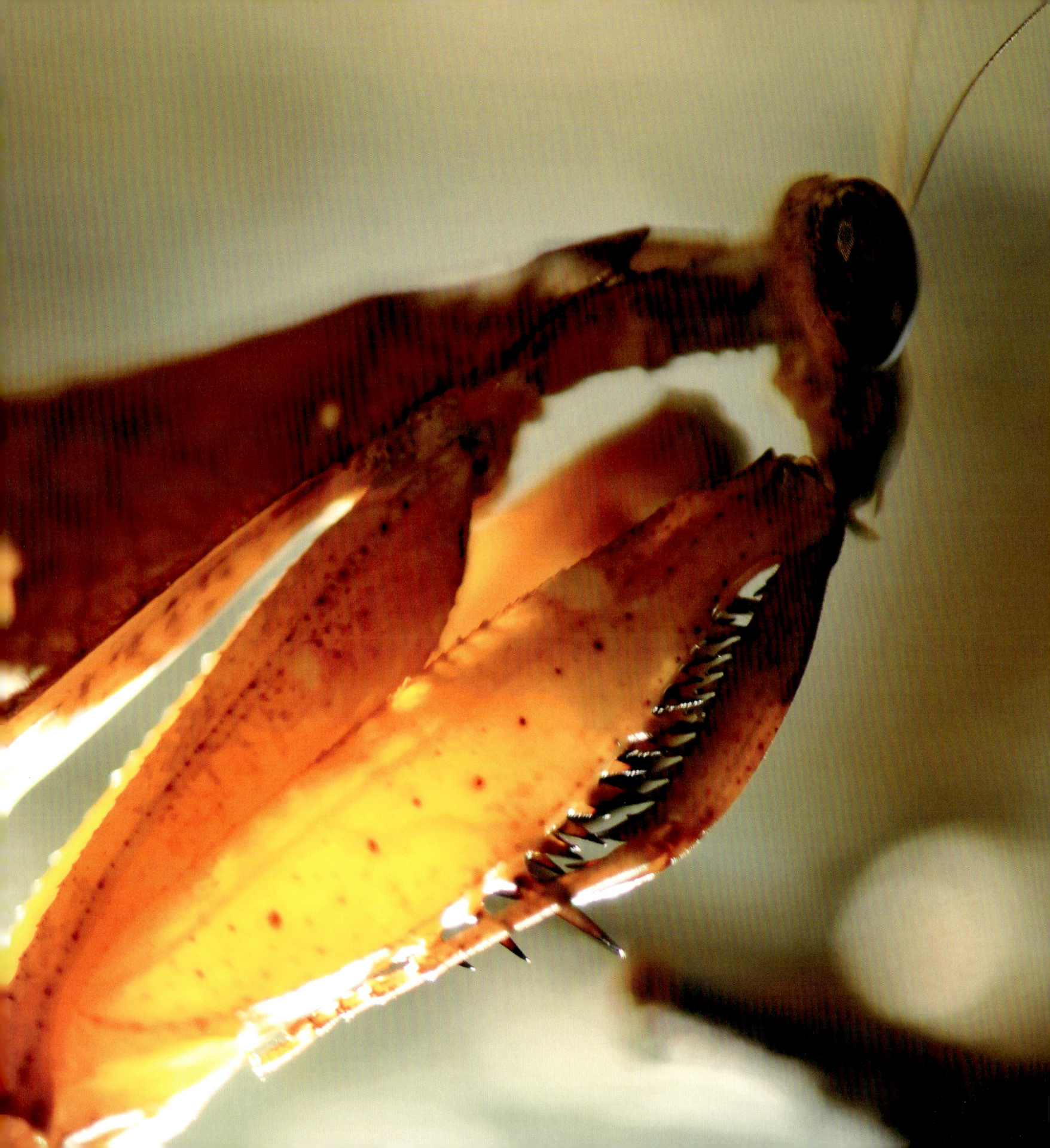

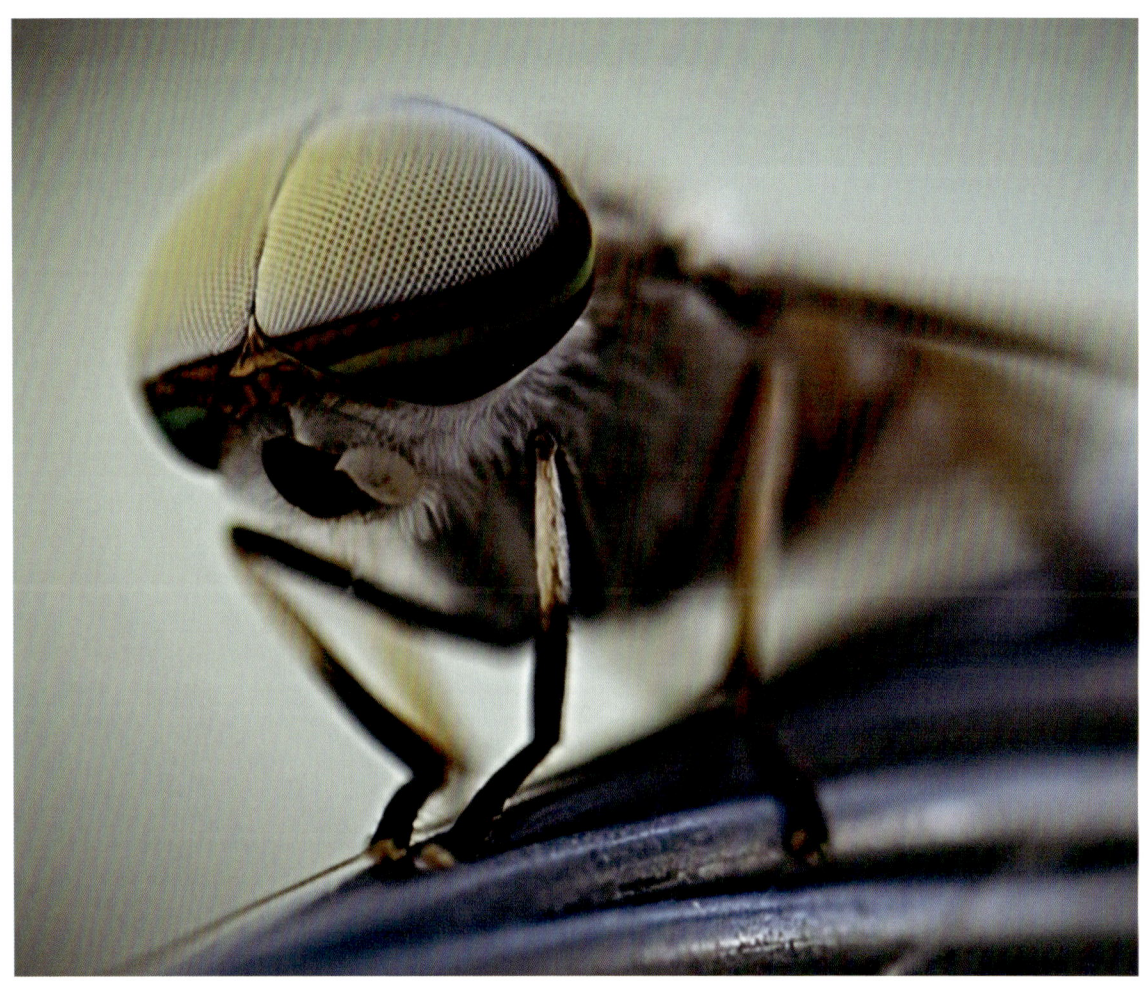

If ever there was an insect that piqued my interest and captivated my imagination, it would be the praying mantis. Its stealth, speed, and reflexes are unparalleled, and when one looks at you, it's difficult not to feel a little intimidated, despite its small size.

Above: Horse Fly, Texas /Nikon D810
Opposite: Praying Mantis, Texas /Nikon D300

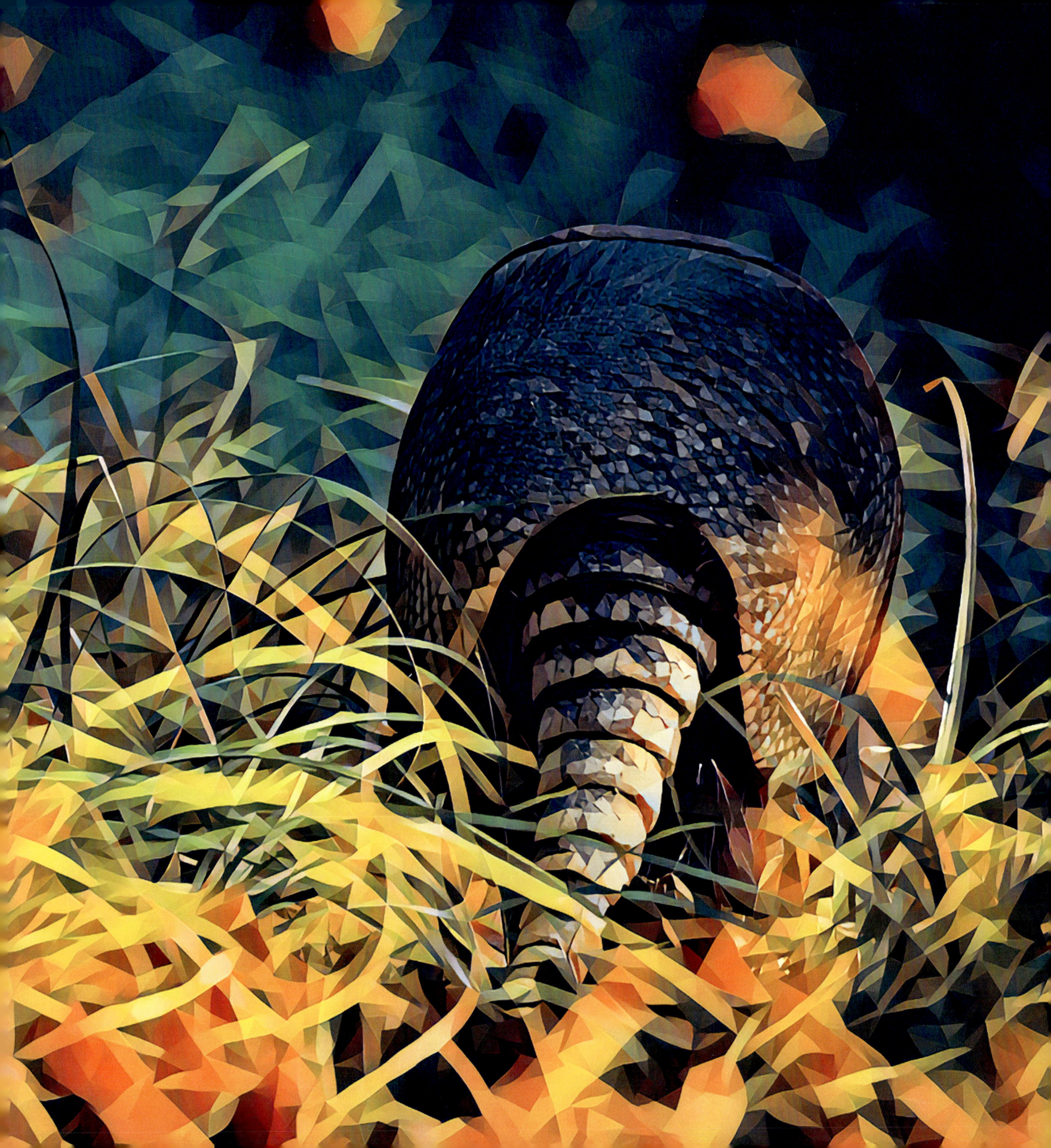

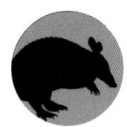

TEXAS WILD

Texas is a land of legend, plenty, and extremes. Where the Old West began, and historic figures such as Davey Crockett, Sam Houston, and James Bowie still resonate in the hearts of many Texans, both young and old. As the saying goes, "Everything's BIGGER in Texas," and they ain't kidding! From the Pine Curtain in the east to the majestic Guadalupe Mountains in the west, the Texas landscape stretches over 268 thousand square miles. It is a wondrous place of natural beauty, rich in wildlife, which on occasion produces dramatic weather patterns that will undoubtedly test your "True Grit" like no other place on Planet Earth! Winter and spring thunderstorms feed the rivers and dry tributaries that thirst for water for most of the year, producing fields of Texas wildflowers, providing vital sustenance to the bees, bats, birds, and other pollinators we depend upon so dearly. Texas is home to over 540 species of birds, 142 species of mammals, amphibians, and other animals, highly diverse ecosystems and wildlife habitats like no other state in our great union. Migratory birds nest here in the hundreds of thousands each spring and use Texas as a resting stop each fall as they head back south for the winter. No image can ever replace "seeing wild" with your own eyes, but I am hopeful that my photography will transport you "Deep into the Heart of Texas," where I have been for so many years.

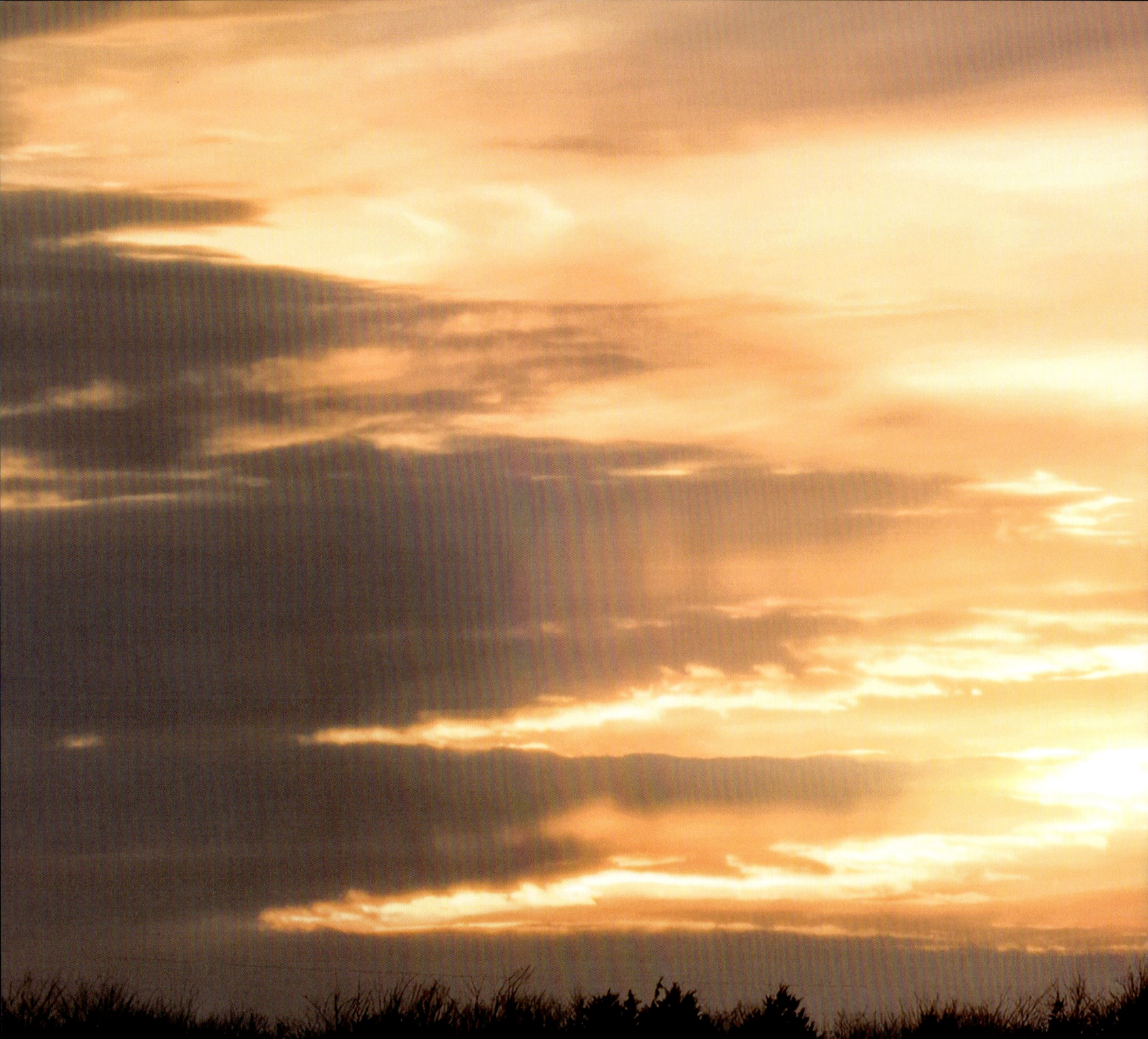

As the sun lowers into the western horizon of Texas, a small flock of white pelicans appears in the sky as they make their way toward their lakeside rendezvous for the evening.

White Pelicans, Texas / Nikon D810

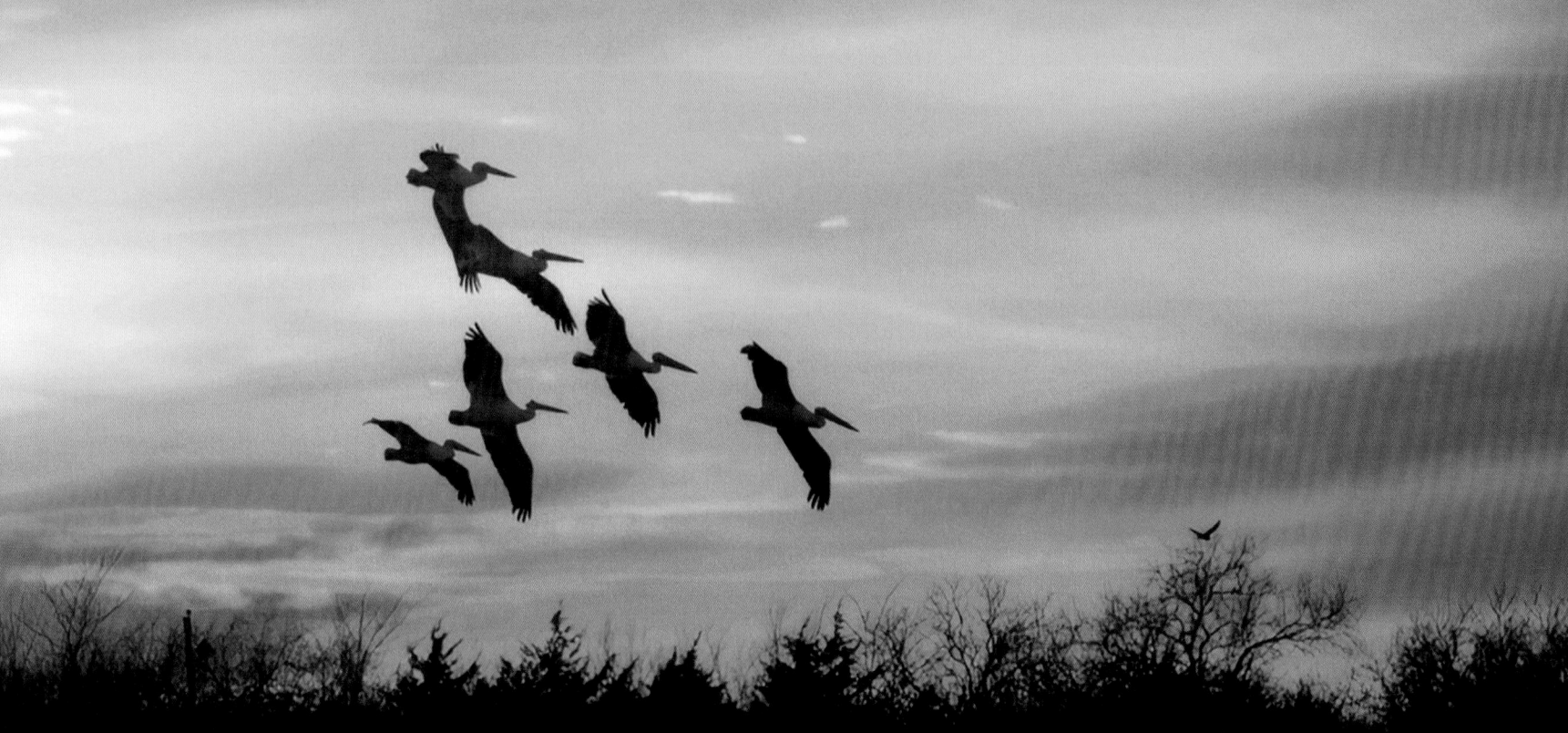

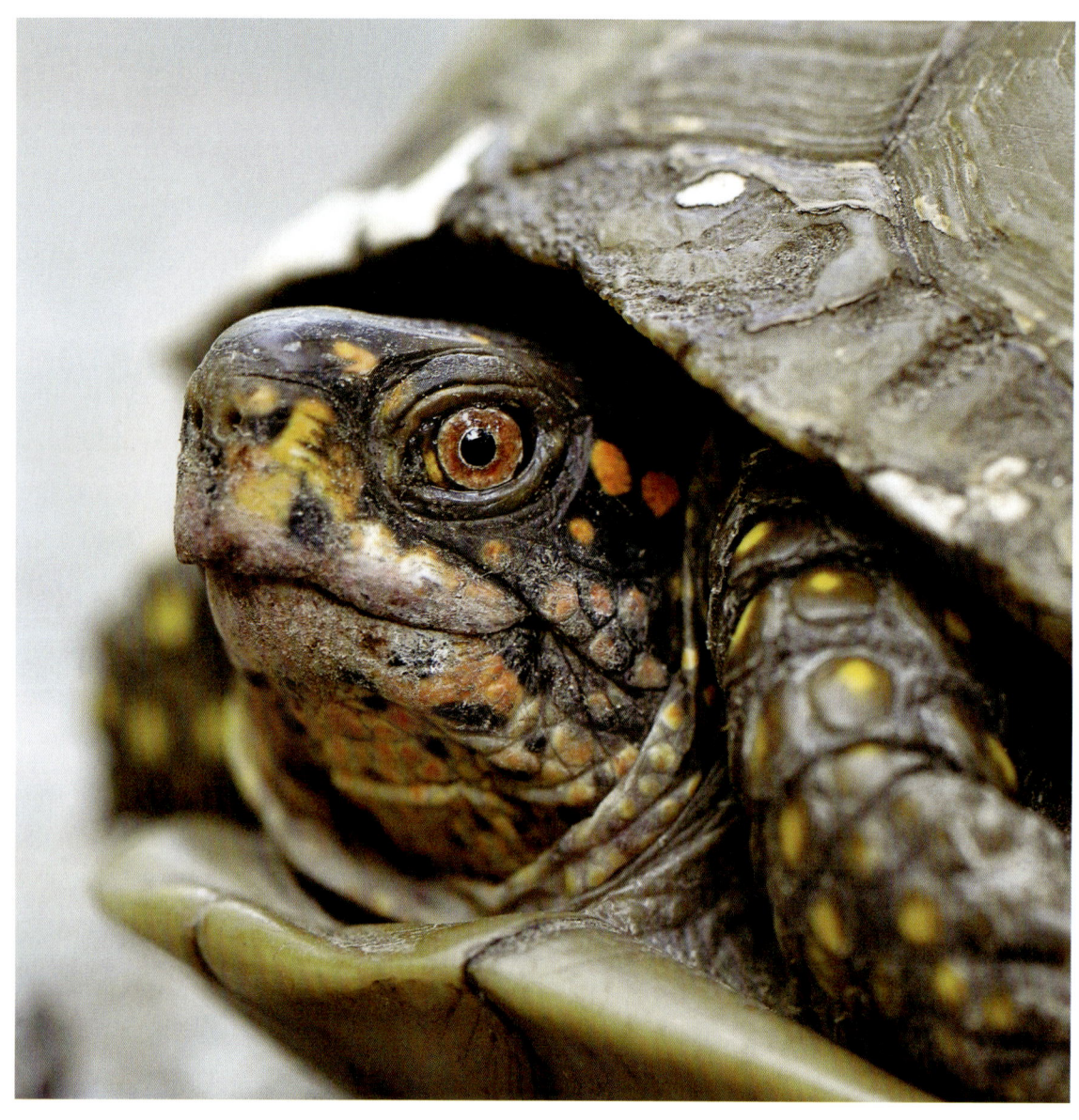

Two unique and distinct species, both exhibiting similar earth-tone coloration to allow them to blend into the natural world around them.

Above: Box Turtle, Texas / Nikon D810

Opposite: American Kestrel, Texas / Nikon D810

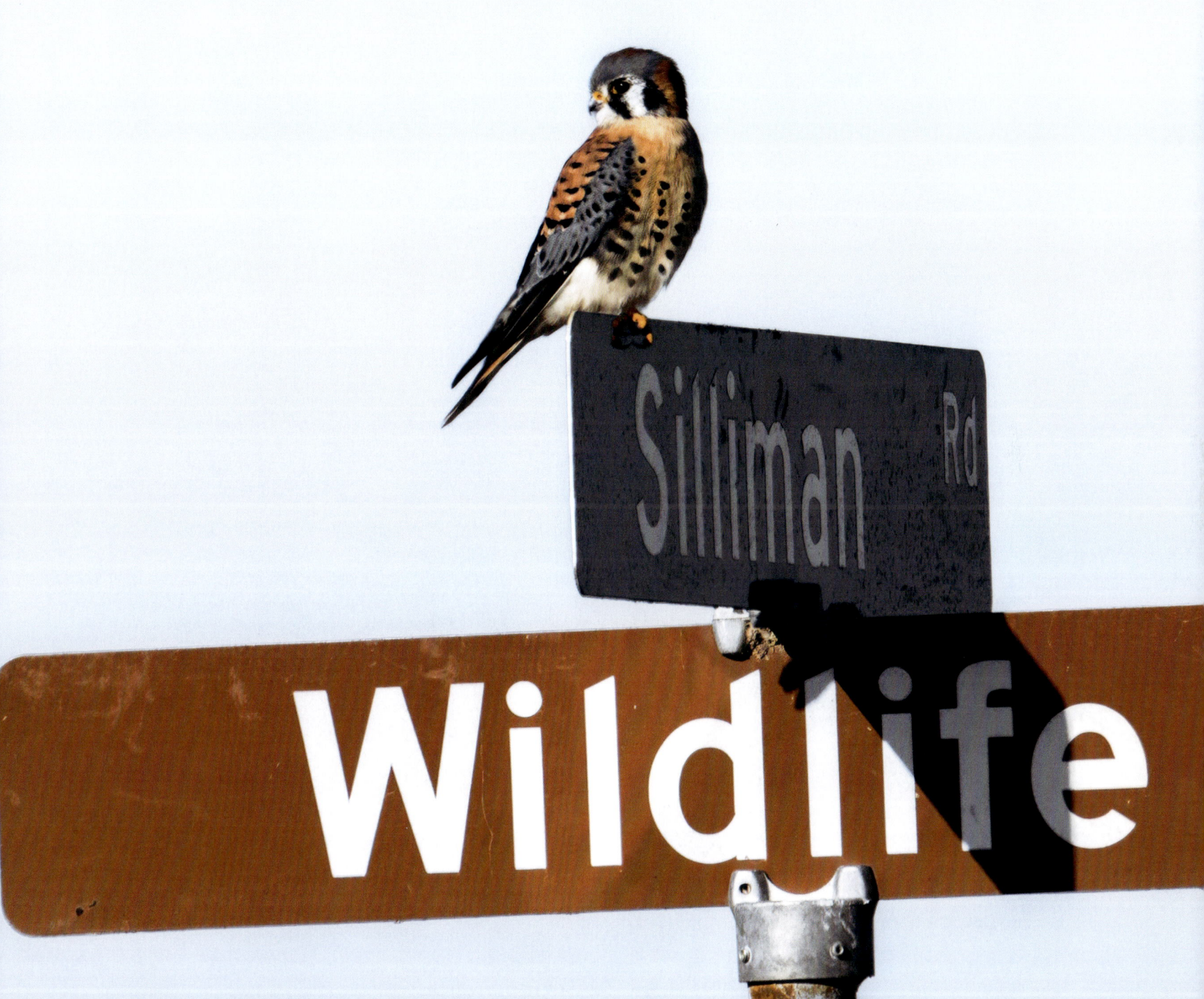

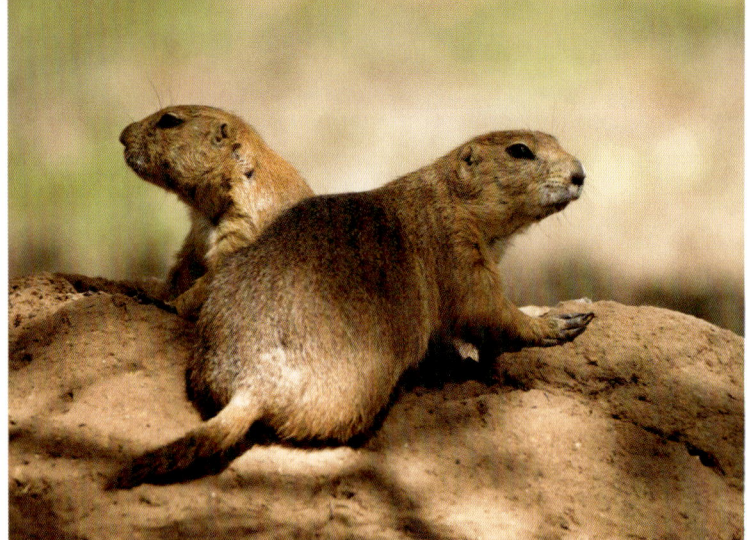

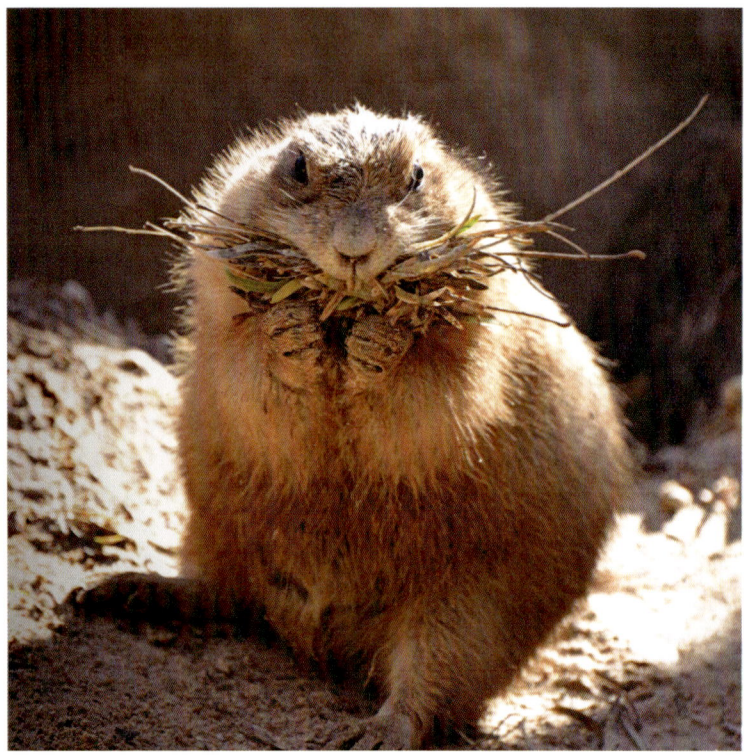

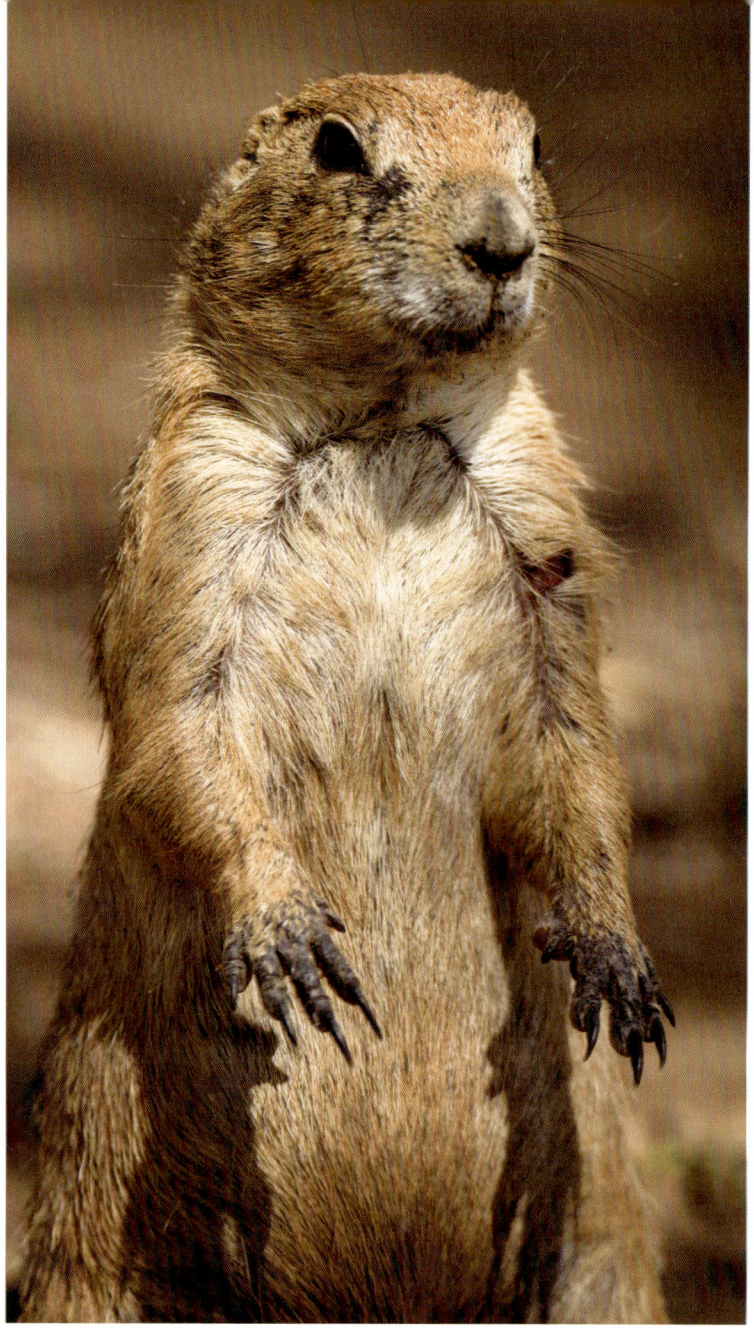

Always seemingly on the move and on high alert for danger, prairie dogs are symbolic of the American west. Their family frolics can lead one to spend countless hours simply observing and enjoying their company.

Above and opposite: Prairie Dogs, Texas /Nikon D600 & D810

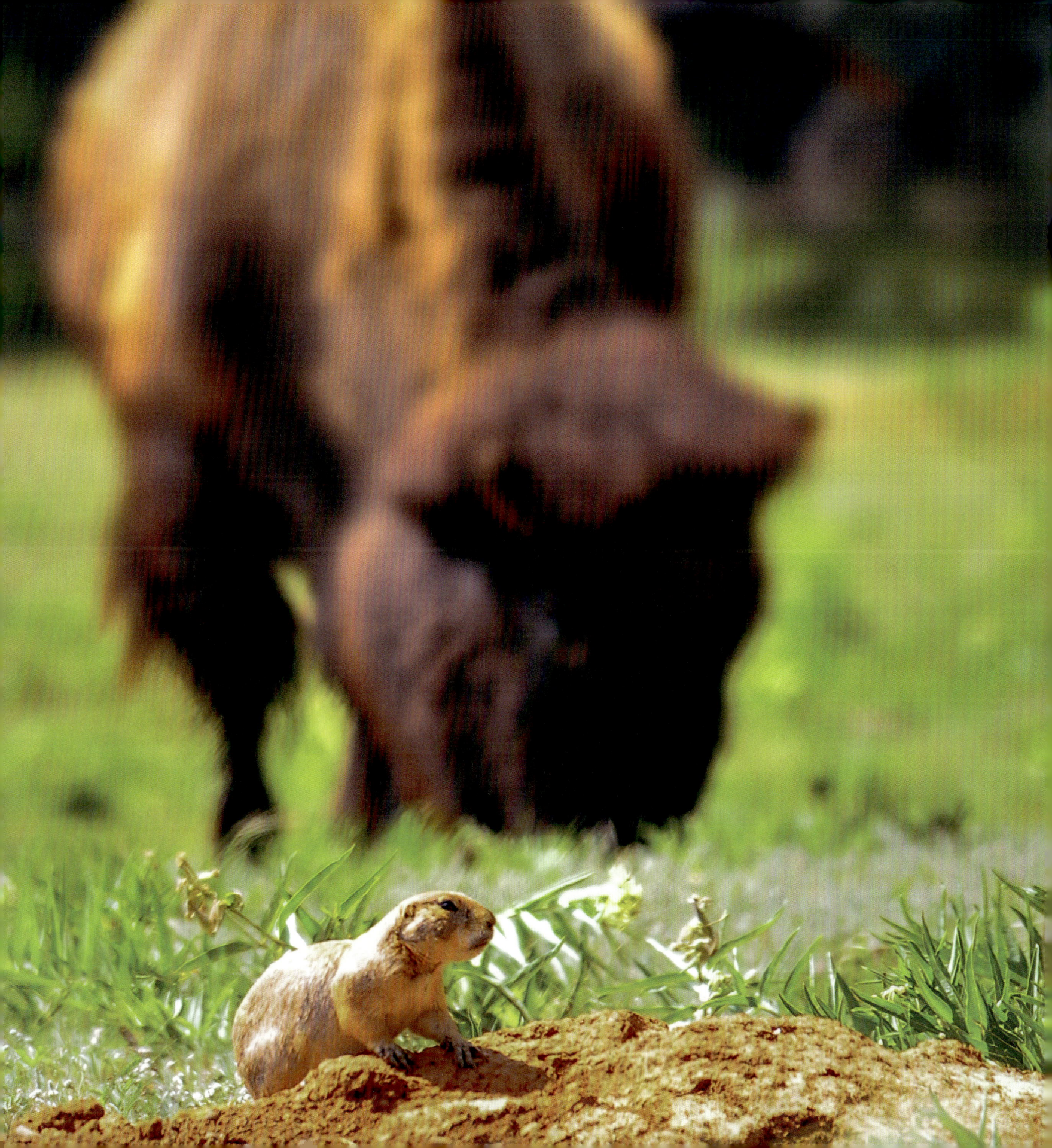

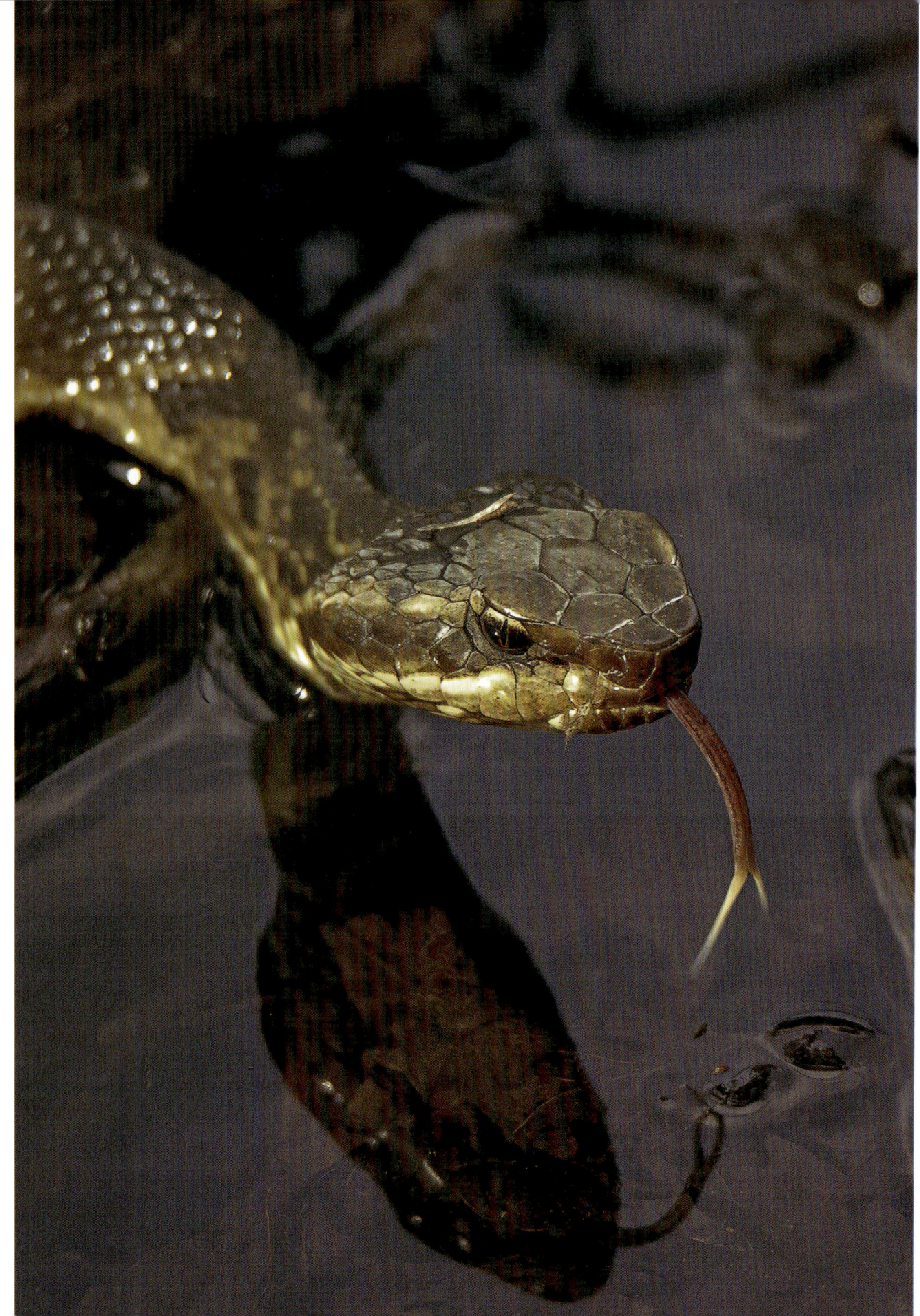

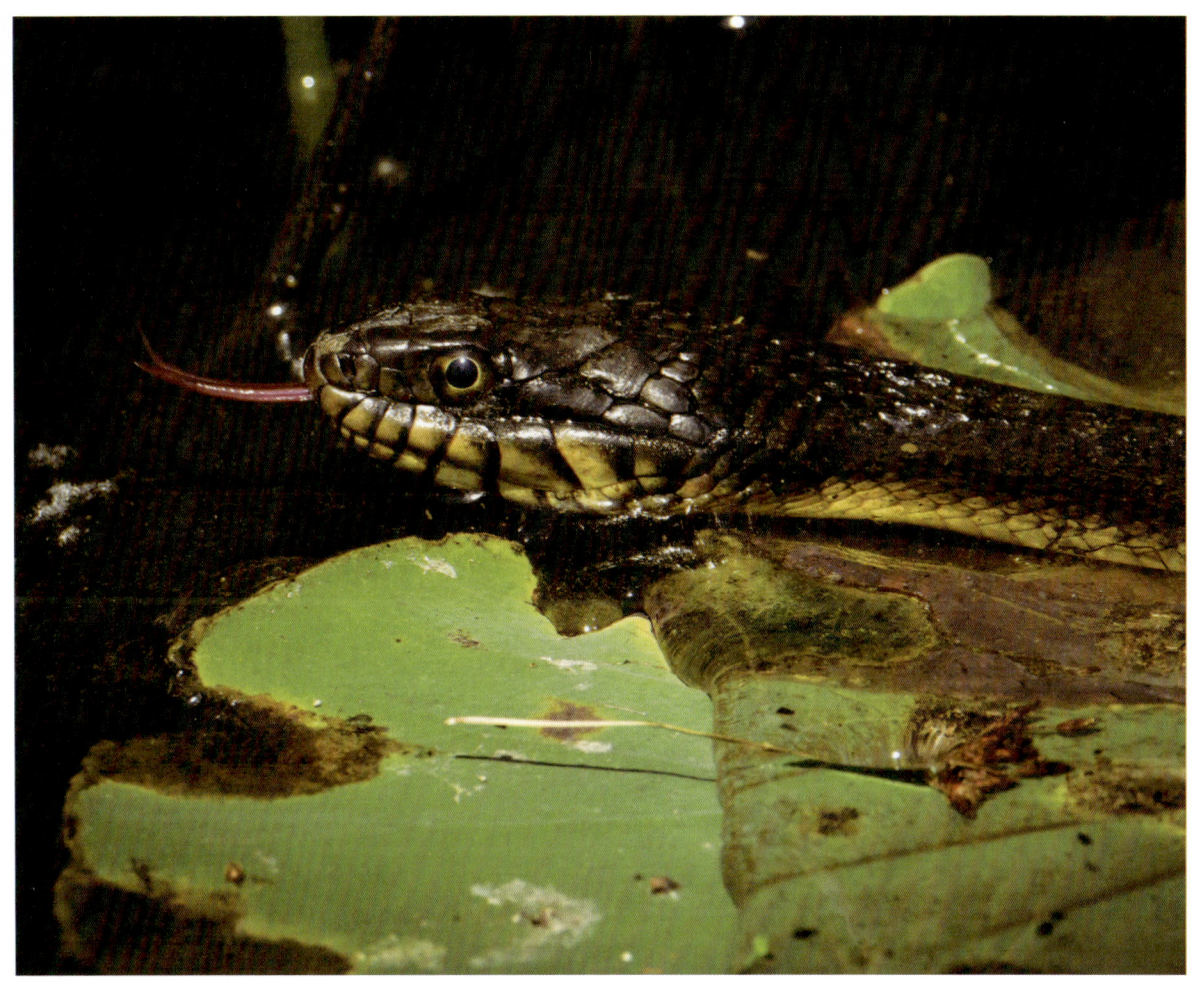

Although they frighten many people, snakes play an important role in the natural world, as their presence helps maintain a healthy ecosystem, and I, for one, enjoy observing them whenever I come across them.

Above: Yellow-Bellied Water Snake, Texas /Nikon D810
Opposite: Cottonmouth, Texas /Nikon D600

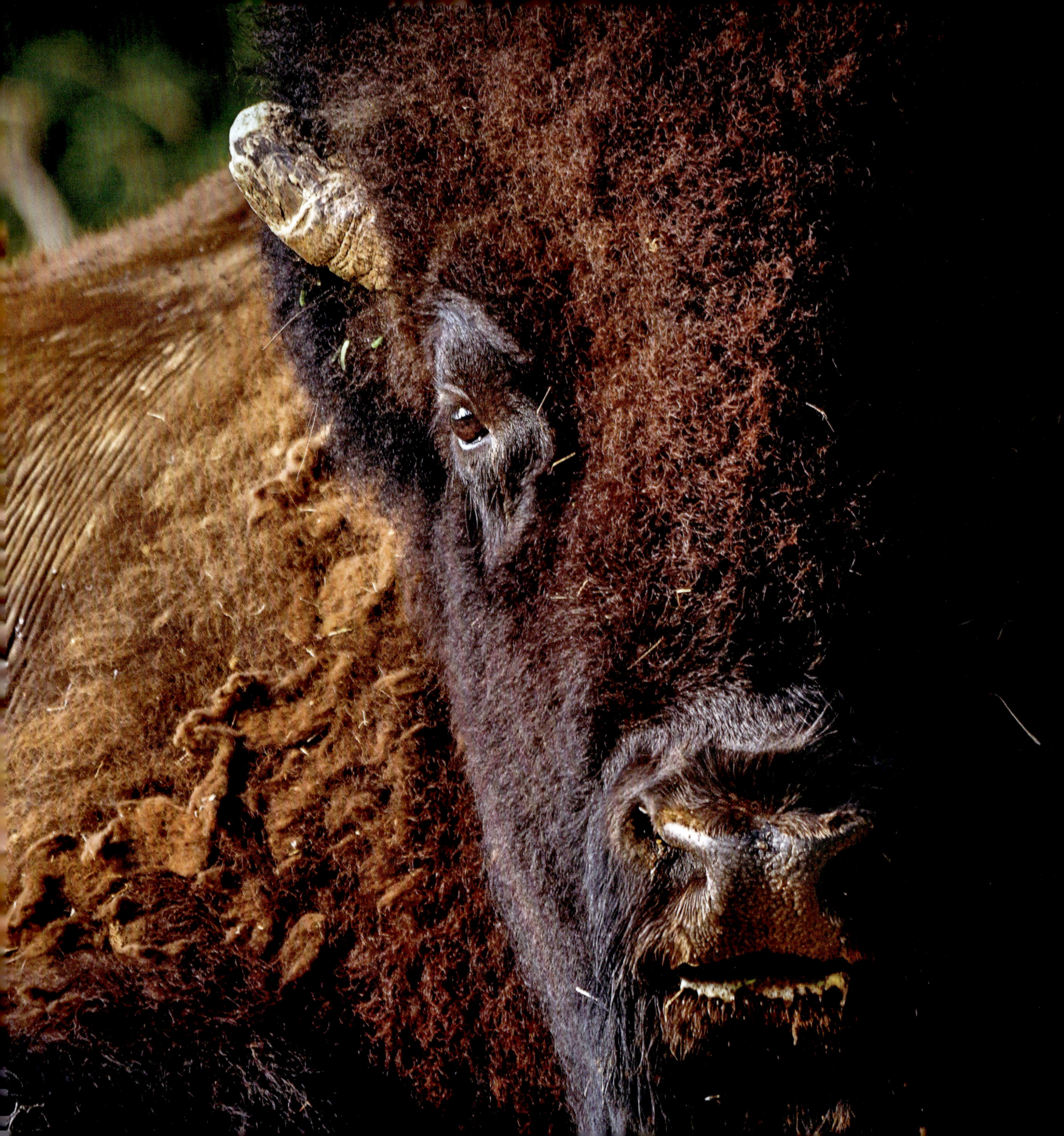

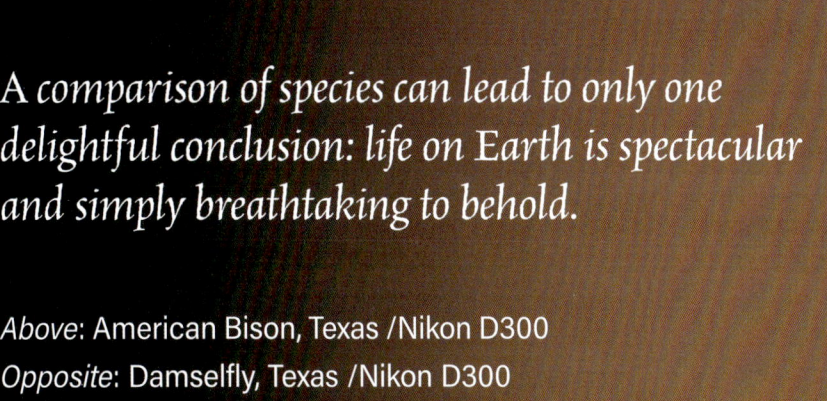

A comparison of species can lead to only one delightful conclusion: life on Earth is spectacular and simply breathtaking to behold.

Above: American Bison, Texas / Nikon D300
Opposite: Damselfly, Texas / Nikon D300

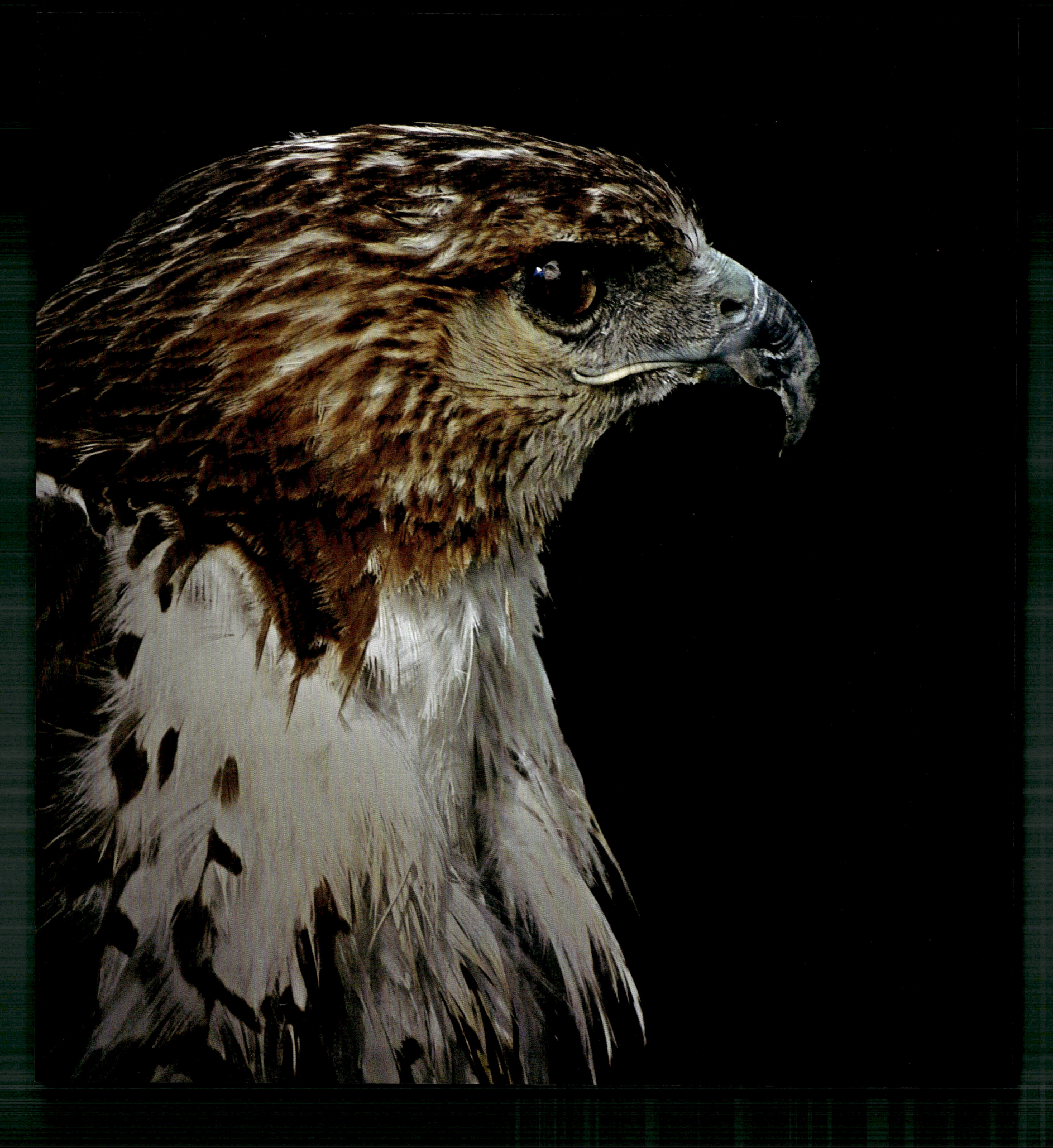

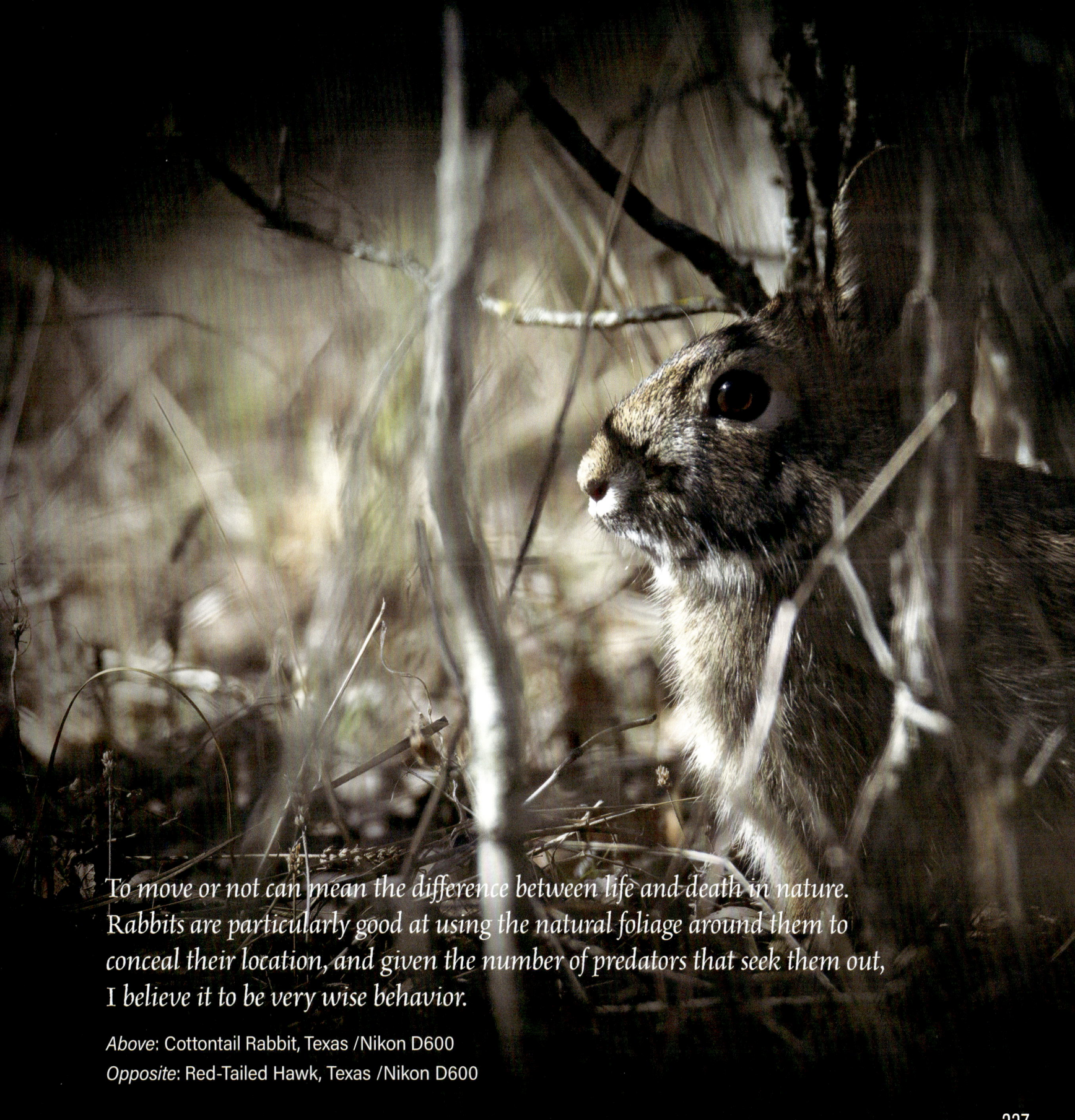

To move or not can mean the difference between life and death in nature. Rabbits are particularly good at using the natural foliage around them to conceal their location, and given the number of predators that seek them out, I believe it to be very wise behavior.

Above: Cottontail Rabbit, Texas /Nikon D600
Opposite: Red-Tailed Hawk, Texas /Nikon D600

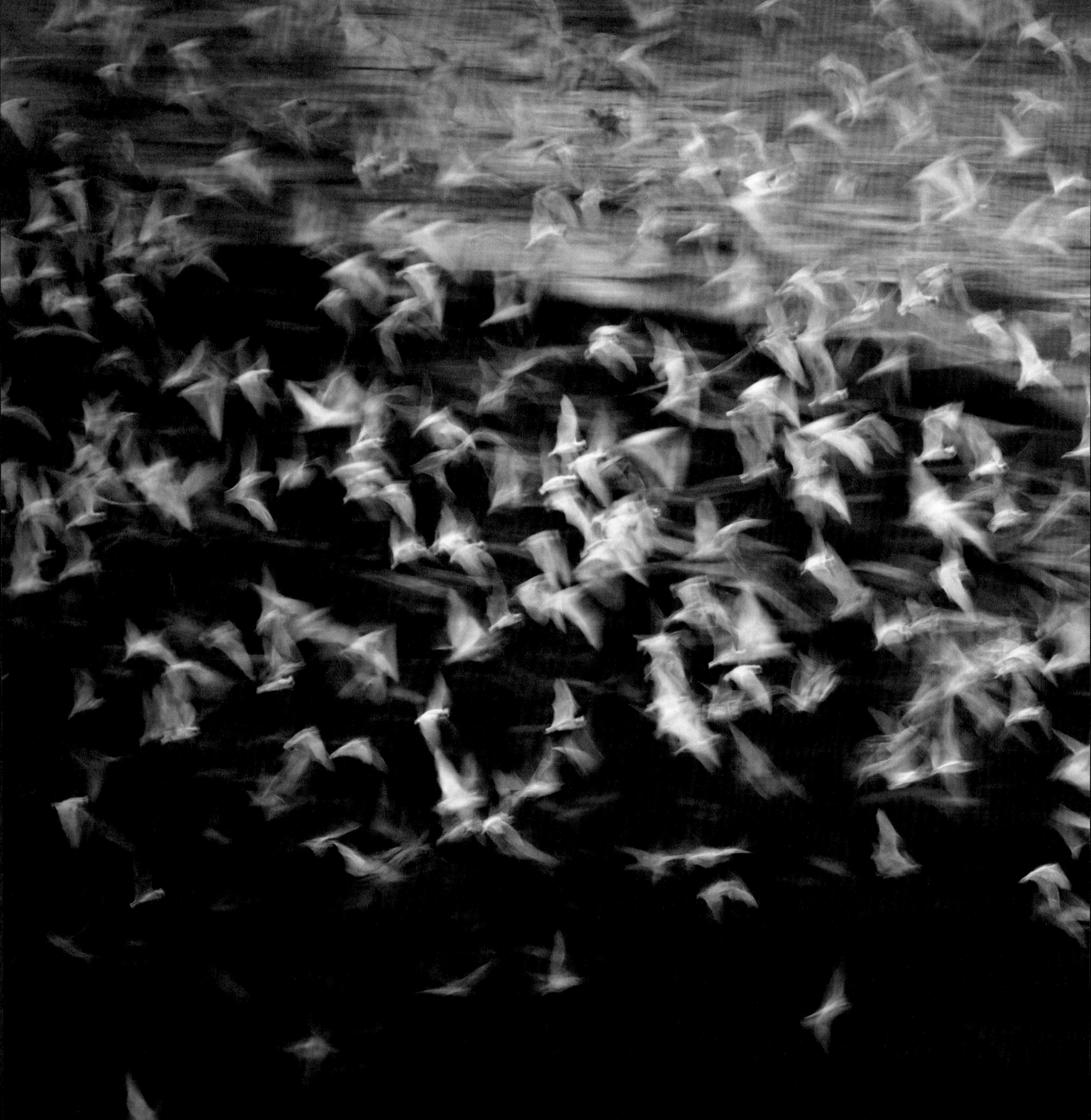

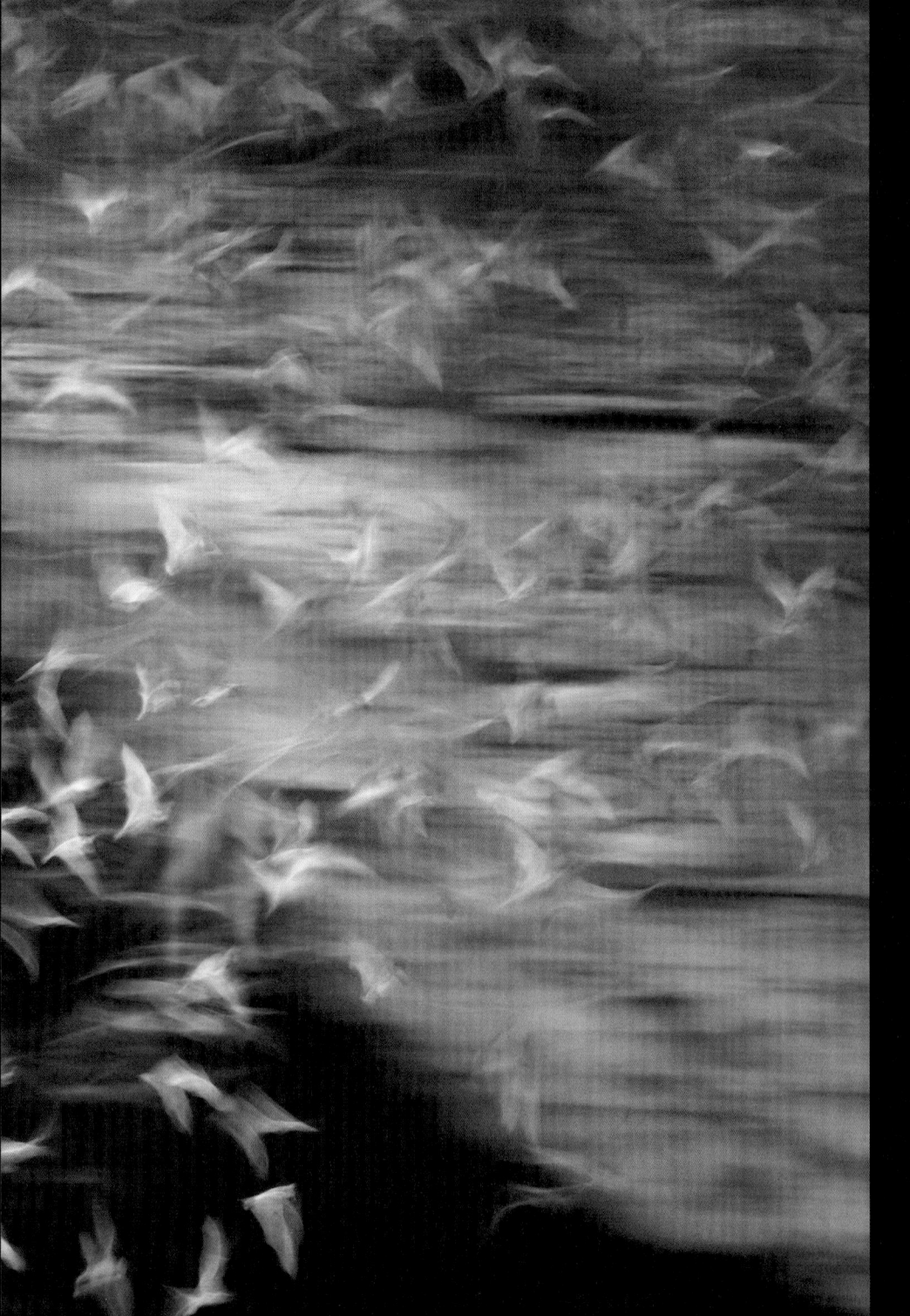

A long exposure reveals the incredible nightly exodus of millions of Mexican free-tailed bats into the surrounding Texas hill country. They will return by dawn, their hunger now satisfied after feasting on all manner of insects throughout the night.

Mexican Free-Tailed Bats, Texas / Nikon D600

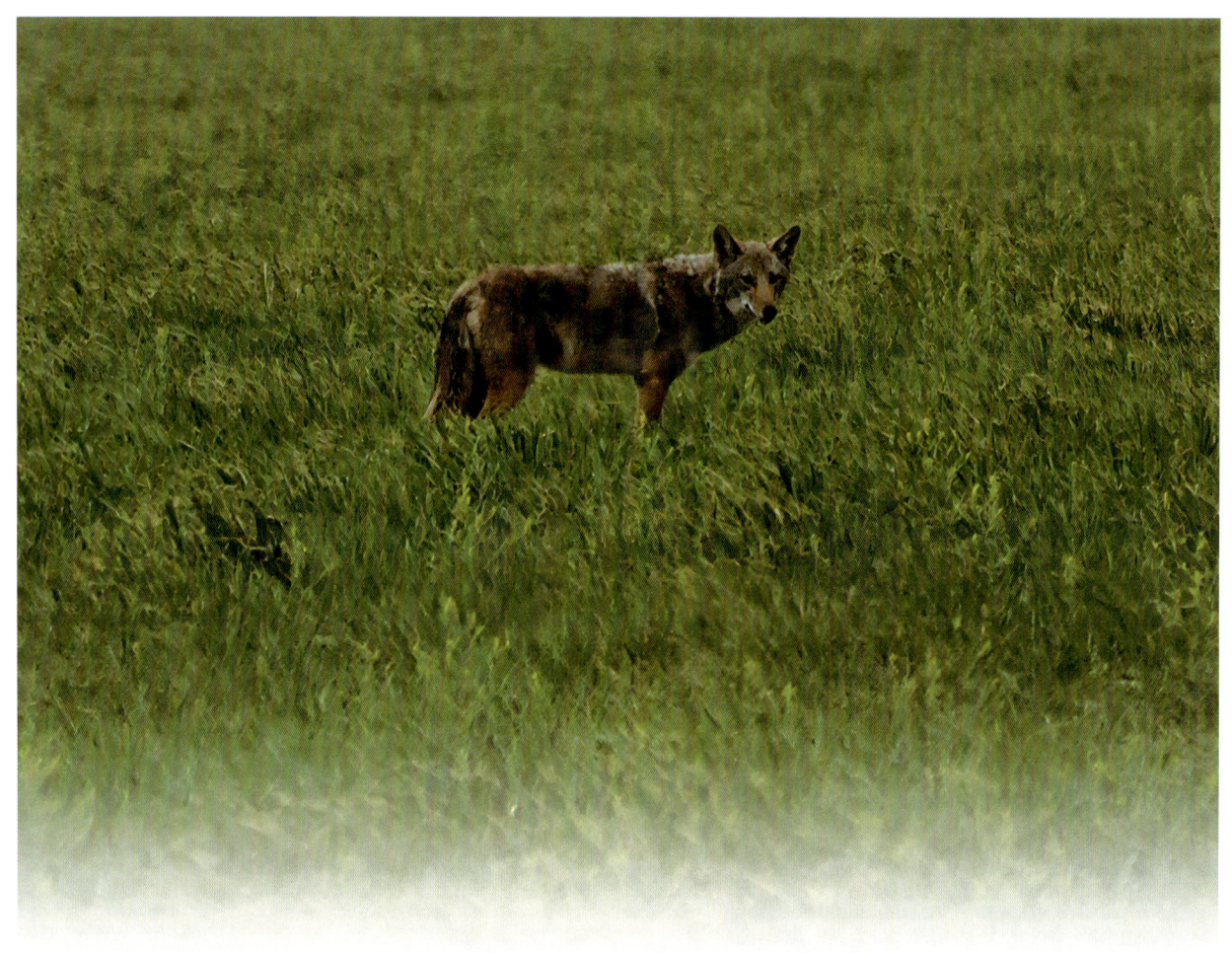

In a tale as old as Texas, the wily coyote takes aim at the ever-quick and ever-observant roadrunner, who is always, it seems, a step ahead no matter how hard he tries. "Beep beep!"

Above: Coyote, Texas /Nikon D300
Opposite: Greater Roadrunner, Texas /Nikon D810

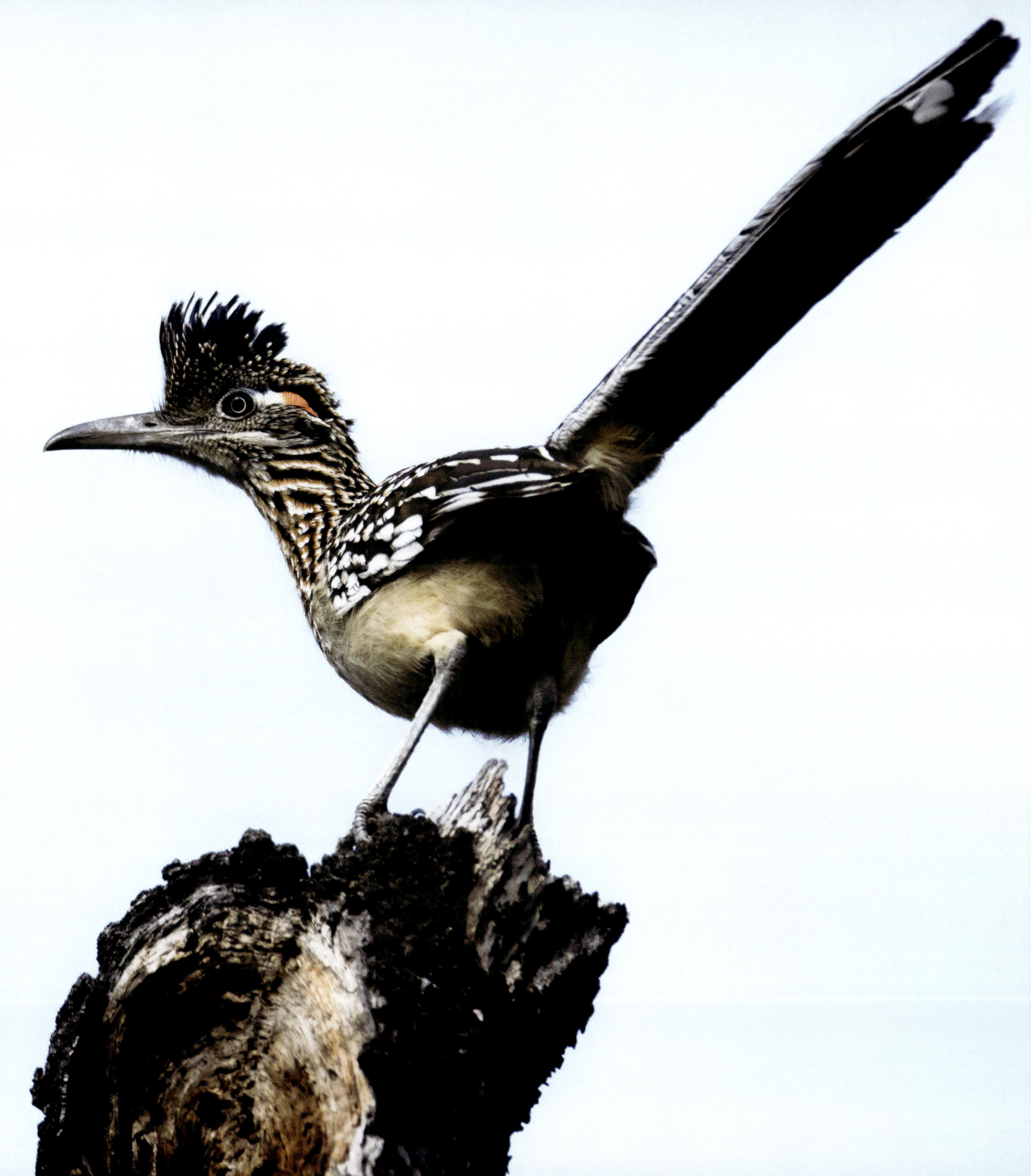

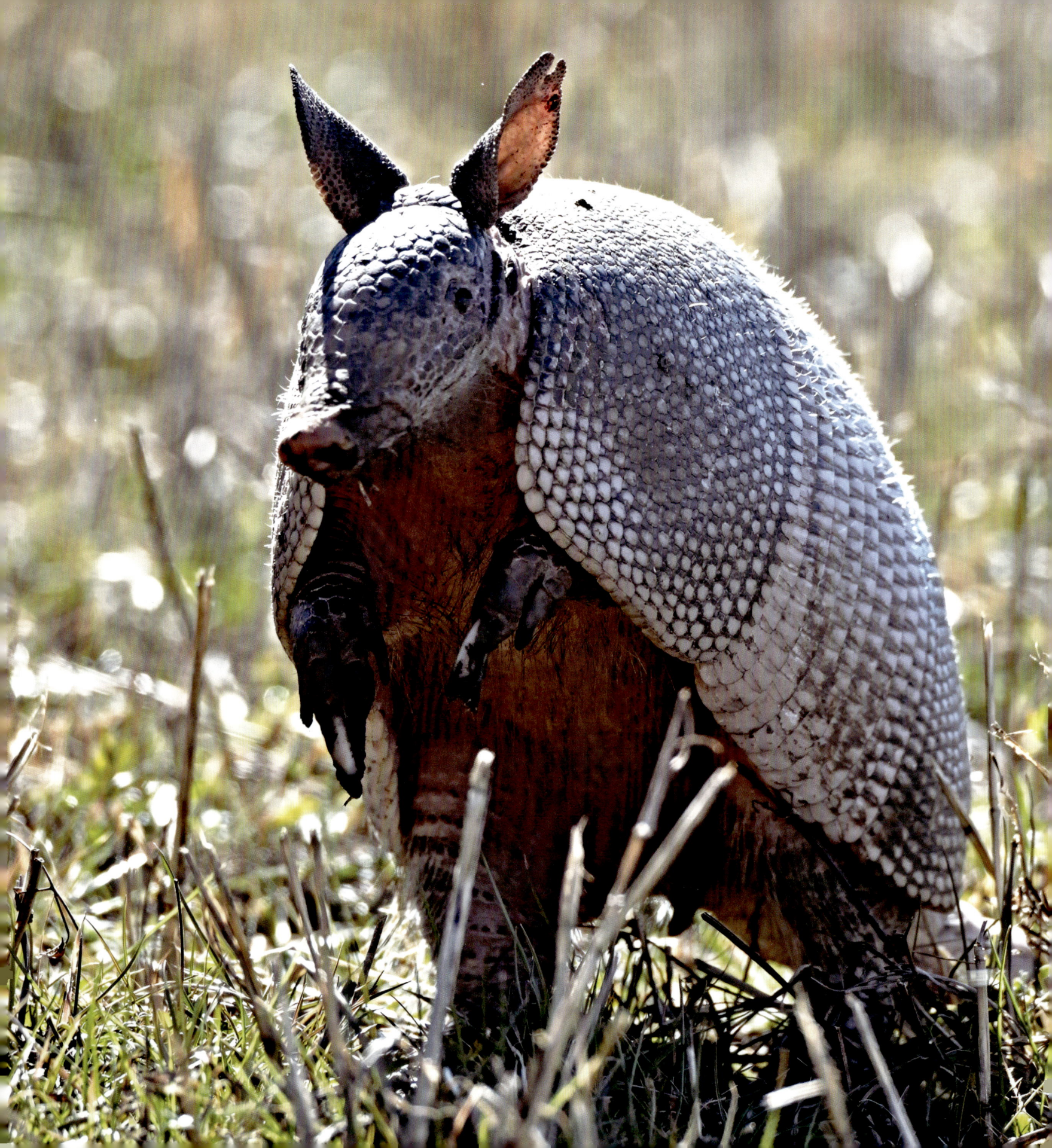

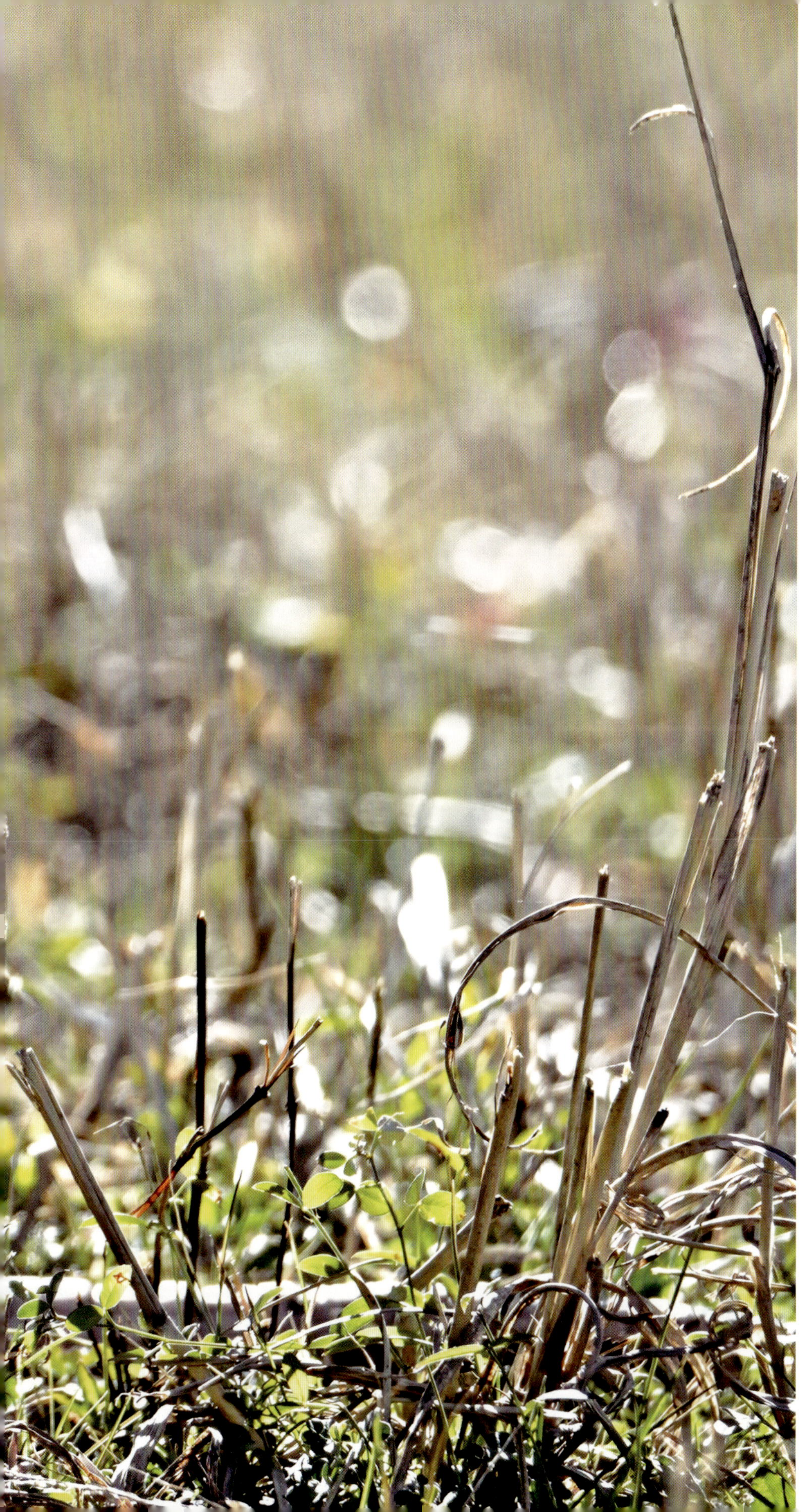

Her vision may be limited, but her sense of smell is extraordinary, alerting her to danger all around. Standing tall, she carefully tests the air, relying on her heightened senses to plan her next move.

Nine-Banded Armadillo, Texas / Nikon D600

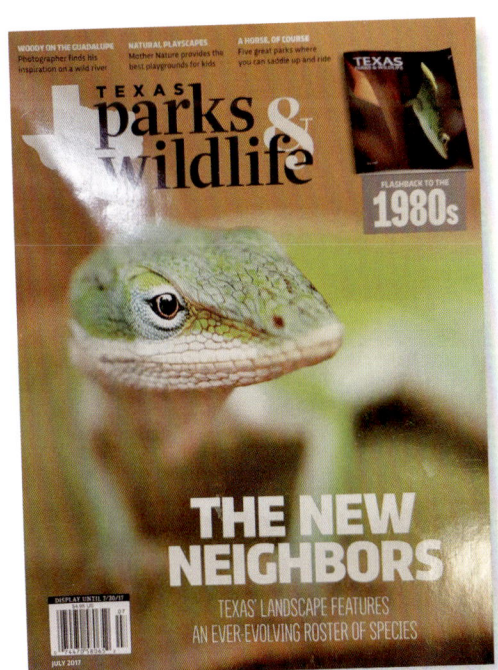

This image was published in *Texas Parks and Wildlife* magazine in the July 2017 issue.

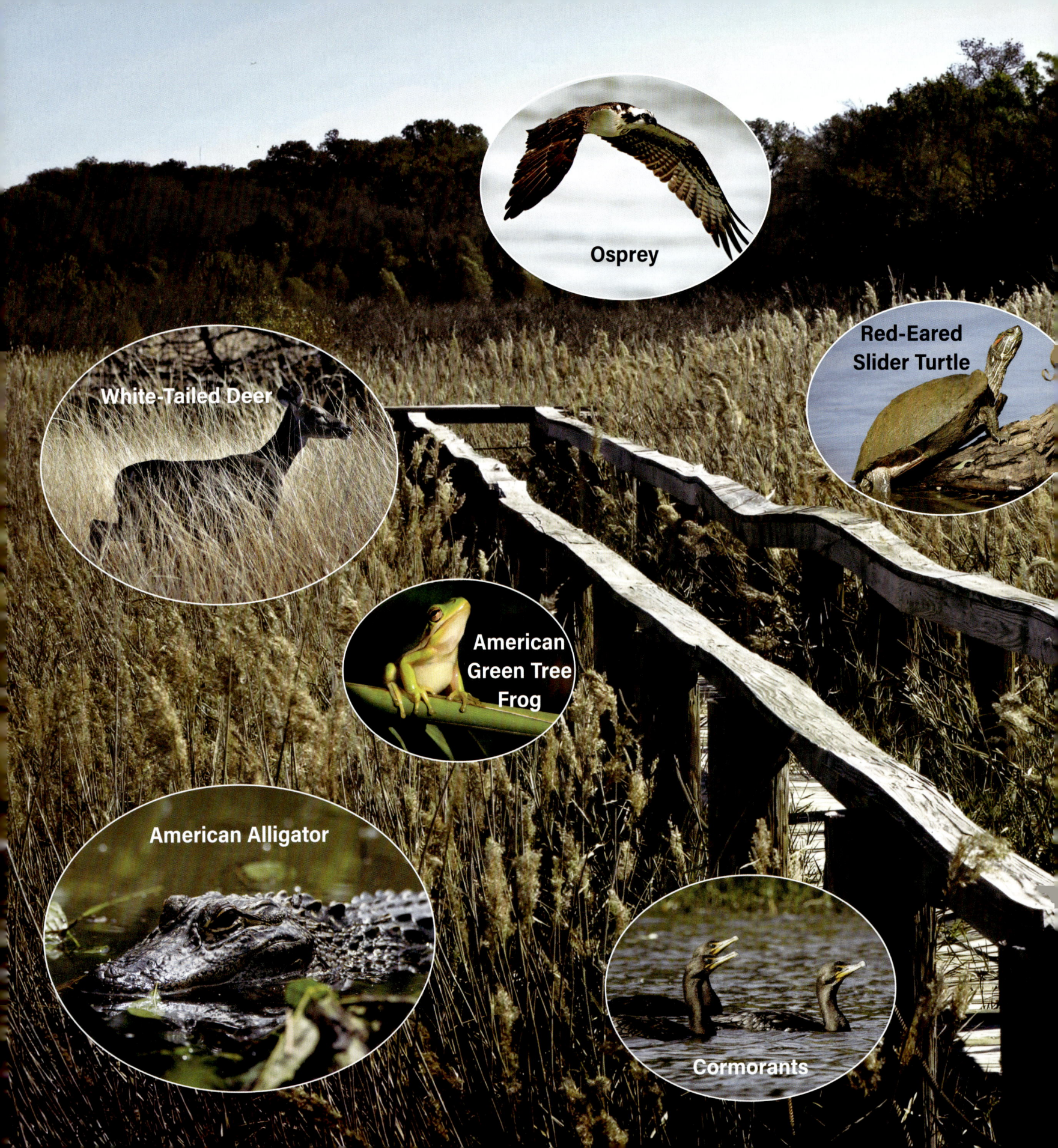

Osprey

Red-Eared Slider Turtle

White-Tailed Deer

American Green Tree Frog

American Alligator

Cormorants

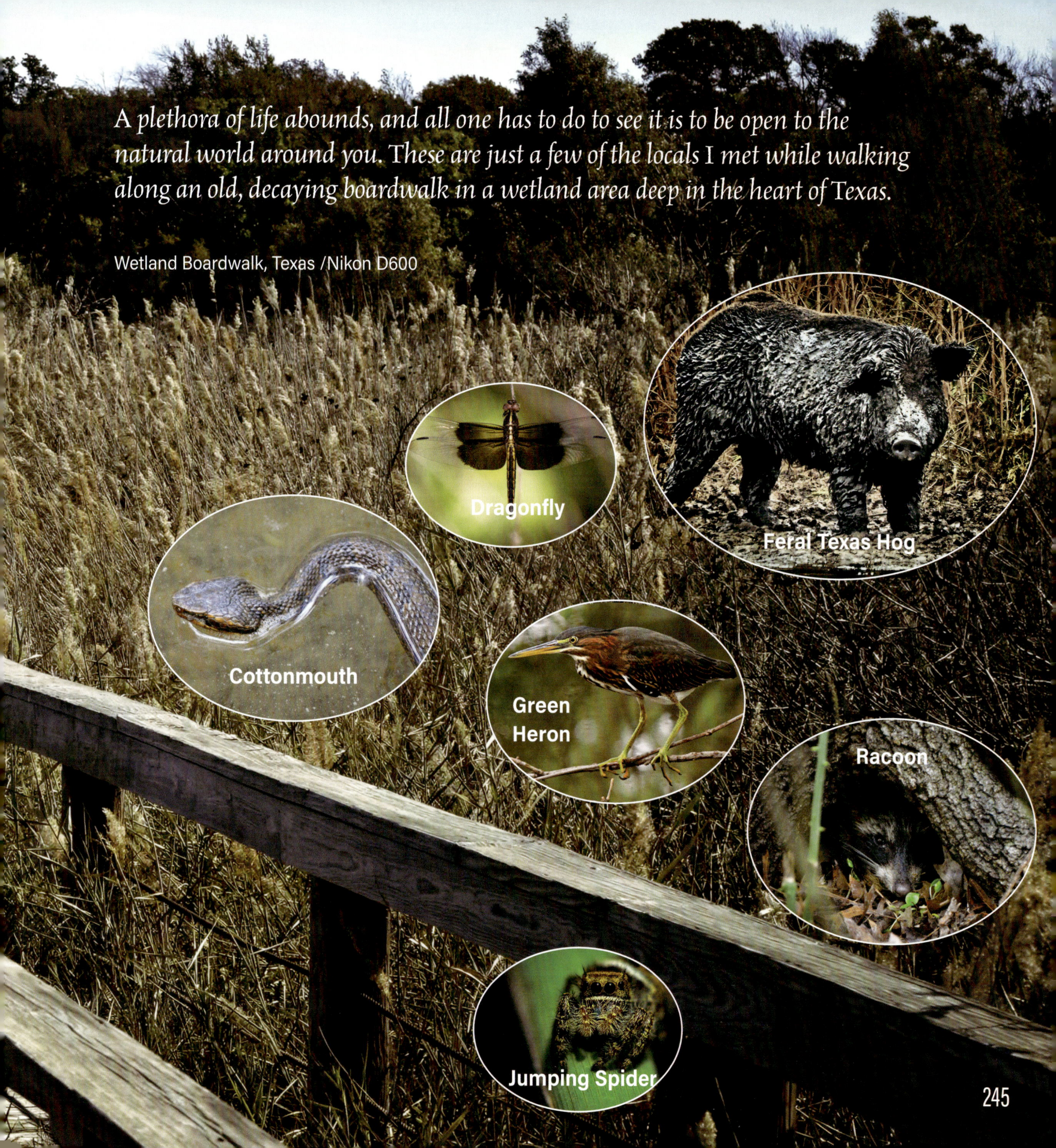

A plethora of life abounds, and all one has to do to see it is to be open to the natural world around you. These are just a few of the locals I met while walking along an old, decaying boardwalk in a wetland area deep in the heart of Texas.

Wetland Boardwalk, Texas / Nikon D600

Dragonfly

Feral Texas Hog

Cottonmouth

Green Heron

Racoon

Jumping Spider

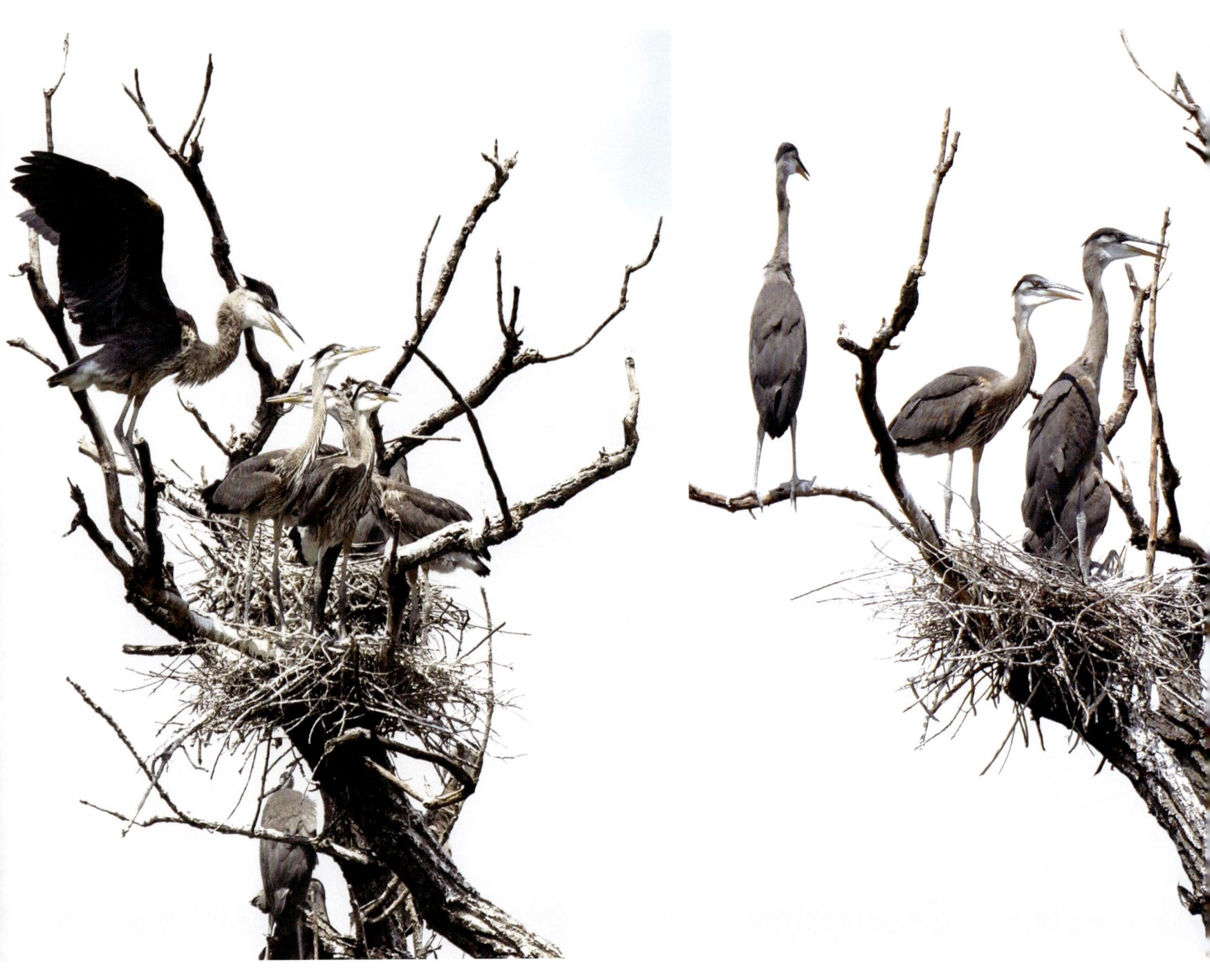

Located high above the meandering west fork of the Trinity River, a large rookery of great blue herons attempts to stay cool as the Texas sun heats up the afternoon sky.

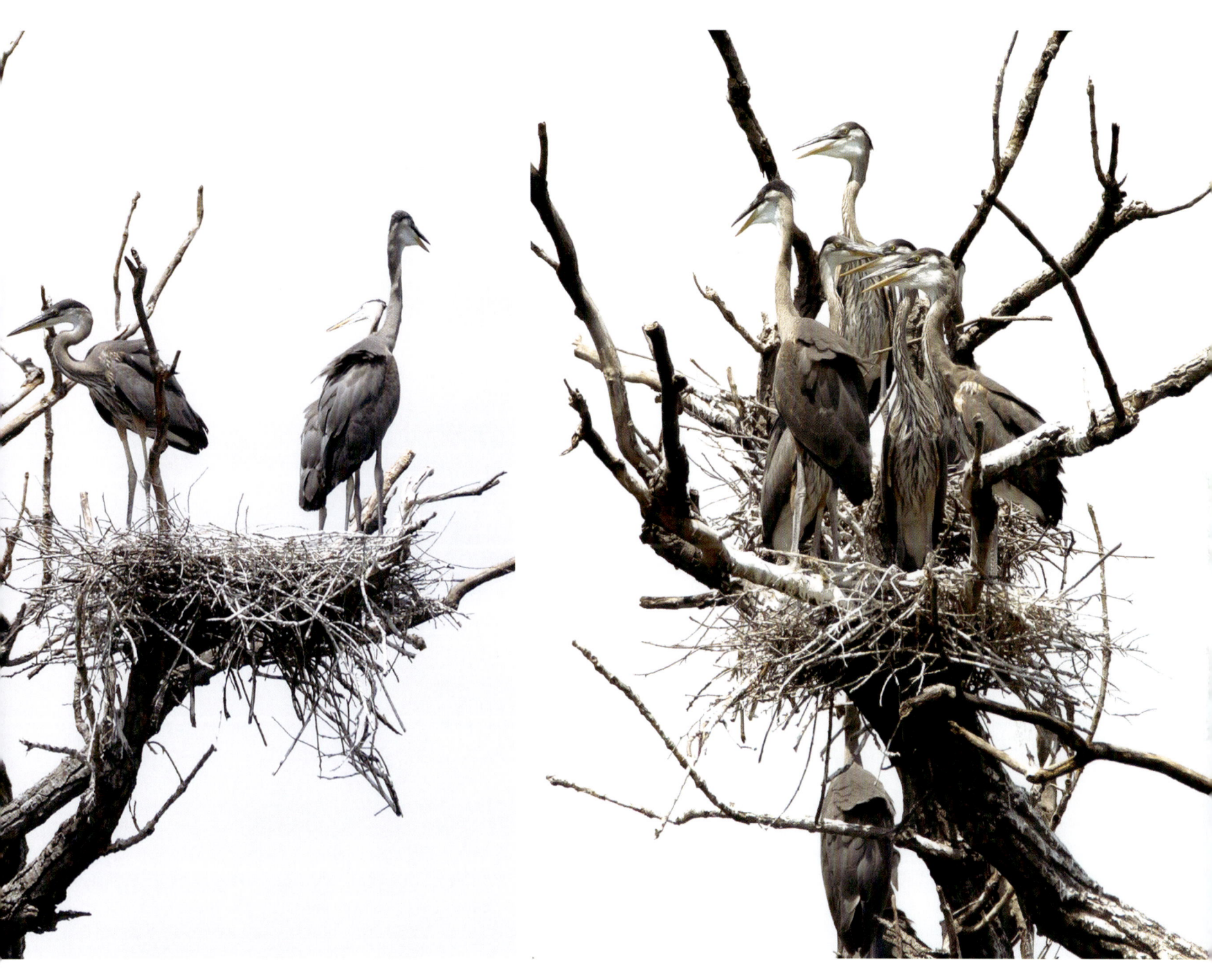

Great Blue Rookery, Texas /Nikon D600

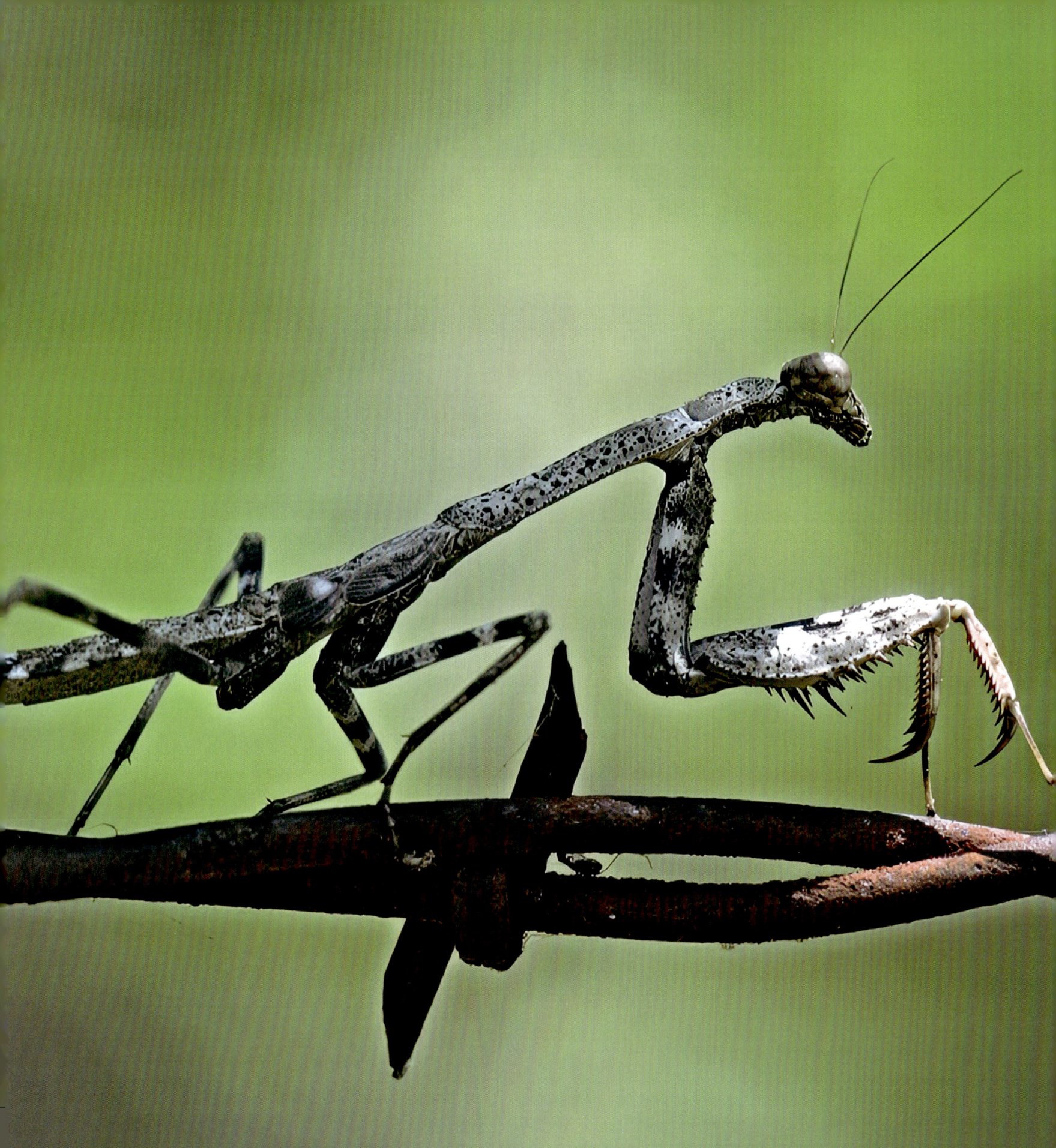

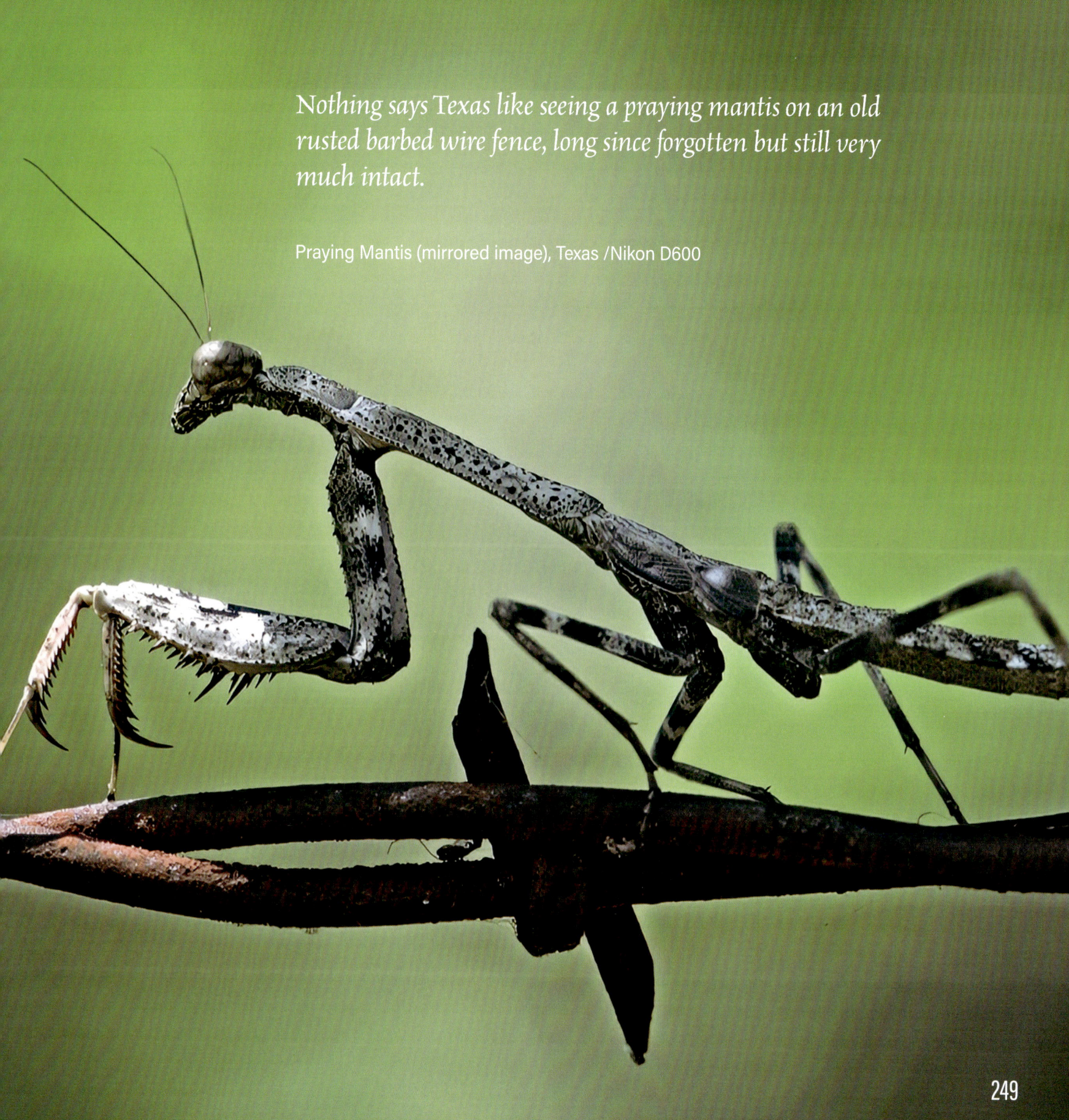

Nothing says Texas like seeing a praying mantis on an old rusted barbed wire fence, long since forgotten but still very much intact.

Praying Mantis (mirrored image), Texas /Nikon D600

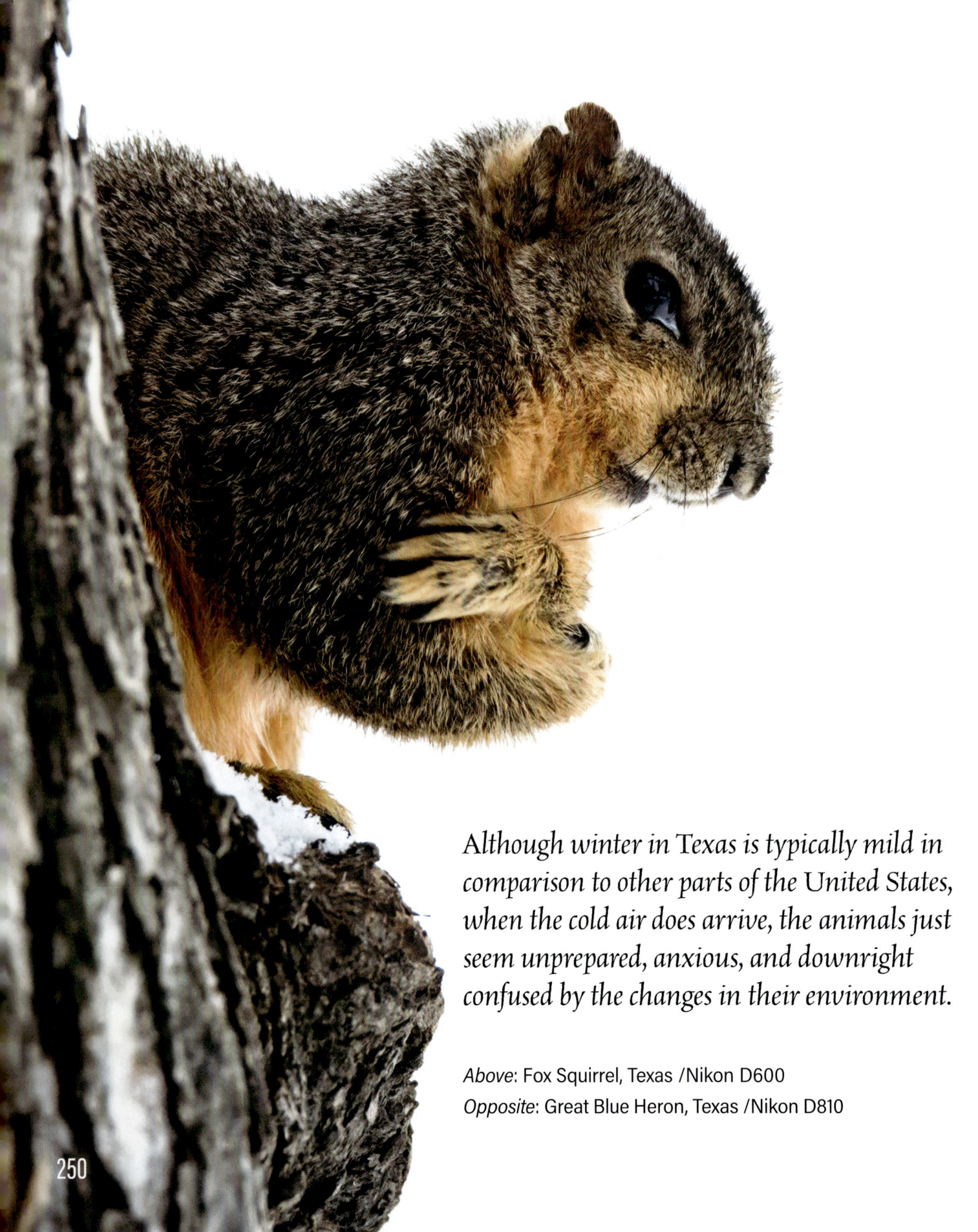

Although winter in Texas is typically mild in comparison to other parts of the United States, when the cold air does arrive, the animals just seem unprepared, anxious, and downright confused by the changes in their environment.

Above: Fox Squirrel, Texas /Nikon D600
Opposite: Great Blue Heron, Texas /Nikon D810

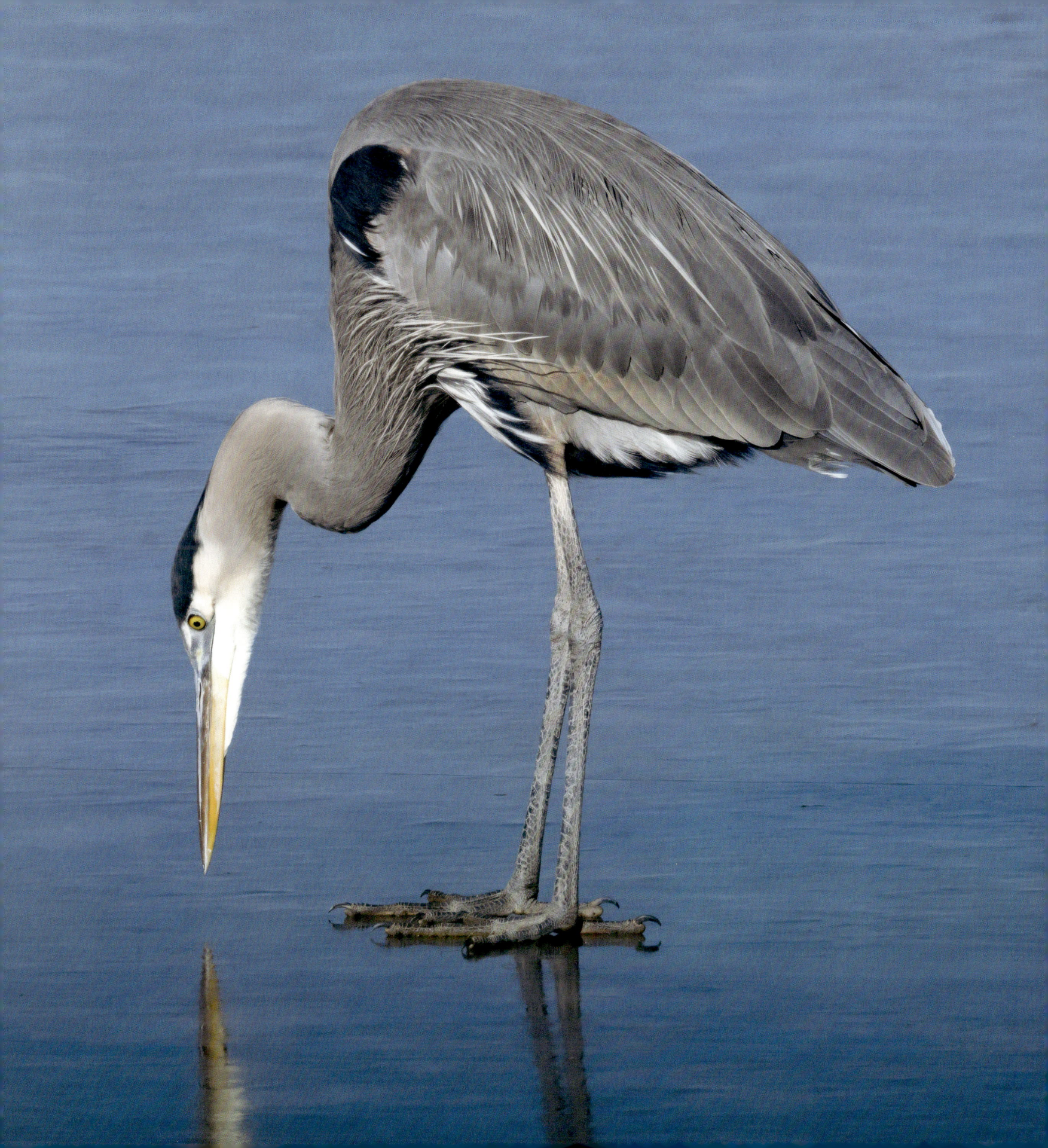

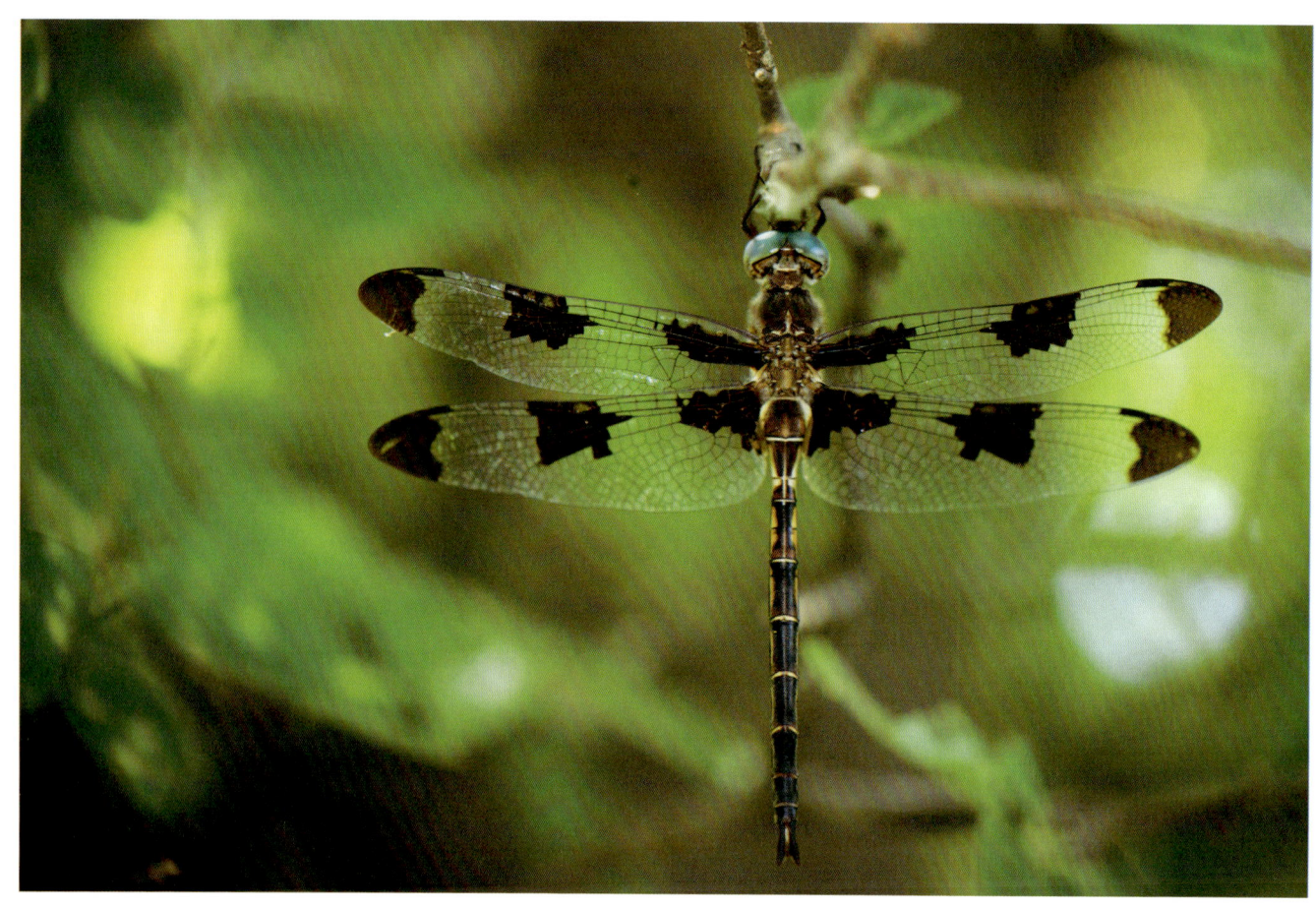

The afternoon heat rises and a peaceful stillness pervades the Texas landscape before me as I carefully make my way over an old, long-forgotten trail with only a few dragonflies and turtles to keep me company.

Above: Resting Dragonfly, Texas /Nikon D810
Opposite: Red-Eared Slider Turtle, Texas /Nikon D810

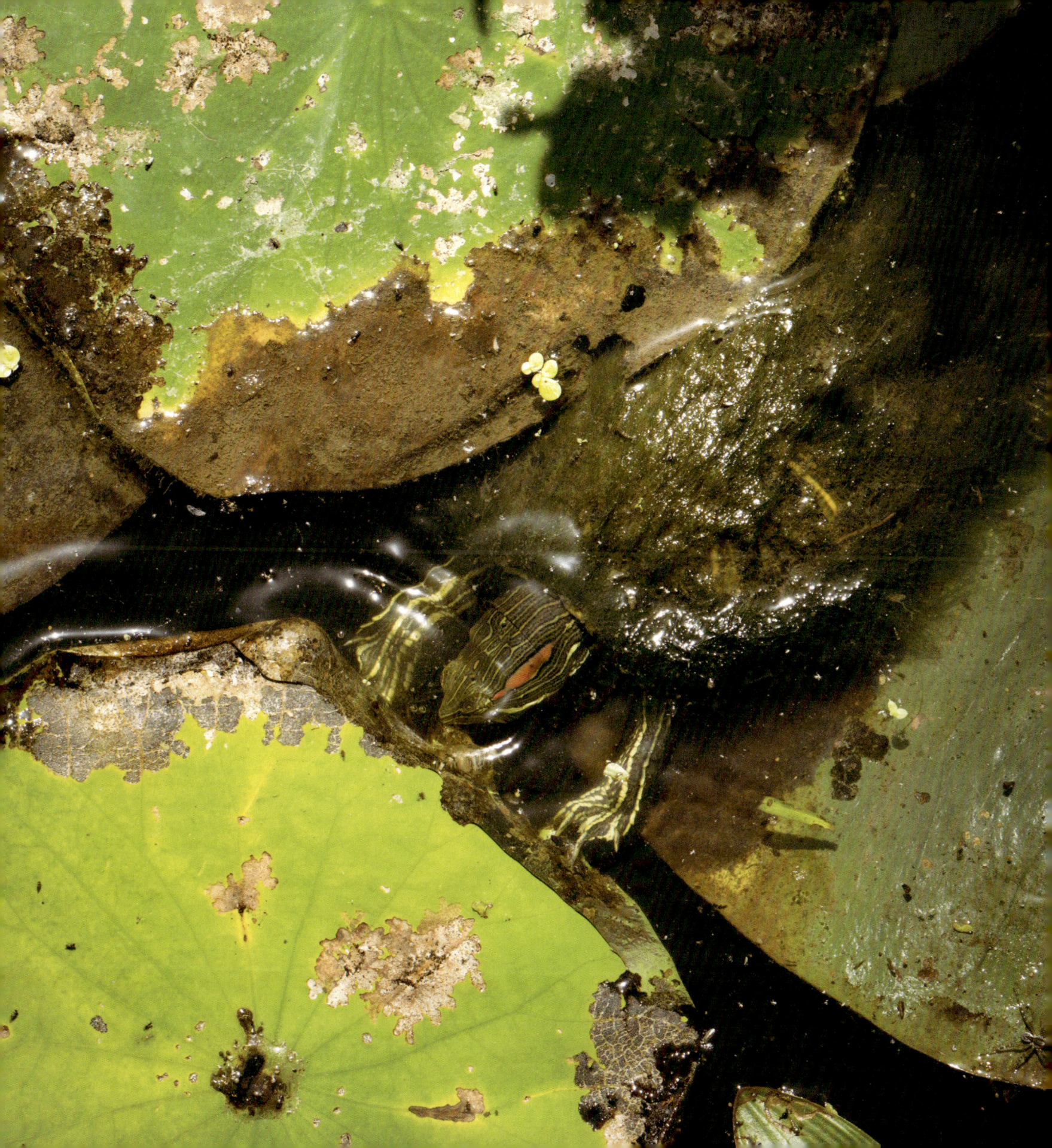

Underappreciated and definitely not the most attractive bird species in the world, the turkey vulture is a tenacious scavenger that can typically be seen soaring high above us, searching the landscape for any signs of carrion that his keen sense of sight and smell can detect.

Turkey Vulture, Texas /Nikon D300

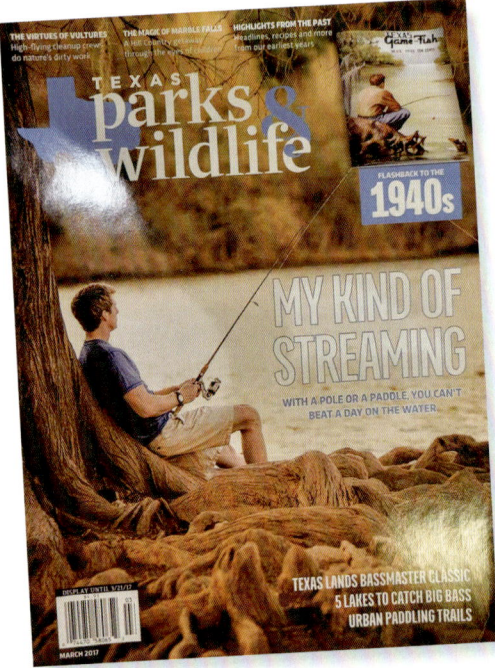

This image was published in *Texas Parks & Wildlife* magazine in the March 2017 issue.

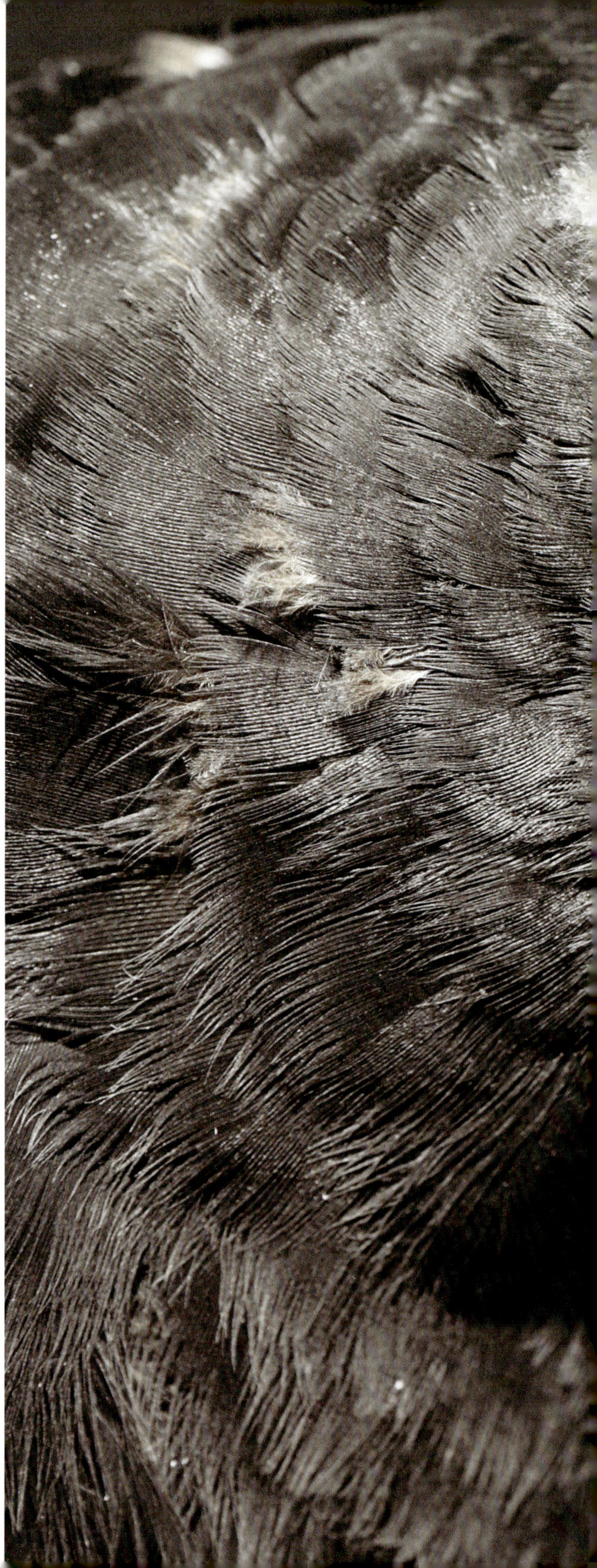

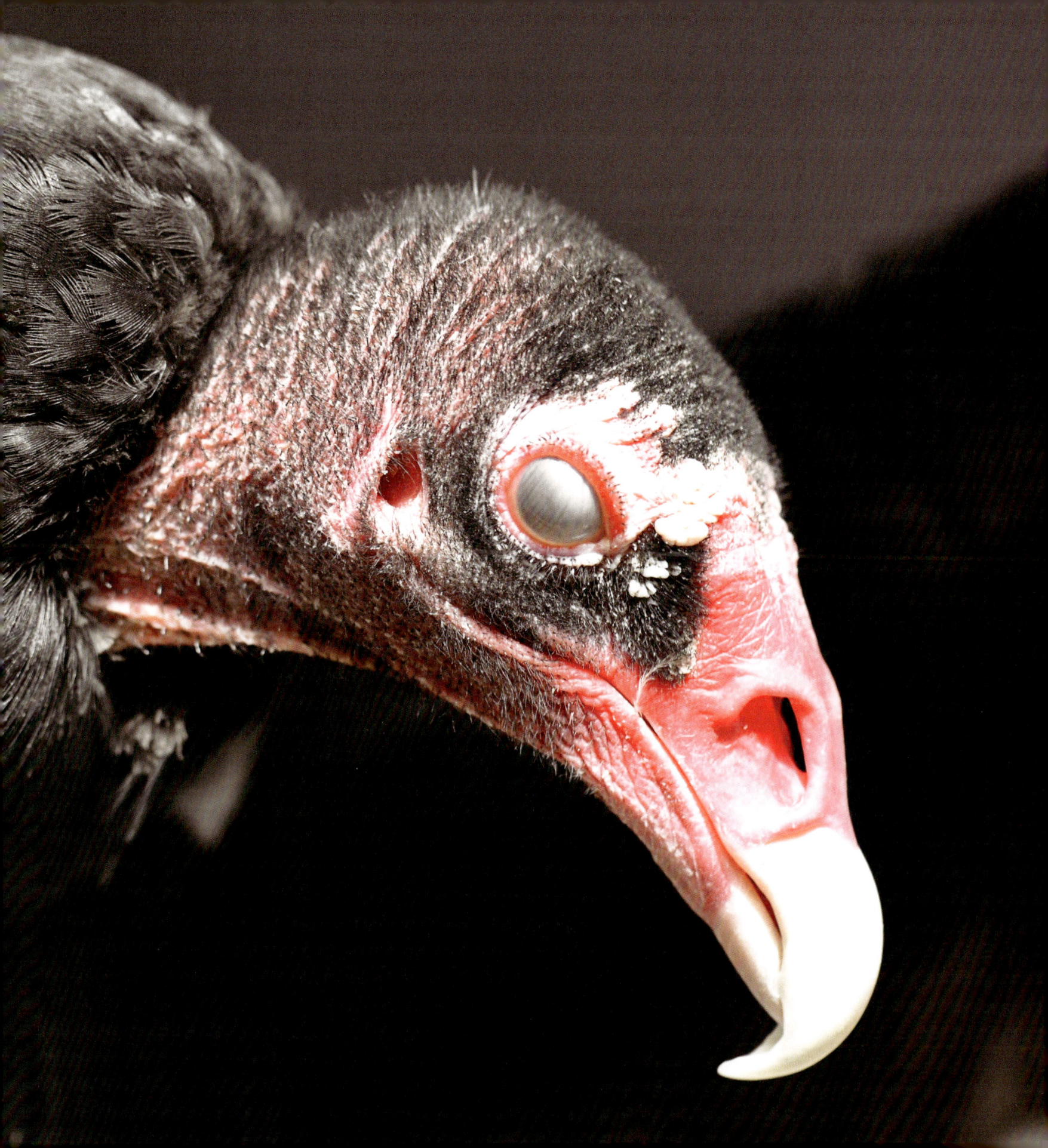

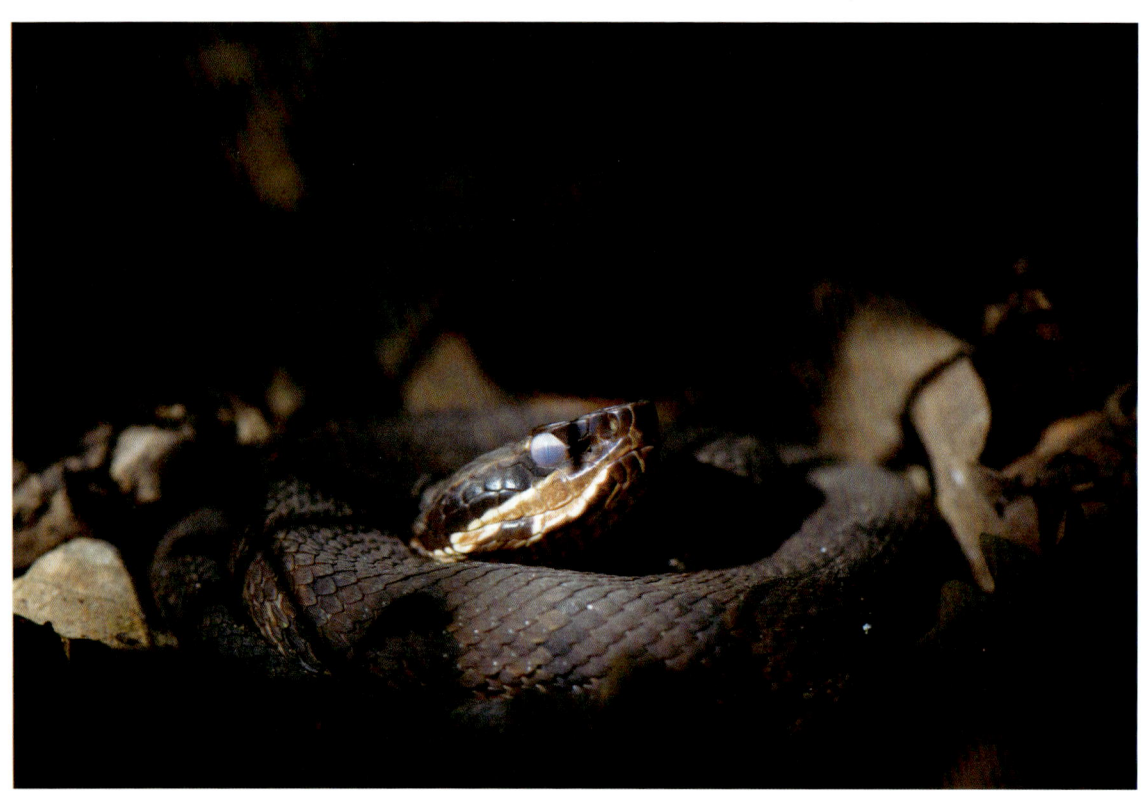

Traversing the water's edge always allows me to visit some of my fellow Texas residents that tend to keep to themselves as they go about their daily lives.

Above: Cottonmouth, Texas /Nikon D810
Opposite: Nutria, Texas /Nikon D810

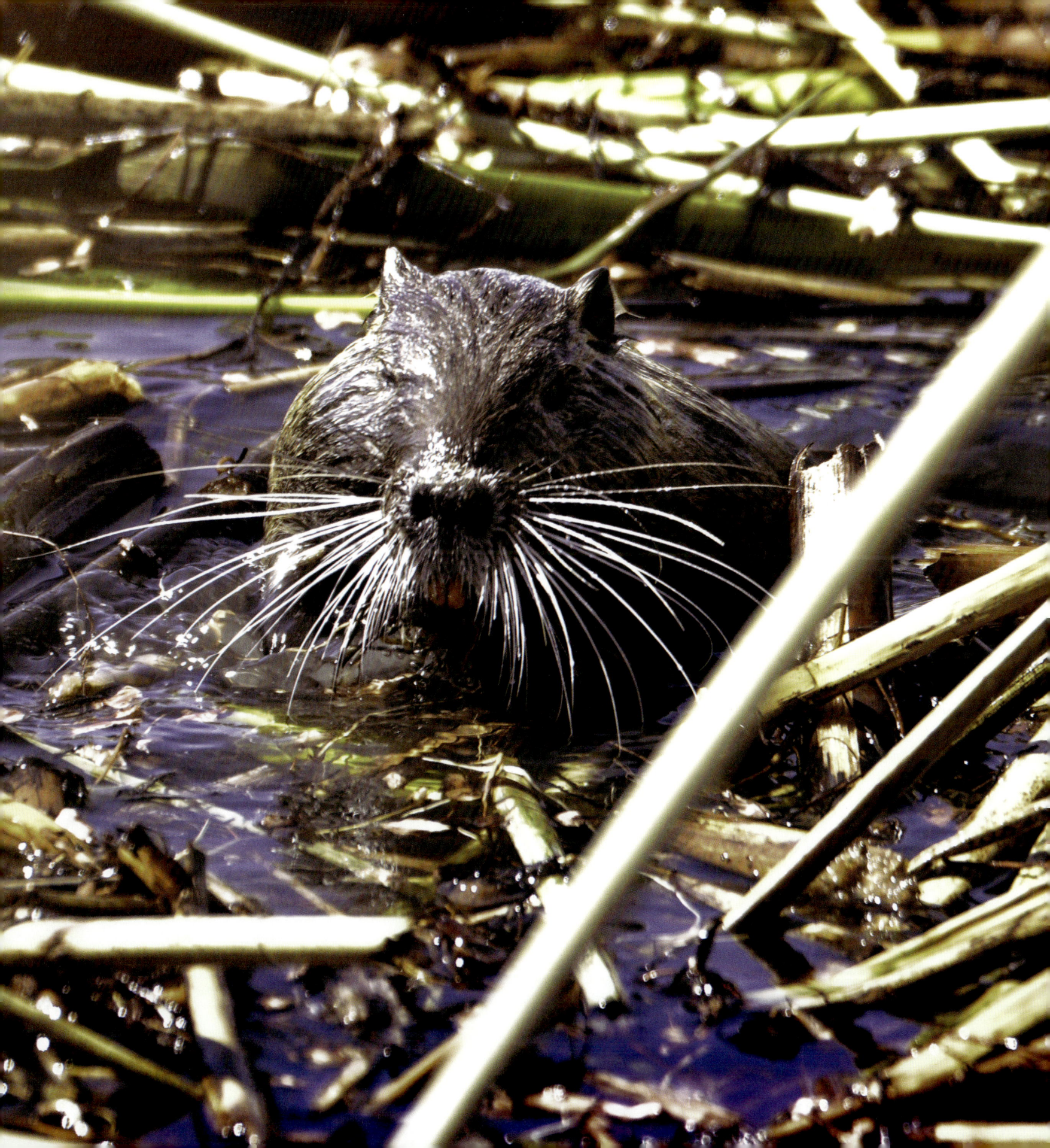

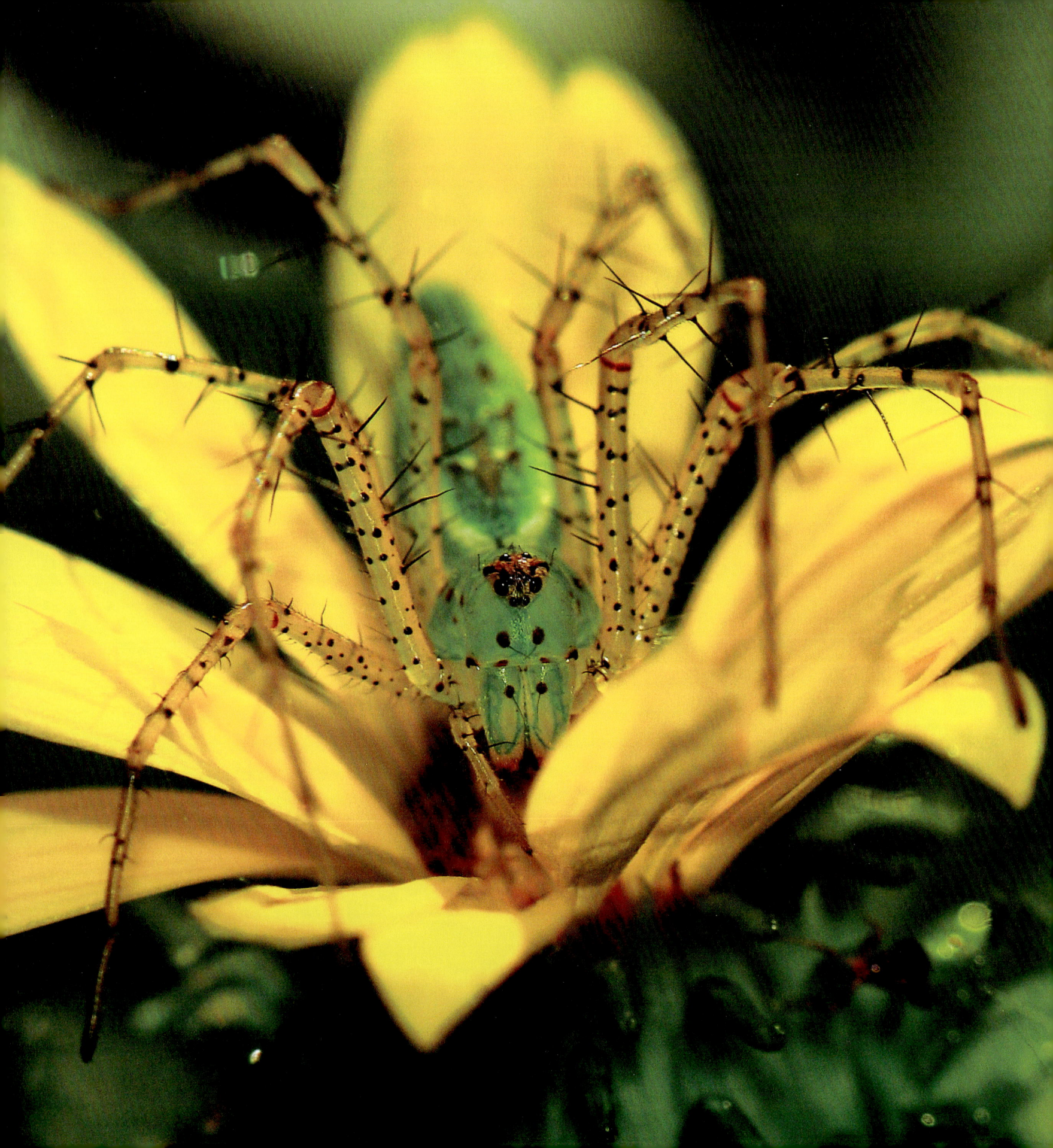

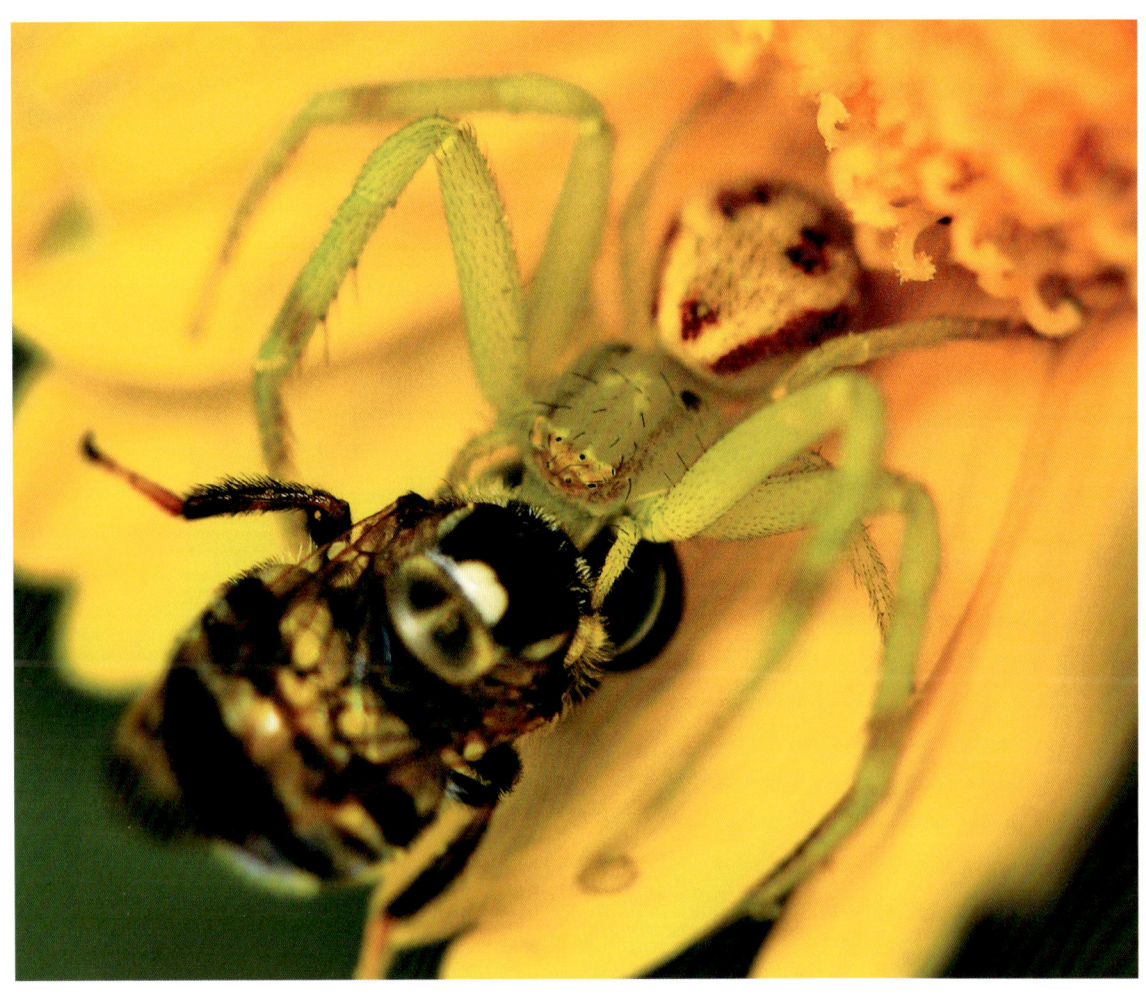

Observing the natural world can be both breathtaking and disconcerting, as the proverbial circle of life plays itself out every second of every hour all around us. Arachnids are consummate predators of nature, and they never cease to fascinate me whenever I come across them, even in the most unlikely of places.

Above: Green Crab Spider, Texas /Nikon D300
Opposite: Green Lynx Spider, Texas /Nikon D300

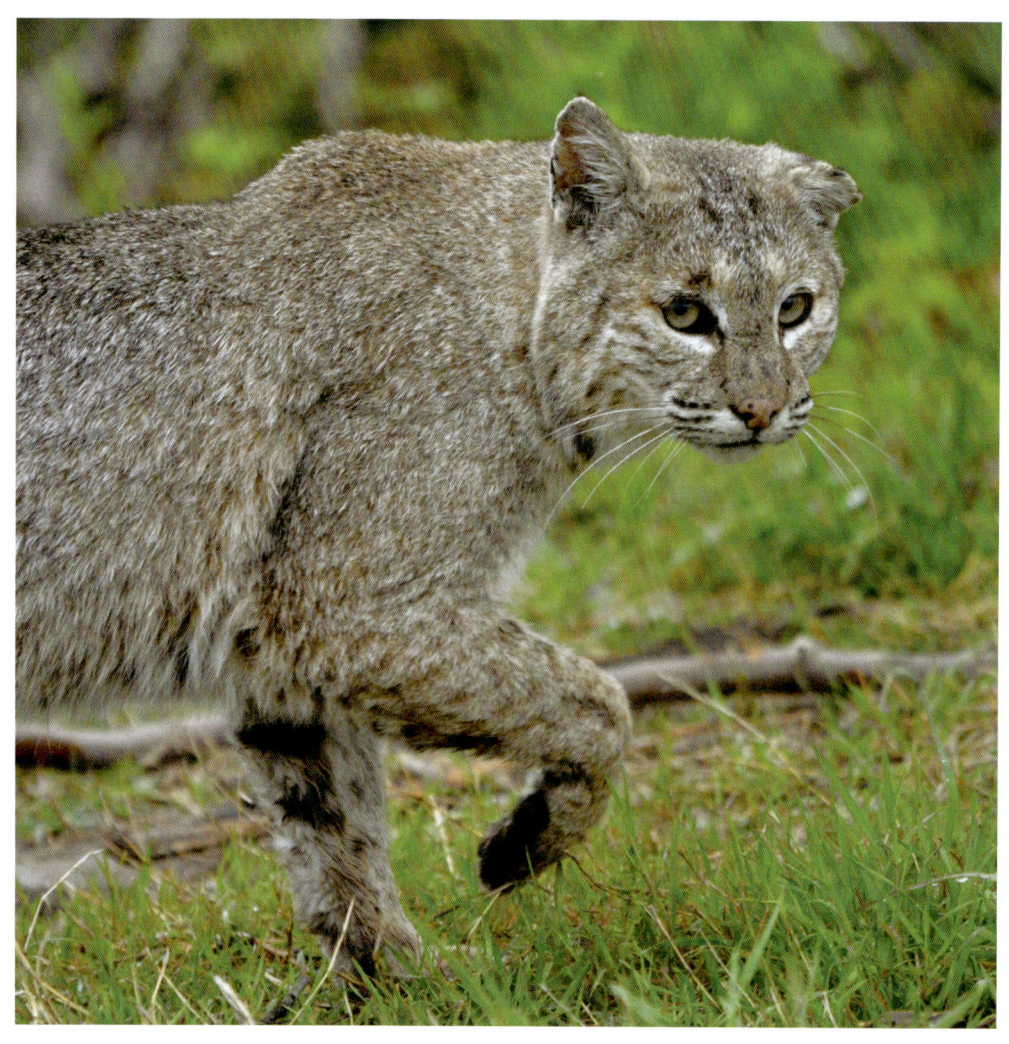

Now that the rain has subsided, a scruffy-looking bobcat decides to patrol the lakeshore in search of an easy meal. Egrets are always on the menu, but catching them unaware is an altogether different story.

Above: Bobcat, Texas /Nikon D600
Opposite: Snowy Egret, Texas /Nikon D810

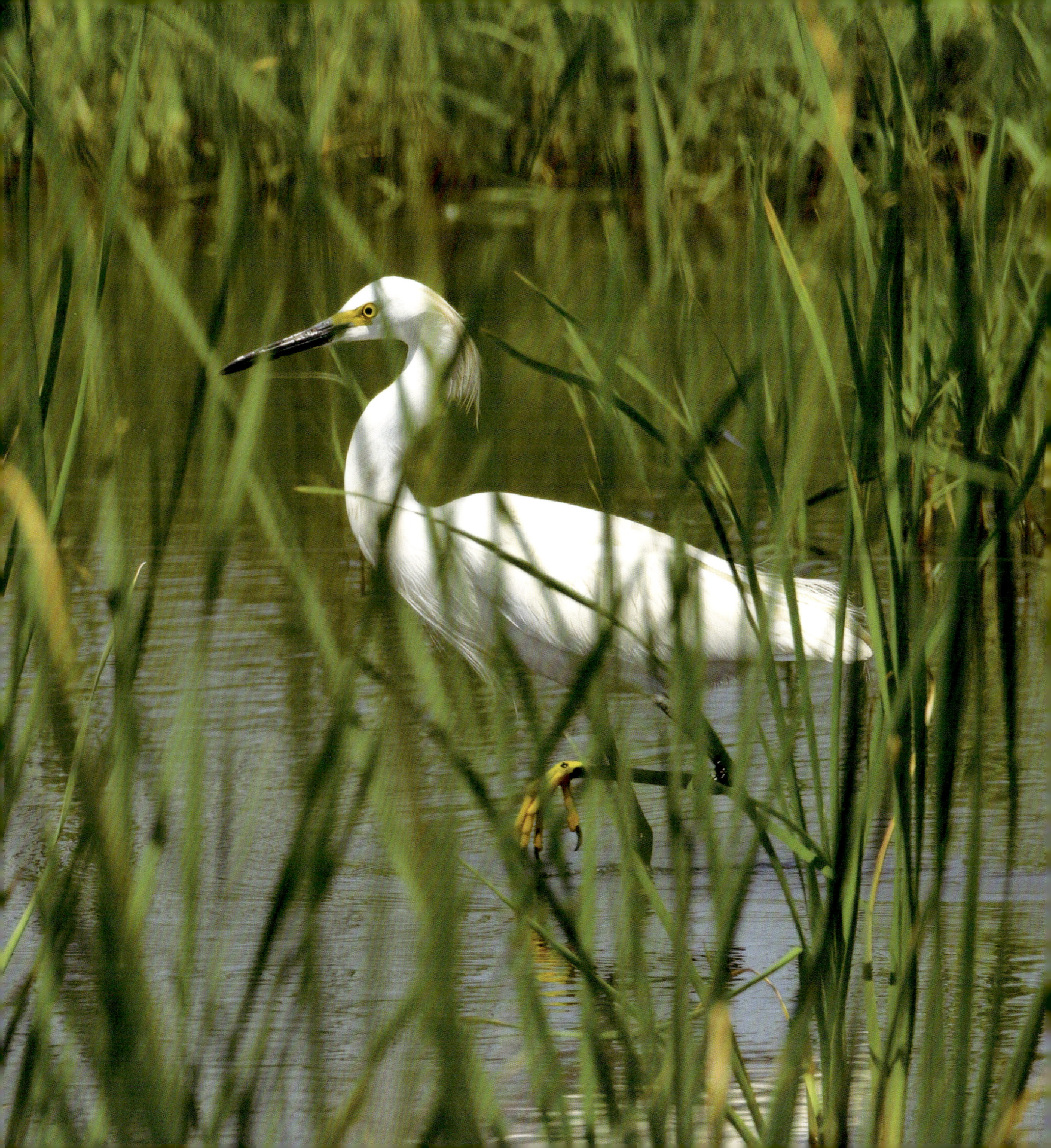

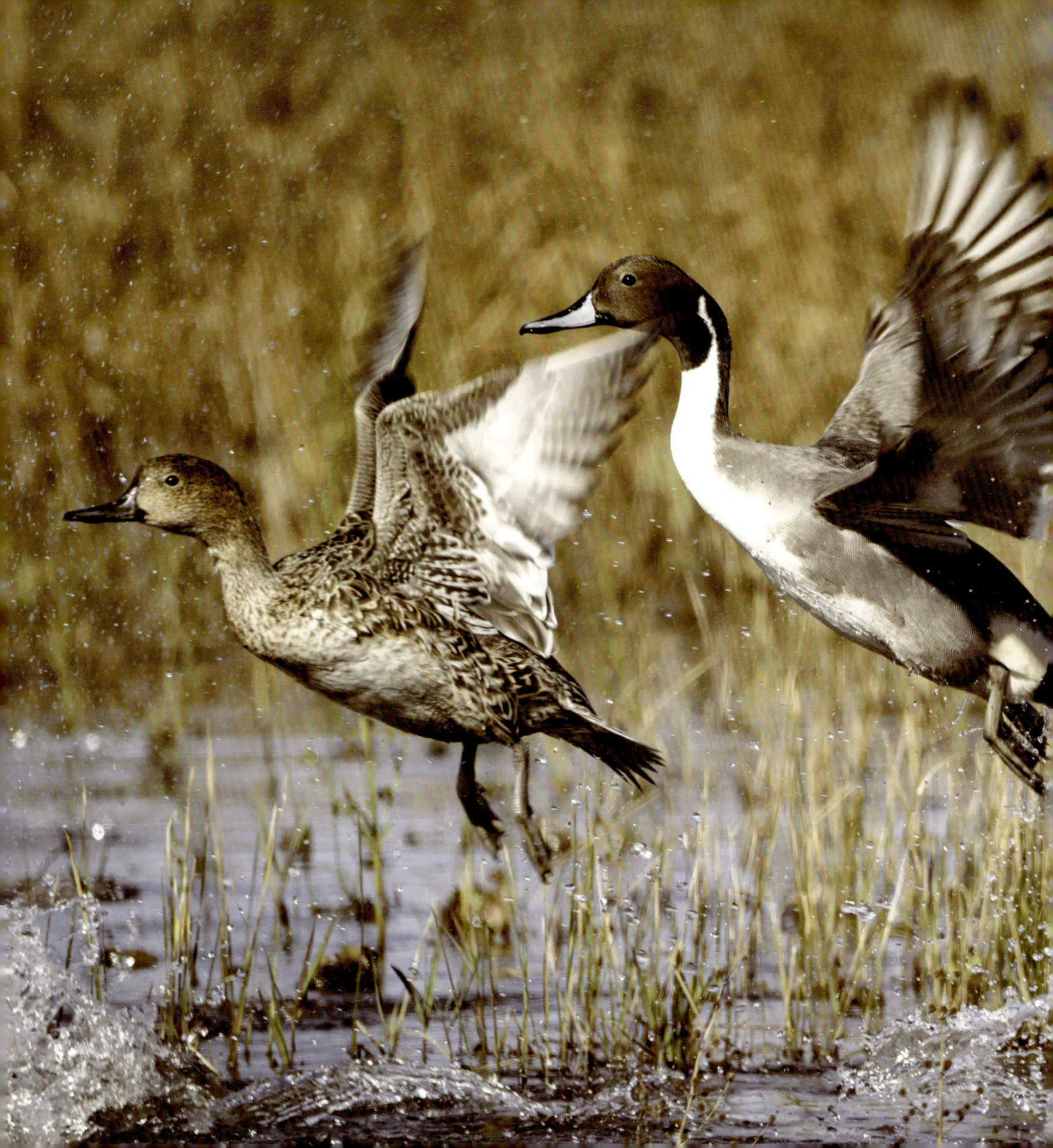

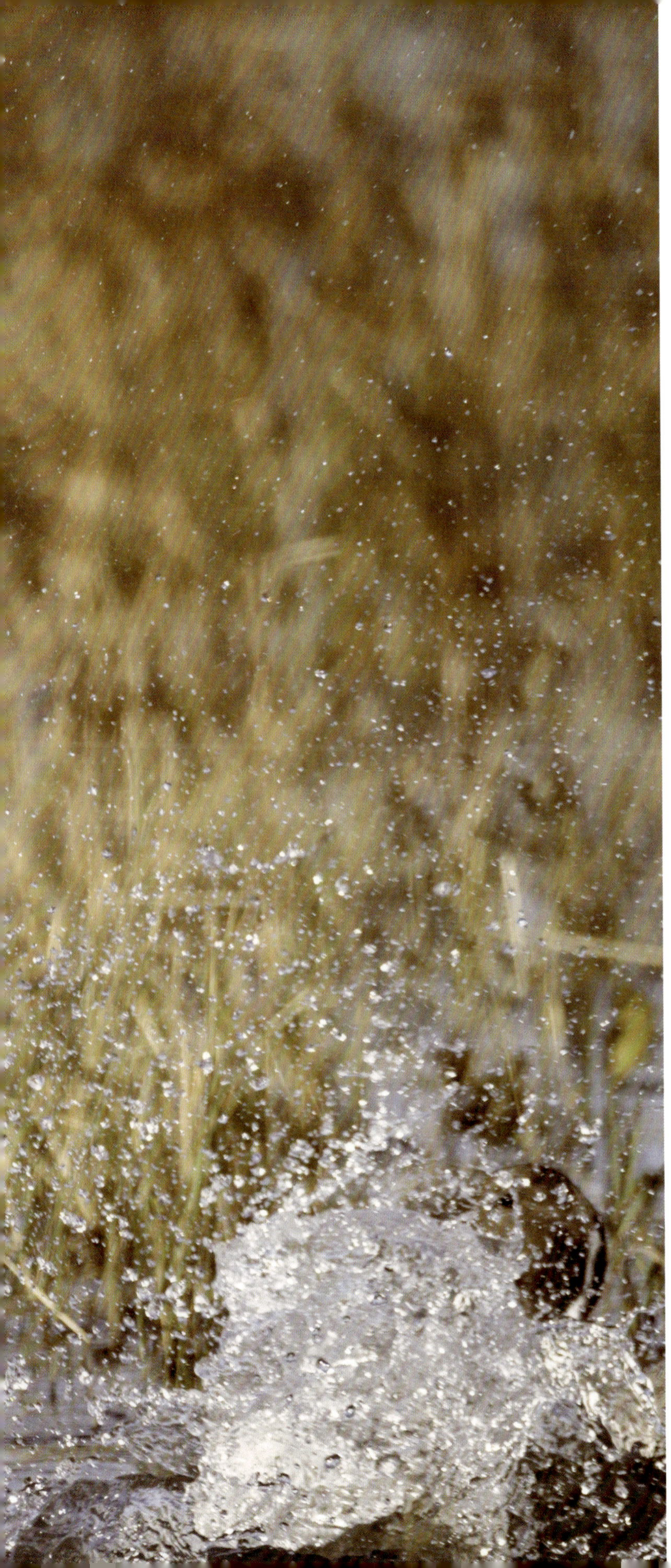

A pair of majestic northern pintail ducks jettison into the air, leaving only a cascade of unsettled water in their wake.

Northern Pintail Duck, Texas /Nikon D810

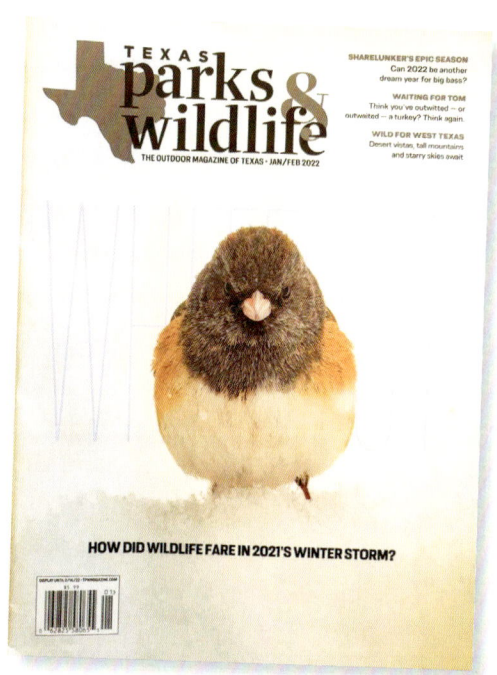

This image was published in *Texas Parks & Wildlife* magazine in the Jan/Feb 2022 issue.

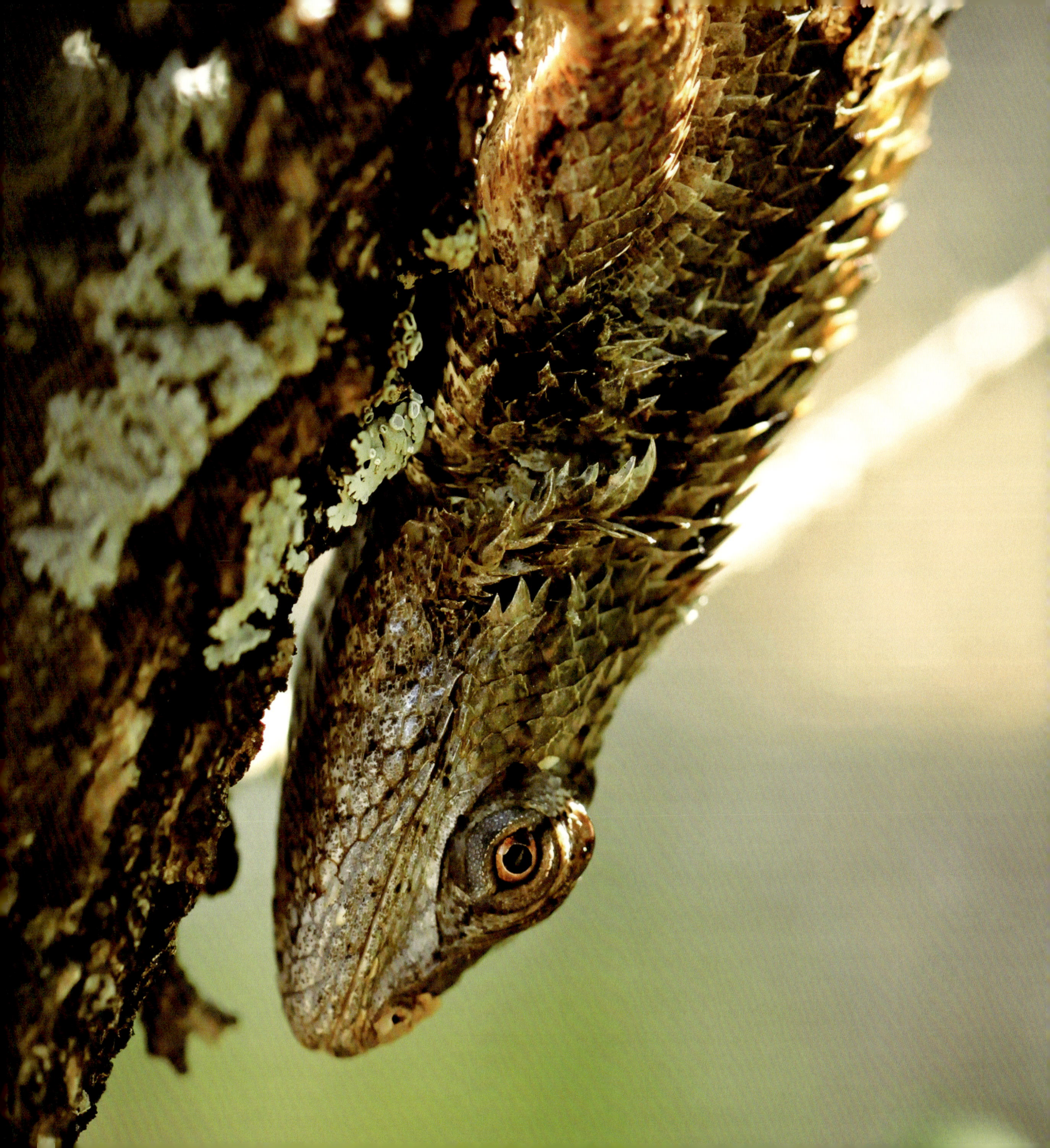

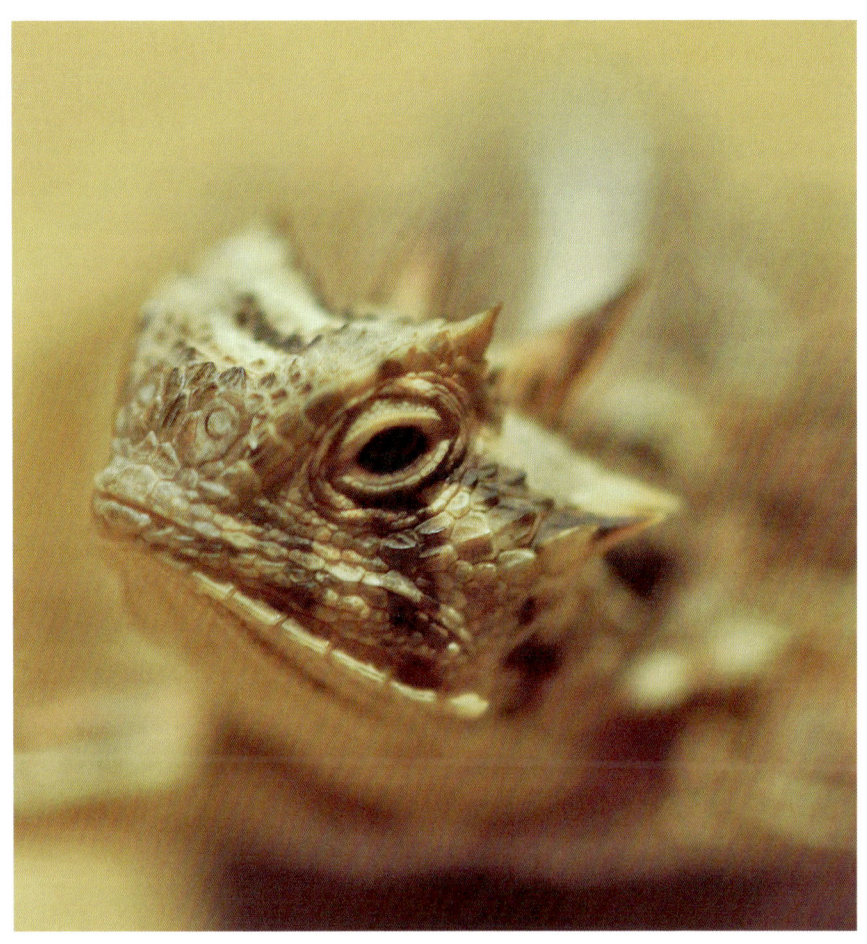

They are small in size, but to see them in the wild reminds me of a long-ago time when reptiles ruled this world, and their presence would have been much more noticeable. Today, they blend so well into the Texas landscape that finding them can be both a challenge and an adventure.

Above: Texas Horned Lizard, Texas /Nikon D300
Opposite: Texas Spiny Lizard, Texas /Nikon D600

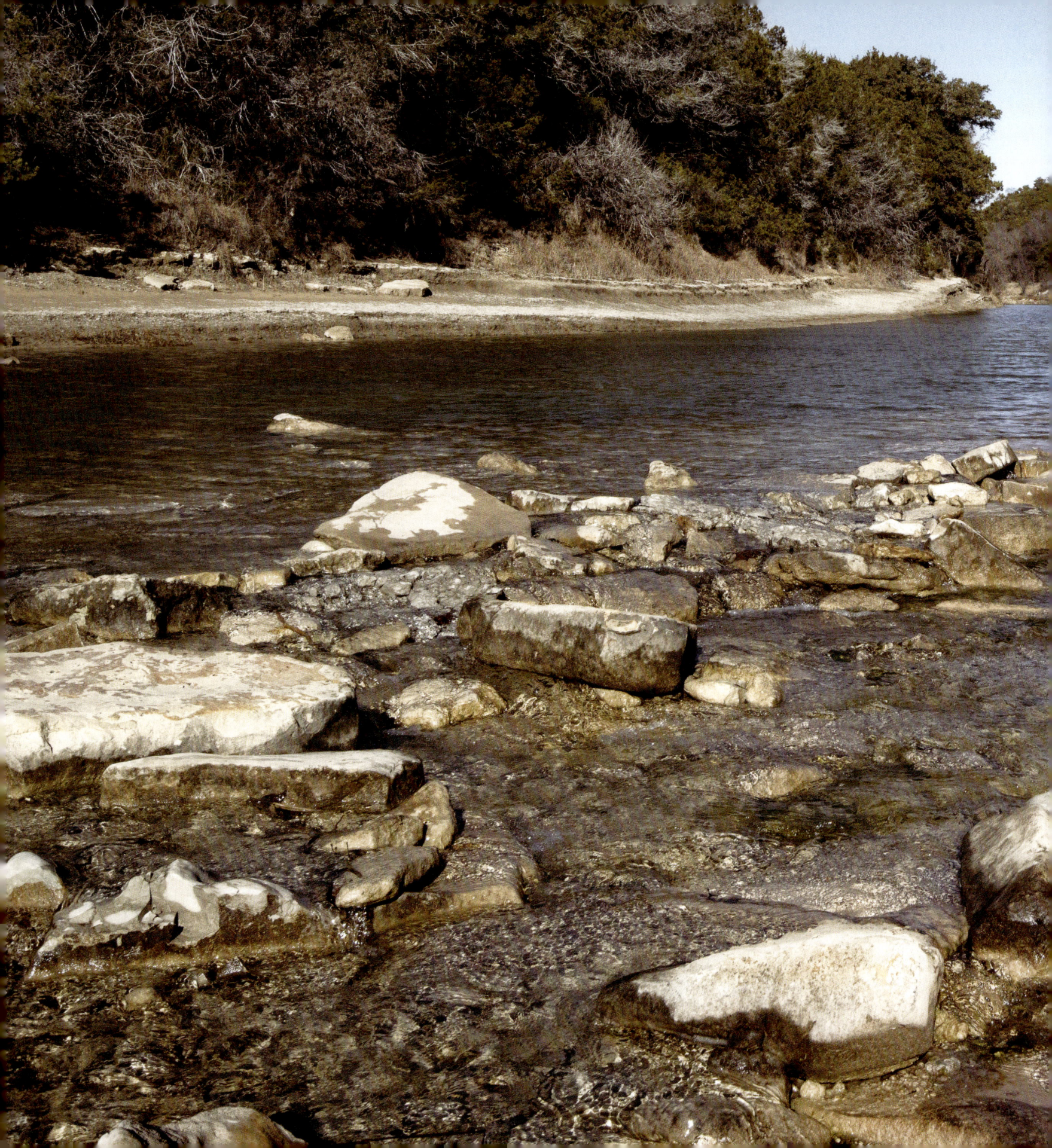

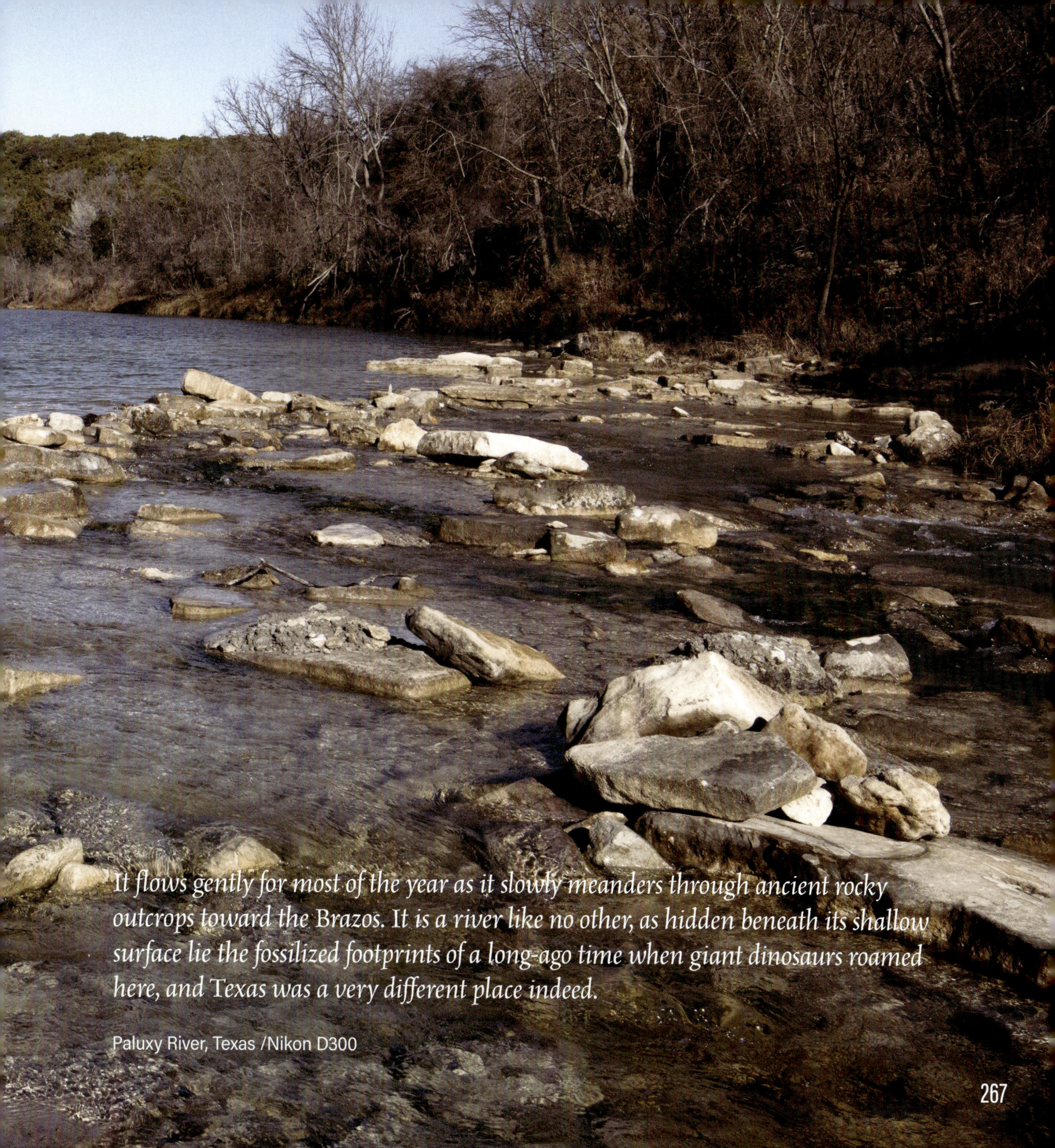

It flows gently for most of the year as it slowly meanders through ancient rocky outcrops toward the Brazos. It is a river like no other, as hidden beneath its shallow surface lie the fossilized footprints of a long-ago time when giant dinosaurs roamed here, and Texas was a very different place indeed.

Paluxy River, Texas /Nikon D300

Baby bison enjoy a Texas spring morning together. Their reddish coat gets them the nickname "Red-dogs," which they will only have for a few months before it darkens with age. Today, Caprock Canyons State Park is one of the few places in Texas where you may view these bison, though there are other populations on private ranches and preserves throughout the state.

The buffalo of Caprock Canyons are designated Texas's official bison herd.

Baby Bison, Texas /Nikon D600

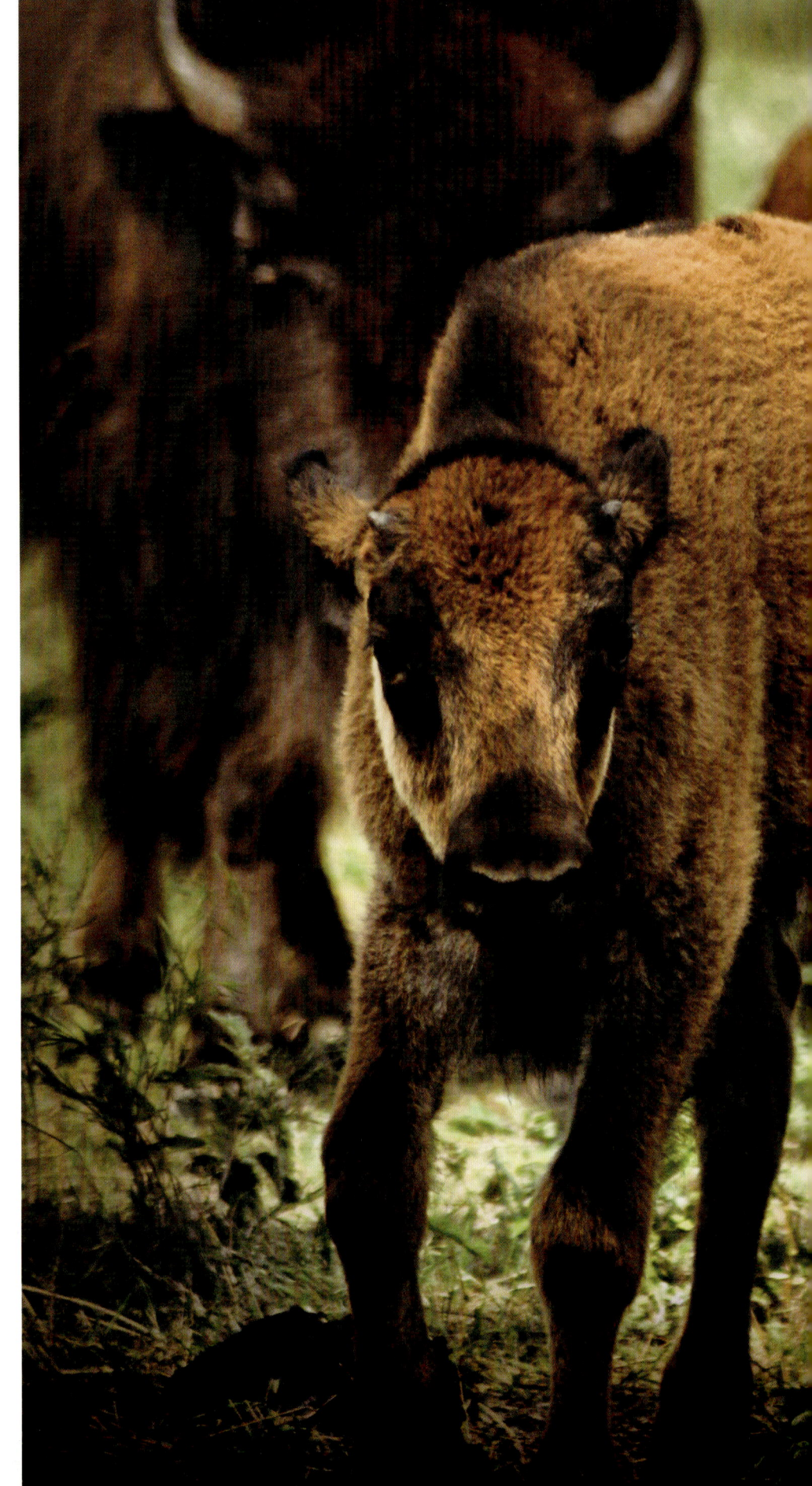

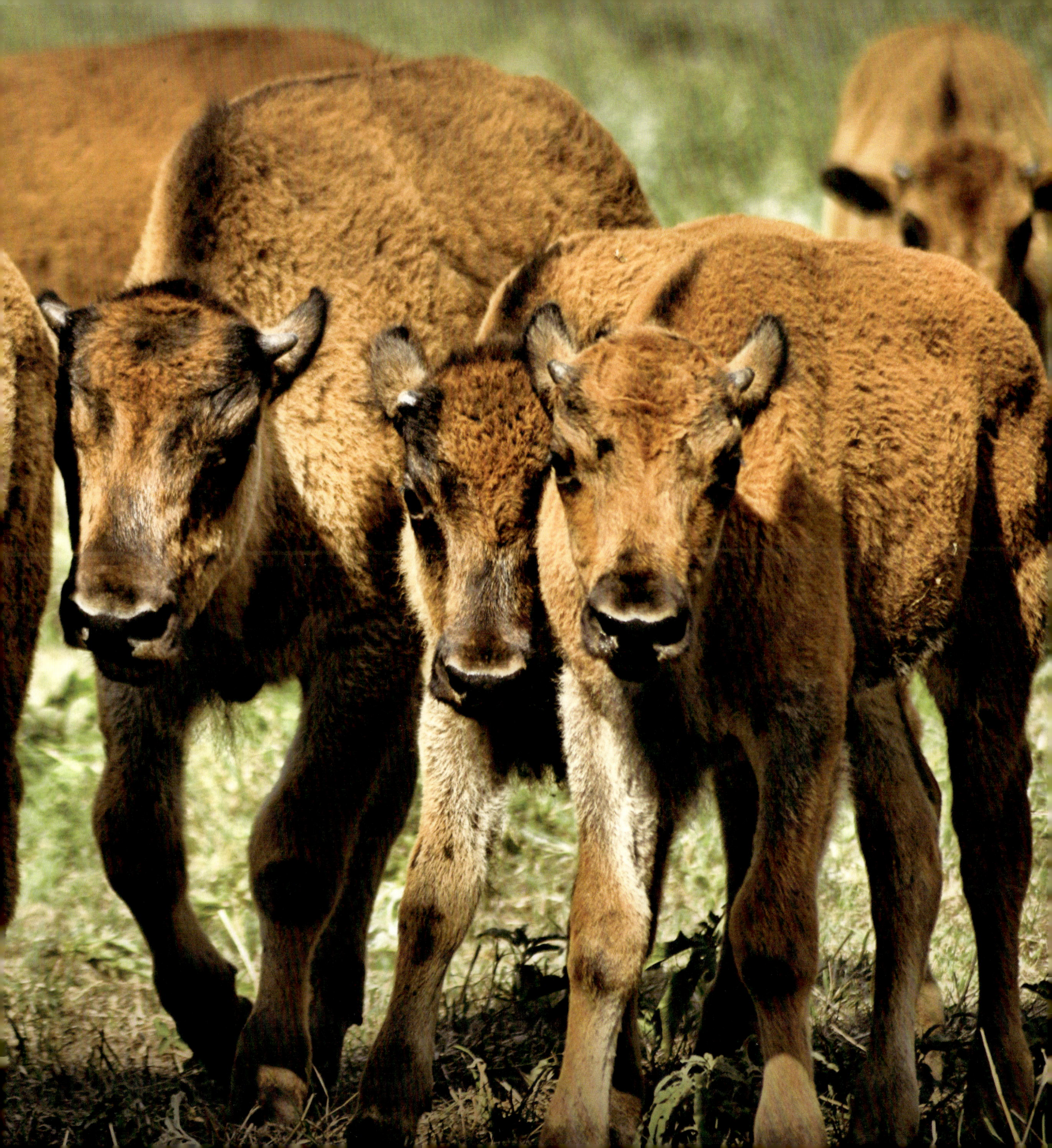

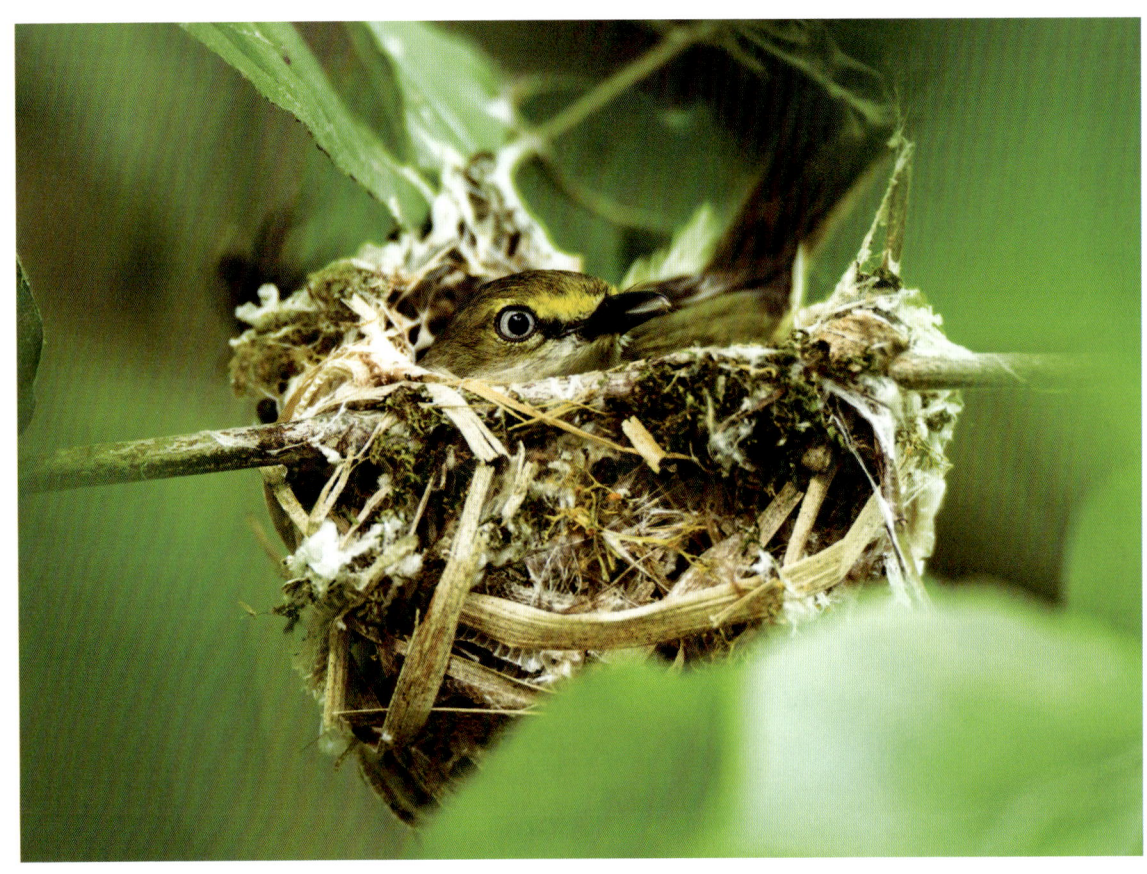

Spring in Texas can be brief, as summer often arrives early and stays late for most of the year. Wildflowers only get a few months to show off their beauty, and what beauty it is.

Above: Yellow-Throated Vireo, Texas /Nikon D810

Opposite: Texas Firewheel Flower, Texas /Nikon D810

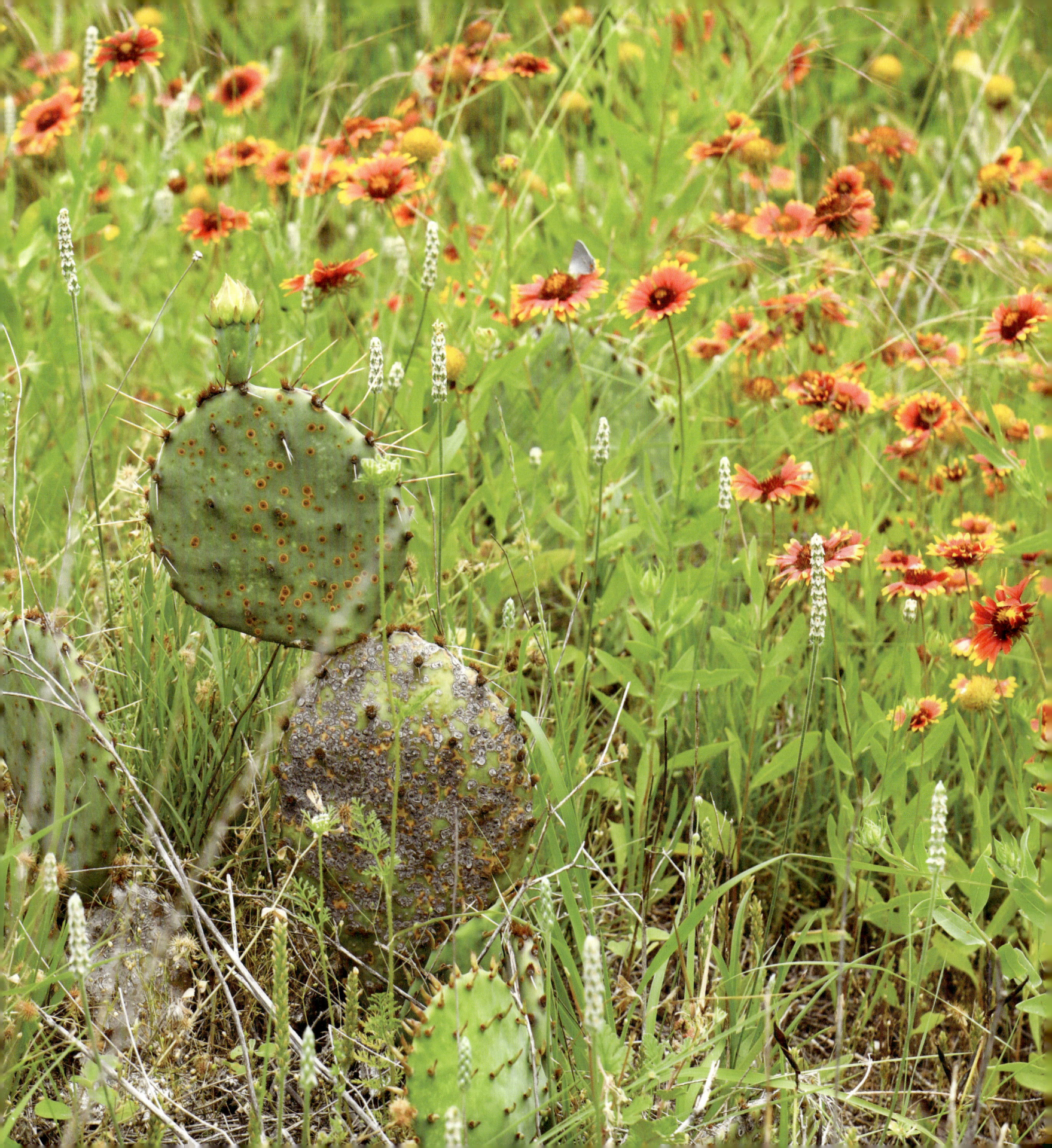

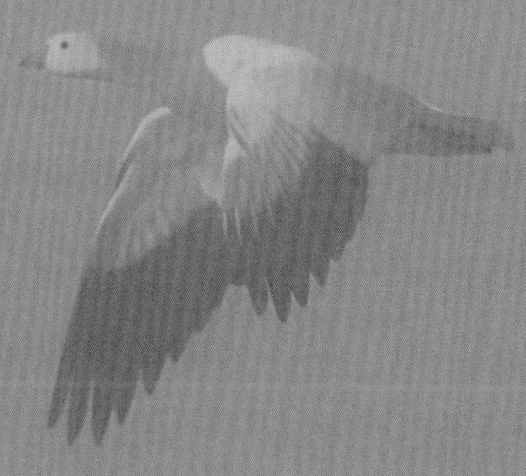

Snow geese arrive before a backdrop of old oil derricks that stand as sentinels of a past time and an uncertain future as an early morning fog blankets a revitalized Texas wetland.

Snow-Geese and Oil Derricks, Texas /Nikon D810

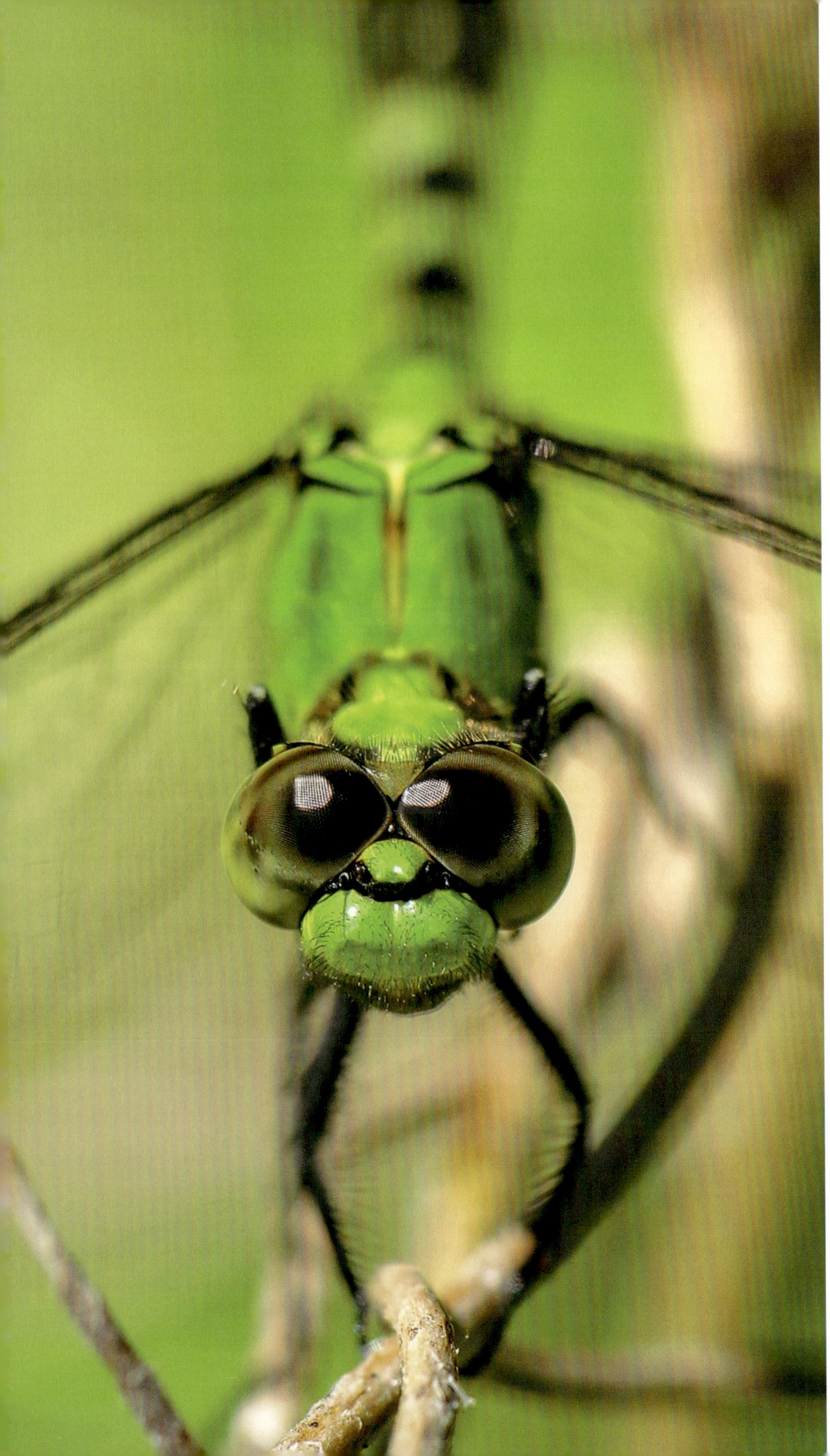

To bridge the eons of time, one must only seek out the company of the dragonfly who has changed little in a world changed much. Accurately named nature's perfect design, it will undoubtedly be here long after we are gone.

Eastern Pondhawk Dragonfly, Texas / Nikon D300

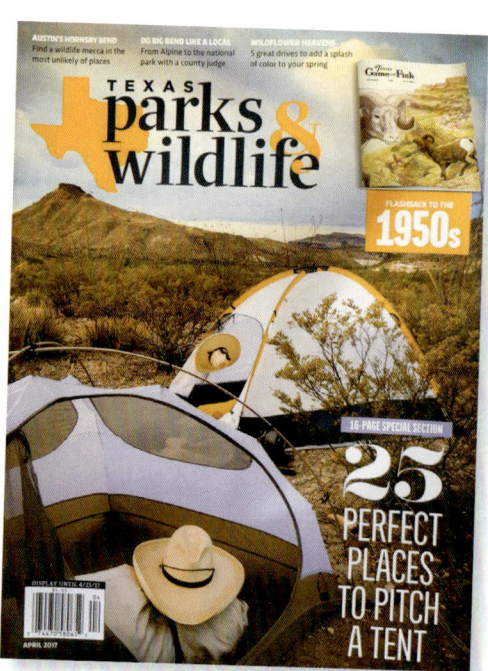

This image was published in *Texas Parks and Wildlife* magazine, April 2017

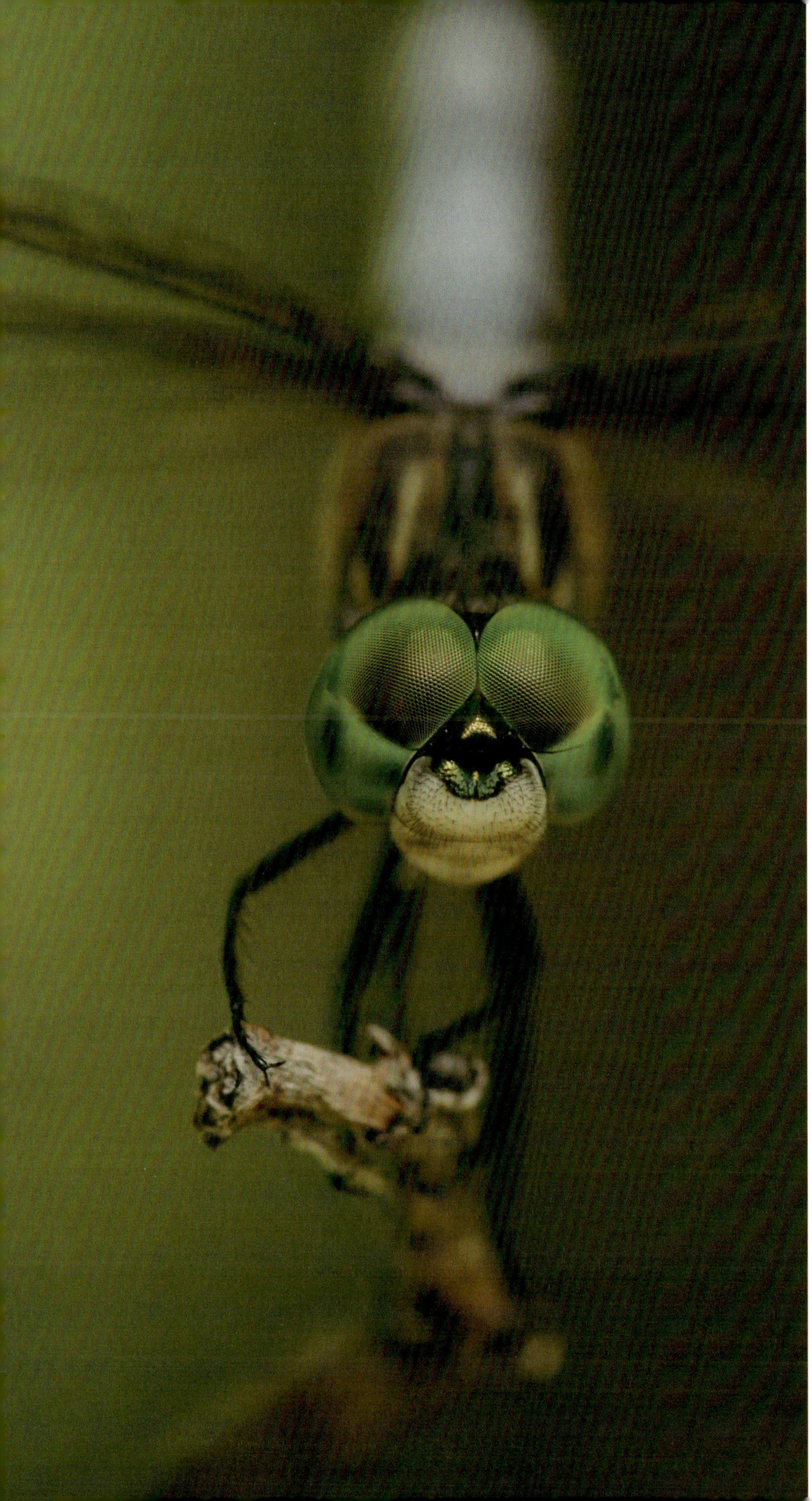

When I stare into the eyes of a dragonfly, I see an alien species of unfathomable complexity, curiosity, and wonder.

Blue Dasher Dragonfly, Texas / Nikon D810

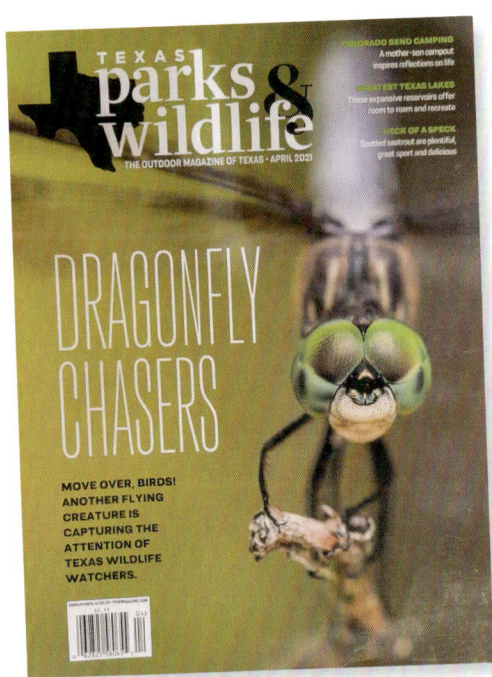

This image was the cover image of the *Texas Parks and Wildlife* magazine, April 2021.

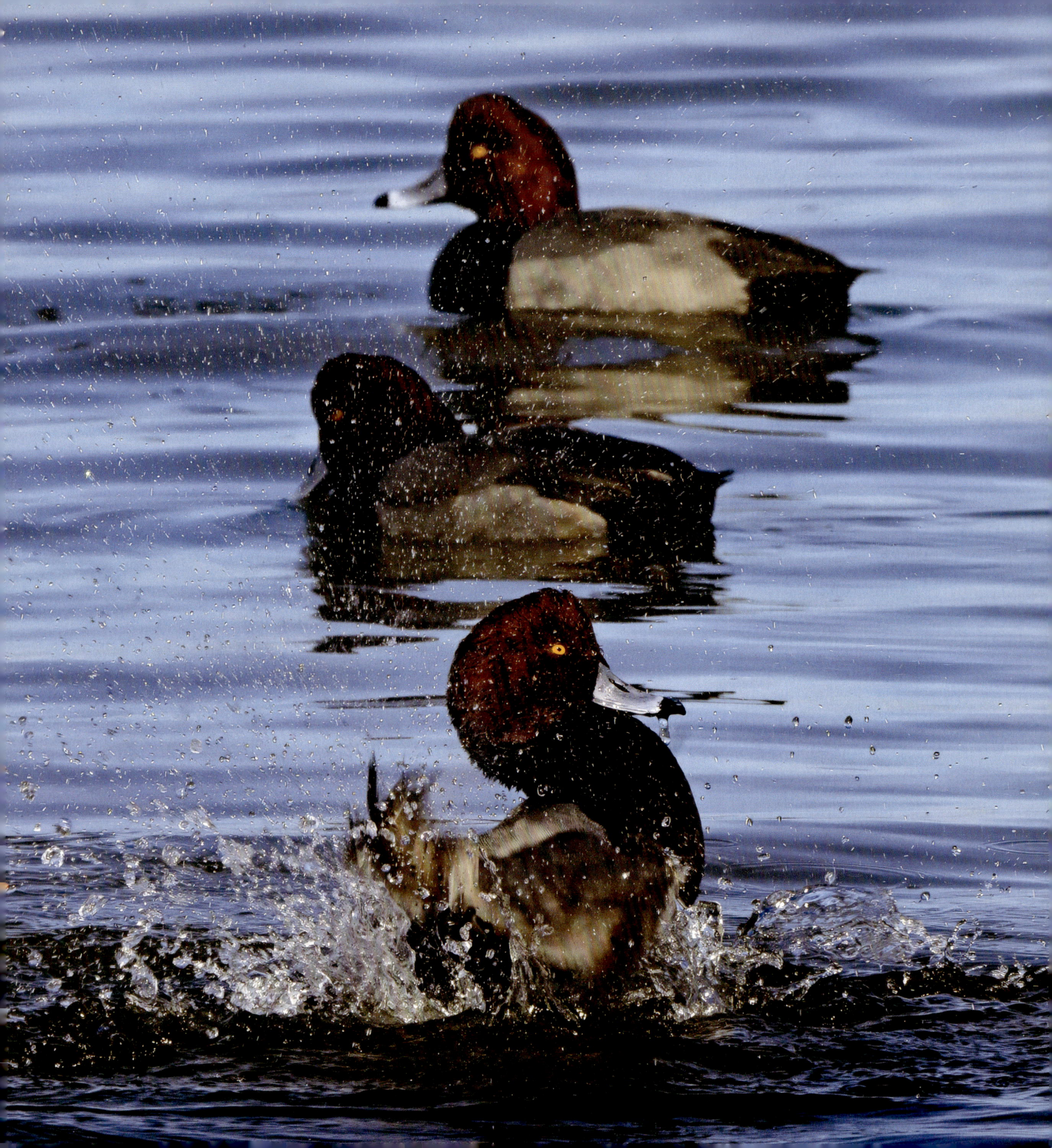

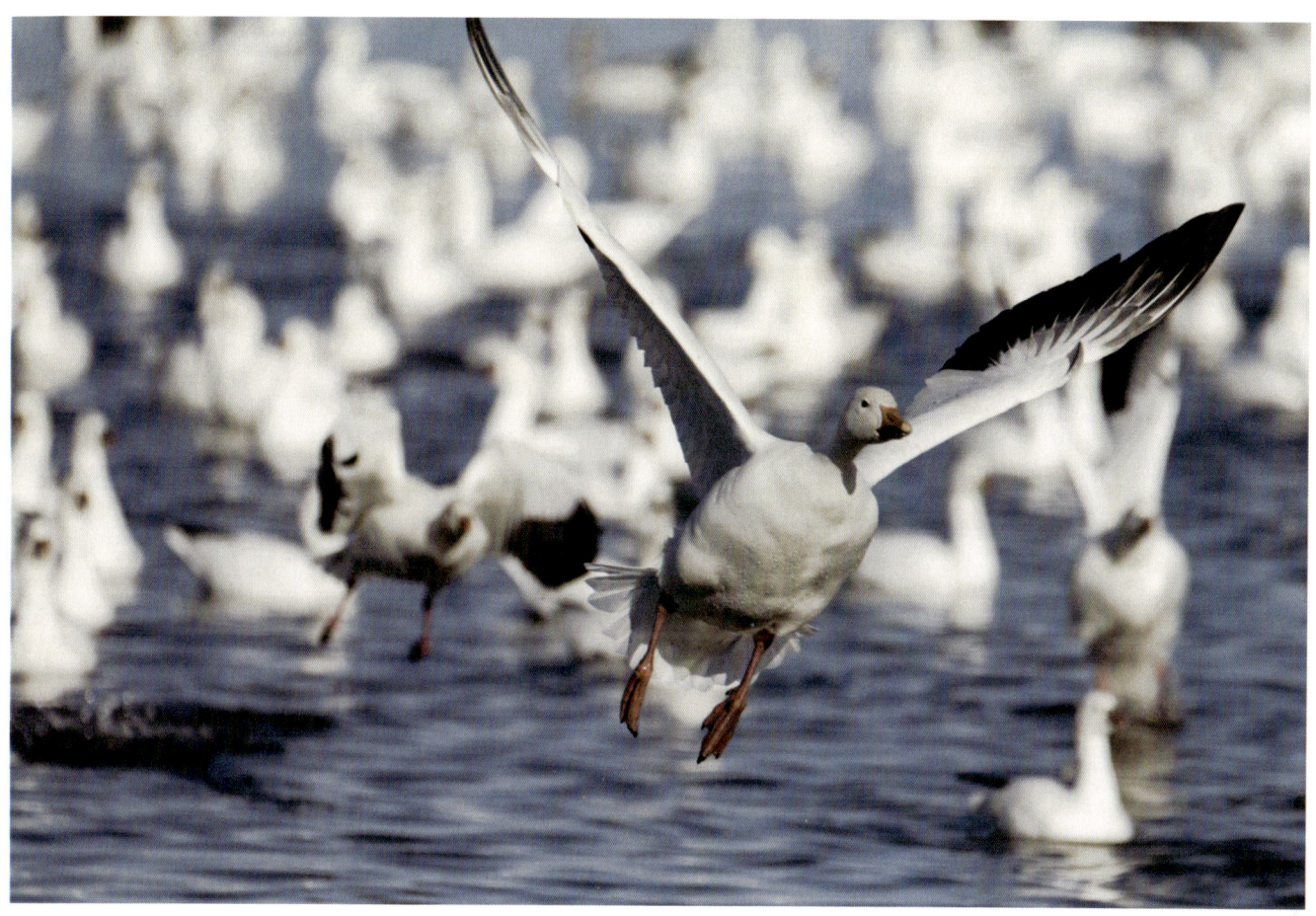

Thousands of birds of all species congregate within a Texas wetland sanctuary as the oppressive heat of summer finally relents and the cooler winds of autumn take hold.

Above: Snow Geese, Texas /Nikon D810
Opposite: Red-Headed Ducks, Texas /Nikon D810

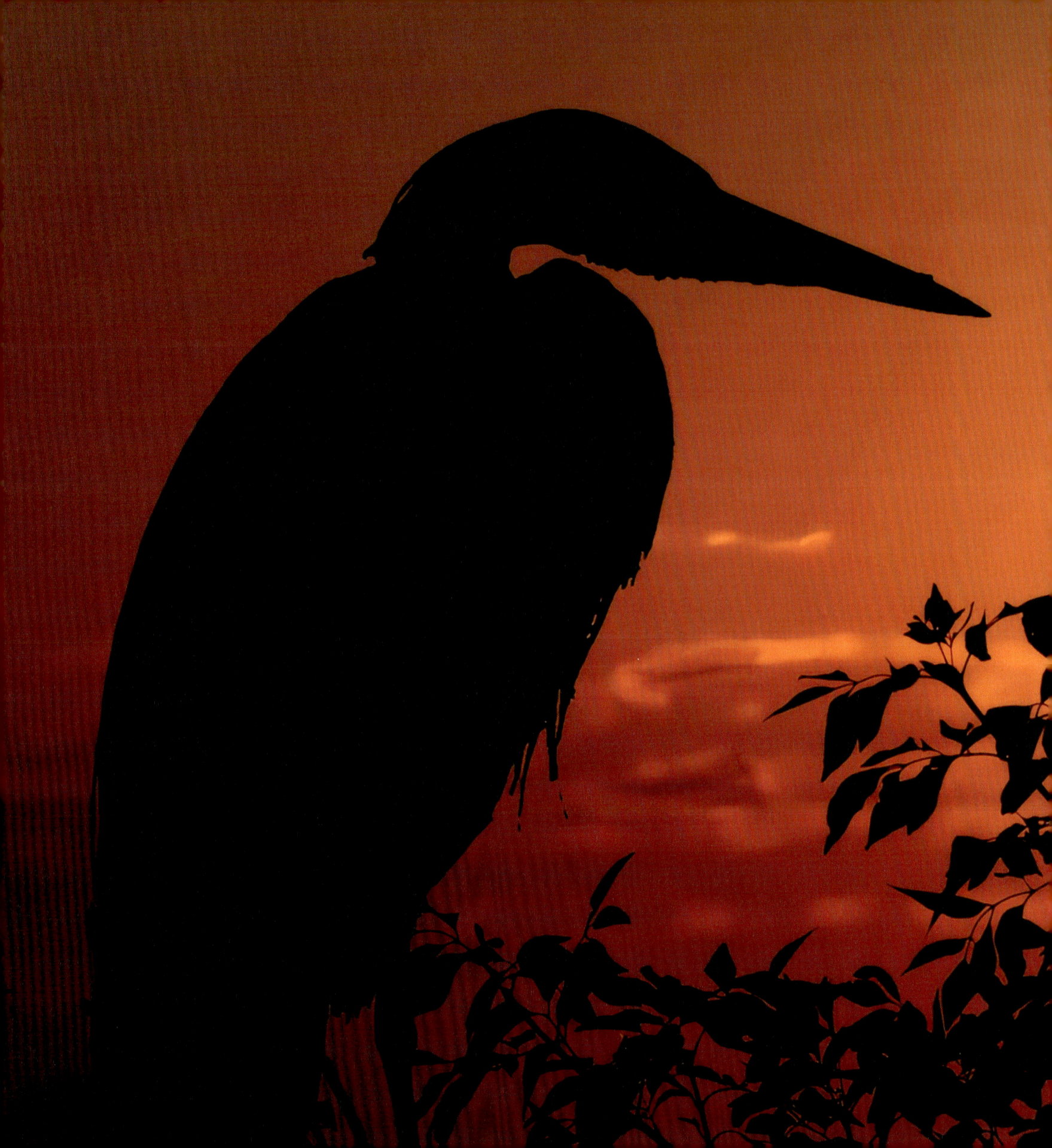

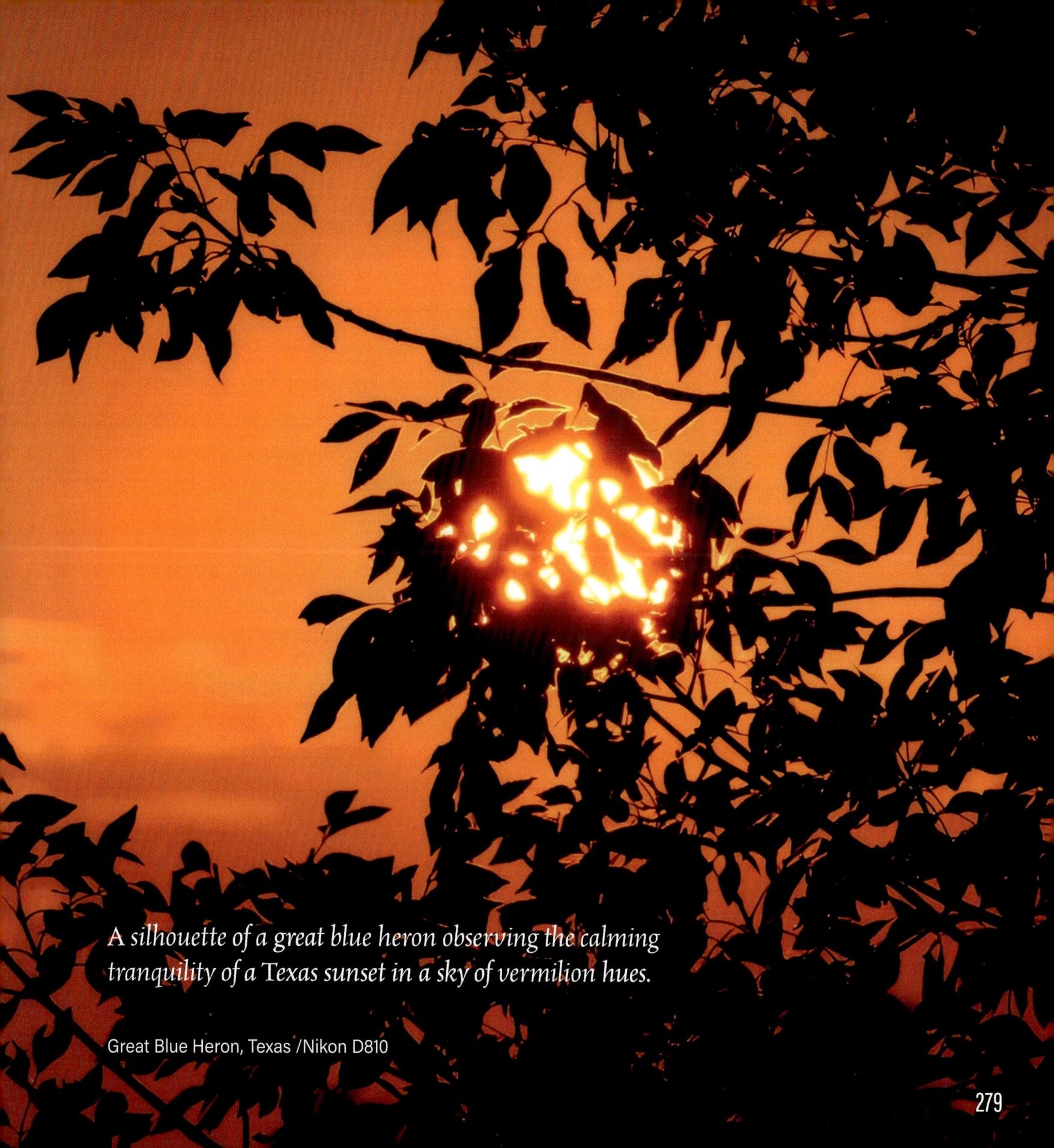

A silhouette of a great blue heron observing the calming tranquility of a Texas sunset in a sky of vermilion hues.

Great Blue Heron, Texas /Nikon D810

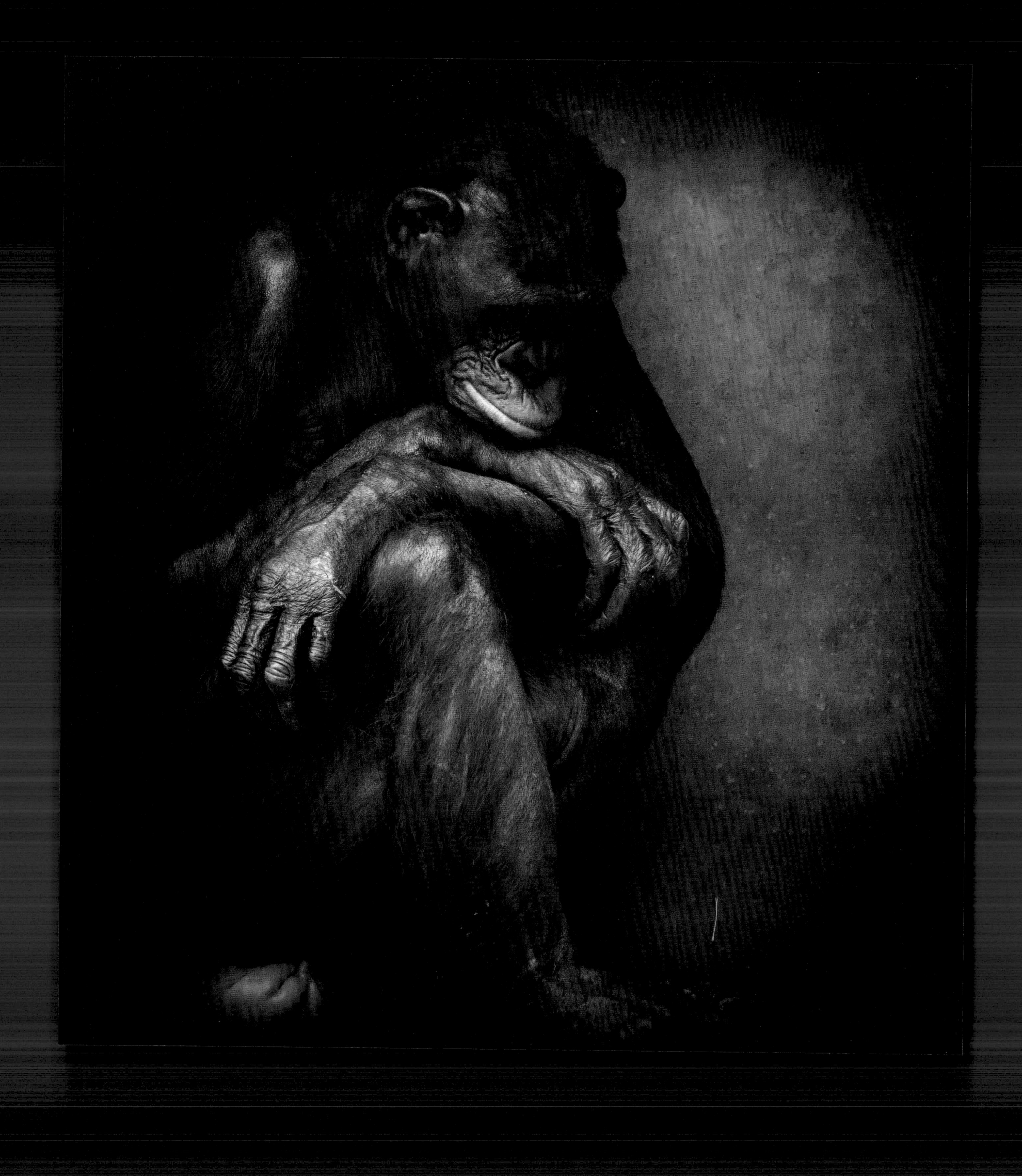

ENDANGERED

What is lost will never be found. A very powerful statement that rings so very true to so many wildlife species now extinct, lost forever over time with only our imagination left to remember them. The word "extinction" is an ugly word to me, and it has been since my early childhood, when I first visited a memorial exhibit at the Cincinnati Zoo and saw Martha, the last passenger pigeon on Earth, who died there in 1914. It was a defining moment in my life, as I simply could not understand the reasons why. I believe my love of animals and the natural world started on this day, and over time, I have endeavored through my photography to provide moving images of wildlife to help others see, truly see, how utterly amazing the world around us is, and hopefully will always be.

Ignoring endangered wildlife invites their extinction, and that must never happen. The premise that many species on the edge of extinction can survive without our help is not plausible. Over the last century alone, hundreds of thousands of African elephants have been illegally killed by poachers. So many of the large male "tuskers," as they are commonly known, have long since perished, their faces cut off, tusks removed, and their corpses left to rot in the harsh African sun. It is difficult to fathom that magnificent species such as the elephant, the rhino, and so many, many others may someday disappear altogether from memory simply because someone wanted to have a piece of jewelry or ornament made of ivory to adorn their mantelpiece. We are better than this. We have to be.

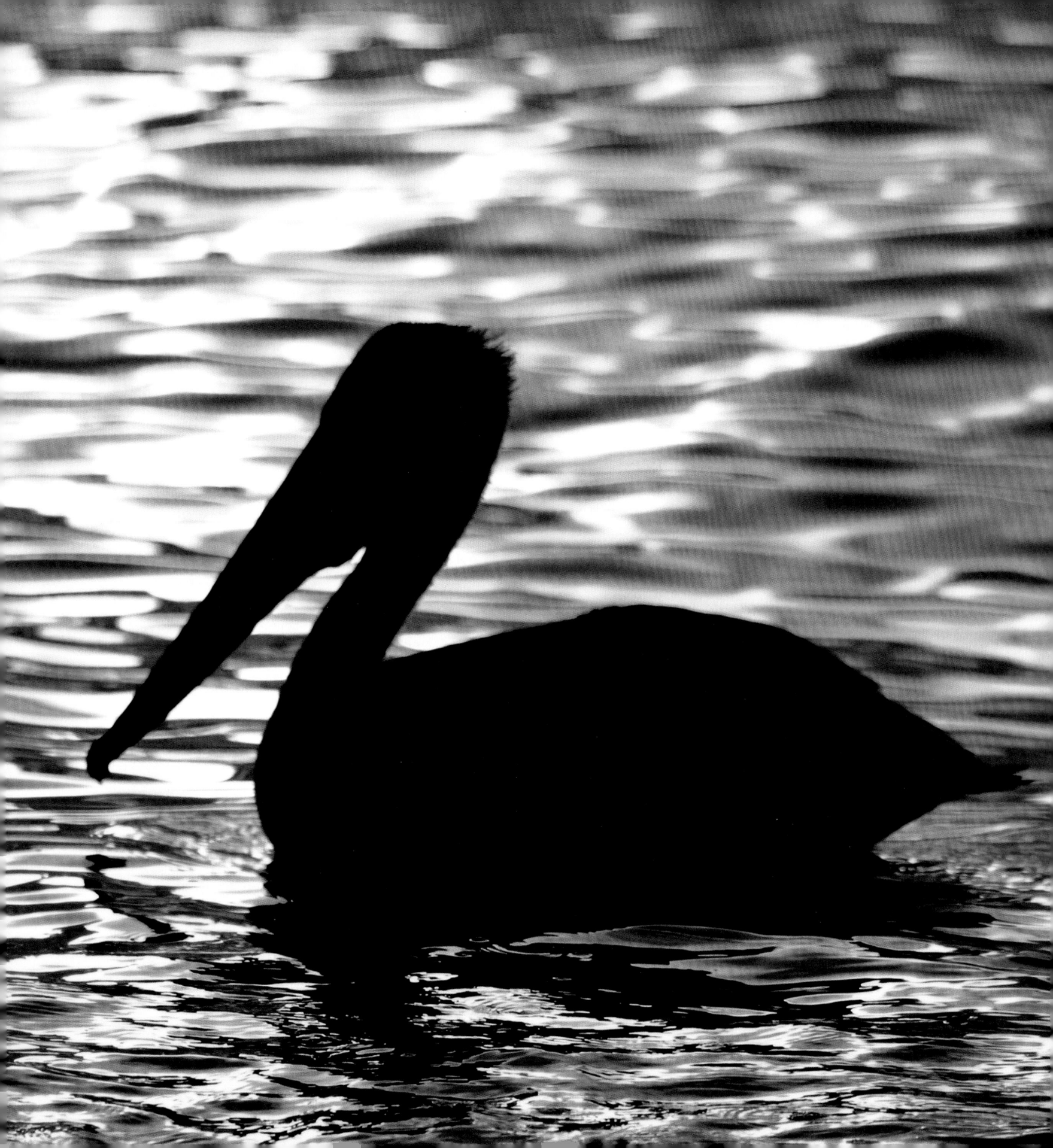

CONSERVATION

A day like no other. Walking along a pristine white sandy beach, with a tranquil tropical breeze in the air, with the setting sun slowly descending behind the horizon, illuminating the ocean surface with a symphony of sparkling lights. Sandpipers scurry about the shoreline, moving with the constant rhythm of the tidal waves, always one step ahead of getting washed away. A wondrous place, a magical day forever etched in my memory, but not for the reasons you might imagine. This day, on this same tranquil beach, I came across a solitary pelican perched atop a lonely rocky outcrop. His leg was tangled terribly in a fishing line, from which he was desperately trying to be free. Helping him was not possible, and all I could do was observe from a distance, hoping he would prevail. As the sun descended, I watched him drift back into the ocean currents with only his shadowy outline barely visible, soon to disappear completely as darkness enveloped us. Conservation is a big word and a responsibility that we all share, but it truly starts and ends with you. Your actions, multiplied by a billion others, can and do make a difference. The natural world is a very fragile place: it can be hurt, it can suffer, and it can die. I often wonder about my pelican friend. I wonder if he was able to free himself and live the life he deserved. I wonder how many others have suffered a similar fate. I wonder . . .

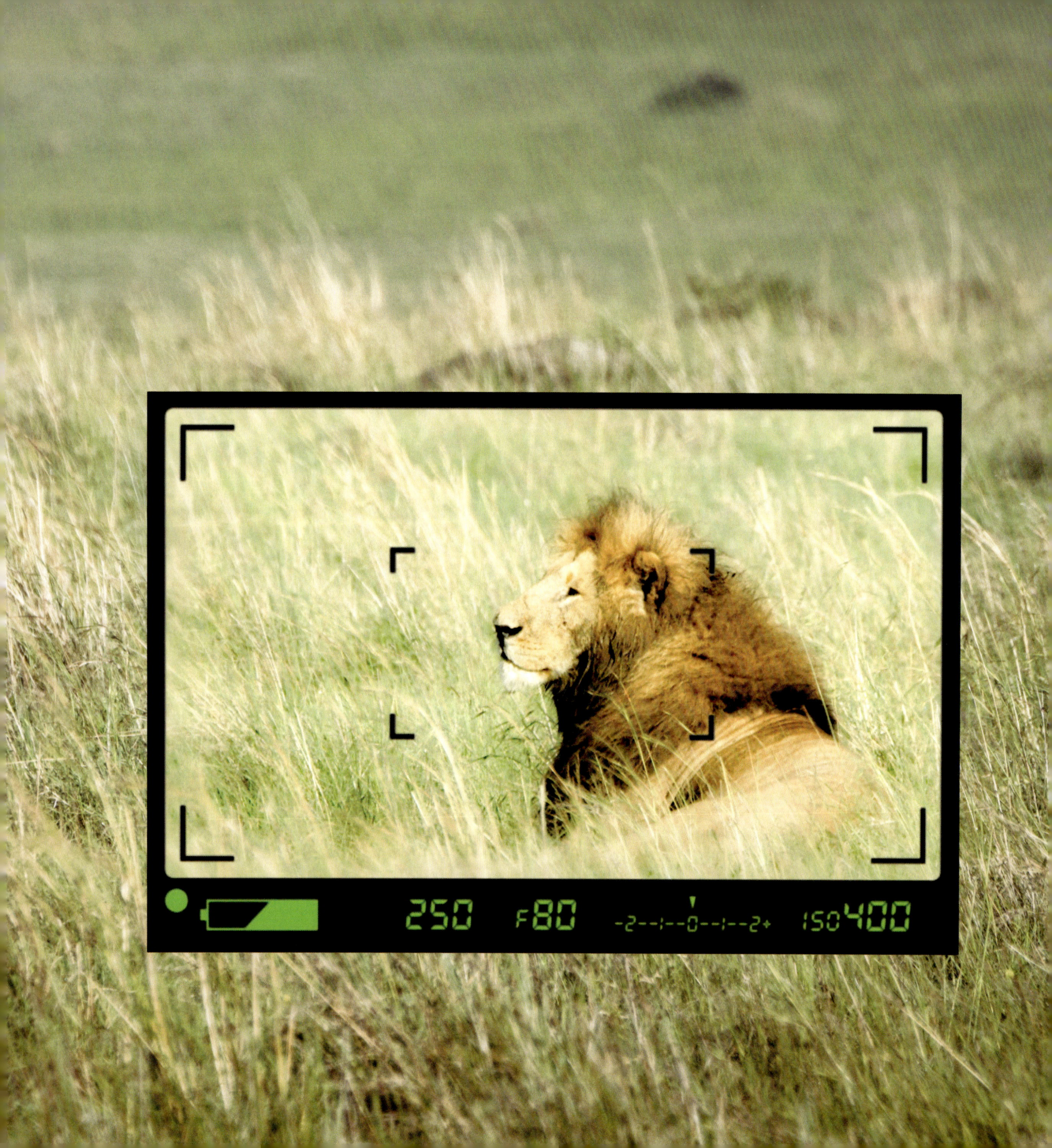

SEEING WILD

What makes a good wildlife photographer is being able to sense the world all around you that many others simply do not: The fluttering of a monarch butterfly high in the treetops above. A praying mantis sitting motionless on a leaf. The distant chirping of a cardinal feeding on a berry bush at the edge of the forest. There is a chorus of sights and sounds in nature that exist, but to learn and master them is a lifetime tutorial of patience, practice, and accumulated knowledge for which there is no diploma nor certification ever to be given. As the pen is to the writer, the camera is to the wildlife photographer. It's intimidating at first, but it quickly becomes a part of you wherever you go. In today's world, cameras are everywhere. Learning to use them can be as easy as clicking a button on your smartphone or as difficult as absorbing the 300-plus-page technical manual that came in the box with your new DSLR camera. Composition, lighting, and focus should forever be your top priorities, and learning how your camera can best support that outcome should be your never-ending quest. I try to stay as true to the wildlife moment as possible without adding questionable enhancements that might deceive the viewer. Starting out, you will miss many great shots; you might curse, you might cry, but through lots of trial and error, like everything else in life, the more you persevere, the better you will eventually become.

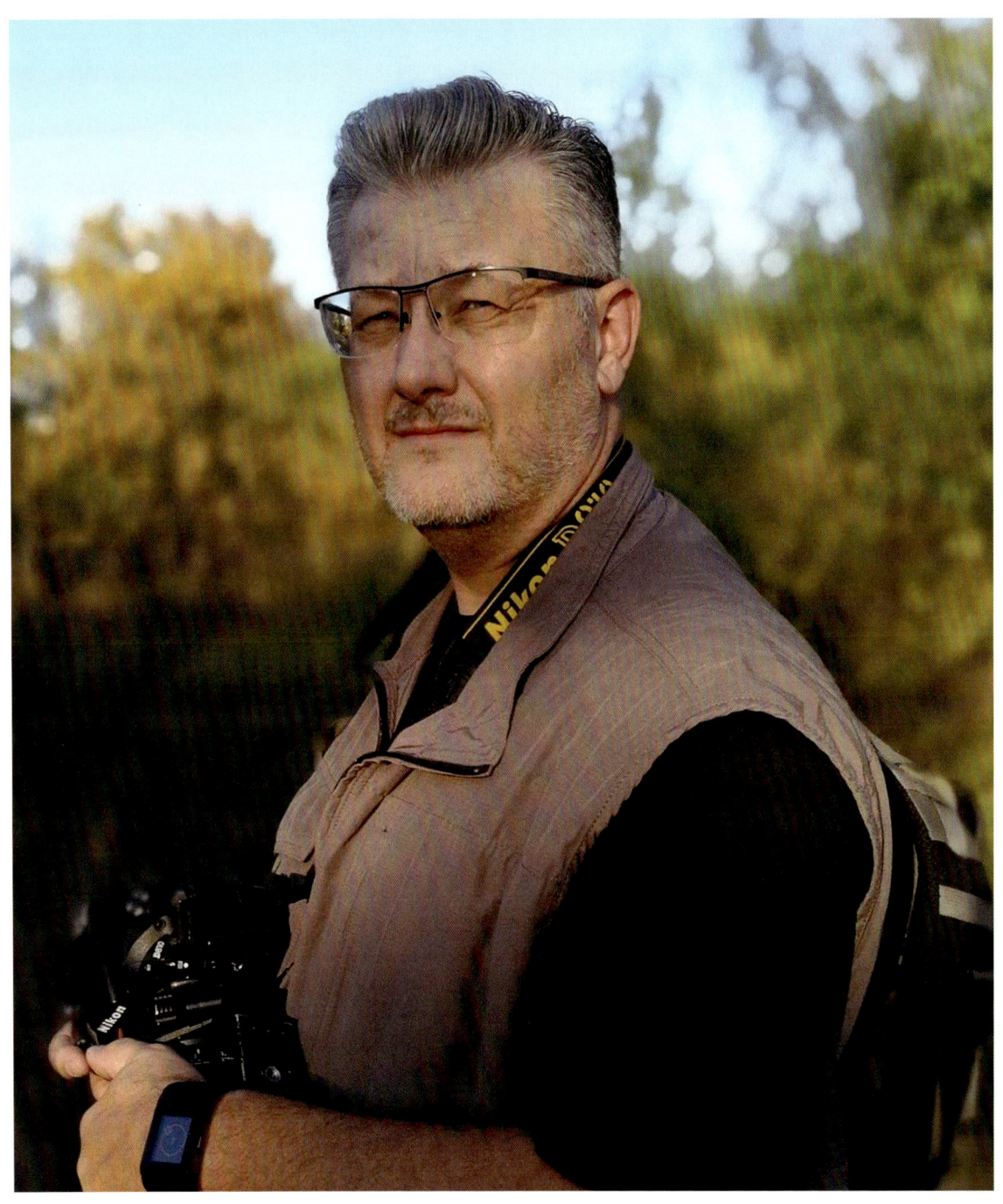

BIOGRAPHY

When you live in places where urban sprawl surrounds you, immersing yourself in nature can be a daunting challenge, to say the least. As a kid, I can vividly remember spending endless hours exploring my backyard with the same excitement, curiosity, and wonderment as Lewis and Clark must have had traversing the great western expanses of the United States in the early 19th century. My backyard was my refuge: a very small yard in a decaying alleyway surrounded by an urban jungle of brick and concrete. My fascination with spiders, ants, and other types of creepy crawlies became my first fascination, as they still are to this day. My passion for wildlife photography started when my wife bought a small film camera for me to take on my frequent hikes through the swamps of the Florida Everglades. I think she really just wanted to see some of the wildlife I had often described to her without experiencing the humidity, mosquitoes, and danger of trekking with me. My early images were, in truth, mostly dreadful. But I was excited to be able to capture a brief moment in time to be remembered forever without a single word ever needing to be said. Helping others to see and appreciate wildlife through my photography is an integral part of who I am today. If I can inspire the next generation to continue to preserve our natural world, I will be content that my images made a difference.

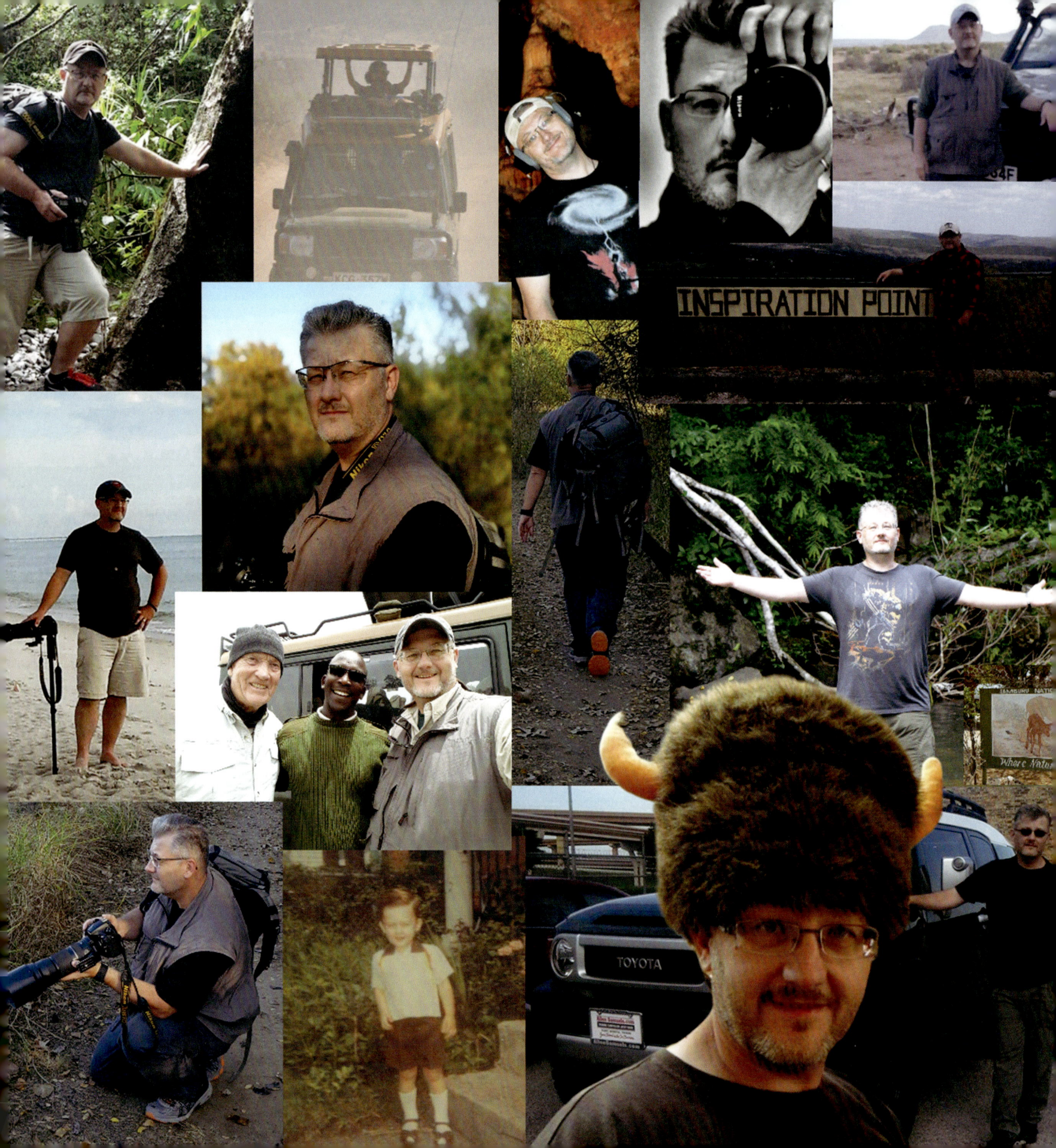

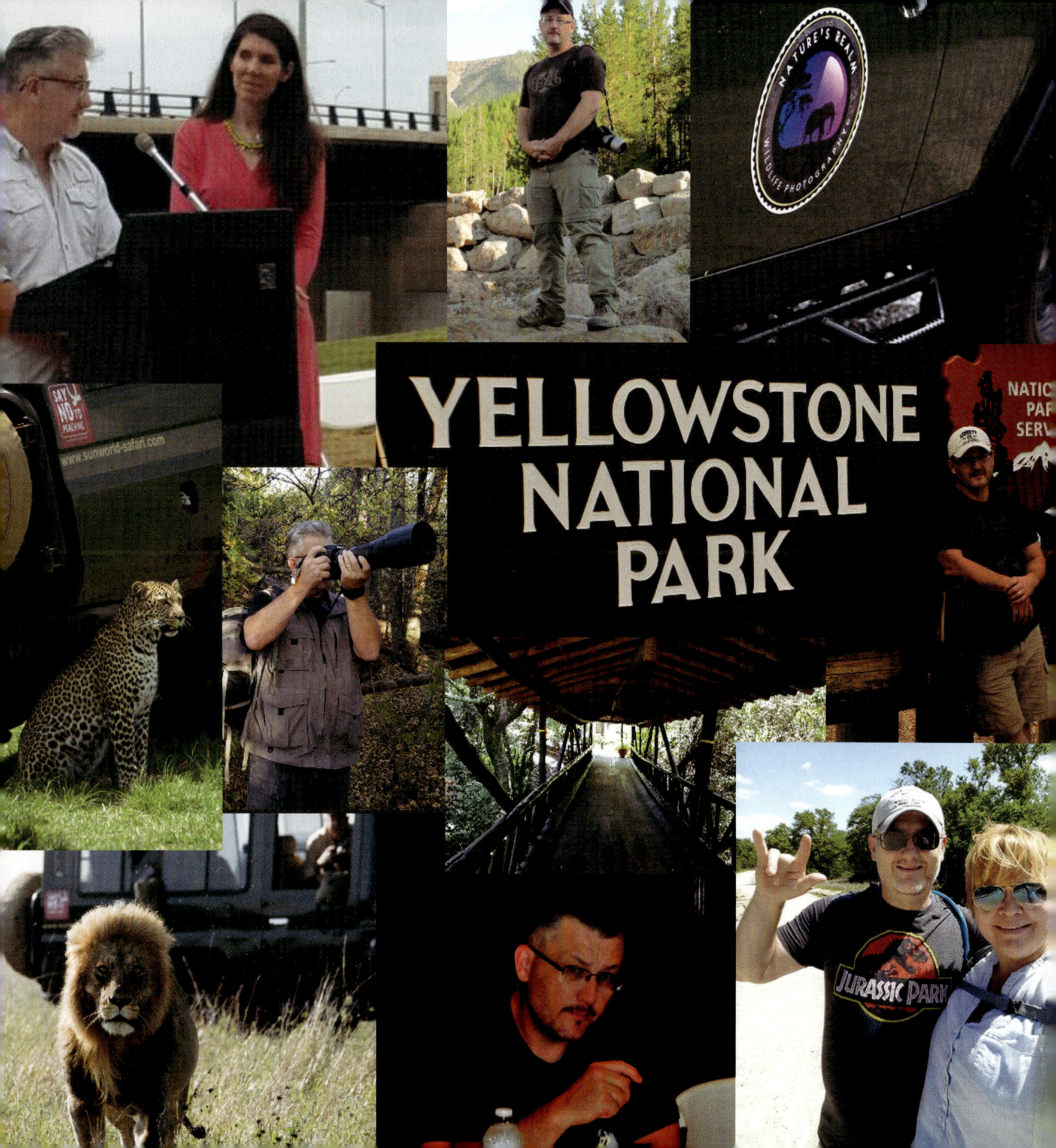

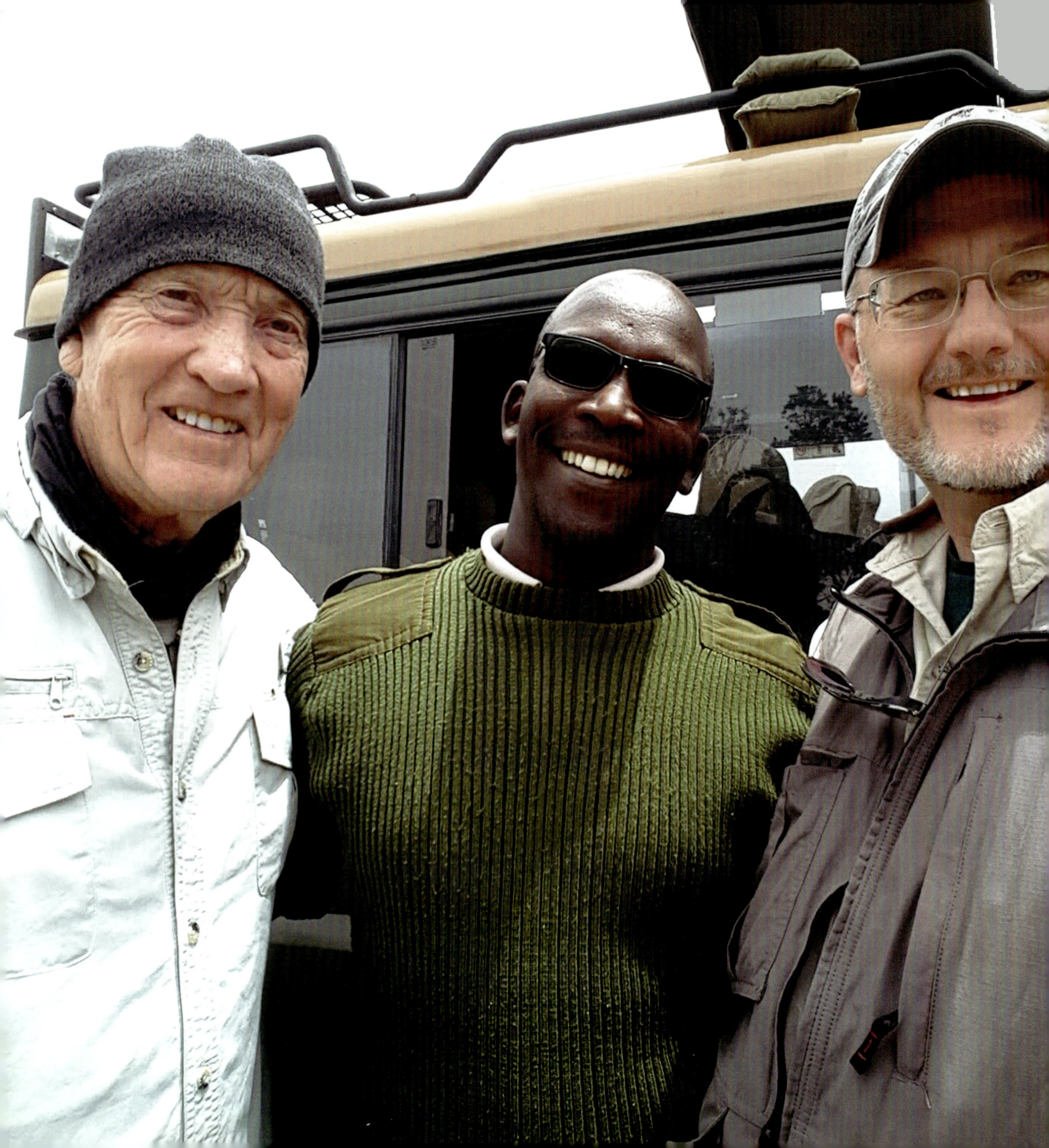

ACKNOWLEDGMENTS

Over the course of the last thirty years, I have met more people than I can remember who have truly helped me along the way. From the camera store manager explaining how to use the features on my new camera, to the young hikers I met in Texas taking the time to show me where they spotted an armadillo foraging in the forest. Photographers, hikers, naturalists, fishermen, hunters, and so many other ordinary—yet extraordinary—people are within the unseen pages of this book, and I am so very thankful for their wisdom, guidance, and friendship along the way. In Africa, my guide Eric was simply the best, and I shall forever remember our many bird conversations we had while on the rough roads of the Mara in search of extraordinary wildlife. I recall chatting with a park ranger in Yellowstone, who directed my wife and me to an American bald eagle's nest high atop a lodgepole pine, where we were greeted by a pair of young eaglets awaiting their mother's return. The list goes on and on, but most importantly, I want to thank my wife, Rebecca, and my three children, who have supported my passion for nature and wildlife photography from the very beginning and have always been there for me. This book is for you. I love you more!

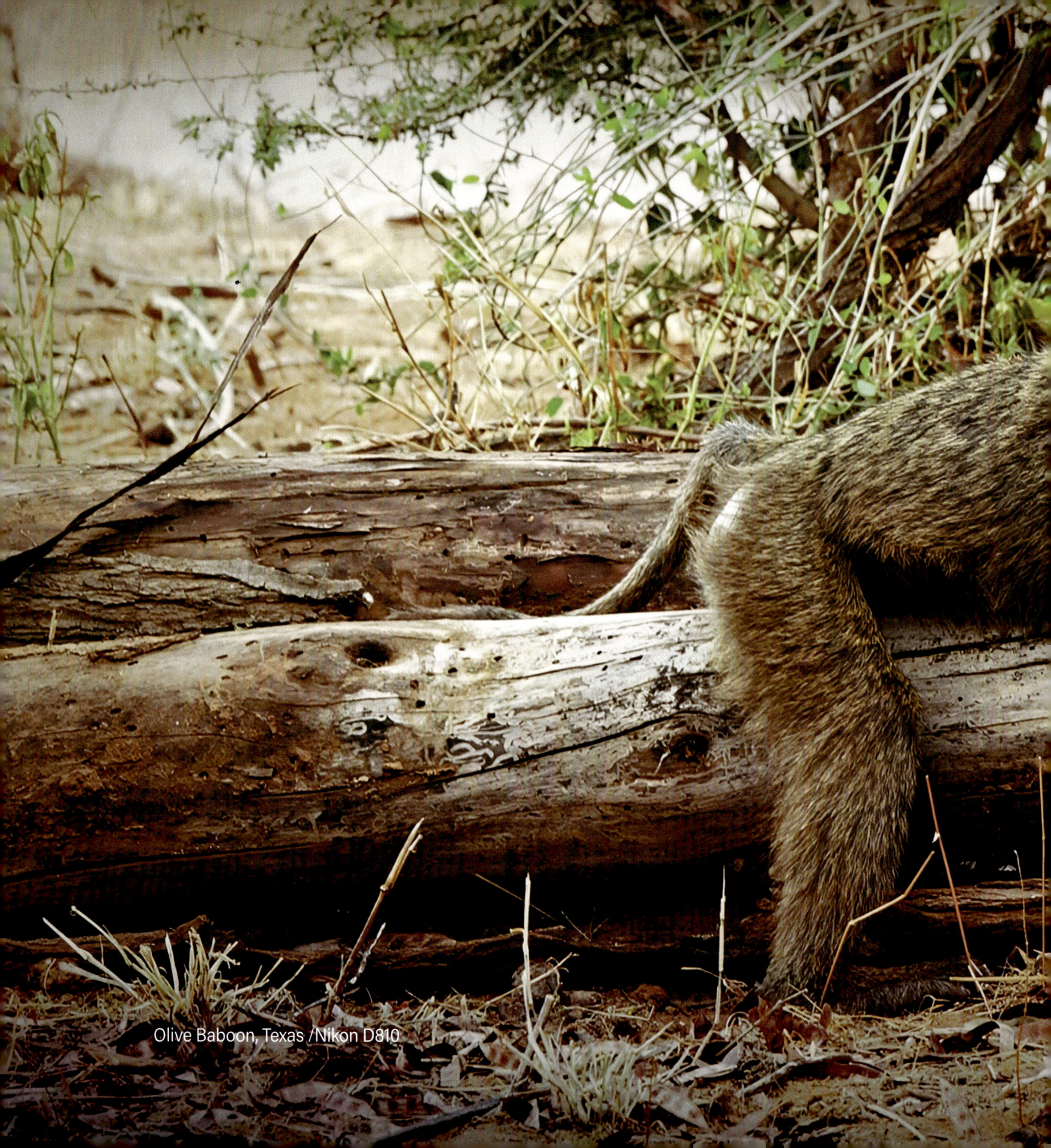

Olive Baboon, Texas /Nikon D810

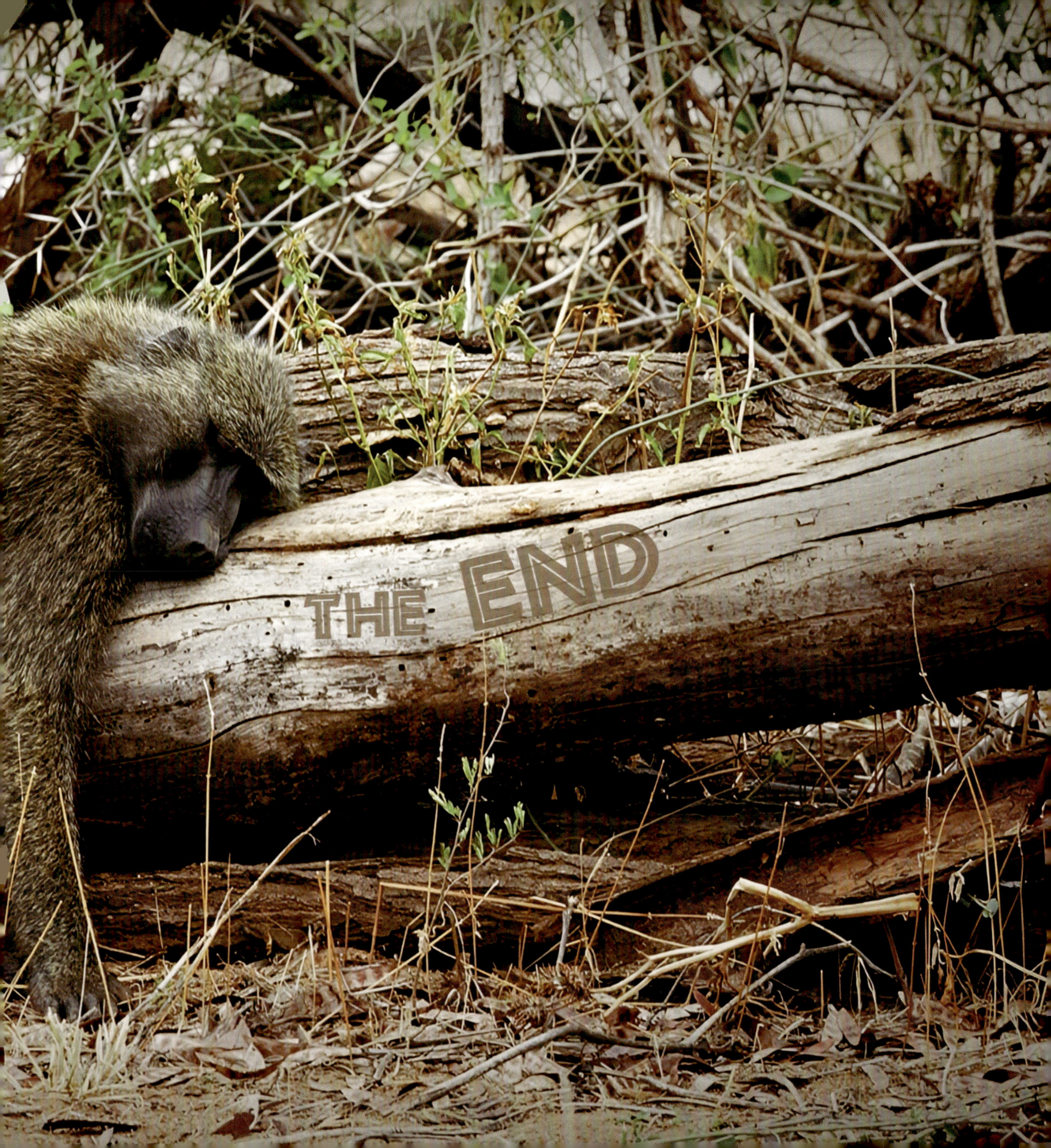

WAIT . . . HOW ABOUT
A CURTAIN CALL?

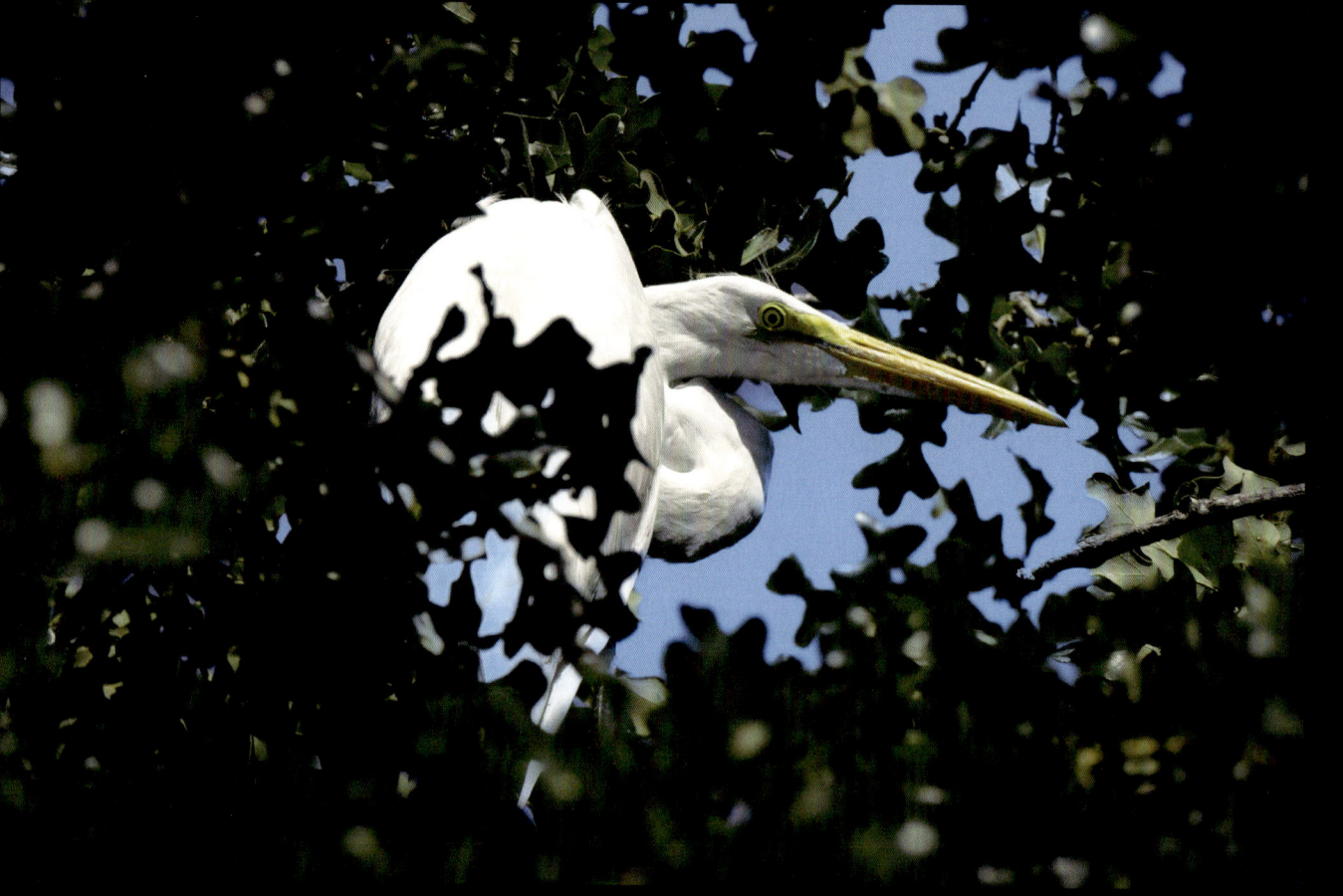

High in the canopy above, within its many hidden corridors, life abounds in absolute wonder. Animals of all sizes seek refuge, raise their young, and thrive in this vibrant sea of green. Dappled sunlight creates a mesmerizing kaleidoscope of color, constantly transforming the moment into an ever changing masterpiece of the natural world.

Above: Great Egret, Texas /Nikon D850
Opposite: Barred Owl, Texas /Nikon D850

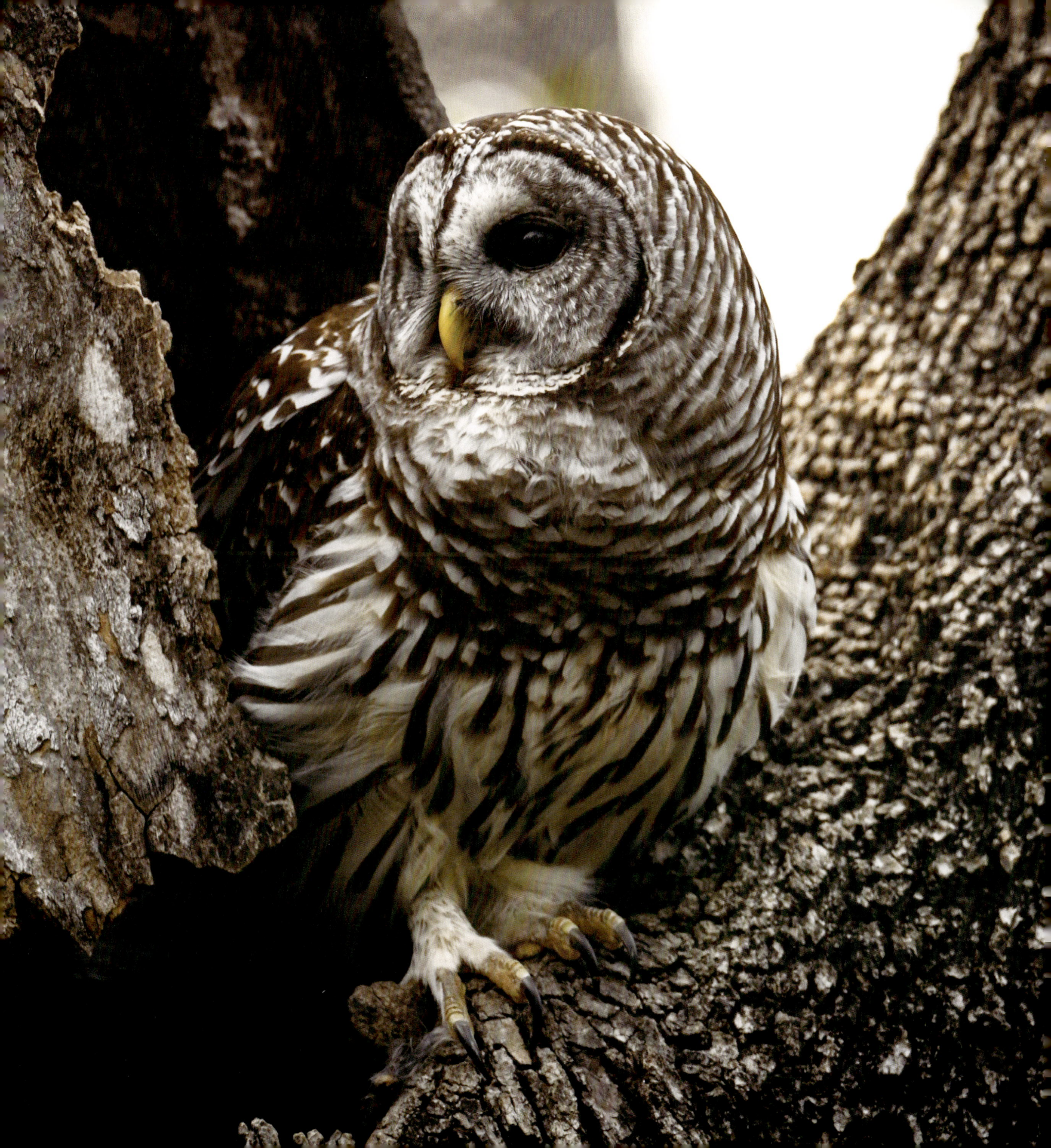

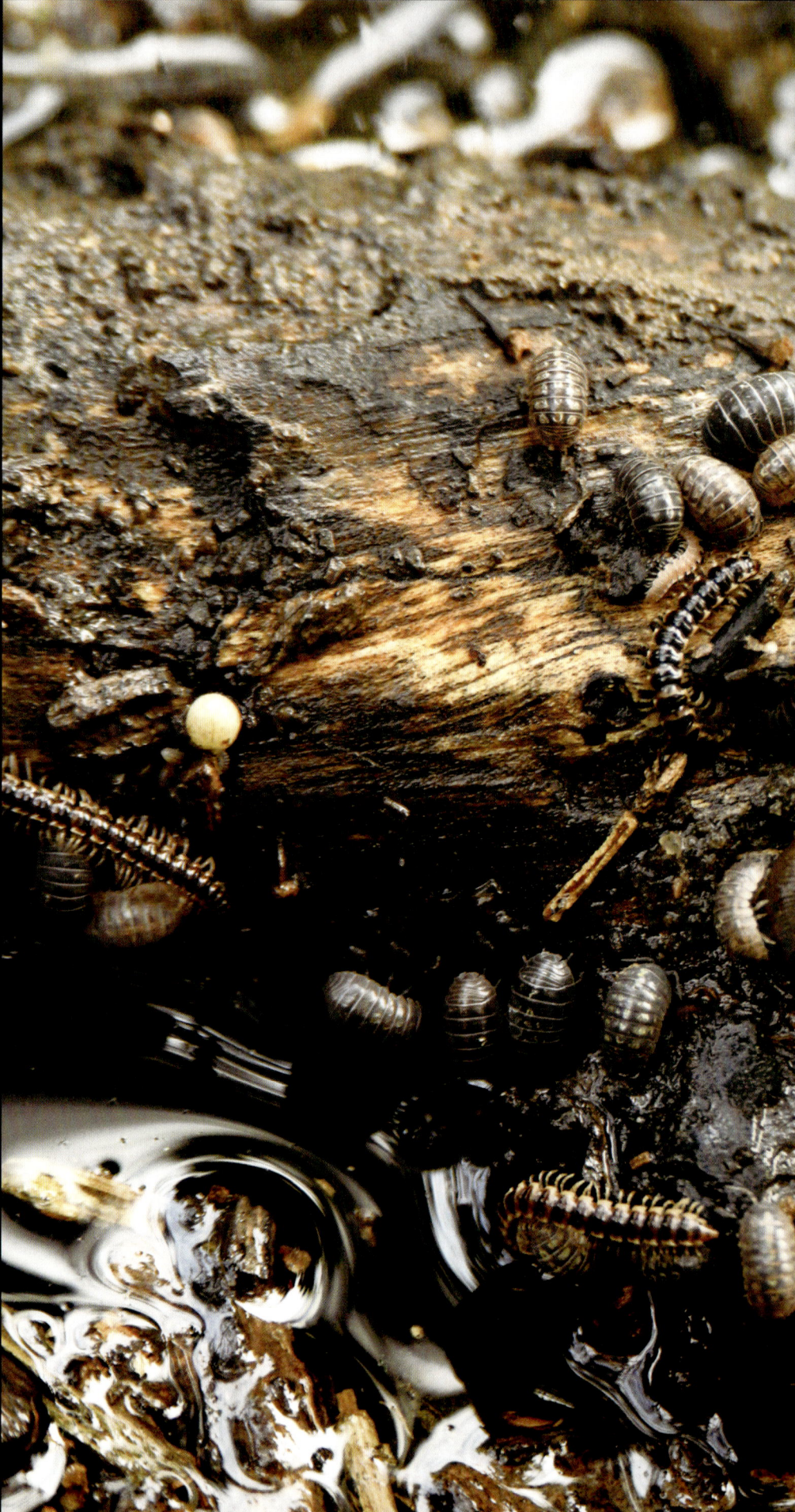

As the floodwaters rise, a single wooden log becomes a floating refuge for all manner of life to cling to together. In these moments of natural upheaval, insects, plants, and small animals find a temporary sanctuary on this unlikely vessel, showcasing the resilience and adaptability of nature.

The Ark of the Floodplain, Texas /
Nikon D850

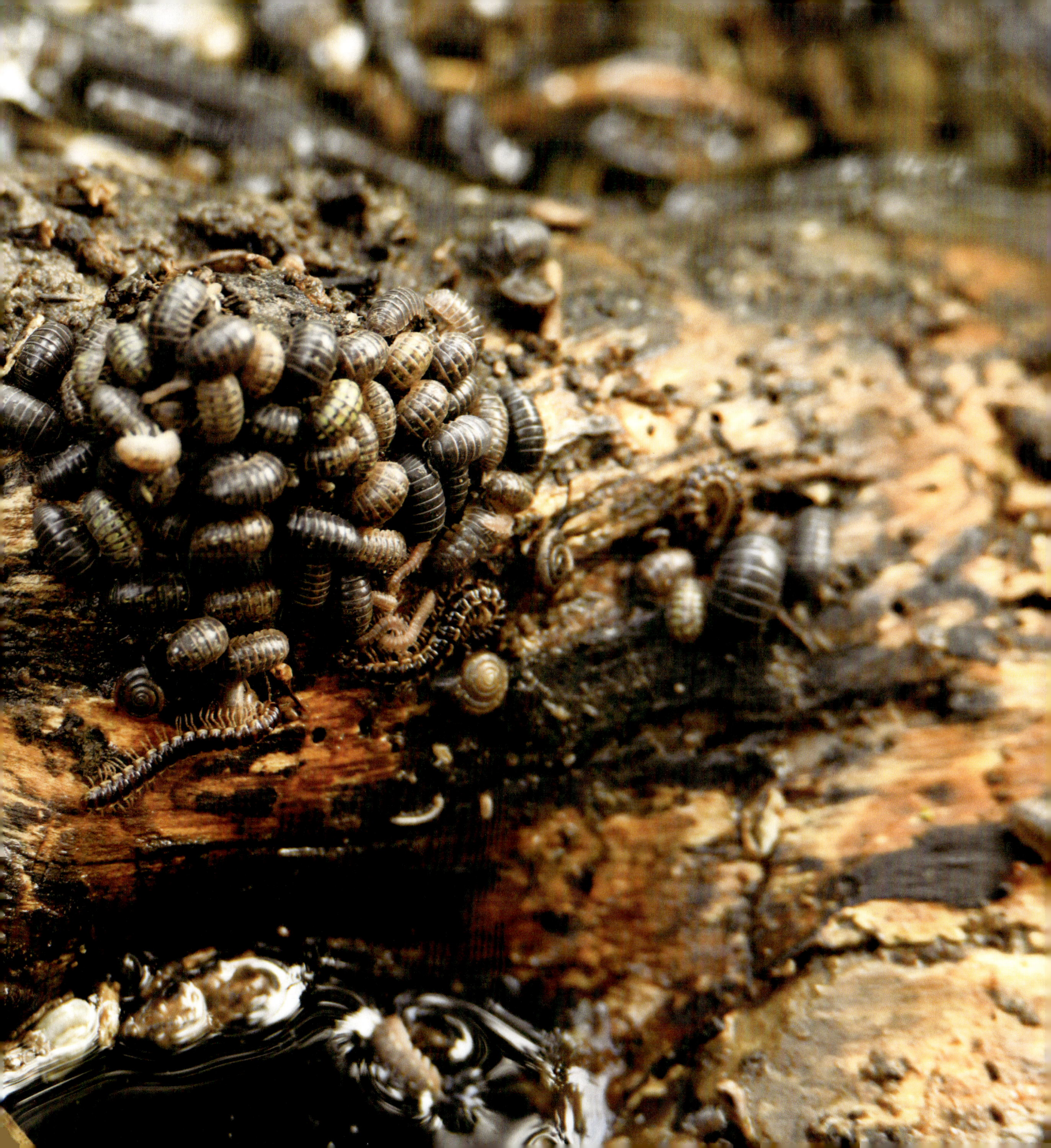

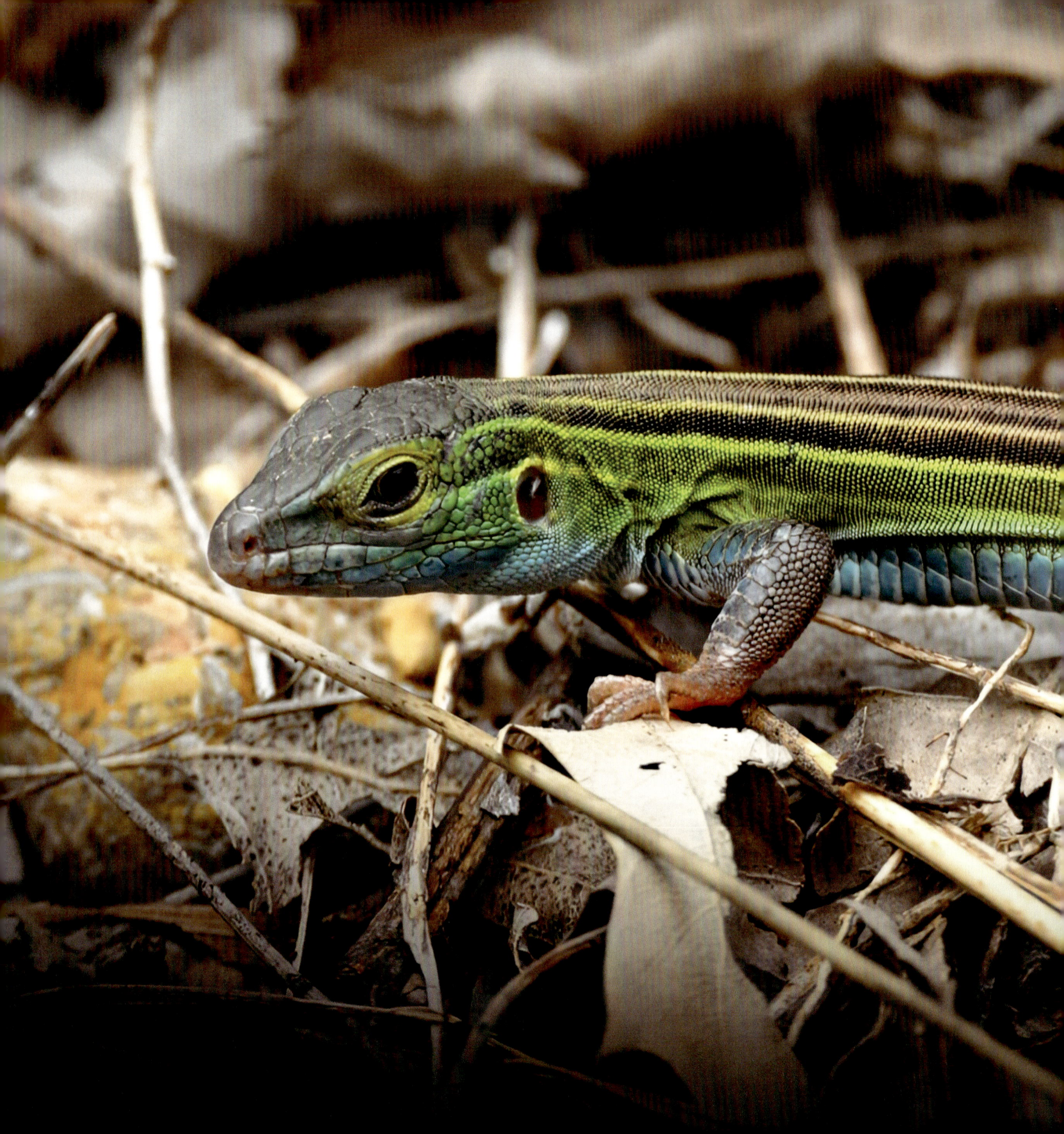

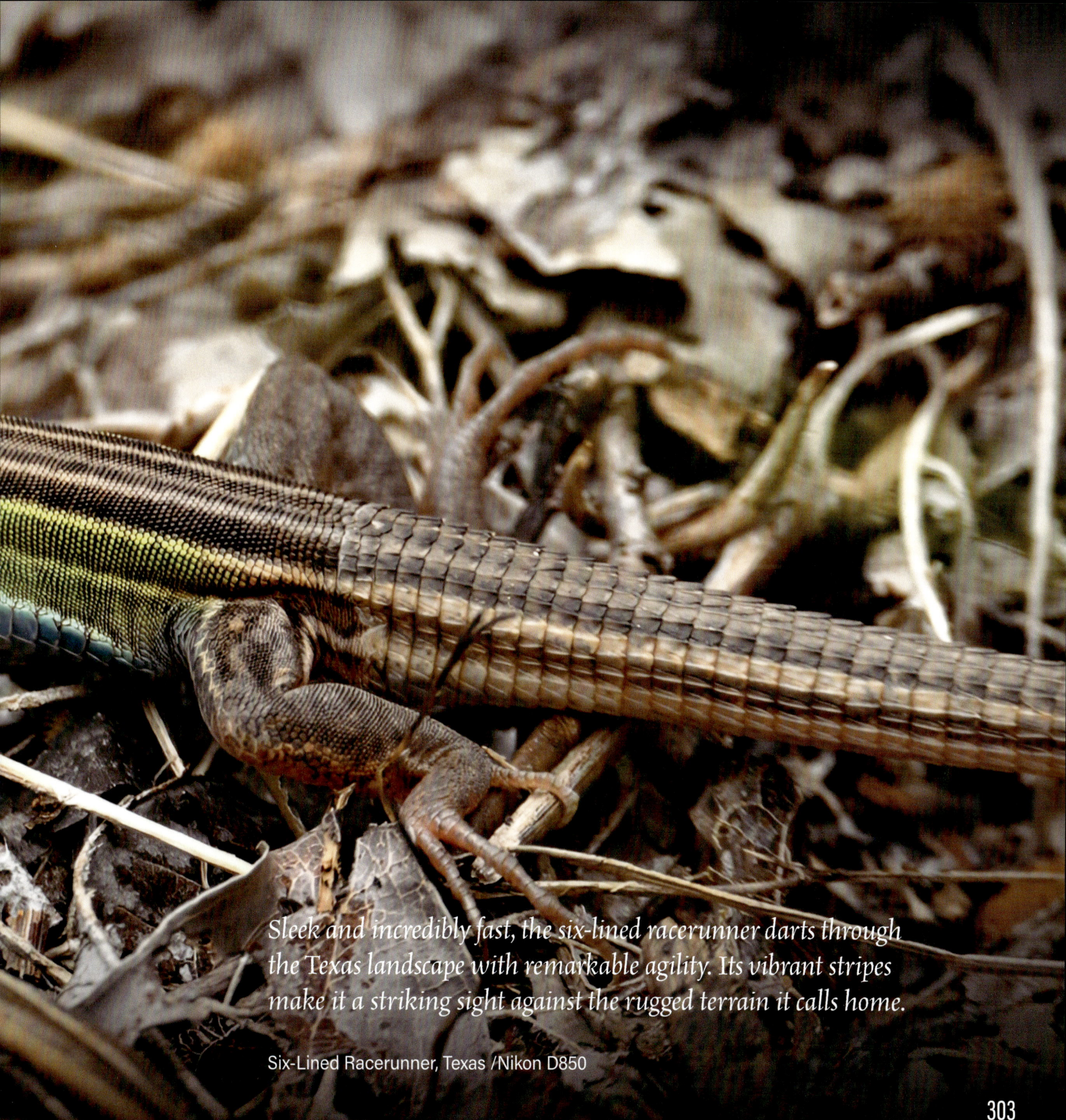

Sleek and incredibly fast, the six-lined racerunner darts through the Texas landscape with remarkable agility. Its vibrant stripes make it a striking sight against the rugged terrain it calls home.

Six-Lined Racerunner, Texas /Nikon D850

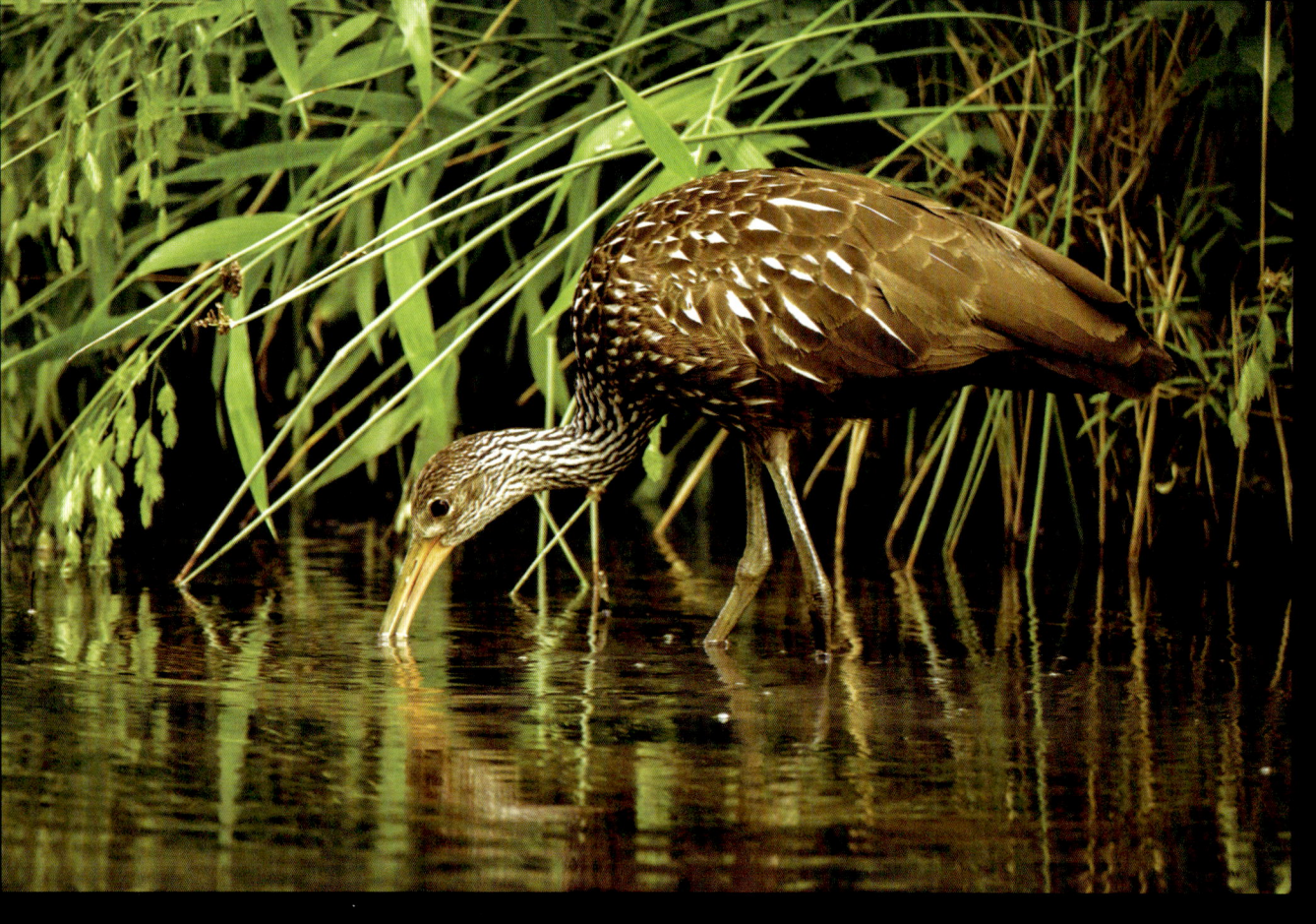

Wetland areas across the world are teeming with life. Herons, ducks, and so many other bird species grace the waters and shores with their vibrant colors and lively presence. All one has to do is observe long enough, and wonders will appear.

Below: Limpkin, Texas /Nikon D850
Opposite: Yellow-Crowned Night Heron, Texas /Nikon D850

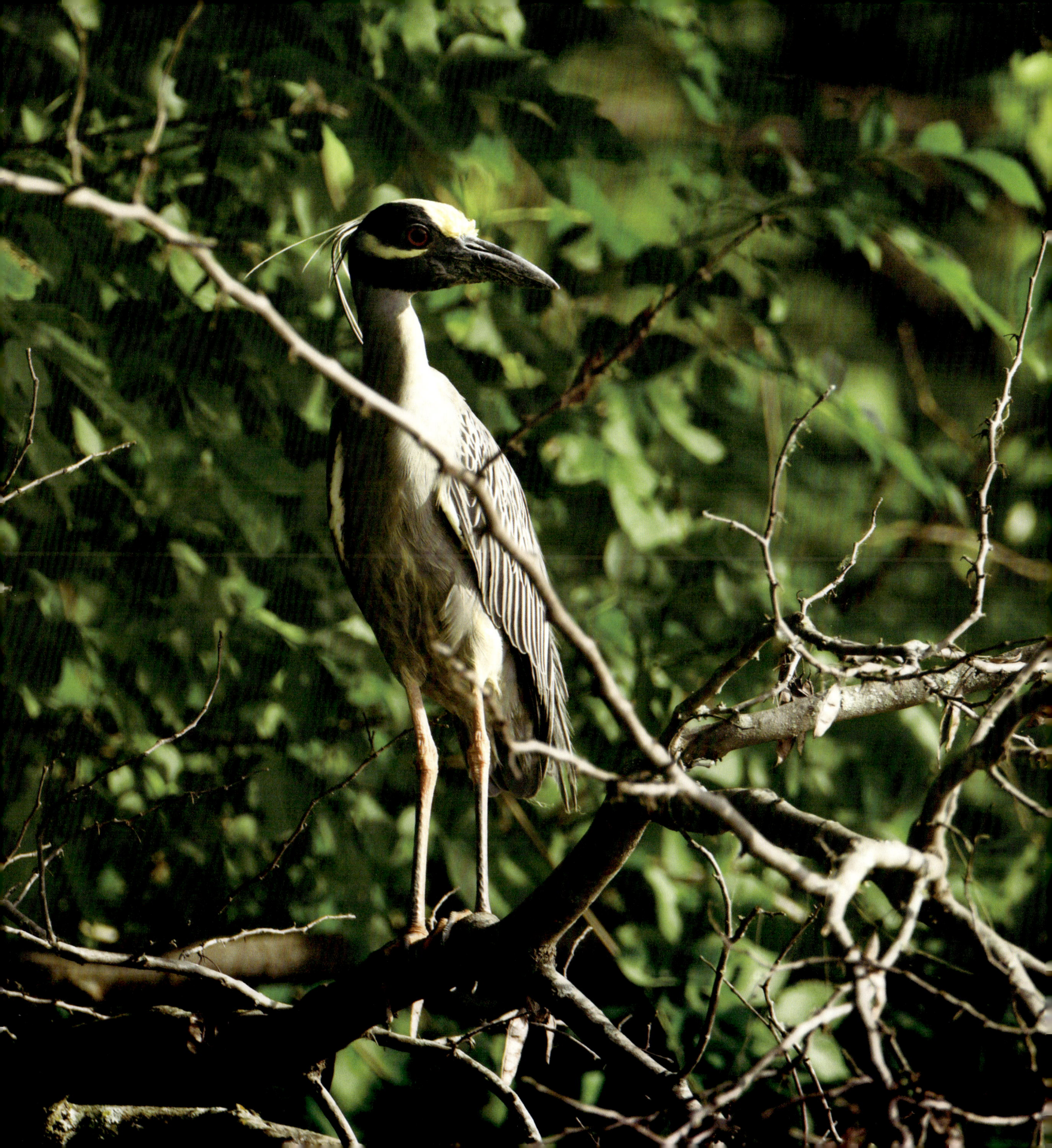

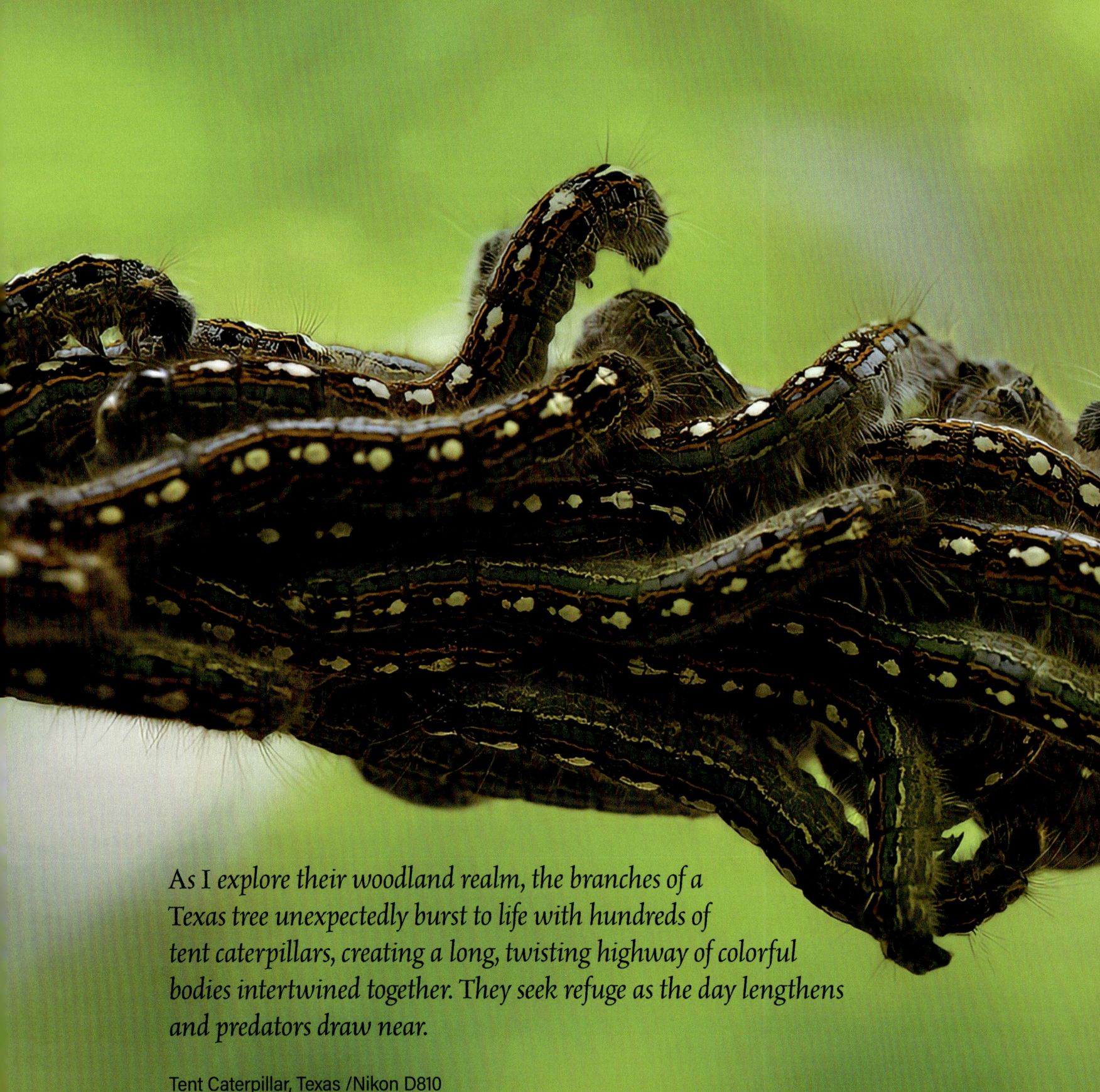

As I explore their woodland realm, the branches of a Texas tree unexpectedly burst to life with hundreds of tent caterpillars, creating a long, twisting highway of colorful bodies intertwined together. They seek refuge as the day lengthens and predators draw near.

Tent Caterpillar, Texas / Nikon D810

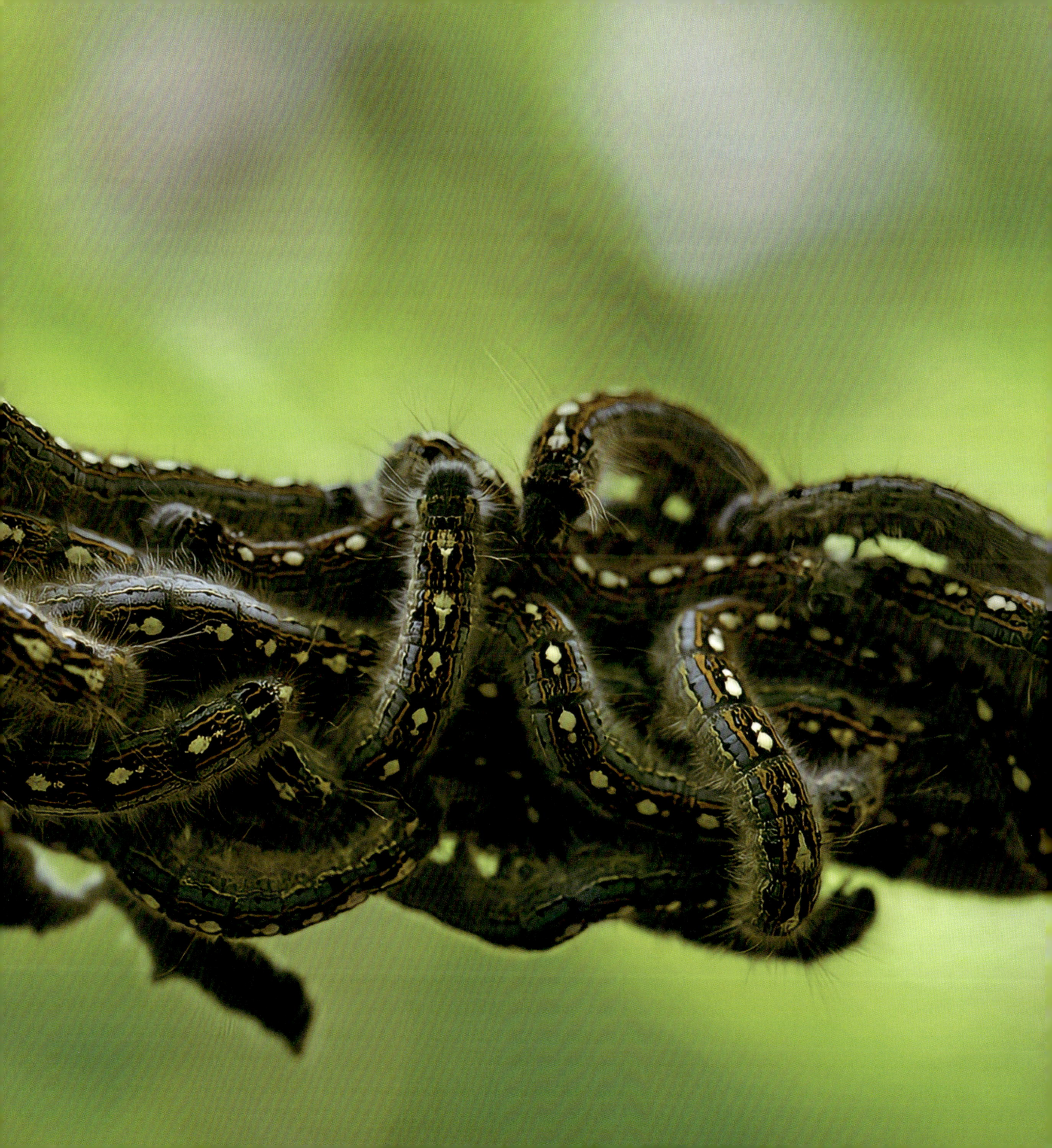

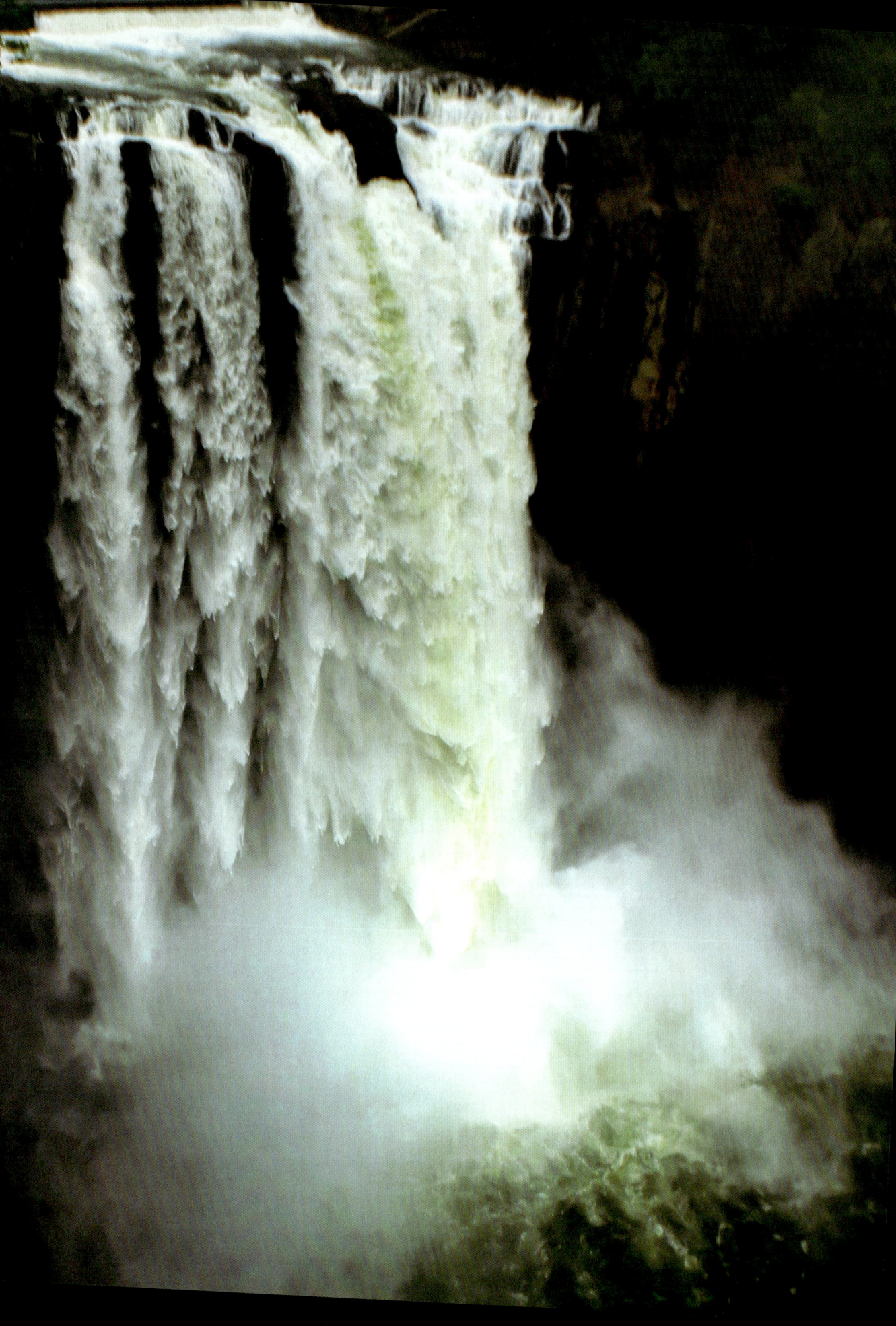

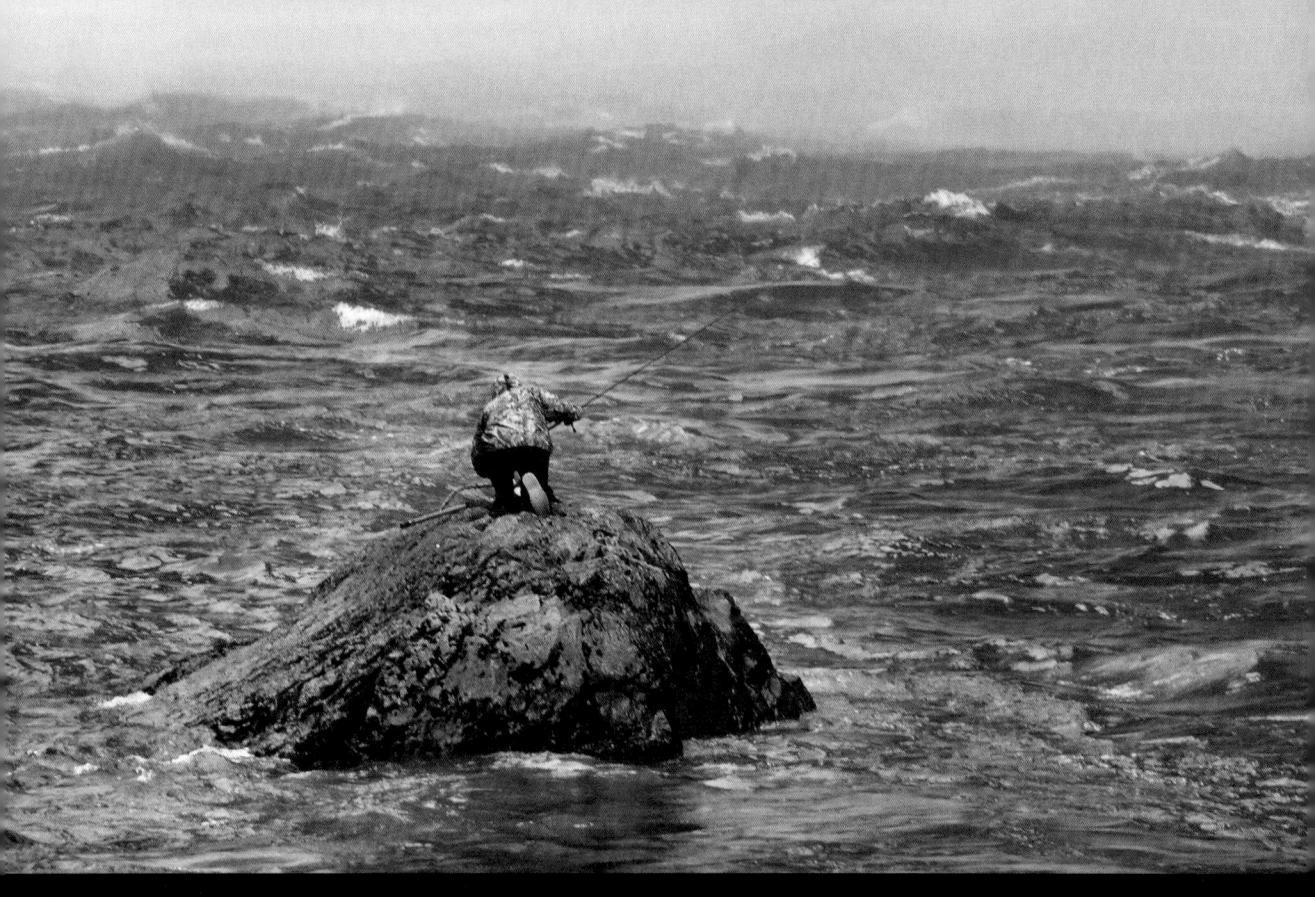

Perched on a massive boulder amindst rising waters, a lone fisherman defies the might of Snoqualmie Falls, casting his line into the roaring cascade.

Above and opposite: Snoqualmie Falls, Washington /Nikon D300.

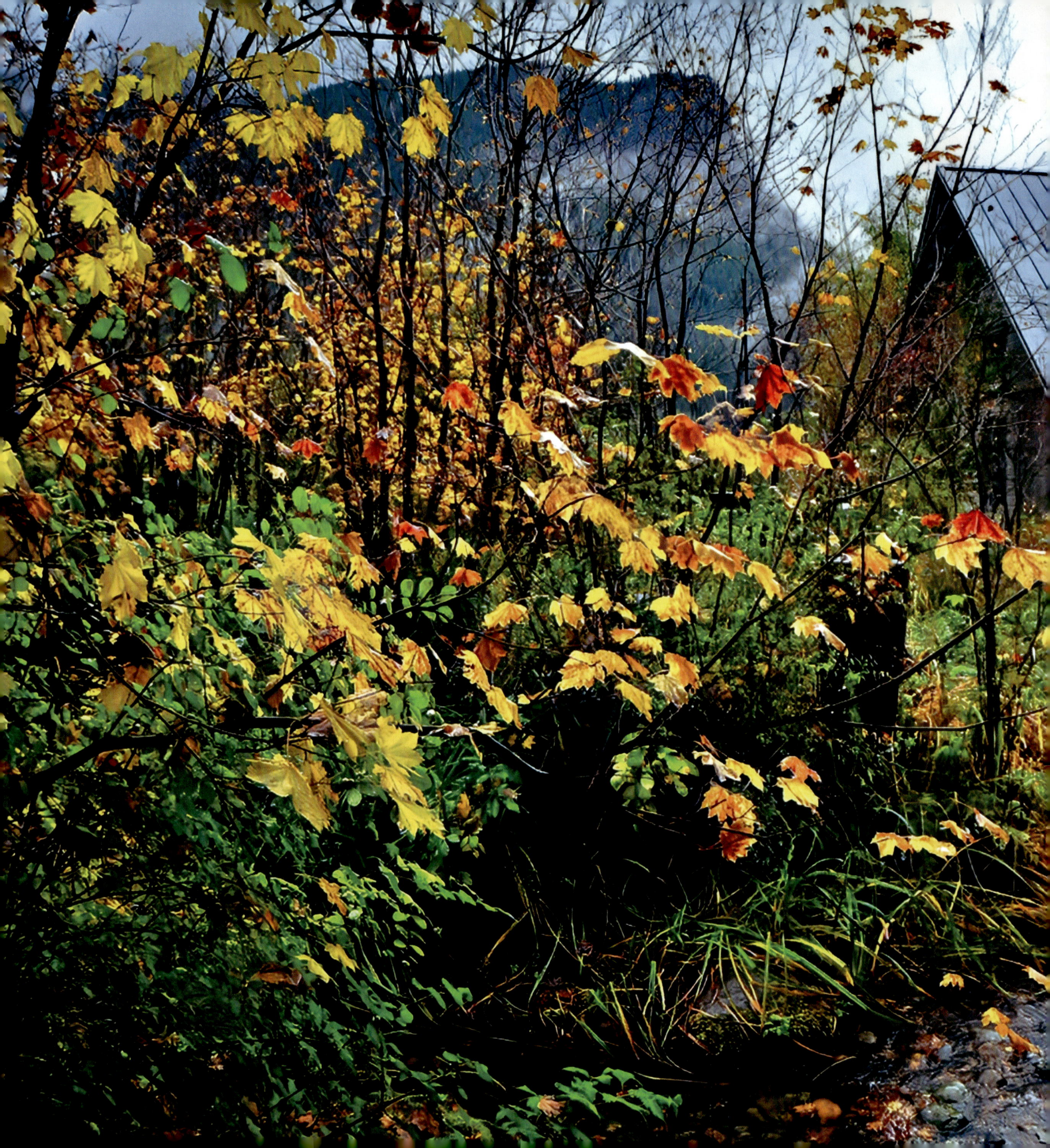

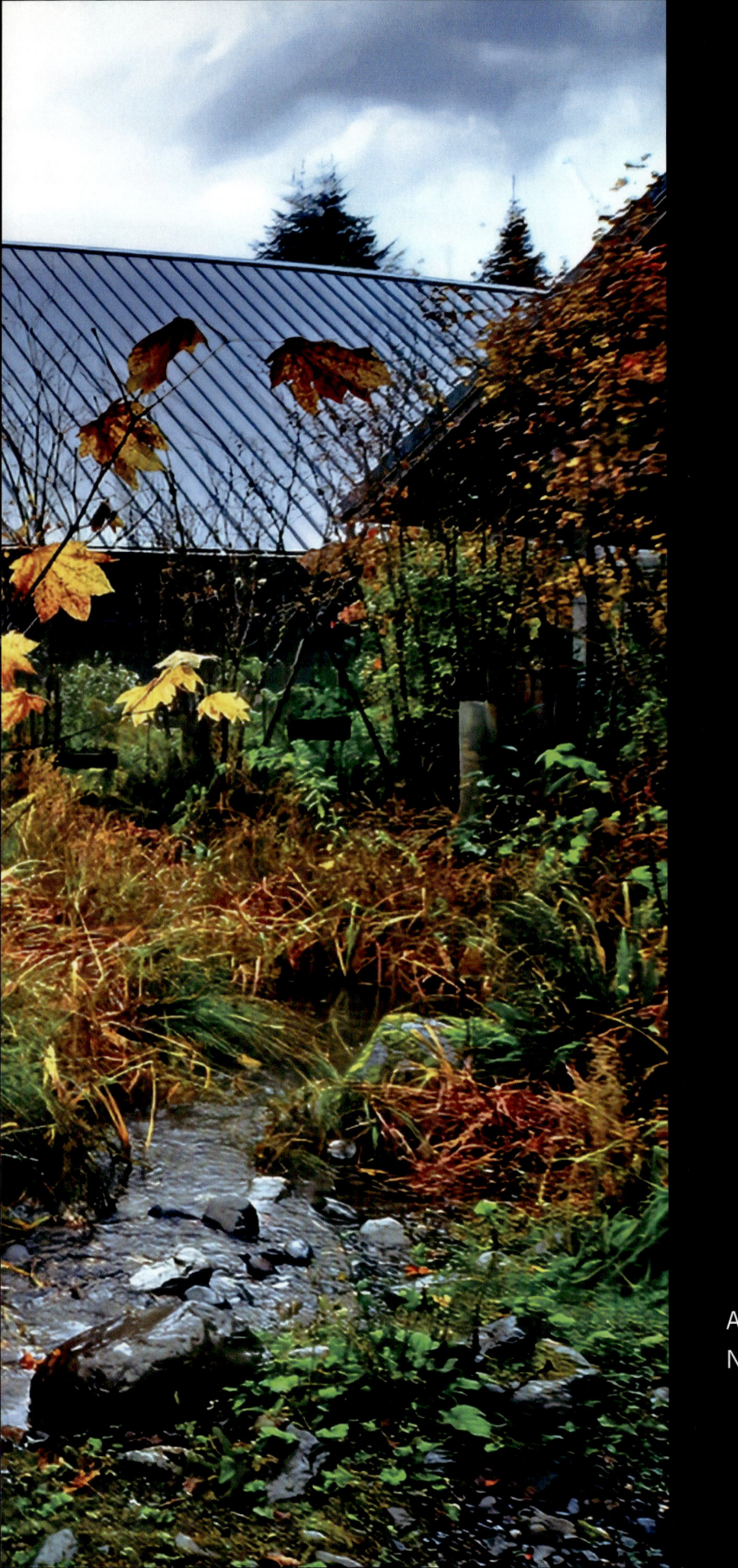

As the Season
Nikon D300

Mya was my best friend, and I miss her so . . .

IN MEMORIAM

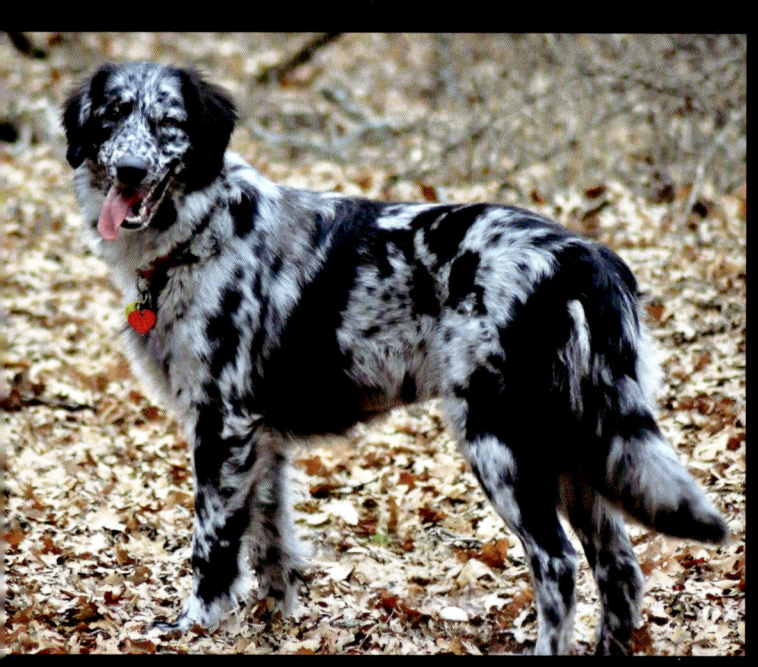

2007–2020

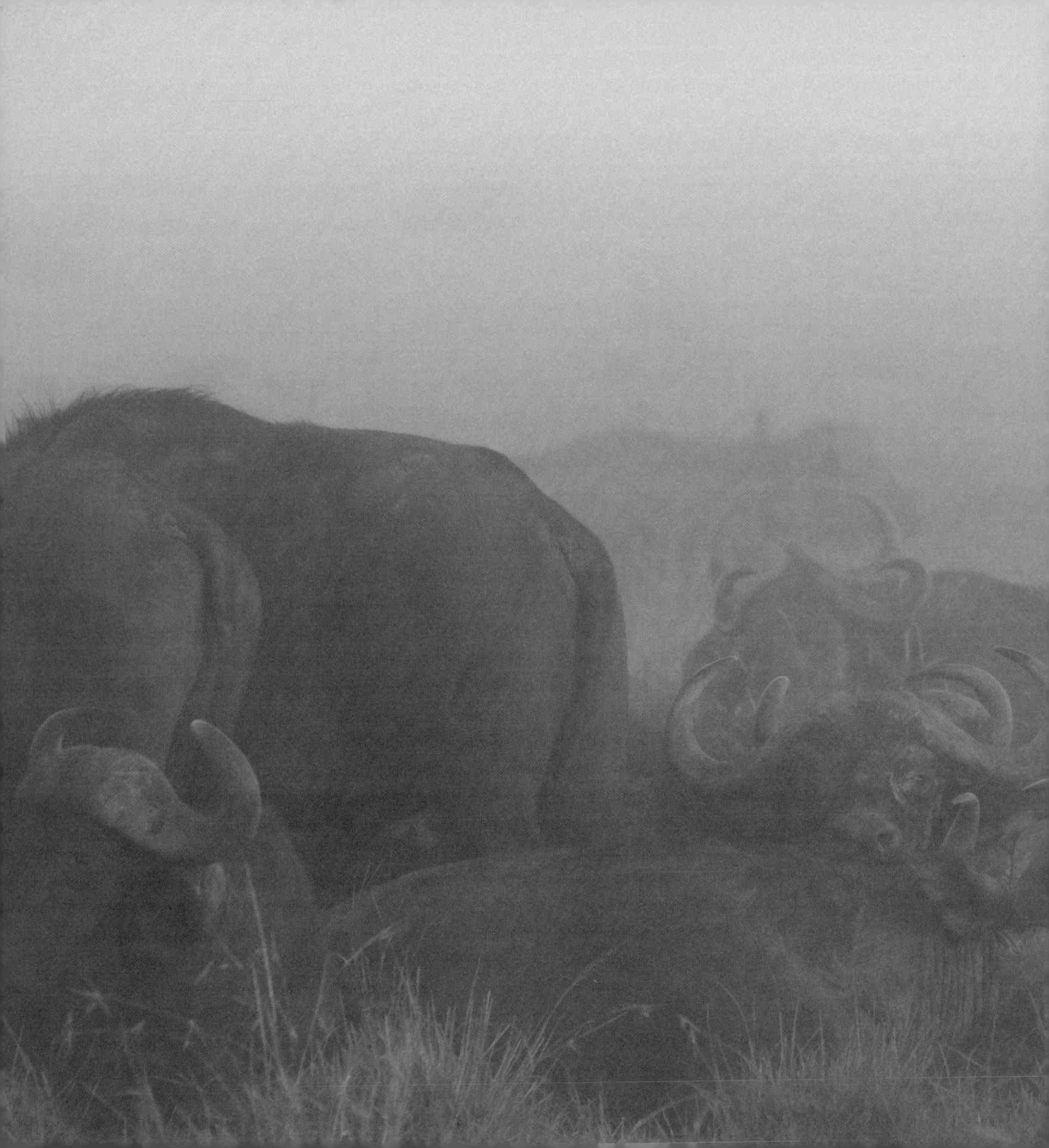